FILM ART

AN INTRODUCTION

ELEVENTH EDITION

FILM ART

AN INTRODUCTION

David Bordwell
University of Wisconsin—Madison

Kristin Thompson
University of Wisconsin—Madison

Jeff Smith
University of Wisconsin—Madison

McGraw Hill Education

FILM ART: AN INTRODUCTION, ELEVENTH EDITION

Published by McGraw-Hill Education, 2 Penn Plaza, New York, NY 10121. Copyright © 2017 by McGraw-Hill Education. All rights reserved. Printed in the United States of America. Previous editions © 2013, 2010, and 2008. No part of this publication may be reproduced or distributed in any form or by any means, or stored in a database or retrieval system, without the prior written consent of McGraw-Hill Education, including, but not limited to, in any network or other electronic storage or transmission, or broadcast for distance learning.

Some ancillaries, including electronic and print components, may not be available to customers outside the United States.

This book is printed on acid-free paper.

2 3 4 5 6 7 8 9 10 DOW 21 20 19 18 17 16

ISBN 978-1-259-53495-9
MHID 1-259-53495-2

Senior Vice President, Products & Markets: *Kurt L. Strand*
Vice President, General Manager, Products & Markets: *Michael Ryan*
Vice President, Content Design & Delivery: *Kimberly Meriwether David*
Managing Director: *William Glass*
Brand Manager: *Sarah Remington*
Lead Product Developer: *Dawn Groundwater*
Marketing Manager: *Kelly Odom*
Editorial Coordinator: *Christina Grimm*
Director, Content Design & Delivery: *Terri Schiesl*
Program Manager: *Debra Hash*
Content Project Managers: *Sandy Wille; Jodi Banowetz*
Buyer: *Susan K. Culbertson*
Designer: *Srdjan Savanovic*
Content Licensing Specialists: (photo) *Shawntel Schmitt*; (text) *Ann Marie Jannette*
Cover Image: *Courtesy of Universal Studios Licensing LLC and Moonrise LLC*
Compositor: *MPS Limited*
Printer: *R. R. Donnelley*

All credits appearing on page or at the end of the book are considered to be an extension of the copyright page.

Library of Congress Cataloging-in-Publication Data

Bordwell, David.
    Film art : an introduction / David Bordwell, Kristin Thompson, Jeff Smith, University of Wisconsin, Madison.—11
        pages cm
    Includes bibliographical references and index.
    ISBN 978-1-259-53495-9 (paperback)
    1. Motion pictures—Aesthetics. I. Thompson, Kristin, 1950- II. Title.
    PN1995.B617 2015
    791.4301—dc23

                        2015032809

mheducation.com/highered

ABOUT THE AUTHORS

David Bordwell is Jacques Ledoux Professor Emeritus of Film Studies at the University of Wisconsin–Madison. He holds a master's degree and a doctorate in film from the University of Iowa. His books include *The Films of Carl-Theodor Dreyer* (University of California Press, 1981), *Narration in the Fiction Film* (University of Wisconsin Press, 1985), *Ozu and the Poetics of Cinema* (Princeton University Press, 1988), *Making Meaning: Inference and Rhetoric in the Interpretation of Cinema* (Harvard University Press, 1989), *The Cinema of Eisenstein* (Harvard University Press, 1993), *On the History of Film Style* (Harvard University Press, 1997), *Planet Hong Kong: Popular Cinema and the Art of Entertainment* (Harvard University Press, 2000), *Figures Traced in Light: On Cinematic Staging* (University of California Press, 2005), *The Way Hollywood Tells It: Story and Style in Modern Movies* (University of California Press, 2006), *Poetics of Cinema* (Routledge, 2008), *Pandora's Digital Box: Films, Files, and the Future of Movies* (Irvington Way Institute Press, 2012), and *The Rhapsodes: How 1940s Critics Changed American Film Culture* (University of Chicago Press, 2016). He has won a University Distinguished Teaching Award and was awarded an honorary degree by the University of Copenhagen. His website is www.davidbordwell.net.

Kristin Thompson is an Honorary Fellow at the University of Wisconsin–Madison. She holds a master's degree in film from the University of Iowa and a doctorate in film from the University of Wisconsin–Madison. She has published *Eisenstein's Ivan the Terrible: A Neoformalist Analysis* (Princeton University Press, 1981), *Exporting Entertainment: America in the World Film Market 1907–1934* (British Film Institute, 1985), *Breaking the Glass Armor: Neoformalist Film Analysis* (Princeton University Press, 1988), *Wooster Proposes, Jeeves Disposes, or, Le Mot Juste* (James H. Heineman, 1992), *Storytelling in the New Hollywood: Understanding Classical Narrative Technique* (Harvard University Press, 1999), *Storytelling in Film and Television* (Harvard University Press, 2003), *Herr Lubitsch Goes To Hollywood: German and American Film After World War I* (Amsterdam University Press, 2005), and *The Frodo Franchise: The Lord of the Rings and Modern Hollywood* (University of California Press, 2007). She blogs with David at www.davidbordwell.net/blog, and is a contributor to TheOneRing.net. In her spare time, she studies Egyptology.

David Bordwell and Kristin Thompson have also collaborated on *Film History: An Introduction* (McGraw-Hill, 3d ed., 2010), *Minding Movies: Observations of the Art, Craft, and Business of Filmmaking* (University of Chicago Press, 2011), *Christopher Nolan: A Labyrinth of Linkages* (Irvington Way Institute Press, 2013), and, with Janet Staiger, on *The Classical Hollywood Cinema: Film Style and Mode of Production to 1960* (Columbia University Press, 1985).

Jeff Smith is a professor in the Communication Arts Department at the University of Wisconsin–Madison and the author of two books: *The Sounds of Commerce: Marketing Popular Film Music* (Columbia University Press, 1998) and *Film Criticism, the Cold War, and the Blacklist: Reading the Hollywood Reds* (University of California Press, 2014).

To our parents,

Marjorie and Jay Bordwell

and Jean and Roger Thompson

FILM ART—A PERSONALIZED LEARNING AND TEACHING EXPERIENCE IN FILM APPRECIATION

Film Art helps students master the skills of film appreciation by teaching them to analyze and appreciate classic and contemporary films. Enhanced by McGraw-Hill Education's SmartBook®, *Film Art* delivers a learning and teaching experience tailored to the needs of each institution, instructor, and student.

PERSONALIZING FILM LEARNING

For nearly a generation, *Film Art* has helped students become informed viewers of classic and contemporary films by explaining key vocabulary and concepts of film forms, techniques, and history. And now, with the introduction of McGraw-Hill Education's SmartBook students are better equipped to understand and retain these basic concepts.

SmartBook is an adaptive learning program proven to help students learn faster, study smarter, and retain more knowledge for greater success. Distinguishing what students know from what they don't, and focusing on concepts they are most likely to forget, SmartBook continuously adapts to each student's needs by building a personalized learning path. An intelligent, adaptive study tool, SmartBook is proven to strengthen memory recall, keep students in class, and boost grades.

Enhanced by McGraw-Hill Education's SmartBook, *Film Art* delivers the first and only adaptive reading experience currently available.

- **Make It Effective.** SmartBook creates a personalized reading experience by highlighting the most impactful concepts a student needs to learn at that moment in time. This ensures that every minute spent with SmartBook is returned to the student as the most valuable minute possible.

- **Make It Informed.** Real-time reports quickly identify the concepts that require more attention from individual students—or the entire class.

ANALYZING AND CRITIQUING FILM

Studying film isn't just about learning the facts; it's also about the skills of watching and listening closely. Together with the Criterion Collection, we've developed Connect Film to introduce students to the world of film and challenge them to develop the critical-analysis skills necessary to become informed viewers.

The authors have partnered with the Criterion Collection to create brief video tutorials, available exclusively in Connect Film. The tutorials use film clips to clarify and reinforce key concepts and model the critical skills necessary to become informed viewers. They can be shown in class or assigned for students to view outside class, with brief optional follow-up quizzes. Below is a list of Criterion Collection tutorial selections available in Connect Film:

Light Sources: *Ashes and Diamonds* (1958)

Available Lighting: *Breathless* (1960)

Staging in Depth: *Mr. Hulot's Holiday* (1953)

Color Motifs: *The Spirit of the Beehive* (1973)

Tracking Shots Structure a Scene: *Ugetsu* (1953)

Tracking Shot to Reveal: *The 400 Blows* (1959)

Style Creates Parallelism: *Day of Wrath* (1943)

Staging and Camera Movement in a Long Take: *The Rules of the Game* (1939)

Editing with Graphic Matches: *Seven Samurai* (1954)

Shifting the Axis of Action: *Shaun of the Dead* (2004)

Crossing the Axis of Action: *Early Summer* (1951)

Crosscutting: *M* (1931)

Elliptical Editing: *Vagabond* (1985)

Jump Cuts: *Breathless* (1960)

Sound Mixing: *Seven Samurai* (1954)

Contrasting Rhythms of Sound and Image: *Mr. Hulot's Holiday* (1953)

Offscreen Sound: *M* (1931)

What Comes Out Must Go In: 2D Computer Animation

Lens and Camera Movement

Film Lighting

Below are several Criterion Tutorials new to the eleventh edition:

Contrasting Style for Objective and Subjective Narration: *Journey to Italy* (1954)

Diegetic narration by an Unidentified Character: *I Vitelloni* (1953)

Setting and Costume Play an Active Role: *Ivan the Terrible, Part II* (1958)

Two Ways of Staging for Humor: *The Gold Rush* (1925)

The Long Lens and Zooming: *Close-up* (1990)

Playing with Unrealistic Sound: *Daisies* (1966)

Staging with the Main Characters' Backs toward the Camera: *L'Avventura* (1960)

Authenticity in Documentaries: *Nanook of the North* (1922)

Surrealism in Experimental Film: *Un Chien andalou* (1929)

Post Production Sound

In addition, Connect Film features **Film Analysis Assignments** with additional clips, film stills, and links to movie clips to help students practice analyzing aspects of each film and prepare them for their longer written assignments. These include clips from the following films:

Battleship Potemkin (1925)

D.O.A. (1950)

The General (1926)

His Girl Friday (1940)

The Lady Vanishes (1938)

M (1931)

Man with a Movie Camera (1929)

Meet John Doe (1941)

Night of the Living Dead (1968)

Nosferatu (1922)

Scarlet Street (1945)

Sita Sings the Blues (2008)

Wackiki Wabbit (1943)

APPRECIATING FILM

Film Art provides the respected scholarship and analytic tools students need to understand key vocabulary and concepts of film forms, techniques, and history; appreciate a wide variety of classic and contemporary films and the creative choices made by filmmakers to shape the experience of viewers; and analyze films critically and systematically to enrich their understanding and appreciation of any film, in any genre.

"Creative Decision" sections provide in-depth examples to deepen students' appreciation for how creative choices by filmmakers affect how viewers respond. Discussions include, for example, performance and camera positioning in *The Social Network*, editing in *The Birds*, and overlapping dialogue cuts in *The Hunt for Red October*.

"Closer Look" features examine important issues in contemporary cinema and provide detailed looks at such topics as computer-generated imagery (CGI) in *The Lord of the Rings*, editing in *L. A. Confidential*, and motifs in *The Shining*.

Authors' blog, "Observations on Film Art." In what Roger Ebert called "the most knowledgeable film blog on the web," David Bordwell and Kristin Thompson share their ideas and experiences with instructors and students (http://www.davidbordwell.net/blog). Throughout the text, "Connect to the Blog" references point to blog entries with relevant ideas, terms, and film examples, connecting ideas in *Film Art* to the current film scene in an accessible way.

PERSONALIZING FILM TEACHING

Through **McGraw-Hill Education's Create**, a new chapter on Film Adaptations, written by Jeff Smith of the University of Wisconsin, is available for instructors to better customize and personalize their film appreciation course. In addition, an appendix on "Writing a Critical Analysis" is available for instructors who require written film critiques, and DVD Recommendations provide particularly effective resources related to key topics.

McGraw-Hill Create allows you to create a customized print book or eBook tailored to your course and syllabus. You can search through thousands of McGraw-Hill Education texts, rearrange chapters, combine material from other content sources, and include your own content or teaching notes. Create even allows you to personalize your book's appearance by selecting the cover and adding your name, school, and course information. To register and to get more information, go to http://create.mheducation.com.

Chapter-by-Chapter Changes

Chapter 1   Updated and expanded information on digital production, distribution, and exhibition, with examples of special effects from *Pacific Rim*. New information on contemporary theater sound systems, as exemplified by Atmos and *Brave*. New references to *Middle of Nowhere* and *Nightcrawler*. Examination of marketing campaigns for *The Dark Knight*, the *Transformers* series, and *The Grand Budapest Hotel*. Enhanced references to blog "Observations on Film Art."

Chapter 2   Enhanced references to blog "Observations on Film Art."

Chapter 3   Enhanced references to blog "Observations on Film Art."

Chapter 4   New references to mise-en-scene in *Watchmen*, *Snowpiercer*, and *Laura*. Enhanced references to blog "Observations on Film Art."

Chapter 5   Updated information on digital color grading. Discussion of 3D in *Life of Pi*. Discussions of *Family Plot* and *Leviathan*. Enhanced references to blog "Observations on Film Art."

Chapter 6   New examples from *Wolf of Wall Street* and *Lucy*. Enhanced references to blog "Observations on Film Art."

Chapter 7   Extensively revised sound chapter, with new material on sound perspective in the theater space.

New analyses of sound techniques in *The Magnificent Ambersons, Blow-Out, Norma Rae, Interstellar, Breakfast at Tiffany's, Reservoir Dogs, The Nutty Professor, Vicki Cristina Barcelona, Gosford Park, 12 Monkeys,* and *Accident*, along with an expanded consideration of *The Conversation*. Enhanced references to blog "Observations on Film Art."

Chapter 8   Extensive new section on *Gravity* and film style in the digital age. Enhanced references to blog "Observations on Film Art."

Chapter 9   New section on sports film as genre, with new examples from *My Sweet Pepper Land, The World's Fastest Indian, Fever Pitch*, and *Offside*. Enhanced references to blog "Observations on Film Art."

Chapter 10   New examples from *The Act of Killing, Searching for Sugar Man*, and *Rango*. Enhanced references to blog "Observations on Film Art."

Chapter 11   New detailed analysis of *Moonrise Kingdom*. Enhanced references to blog "Observations on Film Art."

Chapter 12   Update on contemporary Hollywood industry and technology, including sound systems and Video on Demand. New examples from *Beetlejuice, Ben-Hur, The Apple*, and *Beasts of the Southern Wild*. Enhanced references to blog "Observations on Film Art."

FROM THE AUTHORS

If you're in your late teens or early twenties, we have something in common with you. That was the age when we became curious about—some would say, obsessed with—film, cinema, movies.

What fueled our enthusiasm was a simple love of this medium and the great films we saw. For us, films that are classics today, from *Alphaville, 2001,* and *The Godfather* through *Jaws* and *Nashville* to *Pulp Fiction* and *Chungking Express,* were new movies. Over the years, we've watched film history unfold, and our excitement at new developments hasn't flagged.

Of course, we loved particular films and admired particular filmmakers. At the same time, we were entranced by the artistic possibilities of film as an art form. As teachers and writers, we roamed widely, trying to understand films from very different traditions—from silent avant-garde cinema to modern Hong Kong film, from Los Angeles to Paris to Tokyo. We've written about modern Hollywood, including *The Lord of the Rings,* and filmmakers working outside Hollywood—for example, Carl Dreyer, Sergei Eisenstein, and Yasujiro Ozu. In the past ten years, we've extended our explorations to the Web, where we blog regularly about the many things that interest us in film.

Studying the arts isn't just about learning facts. That's why in *Film Art* we have always emphasized the skills of watching and listening closely. With the tenth edition we partnered with the prestigious Criterion Collection of DVDs and Blu-ray discs in our new Connect Film digital program (see pp. vi–vii). The Criterion Collection is dedicated to gathering many of the greatest classic and contemporary films from around the world. Criterion editions provide the highest technical quality and include award-winning supplements. They are a natural partner in introducing a new generation to cinema studies. We've created a series of clips that model the critical viewing skills that will help you become informed viewers. For this eleventh edition, we've added to our first set of clips, and we hope that these will continue to help you become critical, informed viewers.

Filmmaking has undergone a continuous change since we launched this book in 1979. Digital technology has given many people access to filmmaking tools, and it has changed film distribution and exhibition. You can watch movies on your laptop or mobile phone, and films now arrive at theaters on hard drives rather than film reels. Because we focus on concepts, and because the techniques we study remain central to all sorts of moving-image media, much of what we studied in earlier editions remains valid. Still, we've expanded our discussion to include the creative choices opened up by digital cinema.

Studying the arts isn't only about learning facts and concepts either, although both are important. In addition, studying the arts broadens our tastes. In eleven editions of *Film Art,* we've made reference to many well-known films but also to many that you've probably never heard of. This is part of our plan. We want to show that the world of cinema teems with a great many unexpected pleasures, and we hope to get you curious.

In surveying film art through such concepts as form, style, and genre, we aren't trying to wrap movies in abstractions. We're trying to show that there are principles that can shed light on a variety of films. We'd be happy if our ideas can help you to understand the films that you enjoy. And we hope that you'll seek out films that will stimulate your mind, your feelings, and your imagination in unpredictable ways. For us, this is what education is all about.

Acknowledgments

Over the 40 years of preparing editions of *Film Art: An Introduction* we have incurred many debts to hundreds of individuals, and it's impossible to thank them all individually. We do, however, want to thank certain people for their long-term support. Our colleagues at the University of Wisconsin–Madison: Tino Balio, Maria Belodubrovskaya, Ben Brewster, Noël Carroll, Kelley Conway, Kaitlin Fyfe, Maxine Fleckner-Ducey, Erik Gunneson, Vance Kepley, Mike King, Lea Jacobs, J. J. Murphy, Peter Sengstock, and Ben Singer have helped us in many ways. Archivists have also been exceptionally cooperative, so we thank Eileen Bowser, Elaine Burrows, Mary Corliss, the late Susan Dalton, the late Jacques Ledoux, Jan-Christopher Horak, Patrick Loughney, Nicola Mazzanti, Jackie Morris, Charles Silver, Paolo Cherchi Usai, and especially Gabrielle Claes for giving us access to films and materials in their collections. Thanks as well to Michael Barker of Sony Pictures Classics, Dan Talbot and José Lopez of New Yorker Films, and James Schamus, formerly of Focus Features. Thanks as well to Michael Barker of Sony Pictures Classics, Roni Lubliner of NBC–Universal, Peter McPartlin of Indian Paintbrush, and Matt Zoller Seitz of Rogerebert.com, who initiated our contact with Mr. McPartlin. Finally, we appreciate the kind cooperation of several filmmakers, including the late Les Blank, Bruce Conner, and Norman McLaren, as well as Ernie Gehr, Michael Snow, and Frederick Wiseman.

As the new contributor to this edition, Jeff Smith would like to thank Eric Dienstfrey for his valuable advice about the history of film sound technologies, Michele Smith for her helpful recommendations of new film examples, and Megan Lacroix, personal consultant for all things Harry Potter.

In preparing this edition, we're grateful to Aaron Adair, Southeastern Oklahoma State University; Laura Bouza, Moorpark College; Domenic Bruni, University of Wisconsin–Oshkosh; Maria Elena de las Carreras, California State University–Northridge; Shawn Cheatham, University of South Florida–Tampa; John Claborn, University of Illinois–Champaign; Megan Condis, University of Illinois–Champaign; Steve Gilliland, West Virginia State University; Lucinda McNamara, Cape Fear Community College; James McWard, Johnson County Community College; Barbara Multer-Wellin, New York Film Academy; Deron Overpeck, Auburn University; Lisa Peterson, University of Central Florida–Orlando; Syd Slobodnik, University of Illinois–Champaign; Jared Saltzman, Bergen Community College; and Susan Tavernetti, Deanza College.

We owe special thanks to Erik Gunneson, producer and director of our video supplements, and Petra Dominkova, whose eagle eye scanned for slips, misprints, and inconsistencies. Warm thanks as well go to Peter Becker and Kim Hendrickson of the Criterion Collection for their generosity in cooperating with us on the video extracts.

As ever, we're grateful to the McGraw-Hill Education publishing team, particularly Dawn Groundwater, Sarah Remington, Sandy Wille, Shawntel Schmitt, Susan Messer, and Carey Lange.

David Bordwell
Kristin Thompson
Jeff Smith

BRIEF CONTENTS

CONTENTS

PART THREE • Film Style

CHAPTER 4   The Shot: Mise-en-Scene   112

CHAPTER 5   The Shot: Cinematography   159

CHAPTER 6   The Relation of Shot to Shot: Editing   216

CHAPTER 7   Sound in the Cinema   263

CHAPTER 8   Summary: Style and Film Form   303

PART FOUR • Types of Films

CHAPTER 9   Film Genres   326

create™ **FILM ADAPTATIONS**

create™ **WRITING A CRITICAL ANALYSIS OF A FILM**

create™ **ADDITIONAL RESOURCES FOR FILM ART**

PART 1

Film is a young medium. Painting, literature, dance, and theater have existed for thousands of years, but cinema was invented only a little more than a century ago. Yet in its comparatively short span, the newcomer has established itself as an energetic and powerful art.

It's this art that we explore in this book. The chapters that follow show how creative people have used moving pictures to give us experiences that we value. We examine the principles and techniques that give film its power to tell stories, express emotions, and convey ideas.

But this art has some unusual features we should note from the start. More than most arts, film depends on complex technology. Without machines, movies wouldn't move. In addition, film art usually requires collaboration among many participants, people who follow well-proven work routines. Films are not only created but produced. Just as important, they are firmly tied to their social and economic context. Films are distributed and exhibited for audiences, and money matters at every step.

Film Art and Filmmaking

Chapter 1 surveys all these aspects of the filmmaking process. We examine the technology, the work practices, and the business side of cinema. All these components shape and sustain film as an art.

1

Film as Art: Creativity, Technology, and Business

Motion pictures are so much a part of our lives that it's hard to imagine a world without them. We enjoy them in theaters, at home, in offices, in cars and buses, and on airplanes. We carry films with us in our laptops, tablets, and cellphones. Press a button, and a machine conjures up movies for your pleasure.

Films communicate information and ideas, and they show us places and ways of life we might not otherwise know. Important as these benefits are, though, something more is at stake. Films offer us ways of seeing and feeling that we find deeply gratifying. They take us through experiences. The experiences are often driven by stories centering on characters we come to care about, but a film might also develop an idea or explore visual qualities or sound textures.

Such things don't happen by accident. Films are *designed* to create experiences for viewers. To gain an understanding of film as an art, we should ask why a film is designed the way it is. When a scene frightens or excites us, when an ending makes us laugh or cry, we can ask how the filmmakers have achieved those effects.

It helps to imagine that we're filmmakers, too. Throughout this book, we'll be asking you to put yourself in the filmmaker's shoes.

This shouldn't be a great stretch. You've taken still photos with a camera or a mobile phone. Very likely you've made some videos, perhaps just to record a moment in your life—a party, a wedding, your cat creeping into a paper bag. And central to filmmaking is the act of choice. You may not have realized it at the moment, but every time you framed a shot, shifted your position, told people not to blink, or tried to keep up with a dog chasing a Frisbee, you were making choices.

You might take the next step and make a more ambitious, more controlled film. You might compile clips into a YouTube video, or document your friend's musical performance. Again, at every stage you make design decisions, based on how you think this image or that sound will affect your viewers' experience. What if you start your music video with a black screen that gradually brightens as the music fades in? That will have a different effect than starting it with a sudden cut to a bright screen and a blast of music.

At each instant, the filmmaker can't avoid making creative decisions about how viewers will respond. Every moviemaker is also a movie viewer, and the choices are considered from the standpoint of the end user. Filmmakers constantly ask themselves: *If I do this, as opposed to that, how will viewers react?*

The menu of filmmaking choices has developed over time. Late in the 19th century, moving pictures emerged as a public amusement. They succeeded because they spoke to the imaginative needs of a broad-based audience. All the traditions that emerged—telling fictional stories, recording actual events, animating objects or drawings, experimenting with pure form—aimed to give viewers experiences they couldn't get from other media. Men and women discovered that they could use cinema to shape those experiences in various ways. Suppose we center the actors so they command the frame space? Suppose we cut up a scene into shots taken from several angles? Suppose we move the camera to follow the actors? Learning from one another, testing and refining new choices, filmmakers developed skills that became the basis of the art form we have today.

Thinking like a filmmaker is all very well, you might say, if you want a career in the business. What if you just want to enjoy movies? We think that you can appreciate films more fully if you're aware of how creative choices shape your experience. You've probably looked at some making-of bonuses on DVD versions of films you love, and some of those supplements have increased your enjoyment. We enhance our appreciation of *The Social Network* or *Inception* when we know something of the filmmakers' behind-the-scenes discussion of character motivation and specific line readings. We can always get more out of the films we see, and thinking about the filmmakers' choices helps us to understand why we respond as we do.

This is why we start our survey of film art by looking at the process of film production. Here we can see, in very tangible ways, the sorts of options available to people working in this medium. In every chapter that follows, we invoke what film artists have said about the ways they've chosen to solve creative problems.

Throughout this book, we focus on the two basic areas of choice and control in the art of film: form and style. **Form** is the overall patterning of a film, the ways its parts work together to create specific effects (Chapters 2 and 3). **Style** involves the film's use of cinematic techniques. Those techniques fall into four categories: mise-en-scene, or the arrangement of people, places, and objects to be filmed (Chapter 4); cinematography, the use of cameras and other machines to record images and sounds (Chapter 5); editing, the piecing together of individual shots (Chapter 6); and sound, the voices, effects, and music that blend on a film's audio track (Chapter 7). After examining the various techniques, Chapter 8 integrates them in an overview of film style.

In later chapters, we discuss how form and style differ among genres and other types of films (Chapters 9–10). We consider how we can analyze films critically (Chapter 11) and how film form and style have changed across history, offering filmmakers different sets of creative choices (Chapter 12). In all, we'll see how through choice and control, film artists create movies that entertain us, inform us, and engage our imaginations.

Art vs. Entertainment? Art vs. Business?

The term "art" might put some readers off. If cinema originated as a mass medium, should we even use the word? Are Hollywood directors "artists"? Some people would say that the blockbusters playing at the multiplex are merely "entertainment," but films for a narrower public—perhaps independent films, or foreign-language fare, or experimental works—are true art.

Usually the art/entertainment split rests on a value judgment: Art is serious and worthy; entertainment is superficial. Yet things aren't that simple. Many of the artistic resources of cinema were discovered by filmmakers working for the general public. During the 1910s and 1920s, for instance, many filmmakers who simply aimed to be entertaining pioneered new possibilities for film editing.

As for the matter of value, it's clear that popular traditions can foster art of high quality. Shakespeare and Dickens wrote for broad audiences. Much of the greatest 20th-century music, including jazz and the blues, was rooted in popular traditions. Cinema is an art because it offers filmmakers ways to design experiences for viewers, and those experiences can be valuable regardless of their pedigree. Films for audiences both small and large belong to that very inclusive art we call film or cinema.

Sometimes, too, people consider film *art* to be opposed to film as a *business*. This split is related to the issue of entertainment, since entertainment generally is sold to a mass audience. In most modern societies, however, no art floats free from economic ties. Novels good, bad, and indifferent are published because publishers and authors expect to sell them. Painters hope that collectors and museums will acquire their work. True, some artworks are funded through subsidy or private donations, but that process, too, involves the artists in financial transactions.

Films are no different. Some movies are made in the hope that consumers will pay to see them. Others are funded by patronage (an investor or organization wants to see the film made) or public money. (France, for instance, generously subsidizes film projects.) Crowdfunding sites such as Kickstarter offer another alternative. You might make short videos for YouTube or Vimeo at little cost, but if you hope to make a feature-length digital movie, you face the problem of paying for it. If you can't profit from your film, you may still hope that the project will lead to a job.

The crucial point is that considerations of business don't necessarily make the artist less creative or the project less worthwhile. Money can corrupt any activity, but it doesn't have to. In Renaissance Italy, painters were commissioned by the Catholic Church to illustrate events from the Bible. Michelangelo and Leonardo da Vinci worked for hire, but we revere their artistry.

In this book we won't assume that film art precludes entertainment. We won't take the opposite position either, claiming that only Hollywood mass-market movies are worth our attention. Similarly, we don't think that film art rises above commercial demands, but we also won't assume that money rules everything. Any art form offers a vast range of creative possibilities.

As an art, film offers experiences that viewers find worthwhile—diverting, provocative, puzzling, or rapturous. But how do films do that? To answer that question, let's go back a step and ask: Where do movies come from?

They come from three places. They come from the imagination and hard work of the filmmakers who create them. They come from a complex set of machines that capture and transform images and sounds. And they come from companies or individuals who pay for the filmmakers and the technology. This chapter examines the artistic, technological, and business sides of how films come into being.

CONNECT TO THE BLOG
www.davidbordwell.net/blog

We examine an unusual problem and a director's unusual solution in "Problems, problems, Wyler's workaround."

Creative Decisions in Filmmaking

In *Day for Night,* French filmmaker François Truffaut plays a director making a movie called *Meet Pamela.* Crew members bring set designs, wigs, cars, and prop pistols to him, and we hear his voice telling us his thoughts: "What is a director? A director is someone who is asked questions about everything."

Making a film can be seen as a long process of decision making, not just by the director but by all the specialists who work on the production team. Screenwriters, producers, directors, performers, and technicians are constantly solving problems and making choices. A great many of those decisions affect what we see and hear on the screen. There are business choices about the budget, marketing, distribution, and payments. Connected to those choices are the artistic ones. What lighting will enhance the atmosphere of a love scene? Given the kind of story being told, would it be better to let the audience know what the central character is thinking or to keep her enigmatic? When a scene opens, what is the most economical way of letting the audience identify the time and place? We can see how decisions shape the process by looking in more detail at a single production.

■■
CREATIVE DECISIONS
■■

To See into the Night in Collateral

Michael Mann's *Collateral,* released in 2004, is a visually striking psychological thriller set in Los Angeles in a single night. The mysterious Vincent (Tom Cruise) hires a cab driver, Max (Jamie Foxx), to drive him to several appointments. When Max learns that Vincent is a hired killer, he struggles to break their bargain and escape. But Vincent forces him to carry on as a getaway driver. In the course of the evening, the two men spar verbally and move toward a climactic chase and confrontation.

Mann and his crew made thousands of decisions during the making of *Collateral.* Here we look at five important choices: one that influenced the film's form and one each for our four categories of mise-en-scene, cinematography, editing, and sound. Several of these decisions involved new technologies that became standard production tools.

Scriptwriter Stuart Beattie originally set *Collateral* in New York City. In the screenplay, Max was a loser, hiding from the world in his cab and getting little out of life. Vincent was to goad him about his failures until Max had finally had enough and stood up to him. Once Mann came on board as director, he altered the plot in several ways. The setting became Los Angeles. Max became less a loser and more a laid-back, intelligent man content to observe the world from behind a steering wheel, endlessly delaying his plans to start his own limousine service. This more appealing Max becomes our point-of-view figure for most of the film. For example, we don't see the first murder but stay with Max in the cab until the shocking moment when a body hurtles down onto his cab roof. The story largely consists of Max's conflict with Vincent, so Mann's decision to change Max's traits altered their confrontations as well. In the finished film, moments of reluctant mutual respect and even hints of friendship complicate the men's relationship. Such decisions as these reshaped the film's overall narrative form.

The switch to Los Angeles profoundly affected the film's style. For Mann, one of the attractions was that this tale of randomly crossing destinies took place almost entirely at night, from 6:04 P.M. to 4:20 A.M. He wanted to portray the atmospheric Los Angeles night, where haze and cloud cover reflect the city's lights back to the vast grid of streets. According to cinematographer Paul Cameron, "The goal was to make the L.A. night as much of a character in the story as Vincent and Max were."

This was a major decision that created the film's look. Mann was determined not to use more artificial light than was absolutely necessary. He relied to a considerable degree on street lights, neon signs, vehicle headlights, and other sources in the locations where filming took place. To achieve an eerie radiance, his team came up with a cutting-edge combination of tools.

Digital Cinematography Certain choices about photographing *Collateral* were central to its final look and also dictated many other decisions. For example, at that time Hollywood productions employed cameras loaded with rolls of photographic film. Night scenes were shot using large banks of specialized spot- and floodlights. If the light was too weak, dark areas would tend to go a uniform black.

Mann and his cinematographers decided to shoot portions of *Collateral* on recently developed high-definition (HD) digital cameras. Those cameras could shoot on location with little or no light added to the scene **(1.1).** They could also capture the distinctive night glow of Los Angeles. As Mann put it, "Film doesn't record what our eyes can see at night. That's why I moved into shooting digital video in high definition—to see into the night, to see everything the naked eye can see and more. You see this moody landscape with hills and trees and strange light patterns. I wanted that to be the world that Vincent and Max are moving through."

1.1–1.3 Digital filming for *Collateral.* A digital camera shoots in a dim alley. As in many shots, the skyline of downtown Los Angeles figures prominently (1.1). An eerily glowing cityscape, with digital cinematography making a row of palm trees stand out against a dark sky (1.2). Vincent stalks one of his victims in a law library with huge windows overlooking the city (1.3). On regular photographic film, the streets and buildings would go uniformly dark, with only points of light visible.

1.1

1.2

1.3

Cinematographer Dion Beebe enthused, "The format's strong point is its incredible sensitivity to light. We were able to shoot Los Angeles at night and actually see silhouettes of palm trees against the night sky, which was very exciting" **(1.2).** In a particularly dark scene at the climax, the characters become visible only as black shapes outlined by the myriad lights behind them **(1.3).** The suspense is heightened as we strain to see the figures.

Custom-Made Lights Though digital cameras could pick up a great deal in dark situations, the audience needed to see the faces of the actors clearly. Much of the action takes place inside the taxi as Max and Vincent ride and talk. The actors' faces had to be lit, but the filmmakers wanted to avoid the sense that there was artificial light in the cab.

To create a soft, diffuse light, the filmmakers tried an innovative approach: electroluminescent display (ELD) panels. The technology had been used in digital watches and cellphones, but it had never been employed in filming. Flexible plastic panels of various sizes were custom made, all with Velcro backings that would stick to the seats and ceiling of the cab **(1.4, 1.5).** These ELD panels could then be turned on in various combinations. Although they look bright in Figure 1.5, the effect on the screen was a soft glow on the actors. In a shot like Figure **1.6,** we might simply take it for granted that the light coming through the windows and the glow of the dashboard panel are all that shines on the characters. Such dim illumination on the faces allows the lights visible through the windows to be brighter than they are, helping to keeping the city "as much of a character in the story as Vincent and Max were."

Here's a case where an artistic decision led to new technology. Since *Collateral* was made, a similar lighting technology, the light-emitting diode (LED) has become common in flashlights, auto tail lights, scoreboard displays, and computer monitors. Specially designed LED units have become central to film production. Mann's team solved a problem in mise-en-scene, and a new option was added to the menu available to other filmmakers.

1.4

1.5

1.6

1.4–1.6 Unobtrusive lighting. One of the ELD panels specially made for illuminating the cab interior (1.4). Several ELD panels were attached to the back of a seat to shine on Tom Cruise as Vincent (1.5). The units created a dim glow on the actors (1.6).

Seamless Editing   *Collateral* contains several dynamic action scenes, including a spectacular car crash. The plan was for a cab going nearly 60 miles per hour to flip, then bounce and roll several times before coming to rest upside down. If we put ourselves in the filmmakers' place, we can imagine their options about how to show the crash.

Mann's team could have put the camera in a single spot and swiveled it to follow the car rolling past. That might have been a good idea if the scene showed us the crash through the eyes of an onlooker whose head turns to watch it. But there is no character witnessing the crash.

The filmmakers decided to generate excitement by showing several shots of the car rolling, each taken from a different point along the trajectory of the crash. One option would have been to use several cabs and execute numerous similar crashes, each time filmed by a single camera that would be moved between crashes from place to place to record the action from a new vantage point. Such a procedure would have been very expensive, however, and no two crashes would have taken place in exactly the same way. Splicing together shots from each crash might have created discrepancies in the car's position, resulting in poor "matches on action," as we'll term this technique in Chapter 6.

Instead, the team settled on a technique commonly used for big action scenes. Along the cab's path were stationed multiple cameras, all filming at once **(1.7).** The economic benefits were that only one car had to be crashed and the high expense of keeping many crew members working on retakes was reduced. Artistically, the resulting footage allowed the editing team to choose portions of many shots and splice them together in precise ways **(1.8, 1.9).** The result is an exciting stream of shots, each taken from farther along the taxi's path.

Music in Movements   Composers are fond of saying that their music for a film should serve the story so well that the audience doesn't notice it. For *Collateral*, Mann wanted James Newton Howard to score the climax so as to not

1.7–1.9 Editing a car crash. On location after the execution of the car crash in *Collateral,* director Michael Mann surveys digital monitors displaying shots taken by multiple cameras covering the action (1.7). The result: A seamless continuation of the cab's movement. A shot taken from one camera shows the car flipping over, its hood flapping wildly (1.8) is followed by a cut to another shot, taken from a camera placed on the ground and continuing the same movement, now with the vehicle rolling toward the viewer (1.9). This particular camera was placed in a very thick metal case.

1.7

1.8

1.9

build up excitement too quickly. According to Howard, "Michael was very clear about the climax taking place in three movements." "Movements" as a term is usually applied to the parts of a symphony, a concerto, or a sonata. Thus the idea was that the score for this last part of the film should play a major role in shaping the progression and rhythm of the action.

At the climax, Vincent is trying to kill a character who is important to Max, while Max tries frantically to save both himself and the other character. Howard and Mann called the first musical movement "The Race to Warn," since Vincent gets ahead of Max in running to the building where the potential victim is located. Despite the fact that both men are running and the situation is suspenseful, Howard avoids rapid rhythms. He begins with long-held string chords over a deep, rumbling sound, then adds sustained brass chords with a strong beat accompanying them. The music is dynamic but doesn't reach a high pitch of excitement.

The second movement, "The Cat and Mouse," accompanies Vincent getting into the building, turning off the electricity, and stalking his victim in near darkness (1.3). Again, the chords are slow, with ominous undertones, dissonant glides, and, at a few points, fast, eerie high-string figures as Vincent nears his goal. During the most suspenseful moments in the scene, when Vincent and his prey are in the darkened room, strings and soft, clicking percussion accompany their cautious, hesitant movements.

Finally, there is a swift chase sequence, and here Howard's score is louder and faster, with driving tympani in very quick rhythm as the danger grows. Once the chase tapers off, the percussion ends, and slow, low strings accompany the final quiet shots.

These decisions and many others affect our experience of *Collateral.* Thanks to the digital imagery and innovative lighting, we have a sense of characters moving through an eerie, unfamiliar-looking world. The editing of the crash allows the taxi to come hurtling toward the camera several times. The music accompanying the fast-chase/slow-stalking/fast-chase climax helps heighten the suspense and build the excitement. Creative decision making is central to every film, and *Collateral*

1.10 The legacy of *Collateral.* The sleazy news photographer protagonist of *Nightcrawler* pauses on the street to check some footage he has just shot. The dim light on his face comes entirely from the glow of his laptop and street lamps reflecting off his car.

stands out for making several unusual choices. *Collateral*'s innovative visual style showed later filmmakers what digital tools could do. Director Tony Scott replicated the HD sheen of the film in his *Déjà vu*. Cinematographer Robert Elswit's half-beautiful, half-creepy images for *Nightcrawler* (**1.10**) provide a similar look into the Los Angeles night.

Mechanics of the Movies

Filmmaking relies on technology and financing. First, filmmakers need fairly complicated machines. Anyone with a pen and paper can write a novel, and a talented kid with a guitar can become a musician. Movies demand much more. Even the simplest home video camera is based on fiendishly complex technology. A major film involves elaborate cameras, lighting equipment, multitrack sound-mixing studios, sophisticated laboratories, and computer-generated special effects.

Partly because of the technology, making a movie also involves businesses. Companies manufacture the equipment, other companies provide funding for the film, still others distribute it, and finally theaters and other venues present the result to an audience. In the rest of this chapter, we consider how these two sides of making movies—technology and business—shape film as an art.

Illusion Machines

Moving-image media such as film and video couldn't exist if human vision were perfect. Our eyes are very sensitive, but they can be tricked. As anyone who has paused a DVD knows, a film consists of a series of *frames,* or still pictures. Yet we don't perceive the separate frames. Instead, we see continuous light and movement. What creates this impression?

For a long time people thought that the effect results from "persistence of vision," the tendency of an image to linger briefly on our retina. Yet if this were the cause, we'd see a bewildering blur of superimposed stills instead of smooth action. At present, researchers believe that two psychological processes are involved in cinematic motion: critical flicker fusion and apparent motion.

If you flash a light faster and faster, at a certain point (around 50 flashes per second), you see not a pulsating light but a continuous beam. A film is usually shot and projected at 24 still frames per second. The projector shutter breaks the light beam once as a new image is slid into place and once while it is held in place. Thus each

1.11

1.12

1.11–1.12 Early moving-image gadgets. The Zoetrope, which dates back to 1834, spun its images on a strip of paper in a rotating drum (1.11). The Mutoscope, an early-20th-century entertainment, displayed images by flipping a row of cards in front of a peephole (1.12).

frame is actually projected on the screen twice. This raises the number of flashes to 48, the threshold of what is called *critical flicker fusion.* Early silent films were shot at a lower rate (often 16 or 20 images per second), and projectors broke the beam only once per image. The picture had a pronounced flicker—hence an early slang term for movies, "flickers," which survives today when people call a film a "flick."

Apparent motion is a second factor in creating cinema's illusion. If a visual display is changed rapidly enough, our eye can be fooled into seeing movement. Neon advertising signs often seem to show a thrusting arrow, but that illusion is created simply by static lights flashing on and off at a particular rate. Certain cells in our eyes and brain are devoted to analyzing motion, brightness, and edges. Any stimulus presenting changes in those features tricks those cells into sending the wrong message.

Apparent motion and critical flicker fusion are quirks in our visual system, and technology can exploit those quirks to produce illusions. Some moving-image machines predate the invention of film **(1.11, 1.12).** Film as we know it came into being when photographic images were first imprinted on strips of flexible celluloid.

Making Films with Photographic Film

Until the 2000s, cinema was almost entirely a photochemical medium. Most of the movies we use as examples in this book were shot on photographic film, as were nearly all the films that you watch on DVD or streaming. Although digital production has become common, some directors and cinematographers still prefer photochemical media. So we'll look first at motion pictures shot on film.

Physically, a photographically based film is a ribbon of still images, each one slightly different from its mates. That ribbon starts life as unexposed film stock in a camera. Eventually the finished movie is another strip of film run through a projector. Both the camera and the projector move the film strip one frame at a time past a light source. For a fraction of a second, the image is held in place before the next one replaces it. In a camera, the lens gathers light from the scene photographed, while a projector uses a light source to cast the images on the screen. In a sense, the projector is just an inverted camera **(1.13, 1.14).**

In filming, the most common shooting rate is 24 frames per second (fps), and in projection the same rate is usually maintained. In the 35mm format, the film whizzes through the projector at 90 feet per minute, meaning that a two-hour feature will consist of about two miles of film.

The film strip that emerges from the camera is usually a *negative.* That is, its colors and light values are the opposite of those in the original scene. For the images to be projected, a *positive* print must be made. This is done on another machine, the *printer,* which duplicates or modifies the footage from the camera. Like a projector, the printer controls the passage of light through film—in this case, a negative. Like a camera, it focuses light to form an image—in this case, on the unexposed roll of film. Although the filmmaker can create nonphotographic images on the film strip by drawing, painting, or scratching, most filmmakers in the predigital era have relied on the camera, the printer, and other photographic technology.

If you were to handle the film that runs through these machines, you'd notice several things. One side is much shinier than the other. Motion picture film consists of a transparent plastic *base* (the shiny side), which supports an *emulsion,* layers of gelatin containing light-sensitive materials. On a black-and-white film strip, the emulsion contains grains of silver halide. Color film emulsion adds layers of chemical dyes that react with the silver halide components. In both cases, billions of microscopic particles form clusters of light, dark, and color corresponding to the scene photographed.

What enables film to run through a camera, a printer, and a projector? The strip is perforated along both edges, so that small teeth (called *sprockets*) in the machines can seize the perforations (sprocket holes) and pull the film at a uniform rate and smoothness. The strip also reserves space for a sound track.

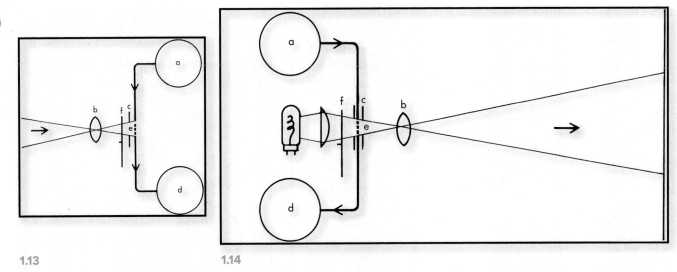

1.13–1.14 Moving the film: Camera and projector. In a light-tight chamber (1.13), a drive mechanism feeds the unexposed motion picture film from a reel (a) past a lens (b) and aperture (c) to a take-up reel (d). The lens focuses light reflected from a scene onto each frame of film (e). The mechanism moves the film intermittently, with a brief pause while each frame is held in the aperture. A shutter (f) admits light through the lens only when each frame is unmoving and ready for exposure. The projector is basically an inverted camera, with the light source inside the machine rather than in the world outside (1.14). A drive mechanism feeds the film from a reel (a) past a lens (b) and aperture (c) to a take-up reel (d). Light is beamed through the images (e) and magnified by the lens for projection on a screen. Again, a mechanism moves the film intermittently past the aperture, while a shutter (f) admits light only when each frame is pausing.

The size and placement of the perforations and the area occupied by the sound track have been standardized around the world. So, too, has the width of the film strip, which is called the *gauge* and is measured in millimeters. For most of cinema history, commercial theaters used 35mm film, but other gauges also have been standardized internationally: Super 8mm, 16mm, and 70mm **(1.15–1.19).**

Usually image quality increases with the width of the film because the greater picture area gives the images better definition and detail. All other things being equal, 35mm provides significantly better picture quality than 16mm, and 70mm is superior to both. The finest photographic quality currently available for public screenings is that offered by the Imax system **(1.20).**

With the rise of digital filmmaking, 16mm has declined as an amateur gauge. If you take an introductory production course, you are more likely to shoot with a digital camera than a 16mm one. Yet a higher-quality version of the gauge, Super 16mm, still gets used in commercial films seeking to economize or to achieve a "documentary look." Recent films utilizing Super 16mm include *The Wrestler, The Hurt Locker, Black Swan,* and *Moonrise Kingdom.* The comedy *The World's End* combined 35mm and regular 16mm. Super 8 film is still occasionally used in professional production, usually to simulate home movies or television images; *Super 8* used both Super 16 and Super 8 to present the amateur footage shot by its young protagonists. Imax and other cameras employing 65mm film have been used for fiction films, including some scenes in *The Dark Knight, Inception, Mission Impossible: Ghost Protocol, Gravity,* and *Interstellar.*

The sound track runs along the side of the film strip. Magnetic tracks, consisting of magnetic tape running along the film strip (1.19), have virtually vanished. Most films today have an optical sound track, which encodes sonic information in the form of patches of light and dark running along the frames. During production, electrical impulses from a microphone are translated into pulsations of light, which are photographically inscribed on the moving film strip. When the film is projected, the optical track produces varying intensities of light that are translated back into electrical impulses and then into sound waves. The optical sound track of 16mm

1.15 Super 8mm   **1.16** 16mm   **1.17** 35mm   **1.18** 35mm   **1.19** 70mm

1.15–1.19 Film gauges. Super 8mm (1.15) has been a popular gauge for amateurs and experimental filmmakers. *Year of the Horse*, a concert film featuring Neil Young, was shot partly on Super 8. 16mm film (1.16) has been used for both amateur and professional film work. A variable-area optical sound track (p. 13) runs down the right side. 35mm film (1.17) is the standard theatrical film gauge. In this sample a variable-area sound track runs down the side of the strip. A 35mm strip from *Jurassic Park* (1.18) shows an optical (analog) stereophonic sound track (p. 13) on the left of the images, encoded as two parallel squiggles. The Morse code–like dots between the stereophonic track and the picture area are a timecode to sync the film with DTS files on a CD-ROM. 70mm film (1.19), another theatrical gauge, was used for historical spectacles and epic action films into the 1990s. In this strip from *The Hunt for Red October,* a stereophonic magnetic sound track runs along both edges of the film strip and between the edges of the picture and the sprocket holes, allowing for six discrete channels of sound.

1.20 **Imax film.** The Imax image is printed on 70mm film but runs horizontally along the strip, allowing each image to be 10 times larger than 35mm and triple the size of 70mm. The Imax film can be projected on a very large screen with no loss of detail.

film is on the right side (1.16), whereas 35mm puts an optical track on the left (1.17, 1.18). In each, the sound is usually encoded as *variable area,* a wavy contour of black and white along the picture strip.

A film's sound track may be *monophonic* or *stereophonic.* The 16mm film strip (1.16) and the first 35mm film strip (1.17) have monophonic optical tracks. Stereophonic optical sound is registered as a pair of squiggles running down the left side (1.18). For digital sound, a string of dots and dashes running along the film's perforations, or between the perforations, or close to the very left edge of the frames provides the sound-track information. The projector scans these marks as if reading a bar code.

Filmmaking with Digital Media

Digital information technology gave filmmakers a set of new tools. Computers first came into use in editing and in special-effects processes, and eventually digital shooting and projection became feasible. The term "digital film" may seem contradictory, but almost immediately everyone understood it. Just as audio books and e-books were still called books, digital films counted as films, even though they never involved light hitting celluloid. Some people prefer to speak of "digital capture" rather than "digital filming," but most call digital image-creators "filmmakers." So will we.

Digital Filming To some extent a professional digital motion picture camera functions in the same way as the 35mm camera. The camera operator uses a viewfinder to frame a scene. There are controls to manipulate exposure and the speed of recording. At the front, a lens gathers and focuses light reflected from the scene. A shutterlike mechanism breaks the input into frames, usually 24 per second. A professional digital camera also looks very much like a traditional 35mm camera **(1.21).** The design reflects manufacturers' effort to make the new device feel familiar to cinematographers. Some digital cameras can accept lenses designated for 35mm machines.

Instead of a strip of film whizzing through a gate behind the lens, the digital camera has a fixed sensor. The sensor is covered with a grid of millions of microscopic diodes, or photosites. Each of these diodes measures a tiny portion of the light. The diodes create pixels (short for "picture elements") in the final image. The sensor converts these

1.21 **Digital motion picture camera.** An operator with an Arri Alexa, one of the most widely used professional digital cameras, mounted on a Steadicam support. The operator watches the image being filmed on a monitor rather than through a viewfinder. The back of the camera and the bottom of the Steadicam have batteries attached, and the attachment at the middle right is a gimbal to stabilize the camera as the operator moves.

1.22 Combining digital video and film. In *julien donkey-boy*, pixels and grain yield a unique texture, and the high contrast exaggerates pure colors and shapes to create a hallucinatory image.

patterns of light into electrical impulses that are sent to a recording medium and registered as files of ones and zeroes. A similar process of sampling and digital conversion occurs while recording sound.

A frame of photographic film holds billions of specks carrying visual information. But pixels are much larger than photographic molecules, so making digital imagery as finely detailed as 35mm is a challenge. Digital image quality depends on several factors, including the size of the sensor, the number of pixels, and the type of compression applied to the files. As a result, several formats of digital image recording emerged. The first wave in the 1990s utilized the format known as digital video (DV). The images were quite low resolution (about 350,000 pixels), but lit by an experienced cinematographer they could be attractive, as in Spike Lee's *Bamboozled,* shot by Ellen Kuras. Some filmmakers played up the pebbly textures of DV imagery. *Dancer in the Dark* uses saturated DV imagery to suggest the fantasy world of a young mother going blind, while *28 Days Later* fitted the rough-edged format to a horror film. Harmony Korine shot *julien donkey-boy* with mini-DV consumer cameras, transferred the footage to film, and reprinted it several times **(1.22).**

As digital photography improved in the 2000s, *high-definition (HD) video* emerged as a preferred choice for digital filmmaking, amateur or professional. Today HD video usually refers to digital formats of 720p and 1080p. The numbers refer to the number of horizontal lines in the display, and "p" stands for progressive scan, which refreshes each frame in the manner of a computer monitor; 720p images contain about 921,000 pixels, and 1080p images have nearly 2.1 million.

Further innovations have led to images that are sharper, more detailed, and freer of artifacts. The newer formats, often known as "digital cinema," were standardized at 2K (usually rated at 2,048 pixels across, or about 3.2 million pixels in all) and 4K (4,096 pixels across, or over 12.7 million pixels). The rectangles in Figure **1.23** represent the numbered pixels in each of these formats. The images as projected on

1.23 Pixel size of sensors in four standard digital formats. The lowest resolution digital moving image system in common use, 720p, contains 1,280 (width) by 720 (height) pixels, yielding 0.92 megapixels. (A megapixel is 1 million pixels.) 720p is used primarily for U.S. broadcast and cable television and for Internet video. The next step up is 1080 HD, with either progressive or interlaced scanning. HD commonly measures 1,920 by 1,080 pixels, for a total of 2.1 megapixels. The 2K format typically supports 1,998 by 1,080 pixels, yielding 2.2 megapixels. A typical 4K image measures 4,096 by 2,160 pixels, yielding 8.8 megapixels.

a screen would all be the same size, but the density of visual information increases proportionately with the number of pixels. Since the information carried on each image increases both vertically and horizontally, each step up multiplies the resolution: 4K carries not twice but four times the amount of information in 2K. Each format can produce images in different proportions, or aspect ratios, and these make the pixel count vary somewhat. (More on aspect ratios in Chapter 5.) Sensors come formatted for these various image sizes.

The moving images are stored on memory cards, large versions of the sort of card used in digital still photography. For more space and longer recording capacity, filmmakers turn to hard drives **(1.24).** When the images are downloaded and backed up, the capture medium is wiped clean for reuse. The great advantage of this system is that digital media cost much less than raw film stock, an expensive component of a traditional film's budget. The downside is that such huge amounts of data require a lot of storage space. A finished feature film may consist of 10 to 12 terabytes (TB) of data, and the amount shot may consume 350 TB. For this reason, digital imagery is subjected to many compression and decompression processes from production through to final projection. A feature film projected at your local multiplex probably takes up no more than 100 to 350 gigabytes (GB) on the hard drive file that is fed to the projector.

In the late 1990s, George Lucas commissioned Sony to make a high-quality digital camera, which he utilized on *Star Wars: Episode II—Attack of the Clones* (2002). It used the 1080p format. Michael Mann's digital camera on *Collateral* also delivered 2K-resolution images. More and more big-budget directors embraced HD digital formats, particularly for their price and convenience. Lucas claimed that apart from creating spectacular special effects, using HD for *Attack of the Clones* and *Revenge of the Sith* saved millions of dollars. A comparable system was employed on *Sin City,* which combined HD footage of the actors with graphic landscapes created in postproduction. Basing the entire project on digital technology allowed director Robert Rodriguez to edit, mix sound, and create special effects in his home studio in Austin, Texas.

Shooting in the 2K format quickly became widespread. In 2009, a few films, including *District 9, Che,* and *Knowing,* used 4K systems. Many have claimed that

1.24 Two types of hard-drive recording media. A recorder containing a high-capacity hard drive or "RAID unit" may be attached directly to the camera. Smaller hard drives, like the unit sitting by the camera, can be loaded into the machine. Both types may be used in combination to increase recording time.

4K images are the equal in visual quality to those of 35mm, and the format has become increasingly popular. Prestigious films such as David Fincher's *Zodiac* and *The Social Network* showed that high-resolution capture could in many respects rival 35mm film while harboring its own artistic possibilities. Fincher continued to push digital filmmaking in 2014, when *Gone Girl* became the first commercial feature to be shot in 6K. This larger format is 6,144 by 3,160 pixels in size, yielding 2.2 times as many pixels as 4K.

Most professional cameras have two big advantages over lower-cost models. They employ minimal data compression, and they tend to have larger sensors, ones about the same size as a frame of 35mm film. Both factors make for higher image quality. But consumer and "prosumer" cameras have also found roles in professional production. Filmmakers working on low budgets have discovered that not only dedicated video cameras but digital single-lens reflex still cameras (DSLRs) can yield high-quality video imagery. Stop-motion films made with puppets or clay figures often use DSLRs rather than exposing single frames with motion picture cameras. Even some cellphone cameras have the capacity for 1080p recording. Park Chan-wook, the Korean director of *Oldboy,* shot a prize-winning short film on his iPhone. These paraprofessional tools have proved particularly valuable for documentary filmmakers, who need to shoot hours of footage cheaply.

Digital Projection For some years, films shot on digital video were transferred to photographic film and sent to theaters as 35mm prints. After rather slow growth, digital projection exploded in 2010–2011 and by 2013 had almost entirely replaced 35mm projection in most commercial venues around the world.

Digital theatrical projection is usually in either the 2K or 4K format. The most common projection hardware employs microscopic mirrors and is manufactured in various designs by several companies. Running speeds are standardized at 24 fps and 48 fps. The film is encoded as a Digital Cinema Package (DCP), a set of files containing images, sound, subtitles, and other information. The DCP, delivered on a hard drive and heavily encrypted, provides a compressed version of the film **(1.25).** The DCP loads into a server that feeds one or more projectors in a theater complex **(1.26).**

CONNECT TO THE BLOG
www.davidbordwell.net/blog

We survey the development of digital projection in our series "Pandora's digital box."

1.25

1.26

1.25–1.26 Digital theatrical projection. Films are shipped to theaters on hard drives (1.25). Figure 1.26 shows a Sony digital projection system. The projector is run from a server that stores films and trailer files loaded from the Digital Cinema Package. The touch-screen monitor on the left allows the operator to control the screening through a playlist. The dual lenses on the upper right are used for 3D screenings.

The new filmmaking and projection technology was given a boost by the resurgence of 3D films in the mid-2000s. Digital filming proved more reliable and efficient for stereoscopic movies, which were almost always projected digitally. (Imax retained some theaters that projected 3D on two strips of 70mm film.) James Cameron's colossal hit *Avatar* served as a showcase not just for 3D but for digital filmmaking in general.

Whether shooting on film or on video, the filmmaker faces comparable artistic choices. Now that we have a sense of the technical tools available, we can turn to the ways filmmakers work with them.

Making the Movie: Film Production

Important as technology is, films are part of social institutions as well. Sometimes the social context is intimate, as when a family records their lives to show friends and relations. But films that aim at the public enter a wider range of institutions.

A movie typically goes through three phases: *production, distribution,* and *exhibition.* An individual, group, or company makes the film. A distribution company rents copies to theater chains, and theaters exhibit the film. Later, DVD and Blu-ray versions are distributed to chain stores or rental shops; and the movie is then exhibited on TV monitors, computer screens, or portable displays. For video on demand, streaming, and websites such as YouTube, the Internet serves as both a distribution and an exhibition medium.

The whole system depends on having movies to circulate, so let's start by considering the process of production. Most films go through four distinct phases:

1. *Scriptwriting and funding.* The idea for the film is developed and a screenplay is written. The filmmakers also acquire financial support for the project.

2. *Preparation for filming.* Once a script is more or less complete and at least some funding is assured, the filmmakers plan the physical production.

3. *Shooting.* The filmmakers create the film's images and sounds.

4. *Assembly.* The images and sounds are combined in their final form. This involves cutting picture and sound, executing special effects, inserting music or extra dialogue, and adding titles.

The phases can overlap. Filmmakers may be scrambling for funding while shooting and assembling the film, and some assembly is usually taking place during filming. In addition, each stage modifies what went before. The idea for the film may be radically altered when the script is hammered out; the script's presentation of the action may be drastically changed in shooting; and the material that is shot takes on new significance in the process of assembly. As the French director Robert Bresson puts it: "A film is born in my head and I kill it on paper. It is brought back to life by the actors and then killed in the camera. It is then resurrected into a third and final life in the editing room where the dismembered pieces are assembled into their finished form."

These four phases include many particular jobs. Most theatrical releases result from dozens of specialized tasks carried out by hundreds of experts. This fine-grained division of labor has proved a reliable way to prepare, shoot, and assemble large-budget movies. On smaller productions, individuals perform several roles. A director might also edit the film, or the principal sound recordist on the set might also oversee the sound mixing. For *Tarnation,* a memoir of growing up in a troubled family, Jonathan Caouette assembled 19 years worth of photographs, audiotape, home movies, and videotape. Some of the footage was filmed by his parents, and some by him as a boy. Caouette shot new scenes, edited everything on iMovie, mixed the sound, and transferred the result to digital video. In making this personal documentary, Caouette executed virtually all the phases of film production himself.

> " We don't shy away from all-digital filmmakers. We just happen to really, really love film. With artists who are passionate about image making, you don't hear, 'I want to make film look like digital!' You hear, 'I want digital to look like film.'"
>
> —Paul Korver, head of the Cinelicious postproduction company, Hollywood

CONNECT TO THE BLOG
www.davidbordwell.net/blog

The study of the film industry as a business was a major research focus at our university, the University of Wisconsin–Madison. We look back at the innovative work of our colleagues in "Industrial Strength."

CONNECT TO THE BLOG
www.davidbordwell.net/blog

We discuss one producer who exerted an exceptional degree of control over his projects (*Gone with the Wind, Rebecca, Duel in the Sun*) in "A Dose of DOS: Trade secrets from David O. Selznick."

> 66 A screenplay bears somewhat the same relationship to a movie as the musical score does to a symphonic performance. There are people who can read a musical score and 'hear' the symphony—but no two directors will see the same images when they read a movie script. The two-dimensional patterns of colored light involved are far more complex than the one-dimensional thread of sound."
>
> —Arthur C. Clarke, co-screenwriter, *2001: A Space Odyssey*

CONNECT TO THE BLOG
www.davidbordwell.net/blog

We consider the art of the screenwriter in two entries: "JCC" and "Scriptography." Other entries consider major screenwriter-directors: David Koepp (*Jurassic Park, Premium Rush*) in "David Koepp: Making the world movie-sized," and Alexander Payne (*Sideways, Nebraska*) in "Alexander Payne's vividly shot reality."

The Scriptwriting and Funding Phase

Two roles are central in this phase: producer and screenwriter. The tasks of the *producer* are chiefly financial and organizational. This person may be an "independent" producer, unearthing film projects and trying to convince production companies or distributors to finance the film. Or the producer may work for a distribution company and generate ideas for films. A studio may also hire a producer to put together a particular package.

The producer nurses the project through the scriptwriting process, obtains financial support, and arranges to hire the personnel who will work on the film. During shooting and assembly, the producer usually acts as the liaison between the writer or director and the company that is financing the film. After the film is completed, the producer often has the task of arranging the distribution, promotion, and marketing of the film. The producer is usually responsible as well for paying back the money invested in the production.

A single producer may take on all these tasks, but in the contemporary American film industry, the producer's work is further subdivided. The *executive producer* is often the person who arranges the financing for the project or obtains the literary rights. Once the production is underway, the *line producer* oversees the day-to-day activities of director, cast, and crew. The line producer is assisted by an *associate producer,* who acts as a liaison with laboratories or technical personnel.

The chief task of the *screenwriter* is to prepare the *screenplay* (or script). Sometimes the writer will compose an original screenplay and send it to an agent, who submits it to a production company. Or an experienced screenwriter meets with a producer in a "pitch session," where the writer can propose ideas for scripts. The first scene of Robert Altman's *The Player* mocks pitch sessions by showing screenwriters proposing strained ideas like "*Pretty Woman* meets *Out of Africa.*" Alternatively, the producer may have an idea and hire a screenwriter to develop it. This approach is common if the producer has bought the rights to a novel or play and wants to adapt it for the screen. Since 2004, a service called "The Black List" has featured promising scripts by both new and experienced writers. These have been voted as favorites by industry professionals and offered for perusal by potential financial backers. Of the 970 scripts chosen during the List's first decade, 270 were produced, of which nearly 200 received Oscar nominations and wins. Titles included *Little Miss Sunshine, Inglourious Basterds,* and *Nebraska.* Thanks to the Internet, the Black List allows talented writers to bring their work to potential producers.

The screenplay usually goes through several stages. These include a *treatment,* a synopsis of the action; then one or more full-length scripts; and a final version, the *shooting script.* Extensive rewriting is common, and writers often must revise their work several times.

If the producer or director finds one writer's screenplay unsatisfactory, other writers may be hired to revise it. Most Hollywood screenwriters earn their living by rewriting other writers' scripts. As you can imagine, this often leads to conflicts about which writer or writers deserve onscreen credit for the film. In the American film industry, these disputes are adjudicated by the Screen Writers' Guild.

Shooting scripts are constantly changed, too. Some directors allow actors to modify the dialogue, and problems on location or on a set may necessitate changes in the scene. In the assembly stage, script scenes that have been shot are often condensed, rearranged, or dropped entirely.

As the screenplay is being prepared, the producer is planning the film's finances. This person has sought out a director and stars to make the package seem a promising investment. The producer must prepare a budget spelling out *above-the-line costs* (the costs of literary property, scriptwriter, director, and major cast) and *below-the-line costs* (the expenses allotted to the crew, secondary cast, the shooting and assembly phases, insurance, and publicity). The sum of above- and below-the-line costs is called the *negative cost* (that is, the total cost of producing the film's master negative).

Some films don't follow a full-blown screenplay. Documentaries, for instance, are difficult to script fully in advance. In order to get funding, however, the projects typically require a summary or an outline, and some documentarists prefer to have a written plan even if they recognize that the film will evolve in the course of production. When compiling a documentary from existing footage, the filmmakers often write the final voice-over commentary after assembling most of the sequences.

The Preparation Phase

When funding is more or less secure and the script is solid enough to start filming, the filmmakers can prepare for the physical production. In commercial filmmaking, this stage of activity is called **preproduction.** The *director,* who may have come on board the project at an earlier point, plays a central role in this and later phases. The director coordinates the staff to create the film. Although the director's authority isn't absolute, he or she is usually considered the person most responsible for the final look and sound of the film.

At this point, the producer and the director hire crew and cast the roles, and scout locations for filming. They also prepare a daily schedule for shooting. This is done with an eye on the budget. The producer assumes that the separate shots will be made "out of continuity"—that is, in the most convenient order for production—and put in proper order in the editing room. Since transporting equipment and personnel to a location is a major expense, producers usually prefer to shoot all the scenes taking place in one location at one time. For *Jurassic Park,* the main characters' arrival on the island and their departure at the end of the film were both shot at the start of production, during the three weeks on location in Hawaii. A producer must also plan to shoot around actors who can't be on the set every day. Many producers try to schedule the most difficult scenes early, before cast and crew begin to tire. The complex prizefight sequences of *Raging Bull* were filmed first, with the dialogue scenes shot later. Keeping all such contingencies in mind, the producer comes up with a schedule that juggles cast, crew, locations, and even seasons most efficiently.

During preproduction, several things are happening at the same time under the supervision of the director and producer. A writer may be revising the screenplay while a casting supervisor is searching out actors. In large-scale production, the director orchestrates the contributions of specialists in several units. He or she works with the *set unit,* or *production design unit,* headed by a *production designer.* The production designer is in charge of visualizing the film's settings. This unit creates drawings and plans that determine the architecture and the color schemes of the sets. Under the production designer's supervision, an *art director* oversees the construction and painting of the sets. The *set decorator,* often someone with experience in interior decoration, modifies the sets for specific filming purposes, supervising workers who find props and a *set dresser* who arranges things on the set during shooting. The *costume designer* is in charge of planning and executing the wardrobe for the production.

Working with the production designer, a *graphic artist* may be assigned to produce a **storyboard,** a series of comic strip–like sketches of the shots in each scene, including notations about costume, lighting, and camera work **(1.27).** Most directors do not demand a storyboard for every scene, but action sequences and shots using special effects or complicated camera work tend to be storyboarded in detail. The storyboard gives the cinematography unit and the special-effects unit a preliminary sense of what the finished shots should look like. The storyboard images may be filmed, cut together, and played with sound to help visualize the scene. This is one form of *animatics.*

Computer graphics can take planning further. The process of *previsualization,* or "previs," reworks the storyboards into three-dimensional animation, complete

66 Many, many novelists fail when they try to become screenwriters because they really believe writing for film is writing. It's not. Writing for a film is filming."
—Jean-Claude Carrière, screenwriter

1.28

1.27–1.28 Planning the movie visually. A page from the storyboard for Hitchcock's *The Birds* (1.27). Simple computer-animated previsualization from *Pacific Rim* (1.28).

with moving figures, dialogue, sound effects, and music. Contemporary software can create settings and characters reasonably close to what will be filmed, and textures and shading can be added. Previsualization animatics are most often used to plan complicated action scenes or special effects **(1.28),** but they can also help the director to test options for staging scenes, moving cameras, and timing sequences. A substantial previs, complete with a temporary sound track, was made for *The Last Airbender.* Cinematographer Andrew Lesnie suggests how widely it was used from preplanning to postproduction: "It proved invaluable to the visual-effect, special-effects, stunt, lighting, production and art departments, and made the whole production a lot more cost efficient."

Sometimes storyboards or short previs films are made before the preproduction begins, to find financial backing. Director Angelina Jolie created homemade storyboards for *Unbroken* and successfully used them to pitch the film to Universal.

The Shooting Phase

Although the term "production" refers to the entire process of making a film, Hollywood filmmakers also use it to refer to the *shooting phase.* Shooting is also known as *principal photography.*

Units and Personnel   During shooting, the director supervises what is called the *director's crew,* consisting of these personnel:

- The *script supervisor,* known in the classic studio era as a "script girl." (Today one-fifth of Hollywood script supervisors are male.) The script supervisor is in charge of all details of *continuity* from shot to shot. The supervisor checks details of performers' appearances (in the last scene, was the character's coat buttoned or not), props, lighting, movement, camera position, and the running time of each shot.

- The *first assistant director (AD),* a jack-of-all-trades who, with the director, plans each day's shooting schedule. The AD sets up each shot for the director's approval while keeping track of the actors, monitoring safety conditions, and keeping the energy level high.

❝ If you wander unbidden onto a set, you'll always know the AD because he or she is the one who'll probably throw you off. That's the AD yelling, 'Places!' 'Quiet on the set!' 'Lunch—one-half hour!' and 'That's a wrap, people!' It's all very ritualistic, like reveille and taps on a military base, at once grating and oddly comforting."

—Christine Vachon, independent producer, on assistant directors

- The *second assistant director,* who is the liaison among the first AD, the camera crew, and the electricians' crew.

- The *third assistant director,* who serves as messenger for director and staff.

- The *dialogue coach,* who feeds performers their lines and speaks the lines of offscreen characters during shots of other performers.

- The *second unit director,* who films stunts, location footage, action scenes, and the like at a distance from where principal shooting is taking place.

The most visible group of workers is the *cast.* The cast may include *stars*—well-known players assigned to major roles and likely to attract audiences. The cast also includes *supporting players,* or performers in secondary roles; *minor players;* and *extras,* those anonymous persons who pass by in the street and occupy distant desks in large office sets. One of the director's major jobs is to elicit performances from the cast. The first AD usually works with the extras and takes charge of arranging crowd scenes.

On some productions, there are still more specialized roles. *Stunt artists* are supervised by a *stunt coordinator;* professional dancers work with a *choreographer.* If animals join the cast, they are handled by a *wrangler.* There have been pig wranglers (*Mad Max Beyond Thunder Dome*), snake wranglers (*Raiders of the Lost Ark*), and spider wranglers (*Arachnophobia*).

Another unit of specialized labor is the *photography unit.* The leader is the *cinematographer,* also known as the *director of photography* (or *DP*). The cinematographer is an expert on photographic processes, lighting, and camera technique. We have already seen how important Michael Mann's two DPs, Dion Beebe and Paul Cameron, were in achieving the desired look for *Collateral* (pp. 5–6). The cinematographer consults with the director on how each scene will be lit and filmed **(1.29).** The cinematographer supervises these workers:

- The *camera operator,* who runs the machine and who may also have assistants to load the camera, adjust and follow focus, push a dolly, and so on.

1.29 Shooting phase of production. On the set of *Citizen Kane*, Orson Welles directs from his wheelchair on the far right, cinematographer Gregg Toland crouches below the camera, and actress Dorothy Comingore kneels at the left. The script supervisor is seated in the left background.

- The *key grip,* who supervises the *grips.* These workers carry and arrange equipment, props, and elements of the setting and lighting.
- The *gaffer,* the head electrician who supervises the placement and rigging of the lights.

Parallel to the photography unit is the *sound unit.* This is headed by the *production recordist* (also called the *sound mixer*). The recordist's principal responsibility is to record dialogue during shooting. Typically, the recordist uses a tape or digital recorder, several sorts of microphones, and a console to balance and combine the inputs. The recordist also tries to capture some ambient sound when no actors are speaking. These bits of room tone are later inserted to fill pauses in the dialogue. The recordist's staff includes:

- The *boom operator,* who manipulates the boom microphone and conceals radio microphones on the actors.
- The *third man,* who places other microphones, lays sound cables and is in charge of controlling ambient sound.

Some productions also have a *sound designer,* who enters the process during the preparation phase and who plans a sonic style appropriate for the entire film.

A *visual-effects unit,* overseen by the *visual-effects supervisor,* is charged with preparing and executing process shots, miniatures, matte work, computer-generated graphics, and other technical shots **(1.30).** During the planning phase, the director and the production designer have determined what effects are needed, and the supervisor consults with the director and the cinematographer on an ongoing basis. The visual-effects unit can number hundreds of workers, from puppet- and model-makers to specialists in digital compositing. On effects-heavy films, work is usually turned over to specialist firms.

A miscellaneous unit includes a *makeup staff,* a *costume staff, hairdressers,* and *drivers,* who transport cast and crew. During shooting, the producer is represented by a unit called the *producer's crew.* Central here is the *line producer,* who manages daily organizational business, such as arranging for meals and accommodations. A *production accountant* (or *production auditor*) monitors expenditures, a *production secretary* coordinates telephone communications among units and with the producer, and *production assistants* (or *PAs*) run errands. Newcomers to the film industry often start out working as production assistants.

1.30 Creating special effects. Sculpting a model dinosaur for *The Lost World: Jurassic Park.* The model was scanned into a computer for digital manipulation.

Scenes and Takes All this coordinated effort results in many hours of footage and recorded sound. For each shot called for in the script or storyboard, the director usually does several *takes,* or versions. For instance, if the finished film requires one shot of an actor saying a line, the director may do several takes of that speech, each time asking the actor to vary the delivery. Only one take, or even one part of the take, becomes the shot included in the finished film. Left-over footage can be used in coming-attractions trailers and electronic press kits.

Because scenes seldom are filmed in plot order, the director and the crew must have some way of labeling each take. As soon as the camera starts, one of the cinematographer's staff holds up a *clapperboard* before the lens. On the clapperboard are written the production, scene, shot, and take. A hinged arm at the top, the clapboard, makes a sharp clack that allows the recordist to synchronize the sound track with the footage in the assembly phase **(1.31).** Thus every take is identified for future reference.

In filming a scene, most directors and technicians follow an organized procedure. While crews set up the lighting and test the sound recording, the director rehearses the actors and instructs the cinematographer. The director then usually supervises the filming of a *master shot.* The master shot typically records the entire action and dialogue of the scene. There may be several takes of the master shot. Then portions of the scene are restaged and shot in closer views or from different angles. These shots are called *coverage,* and each one may require many takes. Today most directors shoot a great deal of coverage. The script supervisor checks to ensure that details are consistent within all these shots.

For most of film history, scenes were shot with a single camera, which was moved to different points for different setups. More recently, under pressure to finish principal photography as quickly as possible, the director and the camera unit often use two or more cameras, even for routine coverage. Action scenes like the taxi smashup in *Collateral* are usually shot from several angles simultaneously, because chases, crashes, and explosions are difficult to repeat for retakes. The battle scenes in *Gladiator* were filmed by 7 cameras, while 13 cameras were used for stunts in *XXX.*

For dialogue scenes, a common tactic is to film with an A camera and a B camera, an arrangement that can capture two actors in alternating shots. Still, some directors prefer the single-camera method. The camera assistant on Quentin Tarantino's *Inglourious Basterds* sums up the artistic advantages: "You get such a hand-crafted movie. The actors know they're going to do a lot of setups because it's only one camera, but they get to perfect their craft. The camera rolls for as many takes as necessary to perfect each shot."

When special effects are to be included, the shooting phase must carefully plan for them. In many cases, actors will be filmed against blue or green backgrounds so that their figures can be inserted into computer-created settings. Or the director may film performers with the understanding that other material will be composited into the frame **(1.32).** If a moving person or animal needs to be created by computer, a specialized unit will use *motion capture.* Here small sensors are attached all over the body of the subject, and as that subject moves against a blank background or a set,

1.31 Labeling takes. A clapperboard on a set of *Argo* features an electronic time readout and an erasable acrylic board for information on the scene, camera roll, and take. The title and the names of the director and cinematographer have been permanently printed on the board, with the date applied with tape at the bottom.

1.32 **Combining actors and special effects.** For the climax of *Jurassic Park,* the actors were shot in the set of the visitor's center, but the velociraptors and the *Tyrannosaurus rex* were computer-generated images added later.

1.33

1.34

1.33–1.34 Motion capture. For *Iron Man,* Robert Downey Jr. performed in a motion-capture suit covered with sensors (1.33). The same scene with a computer-animated suit partially added (1.34).

a special camera records the movement **(1.33, 1.34).** Each sensor provides a point in a wire-frame figure on a computer. That image can then be animated and built up to a completely rendered person or animal to be inserted digitally into the film.

The Assembly Phase

Filmmakers call the assembly phase **postproduction.** Yet this phase doesn't begin after the shooting is finished. Typically, postproduction staff members work behind the scenes throughout shooting. Since the advent of digital postproduction tools, many filmmakers prefer to start editing, sound mixing, special effects, and other important tasks immediately after the first footage is shot.

Picture Editing Before the shooting begins, the director or producer probably hires an *editor* (also known as the *supervising editor*). This person catalogues and assembles the takes produced during shooting. The editor also works with the director to make creative decisions about how the footage can best be cut together.

A CLOSER LOOK

Some Terms and Roles in Film Production

The rise of packaged productions, the use of freelance workers, and other factors have led producers to credit everyone who worked on a film. Meanwhile, the specialization of large-scale filmmaking has created its own jargon. We have explained some of the most colorful terms in the text. Here are some other terms that you may see in a film's credits.

ACE: After the name of the editor; abbreviation for the American Cinema Editors, a professional association.

ASC: After the name of the director of photography; abbreviation for the American Society of Cinematographers, a professional association. The British equivalent is the BSC.

Additional photography: Crew shooting footage apart from the *principal photography,* typically supervised by the director of photography.

Best boy: Term from the classic studio years, originally applied to the gaffer's assistant. Today film credits may list both a *best boy electric* and a *best boy grip,* the assistant to the key grip.

Casting director: Member who searches for and auditions performers for the film, and suggests actors for *leading roles* (principal characters) and *character parts* (fairly standardized or stereotyped roles). She or he may also cast *extras* (background or nonspeaking roles).

Clapper boy: Crew member who operates the clapboard that identifies each take.

Concept artist: Designer who creates illustrations of the settings and costumes that the director has in mind for the film.

Dialogue editor: Sound editor specializing in making sure recorded speech is audible.

Digital colorist: In postproduction, the colorist works on a digital copy of the film, manipulating the color, light levels, and other pictorial aspects. The colorist creates a consistent look for all the shots in a scene, corrects mistakes made in shooting, and makes shots more visually appealing.

Digital imaging technician: A specialist who advises on the choice of camera and other digital equipment, calibrates monitors during shooting, downloads and checks image files, and ensures that the postproduction workflow proceeds smoothly.

Dolly grip: Crew member who pushes the dolly that carries the camera, either from one setup to another or during a take for moving camera shots.

Foley artist: Sound-effects specialist who creates sounds of movement by walking or by shifting materials across large trays of different substances (sand, earth, glass, for example). Named for Jack Foley, a pioneer in postproduction sound.

Greenery man: Crew member who chooses and maintains trees, shrubs, and grass in settings.

Lead man: Member of set crew responsible for tracking down various props and items of decor.

Loader: On a production using film, this person inserts and unloads the camera magazines, keeps a log of shots taken, labels the cans of film, and sends them to the laboratory. A digital loader works alongside the digital imaging technician, putting the memory cards or drives in the camera, inventorying the contents of the recording media, and backing up the image files.

Matte artist: Member of special-effects unit who paints backdrops that are then photographically or digitally incorporated into a shot to indicate a setting.

Model maker: (1) Member of production design unit who prepares architectural models for sets to be built. (2) Member of the special-effects unit who fabricates scale models of locales, vehicles, or characters to be filmed or scanned as substitutes for full-size ones.

Property master: Member of set crew who supervises the use of all props, or movable objects in the film.

Publicist, unit publicist: Member of producer's crew who creates promotional material regarding the production. The publicist may arrange for press and television interviews with the director and cast and for coverage of the production in the mass media.

Scenic artist: Member of set crew responsible for painting surfaces of set.

Still photographer: Member of crew who takes photographs of scenes and behind-the-scenes shots of cast members and others. These photographs may be used to check lighting or set design or color, and some will be used in publicizing the film.

Video assist: A video camera attached to the motion picture camera that allows immediate playback of a shot. This allows the director and cinematographer to check lighting, framing, or performances.

> **"** A couple of guys in a coffee shop set out to write a gag; a couple of guys with a camera set out to film a gag; a couple of guys in an editing room set out to make sense of the trash that's been dumped on their desks."
>
> —David Mamet, director, *The Spanish Prisoner* and *Redbelt*

Because each shot usually exists in several takes, because the film is shot out of plot order, and because the master-shot/coverage approach yields so much footage, the editor's job can be a daunting one. A 100-minute feature, which amounts to about 9,000 feet of 35mm film, may have been carved out of 500,000 feet of raw footage. Shooting on video can also generate a huge amount of material to be edited. Over 286 hours of footage were sent to postproduction for *The Social Network.* For this reason, postproduction on major Hollywood pictures often takes up to seven months. Sometimes several editors and assistants are brought in.

Typically, the editor receives filmed material as quickly as possible. This footage is known as the *dailies* or the *rushes.* The editor inspects the dailies, leaving it to the *assistant editor* to synchronize image and sound and to sort the takes by scene. The editor meets with the director to examine the dailies, or if the production is filming far away, the editor informs the director of how the footage looks. Since retaking shots is costly and troublesome, constant checking of the dailies is important for spotting any problems with focus, exposure, framing, or other visual factors. From the dailies, the director selects the best takes, and the editor records the choices. To save money, "digital dailies" are often shown to the producer and director, but since video playback on small monitors can conceal defects in the original footage, many editors prefer to check the shots on a big screen before.

As the footage accumulates, the editor assembles it into a *rough cut*—the shots loosely strung in sequence, without sound effects or music. Rough cuts tend to run long—the rough cut for *Apocalypse Now* ran 7½ hours. From the rough cut, the editor, in consultation with the director, builds toward a *fine cut* or *final cut.* The unused shots constitute the *outtakes.* While the final cut is being prepared, a *second unit* may be shooting *inserts,* footage to fill in at certain places. These are typically long shots of cities or airports or close-ups of objects. At this point, *pickups* are also shot. These are retakes and additional footage not made during principal photography. Then, titles are prepared, and further laboratory work or special-effects work may be done.

Until the mid-1980s, editors cut and spliced the *work print,* footage printed from the camera negative. In trying out their options, editors were obliged to rearrange the shots physically. Now virtually all commercial films are edited digitally. Any footage shot on film is transferred to a hard drive. The editor enters notes on each take directly into a computer database. From these, the editor can call up any shot, join it to another shot, trim it, or junk it. Special effects and music can be tried out as well.

As the editing team puts the footage in order, other members of the team manipulate the look of the shots via computer. If the footage has been shot on film, it may be scanned frame by frame into computer files to create a *digital intermediate* (DI). The DI is manipulated in many ways, most importantly to change light levels and to alter colors. The purpose is to make sure that shots made at different times of day or in different locales can be cut together to create a consistent look throughout a scene. Such tasks are handled by *digital color grading,* and the job is done by the *colorist.* To some extent the colorist takes over tasks that a cinematographer and traditional grader would originally have performed in the photographic laboratory, and the two may work together on the DI. Nowadays if a problem arises on set, the filming continues, with the crew deciding, "we'll fix it in post." As we'll see in Chapter 5, digital tools can make precise changes in portions of the image.

Ironically, the use of digital intermediates has encouraged some filmmakers to continue working on 35mm photographic film stock. They believe that they can best exploit the visual richness of film by digital manipulation. Jacques Audiard's *A Prophet* was shot on 35mm, but after transfer to a DI it was shown at the Cannes Film Festival as a 2K version. Audiard was thrilled with the way it looked on the screen: "It's a miraculous hybrid that magnifies the beauty of 35mm." Several directors and cinematographers share Audiard's enthusiasm for this "hybrid" approach.

1.35 Computer-generated imagery. In the chase through the airways of Coruscant in *Attack of the Clones,* the actor was shot against a blue or green screen, and the backgrounds and moving vehicles were created through CGI.

Special Effects For special effects, filmmakers turn to computer-generated imagery (CGI). Their tasks may be as simple as deleting distracting background elements or building a crowd out of a few spectators. George Lucas has claimed that if an actor blinked at the wrong time, he just erased the blink digitally. CGI can also create imagery that would be virtually impossible with photographic film **(1.35).** Computers can conjure up photorealistic characters such as Gollum in *The Hobbit* and *The Lord of the Rings.* (See pp. 165–166.) Fantasy and science fiction have fostered the development of CGI, but all genres have benefited, from the comic multiplication of a single actor in *Charlie and the Chocolate Factory* to the grisly realism of the digitally enhanced Omaha Beach assault in *Saving Private Ryan.* In *The Curious Case of Benjamin Button,* CGI substituted for makeup, allowing Brad Pitt and Cate Blanchett to plausibly portray their characters through youth to old age.

Sound Editing Once the shots are arranged in something approaching final form, the *sound editor* takes charge of building up the sound track. The director, the composer, the picture editor, and the sound editor view the film and agree on where music and effects will be placed, a process known as *spotting.* The sound editor may have a staff whose members specialize in mixing dialogue, music, or sound effects.

Surprisingly little of the sound recorded during filming winds up in the finished movie. Often half or more of the dialogue is rerecorded in postproduction, using a process known as *automated dialogue replacement* (*ADR*). ADR usually yields better quality than location sound does. With the on-set recording serving as a *guide track,* the sound editor records actors in the studio speaking their lines (called *dubbing* or *looping*). Nonsynchronized dialogue such as the babble of a crowd (known in Hollywood as "walla") is added by ADR as well.

Similarly, very few of the noises we hear in a film were recorded during filming. A sound editor adds sound effects, drawing on a library of stock sounds or creating particular effects for the film. Sound editors routinely manufacture footsteps, car crashes, pistol shots, and fists thudding into flesh (often produced by whacking a watermelon with an axe). In *Terminator 2,* the sound of the T-1000 cyborg passing through jail cell bars is that of dog food sliding slowly out of a can. Sound-effects technicians have sensitive hearing. One veteran noted the differences among doors: "The bathroom door has a little air as opposed to the closet door. The front door has to sound solid; you have to hear the latch sound. . . . Don't just put in any door, make sure it's right."

Like picture editing, modern sound editing relies on computer technology. The editor can store recorded sounds in a database, classifying and rearranging them in

> " [ADR for *Apocalypse Now*] was tremendously wearing on the actors because the entire film is looped, and of course all of the sound for everything had to be redone. So the actors were locked in a room for days and days on end shouting. Either they're shouting over the noise of the helicopter, or they're shouting over the noise of the boat."
> —Walter Murch, sound designer

any way desired. A sound's qualities can be modified digitally—clipping off high or low frequencies and changing pitch, reverberation, equalization, or speed. The boom and throb of underwater action in *The Hunt for Red October* were slowed down and reprocessed from such mundane sources as a diver plunging into a swimming pool, water bubbling from a garden hose, and the hum of Disneyland's air-conditioning plant. One technician on the film called digital sound editing "sound sculpting."

During the spotting of the sound track, the film's *composer* enters the assembly phase as well. The composer compiles cue sheets that mark exactly where the music will go and how long it should run. The composer writes the score, although she or he will probably not orchestrate it personally. While the composer is working, the rough cut is synchronized with a *temp dub*—accompaniment pulled from recorded songs or classical pieces. Musicians record the score with the aid of a *click track,* a taped series of metronome beats synchronized with the final cut.

Dialogue, effects, and music are recorded on separate tracks, and each type of sound, however minor, will occupy a separate track. During the mixing, for each scene, the image track is run over, once for each sound, to ensure proper synchronization. The specialist who performs the task is the *rerecording mixer,* usually supervising a team of mixers. Each scene may involve dozens of tracks of individual sounds, which are all mixed together. Equalization, filtering, and other adjustment take place at this stage. The director typically oversees some mixing sessions, particularly the one creating the final mix.

In the era of photochemical filmmaking, the *camera negative,* which was the source of the dailies and the work print, was too precious to serve as the source for final prints. Traditionally, from the negative footage, the laboratory drew an *interpositive,* which in turn provided an *internegative.* The internegative was then assembled in accordance with the final cut, and it served as the primary source of future prints. An alternative, as we've seen, was to create a digital intermediate that could be recorded back to film as an internegative.

Once the internegative was created, the master sound track was synchronized with it. The first positive print, complete with picture and sound, was called the *answer print.* After the director, producer, and cinematographer approved an answer print, *release prints* were made for distribution. Using a digital intermediate made it possible to generate additional internegatives as old ones wore out, all without any damage to the original materials.

Films that are shot digitally may proceed through postproduction without ever being put on photochemical stock. The director and cinematographer approve a master version that will be converted to the Digital Cinema Packages released to theaters. Further conversions will turn out video versions for DVD and Blu-ray, streaming, and other platforms. These transfers often demand new judgments about color quality and sound balance. The master version of the finished film, along with all the footage and materials used in the creation of the movie, will be stored on files. Because digital media have a short life, most film studios arrange for the finished film and the most valuable supplementary footage to be saved on 35mm film as well.

Special Versions   The work of production does not end when the final theatrical version has been assembled. In consultation with the producer and director, the postproduction staff prepares airline and broadcast television versions. For a successful film, a director's cut or an extended edition may be released on disc. Different versions may be prepared for different countries. European prints of Stanley Kubrick's *Eyes Wide Shut* featured more nudity than did American ones, in which some naked couples were blocked by digital figures added to the foreground.

Many fictional films have dramatized processes of film production. Federico Fellini's *8½* concerns itself with the preproduction stage of a film that is abandoned before shooting starts. François Truffaut's *Day for Night,* David Mamet's *State and*

Main, Christopher Guest's *For Your Consideration,* and Tom DiCillo's *Living in Oblivion* all center on the shooting phase. The action of Brian De Palma's *Blow Out* occurs while a low-budget thriller is in sound editing. *Singin' in the Rain* follows a single film through the entire process, with a gigantic advertising billboard filling the final shot.

Artistic Implications of the Production Process

Every artist works within constraints of time, money, and opportunity. Of all the arts, filmmaking is one of the most pressurized. Budgets must be maintained, deadlines must be met, weather and locations are unpredictable, and the coordination of any group of people involves unforeseeable twists and turns. Even a Hollywood blockbuster, which might seem to offer unlimited freedom, is actually confining on many levels. Big-budget filmmakers sometimes get tired of coordinating hundreds of staff and wrestling with million-dollar decisions, and they start to long for more relaxed productions. Steven Soderbergh has swung between high-profile projects like the star-packed *Ocean's 11* franchise and smaller projects like *Bubble,* shot with nonprofessional actors on 1080p HD.

We appreciate films more when we realize that in production, every film is a compromise made within constraints. When Mark and Michael Polish conceived their independent film *Twin Falls Idaho,* they had planned for the story to unfold in several countries. But the cost of travel and location shooting forced them to rethink the film's plot: "We had to decide whether the film was about twins or travel."

Similarly, the involvement of a powerful director can reshape the film at the screenplay stage. In the original screenplay of *Witness,* the protagonist was Rachel, the Amish widow with whom John Book falls in love. The romance and Rachel's confused feelings about Book formed the central plot line. But the director, Peter Weir, wanted to emphasize the clash between pacifism and violence. So William Kelley and Earl Wallace revised their screenplay to stress the mystery plot line and to center the action on Book and the introduction of urban crime into the peaceful Amish community. Given the new constraints, the screenwriters found a new form for *Witness.*

Some filmmakers struggle against their constraints, pushing the limits of what's considered possible. The production of a film we'll study in upcoming chapters, *Citizen Kane,* was highly innovative on many fronts. Yet even this project had to accept studio routines and the limits of current technology. More commonly, a filmmaker works with the same menu of choices available to others. In directing *Collateral,* Michael Mann made creative choices about how to use digital cameras and low lighting levels. Other filmmakers working in 2004 could have taken the same risks, but Mann saw new ways of employing such techniques. The overall result was a visual style that no other film had achieved, though others imitated it.

Starting our study of film art with a survey of production allows us to understand some of the possibilities offered by images and sounds. It also helps put us in the filmmaker's shoes: We can see the decisions from the inside. We realize that everything in the finished movie springs from choices that we too would face. Later chapters will discuss the artistic consequences of decisions made in production—everything from storytelling strategies to techniques of staging, shooting, editing, and sound work. By choosing within production constraints, and sometimes pushing against them, filmmakers create film form and style.

Modes of Production

The scale and type of production varies from large-scale studio filmmaking involving hundreds of people to do-it-yourself productions completed by a single filmmaker. The different modes of production shape the final film.

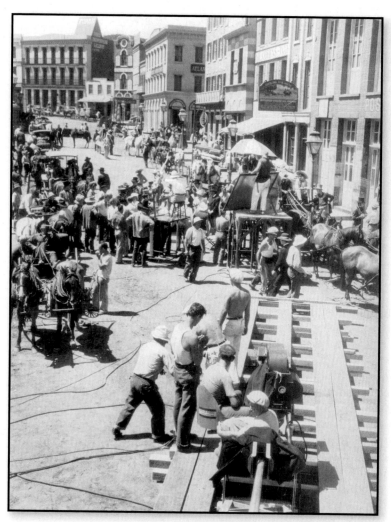

1.36 Large-scale production. Studio production was characterized by a large number of highly specialized production roles. Here several units prepare a moving-camera shot for *Wells Fargo* (1937).

Large-Scale Production

The fine-grained division of labor we've been describing is characteristic of *studio* filmmaking. A studio is a company in the business of creating films. The most famous studios flourished in Hollywood from the 1920s to the 1960s—Paramount, Warner Bros., Columbia, and so on. These companies owned equipment and extensive physical plants, and they retained most of their workers on long-term contracts. Each studio's central management planned all projects, then delegated authority to supervising producers, who in turn assembled casts and crews from the studio's pool of workers.

Organized as efficient businesses, the studios created a tradition of carefully tracking the entire process through paper records. At the start, there were versions of the script. During shooting, reports were written about camera footage, sound recording, special-effects work, and laboratory results. In the assembly phase, there were logs of shots catalogued in editing and a variety of cue sheets for music, mixing, looping, and title layout. This sort of record keeping has remained a part of large-scale filmmaking, though now it is done mostly on computer.

Although studio production might seem to resemble a factory's assembly line, it was always more creative, collaborative, and chaotic than turning out cars or microchips. Each film is a unique product, not a replica of a prototype. In studio filmmaking, skilled specialists collaborated to create such a product while still adhering to a "blueprint" prepared by management (**1.36**).

The centralized production system has virtually disappeared. The giant studios of Hollywood's golden age have become distribution companies, although they may initiate, fund, and oversee the making of some of the films they distribute. The old studios had stars and staff under contract, so the same group of people might work together on film after film. Now each film is planned as a distinct package, with director, actors, staff, and technicians brought together for the project. The studio may provide its own sound stages, sets, and offices for the production, but in most cases, the producer arranges with outside firms to supply cameras, catering, locations, special effects, and anything else required.

In recent years, each phase of filmmaking has encompassed more and more specialized tasks. This trend is largely due to bigger budgets and greater reliance on digital special effects. Still, the basic production stages and division of labor remain similar to what they were in the years of classic studio moviemaking.

Exploitation, Independent Production, and DIY

Not all films using the division of labor we have outlined are big-budget projects financed by major companies. There are also low-budget *exploitation* products tailored to a particular market—in earlier decades, fringe theaters and drive-ins; now, video rentals and sales. Troma Films, maker of *The Toxic Avenger,* is probably the most

> 66 Deep down inside, everybody in the United States has a desperate need to believe that some day, if the breaks fall their way, they can quit their jobs as claims adjusters, legal secretaries, certified public accountants, or mobsters, and go out and make their own low-budget movie. Otherwise, the future is just too bleak."
>
> —Joe Queenan, critic and independent filmmaker

famous exploitation company, turning out horror movies and teen sex comedies for $100,000 or less. Nonetheless, exploitation filmmakers usually divide the labor along studio lines. There is the producer's role, the director's role, and so on, and the production tasks are parceled out in ways that roughly conform to mass-production practices.

Exploitation production often forces people to double up on jobs. Robert Rodriguez made *El Mariachi* as an exploitation film for the Spanish-language video market. The 21-year-old director also functioned as producer, scriptwriter, cinematographer, camera operator, still photographer, and sound recordist and mixer. Rodriguez's friend Carlos Gallardo starred, coproduced, and coscripted; he also served as unit production manager and grip. Gallardo's mother fed the cast and crew. *El Mariachi* wound up costing only about $7,000.

Unlike *El Mariachi,* most exploitation films don't enter the theatrical market, but other low-budget productions, loosely known as *independent* films, may. Independent films are made for the theatrical market but usually without major distributor financing. Some independent filmmakers are well known, such as Spike Lee, David Cronenberg, and Joel and Ethan Coen, who prefer to work with budgets significantly below the industry norm. In such cases, the director usually initiates the project and partners with a producer to get it realized. Financing may come from television firms, with major U.S. distributors buying the rights if the project seems to have good prospects. Or private investors may provide funding, as Megan Ellison has done for *Zero Dark Thirty, Spring Breakers*, and *American Hustle.*

As we would expect, these industry-based independents organize production in ways close to the full-fledged studio mode. Nonetheless, because these projects require less financing, the directors can demand more control over the production process. For *Slumdog Millionaire,* a relatively low-cost project, director Danny Boyle had the freedom to shoot some of the film on 35mm and other portions on smaller 2K digital cameras, which were easier to maneuver in the crowded streets of Mumbai.

The category of independent production is a roomy one, and it also includes more modest projects by less well-known filmmakers. Examples are Victor Nuñez's *Ulee's Gold,* Phil Morrison's *Junebug,* and Miranda July's *Me and You and Everyone We Know.* Even though they are far less costly than studio projects, independent productions face many obstacles. Filmmakers may have to finance the project themselves, with the help of relatives and friendly investors; they must also find a distributor specializing in independent and low-budget films. Festivals and networking are important for independent filmmakers. Ava DuVernay, who had started her career as a publicist, was inspired to become a director when working on *Collateral.* Her second low-budget feature, *Middle of Nowhere* (**1.37**), was shown at the Sundance Film Festival, and she became the first African-American woman to win its best-director prize. When there were problems finding a director for *Selma,* actor David Oyelowo, who had a leading role in *Middle of Nowhere,* suggested DuVernay. Her work on *Selma* led to an Academy Award nomination. DuVernay also founded the African-American Film Festival Releasing Movement to distribute independent work by black filmmakers. If you were an independent filmmaker, you might believe the advantages are worth the struggle. Independent production can treat subjects that large-scale studio production ignores. No film studios would probably have supported Kevin Smith's *Clerks* or Lena Dunham's *Tiny Furniture* or Richard Linklater's *Boyhood.* Because the independent film does not need as large an audience to repay its costs, it can be more personal and controversial. And the production process, no matter how low the budget, still relies on the basic roles and phases established by the studio tradition.

Small-Scale Production

In large-scale and independent production, many people work on the film, each one a specialist in a particular task. Even on *Boyhood,* which was a relatively small production, there were about 45 crew members on set each day. But there's also a tradition of a single filmmaker assuming all or many of the roles: planning the film,

CONNECT TO THE BLOG
www.davidbordwell.net/blog

Studio films and independent ones aren't always that far apart, as we suggest in "Independent film: How different?"

1.37 The heroine of *Middle of Nowhere* puts her life on hold when her husband is imprisoned. The tedium of her long bus rides to visit him is suggested by several shots at intervals in the film.

1.38 Small-scale production. In *The Riddle of Lumen,* Stan Brakhage turns shadows and everyday objects into vivid patterns.

1.39

1.40

1.39–1.40 Handmade movies. In *Meshes of the Afternoon,* multiple versions of the protagonist were played by the filmmaker, Maya Deren (1.39). For *Empire II,* Amos Poe digitally manipulated this tantalizing glimpse of the Manhattan skyline (1.40).

1.41 Small-scale documentary filmmaking. In *Harlan County, U.S.A.,* the driver of a passing truck fires at the film crew. Working organically within the community, the filmmakers were threatened with violence similar to that experienced by the striking coal miners they were filming.

financing it, performing in it, running the camera, recording the sound, and putting it all together. For his low-budget horror film *Monsters,* Gareth Edwards acted as writer, director, cinematographer, and special-effects supervisor. He did his own location scouting from his computer, using Google Earth to survey Mexico, Belize, and Guatemala.

Experimental and documentary traditions have given great weight to the film dominated by a single person's efforts. Consider Stan Brakhage, whose films are among the most directly personal ever made. Some, such as *Window Water Baby Moving,* are lyrical studies of his home and family (**1.38**). Others, such as *Dog Star Man,* are mythic treatments of nature; still others, such as *23rd Psalm Branch,* are quasi-documentary studies of war and death. Funded by grants and his personal finances, Brakhage prepared, shot, and edited his films virtually unaided. While he was working in a film laboratory, he also developed and printed his footage. With over 150 films to his credit, Brakhage proved that the individual filmmaker can become an artisan, executing all the basic production tasks.

The 16mm and less costly digital video formats are customary for small-scale production of this sort. Financial backing often comes from the filmmaker, from grants, and perhaps from obliging friends and relatives. There is very little division of labor: The filmmaker oversees every production task and performs many of them. Although technicians or performers may help out, the creative decisions rest with the filmmaker. Experimentalist Maya Deren's *Meshes of the Afternoon* was shot by her husband, Alexander Hammid, but she scripted, directed, and edited it and performed in the central role (**1.39**). Amos Poe made his lengthy, evocative experimental film *Empire II* by placing a small digital camera in a window of his Manhattan apartment and exposing single frames in bursts at intervals over an entire year (**1.40**). Poe edited the film himself, reworked the images digitally, and assembled the sound track from existing songs and original music.

Such small-scale production is common in documentary filmmaking as well. Jean Rouch, a French anthropologist, made several films alone or with a small crew in his efforts to record the lives of marginal people living in alien cultures. Rouch wrote, directed, and photographed *Les Maîtres fous* (1955), his first widely seen film. He examined the ceremonies of a Ghanaian cult whose members lived a double life: Most of the time they worked as low-paid laborers, but in their rituals, they passed into a frenzied trance and assumed the identities of their colonial rulers.

Similarly, Barbara Kopple devoted four years to making *Harlan County, U.S.A.,* a record of Kentucky coal miners' struggles for union representation. After eventually obtaining funding from several foundations, she and a small crew spent 13 months living with miners during the workers' strike. During filming, Kopple acted as sound recordist, working with cameraman Hart Perry and sometimes also a lighting person. A large crew was ruled out not only by Kopple's budget but also by the need to fit naturally into the community. Like the miners, the filmmakers were constantly threatened with violence from strikebreakers (**1.41**).

On rare occasions small-scale production becomes *collective* production. Here, instead of a single filmmaker shaping the project, several film workers participate equally. The group shares common goals and makes production decisions democratically. Roles may also be rotated: The sound recordist on one day may serve as cinematographer on the next. One instance is the Canadian film *Atanarjuat: The Fast Runner.* Three Inuits (Zacharias Kunuk, Paul Apak Angilirq, and Paul Qulitalik) and one New Yorker (Norman Cohn) composed a screenplay based on an oral tale about love, murder, and revenge. Cast and crew spent six months shooting in the Arctic, camping in tents and eating seal meat. "We don't have a hierarchy," Cohn explained. "There's no director, second, third or fourth assistant director. We have a team of people trying to figure out how to make this work." Because of the communal nature of Inuit life, the Igloolik team expanded the collective effort by bringing local people into the project. An early showcase for the strengths of digital video **(1.42)**, *Atanarjuat: The Fast Runner* won a prize at the 2002 Cannes Film Festival. YouTube and other media-sharing sites have popularized collective production by encouraging high school classes to make films together.

Small-scale production allows the filmmakers to retain tight control of the project. The rise of digital video formats has made small-scale production more visible. *The Gleaners and I* (see p. 174), *The Yes Men, Searching for Sugarman, The Cove, Anvil! The Story of Anvil, Citizenfour,* and other documentaries indicate that the theatrical market and festival circuit have room for works made by single filmmakers or small production units.

1.42 Collective filmmaking. The hero of *Atanarjuat: The Fast Runner* pauses in his flight across the ice. "We made our film in an Inuit way," Norman Cohn explained, "through consensus and collaboration."

Thanks to digital cameras and affordable software for computer postproduction, there has been an explosion of "do it yourself" (DIY) filmmaking. Individuals or small groups of amateurs can make their own films and share them on YouTube, Vimeo, and other websites. An early instance was Arin Crumley and Susan Buice's *Four Eyed Monsters,* a filmed reenactment of the couple's unconventional romance that got some festival exposure before moving to a self-published DVD and YouTube. This project was an early example of crowdfunding before such resources as Indiegogo and Kickstarter existed.

Artistic Implications of Different Modes of Production

Production and Film Categories   We sometimes categorize films on the basis of how they were made. We can distinguish a *fiction* film from a *documentary* on the basis of production phases.

The fiction film is characterized by much more control over the preparation and shooting phases. By contrast, the documentary filmmaker usually controls only certain portions of preparation, shooting, and assembly. Some stages (script and rehearsal) may be omitted, whereas others (setting, lighting, and performance) are present but often uncontrolled. In interviewing an eyewitness to an event, the filmmaker typically controls camera work and editing but does not tell the witness what to say or how to act. For example, there was no script for the documentary *Manufacturing Consent: Noam Chomsky and the Media.* Filmmakers Mark Achbar and Peter Wintonick instead shot long interviews in which Chomsky explained his ideas.

Similarly, a *compilation* film assembles existing images and sounds that provide historical evidence on a topic. The compilation filmmaker may minimize the shooting stage and create a story from archival footage. For *The Power of Nightmares,* Adam Curtis gathered newsreel and television footage, television commercials, and clips from fiction films to track the rise of fundamentalist politics and religion after World War II.

One more kind of film is distinguished by the way it's produced. The *animated* film is created frame by frame. Images may be drawn directly on the film strip, or the camera may photograph drawings or three-dimensional models, as in the *Wallace and Gromit* movies. *Corpse Bride* was created without using motion picture cameras; instead, each frame was registered by a digital still camera and transferred to film. Today most animated films, both for theater screens and for the Internet, are created directly on computer with imaging software.

> One of the best things about directing is that there's no confusion about who's to blame: You are."
>
> —Nora Ephron, director, *Julie & Julia*

Production and Authorship Production practices have another implication for film as an art form. Who, it is often asked, is the "author," the person responsible for the film? In individual production, the author must be the solitary filmmaker—Stan Brakhage or perhaps you. Collective film production creates collective authorship: The author is the entire group. The question of authorship becomes difficult to answer only when asked about large-scale production, particularly in the studio mode.

Studio film production assigns tasks to so many individuals that it is often difficult to determine who controls or decides what. Is the producer the author? In the prime years of the Hollywood system, the producer might have had nothing to do with shooting. The writer? The writer's script might be completely transformed in shooting and editing. So is this situation like collective production, with group authorship? No, because there is a hierarchy in which a few main players make the key decisions.

Moreover, if we consider not only control and decision making but also individual style, it seems certain that some studio workers leave recognizable and unique traces on the films they make. Cinematographers such as Gregg Toland, set designers such as Hermann Warm, costumers such as Edith Head, choreographers such as Gene Kelly—the contributions of these people stand out within the films they made. So where does the studio-produced film leave the idea of authorship?

Most people who study cinema regard the director as the film's primary "author." Although the writer prepares a screenplay, later phases of production can modify it beyond recognition. And although the producer monitors the entire process, he or she seldom controls moment-by-moment activity on the set. It is the director who makes the crucial decisions about performance, staging, lighting, framing, cutting, and sound. On the whole, the director usually has most control over how a movie looks and sounds.

This doesn't mean that the director is an expert at every job or dictates every detail. The director can delegate tasks to trusted personnel, and directors often work habitually with certain actors, cinematographers, composers, and editors. In the days of studio filmmaking, directors learned how to blend the distinctive talents of cast and crew into the overall movie. Humphrey Bogart's unique talents were used very differently by Michael Curtiz in *Casablanca,* John Huston in *The Maltese Falcon,* and Howard Hawks in *The Big Sleep.* Gregg Toland's cinematography was pushed in different directions by Orson Welles (*Citizen Kane*) and William Wyler (*The Best Years of Our Lives*).

During the 1950s, young French critics applied the word *auteur* (author) to Hollywood directors who they felt had created a distinctive approach to filmmaking while working within the Hollywood studio system. Soon American critics picked up the "auteur theory," which remained a central idea for film academics and students. Now you will occasionally read reviews or see spots on television that use the term to refer to a respected and distinctive director.

Today well-established directors can control large-scale production to a remarkable degree. Until 2011, Steven Spielberg resisted using digital editing. The late Robert Altman disliked ADR and used much of the casual on-set dialogue in the finished film. In the days of Hollywood's studio system, some directors exercised power more indirectly. Most studios did not permit the director to supervise editing, but John Ford often made only one take of each shot. Precutting the film "in his head," Ford virtually forced the editor to put the shots together as he had planned.

Around the world, the director is generally recognized as the key player. In Europe, Asia, and South America, directors frequently initiate the film and work closely with scriptwriters. In Hollywood, directors usually operate on a freelance basis, and the top ones select their own projects. To a great extent, it is the director who shapes the film's unique form and style, and these two components are central to cinema as an art.

❝ The times when [our job] is most satisfying are when you really are in sync with the director. It is almost like you are trying to crawl into their brain, and it is about fulfilling their vision, which is what everybody's role on a film is."
—Ellen Lewis, casting director

CONNECT TO THE BLOG
www.davidbordwell.net/blog

Screenwriters often take issue with the idea of directorial authorship, but we defend it in "Who the devil wrote it? (Apologies to Peter Bogdanovich.)"

Bringing the Film to the Audience: Distribution and Exhibition

We've spent some time considering film production because that's where film art begins. What of the other two phases of filmmaking? As in production, money plays a significant role in both distribution and exhibition. We'll see as well that these phases have effects on film art and viewers' experiences of particular films.

Distribution: The Center of Power

Distribution companies form the core of economic power in the commercial film industry. Filmmakers need distributors to circulate their work; exhibitors need them to supply their screens. Europe and Asia are home to some significant media companies, but six Hollywood firms remain the world's major distributors. You recognize the names: Warner Bros., Paramount, Walt Disney/Buena Vista, Universal, Sony/Columbia, and Twentieth Century Fox.

These firms provide mainstream entertainment to theaters around the world. The films they release account for 95 percent of ticket sales in the United States and Canada, and about half of the overseas market. In world capitals, the majors maintain branch offices that advertise films, schedule releases, and arrange for prints to be made in local languages (either dubbing dialogue or adding subtitling). With vigorous marketing units in every region, the majors can distribute non-U.S. films as well as Hollywood titles. For example, Hayao Miyazaki's popular animated films (*Spirited Away, Howl's Moving Castle*) are distributed on video by Disney's Buena Vista arm, even in Miyazaki's homeland of Japan.

The major distributors have won such power because large companies can best endure the risks of theatrical moviemaking. Filmmaking is costly, and most films don't earn profits in theatrical release. Worldwide, the top 10 percent of all films released garner 50 percent of all box office receipts. The most popular 30 percent of films account for 80 percent of receipts. Distributors are in a position to move films smoothly from theatrical runs to cable TV, DVD, and other platforms. Typically, a film breaks even or shows a profit only after it has been released in these ancillary markets.

In the United States, theater owners bid for each film a distributor releases, and in most states, they must be allowed to see the film before bidding. Elsewhere in the world, distributors may force exhibitors to rent a film without seeing it (called *blind booking*), perhaps even before it has been completed. Exhibitors may also be pressured to rent a package of films in order to get a few desirable items (*block booking*).

Once the exhibitor has contracted to screen the film, the distributor can demand stiff terms. The theater keeps a surprisingly small percentage of total box office receipts (known as the *gross* or *grosses*). One standard U.S. arrangement guarantees the distributor a minimum of 90 percent of the first week's gross, dropping gradually to 30 percent after several weeks.

These terms aren't favorable to the exhibitor. A failure that closes quickly will yield almost nothing to the theater, and even a successful film will make most of its money in the first two or three weeks of release, when the exhibitor gets less of the revenue. Averaged out, a long-running success will likely yield no more than 50 percent of the gross to the theater.

To make up for this drawback, the distributor allows the exhibitor to deduct from the gross the expenses of running the theater (a negotiated figure called the *house nut*). In addition, the exhibitor gets all the cash from the concession stand, which may deliver up to 70 percent of the theater's profits. Without high-priced snacks, movie houses couldn't survive.

After the grosses are split with the exhibitor, the distribution company receives its share (the *rentals*) and divides it further. A major U.S. distributor typically takes 35 percent of the rentals as its distribution fee. If the distributor helped finance the

66 Selling food is my job. I just happen to work in a theater."
—Theater manager in upstate New York

CONNECT TO THE BLOG
www.davidbordwell.net/blog

Every Monday, the weekend box office figures are news, but what do they mean? We add some nuance in "What won the weekend? Or how to understand box-office figures."

CONNECT TO THE BLOG
www.davidbordwell.net/blog

James Schamus, then head of Focus Features, shares thoughts on independent distribution in "A man and his focus."

“ Our underlying philosophy is that all media are one."

—Rupert Murdoch, owner of News Corp and Twentieth Century Fox

film, it takes another percentage off the top. The costs of prints and advertising are deducted as well. What remains comes back to the filmmakers. Out of the proceeds, the producer must pay all *profit participants*—the directors, actors, executives, and investors who have negotiated a share of the rental returns.

For most films, the amount returned to the production company is relatively small. Once the salaried workers have been paid, the producer and other major players usually must wait to receive their share from video and other ancillary markets. Because of this delay, and the suspicion that the major distributors practice misleading accounting, powerful actors and directors may demand "first-dollar" participation. In that case, their share will derive from the earliest money the picture returns to the distributor.

Majors and Minors   The major distributors all belong to multinational corporations devoted to leisure activities. For example, Paramount Pictures, which produces and distributes films, is owned by Viacom, which controls Comedy Central, MTV, and other cable channels. Time Warner not only owns Warner Bros. but also has broadcast and cable services (CNN, HBO, Turner Classic Movies, and the Cartoon Network) along with publishing houses and magazines (*Time, Sports Illustrated, People,* and DC Comics). Twentieth Century Fox is a subsidiary of News Corp, which owns many newspapers, book publishers, cable news and sports channels, and half-interest in Australia's National Rugby League. Columbia Pictures is an arm of Sony, which has extensive holdings in electronics, recorded music, and mobile communications.

Independent and overseas filmmakers usually don't have access to direct funding from major distribution companies, so they try to presell distribution rights to finance production. Sometimes the distribution rights are sold in advance of production and provide some of the film's budget. Alternatively, once a film is finished, a producer may try to attract distributors' attention at film festivals. In 2012, *Beasts of the Southern Wild* won an award at the Sundance Film Festival and was bought by Fox Searchlight. It went on to win a major prize at the Cannes Film Festival and was nominated for four Academy Awards.

More specialized distributors, such as the New York firms Kino Lorber and Milestone, acquire rights to foreign and independent films for rental to art cinemas, colleges, and museums. As the audience for these films grew during the 1990s, major distributors sought to enter this market. The independent firm Miramax generated enough low-budget hits to be purchased by the Disney corporation. With the benefit of Disney's funding and wider distribution reach, Miramax movies such as *Pulp Fiction, Scream, Shakespeare in Love,* and *Hero* earned even bigger box office receipts. Sony Pictures Classics funded art house fare that sometimes crossed over to the multiplexes, as *Crouching Tiger, Hidden Dragon* did.

By belonging to multinational conglomerates, the big film distributors gain access to private investors, bank financing, and other sources of funding. Branch offices in major countries can carry a film into worldwide markets. Sony's global reach allowed it to release 11 different soundtrack CDs for *Spider-Man 2,* each one featuring artists famous in local territories. Just as important, media conglomerates can build *synergy*—focusing the film, music, television, and publishing sectors of the company on promoting a piece of "branded content." The Disney company followed the release of *Frozen* with a soundtrack album, books, a ride at Disney theme parks, a Broadway show, and a *Frozen* storyline in a television series on ABC (a network owned by Disney). Every product promotes the others, and each wing of the parent company gets more business. One film can even advertise another within its story **(1.43).** Although synergy sometimes fails, multimedia giants are in the best position to take advantage of it.

Distributors arrange release dates, make prints, and launch advertising campaigns. For big companies, distribution can be efficient because the costs can be spread out over many units. One poster design can be used in several markets, and

1.43 Product placement. In *Lethal Weapon,* as Murtaugh and Riggs leave a hotdog stand, they pass in front of a movie theater. The shot provides advance publicity for *The Lost Boys,* another Warner Bros. film released four months after *Lethal Weapon.* The prominence of Pepsi-Cola in this shot is an example of *product placement*—featuring well-known brands in a film in exchange for payment or cross-promotional services.

a distributor who orders a thousand prints from a laboratory will pay less per print than the filmmaker who orders one. Large companies are also in the best position to cope with the rise of distribution costs. Today, the average Hollywood film is estimated to cost over $100 million to make and an additional $50 million to distribute.

Release Patterns   The risky nature of mass-market filmmaking has led the majors to two distribution strategies: *platforming* and *wide release.* With platforming, the film opens first in a few big cities. It then gradually expands to theaters around the country, although it may never play in every community. If the strategy is successful, anticipation for the film builds, and it remains a point of discussion for months. The major distributors tend to use platforming for unusual films, such as *Tinker Tailor Soldier Spy* and *Selma,* which need time to accumulate critical support and positive word-of-mouth. Smaller distributors use platforming out of necessity, since they can't afford to make enough prints to open wide, but the gradual accumulation of buzz can work in their favor, too.

In wide release, a film opens at the same time in many cities and towns. In the United States, this requires that thousands of copies be shipped out, so wide release is available only to the deep-pocketed major distributors. Wide release is the typical strategy for mainstream films, with two or three new titles opening each weekend on 2,000–4,000 screens. A film in wide release may be a midbudget one—a comedy, an action picture, a horror or science fiction film, or a children's animated movie. Or it may be a very big-budget item, a *tentpole* picture such as *The Dark Knight Rises* or a *Hunger Games* installment.

Distributors hope that a wide opening signals a "must-see" film, the latest big thing. Just as important, opening wide helps to recoup costs faster, since the distributor gets a larger portion of box office receipts early in the run. Still, it's a gamble. If a film fails in its first weekend, it almost never recovers momentum and can lose money very quickly. Even successful films usually lose revenues by 40 percent or more every week they run. So when two high-budget films open wide the same weekend, the competition is harmful to all. Companies tend to plan their tentpole release dates to avoid head-to-head conflict.

Wide releasing has extended across the world. As video piracy has spread, distribution companies have realized the risks of opening wide in the United States

CONNECT TO THE BLOG
www.davidbordwell.net/blog

With help from some colleagues, we defend movie franchises in "Live with it! There'll always be movie sequels. Good thing, too."

CONNECT TO THE BLOG
www.davidbordwell.net/blog

Fan events like Comic-Con have become a new way for Hollywood distributors to promote popular films directly to moviegoers, as we discuss in "Comic-Con 2008, Part 2."

and then waiting weeks or months before opening overseas. By then, illegal DVDs and Internet downloads would stifle the theatrical release. As a result, U.S. companies undertake *day-and-date* releasing for their biggest tentpole pictures. *Matrix: Revolutions* opened simultaneously on 8,000 screens in the United States and 10,000 screens in 107 other countries. In a stroke of showmanship, the first screening was synchronized to start at the same minute across all time zones.

Selling the Film   The distributor provides not only the movie but a publicity campaign. The theater is sent a *trailer,* a short preview of the upcoming film. Many executives believe that a trailer is the single most effective piece of advertising. Shown in theaters, it gets the attention of confirmed moviegoers. Posted on websites, a trailer gains mass viewership.

Publicists run press junkets, bringing entertainment reporters to interview the stars and principal filmmakers. "Infotainment" coverage in print, broadcast media, and online builds audience awareness. A making-of documentary, commissioned by the studio, may be shown on cable channels. A prominent film's premiere creates an occasion for further press coverage **(1.44).** For journalists, the distributor provides electronic press kits (EPKs), complete with photos, background information, star interviews, and clips of key scenes. Even a modestly budgeted production such as *Waiting to Exhale* had heavy promotion: five separate music videos, star visits to Oprah Winfrey, and displays in thousands of bookstores and beauty salons. Marketing costs for summer blockbusters may run as high as $200 million.

Most of those costs will go toward TV advertisements and outdoor displays such as billboards and bus-shelter posters. Less expensive, but for young audiences more attractive, is marketing on the Internet. In 1999, two young directors found their target audience by creating a website purporting to investigate sightings of the Blair Witch. "The movie was an extension of the website," noted a studio executive. When *The Blair Witch Project* earned over $130 million in the United States, distributors woke up to the power of the Internet. Now every film has a webpage, enticing viewers with plot information, star biographies, games, screen savers, and links to merchandise.

Distributors have realized that young Web surfers will eagerly promote a film if they're allowed to participate in getting the word out. Fan sites such as Harry Knowles's *Ain't It Cool News* publicize upcoming films through steady leaks and exclusive access. Every few days during the production of *King Kong*, Peter Jackson sent brief "Production Diaries" to a fan site; the full set of 90 "entries" were later released as an elaborate DVD boxed set. Social networking sites such as Facebook and services such as Twitter are filled with Hollywood publicity. When filming outdoor chase scenes for *Transformers: Age of Extinction*, the crew permitted onlookers to use their smartphones to shoot what they saw and post amateur making-of clips online.

Audience participation went further in a publicity campaign that has become a model of cyber-marketing. For *The Dark Knight*, a consulting firm created an alternate reality game (ARG) called "Why So Serious?" The premise was that Batman's adversary, the Joker, was recruiting gang members. On websites and social media, fans found clues that sent them racing to real street addresses. There they found coded instructions for getting closer to the master criminal. In the most famous phase,

1.44 Publicity builds audience awareness. A press conference held at Te Papa Museum in Wellington, New Zealand, as part of the December 1, 2003, world premiere of *The Lord of the Rings: The Return of the King.*

people who decoded a cryptic message were sent to bakeries, where they found chocolate cakes containing cellphones (with new information) and a playing card, the joker. The trails of clues took players to websites with trailers, sequences from the film, and free tickets. "Why So Serious?" ran over a 14-month period and is said to have engaged 10 million people worldwide (**1.45**).

Merchandising is a form of promotion that pays back its investment directly. Manufacturing companies license the rights to use the film's characters, title, or images on products. These licensing fees defray production and distribution costs. If the merchandise catches on, it can provide the studio with long-term income from an audience that might never have seen the film. Although *Tron* did poorly in theatrical release in 1982, the *Discs of Tron* video game became a popular arcade attraction.

1.45 Why so serious? For the *Dark Knight* alternate reality game, players were encouraged to wear Joker makeup as they gathered on the street and scanned the Net for clues and commands.

Today nearly all major motion pictures rely on merchandising, if only of a novelization or a soundtrack CD. A successful blockbuster can reap a merchandising bonanza. Children's films tend to exploit the gamut of possibilities: toys, games, clothing, lunch boxes, and schoolbags. There were *Shrek* ring tones, bowling balls, and hospital scrubs. George Lucas's entertainment empire was built on his ownership of the licensing rights for *Star Wars* merchandise. The four *Transformers* films grossed about a billion dollars each at theaters, but their toys, video games, and apps have yielded over $7 billion.

Merchandising is not only aimed at children. Given the aging population of Harry Potter readers and the darkening tone of the films, Warner Bros. concentrated on high-end collectibles, such as wool scarves and silk ties based on the characters' costumes. Reportedly, about 70 percent of Potter action figures are bought by college students.

Smaller-budget films can sometimes imitate the big promotional efforts. The campaign for Wes Anderson's *The Grand Budapest Hotel* offered eccentric products, such as mustache wax, on eBay auctions. Videos showing how to create pastries like those in the film went viral. Fans began posting footage of their own creations, and those featured in ads on television cooking shows. The script of the film was published, as was Anderson's curated collection of stories that inspired him. A hefty art book consisting of interviews and essays about the film was published just before the 2015 Academy Awards ceremony. Interestingly, Anderson has permitted fans to make and sell their own merchandise inspired by his films. For big-studio projects, the property is the brand, but for an independent like Anderson, the brand is the filmmaker himself.

In addition to merchandising, there is *cross-promotion*, or *brand partnering*. This tactic allows a film and a product line to be advertised simultaneously. A partner company, in the case of children's films often a fast-food chain or a soft-drinks manufacturer, receives the right to use characters from a film in its advertising. In exchange, the firm commits to spending a certain amount on ads and promotions featuring its products and the film's characters. Such a bargain can shift tens of millions of dollars in publicity costs away from the studios. *How to Train Your Dragon 2* had tie-ins with candy, bubblegum, and McDonald Happy Meals. Other cross-promotional campaigns are designed for adults. The James Bond films have long relied on cobranding, with stars featured in ads and the products appearing in the films. *Skyfall* was cross-promoted with Coke Zero, Heineken beer, Bollinger champagne, Omega watches, Jaguar cars, Range Rover, perfumes, and nail polishes.

CONNECT TO THE BLOG
www.davidbordwell.net/blog

Internet sites don't guarantee success. We speculate on why in "Snakes, no, Borat, yes. Not all Internet publicity is the same."

CONNECT TO THE BLOG
www.davidbordwell.net/blog

Have Hollywood films declined in popularity internationally? We don't think so, as we explain in "World rejects Hollywood blockbusters!?"

CONNECT TO THE BLOG
www.davidbordwell.net/blog

How did theaters convert from 35mm film projection to digital projection? The story is told in our blog series, "Pandora's Digital Box" and in our e-book of the same title.

Exhibition: Theatrical and Nontheatrical

We're most familiar with the exhibition phase of the business, the moment when we pay for a movie ticket or play a DVD or stream a movie. *Theatrical* exhibition involves screening to a public that pays admission, as in commercial movie houses. Other theatrical sites are city art centers, museums, film festivals, and cinema clubs. *Nontheatrical* exhibition includes all other presentations, such as home video, cable transmissions, Internet downloads, and screenings in schools and colleges.

Public movie exhibition centers on the commercial theater. Most theaters screen wide releases from the major distributors, while others specialize in foreign-language or independent films. In all, the theatrical moviegoing audience is not a colossal one. In the United States, admissions average around 30 million per week, which sounds like a huge number until we realize that the weekly television audience numbers about 200 million. Only about 10 percent of the U.S. population visits movie theaters once a month or more; about one-third never goes at all.

The most heavily patronized theaters belong to chains or circuits, and in most countries, these circuits are controlled by a few companies. Until the 1980s, most theaters housed only one screen, but exhibitors began to realize that several screens under one roof could reduce costs. The multiplex theater, containing up to 15 or more screens, lured far bigger crowds than a single-screen cinema could. Centralized projection booths and concession stands also cut costs.

The boom in building multiplexes allowed exhibitors to upgrade the presentation, offering stadium seating, digital sound, and in some cases Imax and 3D. Multiplexes can also devote occasional screenings to niche markets, as when live opera broadcasts are shown digitally. Multiplexes are now the norm in most of the world, with snacks adjusted to local tastes—popcorn and candy nearly everywhere, but also salty licorice (in the Netherlands) and dried squid (in Hong Kong).

The United States is the most lucrative national market, contributing 25 percent of global box office receipts (see "Movies on Screens" chart). China comes in second because of its immense urban population. China's economy and its film industry are still on the rise; in 2014 alone, 15 new screens opened every day. Consequently, the country's share of world revenues will grow even larger. The most important regional market outside North America is Western Europe (including the United Kingdom and the Nordic countries), which provides 25 percent of the global box office. Filmmakers around the world aim for distribution in these lucrative markets.

Overseas multiplexes have yielded great benefits for Hollywood. Some American distributors have invested in foreign chains, thus guaranteeing an outlet for their products. In addition, comfortable multiplexes attract more prosperous viewers. Because multiplexes tend to charge higher prices than older theaters, the cost of tickets has risen throughout the world. Some price hikes are also attributable to 3D and Imax showings, which have proven enormously popular outside the United States.

In 1999, four of the 3,100 theaters in which *Star Wars: Episode I—The Phantom Menace* played had digital projectors. At the end of 2014, there were over 127,000 digital theater screens worldwide—90 percent of all screens. As an exhibition format, 35mm film was confined to countries with struggling economies and, in the rich world, to archives and specialized theaters.

Although films are shown in such venues as museums, archives, and film clubs, the most important theatrical alternative to commercial movie houses has become the *film festival*. The first major annual film festival was held in Venice in 1932, and although it had to be suspended during World War II, it was revived afterward and endures today. Festivals were mounted in Cannes, Berlin, Karlovy Vary, Moscow, Edinburgh, and many other cities. Today there are thousands of festivals all over the world—some large and influential, such as the Toronto Film Festival, and others aimed primarily at bringing unusual films to local audiences.

Movies on Screens: A 2013 Profile of International Theatrical Exhibition

Worldwide production of theatrical motion pictures: **6,300 features**

Worldwide attendance: **6.53 billion admissions**

Worldwide number of screens: **136,497**

Worldwide box office receipts: **$35.4 billion**

U.S. box office receipts: **$9.9 billion**

Western Europe box office receipts: **$8.2 billion**

China box office receipts: **$3.5 billion**

Countries and Numbers of Screens

Highest: USA 39,783; China 18,109; India 11,081; Mexico 5,594; France 5,587; Germany 4,610; Russia 4,119; UK 3,897; Spain 3,675; Japan 3,318; Italy 2,977

Lowest: Malta 37; Netherlands 36; Azerbaijan 29; Macedonia 26; Tunisia 17

Annual Admissions

Highest: India 1.98 billion; USA 1.22 billion; China 610 million; Mexico 257 million; South Korea 213 million; France 190.9 million; Russia 177.1 million; UK 165.5 million; Japan 155.9 million; Brazil 145.9 million

Other: Australia 87 million; New Zealand 14.5 million; Iceland 1.4 million (highest per capita film attendance, with 4.3 visits per year)

Average Ticket Prices in U.S. Dollars

Highest: Switzerland $16.80; Norway $15.80; Sweden $15.20; Denmark $13.80; Japan $12.80

Lowest: Egypt $2.50; Philippines $2.20; Venezuela $.80; India $.60

Others: Australia $12.90; UK $10.20; France $8.60; Canada $8.34; USA $8.00; China $5.80

Sources: *IHS Media Technology Digest and Focus: World Film Market Trends 2014*

Some festivals promote specific genres, such as the Brussels International Festival of Fantastic Film, or specific subject matter, such as the New York Gay and Lesbian Film Festival.

The big festivals may show major Hollywood films. In 2013, *The Great Gatsby* was the opening-night presentation at the Cannes International Film Festival. Usually, however, the focus is on less mainstream cinema. Some festivals, like those in Cannes and Pusan, South Korea, include markets where such films can find distributors. The International Film Festival Rotterdam even helps to finance films made in developing countries. Not all festivals award prizes, but the bigger ones that do—most notably Cannes, Venice, and Berlin—can draw attention to films that might otherwise get lost among the hundreds of movies circulating among festivals.

Festivals offer an outlet for films that might never be picked up for release beyond their country of origin. For example, during the mid-1980s, programmers showcased the films of Abbas Kiarostami, Mohsen Makhmalbaf, and other Iranian directors. By winning prizes and critical acclaim at festivals, Iranian films gained commercial distribution in Europe and North America.

> ❝ I've come to realize that my festival run is my theatrical run."
> —Joe Swanberg, independent film director, *Hannah Takes the Stairs*

CONNECT TO THE BLOG
www.davidbordwell.net/blog

Films may be altered as they move from window to window. We show what happened to the airline version of *The Grand Budapest Hotel* in "Proof! and a minor mystery."

Ancillary Markets: Taking Movies beyond the Theater

When a film leaves theatrical distribution, it lives on. Home video creates a vast array of ancillary markets "downstream," and taken together these return more money than the theatrical release windows and the Web.

Distributors carefully plan the timing of their video releases according to *windows* of scheduling. Typically the video version appears first on hotel pay-television systems, then on pay-per-view cable, then on DVD release, then on pay cable outlets like HBO, and eventually on network broadcast and basic cable. Thanks to greater Internet bandwidth, video on demand (VOD) has become an important window. Sometimes VOD becomes available after a film's theatrical release, sometimes during it, and sometimes even before it.

Each window is delayed by a certain period from the initial release. For example, DVD/Blu-ray releases become available three to six months after the film's theatrical opening. The windows strategy maximizes the income from consumers with different levels of interest. Video has proved a boon to smaller distributors, too. Foreign and independent films yield slim returns in theatrical release, but DVD and VOD can make these items profitable.

With only 10 percent of Americans being regular moviegoers, television, in one form or another, has kept the theatrical market going. During the 1960s, the U.S. television networks began supporting Hollywood production by purchasing broadcast rights to the studios' output. Lower-budget filmmakers depended on sales to European television and U.S. cable outlets. Videocassette versions arrived in the 1980s, and surprisingly they didn't harm the theatrical side of the business. In 1997, when the DVD format was introduced, consumers embraced it as a substitute for VHS tape. In the United States, the Walmart chain became the main purveyor of DVDs, accounting for over a third of all sales.

The major U.S. studios set up home entertainment divisions to sell DVDs. Because the discs cost less than VHS tapes to create, the studios reaped huge rewards. The cable and network television aftermarket remained brisk as well. Currently a studio film earns only a quarter or less of its total income from theatrical screenings. All forms of home video yield about 70 percent, with the remainder coming from licensed merchandise and other income.

Despite the swift success of the DVD format, it caused distributors some worries as well. The discs were easy to copy and manufacture in bulk, so piracy took off worldwide. A bootleg DVD of a Hollywood movie could sell for as little as 80 cents in China. Moreover, with tens of thousands of DVD titles available, shelf space was at a premium, so discount chains dumped slow-moving titles into bargain bins. DVD purchases stalled, and rentals became more popular with the rise of subscription services such as Netflix. The Blu-ray disc, which offered superior quality, was designed to replace the DVD, but sales didn't match the success of the earlier format.

The video market sustains most commercial filmmaking in the long run, but movie theatres remain central to the exhibition system. A theatrical screening focuses public interest. Critics review the film, television and the press publicize it, and people talk about it. The theatrical run usually determines how successful a movie will be in ancillary markets.

Even though the worldwide theatrical audience grew during the 1990s, most of the growth was in developing countries. U.S. and European attendance showed signs of flattening or even declining. Multiplexes were competing with home theaters, video games, and Internet entertainment. Exhibitors tried various ways to keep audiences coming.

One successful strategy involved building Imax screens in multiplexes and showing studio tentpole pictures in that immersive format. A second strategy focused on digital 3D. The push toward 3D production encouraged exhibitors to

CONNECT TO THE BLOG
www.davidbordwell.net/blog

Many movies are available on the Internet, for legal or illegal downloading. That doesn't mean every movie ever made will someday be online. We talk about why with two restoration experts in "The celestial multiplex."

install digital projection systems faster than they probably would have otherwise. In turn, the major studios began tailoring their blockbusters to 3D. Both Imax and 3D screenings charged higher ticket prices, which benefited exhibitor and distributor alike.

The stupendous rise in Internet usage after 2000 transformed distribution and exhibition. As more people acquired high-speed connections, films of any length could be made available online. For the major distributors, the Net offered a chance to resell their product, but without the problems of DVDs. Selling movies as downloads (termed "electronic sell-through" [EST]) or renting them as streaming video eliminated the cost of making discs. Encryption could prevent consumers from copying films. Netflix, Apple's iTunes store, Hulu (a consortium of Hollywood studios), among other smaller companies, launched online distribution services.

In 2013, U.S. digital transactions for film and television shows yielded over $6.5 billion in total revenue. Sales and rentals of DVDs and Blu-ray discs yielded somewhat more,

1.46 **Distributing a film via the Web.** Johan Rijpma's graceful *Tape Generations,* an abstract animation choreographing rolls of transparent tape, was downloaded over half a million times in 17 days.

but viewers were starting to understand the advantages of "always on" media. To make downloading more attractive, media companies let consumers store their purchased films in online lockers that they could access with personal digital devices. Consumers, especially young ones who had grown up with the Net, were shifting away from packaged media and toward utilizing a service that made movies available to them at any moment.

The major distributors were not the only beneficiaries of Web 2.0. The Net offers a far more level playing field than traditional distribution. Films that would never be shown in a multiplex can gain enormous audiences online. Judson Laipply's "Evolution of the Dance" (over 290 million views), "JK Wedding Entrance Dance" (nearly 88 million views), and innumerable pieces starring household pets showed that amateur videos, once limited to family or friends, could become Internet sensations. More carefully made films could get exposure on an unprecedented scale **(1.46).** Rival high schools won millions of viewers with elaborate single-take lipdubs. YouTube and Vimeo revived the short-film format for a new generation, and hopeful filmmakers saw posting a film online as a way to bypass corporate gatekeepers.

Some filmmakers still want to show their work in theaters. To meet that desire, festivals of DIY films have arisen, including the DIY Film Festival, based in Los Angeles and traveling to other cities. Another started in 2001, when 10 small teams of filmmakers in Washington, D.C., accepted a challenge to make a short film in 48 hours. All the completed shorts would be screened as a program immediately after the deadline. The result was the 48 Hour Film Project, which has become popular in dozens of cities around the world and which regularly sends films to international festivals.

DVDs and the Internet, videogame players and cellphones, laptops and tablet computers—all these have revolutionized movie viewing. Today people can watch films, short or long, amateur or professional, virtually anywhere. Digital technology not only changed theatrical exhibition; it redefined nontheatrical distribution and exhibition.

Artistic Implications of Distribution and Exhibition

Grosses, synergy, ticket prices, and movies on game consoles might seem very remote from issues of film as an art. Yet film is a technological medium usually aimed at a broad public, so the ways in which movies are circulated and shown

CONNECT TO THE BLOG
www.davidbordwell.net/blog

We talk about inventive teenage lipdubs as a form of film art in "2-4-6-8, whose lipdub do we appreciate?"

CONNECT TO THE BLOG
www.davidbordwell.net/blog

In this age of new media, have movies lost their importance to audiences? Some would say yes, but we argue against that idea in "Movies still matter."

can affect viewers' experiences. Home video turns viewing into a small-group or individual activity, but seeing a film in a packed theater yields a different response. Comedies, most people feel, seem funnier in a theater, where infectious laughter can ripple through a crowd. Filmmakers are aware of this difference, so they preview comedies many times to test audience reactions.

New Narrative Possibilities   Video distribution and exhibition have created new choices in the realm of storytelling. Until the 1980s, people couldn't rewatch a movie whenever they wished. With videotape and then DVDs viewers can pore over a film. Bonus materials encourage them to rerun the movie to spot things they missed. Some filmmakers have taken advantage of this opportunity by creating *puzzle films* such as *Memento, Donnie Darko,* and *Inception,* which fans scrutinize for clues to plot enigmas **(1.47, 1.48).** Video versions can deviate from and complicate the theatrical release version, as the extra ending of *The Butterfly Effect* does. Some interactive DVD movies permit the viewers to choose how the plot develops. The DVD of Greg Marcks's *11:14* allows you to enter parallel storylines at various points, in effect recasting the film's overall form.

With the Internet as a major distribution platform, we should expect variations in narrative form. Short-form storytelling is already in full bloom online. Events like the festivals run by the 48 Hour Film Project also encourage the making of short films, especially given the assumption that most of the films will later be posted on the Internet. We're likely to find movies designed specifically for mobile phones; television series are already creating "mobisodes" branching off the broadcast storyline. The Web is the logical place for interactive films that use hyperlinks to amplify or detour a line of action.

CONNECT TO THE BLOG
www.davidbordwell.net/blog

Have DVDs radically changed the way movies tell their stories? Mostly not, we argue in "New media and old storytelling."

❝ *The Matrix* is entertainment for the age of media convergence, integrating multiple texts to create a narrative so large that it cannot be contained within a single medium."
—Henry Jenkins, media analyst

1.47–1.48 Planting clues for DVD rewatching. A viewer scrutinizing *Magnolia* on DVD would notice that the extraordinary meteorological event at the climax is predicted by the recurring numerals 82, referring to chapter and verse in the biblical book of Exodus (1.47). Elsewhere, the figure 82 appears as coils in the rooftop hose (1.48).

1.47

1.48

Marketing and merchandising can extend a theatrical film's story in intriguing ways. The *Star Wars* novels and video games give the characters more adventures and expand spectators' engagement with the movies. The *Memento* website hinted at ways to interpret the film. The *Matrix* video games supplied key information for the films' plots, while the second movie in the trilogy sneaked in hints for playing the games. As a story world shifts from platform to platform, a multimedia saga is created, and viewers' experiences will shift accordingly. *Matrix* viewers who have never played the games understand the story somewhat differently from those who have.

Even product placement offers some artistic opportunities. We're usually distracted when a Toyota truck or a box of Frosted Flakes pops up on the screen, but *Back to the Future* cleverly integrates brands into its story. Marty McFly is catapulted from 1985 to 1955. Trapped in a period when diet soda didn't exist, he asks for a Pepsi Free, but the counterman says he'll have to pay for it. Later, buying a bottle of Pepsi from a vending machine, Marty tries frantically to twist off the cap, but his father-to-be George McFly casually pops it off at the machine's built-in opener. Pepsi soft drinks weave through the movie, reasserting Marty's comic inability to adjust to his parents' era, and perhaps stirring some nostalgia in viewers who remember how teenage life has changed since their youth.

Screens and Sounds: Stylistic Opportunities and Challenges

Distribution and exhibition can affect a filmmaker's stylistic choices as well. Consider modern sound systems. Today almost all multiplex theaters are equipped with some type of surround system such as Dolby Digital 5.1. In a 5.1 configuration, the first digit refers to the number of channels used (5), and the second (.1) refers to the use of a large subwoofer to reproduce low-frequency effects. Three speakers behind the screen are aligned with the left, center, and right areas of the image. The remaining two channels transmit sounds to the surround speakers. These are further split into left and right halves and are grouped along the side and back walls of the auditorium.

The center speaker emits most of the onscreen dialogue, as well as the most important sound effects. The left and right speakers are stereophonic, adding sound effects, music, and minor dialogue. These channels can suggest sound events within the frame or just off screen. The surround channels carry ambient sounds, music, and reverberation—that is, slightly delayed repetitions of sounds from other speakers.

Dolby 5.1 is currently the global standard for multichannel sound recording and reproduction. Whether the film is a visual-effects-heavy blockbuster, like *Transformers: Age of Extinction*, or a more modest psychological thriller, like *Black Swan*, most commercial theaters will present the film mixed in that format.

If you're a filmmaker, Dolby 5.1 gives you many creative opportunities. You can set visual action directly in front of your viewers, or you can surround them with a busy auditory environment similar to real life. The immersive effect is intensified by Dolby Atmos, a recently developed system that accommodates up to 64 distinct channels, some of them in the ceiling. Directors and supervising sound editors can now place sounds precisely within the theater space.

Brave, the first film mixed in Atmos, exploits this possibility in a scene where Merida receives "princess training" from her mother (**1.49**).

CONNECT TO THE BLOG
www.davidbordwell.net/blog

The concept of "transmedia storytelling"—shifting a story world's action across media platforms—was formulated by scholar Henry Jenkins. We discuss his ideas in "Now leaving from platform 1."

" Not until seeing [*North by Northwest*] again on the big screen did I realize conclusively what a gigantic difference screen size does make. . . . This may be yet another reason why younger people have a hard time with older pictures: they've only seen them on the tube, and that reduces films' mystery and mythic impact."

—Peter Bogdanovich, director, *The Last Picture Show* and *Mask*

1.49 Surround-sound precision. As Merida recites a poem, the Queen says, "Enunciate! You must be understood from anywhere in the room, or it's all for naught." When Merida says under her breath, "This is all for naught," the camera briefly holds on her. The off-screen Queen's snappish reply, "I heard that!" comes from one of the left rear speakers. Her Majesty's demand that Merida project her voice to the entire room seems to be a boastful display of the power of the Atmos multichannel system.

1.50

1.51

1.50–1.51 Shot scale adjusted for image display. On the large screen of a CinemaScope theater, the faces of these characters in *How to Marry a Millionaire* would have been quite visible (1.50). Early television relied heavily on close-ups because of the small screen size, as in this shot from a 1953 *Dragnet* episode (1.51).

CONNECT TO THE BLOG
www.davidbordwell.net/blog

We explore another peril of watching films on video—logos superimposed on films—in "Bugs: the secret history."

1.52–1.53 Close-up or long shot?
Extreme close-ups of actors' faces are common in modern cinema, as in this shot from *Red Eye*. Filmmakers are adjusting their style to the fact that most viewing takes place on video formats (1.52). In *Flowers of Shanghai,* director Hou Hsiao-hsien builds every scene out of full shots of several characters. The result loses information on a small display and is best seen on a theater screen (1.53).

Brave also showcases Atmos's ability to create an overhead zone. Describing a scene where Merida goes to retrieve an arrow, *Brave*'s sound designer, Gary Rydstrom, says, "I love putting sound in the ceiling, things like scary forest birds. For a little girl, the forest feels even taller and more imposing if you can have weird sounds way up high."

Filmmakers have likewise responded to changes in image displays. In the early 1950s, new aspect ratios like CinemaScope made theater screens both wider and bigger overall. A common size was 24 feet by 64 feet. Many directors and producers believed that these screens made close-ups unnecessary, perhaps too aggressive. The new exhibition demands pushed many filmmakers toward distant framings and full-size figures **(1.50).**

By contrast, television of the same period displayed a small, rather unclear image, in some cases only 10 inches diagonally. If you were a filmmaker obliged to fill the fuzzy little frame, you'd probably do what TV directors did. They tended to rely on close shots, which were more visible on the monitor **(1.51).**

Today both extremes exist. Modern multiplex screens can be quite large, but most people will see a film on a video monitor or a computer screen. Accordingly, commercial films tend to favor medium and close views, which are more readable on small displays **(1.52).** Yet some contemporary filmmakers have picked the alternative option, designing their films for the scale of a theater screen **(1.53).**

Every change in technology and exhibition has forced filmmakers to make tough choices. For example, many films contain images wider than nearly all video

1.52

1.53

1.54   **1.55**

1.54–1.55 Changing compositions in video distribution. In *Jaws,* a wide image in the original (1.54) is cropped to fit 16 × 9 TV monitors for a cable airing (1.55).

and computer monitors. How can these small displays respect the filmmaker's intentions?

The best solution, seen on DVDs and many cable and streaming services, is *letterboxing*. With letterboxing, dark bands at the top and bottom of the screen allow for the whole image to be shown. If the image isn't letterboxed, then parts of it must be cut off to make it fit the monitor **(1.54, 1.55).** This process, called *pan-and-scan,* was common with consumer videotapes and can still be seen on some cable and streaming services, as well as on airplane in-flight monitors. Often these versions are prefaced by the comment that the film has been "adjusted to fit your screen."

Again, an exhibition format has affected filmmakers' creative choices. Because home video might crop part of the image, some directors compose their shots so that the key action is concentrated in an area that will fit smaller displays **(1.56).**

Other problems with consumer video displays can't be solved by the filmmaker. Older films were designed in an approximately 4 × 3 ratio, and traditional television monitors were in accord with that. The introduction of widescreen TV monitors has created a new problem for film images. Monitors with a 16 × 9 ratio can reproduce some modern films faithfully, but older material can suffer by being stretched and distorted **(1.57).** Some monitors allow adjusting the ratio by creating black bands on the sides to provide "windowboxing." In this case, the viewer must take the initiative and respect the intentions of the filmmakers.

 CONNECT TO THE BLOG
www.davidbordwell.net/blog

Jean-Luc Godard's films present special challenges to the projectionist and DVD producer, as we show in "Godard comes in many shapes and sizes."

1.56 Adjusting composition for the television frame. As with many modern wide-screen films, the essential information on screen left in this shot from *Catch Me If You Can* would fit within squarer video displays. Still, cropping out the right half would lose a secondary piece of information—the pile of take-out food cartons that implies that Agent Hanratty has been at his desk for days.

1.57 Incorrect aspect ratio. Here the 4 × 3 image from *Angel Face* (1952) is rendered on an incorrectly set 16 × 9 widescreen television monitor. Many viewers do not know how to change a monitor's ratio, and some monitors make it difficult to correct the problem.

SUMMARY

The art of film depends on technology, from the earliest experiments in apparent motion to the most recent computer programs. It also depends on people who use that technology, who come together to make films, distribute them, and show them. As long as a film is aimed at an audience, however small, it enters into a social dynamic of production, distribution, and exhibition. Out of technology and work processes, filmmakers create an experience for their viewers. Along the way, they inevitably make choices about film form and style. What options are available to them? How might filmmakers organize the film? How might they draw on the techniques of the medium? The next two parts of this book survey the possibilities.

2

Film Form

Chapter 1 outlined some ways in which people, working with technology, make films. Now we can ask more basic questions.

If you were to make a film, what would guide you in putting the whole thing together? How would you fit the various parts to one another? How would you try to shape the viewer's experience of the whole film? Thinking about these questions will help us understand how we respond to individual movies and how cinema works as an artistic medium.

The next two chapters explore questions like these. We assume that a film isn't a random assortment of things. If it were, viewers wouldn't care if they missed a movie's ending, or if scenes were shown out of order. But viewers do care. When you describe a book as hard to put down or a song as engaging, you're implying that a pattern exists there. The pattern is pulling you along. This overall pattern of relationships among parts is called *form*.

Chapter 2 examines form in film. This concept is one key to understanding cinema as an art. Filmmakers are thinking about a film's form at each stage of the production process, and formal matters demand creative decisions at every turn.

Although there are several ways of organizing films into formal wholes, the one that we most commonly encounter involves telling a story. Filmmakers are well aware that narrative form arouses our interest and impels us to follow a series of events from start to finish. Chapter 3 examines how certain principles allow a story to arouse and fulfill our expectations. We consider examples of nonnarrative form in Chapter 10.

2

The Significance
of Film Form

You are a filmmaker. How might you start your movie? With an exciting bit of action that grabs the viewer's interest? Or with something more slowly paced that gradually builds up involvement?

Steven Spielberg's *Jurassic Park* follows option one. Park workers nervously surround a shipping container housing an unseen, thrashing, roaring beast. Workers train their weapons on the case as it's opened to release the creature into the park. The gate slides open, but the heaving cage knocks a worker to the ground. Suddenly he's seized and dragged into the container **(2.1).** The guards fire at the creature, but the man slides into darkness.

The film doesn't present another dinosaur attack for an hour. In the meantime, we get background information about the park, its genetically bred inhabitants, and the characters who have been brought there. Conflicts build and schemes emerge. Yet before all this development of the drama, Spielberg and his screenwriters Michael Crichton and David Koepp have given us a taste of the suspense and physical action coming up later. Since the opening doesn't show us the velociraptor, we look forward to seeing the beast fully, and in action. The filmmakers' creative decisions have shaped our experience—teasing us with the promise of thrills but making us wait while the plot is filled in. Primed by this opening, we'll be vigilant for anything that would put the characters at risk. And of course the violence of the first scene gives the lie to the bland cuteness of the park's publicity rolled out in later scenes. We know, as the visiting scientists don't, that behind the family-friendly surface this is a dangerous place.

Spielberg's *Close Encounters of the Third Kind* begins in a far less aggressive way. During a desert sandstorm, men in goggles and protective suits meet a French scientist. They exchange greetings before pressing forward to check a fleet of vintage airplanes, reported missing in 1945. The man serving as a translator raises a flurry of questions: "Where's the crew? How did they get here?" **(2.2)** The investigative team finds an old man nearby. Although his face is badly sunburned, he's smiling. "He says the sun came out last night. He says it sang to him."

Instead of shocking us with violence, *Close Encounters'* opening poses a series of mysteries. Those will deepen in the scenes to come: a UFO swerves near a commercial jet, a little boy follows unseen home invaders into the night. The calmness of the opening, the friendly professionalism of the scientists, and the joyous reaction of the old man to what he's seen indicate that the film will be gentle, slow-moving, and concerned with characters trying to understand what is making extraordinary things happen. This will be an interplanetary mystery story, not a horror-action-adventure like *Jurassic Park*.

2.1

2.2

2.1–2.2 Hard and soft openings. Grabbing the audience in *Jurassic Park* (2.1) versus enticing the audience in *Close Encounters of the Third Kind* (2.2).

Either strategy for starting a movie, abrupt or gradual, can have a strong effect on the viewer. The choices come down to a matter of *form*—the way parts work together to create an overall effect. If you are a director or screenwriter, you face perpetual choices about form. As a viewer, you are responding to it at every moment.

The Concept of Form in Film

Form as Pattern

The arts offer us intensely involving experiences. We say that movies draw us in or immerse us. We can lose track of time when listening to music, and when we enjoy a novel, we may say, "I really got into it." All these ways of talking suggest that artworks involve us by engaging our senses, feelings, and mind in a *process*. That process sharpens our interest, focuses our attention, urges us forward. How does this happen?

Because the artist has created a pattern. Artists design their works—they give them form—so that we can have a structured experience. For this reason, form is of central importance in film.

> ❝ I believe in soft openings for movies. . . . I think it's almost impossible to lose an audience in the first ten minutes. . . . It's not television. You don't have to grab them. In a movie with a very fast opening, you end up paying for it somewhere along the way— usually by having to explain what happened in the fast and furious action."
>
> —Robert Towne, screenwriter, *Chinatown*

Our minds are very good at finding patterns in things—faces in the clouds, a rhythm in a downpour. Artworks rely on this dynamic, unifying effort of the human mind. Novels present a pattern of events that create suspense or surprise, while paintings expect that we'll be sensitive to composition and color. Artworks in all media ask us to pay attention, to anticipate upcoming events, to construct a whole out of parts, and to feel an emotional response to the pattern that we help create.

In similar ways, a film coaxes us to connect sequences into a larger whole. The savage attack at the start of *Jurassic Park* establishes the park's raptors as a force to be reckoned with later. We'd be disappointed if they never reappeared in the plot. Similarly, *Close Encounters* promises to reveal the fates of the missing World War II pilots and the runaway boy.

Even small details get linked in a pattern. Early in *Collateral*, the taxi driver Max is shown wiping down his cab's dashboard and steering wheel before setting out on his night shift. He then carefully clips a snapshot to his sun visor. For a moment, he gazes at the postcard view of a tropical island (**2.3**). These gestures prompt us to see Max's personality as neat and orderly. They also suggest that in the city's turmoil, he clears a quiet mental space for himself. The next scene's cues reinforce our judgment of Max's character (**2.4, 2.5**). Small or large, local or far-ranging, the patterns we find engage our interest, our minds, and our emotions.

These instances suggest that a film is not simply a random batch of elements. Like all artworks, a film has **form.** By form, in its broadest sense, we mean the overall set of relationships among a film's parts.

This description of form is still very abstract, so let's draw some examples from one movie you've probably seen. In *The Wizard of Oz*, the viewer is expected to follow a story—that is, a pattern of *narrative* elements. These are events that involve the characters. Dorothy dreams that a tornado blows her to Oz. There she encounters other characters, and together they have adventures. Eventually Dorothy awakens from her dream to find herself home in Kansas. Alongside the story, we can also notice *stylistic* elements: the way the camera moves, the arrangements of color in the frame, the use of music, and other devices. Stylistic elements utilize the various film techniques we'll be considering in later chapters.

Because *The Wizard of Oz* is designed to give us a particular experience, we actively relate the elements within each set to one another. We know that the narrative elements form a pattern, a story. We see the tornado as causing Dorothy's trip to Oz, and her adventures there result from her desire to get home. Likewise, we identify the characters in Oz as similar to characters in Dorothy's Kansas life. Various stylistic elements also form patterns. We recognize the "We're Off to See the Wizard" tune whenever Dorothy picks up a new companion. Our experience of the film depends on our recognizing and anticipating how these broad patterns will develop.

Moreover, our minds tie these two sorts of patterning together. In *The Wizard of Oz*, the narrative development can be linked to the stylistic patterning. Colors identify story landmarks, such as Kansas (in black and white) and the Yellow Brick Road. Movements of the camera call our attention to story action. And the music serves to describe certain characters and situations. The relationships among all these elements make up the overall form of *The Wizard of Oz*.

"Form" Versus "Content"

Very often people think of "form" as the opposite of something called "content." This implies that a poem or a musical piece or a film is like a jug. An external shape, the jug, *contains* a liquid that could just as easily be held in a cup or a pail. Under this assumption, form becomes less important than whatever it's presumed to contain.

We don't accept this assumption. We think that every component functions as part of a pattern, big or small, that engages the viewer. So we'll treat as formal elements many things that some people consider content. From our standpoint, subject matter and abstract ideas all enter into the total form of the artwork. They may cue

2.3

2.4

2.5

2.3–2.5 Patterns create character. Max is introduced as able to tune out his environment, thanks to the island on his postcard (2.3). We're reminded of this when in the next scene, as the passengers quarrel, he tips down the visor and stares at the postcard, as if to shut out the unpleasantness in his back seat (2.4, 2.5).

us to frame certain expectations or imagine certain possibilities. The viewer relates these elements to one another dynamically. Consequently, subject matter and ideas become somewhat different from what they might be outside the artwork.

Consider extraterrestrials and UFOs. In popular thinking, aliens can be either peaceful or hostile, but if you were going to make a film about UFOs, you'd have to decide how to treat the subject. That would be a decision about form. In *Independence Day*, presenting the aliens as an invading horde fits well with a story of Americans of all classes uniting to conquer a threat. By contrast, *Close Encounters of the Third*

Kind treats alien visitors as spiritual teachers, creatures who restore people's sense of wonder and promise a better life. The aliens of *Mars Attacks!* pretend to be peaceful but then turn treacherous, and their cunning reveals the ineptitude of the people in power. This treatment suits the film's satire of modern politics and media. In each case, the filmmakers' choices about form have repurposed the basic subject matter of aliens. What we might call the content is governed by the film's formal context.

Formal Expectations

We're now in a better position to see how film form grabs and holds us. It creates expectations and sustains them over time. Suppose that *Jurassic Park* never revealed the raptors, or *Close Encounters* never explained its puzzles. We'd think that something important had been left out, to say the least. Once we're caught up in following the interrelations among elements, we want the patterns to develop and conclude.

Expectations color our everyday experiences. Psychological experiments have shown that if people are told that a cheap wine is expensive, they rate it as tasting better than if they're told its true price. Creating expectations is central to advertising any product. A film's title, its poster, its online promotion, and its trailers aim to set up particular expectations. You would not go to a film called *12 Years a Slave* anticipating a raunchy teen comedy.

Expectation pervades our experience of artworks. In reading a mystery, we expect that a solution will be offered at some point, usually the end. In listening to a piece of music, we expect repetition of a melody or a motif. In looking at a painting, we search for what we expect to be the most significant areas, then scan the less prominent portions. From beginning to end, our involvement with a work of art depends largely on expectations.

We can illustrate this with a little experiment. Assume that "A" is the first letter of a series. What follows?

AB

After seeing A, you probably thought that the next letters would run in alphabetical order. Your expectation was confirmed. What follows AB? Most people would say "C." But form doesn't always follow our initial expectation.

ABA

Here form takes us a little by surprise. If we are puzzled by a formal twist, we readjust our expectations and try again. What follows ABA?

ABAC

Here the main possibilities were either ABAB or ABAC. (Note that your expectations limit possibilities as well as select them.) If you expected ABAC, your expectation was fulfilled, and you can confidently predict the next letter. If you expected ABAB, you still should be able to make a strong guess at the next letter:

ABACA

Simple as this game is, it illustrates the involving power of form. As a viewer or listener you don't simply let the parts parade past you. You enter into an active participation with them, creating and readjusting expectations as the pattern develops over time.

If you're a filmmaker, you want to arouse and shape viewers' expectations. This is what happens in the opening scenes of *Jurassic Park* and *Close Encounters.* Similarly, *The Wizard of Oz* begins with Dorothy running down a road with her dog Toto **(2.6).** Immediately, we form expectations. She seems to be fleeing from someone; will she be caught? Perhaps she will meet another character or arrive at her destination. Even such a simple action asks us to participate in the story's development by adjusting our expectations about what may happen. Much later in the film, we come to expect that Dorothy will get her wish to return to Kansas. Indeed, the settings of the film give *The Wizard of Oz* a large-scale ABA form: Kansas-Oz-Kansas.

CONNECT TO THE BLOG
www.davidbordwell.net/blog

Even at the very beginning of a film, the title can give us clues to its subjects, themes, and form—or baffle us. We consider various options in "Title wave."

2.6 What does the audience expect? Dorothy pauses while fleeing with Toto at the beginning of *The Wizard of Oz.*

You probably noticed that the formal development of *The Wizard of Oz* didn't satisfy our expectations immediately, as our alphabet exercise did. When a filmmaker delays fulfilling an expectation, making us wait to see if the punch comes, the audience feels what we usually call *suspense*. As the term implies, suspense leaves something suspended—not only the next element in a pattern but also our urge for completion. Both the opening raptor attack in *Jurassic Park* and the mysteries in *Close Encounters* leave a pattern uncompleted, and as a result they keep us in suspense.

Expectations may also be cheated, as when we expect ABC but get ABA. In general, *surprise* is a result of an expectation that is revealed to be incorrect. We don't expect that a teenage boy troubled at home and at school will have a friend who has built a time machine. When this happens in *Back to the Future*, we understand that a high school comedy is turning into a science fiction movie.

One more pattern of our expectations needs tracing. Sometimes the filmmaker will cue us to think about what might have come *before* a certain point. When Dorothy runs down the road at the beginning of *The Wizard of Oz,* we wonder not only where she is going but where she's been and what she's fleeing from. In ways like these, filmmakers can arouse *curiosity* about earlier events. As Chapter 3 will show, curiosity is an important factor in narrative form.

Already we have several possible ways in which filmmakers' creative decisions about form can engage us. The filmmaker can cue us to make expectations and then gratify them. The expectations may be gratified quickly, as when we soon learn why Dorothy is running down the road. Or the filmmaker may wait quite a while before fulfilling our expectations, as with the raptors' eventual reappearance in *Jurassic Park*. And the filmmaker may set up expectations and then undercut them, creating surprise.

At a limit, the filmmaker may choose to disturb our expectations. We often associate art with pleasure, but many artworks offer us conflict, tension, and shock. An artwork's form may even strike us as unpleasant because of its imbalances or contradictions. For example, experimental films may jar rather than soothe us. Viewers frequently feel puzzled or shocked by *Eat, Scorpio Rising,* and other avant-garde works (pp. 369–386). We'll encounter similar challenges when we examine the editing of Sergei Eisenstein's *October* (Chapter 6) and the style of Jean-Luc Godard's *Breathless* (Chapter 11).

Yet even when they disturb us, filmmakers still arouse and shape formal expectations. For example, on the basis of our experience of most movie stories, we expect that the main characters introduced in the first half of a film will be present in the second half. Yet Wong Kar-wai punctures this expectation in *Chungking Express* (pp. 428–432). When our expectations are thwarted, we may feel disoriented, but then we adjust them to look for other, more appropriate, ways of engaging with the film's form.

If we can adjust our expectations to a disorienting work, we may find it satisfying in a new way. Hollis Frampton's *Zorns Lemma,* for example, slowly trains the viewer to associate a series of images with the letters of the alphabet **(2.7, 2.8).** Viewers often become quite absorbed in watching the series take shape as a cinematic picture puzzle. As *Chungking Express* and *Zorns Lemma* also suggest, a disturbing work can reveal to us our normal expectations about form. Such films can coax us to reflect on our taken-for-granted assumptions about how a movie must behave.

There is no limit to the number of ways in which a film can be organized. Some filmmakers will ask us to recast our expectations in drastic ways. Still, our enjoyment can increase if we welcome the unfamiliar experiences offered by formally challenging films.

Conventions and Experience

Our ABAC example illustrates still another point. One guide to your expectations is your *prior experience.* Your knowledge of the English alphabet makes ABA an unlikely sequence. This fact suggests that artistic form is not a pure activity isolated from other experiences.

CONNECT TO THE BLOG
www.davidbordwell.net/blog

Why is it that we feel suspense even if we're rewatching a film and know the outcome? We talk about how that happens in "This is your brain on movies, maybe."

❝ Now, if you're going to do action films, a certain amount of repetition, which certainly is a kind of straitjacket, is inevitable. You are going to have to deal with gunfights and chases. . . .

So it becomes a kind of game. The audience knows what the conclusion will be, but you still have to entertain them. So you are always walking on the edge of a precipice—trying to juggle the genre expectations. . . ."
—Walter Hill, director, *The Driver* and *The Warriors*

2.7   2.8

2.7–2.8 *Zorns Lemma* repeats the alphabet over and over, gradually replacing signs beginning with each letter, such as O (2.7), with images that have no relation to the letter (2.8). By the end of the film, we have been taught a new "alphabet" of patterned imagery.

CONNECT TO THE BLOG
www.davidbordwell.net/blog

Slumdog Millionaire uses some conventions in novel ways, as we show in "Slumdogged by the past."

❝ To a story-teller a journey is a marvelous device. It provides a strong thread on which a multitude of things that he has in mind may be strung to make a new thing, various, unpredictable, and yet coherent. My chief reason for using this form was technical."

—J. R. R. Tolkien

Artworks are human creations, and the artist lives in history and society. As a result, the artwork will relate, in some way, to other works and to aspects of the world. A tradition, a dominant style, a popular form—elements like these will be common to several different artworks. These common traits are usually called *conventions.*

For example, the first few scenes of a film often explain background information about the characters and the action; this sort of exposition is a narrative convention. *Genres,* as we will see in Chapter 9, depend heavily on conventions. Urban thrillers tend to feature spectacular car crashes, so Michael Mann's use of the device in *Collateral* (pp. 7–8) accords with that genre convention. It's a convention of the musical film that characters sing and dance, as in *The Wizard of Oz.* It's one convention of narrative form that the conclusion solves the problems that the characters confront, and *Wizard* likewise accepts this convention by letting Dorothy return to Kansas.

If the filmmaker can't avoid connecting to both art and the larger world, neither can the audience. When we respond to cues in the film, we call on our experiences of life and other artworks. You were able to play the ABAC game because you had learned the alphabet. You may have learned it in everyday life (in a classroom or from your parents) or from an artwork (perhaps from a rhyming song or TV cartoons). Similarly, we're able to recognize the journey structure in *The Wizard of Oz* because we've taken trips ourselves. We've also read such books as Homer's *Odyssey* and Tolkien's *The Lord of the Rings,* and we've seen other films organized around the journey pattern.

The filmmaker assumes that we viewers will draw on our knowledge of real life and our experience with artistic conventions. But what if the two principles come into conflict? In ordinary life, people don't simply start to sing and dance, as they do in *The Wizard of Oz.* Very often conventions separate art from life, saying implicitly, "In artworks of this sort, the laws of everyday reality don't operate. By the rules of *this* game, something 'unreal' *can* happen." All stylized art, from opera, ballet, and pantomime to slapstick comedy, depends on the audience's willingness to suspend the laws of ordinary experience and to accept particular conventions.

Why do characters in musicals sing to one another? Why doesn't Buster Keaton smile? It's beside the point to ask such questions. Filmmakers assume that we're familiar with conventions and are willing to go along with the game. You probably haven't met a contract killer in real life, but the cues in the early scenes of *Collateral* prompt you to take Vincent as a movie version of a hit man.

Further, conventions can change. Very brief flashbacks to earlier events in the story are common in today's films, but they would have been considered unusual in the 1930s and 1940s. Similarly, conventions of earlier periods of film history can seem odd to us today. Filmmakers rely on existing conventions, but they also may try to create new ones. For example, some modern directors have deliberately made films that lack the quick turns of events we associate with Hollywood movies. Films like Béla Tarr's *Satan's Tango* move at a solemn pace and ask us to concentrate on details of setting and sound. In other words, we're being asked to summon up an unusual set of expectations. As Tarr's sort of filmmaking attracted interest, other filmmakers explored the approach, so that this trend created its own set of conventions.

Form and Feeling

Filmmakers devote a great deal of effort to infusing emotion into their movies. To see how this happens, let's distinguish between *emotions represented* in the artwork and an *emotional response* felt by the spectator. If an actor grimaces in agony, the emotion of pain is represented within the film. But that emotion might not be felt by us in the audience; if the movie is a comedy, we might laugh. Both presented emotions and emotional responses have formal implications.

Emotions represented within the film play particular roles in the film's overall form. The dinosaur wranglers in the opening of *Jurassic Park* are grim and tense; their emotional attitude fits Spielberg's effort to show the park as a dangerous place. But the little boy in the opening of *Close Encounters* reacts to the offscreen aliens ransacking the kitchen with a smile of delight. This prepares us to expect that in later scenes the visitors will be shown as benevolent.

Form shapes the spectator's emotional response, too. We have just seen how cues in the artwork interact with our prior experience, especially our experience of artistic conventions. At the start of *Jurassic Park*, we're frightened and repelled. That's partly because we're naturally afraid of threatening creatures, but also we know that horror films include monsters that are designed to scare us.

Often, form in artworks appeals to our ready-made emotional responses. All other things being equal, we tend to smile at a gurgling baby and recoil from acts of torture. But form can create new responses instead of harping on old ones. An artwork may lead us to override or suspend our everyday emotional responses. No one wants to meet Hannibal Lecter in real life, but as a film character he may become spellbinding. In the abstract, we might find the land of Oz a child's paradise. But because the film's developing plot leads us to sympathize with Dorothy in her desire to go home, we feel satisfaction when she finally returns to Kansas.

The dynamic aspect of form also engages our feelings. Expectation, for instance, spurs emotion. When the filmmaker gets us wondering about what will happen next, we're likely to invest some emotion in the situation. Delayed fulfillment of an expectation—suspense—may produce anxiety or sympathy. (Will the detective find the criminal? Will boy get girl? Will the melody return?) Gratified expectations may produce a feeling of satisfaction or relief. (The detective solves the mystery; boy does get girl; the melody returns one more time.) Cheated expectations and curiosity about past material may produce puzzlement or keener interest. (So he isn't the detective? This isn't a romance story? Has a second melody replaced the first one?)

Note that all of these possibilities *may* occur. No recipe can guarantee that the filmmaker will achieve a specific emotional response. It is all a matter of context—that is, of each artwork's overall form. All we can say for certain is that the emotion felt by the spectator will emerge from formal patterns that she or he perceives in the work. This is one reason why we should try to notice as many formal relations as possible in a film. The richer our perception, the deeper and more complex our response may become.

The death of a child is perhaps the most sorrowful event that can occur in people's lives. Most films would use this event to summon up the sadness we would also feel in life. But artistic form can alter the emotional tenor of even this unhappy situation. In Jean Renoir's *The Crime of M. Lange,* the cynical publisher Batala rapes and abandons Estelle, a young laundress. After Batala disappears, Estelle

CONNECT TO THE BLOG
www.davidbordwell.net/blog

On slow-moving movies, see "The sarcastic laments of Béla Tarr" and "Tony and Theo."

> " If my film makes one more person feel miserable, I'll feel I've done my job."
> —Woody Allen, director, *Hannah and Her Sisters*

CONNECT TO THE BLOG
www.davidbordwell.net/blog

Scholars have studied the ways in which we respond emotionally to movies. We discuss their lines of argument in "Now you see it, now you can't."

2.9

2.10

2.9–2.10 Context reshaping emotion. In *The Crime of M. Lange*, the neighbors initially display grief at the news of Batala and Estelle's baby (2.9). But in reaction to Batala's cousin's remark, everyone breaks out into smiles (2.10). The film's formal development has rendered appropriate a reaction that might be perverse in ordinary life.

becomes integrated into the neighborhood and returns to her former fiancé. But Estelle is pregnant by Batala and bears his child.

The scene when Estelle's employer, Valentine, announces that the child was born dead is one of the most emotionally complex in cinema. The first reactions expressed by the characters are gravity and sorrow **(2.9).** Suddenly, Batala's cousin remarks, "Too bad. It was a relative." In the film's context, this is taken as a joke **(2.10).** The shift in the emotion represented in the film catches us off guard. Since these characters are not heartless, we must readjust our reaction to the death and respond as they do—with relief. Estelle's survival is far more important than the death of Batala's child. This is a daring, extreme example, but it dramatically illustrates how the emotions presented onscreen and aroused in us depend on the context created by form.

Form and Meaning

Like emotion, **meaning** is important to our experience of artworks. As viewers we are constantly testing the work for larger significance, for what it says or suggests. And filmmakers often create movies to convey their ideas and opinions. They want us to grasp the meanings they've offered.

What sorts of things might filmmakers and spectators think of as meaningful? Let's look at four remarks we might make about the meaning of *The Wizard of Oz*.

1. **Referential meaning.** *During the Depression, a tornado takes a girl from her family's Kansas farm to the mythical land of Oz. After a series of adventures, she returns home.*

This is very concrete, close to a bare-bones plot summary. Here the meaning depends on the spectator's ability to identify specific items: the hard times of America in the 1930s and features of midwestern climate. A viewer unacquainted with such information would miss some of the meanings cued by the film. We can call such tangible meanings *referential,* since the film refers to things or places already invested with significance in the real world.

A film's subject matter—in *The Wizard of Oz,* American farm life in the 1930s—is often established through referential meaning. And, as you might expect, referential meaning plays a role within the film's overall form. Suppose that instead of having Dorothy live in flat, spare, rural Kansas, the film made Dorothy a child living in a posh section of Beverly Hills. When she got to Oz (transported there, perhaps, by a hillside flash flood), the contrast between the crowded opulence of Oz and her home would not have been nearly as sharp. Here the referential meanings of Kansas and the Great Depression play a definite role in the overall contrast of settings that the film's form creates.

2. **Explicit meaning.** *A girl dreams of leaving home to escape her troubles. Only after she leaves does she realize how much she loves her family and friends. Nothing she finds elsewhere can replace them.*

This assertion is still fairly concrete in the meaning it attributes to the film. If someone were to ask you the *point* of the film—what it seems to be trying to get across—you might answer with something like this. Perhaps you would also mention Dorothy's closing line, "There's no place like home," as a summary of what she has learned. Let's call this sort of openly asserted meaning an *explicit meaning.*

Like referential meanings, explicit meanings function within the film's overall form. They are controlled by context. For instance, we might want to take "There's no place like home" as a statement of the meaning of the entire film. But, first, *why* do we take that as a strongly meaningful line? In ordinary conversation, it's a cliché. In context, however, the line gains great force. It's uttered in close-up, it comes at the end of the film (a formally privileged moment), and it refers back to all of Dorothy's desires and ordeals, recalling the film's narrative movement toward her goal. It is the *form* of the film that gives the homily an unfamiliar weight.

This example suggests that we must examine how explicit meanings in a film interact with other elements of the overall form. Usually, we can't isolate a particularly significant moment and declare it to be *the* meaning of the whole film. Dorothy's "There's no place like home" does capture one meaningful element in *The Wizard of Oz.* But her remark is counterbalanced by the entire beguiling Oz fantasy. Oz is attractive but dangerous; home is drab but safe and loving.

In trying to see the meaningful parts within a larger whole, it's useful to set significant moments against one another. Thus Dorothy's final line could be juxtaposed to the scene of the characters getting spruced up after their arrival at the Emerald City. We can try to see the film as about not only Oz or only Kansas, but rather the relation of the two—the delight and risk of a fantasy world versus the comfort and stability of home. Thus the film's total system is larger than any one explicit meaning we can find in it. Instead of asking, "What is this film's meaning?" we can ask, "How do the various meanings relate to one another?"

3. **Implicit meaning.** *An adolescent who must soon face the adult world yearns for a return to the simplicity of childhood, but she eventually accepts the demands of growing up.*

This is more abstract than the first two remarks we've mentioned. This one suggests that *The Wizard of Oz* is about something general, the passage from childhood to adulthood. On this view, the film implies that, as they grow up, people may want to return to the apparently uncomplicated world of childhood. Dorothy's frustration with her aunt and uncle and her urge to flee to a place "over the rainbow" become examples of a general conception of adolescence. Unlike the "no place like home" line, this meaning isn't stated directly. We can call this suggestion an *implicit meaning.* When perceivers ascribe implicit meanings to an artwork, they're usually said to be *interpreting* it.

Clearly, **interpretations** vary. One viewer might propose that *The Wizard of Oz* is really about adolescence. Another might suggest that it is really about courage and persistence, or that it is a satire on the adult world. One of the appeals of artworks is that they ask us to interpret them in several ways at once. Again, the filmmaker invites us to perform certain activities—here, building up implicit meanings, guided by the film's overall form.

Some filmmakers claim to avoid implicit meanings altogether. They leave them to viewers and critics. Of *There Will Be Blood,* director Paul Thomas Anderson said, "It's a slippery slope when you start thinking about something other than just a good battle between two guys. . . . Tell a nasty story and let the rest take care of itself." But other filmmakers try to steer viewers toward implicit meanings, sometimes called *subtexts.* Robert Zemeckis described his *Forrest Gump* as "a movie about grieving." Director Greg Mottola describes the friends' separation at the end of *Superbad* as having several possible subtexts: "It's homosexual panic or it's bravado or it's all these shades of what young men go through to try to appear a certain way to women and to their peers."

Once we identify a film's meaning, either explicit or implicit, we're often tempted to split up the film into the content portion (the meaning) and the form (the vehicle for the content). Explicit and implicit meanings suggest very broad concepts, often called *themes.* A film may have as its theme courage or the power of faithful love. Such descriptions have some value, but they are very general; hundreds of films fit them. To summarize *The Wizard of Oz* as being simply about the problems of adolescence does not do justice to the specific qualities of the film as an experience. We suggest that the search for implicit meanings should not leave behind the *particular* and *concrete* features of a film.

This isn't to say that we should avoid interpreting films. But we should strive to make our interpretations precise by seeing how each film's thematic meanings are suggested by the film's form. In a narrative film, both explicit and implicit meanings depend on the relations between story and style.

> ❝ Critics enable us to see how parts of an artwork serve larger designs. Often this requires that the critics offer interpretations or explications of the larger aims of the work, but these overviews are often introduced, in large measure, in order to explain why the works have the parts they do."
> —Noël Carroll, philosopher of art

CONNECT TO THE BLOG
www.davidbordwell.net/blog

How far can interpretation go? The limits are tested by fans who find a great many implicit and referential meanings in *The Shining.* See our entry "All play and no work? *Room 237.*"

In *The Wizard of Oz,* the Yellow Brick Road has no meaning in and of itself. But if we examine the functions it fulfills in relation to the narrative, the music, the colors, and so on, we can argue that the Yellow Brick Road does suggest meanings. Dorothy's strong desire to go home makes the road represent that desire. At the same time, because it's made of yellow bricks—rare in our everyday world—it partakes of some of the magical qualities of Oz. In a way, the road encapsulates the tension between Oz and Kansas that we see throughout the movie. We want Dorothy to be successful in getting to Oz and going back to Kansas. So the road can suggest the themes of Oz's attraction and the desirability of getting home.

Interpretation need not be an end in itself. It also helps in understanding the overall form of the film. Once we've noticed the Yellow Brick Road as a thematic element, we could analyze its functions in larger patterns. We could see that it gains narrative importance because Dorothy's indecision at a crossroads allows her to meet the Scarecrow. We could work out a color scheme for the film, contrasting the yellow road, the red slippers, the green Emerald City, and so forth. In such ways, when we interpret a film we should try to harmonize the meanings we detect with the film's overall formal development.

> **4. Symptomatic meaning.** *In a society in which human worth is measured by money, the home and the family may seem to be the last refuge of human values. This belief is especially strong in times of economic crisis, such as that in the United States in the 1930s.*

Like statement 3, this is abstract and general. It situates the film within a trend of thought that is assumed to be characteristic of American society during the 1930s. The claim could apply equally well to many other films, as well as to many novels, plays, poems, paintings, advertisements, radio shows, political speeches, and a host of cultural products of the period.

But something else is worth noticing about the statement. It treats an explicit meaning in *The Wizard of Oz* ("There's no place like home") as displaying a set of values characteristic of a whole society. We could treat implicit meanings the same way. If we say the film implies something about adolescence as a crucial time of transition, we could suggest that emphasis on adolescence as a special period of life is also a recurrent concern of American society. So, it's possible to understand a film's explicit or implicit meanings as bearing traces of a particular set of social values. We can call this *symptomatic meaning,* and the set of values that get revealed can be considered a social **ideology.**

Symptomatic meanings remind us that meaning of all sorts is largely a social phenomenon. Many meanings of films are ultimately ideological; that is, they spring from systems of culturally specific beliefs about the world. Religious beliefs, political opinions, conceptions of race or gender or social class, even our most deeply seated notions of life's values—all these constitute our ideological frame of reference. We're tempted to think that our beliefs are the best explanations of how the world is. But if we compare our own ideology with that of another culture or time we see how different many of those views are. In other times and places, *home* and *adolescence* don't carry the meanings they carried in 1930s America. Some cultures don't have the idea of adolescence at all.

Films, like other artworks, can be examined for their symptomatic meanings. Again, however, the abstract and general quality of such meanings can lead us away from the film's concrete form. As in analyzing implicit meanings, we should ground symptomatic meanings in the film's specific aspects. A film *enacts* ideological meanings through its form. We'll see in Chapter 11 how the narrative and stylistic system of *Meet Me in St. Louis* and *Raging Bull* can be analyzed for ideological implications.

To sum up: Films have meaning because we attribute meanings to them. Sometimes the filmmaker guides us toward certain meanings; sometimes we find meanings the filmmaker didn't intend. If we're engaged by a film, we'll search for referential, explicit, implicit, and symptomatic meanings. But a film is a film, not a collection of themes. The filmmaker who wants to make a general statement or suggest implicit meanings will still have to work out the film in concrete terms, through particular choices about form and style. When we look closely at a film, we should keep the same balance in mind, not letting our urge for wider significance outweigh our focus on the film as a dynamic whole.

Evaluation: Good, Bad, or Indifferent?

In talking about an artwork, people often *evaluate* it. They make claims about its goodness or badness. Reviews in print media and on the Internet exist almost solely to tell us whether a film is worth seeing, and our friends often urge us to go to their latest favorite. Some websites rate movies by stars or grades, suggesting that their rankings are fairly precise. What's going on here?

We can start by realizing that there is a difference between *personal taste* and *evaluative judgment.* To say "I liked this film" or "I hated it" is not equal to saying, "It's a good film" or "It's wretched." Most of us want to like good movies and dislike bad ones, but we recognize a range of quality. Very few of us limit our enjoyment to the greatest works. What critics call "guilty pleasures" are movies that are enjoyable despite being bad, maybe even terrible, in some respects.

All this suggests that personal preference need not be the basis for judging a film's quality. Instead, we can try to make a relatively objective evaluation by using specific *criteria.* A criterion is a standard that can be applied in the judgment of many works. By using a criterion, we can compare films for relative quality.

There are many different criteria. Some people evaluate films on *realistic* criteria. Aficionados of military history might judge a film entirely on whether the battle scenes use historically accurate weaponry. Other people condemn films because they don't find the action plausible. They dismiss a scene by saying, "Who'd really believe that X would meet Y just at the right moment?" We have already seen, though, that artworks often violate laws of reality and operate by their own conventions and internal rules. Coincidental encounters, usually at embarrassing moments, are a convention of genres like romantic comedy, as we'll see in Chapter 9. So realism, then, isn't a criterion that we can apply in every case.

Viewers can also use *moral* criteria to evaluate films. Most narrowly, aspects of the film can be judged outside their context in the film. Some viewers might feel that any film with nudity or profanity or violence is bad. Other viewers might defend these aspects as realistic, given the lifestyles of the characters in the story. Likewise, some viewers might condemn Renoir's slightly humorous handling of the baby's death in *The Crime of M. Lange,* regardless of the scene's context. More broadly, viewers and critics may employ moral criteria to evaluate a film's overall significance, and here the film's complete formal system becomes pertinent. We can judge a film good because of its overall view of life, its willingness to show opposing points of view, or its emotional range.

Although realistic and moral criteria are well suited to particular purposes, we should also recognize that there are criteria that assess films as artistic wholes. Such criteria allow us to take each film's form into account as much as possible. *Coherence* is one such criterion. This quality, often referred to as *unity,* has traditionally been held to be a positive feature of artworks. So, too, has *intensity of effect.* If an artwork is vivid, striking, and emotionally engaging, it may be considered more valuable.

Another criterion is *complexity.* We can argue that, all other things being equal, complex films are good. A complex film engages our interest on different levels, and tends to create several patterns of feelings and meanings. Our discussion of *The Wizard of Oz,* so far and going forward, may convince you that it is a more complex film than it might seem at first.

Yet another formal criterion is *originality.* Originality for its own sake is pointless, of course. Just because something is different doesn't mean that it is good. But if an artist takes a familiar convention and uses it in a way that gives viewers a fresh experience, then (all other things being equal) the resulting work may be considered good from an aesthetic standpoint.

Note that all these criteria are matters of degree. One film may be more complex than another. Moreover, there is often a give-and-take among the criteria. A film might be complex but lack coherence or intensity. Ninety minutes of a black screen would make for an original film but not a very complex one. A slasher movie may build up great intensity in certain scenes but may be wholly unoriginal, as well as disorganized and simplistic. In applying the criteria, we often must weigh one against another.

It's fun to share our personal tastes with friends and sometimes vent them in a Tweet or online comment. But a deeper, objective evaluation usually teaches us more about how films work. A considered evaluation can call attention to neglected artworks or make us rethink our attitudes toward accepted classics. Just as the discovery of meanings is not the only purpose of formal analysis, we suggest that evaluation is most fruitful when it is backed up by a close examination of the film. General statements ("*The Wizard of Oz* is a masterpiece") seldom enlighten us very much. Usually, an evaluation is helpful when it points to aspects of the film and shows us relations and qualities we have missed. "*The Wizard of Oz* is more coherent than it looks at first. Look at all the parallels! Miss Gulch's written order to take Toto is echoed by the Wicked Witch's fiery skywriting addressed to the citizens of the Emerald City, 'Surrender Dorothy.'" Like interpretation, evaluation can usefully drive us back to the film's particular formal strategies, helping us to understand them better.

In reading this book, you'll find that we have generally minimized evaluation. We think that most of the films and sequences we analyze are good based on the artistic criteria we mentioned, but the purpose of this book is not to persuade you to accept a list of masterpieces. Instead, by considering how films create our experiences through form and style, you will have an informed basis for whatever evaluations you want to make.

Principles of Film Form

Form doesn't equal formula. Scientists discover powerful laws governing the physical world, but in the arts there are no laws of form that all artists must follow. Artists create within culture, so many principles of artistic form are matters of convention. An outer-space adventure such as Andrei Tarkovsky's *Solaris* isn't faulty because it doesn't follow the conventions at work in *Star Wars: Episode IV—A New Hope*. Still, there are some broad principles that artists, filmmakers included, draw on. These are ideas of function, similarity and repetition, difference and variation, development, and unity and disunity. We'll draw on *The Wizard of Oz* for our main examples.

Function

If form is a pattern of elements, we would expect that those elements fulfill functions. They *do* something in the larger whole. Of any element in a film we can ask, *What are its functions?*

We say "functions" in the plural, because most elements serve several purposes. Perhaps for some MGM executives, the song "Over the Rainbow" had the primary purpose of letting Judy Garland launch a hit tune. Still, the song fits the film because it fulfills certain narrative and stylistic functions. The lyrics establish Dorothy's desire to leave home, and the opening line's reference to the rainbow foreshadows her trip through the sky to colorful Oz. In fact, the "where" in the word "Somewhere" leaps a full octave, creating a musical equivalent of a trip to a distant land. In asking about formal function, therefore, we typically ask not, "How did this element get there?" but rather, "What is this element *doing* there?" and "How does it cue us to respond?"

In *The Wizard of Oz*, every major character fulfills several functions. For instance, Miss Gulch, the woman who wants to take Toto from Dorothy, frightens Dorothy into running away from home. In Oz she reappears as the Wicked Witch who tries to seize the ruby slippers and keep Dorothy from going to the Emerald City and returning home.

Even an element as apparently minor as the dog Toto serves many purposes. The dispute over Toto causes Dorothy to run away from home and to return too late to take shelter from the tornado. Later, when Dorothy is about to leave Oz, Toto's pursuit of a cat makes Dorothy jump out of the ascending balloon. Toto's gray color, set off against the brightness of Oz, recalls the black and white of the Kansas episodes at the film's beginning.

The story goes that when the actress Ingrid Bergman asked Alfred Hitchcock about her motivation in a particular scene, Hitchcock replied: "Your paycheck." But Hitchcock's joke deliberately confused the *actress's* reason for being in the movie (doing her job for pay) with the *character's* reason for doing what she does. Bergman's question can guide us in thinking about the functions of anything in a movie.

For Bergman, as for most actors, the word "motivation" applies to the purposes of a character's actions. But the term doesn't apply only to performance matters. When we speak of *motivation* more generally, we're asking about what justifies anything being in the film. If we see a man in beggar's clothes in the middle of an elegant society ball, we will ask why he's dressed in this way. Is he the victim of practical jokers who have told him that it's a masquerade party? Is he an eccentric millionaire? Such a scene does occur in *My Man Godfrey,* in which the young society people have been assigned to bring back a homeless man as part of a scavenger hunt **(2.11).** The game motivates the presence of an inappropriately dressed character.

2.11 Motivation for formal elements. The heroine of *My Man Godfrey* studies her prize while the well-off crowd urges the unemployed Godfrey to make a speech. A scavenger hunt is the motivation for the homeless man's presence at the elegant society ball.

Motivation points to functions. Throughout *The Wizard of Oz,* one function Toto fulfills is to get Dorothy into scrapes. Since the plot requires that Dorothy run away from home, the screenwriters used her love of Toto to motivate her flight. When Toto jumps from the balloon to chase a cat, we motivate his action by appealing to notions of how dogs are likely to act when cats are around.

Motivation is so common in films that spectators take it for granted, but film-makers must think about it often. A director may decide to let a character's wandering around a room motivate a camera movement. A cinematographer may have to choose between motivated and unmotivated lighting. Gabriel Beristain, who shot *Ring Two,* faced two options in shooting night scenes:

> You could go the straight route and motivate some sort of light through windows, which is the only logical source in play. Or you could decide not to worry about motivation and create chiaroscuro lighting that simulates darkness.

When we study principles of narrative form (Chapter 3) and various types of films (Chapters 9 and 10), we'll look more closely at how motivation gives elements specific functions.

Similarity and Repetition

In our example of the ABACA pattern, we saw how we were able to predict the next steps in the series. One reason for this was a regular pattern of repeated elements. Like beats in music, the repetition of the A's in our pattern established and satisfied formal expectations. Similarity and repetition, then, constitute an important principle of film form.

If you were to make a film, you would rely on repetition constantly. You'd make sure that your main character reappeared often enough for him or her to be seen as central to the plot, and you'd probably have dialogue that reiterated main points about goals, conflicts, and themes. More subtly, you'd probably utilize what are called **motifs.** A motif is *any significant repeated element that contributes to the overall form.*

It may be an object, a color, a place, a person, a sound, or even a character trait. Max's tropical postcard is a motif signaled early in *Collateral.* In *Jurassic Park,* Dr. Alan Grant's dislike of children reappears as a motif—one that alters in the course of the adventure. A lighting scheme or camera position can become

CONNECT TO THE BLOG
www.davidbordwell.net/blog

We discuss George Smiley's eyeglasses as a motif in *"Tinker Tailor:* A guide for the perplexed."

A CLOSER LOOK

Creative Decisions: Picking Out Patterns

In studying film as an art, you might sometimes wonder: Are all the patterns of form and style we notice really in the film? Do filmmakers actually put them there, or are we just reading them in?

Filmmakers often say that their formal and stylistic choices aim to create specific effects. Hitchcock, a director who had an engineering bent, planned his stories carefully and chose techniques in full awareness of their possibilities. His film *Rope* confines the action to a single apartment and presents it in only eleven shots. *Rear Window* limits the action to what the hero can see from his apartment. In these and other films, Hitchcock deliberately set up constraints for himself, inviting his audience to enjoy the way he worked within them.

Filmmakers may work more intuitively than Hitchcock, but they still must choose one story development or another, one technique or another. The finished film can have an overall unity because the choices tend to mesh. Joel and Ethan Coen, the brothers who created *The Big Lebowski, Fargo,* and *True Grit,* don't set out with a particular style in mind. As Ethan puts it, "At the point of making the movie, it's just about making individual choices." Joel picks up the thread:

> . . . about the best way to tell the story, scene by scene. You make specific choices that you think are appropriate or compelling or interesting for that particular scene. Then, at the end of the day, you put it all together and somebody looks at it and, if there's some consistency to it, they say, "Well, that's their style."

Even if the Coens don't map out every option in advance, their films display distinctive patterns of form and style, and those definitely affect our response **(2.12, 2.13).**

Professionals pay attention to other filmmakers' creative decisions about form and style. While watching Stanley Kubrick's *The Shining,* Nicole Kidman pointed out how the composition of one shot had both an immediate point and a long-range story purpose **(2.14):**

> Here, in this scene, look at how there is this rack of knives hanging in the background over the boy's head. . . . It's

> " You can take a movie, for example, like *Angels with Dirty Faces*, where James Cagney is a child and says to his pal Pat O'Brien, 'What do you hear, what do you say?'— cocky kid—and then as a young rough on the way up when things are going great for him he says, 'What do you hear, what do you say?' Then when he is about to be executed in the electric chair and Pat O'Brien is there to hear his confession, he says, 'What do you hear, what do you say?' and the simple repetition of the last line of dialogue in three different places with the same characters brings home the dramatically changed circumstances much more than any extensive diatribe would."
>
> —Robert Towne, screenwriter, *Chinatown*

important because it not only shows that the boy is in danger, but one of those very knives is used later in the story when Wendy takes it to protect herself from her husband **(2.15).**

Kubrick told Kidman that a director had to repeat story information so that the audience could keep up. The knife pattern shaped viewers' experience, although they may not have been aware of it.

Kubrick's comment points up another reason we can have some confidence when we pick out patterns. A filmmaker doesn't create a movie from scratch. All films borrow ideas and storytelling strategies from other movies and other art forms. As we've seen, a lot that happens in films is governed by conventions. When Kubrick shows us the knives behind Danny, he's following a very old storytelling convention: prepare the audience for action that will come later. Similarly, *The Hudsucker Proxy* is a satirical comedy, and the steep perspective in 2.12 and 2.13 follows a convention of using exaggeration to create humor.

Very often, patterns in one film resemble patterns we've seen in other films. Even when filmmakers operate intuitively and don't tell us their trade secrets, we can notice how they treat familiar conventions of form and technique.

2.12

2.13

2.12–2.13 Creating a film's style through compositional motifs. In the *Hudsucker Proxy*, the boss dangles above the street in a very steep, centered-perspective composition (2.12). The same sort of composition is used to show the impersonal layout of desks in the Hudsucker company (2.13).

2.14

2.15

2.14–2.15 Motifs anticipate action. In *The Shining*, an early scene in the Hotel Overlook kitchen displays the telepathic rapport between Halloran and Danny, whose parents are caretaking the hotel for the winter. The knives are a natural part of the kitchen set but are aligned above Danny (2.14). Later Danny's mother, Wendy, goes to the same knife rack, seen from a different angle, to grab a weapon (2.15).

2.16

2.17

2.18

2.19

2.16–2.19 Parallels between frame story and fantasy. The itinerant Kansas fortune-teller, Professor Marvel (2.16), bears a striking resemblance to the old charlatan known as the Wizard of Oz (2.17). Miss Gulch's bicycle in the opening section (2.18) becomes the Witch's broom in Oz (2.19).

2.20

2.21

2.20–2.21 Parallel compositions. As the Lion describes his timidity, the characters are lined up (2.20) to form a mirror reversal of the earlier scene in which the others teased Zeke for being afraid of pigs (2.21).

a motif. (See "A Closer Look," pp. 64–65.) Motifs often reappear at climaxes or highly emotional moments, as happens with the famous line from *Jerry Maguire*, "You complete me."

Motifs are fairly exact repetitions, but a film can chart broader similarities between its ingredients. To understand *The Wizard of Oz*, we must notice that the three Kansas farmhands have counterparts in the Scarecrow, the Tin Man, and the Cowardly Lion. We must notice additional echoes between characters in the frame story and in the fantasy **(2.16–2.19)**. Such similarities are usually called *parallels*. Parallels cue us to compare two or more distinct elements by highlighting some similarity. For example, Dorothy says she feels that she has known the Scarecrow and the Tin Man before. At another point, the staging of a shot reinforces the parallels **(2.20–2.21)**.

Motifs can help create parallels among characters and situations. The viewer will notice, and even come to expect, that every time Dorothy meets a character in Oz, the scene will end with the song "We're Off to See the Wizard." This motif accentuates the broader similarities among Dorothy's encounters. Our recognition of parallelism provides part of our pleasure in watching a film, much as rhymes contribute to the power of poetry.

Difference and Variation

A filmmaker is unlikely to rely only on repetitions. AAAAAA is rather boring. There should also be some changes, or *variations,* however small. So difference, or variation, is another fundamental principle of film form. We've seen this principle at work already, when composer James Newton Howard provided three "movements" for the music accompanying the final scene of *Collateral* (pp. 7–9).

2.22   **2.23**

2.22–2.23 Contrasting settings. Centered in the upper half of the frame, the Emerald City (2.22) creates a striking contrast to the similar composition showing the castle of the Wicked Witch of the West (2.23).

Differences among the elements are most apparent when characters clash. In *The Wizard of Oz,* Dorothy's desires are opposed, at various points, by the differing desires of Aunt Em, Miss Gulch, the Wicked Witch, and the Wizard, so that our experience of the film is engaged through dramatic conflict. But character conflict isn't the only way the formal principle of difference may appear.

If you were making a film, you'd seek out ways to contrast your characters and their environments. Perhaps you'd situate one character in nature and another in busy urban surroundings. You might stress contrasts of costume, or hairstyles, or color. *The Wizard of Oz* presents stark color oppositions: black-and-white Kansas versus colorful Oz; Dorothy in red, white, and blue versus the Witch in black. Settings are opposed as well—not only Oz versus Kansas but also the various locales within Oz (**2.22–2.23**). Voice quality, musical tunes, and a host of other elements play off against one another, demonstrating that any motif may be opposed by any other motif.

Typically, filmmakers vary their motifs and parallels. In *The Wizard of Oz,* the three Kansas hands aren't identical to their counterparts in Oz. When Professor Marvel pretends to read Dorothy's future in a small crystal ball, we see no images in it (2.16). Dorothy's dream transforms the crystal into a large globe in the Witch's castle, where it displays frightening scenes (**2.24**). Similarly, Toto's disruption of a situation is a constant action motif, but it changes its function. In Kansas, he disturbs Miss Gulch and induces Dorothy to take Toto away from home, but in Oz, his disruption prevents Dorothy from returning home.

Not all differences come down to this-versus-that dualities. Dorothy's three Oz friends—the Scarecrow, the Tin Woodman, and the Lion—are distinguished by three things they lack (a brain, a heart, and courage). Other films may rely on less sharp differences, suggesting a scale of gradations among the characters, as in Jean Renoir's *The Rules of the Game.* At the extreme, an abstract film may create minimal variations among its parts, such as in the slight changes that accompany each return of the same footage in J. J. Murphy's *Print Generation* (p. 372).

Repetition and variation are two sides of the same coin. To notice one is to be alert to the other. In thinking about films, we ought to look for similarities *and* differences. Shuttling between the two, we can point out motifs and contrast the changes they undergo, recognize parallelisms as repetition, and still spot crucial variations.

Development

One way to notice how similarity and difference operate in film form is to look for principles of *development* from part to part. Development places similar and different elements within a pattern of change. Our pattern ABACA is based not only on repetition (the recurring motif of A) and difference (the insertion of B and C) but

 CONNECT TO THE BLOG
www.davidbordwell.net/blog

One distinctive type of film form comes in the anthology film, combining short segments by several directors. It's a theme-and-variations approach that we discuss in "Can you spot all the auteurs in this picture?"

2.24 Similarity and difference. Through her crystal ball, the Wicked Witch mocks Dorothy. Contrast it with the earlier scene (2.16) in which the Kansas fortune-teller uses a smaller crystal ball.

2.25 Narrative development: **Starting a journey.** Dorothy puts her feet on the literal beginning of the Yellow Brick Road, as it widens out from a single point.

also on a principle of *progression* that we could state as a rule: Alternate A with successive letters in alphabetical order. Though simple, this is a principle of development, governing the form of the whole series.

Filmmakers often treat formal development as *a progression moving from beginning through middle to end.* The story of *The Wizard of Oz* shows development in many ways. It is, for one thing, a *journey:* from Kansas through Oz to Kansas. The good witch Glinda emphasizes this formal pattern by telling Dorothy that "It's always best to start at the beginning" **(2.25).** Filmmakers often build their plots around journeys. *The Wizard of Oz* is also a *search,* beginning with an initial separation from home, tracing a series of efforts to find a way home, and ending with home being found. Within the film, there is also a pattern of *mystery,* which usually has the same beginning-middle-end pattern. We begin with a question (Who is the Wizard of Oz?), pass through attempts to answer it, and conclude with the question answered. (The Wizard is a fraud.) *Close Encounters of the Third Kind* combines the patterns of journey, search, and mystery, adding the psychological change that occurs in protagonist Roy Neary. As these examples suggest, feature-length films often depend on several developmental patterns.

At some point in making a film, the filmmakers usually prepare a breakdown of its parts. This traces, in sketchy form, the film's pattern of development. When we want to analyze a finished film, we do the same thing. We make what's usually called a *segmentation.*

A segmentation is simply a written outline of the film that breaks it into its major and minor parts, with the parts marked by consecutive numbers or letters. If a narrative film has 40 *scenes,* then we can label each scene with a number running from 1 to 40. It may be useful to divide some parts further (for example, scenes 6a and 6b).

Segmenting a film enables us not only to notice similarities and differences among parts but also to plot the overall development. Following is a segmentation for *The Wizard of Oz* using an outline format. (In segmenting films, we label the opening credits with a "C," the end title with an "E," and all other segments with numbers.)

The Wizard of Oz: Plot Segmentation

C. Credits
1. Kansas
    a. Dorothy is at home, worried about Miss Gulch's threat to Toto.
    b. Running away, Dorothy meets Professor Marvel, who induces her to return home.
    c. A tornado lifts the house, with Dorothy and Toto, into the sky.
2. Munchkin City
    a. After Dorothy's house crashes to earth, she meets Glinda, and the Munchkins celebrate the death of the Wicked Witch of the East.
    b. The Wicked Witch of the West threatens Dorothy over the Ruby Slippers.
    c. Glinda sends Dorothy to seek the Wizard's help.
3. The Yellow Brick Road
    a. Dorothy meets the Scarecrow.
    b. Dorothy meets the Tin Man.
    c. Dorothy meets the Cowardly Lion.
4. The Emerald City
    a. The Witch creates a poppy field near the city, but Glinda rescues the travelers.
    b. The group is welcomed by the city's citizens.
    c. As they wait to see the Wizard, the Lion sings of being king of the forest.

> d. The terrifying Wizard agrees to help the group if they obtain the Wicked Witch's broomstick.

5. The Witch's castle and nearby woods
   a. In the woods, flying monkeys carry off Dorothy and Toto.
   b. The Witch realizes that she must kill Dorothy to get the ruby slippers.
   c. The Scarecrow, Tin Man, and Lion sneak into the Castle; in the ensuing chase, Dorothy kills the Witch.

6. The Emerald City
   a. Although revealed as a humbug, the Wizard grants the wishes of the Scarecrow, Tin Man, and Lion.
   b. Dorothy fails to leave in the Wizard's hot-air balloon but is transported home by the ruby slippers.

7. Kansas—Dorothy describes Oz to her family and friends

E. End credits

Preparing a segmentation may look a little fussy, but in the course of this book, we'll try to convince you that it can shed a lot of light on films. For now, just consider this comparison.

As you walk into a building, your experience develops over time. In many cathedrals, for example, the entryway is fairly narrow. But as you emerge into the open area inside (the nave), space expands outward and upward, your sense of your body seems to shrink, and your attention is directed toward the altar, centrally located in the distance. The somewhat cramped entryway makes you feel a contrast when you enter the broad and soaring space. Your experience has been as carefully planned as any theme park ride. Only by thinking back on it can you realize that the planned progression of the building's different areas shaped your experience. If you could study the builder's blueprints, you'd see the whole layout at a glance. It would be very different from your moment-by-moment experience of it, but it would shed light on how your experience was shaped.

A film works in a similar way. As we watch the film, we're in the thick of it. We follow the formal development moment by moment, and we may get more and more involved. But if we want to study the overall form, we need to stand back a bit. Films don't come with blueprints, but by creating a plot segmentation, we can get a comparable sense of the film's basic design.

In a way, we're recovering the architecture of the movie. A segmentation lets us see the patterning that the filmmakers laid out and that we felt intuitively while watching the film. In Chapters 3 and 10, we consider how to segment different types of films, and several of our sample analyses in Chapter 11 use segmentations to show how the films work.

A quick way to size up how a film develops formally is to *compare the beginning with the ending*. By looking at the similarities and the differences between the beginning and the ending, we can start to understand the overall pattern of the film. We can test this advice on *The Wizard of Oz*. A comparison of the beginning and the ending reveals that Dorothy's journey ends with her return home. The journey, a search for an ideal place "over the rainbow," has turned into a search for a way back to Kansas. The final scene repeats and develops the narrative elements of the opening. Stylistically, the beginning and ending are the only parts that use black-and-white film stock. This repetition supports the contrast the narrative creates between the dreamland of Oz and the bleak landscape of Kansas.

At the film's end, Professor Marvel comes to visit Dorothy (**2.26**), reversing the situation of her visit to him when she had tried to run away. At the beginning, he had convinced her to return home; then, as the Wizard in the Oz section, he had also represented her hopes of returning home. Finally, when she recognizes Professor Marvel and the farmhands as the basis of the characters in her dream, she remembers how much she had wanted to come home from Oz.

CONNECT TO THE BLOG
www.davidbordwell.net/blog

If beginnings are important, then the very beginning is even more important, as "First shots" demonstrates.

2.26 Comparing beginning and ending. The visits of the final scene in *The Wizard of Oz* reverse events at the start of the film; Professor Marvel comes to visit Dorothy at her home, but at the start Dorothy met him after leaving home.

Earlier, we suggested that film form engages our emotions and expectations in a dynamic way. Now we're in a better position to see why. The filmmaker creates a constant interplay between similarity and difference, and repetition and variation. This process leads the viewer to an active engagement with the film's developing system. It is handy to visualize a movie's development in static terms by segmenting it, but we ought not to forget that formal development is a *process* taking place over time. Form shapes our experience of the film.

Unity and Disunity

When all the relationships we perceive within a film are clear and economically interwoven, we say that the film has **unity.** We often call a unified film "tight," because there seem to be no gaps in its overall form. We feel that every element fulfills particular functions, that we understand the similarities and differences among elements, that the form develops logically, and that no element is superfluous. The film's overall unity can give our experience a sense of completeness and fulfillment.

Unity is a matter of degree. Very few films are perfectly tight. For example, at one point in *The Wizard of Oz,* the Witch refers to her having attacked Dorothy and her friends with insects, yet we have never seen them. What is the Witch referring to? In fact, a bee attack was originally shot but then cut from the finished film. The Witch's line about the insect attack now lacks motivation.

More striking is a dangling element at the film's end: We never find out what happens to Miss Gulch. Presumably, she still has her legal order to take Toto away, but no one refers to this in the last scene. The viewer may be inclined to overlook this disunity because Miss Gulch's parallel character, the Witch, has been killed off in the Oz fantasy, and we don't expect to see her alive again. Since perfect unity is scarcely ever achieved, we ought to expect that even a unified film may still contain a few stray elements or unanswered questions.

If we look at unity as a criterion for evaluation, we may judge a film containing several unmotivated elements as a failure. But unity and disunity may be looked at nonevaluatively as well, as the results of particular formal conventions. For example, *Pulp Fiction* lacks a bit of closure in that it never reveals what is inside the briefcase that is at the center of the gangster plot. The contents, however, give off a golden glow, suggesting that they are of very great value (as well as evoking the "whatsit" in *Kiss Me Deadly,* a classic film noir). By not specifying the goods, the film emphasizes characters' reactions to them. For example, in the last scene in the diner, Pumpkin gazes at the mystery object lustfully but the newly spiritual hit man Jules calmly insists that he will deliver it to his boss. In such ways, momentary disunities can fulfill larger functions.

SUMMARY

A filmmaker designs an experience for an audience by shaping the film's form, the overall pattern of parts. Things that are normally considered content—subject matter, or abstract ideas—take on particular functions within the overall form.

Our experience as viewers is shaped by the filmmaker's formal choices. Through the creative decisions they make, filmmakers nudge or thrust us in certain directions. Picking up cues in the work, we frame specific expectations that are aroused, guided, delayed, cheated, satisfied, or disturbed. We feel curiosity, suspense, and surprise. We compare the particular aspects of the artwork with things that we know from life and with conventions found in art.

The concrete context of the artwork expresses and stimulates emotions. It enables us to construct many types of meanings. And even when we apply general criteria in evaluating artworks, we ought to use those criteria to help us discriminate more, to probe more deeply into the particular aspects of the artwork. The rest of this book is devoted to studying these properties of artistic form in cinema.

We can summarize the principles of film form as a set of questions that you can ask about any film:

1. For any element in the film, what are its functions in the overall form? How is it motivated?

2. Are elements or patterns repeated throughout the film? If so, how and at what points? Are motifs and parallelisms asking us to compare elements?

3. How are elements contrasted and differentiated from one another? How are different elements opposed to one another?

4. What principles of progression or development are at work through the form of the film? Does a comparison of the beginning and ending point toward the film's overall form?

5. What degree of unity is present in the film's overall form?

In this chapter, we examined some major ways in which films as artworks can engage us as spectators. We also reviewed some broad principles of film form. Armed with these general principles, we can press on to distinguish more specific types of form that are central to understanding film art.

3

Narrative Form

Humans have an endless appetite for stories. As children, we devour fairy tales and myths; we like to watch the same cartoons over and over. As we get older, we become captivated by other stories—in religion and history, in novels and comic books and video games and, of course, movies. We recount our lives, or just what happened at work today, to anyone who'll listen. Politicians and journalists talk about "changing the narrative." In the courtroom the jury hears competing stories, and in our dreams we imagine ourselves in scenes and situations. Narrative is a fundamental way that humans make sense of the world.

Stories grab and hold us. In Chapter 2 we considered how a sequence of items, even letters of the alphabet, can prod us to ask what comes next. A story, filled out with characters and their actions, intensifies that urge to the maximum. In 1841, Charles Dickens serialized his novel *The Old Curiosity Shop* in magazine installments. When ships brought the latest installment to America, crowds of readers packed the wharf crying out, "Is Little Nell dead?" Almost two centuries later, children and their parents lined up for hours outside bookstores to buy the newest Harry Potter novel. Many of those youngsters rushed home and started reading it immediately.

They were not that different from fans binge-watching a whole season of a TV show, or from fans eagerly waiting for the next installment of a movie franchise and speculating online about upcoming plot twists. Whether the story is fictional or factual, we feel driven to know how the action develops, how the characters react, and how it all comes out in the end.

Because storytelling is so common and so powerful, we need to take a close look at how films—both fictional and nonfictional—embody **narrative form.**

Principles of Narrative Form

Because stories are all around us, spectators approach a narrative film with definite expectations. We may know a great deal about the particular story the film will tell. Perhaps we've read the book that the film is based on, or this is a sequel to a movie we've seen.

Even if we aren't already acquainted with the story's particular world, though, we have expectations that are characteristic of narrative form itself. We assume that there will be characters and that the actions they take will involve them with one another. We expect a series of incidents that will be connected in some way. We usually expect that the problems or conflicts that arise will somehow be settled—either they will be resolved or, at least, a new light will be cast on them. A spectator comes prepared to make sense of a narrative film.

While watching the film, the viewer picks up cues, recalls information, anticipates what will follow, and generally participates in the creation of the film's form. As we suggested in Chapter 2 (pp. 54-55), the film shapes our expectations by summoning up curiosity, suspense, surprise, and other emotional qualities. The ending has the task of satisfying or cheating the expectations prompted by the film as a whole. The ending may also activate memory by cueing the spectator to review earlier events, possibly considering them in a new light. When *The Sixth Sense* was released in 1999, many moviegoers were so intrigued by the surprise twist at the end that they returned to see the film again and trace how their expectations had been manipulated. Something similar happened with *The Conversation* (see pp. 300-302). As we examine narrative form, we need to recognize how it engages the viewer in a dynamic activity.

It's the filmmaker's task to create this engagement. How does this happen? We can start to understand the filmmaker's creative choices and the viewer's activity by looking a little more closely at what narrative is and does.

What Is Narrative?

We can consider a *narrative* to be *a chain of events linked by cause and effect and occurring in time and space*. A narrative is what we usually mean by the term "story," although we'll be using that term in a slightly different way later. Typically, a narrative begins with one situation; a series of changes occurs according to a pattern of cause and effect; finally, a new situation arises that brings about the end of the narrative. Our engagement with the story depends on our understanding of the pattern of change and stability, cause and effect, time and space.

A random string of events is hard to understand as a story. Consider the following actions: "A man tosses and turns, unable to sleep. A mirror breaks. A telephone rings." We have trouble grasping this as a narrative because we are unable to determine how the events are connected by causality or time or space.

Consider a new description of these same events: "A man has a fight with his boss. He tosses and turns that night, unable to sleep. In the morning, he is still so angry that he smashes the mirror while shaving. Then his telephone rings; his boss has called to apologize."

We now have a narrative, unexciting though it is. We can connect the events spatially. The man is in the office, then in his bed; the mirror is in the bathroom; the phone is somewhere else in his home. Time is important as well. The fight starts things off, and the sleepless night, the broken mirror, and the phone call occur one after the other. The action runs from one day to the following morning. Above all, we can understand that the three events are part of a pattern of causes and effects. The argument with the boss causes the sleeplessness and the broken mirror. The phone call from the boss resolves the conflict, so the narrative ends. The narrative develops from an initial situation of conflict between employee and boss, through a series of events caused by the conflict, to the resolution of the conflict. Simple and minimal as our example is, it shows how important causality, space, and time are to narrative form.

The fact that a narrative relies on causality, time, and space doesn't mean that other formal principles can't govern the film. For instance, a narrative may make use of parallelism. As Chapter 2 points out (p. 66), parallelism points up a similarity among story elements. Our example was the way *The Wizard of Oz* paralleled the three Kansas farmhands with Dorothy's three Oz companions.

A narrative may cue us to draw parallels among characters, settings, situations, times of day, or any other elements. *Julie & Julia* parallels two women, living in different periods, trying to juggle their marriages and their passion for cuisine (**3.1, 3.2**). Julie never meets her idol Julia Child, but there is still a cause-effect link: Julie is inspired by the older woman's life. Sometimes a filmmaker goes further and doesn't link the parallel stories causally. Veřá Chytilová's *Something Different* alternates scenes from the life of a housewife and scenes from the career of a gymnast. Since the two women lead entirely separate lives, there are no causal connections between them. The parallel patterning encourages us to compare the women's life decisions.

CONNECT TO THE BLOG
www.davidbordwell.net/blog

When filmmakers create a prequel to an existing film story, they need to weave new patterns of cause and effect that lead to the story we already know. We discuss how prequels manage this task in "Originality and origin stories."

CONNECT TO THE BLOG
www.davidbordwell.net/blog

We analyze *Julie & Julia* in more depth, along with the parallel plot in *Enchantment*, in "Julie, Julia & the house that talked."

3.1   3.2

3.1–3.2 Narrative parallels. *Julie & Julia*: Staging and composition emphasize similarities between the two women's stories.

The documentary *Hoop Dreams* makes a similar use of parallels. Two high school students from a black neighborhood in Chicago dream of becoming professional basketball players, and the film follows each one's pursuit of an athletic career. The film's form invites us to compare their personalities, the obstacles they face, and the choices they make. In addition, the film creates parallels between their high schools, their coaches, their parents, and older male relatives who vicariously pursue their own dreams of athletic glory. *Hoop Dreams,* like *Julie & Julia* and *Something Different,* remains a narrative film. Each of the parallel lines of action is organized by time, space, and causality. But parallelism allows the film to become more complex than it might have been had it concentrated on only one protagonist.

Telling the Story

We make sense of a narrative, then, by identifying its events and linking them by cause and effect, time, and space. We also look out for parallels that can shed light on the ongoing action. But there's a lot more to narrative than this bare-bones account. To dig deeper, let's again try to think like a filmmaker.

CREATIVE DECISIONS

How Would You Tell the Story?

You have a story. Let's say it's a romantic comedy following the development of a love affair. Your problem is: How to tell it?

For example, should you start at the beginning of the story, when the partners meet? You could trace the action chronologically from there, showing them falling in love, being separated, meeting other people, remeeting, and eventually being reunited as a couple in marriage. But you might consider another option. Suppose you break chronology and start your film with the couple's wedding day. Then you might flash back to the beginning, showing how they met, and then trace the love affair through its ups and downs.

But why stop your rearranging there? Why not start with the wedding day, flash back to the first meeting, then return to the wedding day, then flash back to the budding romance, then return to the wedding day, and so on? Instead of one long flashback framed by the wedding, you have several shorter ones that keep interrupting the wedding.

Then you might ask: Who says the love-affair flashbacks have to be presented in chronological order? Maybe I can create more curiosity, or suspense, or surprise, or emotional engagement if I show the first meeting later in the film, out of chronological order. Perhaps just before the wedding, or just after their big bust-up? Although one event causes another, you don't have to respect 1-2-3 order.

While you're speculating about shuffling time periods, you might pause again. Wouldn't it be more engaging to start not with the wedding but with the couple's "darkest moment," the scene in which it seems they're never going to get together? Then flashing back to earlier, happier days could increase the suspense. Will they be reunited? That makes the wedding a sort of epilogue rather than the big event framing the overall action.

Each choice brings up further choices. If your flashbacks skip around a lot, you might worry about viewers' losing their bearings. So to help out, you might add superimposed titles identifying the time and place of the scene.

Time structure is only one of the storytelling choices you face. If you're planning the romantic comedy we sketched, from whose viewpoint will the tale be told? You could limit things to one character's standpoint, showing only what she or he knows about the unfolding action. *(500) Days of Summer* puts us firmly with the man who has fallen in love with the mysterious Summer. Alternatively, you could follow the more common convention of showing both members of the couple when they're alone or with other friends. You could mix in scenes of parents, coworkers, and the like. This asks your viewer to see the central relationship in a wider context.

Storytelling decisions about viewpoint involve what we'll be calling *narration*. Whatever the area of choice you face, you'll want to consider how the options affect the viewer. As we saw, presenting the story out of order could trigger curiosity or suspense. Confining us to what one character knows can enhance surprise, so that we learn new information only when he or she does.

■■■

Our romantic comedy is deeply unoriginal, but the point is just to show how filmmakers face choices in planning narrative form. Those choices involve time structure, narration, and other possibilities we'll examine.

Plot and Story

In our hypothetical movie, the love affair that runs from first meeting to wedding is what we'll be calling the **story.** The story is the chain of events in chronological order. But as we've seen, that story may be presented in various ways. If we use flashbacks instead of linear time, or if we decide to organize events around one character rather than another, or if we make other choices about presentation, we will be creating a different **plot.** As we've just seen, the same story can be presented in different ways—rendered as different plots—and each variant is likely to have different effects on the audience.

As viewers, we have direct access only to the plot that the filmmakers finally decided on. Yet eventually we arrive at an understanding of the underlying story. The filmmakers have built the plot from the story, but viewers build the story from the plot.

How do viewers do that? By making assumptions and inferences about what's presented. At the start of Alfred Hitchcock's *North by Northwest,* we know we are in Manhattan at rush hour. The cues stand out clearly: skyscrapers, bustling pedestrians, congested traffic **(3.3).** Then we watch Roger Thornhill as he leaves an elevator with his secretary, Maggie, and strides through the lobby, dictating memos **(3.4).**

Already we can draw some conclusions. Thornhill is an executive who leads a busy life. We assume that before we saw Thornhill and Maggie, he was also dictating to her; we have come in on the middle of a string of events in time. We also assume that the dictating began in the office, before they got on the elevator. In other words, we infer causes, a temporal sequence, and another locale even though none of this information has been directly presented. We're probably not aware of making these inferences, but insofar as we understand what we see and hear, we are making them. The filmmaker has steered us to make them.

3.3

3.4

3.3–3.4 Depicted and inferred story events. Shots of hurrying Manhattan pedestrians in *North by Northwest* are followed by a shot introducing us to Roger Thornhill and his secretary. Viewers make inferences about the story and characters based on the information that is presented onscreen.

So the plot guides the viewer in building up a sense of all the relevant events, both the ones explicitly presented and those that must be inferred. In our *North by Northwest* example, the story would consist of at least two depicted events and two inferred ones. We can list them, putting the inferred events in parentheses:

(Roger Thornhill has a busy day at his office.)

Rush hour hits Manhattan.

(While dictating to his secretary, Maggie, Roger leaves the office, and they take the elevator.)

Still dictating, Roger gets off the elevator with Maggie and they stride through the lobby.

CONNECT TO THE BLOG
www.davidbordwell.net/blog

Can you make a plot out of several stories? Yes. "Pulverizing plots: Into the woods with Sondheim, Shklovsky, and David O. Russell" shows how.

The total world of the story action is sometimes called the film's *diegesis* (the Greek word for "recounted story"). In the opening of *North by Northwest,* the traffic, streets, skyscrapers, and people we see, as well as the traffic, streets, skyscrapers, and people we assume to be offscreen, are all diegetic because they are assumed to exist in the world that the film depicts.

From the viewer's perspective, the *plot* consists of the action visibly and audibly present in the film before us. The plot includes, most centrally, all the story events that are directly depicted. In our *North by Northwest* example, only two story events are explicitly presented in the plot: rush hour and Roger Thornhill's dictating to Maggie as they leave the elevator. The plot also includes the information that characters may supply about earlier events in the story world, as when Roger mentions his many marriages.

Note, though, that the filmmaker may include material that lies *outside* the story world. For example, while the opening of *North by Northwest* is portraying rush hour in Manhattan, we also see the film's credits and hear orchestral music. Neither of these elements is diegetic, since they are brought in from outside the story world. The characters can't read the credits or hear the music.

Credits and a film's score are thus *nondiegetic* elements. Similarly, in silent films, many of the intertitles don't report dialogue but rather comment on the characters or describe the location. These intertitles are nondiegetic. In Chapters 6 and 7, we consider how editing and sound can function nondiegetically.

Suppose Hitchcock had superimposed the words "New York City" over the traffic shots at the start of *North by Northwest,* in the way we considered adding dates to the scrambled scenes of our hypothetical rom-com. Such titles would be nondiegetic as well. (They aren't part of the story world; the characters couldn't read them.) Today superimposed titles are the most common sorts of nondiegetic inserts, but we can find more unusual ones. In *The Band Wagon,* we see the premiere of a hopelessly pretentious musical play. Through nondiegetic images, accompanied by a brooding chorus, the plot signals that the production bombed **(3.5–3.9).** The filmmakers have added nondiegetic material to the plot for comic effect.

From the standpoint of the filmmaker, the story is the sum total of all the events in the narrative. As the storyteller, you could present some of these events directly (that is, display or mention them in the plot), hint at events that are not presented, and simply ignore other events. For instance, though we learn later in *North by Northwest* that Roger's mother is still close to him, we never learn what happened to his father. You, the filmmaker, could also add nondiegetic material, as in the example from *The Band Wagon.* This is why we can say that the filmmaker makes a story into a plot.

The spectator's task is quite different. All we have before us is the plot—the arrangement of material in the film as it stands. We create the story in our minds, thanks to cues in the plot. And in telling someone about the movie we've just seen, we can summarize it in two ways: We can recap the story, or recap the plot.

We'll see that the story–plot distinction affects all three aspects of narrative: causality, time, and space. Each offers the filmmaker a huge array of choice for guiding the viewer's experience of the film.

3.5

3.6

3.7

3.8

3.9

3.5–3.9 Nondiegetic imagery in *The Band Wagon*. A hopeful investor in the play enters the theater (3.5), and the camera moves in on a poster predicting success for the musical (3.6). But three comic nondiegetic images reveal it to be a flop: ghostly figures on a boat (3.7), a skull in a desert (3.8), and an image referring to the slang expression that the play "laid an egg" (3.9).

Cause and Effect

If narrative depends on changes created by cause and effect, what kinds of things can function as causes? Most often, characters. By triggering events and reacting to them, characters play causal roles within the film's narrative form.

Characters as Causes Most often, characters are persons, or at least entities like persons—Bugs Bunny or E.T. the extraterrestrial or the singing teapot in *Beauty and the Beast.* For our purposes here, Michael Moore is a character in *Roger and Me* no less than Roger Thornhill is in *North by Northwest,* even though Moore is a real person and Thornhill is fictional. In any narrative film, either fictional or documentary, characters create causes and register effects. Within the film's overall form, they make things happen and respond to events. Their actions and reactions contribute strongly to our engagement with the film.

Unlike characters in novels, film characters typically have a visible body. This is such a basic convention that we take it for granted, but it can be contested. Occasionally, a character is only a voice, as in *A Letter to Three Wives,* a film narrated by the woman who has sent a letter to three of her rivals. More disturbingly, in Luis Buñuel's *That Obscure Object of Desire,* one woman is portrayed by two actresses, and the physical differences between them may suggest different sides of her character. Todd Haynes takes this innovation further in *I'm Not There,* in which a folksinger is portrayed by actors of different ages, genders, and races.

Along with a body, a character has *traits:* attitudes, skills, habits, tastes, psychological drives, and any other qualities that distinguish him or her. Some characters, such as Mickey Mouse, may have only a few traits. When we say a character possesses several varying traits, some at odds with others, we tend to call that character complex, or three dimensional, or well developed. Sherlock Holmes, for instance, is a mass of traits. Some stem from his habits, such as his love of music or his addiction to cocaine, while others reflect his basic nature: his arrogance, his penetrating intelligence, his disdain for stupidity, his professional pride, his occasional gallantry.

As our love of gossip shows, we're curious about other humans, and we bring our people-watching skills to narratives. We're quick to assign traits to the characters onscreen, and usually the movie helps us out. Most characters wear their traits far more openly than people do in real life, and the plot presents situations that swiftly reveal them to us.

The opening scene of *Raiders of the Lost Ark* throws Indiana Jones's personality into high relief. We see immediately that he's bold and resourceful, even a little impetuous. He's courageous, but he can feel fear. By unearthing ancient treasures for museums, he shows an admirable devotion to scientific knowledge. In a few minutes, his essential traits are presented straightforwardly, and we come to know and sympathize with him.

All the traits that Indiana Jones displays in the opening scene are relevant to later scenes in *Raiders.* In general, a character is given traits that will play causal roles in the overall story action. The second scene of Alfred Hitchcock's *The Man Who Knew Too Much* (1934) shows that the heroine, Jill, is an excellent shot with a rifle. For much of the film, this trait seems irrelevant to the action, but in the last scene, Jill is able to shoot one of the villains when a police marksman cannot manage it. Like most qualities assigned to characters, Jill's marksmanship serves a particular narrative function.

Not all causes and effects in narratives originate with characters. In the so-called disaster movies, an earthquake or tidal wave may precipitate a series of actions on the parts of the characters. The same principle holds when the shark in *Jaws* terrorizes a community. Still, once these natural occurrences set the situation up, human desires and goals usually enter the action to develop the narrative. In *Jaws,* the townspeople pursue a variety of strategies to deal with the shark, propelling the plot as they do so. The primary cause of the action in *Contagion* is a lethal virus spreading across the world, but the action concentrates on individual researchers struggling to find an antidote and on ordinary citizens trying to survive.

Hiding Causes, Hiding Effects   As viewers we try to connect events by means of cause and effect. Given an incident, we tend to imagine what might have caused it or what it might in turn cause. That is, we look for causal motivation. We have mentioned an instance of this in Chapter 2: In the scene from *My Man Godfrey,* a scavenger hunt serves as a cause that justifies the presence of a beggar at a society ball (see p. 63).

Causal motivation often involves the planting of information in advance of a scene, as we saw in the kitchen scene of *The Shining* (2.14, 2.15). In *L.A. Confidential,* the idealistic detective Exley confides in his cynical colleague Vincennes that the murder of his father had driven him to enter law enforcement. He had privately named the unknown killer "Rollo Tomasi," a name that he has turned into an emblem of all unpunished evil. This conversation may seem to offer only an insight into Exley's personality. Yet later, when the corrupt police chief Smith shoots Vincennes, the latter mutters "Rollo Tomasi" with his last breath. Later, the puzzled Smith asks Exley who Rollo Tomasi is. Exley's earlier conversation with Vincennes motivates his shocked realization that the dead Vincennes has fingered Smith as his killer. Near the end, when Smith is about to shoot Exley, Exley says that the chief is Rollo Tomasi. Thus an apparently minor detail returns as a major causal and thematic motif.

Most of what we have said about causality pertains to the plot's direct presentation of causes and effects. In *The Man Who Knew Too Much,* Jill is shown to be a good shot, and because of this, she can save her daughter. But the plot can also lead us to *infer* causes and effects, and thus build up a total story.

Consider the mystery story. A murder has been committed. That is, we know an effect but not the causes—the killer, the motive, and perhaps also the method. The mystery tale thus depends strongly on curiosity. We want to know about things that happened before the events that the plot presents to us. It's the detective's job to disclose, at the end, the missing causes—to name the killer, explain the motive, and reveal the method. That is, in the detective film, the climax of the plot (the action we see) is a revelation of prior incidents in the story (events we didn't see).

Although this pattern is most common in detective narratives, any film's plot can withhold causes and thus arouse our curiosity. Horror and science fiction films often leave us temporarily in the dark about what forces lurk behind certain events. Not until three-quarters of the way through *Alien* do we learn that the science officer Ash is a robot conspiring to protect the creature. In *Caché,* a married couple receives an anonymous videotape recording their daily lives. The film's plot shows them trying to discover who made it and why it was made. In general, whenever any film creates a mystery, the plot initially suppresses certain story causes and presents only enigmatic effects.

3.10 Withholding story effects. The final image of *The 400 Blows* leaves Antoine's future uncertain.

The plot may also present causes but withhold story *effects,* prompting suspense and uncertainty in the viewer. After Hannibal Lecter's attack on his guards in the Tennessee prison in *The Silence of the Lambs,* the police search of the building raises the possibility that a body lying on top of an elevator is the wounded Lecter. After an extended suspense scene, we learn that Lecter has switched clothes with a dead guard and escaped.

When a plot withholds crucial consequences at the ending, it can ask us to ponder possible outcomes. In the final moments of François Truffaut's *The 400 Blows,* the boy Antoine has escaped from a reformatory and runs to the seashore. The camera zooms in on his face, and the frame freezes **(3.10).** The plot does not reveal if Antoine is captured and brought back, leaving us to speculate on what might happen in his future. As in *Rome Open City* (pp. 478–479), the story of *400 Blows* is, by the conventions of mainstream cinema, incomplete.

CONNECT TO THE BLOG
www.davidbordwell.net/blog

For examples of plots that keep causes secret from the audience, see "Side effects, safe haven: Out of the past" and "Gone grrrl."

Time

Causes and their effects are basic to narrative, but they take place in time. Our story–plot distinction helps us to understand how filmmakers use narrative form to manipulate time.

As we watch a film, we construct story time on the basis of what the plot presents. For instance, a plot may present story events out of chronological order. In *Citizen Kane,* we see a man's death before we see his youth, and we must build up a chronological version of his life. Even if events are shown in chronological order, most plots don't show every detail from beginning to end. We assume that the characters spend uneventful time sleeping, eating, traveling, and so forth, so the periods containing such irrelevant action can be skipped over. Another possibility is to have the plot present the same story event more than once, as when a character recalls a traumatic incident. In John Woo's *The Killer,* an accident in the opening scene blinds a singer, and later we see the same event again and again as the protagonist regretfully thinks back to it.

In short, filmmakers must decide how the film's plot will treat chronological *order* and temporal *duration* and *frequency.* In turn, the viewer must actively pick up the cues about these time-based factors. Each one harbors important artistic possibilities.

Temporal Order: How Are Events Sequenced?   Filmmakers can choose to present events out of story **order.** A flashback, like the ones we proposed for our hypothetical romantic comedy, is simply a portion of the story that the plot presents out of chronological sequence. In *Edward Scissorhands,* we first see the Winona Ryder character as an old woman telling her granddaughter a bedtime story. Most of the film then shows events that occurred when the old lady was in high school. Likewise,

The Hangover starts at a point of crisis, when the bridegroom's buddies report that he's missing. The plot then flashes back to them assembling for their bachelor party.

Flashbacks usually don't confuse us, because we mentally rearrange the events into chronological order: teenage years precede old age, the hangover comes after a night of partying. If story events can be thought of as 1-2-3-4, then the plot that uses a *flashback* presents something like 2-1-3-4, or 3-1-2-4. The filmmaker can also shuffle story order by employing a *flashforward.* This pattern moves from present to future, then back to the present, and could be represented as 1-2-4-3. In either case, given the plot order we figure out story order.

Even a simple reordering of scenes can create complex effects. The plot of Quentin Tarantino's *Pulp Fiction* begins with a couple deciding to rob the diner they're sitting in. This scene actually takes place somewhat late in the story's chronology, but the viewer doesn't learn this until the final scene. At that point, the robbery interrupts a dialogue involving other, more central, characters eating in the same diner. Just by taking a scene that occurs late in the story and placing it at the start of the plot, Tarantino creates a surprise that maintains our interest through the film's last moments.

Tarantino was influenced by the film noir trend of the 1940s and 1950s, which exploited time ordering in ingenious ways. *D.O.A.* (1949) shows how flashbacks can shape the viewer's expectations across a whole film. A man strides into a police station to report a murder. "Who was murdered?" asks the officer. The man replies: "I was." As he starts to explain, we move into an extended flashback. The earliest story action in the past is rather innocuous and slowly paced. Had the plot presented the story in chronological order, viewers might have found these scenes flat. But knowing that the protagonist is dying makes us vigilant. Every encounter he has puts us on the alert: Is this what will kill him? Our anticipation wouldn't have been aroused so keenly if the story had been told in 1-2-3 order.

Temporal Duration: How Long Do the Events Take?

The plot of *North by Northwest* presents four crowded days and nights in the life of Roger Thornhill. But the story stretches back far before that, indicated by the information about the past that is revealed in the course of the plot. The story events include Roger's past marriages, the U.S. Intelligence Agency's plot to create a false agent named George Kaplan, and the villain Van Damm's smuggling activities.

In general, a film's plot selects only certain stretches of story **duration.** As a filmmaker you might decide to concentrate on a short, relatively cohesive time span, as *North by Northwest* does. Or you might let your plot unfold across many years, highlighting significant stretches of time in that period. *Citizen Kane* shows us the protagonist in his youth, skips over some time to show him as a young man, skips over more time to show him middle-aged, and so forth. The sum of all these slices of *story* duration yields an overall *plot* duration.

But we need one more distinction. Watching a movie takes time—20 minutes or two hours or seven-plus hours (as Béla Tarr's *Satan's Tango* does). So there's a third duration involved in a narrative film, which we can call *screen* duration.

The relationships among story duration, plot duration, and screen duration are complicated, but for our purposes, we can say this. The filmmaker can manipulate screen duration independently of the overall story duration and plot duration. For example, *North by Northwest* has an overall story duration of several years (including all relevant story events), an overall plot duration of four days and nights, and a screen duration of about 136 minutes.

Just as plot duration selects from story duration, so screen duration selects from overall plot duration. In *North by Northwest,* only portions of the plot's four days and nights are shown to us. An interesting counterexample is *Twelve Angry Men,* the story of a jury deliberating a murder case. The 95 minutes of the movie approximate the same stretch of time in its characters' lives.

At a more specific level, the filmmaker can use screen duration to override story time. For example, screen duration can *expand* story duration. A famous

CONNECT TO THE BLOG
www.davidbordwell.net/blog

Mark Romanek learned the *D.O.A.* lesson in directing *One Hour Photo.* "Creating suspense through film form" discusses how, after preview screenings fizzled, Romanek rearranged his plot to start late in the story action and to flash back to the beginning. "Now the audience is paying closer attention."

instance is that of the raising of the bridges in Sergei Eisenstein's *October*. Here an event that takes only a few moments in the story is stretched out to several minutes of screen time by means of the technique of film editing. As a result, this action gains a tremendous emphasis. The plot can also use screen duration to compress story time. A process taking hours or days is often condensed into a few swift shots. These examples suggest that film techniques play a central role in creating screen duration, and we'll see how in Chapters 5 and 6.

Temporal Frequency: How Often Do We See or Hear an Event?

Most commonly, a story event is presented only once in the plot. Occasionally, however, a single story event may appear twice or even more in the plot treatment. If we see an event early in a film's plot, and then, later in the plot, there is a flashback to that event, we see that same event twice. Some films use multiple narrators, each of whom describes the same event; again, we see it take place several times. This increased **frequency** may allow us to see the same action in several ways. Repetition can take place simply on the soundtrack. Sometimes only a single line of dialogue will reappear, haunting a character who can't escape the memory of that moment.

Why would a filmmaker want to repeat a story event in the plot? Sometimes it's to remind the audience of something. Or the repetition reveals new information. This occurs in *For a Few Dollars More,* in which the repeated scene gets expanded more fully each time that characters recall it. In *Amores Perros,* a traffic accident is shown three times, and each iteration reveals how a different person is affected by the crash.

The manipulations of story order, duration, and frequency in the plot illustrate how viewers actively participate in making sense of the narrative film. The filmmaker designs the plot to prompt us about chronological sequence, the time span of the actions, and the number of times an event occurs. It's up to the viewer to make assumptions and inferences and to form expectations. Fortunately, we can usually put things together by appealing to our ordinary sense of time and cause and effect. A flashback, for instance, is often motivated as a character's memory. Other cues, such as clothing, age, settings, and the like can help us sort out a film's story time.

Still, some filmmakers have offered quite complicated time schemes. In *The Usual Suspects,* a petty criminal spins an elaborate tale of his gang's activities to an FBI agent. His recounting unfolds in many flashbacks, some of which repeat events we witnessed in the opening scene. Yet a final twist reveals that some of the flashbacks must have contained lies, and we must piece together both the chronology of events and the story's real cause-effect chain. Christopher Nolan's *Inception* creates several stories-within-stories, all unfolding simultaneously in dream-time, but the plot makes each one take place at a different rate. One second in one dream might last many minutes in another, so that we have several scales of plot duration. Through magic, *Harry Potter and the Prisoner of Azkaban* permits action we've already seen to run again, with different results **(3.11).**

CONNECT TO THE BLOG
www.davidbordwell.net/blog

A repeated scene is used to convey fuller story information at the climax of *Mildred Pierce*. To accomplish this, however, the film plays a further trick with story time. See our "Twice told tales: *Mildred Pierce*." Repetition may mislead us in other ways, as we try to show in "Memories are unmade by this."

" The multiple points of view replaced the linear story. Watching a repeated action or an intersection happen again and again . . . they hold the audience in the story. It's like watching a puzzle unfold."
—Gus van Sant, director, on *Elephant*

3.11 Creating complex time schemes. In *Harry Potter and the Prisoner of Azkaban*, Harry and his friend Hermione use a magical device to go back in time. Here they watch themselves playing out the action from a scene we had witnessed earlier in the film.

A CLOSER LOOK

Playing Games with Story Time

For both filmmakers and viewers, reconstructing story time on the basis of the plot might be seen as a sort of game. Most Hollywood films make this game fairly simple. Still, just as we enjoy learning the rules of new games, in unusual films, we can enjoy the challenge of unpredictable orderings of story events.

Pulp Fiction (1994) popularized "broken timelines" for a new generation of filmmakers and moviegoers. The film's plot begins and ends with stages of a restaurant holdup, seemingly a conventional frame situation in the present. Yet in fact the final event in the story, the flight of the Bruce Willis character and his girlfriend from Los Angeles, is not the final scene in the plot. The reordering of events is startling and confusing at first, but it becomes dramatically effective in forcing us to rethink scenes we have seen earlier.

The success of *Pulp Fiction* encouraged American filmmakers to play more freely with story time. *Go* (1999) presents the events of a single night three times, each time from a different character's point of view. We cannot figure out what happened until the end, since various events are withheld from the first version and shown in the second or third. Ten years later, audiences had become quite familiar with such "replay" plots. *Vantage Point* repeats an assassination and bombing, with each version clarifying a bit more of what actually happened in the story.

Replay plots can tease the viewer into fitting everything together. *Out of Sight* begins with an inept bank robber who falls in love with the FBI agent who pursues him. As their oddball romance proceeds, there is a string of flashbacks not motivated by any character's memory. These seem to involve a separate story line, and their purpose is puzzling until the film's second half. Then the last flashback, perhaps a character's recollection, loops back to the action that had begun the film and explains the main events. As often happens, the filmmaker uses cause-effect cues to help the viewer straighten out the broken timeline.

If replay films work to tease us with what happened in the past, filmmakers can use science fiction or fantasy premises to present alternative futures. These are sometimes called "what if?" narratives. Such films typically present a situation, then show how the story might proceed along different cause-effect chains if one factor is changed.

Sliding Doors shows the heroine, Helen, fired from her job and heading home to her apartment, where her boyfriend is in bed with another woman. We see Helen entering the subway and catching her train, but then the action runs backward and she arrives on the platform again, this time bumping into a child on the stairs and missing the train. The rest of the film's plot moves between two alternative futures for Helen. By catching the train, Helen arrives in time to discover her boyfriend's affair and moves out. By missing the train, Helen arrives after the other woman has left and stays with her faithless lover. The plot shifts back and forth between these alternative cause-effect chains before dovetailing them at the end.

Groundhog Day (1993) helped popularize what-if plots. On February 1, an obnoxious weatherman, Phil Connor, travels to Punxsutawney to cover the famous Groundhog Day ceremonies. He then finds himself trapped in February 2, which repeats over and over. The variants depend on how Phil acts—some days behaving frivolously, some days breaking laws **(3.12, 3.13),** and later trying to improve himself. Only after many such days does he become an admirable character, and the repetitions mysteriously stop.

Neither *Sliding Doors* nor *Groundhog Day* provides any explanation for the forking of its protagonist's life into various paths. We simply must assume that some higher power has intervened to improve the character's situation. Other films motivate the alternative futures by a piece of technology. The three *Back to the Future* films (1985, 1989,

3.12

3.13

3.12–3.13 "What if?" narrative—replaying the same day. During one repetition of February 2 in *Groundhog Day*, Phil tests whether he can commit crimes. He's tossed in jail in the evening (3.12), only to wake up, as on other Groundhog Days, back at the bed-and-breakfast inn (3.13).

1990) posit that Marty's friend Doc has invented a time-travel machine, and this gadget permits complicated criss-crossings of cause and effect. In the first film, the machine accidentally transports Marty back to 1955. By accidentally thwarting his parents' romance, Marty endangers his own existence in 1985. Eventually, Marty induces his parents to fall in love and returns safely to 1985, where his life has been improved as a result of his first time trip.

But in the second *Back to the Future* installment, events in Marty's life in 2015 have effects in 1955. The villain Biff uses the time machine to travel back and change what happened then. In the process he wreaks harm on Doc and Marty's family. Marty must again travel back to 1955 to stop Biff from changing events. At the end of Part II, Marty becomes trapped in 1955, while Doc is accidentally sent back to 1885. Marty joins him there in Part III for another set of threatened changes to the future. Although the films maintain a unified cause-effect chain, the story becomes so convoluted that at one point Doc diagrams events for Marty (and us) on a blackboard. Variations on Doc's time-machine device for creating alternative futures can be found in *Déjà vu, Source Code*, and *Project Almanac*.

The game of what-if emerged outside the United States as well. In *Run Lola Run*, the heroine's desperate attempts to replace a large sum that her inept boyfriend owes to drug dealers are shown as three alternative stories. Each one ends very differently because of small changes of action on Lola's part.

Although what-if premises make it more difficult for us to piece story events together, film-makers usually give us enough clues along the way to keep us from frustration. Usually, the film does not provide a huge number of alternative futures—perhaps only two or three. Within these futures, the cause-effect chain remains linear, so we can piece it together. Characters sometimes point out the events that have changed their lives, as with Doc's blackboard explanation in *Back to the Future II*. In *Sliding Doors*, Helen remarks: "If only I had just caught that bloody train, it'd never have happened." The characters and settings tend to remain quite consistent for all the alternative story lines—though often differences of appearance are introduced to help us keep track of events **(3.14, 3.15)**.

CONNECT TO THE BLOG
www.davidbordwell.net/blog

We examine what-if narratives in "Forking tracks: *Source Code*" and "What-if movies: Forking paths in the drawing room." *Inception* presents a complex plot involving dreams within dreams. We look at its exposition, motivation, and embedded plotlines in "*Inception*: Dream a little dream within a dream with me" and a follow-up, "Revisiting *Inception*."

Moreover, the individual story lines tend to parallel one another. In all three presentations of events in *Run Lola Run*, the goal of getting money is the same, even though the progression and outcomes are different. The final version of events tends to give us the impression of being the definitive one, and so what-if films usually achieve a sense of closure.

Replay and what-if films appeal to the way we think in ordinary life. Our minds sometimes revisit certain events, and we speculate about how our lives would have changed if a single moment had been different. We easily understand the sort of game that these films proffer, and we're willing to play it.

3.14

3.15

3.14–3.15 Cues for alternative futures in *Sliding Doors*. In one story line Helen gets her hair cut short (3.14). This helps distinguish her from the Helen of the other story line, who keeps her hair long (3.15). Before the haircut, a forehead bandage was a crucial cue.

A CLOSER LOOK

Continued

More and more, however, *puzzle films* have denied us this degree of unity and clarity. Here filmmakers create perplexing patterns of story time or causality, trusting that viewers will search for clues by rewatching the movie. An example is *Memento*, which presents the hero's investigation along two time tracks. Brief black-and-white scenes show an ongoing present, with story action moving forward chronologically. The more extensive scenes, which are in color, move *backward* through time, so the first plot event we see is the final story event, the second plot event is the next-to-last story event, and so on. This tactic reflects the hero's loss of short-term memory, but it also challenges viewers to piece everything together. At the same time, there are enough uncertainties about the hero's memories to lead viewers to speculate that some mysteries remain unresolved at the close.

The DVD format, which allows random access to scenes, encouraged filmmakers along this path. So did the Internet. Websites still buzz with speculations about what really happened in *Donnie Darko, Identity, Primer, The Butterfly Effect*, and *Inception*. Like other films that twist or break up story time, puzzle movies seek to engross us in the dynamic game of narrative form.

Space

In film narrative, space is usually an important factor. Events occur in particular locales, such as Kansas or Oz; the Flint, Michigan, of *Roger and Me;* or the Manhattan of *North by Northwest.* We'll consider setting in more detail when we examine mise-en-scene in Chapter 4, but we ought briefly to note how plot and story can manipulate space.

Normally, the locale of the story action is also that of the plot, but sometimes the plot leads us to imagine story spaces that are never shown. In Otto Preminger's *Exodus,* one scene is devoted to Dov Landau's interrogation by a terrorist organization he wants to join. Dov reluctantly tells his questioners of his duties in a Nazi concentration camp **(3.16).** Although the film never shows this locale through a flashback, much of the scene's emotional power depends on our using our imagination to fill in Dov's sketchy description of how he survived.

Further, we can introduce an idea akin to the concept of screen duration. Besides story space and plot space, cinema employs screen space: the visible space within the frame. Just as screen duration selects certain plot spans for presentation, so screen space selects portions of plot space. We'll consider screen space and offscreen space when we analyze framing in Chapter 5.

3.16 Imagining offscreen locales. In *Exodus*, Dov Landau recounts his traumatic stay in a concentration camp. Instead of presenting this through a flashback, the narration dwells on his face, leaving us to visualize his ordeal.

Openings, Closings, and Patterns of Development

Our early experiment in romantic-comedy plotting began with beginnings and endings: How will you start your film? How will you conclude it? This echoed our discussion of formal development in Chapter 2, where we suggested that it's often useful to compare beginnings and endings. A narrative usually presents a series of changes from an initial situation to a final situation, and by considering how that pattern works, we can better understand the film.

Openings   A film does not just start, it *begins.* The opening provides a basis for what is to come and initiates us into the narrative. It raises our expectations by setting up a specific range of possible causes for what we see. Indeed, the first quarter or so of a film's plot is sometimes referred to as the *setup.*

Very often, the film begins by telling us about the characters and their situations before any major actions occur. Alternatively, the plot may seek to arouse curiosity by bringing us into a series of actions that has already started. (This is called opening *in medias res,* a Latin phrase meaning "in the middle of things.") The viewer speculates on possible causes of the events presented. *Close Encounters of the Third Kind* begins with investigators arriving in the desert to study World War II airplanes. An *in medias res* opening grabs our interest, but as Robert Towne notes (p. 51), sooner or later the filmmaker has to explain what led up to these events.

In either case, some of the actions that took place before the plot started—often called the *backstory*—will be stated or suggested so that we can understand what's coming later. The portion of the plot that lays out the backstory and the initial situation is called the *exposition.* Usually exposition takes place early in the film, but the filmmaker may postpone chunks of exposition for the sake of suspense and more immediate impact. James Cameron and Gale Anne Hurd did this in their screenplay for *The Terminator.* For nearly 40 minutes the plot provides chases, gunplay, and glimpses of a war-torn future before the fighter Reese explains what has caused the plight that he and Sarah Connor are in.

Development Sections   As a film's plot proceeds, the causes and effects create patterns of development. Some patterns are quite common. Change is essential to narrative, and a common pattern traces a *change in knowledge.* Very often, a character learns something in the course of the action, with the most crucial knowledge coming at the final turning point of the plot. In *Witness,* John Book, hiding out on an Amish farm, learns that his partner has been killed and his boss has betrayed him. His rage leads to a climactic shoot-out.

Another common pattern of development is the *goal-oriented* plot, in which a character takes steps to achieve an object or condition. Plots based on *searches* would be instances of the goal plot. In *Raiders of the Lost Ark,* the protagonists try to find the Ark of the Covenant; in *North by Northwest,* Roger Thornhill looks for George Kaplan. The goal-oriented plot pattern often takes the shape of *investigation,* itself a kind of search. Here the protagonist's goal is not an object, but information, usually about mysterious causes.

Time may also provide plot patterns. A framing situation in the present may initiate a series of flashbacks showing how events led up to the present situation, as in *The Usual Suspects'* flashbacks. *Hoop Dreams* is organized around the two main characters' high school careers, with each part of the film devoted to a year of their lives. The plot may also create a specific duration for the action—a *deadline.* In *Back to the Future,* the hero must synchronize his time machine with a bolt of lightning at a specific moment in order to return to 1985. This creates a goal toward which he must struggle. Space can structure plot development, too. The filmmaker might confine the action to a single locale, such as a home (as in the *Paranormal Activity* films). In *Lebanon,* the action is restricted to the inside of a military tank, and the plot develops as the tank moves to different locations. Similarly, in *Locke,* after a brief introduction the plot attaches us to

CONNECT TO THE BLOG
www.davidbordwell.net/blog

Sometimes a film's opening will signal that we are not going to get much exposition. See "How to watch an art movie, reel 1."

66 No exposition except under heat, and break it up at that."
—Raymond Chandler, novelist and screenwriter for *Double Indemnity*

CONNECT TO THE BLOG
www.davidbordwell.net/blog

Some filmmakers develop their plot in large blocks—more or less self-contained episodes or "chapters." We discuss this strategy in "The 1940s are over, and Tarantino's still playing with blocks."

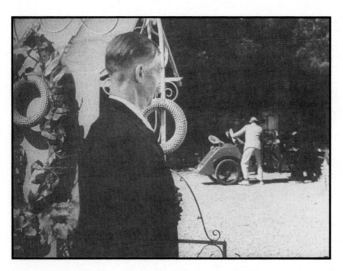

3.17 Time and space in plot patterning. In *Mr. Hulot's Holiday,* Hulot's aged, noisy car has a flat tire that breaks up a funeral—consistent with a comic pattern in which the vacationing Mr. Hulot repeatedly disturbs townspeople and other guests.

the protagonist during his long car drive; the drama arises from several phone calls he conducts on the trip.

A filmmaker can combine any of these plot patterns. Many films built around a journey, such as *The Wizard of Oz* or *North by Northwest,* also involve deadlines. Jacques Tati's *Mr. Hulot's Holiday* uses both spatial and temporal patterns to structure its comic plot. The plot confines itself to a beachside resort and its neighboring areas, and it consumes one week of a summer vacation. Each day certain routines recur: morning exercise, lunch, afternoon outings, dinner, evening entertainment. Much of the film's humor relies on the way that Mr. Hulot disrupts the routines of the guests and townspeople **(3.17).** Although cause and effect still operate in *Mr. Hulot's Holiday,* time and space are central to the plot's formal patterning.

Any pattern of development will encourage the viewer to create specific expectations. As the film trains the viewer in its particular form, these expectations become more and more precise. Dorothy's trip through Oz isn't a casual sightseeing tour. Once we understand her desire to go home, each step of her journey (to the Emerald City, to the Witch's castle, to the Emerald City again) is seen as delaying or furthering her goal.

In any film, the middle portion may delay an expected outcome. When Dorothy at last reaches the Wizard, he sets up a new obstacle for her by demanding the Witch's broom. *North by Northwest*'s journey plot constantly postpones Roger Thornhill's discovery of the Kaplan hoax, and this, too, creates suspense. The pattern of development may also create surprise, the cheating of an expectation, as when Dorothy discovers that the Wizard is a fraud or when Thornhill sees the minion Leonard fire point-blank at his boss Van Damm. Patterns of development encourage the spectator to form long-term expectations that can be delayed, cheated, or gratified.

CONNECT TO THE BLOG
www.davidbordwell.net/blog

How do we learn to recognize that an ending is coming? Starting from an anecdote about a three-year-old watching *Snow White and the Seven Dwarfs,* we speculate on this subject in "Molly wanted more."

CONNECT TO THE BLOG
www.davidbordwell.net/blog

A film is constantly giving us story information. How much do we remember, scene by scene? Some filmmakers exploit our difficulties in remembering what happened earlier, as we show in "Memories are unmade by this."

Climaxes and Closings   A film doesn't simply stop; it *ends.* The plot will typically resolve its causal issues by bringing the development to a high point, or *climax.* In the climax, the action is presented as having a narrow range of possible outcomes. At the climax of *North by Northwest,* Roger and Eve are dangling off Mount Rushmore, and there are only two possibilities: they will fall, or they will be saved.

Because the climax focuses possible outcomes so narrowly, it typically serves to settle the causal issues that have run through the film. In the documentary *Primary,* the climax takes place on election night; both Kennedy and Humphrey await the voters' verdict and finally learn the winner. In *Jaws,* battles with the shark climax in the destruction of the boat, the death of Captain Quint, the apparent death of Hooper, and Brody's final victory. In such films, the ending resolves, or closes off, the chains of cause and effect.

Emotionally, the climax aims to lift the viewer to a high degree of tension. Because the viewer knows that there are relatively few ways the action can be resolved, she or he can hope for a fairly specific outcome. When Brody slays the shark and discovers that Hooper has survived, their relief echoes ours. In the climax of many films, formal resolution coincides with an emotional satisfaction.

A few narratives, however, are deliberately anticlimactic. After creating expectations about how the cause-effect chain will be resolved, the film scotches them by refusing to settle things definitely. One famous example is the last shot of *The 400 Blows* (p. 79). In Michelangelo Antonioni's *L'Eclisse* ("The Eclipse"), the two lovers vow to meet for a final reconciliation but aren't shown doing so. When the filmmaker has chosen to let the ending remain open, the plot leaves us uncertain about the final consequences of the story events. The absence of a clear-cut climax and resolution may encourage us to imagine what might happen next or to reflect on other ways in which our expectations might have been fulfilled.

Narration: The Flow of Story Information

In looking at how a filmmaker tells a story, we've emphasized matters of plot structure: how the parts, from beginning to end, are fitted together to shape the viewer's experience. Filmic storytelling involves decisions about another sort of plot organization. Back when we were sketching alternatives for a romantic comedy (p. 74), we also faced the question of whether to build the scenes around one member of the couple, both members, or the couple and other characters around them. We could tell the same story from different characters' perspectives. The story of Little Red Riding Hood will be very different depending on whether we attach ourselves to the girl or to the wolf.

This means deciding what information to give the spectator, and when to supply it. Thinking like a filmmaker, should you restrict the viewer just to what the character knows? Or should you give the viewer more information than the character has? In a stalking scene, should you show just the person being pursued, watching and listening for a threat we never see? Or should you show both the victim shrinking away and the stalker in pursuit? There is no right or wrong answer. The choice depends on the effect you want to achieve. What is clear is that a filmmaker can't avoid choosing how much information to reveal and when to reveal it.

Similarly, you might ask how objective or subjective your scene should be. Should you show only how characters behave, without any attempt to get inside their heads? Or should you add voice-over monologues that expose what they're thinking, or point-of-view shots that show what they can see? Should you try to dramatize their dreams, fantasies, or hallucinations? Again, it's a forced choice, and again you can imagine presenting the same story in a plot that is deeply subjective or one that is more objective.

These decisions involve **narration,** the plot's way of distributing story information in order to achieve specific effects. Narration is the moment-by-moment process that guides viewers in building the story out of the plot. Many factors enter into narration, but the most important ones for our purposes involve the factors we've just sketched out: the *range* and the *depth* of story information that the plot presents.

Range of Story Information: Restricted or Unrestricted?

D. W. Griffith's *The Birth of a Nation* begins by recounting how slaves were brought to America and how people debated the need to free them. The plot then shows two families, the northern Stoneman family and the southern Camerons. The plot also dwells on political matters, including Lincoln's hope of averting civil war. From the start, then, our range of knowledge is very broad. The plot takes us across historical periods, regions of the country, and various groups of characters. This breadth of story information continues throughout the film. When Ben Cameron founds the Ku Klux Klan, we know about it at the moment the idea strikes him, long before the other characters learn of it. At the climax, we know that the Klan is riding to rescue several characters besieged in a cabin, but the besieged people do not know this.

On the whole, in *The Birth of a Nation,* the narration is *unrestricted.* We know more, we see and hear more, than any of the characters can. Such extremely knowledgeable narration is often called *omniscient* ("all-knowing") narration.

Now consider the plot of Howard Hawks's *The Big Sleep.* The film begins with the detective Philip Marlowe visiting General Sternwood, who wants to hire him. We learn about the case as Marlowe does. Throughout the rest of the film, he is present in every scene. With hardly any exceptions, we don't see or hear anything that he can't see and hear. The narration is *restricted* to what Marlowe knows.

CONNECT TO THE BLOG
www.davidbordwell.net/blog

We examine the idea of restricting the narration to what one character knows in "Alignment, allegiance, and murder."

> **❝** In the first section [of *Reservoir Dogs*], up until Mr. Orange shoots Mr. Blonde, the characters have far more information about what's going on than you have—and they have conflicting information. Then the Mr. Orange sequence happens and that's a great leveler. You start getting caught up with exactly what's going on, and in the third part, when you go back into the warehouse for the climax you are totally ahead of everybody—you know far more than any one of the characters.❞
>
> —Quentin Tarantino, director

Each alternative offers certain advantages. *The Birth of a Nation* seeks to present a panoramic vision of a period in American history (based on a racist ideology). Omniscient narration is thus essential to creating the sense of many destinies intertwined with the fate of the country. Had Griffith restricted narration the way *The Big Sleep* does, we would have learned story information solely through one character—say, Ben Cameron. We could not witness the prologue scene, or the scenes in Lincoln's office, or most of the battle episodes, or the scene of Lincoln's assassination, since Ben is present at none of these events. The plot would now concentrate on one man's experience of the Civil War and Reconstruction.

Similarly, *The Big Sleep* benefits from its restricted narration. By limiting us to Marlowe's range of knowledge, the film can create curiosity and surprise. Restricted narration is important to mystery films, since such films engage our interest by hiding important causes. Confining the plot to an investigator's range of knowledge plausibly motivates concealing important story information. *The Big Sleep* could have been less restricted if the screenwriter had alternated scenes of Marlowe's investigation with scenes that show the gambling boss, Eddie Mars, planning his crimes. But this would have given away some of the mystery. In both *The Birth of a Nation* and *The Big Sleep,* the narration's range of knowledge functions to elicit particular reactions from the viewer.

Range of Knowledge: A Matter of Degree   Unrestricted narration and restricted narration aren't watertight categories but rather two ends of a continuum. A filmmaker may choose to present a broader range of knowledge than does *The Big Sleep* and still not attain the omniscience of *The Birth of a Nation.*

Early scenes of *North by Northwest,* for instance, confine us pretty much to what Roger Thornhill sees and knows. After he flees from the United Nations building, however, the plot takes us to Washington, where the members of the U.S. Intelligence Agency discuss the situation. Here the viewer learns something that Roger won't learn for some time: the man he seeks, George Kaplan, doesn't exist. From then on, we have a greater range of knowledge than Roger does. And we know a bit more than the Agency's staff: we know exactly how the mix-up took place. But we still don't know many other things that the narration could have divulged in the scene in Washington. For instance, the Agency's staff members don't identify the secret agent they have working under Van Damm's nose.

This oscillation between restricted and unrestricted narration is common in films. Typically the plot shifts from character to character, giving us a little more than any one character knows while still withholding some crucial items from us. Even if the plot is focused on a single protagonist, the narration usually includes a few scenes that the character isn't present to witness. *Tootsie's* narration remains almost entirely attached to actor Michael Dorsey, but a few shots show his acquaintances shopping or watching him on television.

Lebanon, set during the June 1982 Israeli-Lebanese war, comes very close to purely restricted narration. Apart from the beginning and ending, the entire film is set inside a tank, where we are limited to what the four team members know. Usually films with such strong attachments to characters cheat a little by cutting to action taking place outside. Here there is no violation of the setting **(3.18, 3.19)**. Necessary information from outside comes via radio communications. Director Samuel Maoz has said that his goal was to make audience members experience young soldiers' sense of the horror of war and their oppressive confinement. "You see only what they see. You know only what they know." Yet there are still moments when one soldier's reactions aren't noticed by the others, so we gain a slightly wider range of knowledge than any one character has.

Analyzing Range of Narration   An easy way to analyze the range of narration is to ask, "Who knows what when?" This question applies to the characters and the spectator as well. At any given moment, we can ask if we the audience knows more than, less than, or as much as the characters do. Sometimes we may get information that *no* character possesses. We shall see this happen at the end of *Citizen Kane.*

CONNECT TO THE BLOG
www.davidbordwell.net/blog

Cloverfield uses an unusually restricted narration, confining itself to a video recording shot by the main characters. See our analysis, "A behemoth from the Dead Zone." As if corresponding to *Cloverfield*, the teenage superhero movie *Chronicle* found ingenious ways to expand the video recording as the plot develops. We discuss this problem of motivation in "Return to paranormalcy."

3.18

3.19

3.18–3.19 Severely restricted range of knowledge. In *Lebanon*, we see the world outside a tank as the characters do, through a gunner's crosshairs (3.18) or when the hatch is briefly opened (3.19).

Filmmakers can achieve powerful effects by manipulating the range of story information. Restricted narration tends to create greater curiosity and surprise for the viewer. For instance, if a character is exploring a sinister house, and we see and hear no more than the character does, a sudden revelation of a hand thrusting out from a doorway will startle us.

In contrast, as Hitchcock pointed out, a dose of unrestricted narration helps to build suspense. He explained it this way to François Truffaut:

> We are now having a very innocent little chat. Let us suppose that there is a bomb underneath this table between us. Nothing happens, and then all of a sudden, "Boom!" There is an explosion. The public is surprised, but prior to this surprise, it has seen an absolutely ordinary scene, of no special consequence. Now, let us take a suspense situation. The bomb is underneath the table and the public knows it, probably because they have seen the anarchist place it there. The public is aware that the bomb is going to explode at one o'clock and there is a clock in the decor. The public can see that it is a quarter to one. In these conditions this innocuous conversation becomes fascinating because the public is participating in the scene. The audience is

66 Narrative tension is primarily about withholding information."
—Ian McEwan, novelist

longing to warn the characters on the screen: "You shouldn't be talking about such trivial matters. There's a bomb beneath you and it's about to explode!"

In the first case we have given the public fifteen seconds of surprise at the moment of the explosion. In the second case we have provided them with fifteen minutes of suspense. The conclusion is that whenever possible the public must be informed.

CONNECT TO THE BLOG
www.davidbordwell.net/blog

In a series of entries starting with "Hitchcock, Lessing, & the bomb under the table," we consider where Hitchcock may have gotten his ideas on suspense and surprise.

Hitchcock put his theory into practice. In *Psycho,* Lila Crane explores the Bates mansion in much the same way as our hypothetical character was doing. There are isolated moments of surprise as she discovers odd information about Norman and his mother. But the overall effect of the sequence is built on suspense because we know, as Lila does not, that Mrs. Bates is in the house. (Actually, as in *North by Northwest,* our knowledge isn't completely accurate, but during Lila's investigation, we believe it to be.) As in Hitchcock's anecdote, our greater range of knowledge creates suspense because we can anticipate events that the character cannot. Once more, the filmmaker guides the viewer's expectations.

Depth of Story Information: Objective or Subjective?

A film's narration manipulates not only the range of knowledge but also the *depth* of our knowledge. The filmmaker must decide how far to plunge into a character's psychological states. As with restricted and unrestricted narration, there is a spectrum between objectivity and subjectivity.

A plot might confine us wholly to information about what characters say and do. Here the narration is relatively *objective.* Or a film's plot may give us access to what characters see and hear. The filmmaker might give us shots taken from a character's optical standpoint, the **point-of-view (POV) shot.** For instance, in *North by Northwest,* point-of-view editing is used as we see Roger Thornhill crawl up to Van Damm's window (**3.20–3.22**). Or we might hear sounds as the character would

3.20

3.21

3.22

3.20–3.22 Perceptual subjectivity in *North by Northwest.* Roger Thornhill looks in Van Damm's window (objective narration; 3.20), and an optical POV shot follows (perceptual subjectivity; 3.21). This is followed by another shot of Roger looking (objectivity again; 3.22).

hear them, what sound recordists call *sound perspective.* In short, through either sight or sound, the filmmaker gives us what we might call *perceptual subjectivity.*

The filmmaker can go deeper, beyond the character's senses and into her or his mind. We can call this *mental subjectivity.* We might hear an internal voice reporting the character's thoughts, or we might see the character's inner images, representing memory, fantasy, dreams, or hallucinations. In *Slumdog Millionaire,* the hero is a contestant on a quiz show, but his concentration is often interrupted by brief shots showing his memories, particularly one image of the woman he loves **(3.23, 3.24).** Here Jamal's memory motivates flashbacks to earlier story events.

Either sort of subjectivity may be signaled through particular film techniques. If a character is drunk, or drugged, the filmmakers may render those perceptual states through slow motion, blurred imagery, or distorted sound. Similar techniques may suggest a dream or hallucination.

But some imaginary actions may not be so strongly marked. Another scene in *Slumdog Millionaire* shows Jamal reuniting with his gangster brother Salim atop a skyscraper under construction. Jamal hurls himself at Salim, and we see shots of both falling from the building **(3.25, 3.26).** But the next shot presents Jamal still on the skyscraper, glaring at Salim **(3.27).** Now we realize that the images of the falling

3.23

3.24

3.23–3.24 Memories motivate flashbacks. Early in *Slumdog Millionaire*, it's established that during the quiz show (3.23) Jamal recalls his past—most often, his glimpse of Latika at the train station (3.24).

3.25

3.26

3.27

3.25–3.27 Suppressed cues for subjectivity in *Slumdog Millionaire*. Furious with Salim, Jamal grabs him and rushes toward the edge of the building (3.25). Several shots present their fall (3.26), but then the narration cuts back to Jamal, glaring at Salim (3.27). This shot reveals that he only imagined killing both of them.

men were purely mental, representing Jamal's rage. Because the shots weren't marked as subjective, we briefly thought that their fall was really taking place.

Typically, moments of perceptual and mental subjectivity come in bursts. They tend to be embedded in a framework of objective narration. POV shots, like those assigned to Roger Thornhill in *North by Northwest,* and flashbacks or fantasies are bracketed by more objective shots. We are able to understand Jamal's memory of Latika and his urge to kill Salim because those images are framed by shots of actions that are really happening in the plot. Other sorts of films, however, may avoid this convention. Fellini's *8½,* Luis Buñuel's *Belle de Jour,* Peter Haneke's *Caché,* and *Memento* mix objectivity and subjectivity in ambiguous ways. *Inception* doesn't signal its dreams with the usual special effects, so that often we're not sure whether we're in reality or a dream (or a dream nested inside another dream).

If a filmmaker restricts our knowledge to a single character, does that restriction create greater subjective depth? Not necessarily. *The Big Sleep* is quite restricted in its range of knowledge, as we've seen. But we very seldom see or hear things from Marlowe's perceptual vantage point, and we never get direct access to his mind. *The Big Sleep* uses almost completely objective narration. The omniscient narration of *The Birth of a Nation,* however, plunges to considerable psychological depth with optical POV shots, flashbacks, and the hero's final fantasy vision of a world without war. To maximize suspense, Hitchcock's films may give us slightly greater knowledge than his characters have. But at certain moments, he confines us to their perceptual subjectivity (usually relying on POV shots). For the filmmaker, range and depth of knowledge are independent variables. These examples show that for the filmmaker, choices about the range of knowledge can be made independently of choices about depth of knowledge.

Incidentally, this is one reason why the term "point of view" is ambiguous. It can refer to range of knowledge (as when a critic speaks of an "omniscient point of view") or to depth (as when speaking of "subjective point of view"). In the rest of this book, we'll use "point of view" only to refer to perceptual subjectivity, as in the phrase "optical point-of-view shot," or POV shot.

Why would a filmmaker manipulate depth of knowledge? Plunging into mental subjectivity can increase our sympathy for a character and can cue stable expectations about what the characters will later say or do. The memory sequences in Alain Resnais's *Hiroshima mon amour* and the fantasy sequences in Federico Fellini's *8½* yield information about the protagonists' traits and possible future actions that would be less vivid if presented objectively. A subjectively motivated flashback can create parallels among characters, as does the flashback shared by mother and son in Kenji Mizoguchi's *Sansho the Bailiff* (**3.28–3.31**). A plot can create curiosity about a character's motives and then use some degree of subjectivity—for example, inner commentary or subjective flashback—to explain what caused the behavior. In *The Sixth Sense,* the child psychologist's odd estrangement from his wife begins to make sense when we hear his inner recollection of something his young patient had told him much earlier.

On the other hand, objectivity can be an effective way of withholding information. One reason that *The Big Sleep* does not treat Marlowe subjectively is that the detective genre demands that the investigator's reasoning be concealed from the viewer. The mystery is more mysterious if we do not know the investigator's hunches and conclusions before he reveals them at the end.

A film need not be in the mystery genre to exploit objective and restricted narration. Julia Loktev's *Day Night Day Night* follows a young woman who has been recruited as a suicide bomber. We see her accepted into the group, awaiting orders, and eventually embarking on the mission. One scene utilizes optical point of view extensively, while another does so briefly. There are a few moments of auditory subjectivity, when the noises of street traffic drop out. Yet these flashes of subjective depth stand out against an overwhelmingly objective presentation. For nearly the entire film, we have to assess the woman's state of mind purely through her

CONNECT TO THE BLOG
www.davidbordwell.net/blog

For more on the distinction between perceptual and mental subjectivity in narration see "Categorical coherence: A closer look at character subjectivity."

3.28

3.29

3.30

3.31

3.28–3.31 Characters sharing memories. One of the early flashbacks in *Sansho the Bailiff* starts with the mother, now living in exile with her children, kneeling by a stream (3.28). Her image is replaced by a shot of her husband in the past, about to summon his son Zushio (3.29). At the climax of the scene in the past, the father gives Zushio an image of the goddess of mercy and admonishes him always to show kindness to others (3.30). Normal procedure would come out of the flashback showing the mother again, emphasizing it as her memory. Instead, we return to the present with a shot of Zushio, bearing the goddess's image (3.31). It is as if he and his mother have shared the memory of the father's gift.

physical behavior. Moreover, our information about the story action is very limited. We are never told what political group has recruited her or why she has volunteered for the task. The woman herself does not know the plan, the members of the terrorist group, or the reasons she was picked. In fact, we know less than she does, because we get only hints about her past life. The impersonal, tightly restricted narration of *Day Night Day Night* not only creates suspense about her mission but also encourages curiosity about a rather large number of story events. These responses make judging her decisions difficult, and they lead us to reflect on why someone would volunteer for a suicide mission.

At any moment in a film, we can ask, "How deeply do I know the characters' perceptions, feelings, and thoughts?" The answer will point directly to how the filmmaker has chosen to present or withhold story information. We can then ask about what effects the narration has on us, the viewers.

The Narrator

Narration, then, is the process by which the plot presents story information to the spectator. The filmmaker may shift between restricted and unrestricted ranges of knowledge and varying degrees of objectivity and subjectivity. The filmmaker may also use a *narrator,* some specific agent who purports to be telling us the story.

The narrator may be a character in the story. We are familiar with this convention from literature, as when Huck Finn or Jane Eyre recounts a novel's action. In *D.O.A.,* the dying man tells his story in flashbacks, addressing the information to inquiring policemen. In the documentary *Roger and Me,* Michael Moore frankly acknowledges his role as a character narrator. He starts the film with his reminiscences of growing up in Flint, Michigan, and he appears on camera in interviews with workers and in confrontations with General Motors security staff. Even an unseen character can serve as a narrator, as an unborn child does in Julie Dash's *Daughters of the Dust.*

A CLOSER LOOK

When the Lights Go Down, the Narration Starts

When we open a novel, we don't expect the story action to start on the copyright page. Nor do we expect to find the story's last scene on the book's back cover. But filmmakers can start giving us narrative information during the credit sequences, and the process can continue to the very last moments we're in the theater.

Credit sequences are nondiegetic material, but they can assist our understanding of the story. Long ago filmmakers realized that credits could be enlivened by drawings and paintings keyed to the action **(3.32)**. Since the 1920s, the credits' graphic design and musical accompaniment have often conjured up the story's time and place **(3.33)**. The breezy credits of Truffaut's *Jules and Jim* offer glimpses of scenes to come while firmly establishing the two young men's friendship in 1910s Paris.

The film can set a mood simply by the music playing over simple titles, as in the nervous score for *The Exorcist*, but the credits can take a more active role through type fonts, color, or movement. Saul Bass, a celebrated designer of corporate logos, gave Alfred Hitchcock's and Otto Preminger's films dynamic geometrical designs **(3.34)**. Rainer Werner Fassbinder was famous for his imaginative credit sequences, some in homage to the 1950s Hollywood melodramas he admired. In a similar vein, the brash collages in Pedro Almodóvar's credit sequences lead us to expect sexy irreverence **(3.35)**.

Plot elements can be announced quite specifically. Illustrations can anticipate particular scenes **(3.36)**. *Goldfinger*'s credits present a key motif, the gold-skinned woman, and anticipate several later scenes **(3.37)**. The

3.32 Incorporating illustration. An early example of illustrated credits for the 1917 comedy *Reaching for the Moon*.

3.35 Setting expectations of tone. A collage design suggesting sophistication and glamorous lifestyles (*Women on the Verge of a Nervous Breakdown*).

3.33 Evoking locations. *Raw Deal*, a crime film from 1948, begins in prison, and the credit sequence suggests the locale before the action begins.

3.36 Anticipating scenes. Some of the stick-figure credits in *Bringing Up Baby* anticipate scenes that will take place in the story action.

3.34 Hinting at actions and themes. Saul Bass's elegantly simple credits for *Advise and Consent* hint that the story will lift the lid off Washington scandals.

plot premises of *Catch Me If You Can* are previewed in the title sequence, which pays affectionate homage to the animated credits of the film's period **(3.38)**. *Se7en*'s scratchy glimpses of cutting, stitching, and defacement launched a cycle of nightmarish credit sequences showing violation and dismemberment. Less overtly, the opening of *The Thomas Crown Affair* hints at the hero's scheme for stealing a painting.

Films often end their plot with an epilogue that celebrates the stable state that the characters have achieved, and

that situation can be presented during the credits **(3.39)**. Sometimes key scenes will be replayed under the final credits, or new plot action will be shown. *Airplane!* began a fashion for weaving running gags into its final credits.

Occasionally, the filmmaker fools us. We think the plot has ended, and a long list of personnel crawls upward. But then the film tacks an image on the very end **(3.40)**. These "credit cookies" remind us that an enterprising filmmaker may exploit every moment of the film's running time to engage our narrative expectations.

3.37 Introducing motifs. *Goldfinger:* The gilded woman will reappear in the film, while other scenes to come, including visions of the villain, are projected on areas of her body.

3.38 Evoking a time period and previewing a story. The streamlined animation of *Catch Me If You Can* evokes 1960s credit sequences while previewing story action and settings. Here the Tom Hanks character starts to trail Leonardo DiCaprio, who plays an impostor pretending to be an airline pilot.

3.39 Presenting an epilogue. In *Slumdog Millionaire*, the dance epilogue in the railway station is intercut with the major credits, which recall scenes from the film.

3.40 Credit cookies. Takeshi Kitano's *Sonatine* follows its final credit sequence with desolate images of a beach, wistfully reminding us of earlier scenes showing childish gangsters at play.

The narrator needn't be a character in the story. Noncharacter narrators are common in documentaries. We never learn who belongs to the anonymous "voice of God" we hear in *The River, Primary,* or *Hoop Dreams.* A fictional film may employ this device as well. *Amélie*'s cozy commentator adds a touch of fantasy, while the urgent voice-over we hear during *The Naked City* suggests that the film has a documentary authenticity.

Either sort of narrator may give us any range or depth of knowledge. A character narrator is not necessarily restricted and very often tells of events that she or he didn't witness. This happens in *The Quiet Man,* when the relatively minor figure of the village priest recounts the action. Likewise, a noncharacter narrator might not be omniscient and could confine the commentary to what a single character knows. A character narrator might be highly subjective, telling us details of his or her inner life, or might be objective, confining the information strictly to externals. A noncharacter narrator might give us access to subjective depths, as in *Jules and Jim,* or might stick simply to surface events, as does the impersonal voice-over commentator in *The Killing.* In any case, the viewer's process of picking up cues, developing expectations, and constructing an ongoing story out of the plot will be partially shaped by what the narrator tells or doesn't tell.

CREATIVE DECISIONS

Choices about Narration in Storytelling

The Road Warrior (also known as *Mad Max 2*) offers a neat summary of how narration contributes to a film's overall effect. At certain points in the film, director George Miller and writers Terry Hayes and Brian Hannant chose to supply information that builds expectations and help us grasp the story. At other points, they decided to withhold information for the sake of surprise.

The plot opens with a voice-over commentary by an elderly male narrator who recalls "the warrior Max." After presenting exposition that tells of the worldwide wars that led society to degenerate into gangs of scavengers, the narrator falls silent. Who is he? We aren't told yet.

The rest of the plot is organized around Max's encounter with a group of peaceful desert settlers. They want to flee to the coast with the gasoline they have refined, but they're under siege by a gang of vicious marauders. Max agrees to work for the settlers in exchange for gasoline. Later, after a brush with the gang leaves him wounded, his dog dead, and his car demolished, Max commits himself to helping the settlers flee their compound. He learns that only by joining them can he hope to survive. The struggle against the encircling gang comes to its climax in Max's attempt to escape with a tanker truck.

Max is the protagonist; his goals and conflicts propel the developing action. After the anonymous narrator's prologue, most of the film is restricted to Max's range of knowledge. Like Philip Marlowe in *The Big Sleep,* Max is present in every scene, and almost everything we learn gets funneled through him. The narration also gives us a degree of subjectivity, again focused on Max. We get optical POV shots as Max drives his car (**3.41**) or watches a skirmish through a telescope. When he is rescued after his car crash, his delirium is rendered as perceptual subjectivity, using the conventional cues of slow motion, superimposed imagery, and sloweddown sound (**3.42**). All of these narrational choices encourage us to sympathize with Max.

At certain points, however, the narration becomes more unrestricted. This occurs principally during chases and battle scenes, when we witness events Max doesn't know about. In such scenes, unrestricted narration builds up suspense by showing both pursuers and pursued or different aspects of the battle. At the climax,

"The whole art of movies and plays is in the control of the flow of information to the audience . . . : how much information, when, how fast it comes. Certain things maybe have to be there three times."

—Tom Stoppard, playwright and screenwriter of *Shakespeare in Love*

CONNECT TO THE BLOG
www.davidbordwell.net/blog

Stretches of unrestricted narration allow a filmmaker to show characters' reactions to a situation. We trace some examples in *Road Warrior* and other films in "They're looking for us."

3.41   3.42

3.41–3.42 Narration in *The Road Warrior*: Optical point of view and perceptual subjectivity. The narration provides a POV shot as Max drives up to an apparently abandoned gyrocopter (3.41). The injured Max's dizzy view of his rescuer uses double exposure to present his delirium as perceptual subjectivity (3.42).

Max's truck successfully draws the gang away from the desert people, who escape to the south. But when his truck overturns, Max—and we—learn that the truck holds only sand. It has been a decoy. Thus our restriction to Max's range of knowledge creates a surprise.

There is still more to learn, however. At the very end, the elderly narrator's voice returns to tell us that he was the feral child whom Max had befriended. The settlers drive off, and Max is left alone in the middle of the highway. The film's final image—a shot of the solitary Max receding into the distance as we pull back (**3.43**)—suggests both a perceptual subjectivity (the boy's point of view as he rides away) and a mental subjectivity (the memory of Max dimming for the dying narrator).

3.43 Mental and perceptual subjectivity. As the camera tracks away from Max, we hear the narrator's voice: "And the Road Warrior? That was the last we ever saw of him. He lives now only in my memories."

The narrative form of *The Road Warrior*, then, rests on decisions about both plot and narration. The plot organizes causality, time, and space through an extended flashback, and it gains further coherence through consistent choices about narration. The main portion of the film channels our expectations through an attachment to Max, alternating with briefer, more unrestricted portions. This main section is in turn framed by the mysterious narrator who puts all the events into the distant past. The narrator's presence at the opening leads us to expect him to return at the end, perhaps explaining who he is. The filmmakers' creative choices have organized narration in order to give us a unified experience.

The Classical Hollywood Cinema

Perhaps you've decided to try your hand at writing a screenplay and you've investigated books and websites that offer advice. *Make sure your main character wants something. Emphasize conflict. Take your character on an emotional journey. Be sure that your ending resolves the initial situation.* Suggestions like these can be valuable, but we need to recognize that they reflect only one tradition. This tradition has often been called that of "classical Hollywood" filmmaking.

The tradition is called "classical" because it has been influential since about 1920 and "Hollywood" because the tradition assumed its most elaborate shape in American studio films. The same mode, however, governs narrative films made in other countries. For example, *The Road Warrior*, although an Australian film, is constructed along classical Hollywood lines. And many documentaries, such as

CONNECT TO THE BLOG
www.davidbordwell.net/blog

David Koepp, screenwriter of *Jurassic Park* and *War of the Worlds*, discusses the cult of storytelling in "David Koepp: Making the world movie-sized." *Premium Rush*, written and directed by Koepp, is a model of a modern film in the classical Hollywood tradition. We discuss it in "Clocked doing 50 in the Dead Zone."

Primary or *Super Size Me* rely on conventions derived from Hollywood's fictional narratives.

This model of narrative form tends to present individual characters making things happen. Large-scale events such as floods, earthquakes, and wars may affect the action, but the story centers on personal psychological causes: decisions, choices, and traits of character.

Typically the plot focuses on one or two central characters who want something. Characters' desires set up a *goal,* and the course of the narrative's development will most likely involve the process of achieving that goal. In *The Wizard of Oz,* Dorothy has a series of goals; at first she wants to save Toto from Miss Gulch, and later she seeks to get home from Oz. Her desire to get home creates short-term goals along the way, such as getting to the Emerald City and then killing the Witch.

If this desire to reach a goal were the only element present, there would be nothing to stop the character from moving quickly to achieve it. But in the classical narrative there's a blocking element: an opposition that creates conflict. Typically, the protagonist comes up against a character with opposing traits and goals. As a result, the protagonist must overcome the opposition. Dorothy's desire to return to Kansas is opposed by the Wicked Witch, whose goal is to obtain the Ruby Slippers. Dorothy must eventually eliminate the Witch before she is able to use the slippers to go home. We shall see in *His Girl Friday* how the two main characters' goals conflict until the final resolution (pp. 401–404).

The classical plot traces a process of change. Often characters achieve their goals by changing their situation—perhaps they gain fame or money or just survival—but they also change their attitudes or values. In *The Road Warrior,* Max comes to appreciate loyalty to a community. At the end of *Jerry Maguire,* the hero has found professional success but also has learned the value of friendship and a loving family.

But don't all narratives tell stories of this sort? Actually, no. In 1920s Soviet films, such as Sergei Eisenstein's *Potemkin, October,* and *Strike,* no individual serves as protagonist. In films by Eisenstein and Yasujiro Ozu, many events are seen as caused not by characters but by larger forces (social dynamics in the former, an overarching rhythm of life in the latter). In narrative films such as Michelangelo Antonioni's *L'Avventura,* the protagonists are not active but rather passive. So a filmmaker need not put the striving, goal-oriented protagonist at the center of a film's story.

Classical Hollywood filmmakers tend to let psychological causes motivate most events. Throughout, motivation in the classical narrative film strives to be as clear and complete as possible—even in the fanciful genre of the musical, in which song-and-dance numbers express the characters' emotions or display stage shows featuring the characters. When there are discontinuities of character traits, those need explaining. In one scene of *Hannah and Her Sisters,* Mickey (played by Woody Allen) is in a suicidal depression. When we next see him several scenes later, he is bubbly and cheerful. What caused the abrupt change? Mickey explains via a flashback that he achieved a serene attitude toward life while watching a Marx Brothers film. Now the cause-effect pattern is clear.

In creating a classical film, the filmmakers adjust time to fit the cause-effect progress of the story. Every instant shows something that contributes to the flow of the story, and stretches of time that don't contribute are skipped over. The hours Dorothy and her entourage spend walking on the Yellow Brick Road are omitted, but the plot dwells on the moments during which she meets a new character. Specific devices such as *appointments* and *deadlines* make plot time depend on the story's cause-effect chain as well. When characters agree to meet and then we see them meeting, the stretch of time between the plan and the meeting becomes

❝❝ Movies to me are about wanting something, a character wanting something that you as the audience desperately want him to have. You, the writer, keep him from getting it for as long as possible, and then, through whatever effort he makes, he gets it."

— Bruce Joel Rubin, screenwriter, *Ghost*

CONNECT TO THE BLOG
www.davidbordwell.net/blog

For a discussion of how characters' goals can be crucial to major transitions in the plot, see "Times go by turns."

insignificant. Similarly, a deadline forces the action to reach a certain stage at a specific time.

Filmmakers working in the classical tradition have a range of choices about narration, but most tend to present the action objectively, in the way discussed on pages 90–92. The film will usually present an objective story reality, against which various degrees of perceptual or mental subjectivity can be measured. Classical filmmakers also tend toward fairly unrestricted narration. Even if we follow a single character, there are portions of the film giving us access to things the character does not see, hear, or know. *North by Northwest* and *The Road Warrior* remain good examples of this tendency. This weighting is overridden only in genres that depend heavily on mystery, such as the detective film, with its reliance on the sort of restrictiveness we saw at work in *The Big Sleep*.

Finally, most classical filmmakers prefer a strong degree of *closure* at the end. Leaving few loose ends unresolved, the films seek to wrap things clearly. We usually learn the fate of each character, the answer to each mystery, and the outcome of each conflict.

Again, none of these features is a law of narrative form in general. There is nothing to prevent a filmmaker from presenting the dead time, or narratively unmotivated intervals between more significant events. Jean-Luc Godard, Carl Dreyer, and Andy Warhol do this frequently, in different ways. The filmmaker's plot can also reorder story chronology to make the causal chain more perplexing. *Love Affair, or the Case of the Missing Switchboard Operator* uses flashforwards interspersed with the main plot action; only gradually do we come to understand the causal relations of these flashforwards to the present-time events. More recently, puzzle films (p. 84) tease the audience to find clues to enigmatic presentation of story events.

The filmmaker can also include material that is unmotivated by narrative cause and effect, such as the chance meetings in Truffaut's films, the political monologues and interviews in Godard's films, the intellectual montage sequences in Eisenstein's films, and the transitional shots in Ozu's work. Narration may be unexpectedly subjective, as in *The Cabinet of Dr. Caligari,* or it may hover ambiguously between objectivity and subjectivity, as in *Last Year at Marienbad.* Finally, the filmmaker need not resolve all of the action at the end; films made outside the classical tradition sometimes have open endings like that of *The 400 Blows* (p. 79).

Great films have been made within the classical tradition. Yet it remains only one way of using narrative form. If we want to gain a wider appreciation of all types of cinema, we can't demand that every movie conform to Hollywood conventions.

CONNECT TO THE BLOG
www.davidbordwell.net/blog

Coincidences supposedly have no place in tight storytelling, but they are more common than you might think. We talk about how filmmakers get away with them in "No coincidence, no story."

CONNECT TO THE BLOG
www.davidbordwell.net/blog

The classical approach to narrative is still very much alive, as we show in "Your trash, my treasure," devoted to *National Treasure*, and "Understanding film narrative: The trailer," on *The Wolf of Wall Street*.

Narrative Form in *Citizen Kane*

Citizen Kane is one of the most original films to come out of Hollywood. It has won praise on many counts, not least its subtle approach to storytelling. Director Orson Welles and screenwriter Herman Mankiewicz made creative choices that continue to influence how films are made today. *Kane* is an ideal occasion to test how principles of film narrative can work in both familiar and fresh ways.

Overall Narrative Expectations in *Citizen Kane*

We saw in Chapter 2 that our experience of a film depends heavily on the expectations we bring to it. Before you saw *Citizen Kane,* you may have known only that it is regarded as a film classic. A 1941 audience would have had a keener sense of anticipation. For one thing, the film was rumored to be a disguised version of the life of the newspaper publisher William Randolph Hearst, a businessman as

CONNECT TO THE BLOG
www.davidbordwell.net/blog

How much variation can classical Hollywood storytelling permit, especially in regard to the plot's ordering of story events? We try for answers in "Innovation by accident" and "What-if movies: Forking paths in the drawing room."

famous as Steve Jobs became. Spectators would thus be looking for events keyed to Hearst's life.

Several minutes into the film, the viewer can form more specific expectations about the relevant genre conventions. The early "News on the March" sequence suggests that this film may be a fictional biography, and this hint is confirmed once the reporter, Thompson, begins his inquiry into Kane's life. In this genre, the plot typically traces an individual's life and dramatizes certain episodes. The most prominent fictional biographies released before *Kane* would include *Anthony Adverse* (1936) and *The Power and the Glory* (1933), about a somewhat Kane-like tycoon.

The viewer can also spot the conventions of the newspaper reporter genre. Thompson's colleagues resemble the wisecracking reporters in *Five Star Final* (1931), *Picture Snatcher* (1933), and *His Girl Friday* (1940). In this genre, the action usually depends on a reporter's dogged pursuit of a story against great odds. We therefore expect not only Thompson's investigation but also his triumphant exposure of the truth.

In the scenes devoted to Susan, there are also some conventions typical of the musical film: frantic rehearsals, backstage preparations, and, most specifically, the montage of her opera career, which parodies the conventional montage of singing success in such films as *Maytime* (1937; p. 253). More broadly, the film evidently owes something to the detective genre, since Thompson is aiming to solve a mystery (Who or what is Rosebud?), and his interviews resemble those of a detective questioning suspects.

Note, however, that *Kane*'s use of genre conventions is somewhat equivocal. Unlike many biographical films, *Kane* is more concerned with psychological states and relationships than with the hero's public deeds or adventures. As a newspaper film, *Kane* is unusual in that the reporter fails to get his story. And *Kane* is not exactly a standard mystery, because it answers some questions but leaves others unanswered. *Citizen Kane* is a good example of a film that relies on genre conventions but often thwarts the expectations they arouse.

The same sort of equivocal qualities can be found in *Kane*'s relation to the classical Hollywood storytelling tradition. Even without specific prior knowledge about this film, we expect that, as an American studio product of 1941, it will follow that tradition. In most ways, it does. We'll see that characters' desires propel the narrative, causality is defined around traits and goals, conflicts lead to consequences, time is motivated by plot necessity, and narration is mostly objective and mixes restricted and unrestricted passages. We'll also see some ways in which *Citizen Kane* is more ambiguous than most films in the classical tradition. Desires, traits, and goals are not always spelled out; the conflicts sometimes have an uncertain outcome; at the end, the narration's omniscience is emphasized to a rare degree. The ending in particular doesn't provide the degree of closure we would expect in a classical film. *Citizen Kane* draws on Hollywood narrative conventions but also violates some of the expectations that we bring to a Hollywood film.

Plot and Story in *Citizen Kane*

After Welles and Mankiewicz decided to tell the life story of a fictional newspaper magnate, Charles Foster Kane, they faced a choice that's familiar to you by now. They could have presented Kane's life story chronologically, letting their plot present incidents in story order as most fictional biographies do. They chose another option. They decided to trace Kane's life through flashbacks, recalled by people who knew him. But Welles and Mankiewicz needed something to motivate the characters' flashbacks. They hit upon the idea of having a media reporter seek the meaning of Kane's dying word, "Rosebud." This generates a second line of action, the reporter Thompson's investigation of Kane's life. The result is a film that creates an unusual relation of plot to story.

We can start to understand this by outlining a segmentation like the one we made for *The Wizard of Oz*. The basic segments are typically scenes, and they form part of a larger section of the film. In the following outline, numerals refer to major parts, some of which are only one scene long. In most cases, however, the major parts consist of several scenes, and each of these is identified by a lowercase letter.

Citizen Kane: **Plot Segmentation**

C. Credit title.
1. Xanadu: Kane dies.
2. Projection room:
    a. "News on the March."
    b. Reporters discuss "Rosebud."
3. El Rancho nightclub: Thompson tries to interview Susan.
4. Thatcher library:
    a. Thompson enters and reads Thatcher's manuscript.

First flashback
    b. Kane's mother sends the boy off with Thatcher.
    c. Kane grows up and buys the *Inquirer*.
    d. Kane launches the *Inquirer*'s attack on big business.
    e. The Depression: Kane sells Thatcher his newspaper chain.

    f. Thompson leaves the library.

5. Bernstein's office:
    a. Thompson visits Bernstein.

Second flashback
    b. Kane takes over the *Inquirer*.
    c. Montage: the *Inquirer*'s growth.
    d. Party: the *Inquirer* celebrates getting the *Chronicle* staff.
    e. Leland and Bernstein discuss Kane's trip abroad.
    f. Kane returns with his fiancée Emily.

    g. Bernstein concludes his reminiscence.

6. Nursing home:
Third flashback
    a. Thompson talks with Leland.
    b. Breakfast table montage: Kane's marriage deteriorates.
    c. Leland continues his recollections.

Fourth flashback
    d. Kane meets Susan and goes to her room.
    e. Kane's political campaign culminates in his speech.
    f. Kane confronts Gettys, Emily, and Susan.

Fourth flashback (cont.)
    g. Kane loses the election, and Leland asks to be transferred.
    h. Kane marries Susan.
    i. Susan has her opera premiere.
    j. Because Leland is drunk, Kane finishes Leland's review.

    k. Leland concludes his reminiscence.

7. El Rancho nightclub:
    a. Thompson talks with Susan.

Fifth flashback
    b. Susan rehearses her singing.
    c. Susan has her opera premiere.
    d. Kane insists that Susan go on singing.
    e. Montage: Susan's opera career.
    f. Susan attempts suicide, and Kane promises she can quit singing.
    g. Xanadu: Susan is bored.
    h. Montage: Susan plays with jigsaw puzzles.
    i. Xanadu: Kane proposes a picnic.
    j. Picnic: Kane slaps Susan.
    k. Xanadu: Susan leaves Kane.

    l. Susan concludes her reminiscence.

8. **Xanadu:**

> *Sixth flashback*

    a. Thompson talks with Raymond.

    b. Kane destroys Susan's room and picks up a paperweight, murmuring "Rosebud."

    c. Raymond concludes his reminiscence; Thompson talks with the other reporters; all leave.

    d. Survey of Kane's possessions leads to a revelation of Rosebud; exterior of gate and of castle; the end.

E. **End credits**.

This sort of outline lets us recover the film's overall architecture. Our segmentation lets us see at a glance the major divisions of the plot and how scenes are organized within them. It also helps us notice how the plot organizes story causality and story time.

Citizen Kane's Causality

Citizen Kane's plot has two main lines of action, but the chain of causality in each one is somewhat unusual. Welles and Mankiewicz give us an investigation—one not conducted by detectives but by reporters. A media company has made a newsreel about tycoon Charles Foster Kane, and that newsreel is already completed when the plot introduces the reporters. But the newsreel fails to satisfy the boss, Rawlston, and his desire to revise the newsreel gets the search for Rosebud underway. He assigns the reporter Thompson a goal, which sets him digging into Kane's past.

Another line of action, Kane's life, has already taken place when the plot begins. Many years before, a poverty-stricken boarder at Kane's mother's boarding-house has paid her with a deed to a gold mine. Thanks to these newfound riches, Mrs. Kane appoints Thatcher as young Charles's guardian. Thatcher's guardianship results in Kane's growing up into a spoiled, rebellious young man.

Usually an investigator searches for an object or a concealed set of facts. In this respect, Thompson's mission is straightforward: Who or what was Rosebud? But Thompson is also looking for a set of character traits. Rawlston's order is clear: "It isn't enough to tell us what a man did, you've got to tell us who he was." So finding the meaning of Rosebud promises to reveal something about Kane's personality. Kane, a rather complex character, has many traits that influence other characters' actions. But, as we'll see, *Citizen Kane*'s narrative leaves some of Kane's character traits uncertain.

Thompson has a goal, then. So does Kane, although his is less well-defined. At various times of his life he seems to be searching for fame, friendship, social justice, or a woman's love. But part of the point of the film is that his real goals are uncertain. At several points, characters speculate that Rosebud was something that Kane lost or was never able to get. Such vagueness about a major character's goal makes this an unusual narrative for the Hollywood tradition.

Thompson and Kane are the prime movers of the action in their plot lines. In Kane's life, other characters come into conflict with him, and he changes their lives. In Thompson's plot line, however, these characters serve to provide information about Kane. Thatcher knew him as a child. Bernstein, his manager, knew his business dealings. His best friend, Leland, had access to his personal life, his first marriage in particular. Susan Alexander, his second wife, knew him in middle age. The butler, Raymond, managed Kane's affairs during his last years. Without these witnesses, Thompson couldn't pursue Rosebud. These secondary characters help us, too, as we reconstruct the progression of story events.

The use of testimony spanning Kane's life solves a major storytelling problem Welles and Mankiewicz faced. But as we've seen, one creative choice often demands others. The film's story includes Kane's wife Emily and his son, so shouldn't they be given a chance to share their impressions of the great man? The problem is that their recollections would largely duplicate what we learn from Leland. Welles and Mankiewicz solve this problem in a simple way. They kill Emily and her son off in an auto accident, which occurs well before Thompson's investigation starts.

Time in *Citizen Kane*

Citizen Kane reshapes time in complex ways, and this gives the film much of its originality, particularly in the Hollywood of 1941.

Duration and Frequency   The most conventional aspect of narrative time in the film involves duration. We know that Kane is 75 years old at his death in 1941, and the earliest scene shows him at around age 10. Thus the plot covers roughly 65 years of his life, plus the week of Thompson's investigation. The only earlier story event is Mrs. Kane's acquisition of the mine deed in 1868, which probably took place shortly before she turned her son over to Thatcher. So the story runs a bit longer than the plot—roughly 73 years. This time span is presented in a screen duration of almost 120 minutes.

Like most films, *Citizen Kane* uses ellipses. The plot skips over years of story time, as well as many hours of Thompson's week of investigations. But plot duration also compresses time through *montage sequences,* such as those showing the *Inquirer*'s campaign against big business (4d), the growth of the paper's circulation (5c), Susan's opera career (7e), and Susan's bored playing with jigsaw puzzles (7h). Montage sequences became conventions of classical Hollywood cinema in the 1920s, and here they have their traditional function of condensing story duration in a comprehensible way. We'll discuss montage sequences in more detail in Chapter 6 (see pp. 252–253).

Kane is a little more unusual in its treatment of temporal frequency. One specific story event appears twice in the plot. In their flashbacks, both Leland and Susan describe her debut in the Chicago premiere of *Salammbo.* Watching Leland's account (6i), we see the performance from the front; we witness the audience reacting with distaste. Susan's version (7c) shows us the performance from behind and on the stage, emphasizing her humiliation. The plot's repeated presentation of Susan's debut doesn't confuse us, for we understand the two scenes as depicting the same story event. ("News on the March" has also referred to Susan's opera career, in parts G and H.) By repeating scenes of her embarrassment, the plot makes vivid the pain that Kane forces her to undergo.

Chronology and Flashbacks   *Kane* presents an unusual ordering of story events. The central structural decision, that of using Thompson's investigation to motivate a series of flashbacks, asks us to put things in chronological order. For example, the earliest *story* event is Mrs. Kane's acquisition of a deed to a valuable mine. We get this information during the newsreel, in the second sequence. But the first event we encounter in the *plot* is Kane's death.

To illustrate the maneuvers that Welles and Mankiewicz ask us to execute, in building up the film's story, let's assume that Kane's life consists of these phases:

Boyhood

Youthful newspaper editing

Life as a newlywed

Middle age

Old age

At first the plot doesn't present these story phases in chronological order. The early portions of the film boldly jump back and forth over many phases of Kane's life. The "News on the March" sequence (2a) gives us glimpses of all periods, and

CONNECT TO THE BLOG
www.davidbordwell.net/blog

Flashbacks were part of filmmaking tradition before *Citizen Kane.* For analysis of flashbacks in Hollywood films during the 1930s, and especially *The Power and the Glory,* which influenced Orson Welles, see "Grandmaster flashback."

Thatcher's manuscript (4) shows us Kane in boyhood, youth, and middle age. In the first flashback, Thatcher's diary tells of a scene in which Kane loses control of his newspapers during the Depression (4e). By this time, Kane is a middle-aged man. Yet in the second flashback, Bernstein describes young Kane's arrival at the *Inquirer* office and his engagement to Emily (5b, 5f). The plot demands that we sort these events into chronological story order.

The film becomes less demanding as it goes along, however. Later portions of the plot tend to concentrate on particular periods, and the flashbacks respect chronological order. Bernstein's recollections (5) concentrate on episodes showing Kane as newspaper editor and fiancé of Emily. Leland's flashbacks (6) run from newly-wed life to middle age. Susan (7) tells of Kane as a middle-aged and an old man. Raymond's brief but significant anecdote (8b) concentrates on Kane in old age.

By getting more linear, the plot helps us grasp the story. If every character's flashback skipped around Kane's life as much as the newsreel and Thatcher's account do, the story would be much harder to reconstruct. As it is, the early portions of the plot show us the results of events we have not seen, while the later portions confirm or modify the expectations that we formed in the more nonlinear scenes. For instance, we know that Kane will lose his newspapers to Thatcher, and that knowledge lends a certain poignancy to Kane's "Declaration of Principles" in which he pledges to fight for the common man.

By arranging story events out of order, the plot cues us to form specific anticipations. In the beginning, with Kane's death and the newsreel version of his life, the plot creates strong curiosity about two issues. What does "Rosebud" mean? And what could have happened to make so powerful a man die alone and, apparently, unmourned?

There is also a degree of suspense. When the plot goes back to the past, we already have quite firm knowledge. We know that neither of Kane's marriages will last and that his friends will drift away. The plot encourages us to focus our interest on *how and when* a particular thing will happen. What will break Leland's friendship with Kane? What will trigger Susan's decision to walk out on him? As Hitchcock pointed out (p. 89), giving us more knowledge than the characters have can promote suspense.

"News on the March" as a Map of the Plot

In 1941, one of the most original sequences of the film was the "News on the March" newsreel. By looking over our segmentation, we can see that the newsreel is not only daring but very helpful. The very first sequence in Xanadu disorients us, for it shows the death of a character about whom we so far know almost nothing. But the newsreel quickly supplies a great deal of information about this mysterious figure. Moreover, by reviewing Kane's life, the newsreel makes it much easier to rearrange the plot events we'll see into linear story order. Here is an outline of "News on the March."

A. Shots of Xanadu.

B. Funeral; headlines announcing Kane's death.

C. Growth of financial empire.

D. Gold mine and Mrs. Kane's boardinghouse.

E. Thatcher testimony at congressional committee.

F. Political career.

G. Private life; weddings, divorces.

H. Opera house and Xanadu.

I. Political campaign.

J. The Depression.

K. 1935: Kane's old age.

L. Isolation of Xanadu.

M. Death announced.

Now we can see that the newsreel offers us a capsule preview of the film's overall plot. "News on the March" begins by emphasizing Kane as "Xanadu's Landlord"; a short segment (A) presents shots of the house and the compound. This is a variation on the opening of the whole film (1), which consisted of a series of shots of the grounds, moving progressively closer to the house. That opening sequence had ended with Kane's death; now the newsreel follows the shots of the house with Kane's funeral (B). Next comes a series of newspaper headlines announcing Kane's death. If we compare this portion with the segmentation of the entire film's plot, we see that these headlines occupy the approximate formal position of the whole newsreel itself (2a). Even the title card that follows the headlines ("To forty-four million U.S. news buyers, more newsworthy than the names in his own headlines was Kane himself. . . .") is a brief parallel to the scene in the projection room, in which the reporters decide that Thompson should continue to investigate Kane's "newsworthy" life.

The order of the newsreel's presentation of Kane's life roughly parallels the order of scenes in the flashbacks told to Thompson. "News on the March" moves from Kane's death to a summary of the building of Kane's newspaper empire (C), with a description of the boarding-house deed and the mine (including an old photograph of Charles with his mother, as well as the first mention of the boy's sled). This bit parallels the first flashback (4), which tells how Thatcher took over the young Kane's guardianship from his mother and how Kane first attempted to run the *Inquirer*. The rough parallels continue: The newsreel tells of Kane's political ambitions (F), his marriages (G), his building of the opera house (H), his political campaign (I), and so on. In the main plot, Thatcher's flashback describes his own clashes with Kane on political matters. Leland's flashbacks (6) cover the first marriage, the affair with Susan, the political campaign, and the premiere of the opera *Salammbo*.

We haven't charted all of the similarities between the newsreel and the overall film. You can tease out many more by comparing the two closely. The crucial point is that the newsreel provides us with a map for the investigation of Kane's life. As we watch scenes in the flashbacks, we already expect certain events and have a rough chronological basis for fitting them into our story reconstruction.

CONNECT TO THE BLOG
www.davidbordwell.net/blog

Citizen Kane helped popularize flashback-based narratives in the 1940s. We look at some less familiar but equally interesting examples in "Chinese boxes, Russian dolls, and Hollywood movies." For more on flashbacks in movies old and new, see "Puppetry and ventriloquism."

Motivation in *Citizen Kane*

Citizen Kane follows classical Hollywood tradition in motivating the causes and effects that push the story forward. Even small details are justified causally. Why did Welles and Mankiewicz decide to make Thatcher a prosperous businessman? Their script could have had Mrs. Kane turn her son over to a kindly but poor family, one that wouldn't treat him as cruelly as apparently his father has. But Thatcher's social position motivates important events. By giving her son to Thatcher, Charles' mother catapults him into a wealthy circle, where he will wield the power we witness across the film. Thatcher's elite standing also makes it easy for Thompson to pursue his initial research on Kane's life. Thatcher is influential enough to testify at a congressional hearing, so he can appear in the newsreel (the first time we encounter him). As a self-important tycoon, he has chronicled his life in a journal, which Thompson can scan for information about Kane's childhood.

A striking instance of motivation involves Thompson's visit to Susan, Kane's second wife at the El Rancho nightclub (3). It's plausible that Thompson would start his search with Kane's ex-wife, presumably the surviving person closest to him. But let's think like a screenwriter. In the story, the young Kane is an audacious editor, thumbing his nose at the stuffed-shirt Thatcher and taking up the cause of the poor. But Susan didn't know Kane then. If she had been given the first flash-back, it would have dwelt on Kane's old age, a period in which he was pompous and self-centered. If Susan had told her story first, showing the elderly Kane, we would not sense his character change gradually. By delaying her flashback, the plot lets Thatcher, Bernstein, and Leland fill in Kane's early, rambunctious years. By then we're prepared to appreciate, from Susan's testimony, how he has decayed into a selfish, aggressive old man.

So the creative problem was, find a way to prevent Susan from telling her story. The solution that Mankiewicz and Welles chose was to make Susan drunk and angry during Thompson's visit. Her refusal to speak to him motivates postponing her flash-back. It also enhances the mystery around Kane—why won't she go on the record?—while her alcoholic haze suggests that he has damaged the people closest to him.

Some critics have argued that the search for Rosebud is a flaw in *Citizen Kane,* because the revelation of the boy's sled is an oversimplification. Does all this come down to the fact that Kane just longs for his lost childhood and his mother's love? If we assume that the point of the plot is simply to identify Rosebud, this charge might be valid. But in fact, Rosebud serves a very important motivating function. It creates Thompson's goal and thus focuses our attention on his digging into the lives of Kane and his associates. *Citizen Kane* becomes a mystery story; but instead of investigating a crime, the reporter investigates a character.

Furthermore, it's not clear that the plot lets us conclude that Rosebud is the final answer to the quest. In the final scene, Thompson gives up the search. He doubts that "any word can explain a man's life." Moreover, in the scene in the newsreel projection room, Rawlston suggests that "maybe he told us all about himself on his deathbed." Immediately, one of the reporters says, "Yeah, and maybe he didn't." Already the suggestion is planted that Rosebud may not provide any adequate answers about Kane. Later Leland scornfully dismisses the Rosebud issue and goes on to talk of other things. Characters' skepticism about the Rosebud clue helps justify Thompson's pessimistic attitude in the final sequence.

Linked to the uncertainties around Rosebud is a degree of ambiguity about psychological motivations. These relate primarily to Kane's character. The charac-ters' varying portraits of Kane don't neatly tally. Bernstein still looks on Kane with sympathy and affection, whereas Leland is cynical about his own relationship with Kane. Likewise, the reasons for some of Kane's actions remain unclear. Does he send Leland the $25,000 check in firing him because of a lingering sentiment over their old friendship or from a proud desire to prove himself more generous than Leland? Why does he insist on stuffing Xanadu with hundreds of artworks that he never even unpacks? By leaving these questions open, the film invites us to specu-late on various facets of Kane's personality. The ambiguities around Rosebud and Kane's character are unusual for the classical Hollywood tradition, which usually prefers more clear-cut explanations of character psychology.

Citizen Kane's Parallelism

Parallelism doesn't provide a major principle of development in *Citizen Kane*'s narrative form, but it crops up more locally. We've already seen important formal parallels between the newsreel and the film's plot as a whole. There is as well a parallel between the two major lines of action: Kane's life and Thompson's search. Both men are searching for Rosebud. Rosebud serves as a summary of the things Kane strives for through his adult life. We see him repeatedly fail to find love and friendship, living alone at Xanadu in the end. His inability to find happiness paral-lels Thompson's failure to locate the significance of the word "Rosebud."

Another narrative parallel juxtaposes Kane's campaign for the governorship with his attempt to build up Susan's career as an opera star. In each case, he seeks to inflate his reputation by influencing public opinion. In trying to achieve success for Susan, Kane forces his newspaper employees to write favorable reviews of her performances. This parallels the moment when he loses the election and the *Inquirer* automatically proclaims a fraud at the polls. In both cases, Kane fails to realize that his power over the public is not great enough to hide the flaws in his projects: first his affair with Susan, which ruins his campaign; then her lack of singing ability, which Kane refuses to admit. The parallels show that Kane continues to make the same kinds of mistakes throughout his life.

Patterns of Plot Development in *Citizen Kane*

The order of Thompson's visits to Kane's acquaintances allows the series of flashbacks to have a clear progression. Thanks to the delay in presenting Susan's flashback, Thompson moves from people who knew Kane early in his life to those who knew him as an old man. Moreover, each flashback contains a distinct type of information about Kane. Bernstein gives an account of the newspaper's growth, and then Leland traces Kane's changing political views. Both men provide the background to Kane's early success and lead into stories of Kane's personal life. Here we get the first real indications of Kane's failure. Susan continues to trace his decline by explaining how he ruled her life. Finally, in Raymond's flashback, Kane becomes a pitiable old man. Thompson's present-day inquiry has its own pattern of development, that of a search. By the ending, this search has failed, as Kane's own search for happiness or personal success had failed.

Because of Thompson's failure, the ending of *Citizen Kane* remains somewhat more open than was the rule in Hollywood in 1941. True, Thompson does resolve the question of Rosebud for himself by saying that it would not have explained Kane's life. To this extent, we have the common pattern showing the protagonist gaining greater knowledge. Still, in most classical narrative films, the main character reaches his or her initial goal, and Thompson, the main character of this line of action, fails to achieve his aim.

The line of action involving Kane himself has even less closure. Not only does Kane apparently not reach his goal, but the film never specifies what that goal is to start with. Most classical narratives create a situation of conflict. The character must struggle with a problem and solve it by the ending. Kane begins his adult life in a highly successful position, happily running the *Inquirer,* and then gradually falls into a barren solitude. His chief conflicts are with his wives and friends; his clash with a political boss rates only one scene. We are invited to speculate about exactly what, if anything, would have made Kane happy. *Citizen Kane*'s lack of closure in this biographical line of action made it a very unusual narrative for its day.

Still, the search for Rosebud does lead to a certain resolution. We the audience discover what Rosebud was. The ending of the film, which follows this discovery, strongly echoes the beginning. The beginning moved past fences toward the mansion. Now a series of shots takes us away from the house and back outside the fences, with the "No Trespassing" sign and large K insignia.

But even at this point, when we learn the answer to Thompson's question, a degree of uncertainty remains. Just because we have learned what Kane's dying word referred to, do we now have the key to his entire character? Or is Thompson's final statement correct—that no one word can explain a person's life? Perhaps the final shot of the "No Trespassing" sign hints that neither Thompson nor we should have expected to know Kane's mind fully. It is tempting to declare that all of Kane's problems arose from the loss of his sled and his childhood home life, but the film also suggests that this is too easy a solution. It is the kind of solution that the slick editor Rawlston would pounce on as an angle for his newsreel.

For years critics have debated whether the Rosebud solution does give us a key that resolves the entire narrative. This debate itself suggests the ambiguity at work in *Citizen Kane*. The film provides much evidence for both views and hence avoids complete closure. We can contrast this somewhat open ending with those of

> " Kane, we are told, loved only his mother—only his newspaper— only his second wife—only himself. Maybe he loved all of these, or none. It is for the audience to judge. Kane was selfish and selfless, an idealist, a scoundrel, a very big man and a very little one. It depends on who's talking about him. He is never judged with the objectivity of an author, and the point of the picture is not so much the solution of the problem as its presentation."
>
> —Orson Welles, director

His Girl Friday and *North by Northwest,* as well as with another open-ended film, *Do The Right Thing.* All are discussed in Chapter 11.

Narration in *Citizen Kane*

In analyzing how *Kane*'s plot manipulates the moment-by-moment flow of story information, it's useful to consider a remarkable fact. The only time we see Kane directly and in the present is when he dies. On all other occasions, he is presented at one remove—in the newsreel or in various characters' memories. This unusual treatment makes the film something of a portrait, a study of a man seen from different perspectives.

The film employs five character narrators, the people whom Thompson tracks down: Thatcher (whose account is in writing), Bernstein, Leland, Susan, and the butler, Raymond. The plot motivates a series of views of Kane that are more or less restricted in their range of knowledge. In Thatcher's account (4b–4e), we see only scenes at which he is present. Even Kane's newspaper crusade is rendered as Thatcher learns of it, through buying copies of the *Inquirer.* In Bernstein's flashback (5b–5f), there is some deviation from what Bernstein witnesses, but in general his range of knowledge is respected. For example, we never see Kane in Europe; we merely hear the contents of Kane's telegram, which Bernstein delivers to Leland.

Leland's flashbacks (6b, 6d–6j) deviate most markedly from the narrator's allotted range of knowledge. Here we see Kane and Emily at a series of morning breakfasts, Kane's meeting with Susan, and the confrontation of Kane with Boss Gettys at Susan's apartment. In scene 6j, Leland is present but in a drunken stupor most of the time. (The plot motivates Leland's knowledge of Kane's affair by having Leland suggest that Kane told him about it, but the scenes present detailed knowledge that Leland probably didn't possess.) By the time we get to Susan's flashback (7b–7k), however, the range of knowledge again fits the character more snugly. (In one scene, 7f, Susan is unconscious for part of the action.) The last flashback (8b) is recounted by Raymond and plausibly accords with his range of knowledge; he is standing in the hallway as Kane wrecks Susan's room.

Using different narrators to transmit story information fulfills several functions. It offers a plausible depiction of the process of investigation, since we expect any reporter to assemble information through interviews. More deeply, the plot's portrayal of Kane himself becomes more complex by showing somewhat different sides of him, depending on who's talking about him. Moreover, the multiple narrators make the film resemble one of Susan's jigsaw puzzles. We must put things together piece by piece. The pattern of gradual revelation enhances curiosity—what is it in Kane's past that he associates with Rosebud?—and suspense—how will he lose his friends and his wives?

This strategy has important implications for film form. While Thompson uses the various witnesses to gather data, the plot uses the narrators both to furnish story information and to *conceal* information. The narration can motivate gaps in knowledge about Kane by appealing to the fact that nobody can know everything about anyone else. If we were able to enter Kane's consciousness, we might discover the meaning of Rosebud much sooner. But Kane is dead. The multiple-narrator format motivates the withholding of key pieces of information, and this in turn arouses curiosity and suspense.

Although each narrator's account is mostly restricted to his or her range of knowledge, the plot doesn't treat each flashback in much subjective depth. Most of the flashbacks are rendered objectively. Some transitions from the framing episodes use a voice-over commentary to lead us into the flashbacks, but these don't represent the narrators' subjective states. Only in Susan's flashbacks are there some attempts to render subjectivity. In scene 7c, we see Leland as if from her optical point of view on stage, and the phantasmagoric montage of her career (7e) reveals her fatigue and frustration. These scenes help make her the most sympathetic narrator, reinforcing our sense that Kane has cruelly forced her to pursue a singing career.

Against the five character narrators, the film's plot sets another source of knowledge, the "News on the March" short. We've already seen the crucial function of the newsreel in introducing us to *Kane*'s plot construction, with the newsreel's sections previewing the parts of the film as a whole. The newsreel also gives us a broad sketch of Kane's life and death that will be filled in by the more restricted behind-the-scenes accounts offered by the narrators. The newsreel is also highly objective, even more so than the rest of the film; it reveals nothing about Kane's inner life. Rawlston's assigns Thompson to add depth to the newsreel's superficial version of Kane.

3.44 Deemphasizing Thompson. Camera angle and selective lighting make the reporter less important than the witnesses he interviews.

Yet we still aren't through with the narrational manipulations in this complex and daring film. For one thing, all the localized sources of knowledge—"News on the March" and the five narrators—are linked together by the shadowy reporter Thompson. To some extent, he is our surrogate in the film, gathering and assembling the puzzle pieces.

It's very striking, especially for a film made over 70 years ago, that Thompson is barely characterized. We can't even identify his face **(3.44).** This, as usual, has a function. If we saw him clearly, if the plot gave him more traits or a background or a past, he would become the central protagonist, as reporters tend to be in the journalism genre. But *Citizen Kane* is less about Thompson the man than about his *search*. The plot's handling of Thompson makes him a neutral channel for the story information that he gathers, even though his conclusion at the end—"I don't think any word can explain a man's life"—suggests that he has been changed by his investigation.

Thompson is not, however, a perfect surrogate for us. That's because the film's narration inserts the newsreel, the narrators, and Thompson within a still broader range of knowledge. The flashback portions are predominantly restricted, but there are other passages that reveal an overall narrational omniscience.

From the very start, we are given a god's-eye view of the action. We move into a mysterious setting that we later learn is Kane's estate, Xanadu. We might have learned about this locale through a character's journey, the way we acquaint ourselves with Oz by means of Dorothy's trip. Here, however, an omniscient narration conducts the tour. Eventually, we enter a darkened bedroom. A hand holds a paperweight, and over this is superimposed a flurry of snow **(3.45).**

The image teases us. Is the narration making a lyrical comment on the action? Or is the image subjective, a glimpse into the dying man's mind or vision? In either case, the narration reveals its ability to command a great deal of story information. Our sense of omniscience is enhanced when, after the man dies, a nurse bustles into the room. Apparently, no character knows what we know.

At other points in the film, the omniscient narration calls attention to itself. During Susan's opera debut in Leland's flashback (6i), we see stagehands high above reacting to her performance. Most vivid is the omniscient narration at the end of the film. Thompson and the other reporters leave, never having learned the meaning of Rosebud. But we linger in the vast storeroom of Xanadu. And, thanks to the narration, we learn that Rosebud is the name of Kane's childhood sled. We can now associate the opening's emphasis on the snowy cottage with the closing scene's revelation of the sled.

3.45 Narrational omniscience in *Citizen Kane*. The elusive image of the paperweight in *Citizen Kane*—seen by film viewers but not by any characters in the film.

This framing narration is truly omniscient. It withholds a key piece of story information at the outset, teases us with hints (the snow, the tiny cottage in the paperweight), and finally reveals at least part of the answer to the initial question. A return to the "No Trespassing" sign reminds us of our point of entry into the film. The film derives its unity not only from systematic choices about causality and time but also from a patterned narration that arouses curiosity and suspense and yields a surprise at the very end.

▶❙ SUMMARY

Not every analysis of a narrative film runs through all the categories we have covered here. Our purpose was as much to illustrate these concepts as to analyze *Citizen Kane*. With practice, you can become more familiar with these analytical tools and can use them flexibly, suiting your approach to the specific film at hand and the things that intrigue you about it. Should you become a filmmaker, all these matters, from cause-effect patterns to narrational organization, will confront you with a cascade of decisions. You may make your choices intuitively or through lots of thought and soul searching, but these remain essential dimensions of storytelling.

In looking at any narrative film, then, asking these questions will help you understand it better:

1. Which story events are directly presented to us in the plot, and which must we assume or infer? Is there any nondiegetic material given in the plot?

2. What is the earliest story event of which we learn? How does it relate to later events through a series of causes and effects?

3. How are story events connected in time? Have the filmmakers manipulated order, frequency, and duration in the plot so as to affect our understanding of events?

4. Does the closing reflect a clear-cut pattern of development that relates it to the opening? Do all narrative lines achieve closure, or are some left open?

5. How does the narration present story information to us? Is it restricted to one or a few characters' knowledge, or does it range freely among the characters in different spaces? Does it give us considerable depth of story information by exploring the characters' mental states?

6. How closely does the film follow the conventions of the classical Hollywood cinema? If it departs significantly from those conventions, what formal principles does it use instead?

Most films that we see employ narrative form, and the great majority of theatrical movies stick to the premises of Hollywood storytelling. Still, there are other formal possibilities. We consider aspects of nonnarrative form in Chapter 10.

In the meantime, other matters will occupy us. In discussing form, we've been examining how we as viewers engage with the film's overall patterning. A film, however, also presents a complex blend of images and sounds. Like the overall architecture of film form, the finer grain of cinematic techniques involves the filmmaker in creative problem solving and decision making. Our experience of the film is shaped by the filmmaker's choice and control and patterning of those techniques. Part Three shows how this all happens.

3

Film Style

We are still trying to understand how a movie creates an absorbing experience for the viewer. Chapter 2 showed that the concept of form offers a way to grasp the film as a whole. Chapter 3 examined how narrative form can shape a film and our response to it. Later we'll see that filmmakers have employed other types of form in documentaries and experimental films.

When we see a film, though, we don't engage only with its overall form. We experience a *film*—not a painting or a novel. A painter knows how to manipulate color, shape, and composition. A novelist lives intimately with language. Likewise, filmmakers work with a distinct medium.

You're already somewhat aware of the creative choices available in the film medium. As a viewer you probably notice performance and color design. If you've made videos, you've become more aware of framing and composition, editing and sound. If you've tried your hand at making a fictional piece, you've already faced problems of staging and acting.

Part Three of this book gives you a chance to learn about film techniques in a systematic way. We look at two techniques governing the shot, mise-en-scene and cinematography. Then we consider the technique that relates shot to shot, editing. Then we consider the role that sound plays in relation to film images. A wrapup chapter returns to *Citizen Kane* and examines how it coordinates all these techniques with its narrative form.

Each chapter introduces a single technique, surveying the choices it offers to the filmmaker. We explore how various filmmakers have used the techniques. Several key questions will guide us: How can a technique shape the viewer's expectations? How may it furnish motifs for the film? How may a technique support the film's overall form—its story/plot relations or its narrational patterning? How may it direct our attention, clarify or emphasize meanings, and shape our emotional response?

The chapters that follow also explore how a film can organize its chosen techniques in consistent ways. This pattern of technical choices we call *style.* Style is what creates a movie's "look and feel." Late in each chapter, we focus on one or two particular films to show how the technique we're studying helps establish a distinctive style.

4

The Shot: Mise-en-Scene

Of all film techniques, **mise-en-scene** is the one that viewers notice most. After seeing a film, we may not recall the cutting or the camera movements, the dissolves or the offscreen sound. But we do remember the costumes in *Gone with the Wind* and the bleak, chilly lighting in Charles Foster Kane's *Xanadu*. We retain vivid impressions of the misty streets in *The Big Sleep* and the labyrinthine, fluorescent-lit lair of Buffalo Bill in *The Silence of the Lambs*. We recall Harpo Marx clambering over Edgar Kennedy's lemonade stand (*Duck Soup*) and Michael J. Fox escaping high-school bullies on an improvised skateboard (*Back to the Future*). Many of our most vivid memories of movies stem from mise-en-scene.

What Is Mise-en-Scene?

Consider this image from Quentin Tarantino's *Inglourious Basterds* **(4.1).** Aldo Raine, a U.S. soldier on a mission to assassinate Hitler, has been captured by SS Colonel Hans Landa. The shot seems a simple one, but if you're starting to think like a filmmaker, you'll notice how Tarantino has shaped the image to accentuate the action and engage our attention.

The shot presents the two men facing each other behind a movie theater. The alley is rendered minimally, in dark colors and subdued lighting. By playing down the setting, Tarantino obliges us to concentrate on the confrontation.

Although both men are positioned in profile, the image doesn't give equal weight to each one. The cowl masks Aldo's face. This costume choice encourages us to concentrate on the face that we can see. The lighting is important as well. A

4.1 What attracts your eye? Elements of mise-en-scene accentuate action and engage attention in this scene from *Inglourious Basterds*, in which Aldo Raine is captured by Colonel Landa.

thread of illumination picks out the edge of Raine's cowl; without it, it would merge into the background. Again, however, it is Landa's face that gets greater emphasis. Strong lighting from above and left sharply outlines his profile, and a less powerful light (what filmmakers call *fill*) reveals his features.

Landa is emphasized in another way, through the actor's dialogue and facial expression. As Landa speaks, he shows delight in the capture of his quarry. His satisfaction bursts out when he chortles: "Alas, you're now in the hands of the SS—my hands, to be exact!" Letting the actor's hands fly up into the center of the frame and emphasizing them by the dialogue, Tarantino reminds us of the officer's florid self-assurance. This hand gesture will be developed when Landa playfully taps Raine's head with a forefinger: "I've been waiting a long time to touch you."

Although Tarantino has made many creative choices in this shot (notably the decision to film in a relatively close framing), certain techniques stand out. Setting, costume, lighting, and performance have all been coordinated to high-

4.2 Unplanned events and mise-en-scene. While filming *She Wore a Yellow Ribbon*, John Ford took advantage of a thunderstorm in Monument Valley.

light Landa's gloating and remind us that he enjoys his cat-and-mouse interrogation tactics. Tarantino has shaped our experience of this story action by his decisions about mise-en-scene.

In the original French, *mise en scène* (pronounced meez-ahn-sen) means "putting into the scene," and it was first applied to the practice of directing plays. Film scholars, extending the term to film direction, use the term to signify the director's control over what appears in the film frame. As you would expect, mise-en-scene includes those aspects of film that overlap with the art of the theater: setting, lighting, costume and makeup, and staging and performance.

As the *Inglourious Basterds* shot suggests, mise-en-scene usually involves planning in advance. But the filmmaker may seize on unplanned events as well. An actor may add a line on the set, or an unexpected change in lighting may enhance a dramatic effect. While filming a cavalry procession through Monument Valley for *She Wore a Yellow Ribbon*, John Ford took advantage of an approaching lightning storm to create a dramatic backdrop for the action (**4.2**). The storm remains part of the film's mise-en-scene even though Ford neither planned it nor controlled it; it was a lucky accident that helped create one of the film's most affecting passages. Jean Renoir, Robert Altman, and other directors have allowed their actors to improvise their performances, making the films' mise-en-scene more spontaneous and unpredictable.

The Power of Mise-en-Scene

Filmmakers can use mise-en-scene to achieve realism, giving settings an authentic look or letting actors perform as naturally as possible. Throughout film history, however, audiences have also been attracted to fantasy, and mise-en-scene has often been used for this purpose. This attraction is evident in the work of cinema's first master of the technique, Georges Méliès. Méliès used highly original mise-en-scene to create an imaginary world on film.

A caricaturist and stage magician, Méliès became fascinated by the Lumière brothers' demonstration of their short films in 1895. (For more on the Lumières, see p. 177.) After building a camera based on an English projector, Méliès began filming unstaged street scenes and moments of passing daily life. One day, the story goes, he was filming at the Place de l'Opéra, but his camera jammed as a bus was passing. By the time he could resume filming, the bus had gone and a hearse was in front of his lens. When Méliès screened the film, he discovered something

CONNECT TO THE BLOG
www.davidbordwell.net/blog

For more on Méliès and his last years, visit our entry "Hugo: Scorsese's birthday present to Georges Méliès."

> ❝ When Buñuel was preparing *The Discreet Charm of the Bourgeoisie,* he chose a tree-lined avenue for the recurring shot of his characters traipsing endlessly down it. The avenue was strangely stranded in open country and it perfectly suggested the idea of these people coming from nowhere and going nowhere. Buñuel's assistant said, 'You can't use that road. It's been used in at least ten other movies.' 'Ten other movies?' said Buñuel, impressed. 'Then it must be good.'❞

unexpected: a moving bus seemed to transform instantly into a hearse. Whether or not the anecdote is true, it at least illustrates Méliès's recognition of the magical powers of mise-en-scene. He would devote most of his efforts to cinematic conjuring.

To do so would require preparation, since Méliès could not count on lucky accidents like the bus–hearse transformation. He would have to plan and stage action for the camera. Drawing on his theatrical experience, Méliès built one of the first film studios—a small, crammed affair bristling with balconies, trapdoors, and sliding backdrops. Total control was necessary to create the fantasy world he envisioned (**4.3–4.6**). He drew shots beforehand, designed sets and costumes, and devised elaborate special effects. As if this were not enough, Méliès starred in his own films (4.6).

Méliès's "Star-Film" studio made hundreds of short fantasy and trick films based on a strict control over every element in the frame, and the first master of mise-en-scene demonstrated the resources of the technique. The legacy of Méliès's magic is a delightfully unreal world wholly obedient to the whims of the imagination.

4.3

4.4

4.5

4.6

4.3–4.6 Méliès and mise-en-scene. Méliès made detailed plans for his shots, as seen in the drawing and final version of the rocket-launching scene in *A Trip to the Moon* (4.3–4.4). For *The Mermaid* (4.5) he summoned up an undersea world by placing a fish tank between the camera and an actress, some backdrops, and "carts for monsters." In *La Lune à une mètre* (4.6) Méliès plays an astronomer. His study and its furnishings, including telescope, globe, and blackboard, are all painted cut-outs.

Components of Mise-en-Scene

Mise-en-scene offers the filmmaker four general areas of choice and control: setting, costumes and makeup, lighting, and staging (which includes acting and movement in the shot).

Setting

Since the earliest days of cinema, critics and audiences have understood that setting plays a more active role in cinema than it usually does in the theater. André Bazin writes:

> The human being is all-important in the theatre. The drama on the screen can exist without actors. A banging door, a leaf in the wind, waves beating on the shore can heighten the dramatic effect. Some film masterpieces use man only as an accessory, like an extra, or in counterpoint to nature, which is the true leading character.

4.7 Setting creates narrative expectations. The railway yard at the opening of *Wendy and Lucy* is a setting that will take on significance later in the film.

In a film, the setting can come to the forefront; it need not be only a container for human events but can dynamically enter the narrative action. Kelly Reichardt's *Wendy and Lucy* begins with shots of a railroad yard as trains pass through (**4.7**). But we don't see any people. Wendy, who is making her way across the United States by car, is later seen walking her dog Lucy in a park. The opening shots of the rail yard suggest the sort of neighborhoods where she must stay. At later points in the film, the roar and whistle of rail traffic will increase suspense, but not until the ending will we come to understand why the opening emphasized the trains.

The filmmaker may select an existing locale for the action. The very early short comedy *L'Arroseur arrosé* ("The Waterer Sprayed," **4.8**) was filmed in a garden. At the close of World War II, Roberto Rossellini shot *Germany Year Zero* in the rubble of Berlin (**4.9**). Alternatively, the filmmaker may construct the setting. Méliès understood that shooting in a studio increased his control, and many filmmakers followed his lead. In France, Germany, and especially the United States, commercial filmmaking became centered on studio facilities in which every aspect of mise-en-scene could be manipulated.

Some directors have emphasized authenticity even in purpose-built settings. For example, Erich von Stroheim prided himself on meticulous research into details of locale for the sets of *Greed* (**4.10**). *All the President's Men* (1976) took a similar tack, seeking to duplicate the *Washington Post* office on a sound stage (**4.11**). Other films have been less committed to accuracy. Though D. W. Griffith studied the various historical periods presented in *Intolerance,* his Babylon constitutes a personal image of that city (**4.12**). Similarly, in *Ivan the Terrible,* Sergei Eisenstein freely stylized the decor of the czar's palace to harmonize with the lighting, costume, and figure movement, so that characters crawl through doorways that resemble mouse-holes and stand frozen before symbolic murals (**4.13**).

Setting can overwhelm the actors, as in Wim Wender's *Wings of Desire* (**4.14**), or it can be reduced to almost nothing, as in Francis Ford Coppola's *Bram Stoker's Dracula* (**4.15**). The overall design of a setting can shape how we understand story action. In Louis Feuillade's silent crime serial *The Vampires,* a criminal gang has killed a courier on his way to a bank. The gang's confederate, Irma Vep, is also a bank employee, and just as she tells her superior that the courier has vanished, an imposter, in beard and bowler hat, strolls in behind them (**4.16**). They turn away from us in surprise as he comes forward (**4.17**). Working in a period when cutting to closer shots was rare in a French film, Feuillade draws our attention to the man by centering him in the doorway.

But suppose a filmmaker is using a more crowded locale. How can a compact setting yield smooth drama? The heroine of Juzo Itami's *Tampopo* is a widow who

4.8

4.9

4.8–4.9 Actual locations used as setting. Although Louis Lumière's cameramen were famous for documentary filming, they also made fictional narratives such as the 1895 *L'Arroseur arrosé* (4.8). Roberto Rossellini's *Germany Year Zero* (4.9) maintained the tradition of staging fictional stories in actual locations.

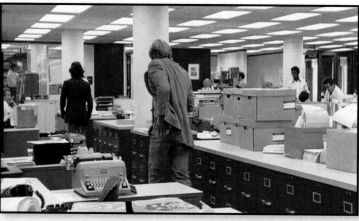

4.10   **4.11**

4.10–4.11 Authenticity in constructed settings. Details such as posters and hanging flypaper create a tavern scene in *Greed* (4.10). To replicate an actual newsroom in *All the President's Men* (4.11), even wastepaper from the actual office was scattered around the set.

4.12   **4.13**

4.12–4.13 Stylized settings. The Babylonian sequences of *Intolerance* (4.12) combined influences from Assyrian history, 19th-century biblical illustration, and modern dance. In *Ivan the Terrible*, Part 2, the décor (4.13) dominates the characters.

4.14   **4.15**

4.14–4.15 The interplay of setting and actors. In *Wings of Desire,* busy, colorful graffiti draw attention away from the man lying on the ground (4.14). In contrast, in *Bram Stoker's Dracula,* apart from the candles, the setting of this scene has been obliterated by darkness (4.15).

is trying to improve the food she serves in her restaurant. In one scene, a cowboy-hatted truck driver takes her to another noodle shop to watch professionals do business. Itami has staged the scene so that the kitchen and the counter serve as two arenas for the action. At first, the widow watches the noodle-man take orders, sitting by her mentor on the edge of the kitchen (**4.18**). Quickly, the counter fills with customers calling out orders. The truck driver challenges her to match the orders with the customers, and she steps closer to the center of the kitchen (**4.19**). After she calls out the orders correctly, she turns her back to us, and our interest shifts to the customers, who applaud her (**4.20**).

As the *Tampopo* example shows, color can be an important component of settings. The dark colors of the kitchen surfaces make the widow's red dress stand out. Robert Bresson's *L'Argent* parallels its settings by drab green backgrounds and cold blue props and costumes (**4.21–4.23**). In contrast, Jacques Tati's *Play Time* displays sharply changing color schemes. In the first portion of *Play Time,* the settings and costumes are mostly gray, brown, and black—cold, steely colors. Later in the film, however, beginning in the restaurant scene, the settings start to sport cheery reds, pinks, and greens. This change in the settings' colors supports a narrative development that shows an inhuman city landscape that is transformed by vitality and spontaneity.

A full-size setting need not always be built. Through much of the history of the cinema, filmmakers have used miniature buildings to create fantasy scenes or simply to economize. Parts of settings could also be rendered as paintings and combined photographically with full-sized sections of the space. Now, digital special effects can conjure up settings in comparable ways. When the makers of *Angels & Demons* were refused permission to shoot in Vatican City, they built partial sets of St. Peter's Square and the Pantheon, then filled in the missing stretches (**4.24, 4.25**).

In manipulating a shot's setting, the filmmaker may use a *prop,* short for *property.* This is another term borrowed from theatrical mise-en-scene. When

4.16

4.17

4.16–4.17 Setting guides attention. In *The Vampires,* a background frame created by a large doorway emphasizes the importance of an entering character.

4.18

4.20

4.19

4.18–4.20 Activating areas of a setting. In *Tampopo,* at the start of the scene (4.18), the noodle counter, with only two customers, occupies the center of the action. The widow and her truck driver mentor stand inconspicuously at the left. After the counter is full (4.19), the dramatic emphasis shifts to the kitchen when the widow rises and takes the challenge to name the customers' orders. Her red dress helps draw attention to her. When she has triumphantly matched the orders, she gets a round of applause (4.20). By turning her away from us, Itami once more emphasizes the rear counter.

4.21

4.22

4.21–4.23 Color creates parallels among settings. Color links the affluent home in *L'Argent* (4.21) to the prison (4.22) and later to the old woman's home (4.23).

4.23

4.24

4.25

4.24–4.25 Digital set replacement. Only a portion of the buildings lining St. Peter's Square were built for *Angels & Demons*. The remainder of the set was covered with greenscreens during filming. Digital matte paintings were added to create major elements like the colonnades at the sides and the tops of the background buildings.

an object in the setting has a function within the ongoing action, we can call it a prop. Films teem with examples: the snowstorm paperweight that shatters at the beginning of *Citizen Kane*, the little girl's balloon in *M*, the cactus rose in *The Man Who Shot Liberty Valance*, Sarah Connor's hospital bed turned exercise machine in *Terminator 2: Judgment Day*. Comedies often use props to create gags **(4.26).**

Over the course of a narrative, a prop may become a motif. In Alexander Payne's *Election*, the fussy, frustrated high school teacher is shown cleaning out spoiled food and hallway litter, and these actions prepare for the climactic moment when he crumples a ballot and secretly disposes of it (**4.27–4.29**). Payne calls this the motif of trash, "of throwing things away, since that's in fact the climax of the film. . . . So we establish it early on." Color may help props become motifs. In some scenes of *Finye* (*The Wind*), the recurrent use of orange creates a cluster of nature motifs (**4.30–4.32**). When we look at *Our Hospitality* later in the chapter, we'll examine how elements of setting, particularly props, can weave through a film to create motifs.

Costume and Makeup

If you were planning a film, you'd probably give as much attention to what your actors wear as you pay to their surroundings. Like setting, costume can have a great variety of specific functions in the film's overall form.

Costumes can play causal roles in film plots. In the runaway bus section of *Speed,* Annie's outfit provides the clue that allows Jack to outwit the bomber Howard. During a phone conversation Howard refers to Annie as a "Wildcat." Noticing Annie's University of Arizona sweater, Jack realizes that Howard must have hidden a video camera on the bus. Less obviously, costumes can become motifs, enhancing characterization and tracing changes in attitude (**4.33–4.36**).

In other films, costumes can be used for their purely graphic qualities. Throughout *Ivan the Terrible,* robes and capes are orchestrated with one another in their colors, their textures, and even the way they flow (**4.37**). *Freak Orlando* boldly uses costumes to display primary colors with maximum intensity (**4.38**).

In these last examples, as well as in *Tampopo* (4.18–4.20) and *L'Argent* (4.21–4.23), costume is coordinated with setting. Since the filmmaker usually wants to emphasize the human figures, setting may provide a more or less neutral background, while costume helps pick out the characters. Color design is particularly

4.26 Comic use of props. The irresponsible protagonist of *Groundhog Day* eats an enormous breakfast; all the dishes serve as props in the diner setting.

> " The best sets are the simplest, most 'decent' ones; everything should contribute to the feeling of the story and anything that does not do this has no place. Reality is usually too complicated. Real locations contain too much that is extreme or contradictory and always require some simplifying: taking things away, unifying colors, etc. This strength through simplicity is much easier to achieve on a built set than in an existing location."
>
> —Stuart Craig, art director, *Notting Hill*

4.27

4.28

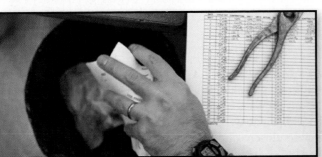

4.29

4.27–4.29 Props as motifs in *Election*. As he discards spoiled leftovers, the teacher is suspiciously watched by the custodian—who will play an important role in his downfall (4.27). He tosses a scrap of paper into the corridor trash bin (4.28). The motif culminates in a close-up of the teacher's hand discarding the crucial vote for student council president (4.29).

4.30

4.31

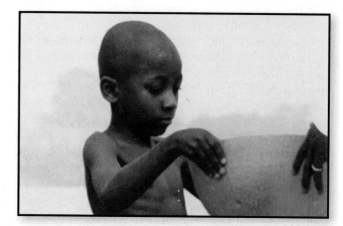

4.32

4.30–4.32 Color as a motif. Souleymane Cissé's *Finye* begins with a woman carrying an orange calabash as the wind rustles through foliage (4.30). Later, the vengeful grandfather prepares to stalk his grandson's persecutor by dressing in orange and making magic before a fire (4.31). At the end, the little boy passes his bowl to someone offscreen (4.32)—possibly a couple seen earlier in the film.

4.33

4.34

4.33–4.34 Costume and character. In a poignant moment in Griffith's *The Birth of a Nation*, the Little Sister decorates her shabby dress with "ermine" made of cotton dotted with spots of soot (4.33). The image suggests both her effort to be elegant and her realization of her poverty. In Fellini's *8½*, the film director Guido persistently uses his dark glasses (4.34) to shield himself from the world.

> " The costume is a very important thing. It speaks before you do. You know what you're looking at. You get a reference and it gives context about the other characters and their relationships."
>
> —Harrison Ford, actor

important here. The *Freak Orlando* costumes (4.38) stand out boldly against the neutral gray background of an artificial lake. In *The Night of the Shooting Stars,* luminous wheat fields set off the hard black-and-blue costumes of the fascists and the peasants **(4.39)**. The director may instead choose to match the color values of setting and costume more closely **(4.40)**. This "bleeding" of the costume into the setting is carried to a kind of limit in the prison scene of *THX 1138,* in which George Lucas strips both locale and clothing to stark white on white **(4.41)**.

4.35   **4.36**

4.35–4.36 Costume and character change. When Hildy Johnson, in *His Girl Friday,* switches from her role of aspiring housewife to that of reporter, her hats change as well—from a stylish number with a low-dipping brim (4.35) to a more "masculine" hat with its brim pushed up, journalist-style (4.36).

4.37   **4.38**

4.37–4.38 Graphic qualities of costumes. In *Ivan the Terrible,* the sweeping folds of a priest's lightweight black robe contrast with the heavy cloak and train of the czar's furs (4.37). In *Freak Orlando,* stylized costumes with intense, primary colors are featured (4.38). The director, Ulrike Ottinger, is a professional costume designer.

Women in Love affords a clear example of how costume and setting can contribute to a film's narrative progression. The opening scenes portray the characters' shallow middle-class life by means of saturated primary and complementary colors in costume and setting **(4.42).** In the middle portions of the film, as the characters discover love on a country estate, pale pastels predominate **(4.43).** The last section of *Women in Love* takes place around the Matterhorn, and the characters' ardor has cooled. Now the colors have almost disappeared, and scenes are dominated by pure black and white **(4.44).** By combining with setting, costumes may reinforce narrative and thematic patterns.

Computer technology can graft virtual costumes onto fully computer-generated characters, like Gollum in *The Lord of the Rings* or the many extras in the backgrounds of big crowd scenes. Entirely digital costumes for human actors are less common, but fantasy and science fiction films use them **(4.45).**

Many of these points about costume apply equally to a closely related area of mise-en-scene, the actors' makeup. In the early days of cinema, makeup was necessary because

4.39 Color contrast of costume and setting. In the climactic skirmish of *The Night of the Shooting Stars,* the dark costumes stand out starkly against the more neutral background.

4.40

4.41

4.40–4.41 Color coordinates costume and setting. Fellini's *Casanova* creates a color gradation that runs from bright red costumes to paler red walls (4.40), the whole composition capped by a small white accent in the distance. In *THX 1138,* heads seem to float in space as white costumes blend into white settings (4.41).

4.42

4.43

4.44

4.42–4.44 Costume, setting, and narrative. Bright colors in an early scene of *Women in Love* (4.42) give way to the softer hues of trees and fields (4.43) and finally to a predominantly white-and-black scheme (4.44), contributing to the progression of the story.

4.45 Virtual costume. *Watchmen's* superhero Rorschach wears a hood with moving black patterns. In postproduction, a digital simulation of ink flowing through the fibers was superimposed on the actor's face.

actors' faces would not register well on film stocks. Over the course of film history, a wide range of possibilities emerged. Dreyer's *La Passion de Jeanne d'Arc* was famous for its complete avoidance of makeup (**4.46**). For *Ivan the Terrible,* however, Nikolai Cherkasov plays the czar wearing a wig and a false beard, nose, and eyebrows (**4.47**). Changing actors to look like historical personages has been one common function of makeup.

Makeup is most noticeable in horror and science fiction films, and the popularity of those genres contributed new technology to the craft. Rubber and plasticine compounds can create bumps, bulges, extra organs, and layers of artificial skin. Now other genres are utilizing those resources (**4.48–4.50**).

Today the hope is for makeup generally to pass unnoticed, and quietly accentuate expressive qualities of the actor's face. Because the camera may record cruel details that we wouldn't notice in ordinary life, unsuitable blemishes, wrinkles, and sagging skin will have to be hidden. The makeup artist can sculpt the face, making it seem narrower or broader by applying blush and shadow. Viewers expect that female performers will wear lipstick and other cosmetics, but the male actors are usually wearing makeup as well.

4.46 Plain faces. Pale backgrounds focus attention on the actors' faces in many shots of *La Passion de Jeanne d'Arc*. The actors wore no makeup, and the director, Carl Dreyer, relied on close-ups and tiny facial changes to create an intense religious drama.

4.47 Makeup interprets a historical figure. In *Ivan the Terrible,* Part 1, makeup shapes the eyebrows and hollows the eye sockets to emphasize Ivan's piercing gaze, a central feature in director Sergei Eisenstein's conception of the all-knowing czar.

4.48

4.49

4.48–4.50 Creative choices in makeup. Tilda Swinton (4.48) is an actor who enjoys experimenting with makeup. In the futuristic fantasy *Snowpiercer,* she and her makeup designer used an artificial nose, protruding teeth, and vibrant lipstick to create a grotesque, tyrannical administrator (4.49). For *The Grand Budapest Hotel,* director Wes Anderson exploited the new makeup technology for grotesque comedy. To portray an elderly woman, Swinton wore 11 pieces of prosthetic makeup on her neck, chin, earlobes, forehead, and nose—along with five wig pieces (4.50).

4.50

4.51

4.52

4.51–4.52 Makeup: Man and woman. In *Speed,* Sandra Bullock's eyeliner, shadow, and arched brows make her eyes vivid and give her an alert expression (4.51). For the same scene, the eyeliner on Keanu Reeves makes the upper edges of his eyes stand out (4.52). Note the somewhat fierce slope of the eyebrows, accentuating his slight frown.

4.53

4.54

4.53–4.54 **Digital makeup.** In *Harry Potter and the Goblet of Fire,* Ralph Fiennes's nose was removed and replaced with nostrils appropriate to the snake-like Lord Voldemort (4.53). When two clones of the same man get into a fight in *Moon,* a stunt man wearing a green hood with motion-capture dots played one of the clones (4.54). Actor Sam Rockwell's head was shot separately and then inserted into the scene.

Film actors rely on their eyes to a great extent (see A Closer Look, p. 134), and makeup artists can often enhance facial performance. Eyeliner and mascara can emphasize the direction of a glance. Nearly every actor will also have expressively shaped eyebrows—lengthened eyebrows can enlarge the face; shorter brows make the face seem more compact. Eyebrows plucked in a slightly rising curve add gaiety to the face, but slightly sloping ones hint at sadness. Thick, straight brows commonly applied to men reinforce the impression of a hard, serious gaze **(4.51, 4.52).**

Although most makeup continues to be physically applied to actors' faces, digital technology can be used as well. Minor cleanups remove flaws or shadows from faces. More drastically, a villain can lose a nose or, via head replacement, an actor can play two roles in the same shot **(4.53, 4.54).** Computer-generated imagery (CGI) has extended the importance of makeup, because now the filmmaker can sculpt entire bodies. Gary Sinise's legs were removed so that he could play an amputee in *Forrest Gump,* and a muscular actor was made to look thin and weak before becoming a superhero in *Captain America: The First Avenger.*

Lighting

If you've shot videos with your cellphone or camera, you may not have thought much about manipulating lighting. Modern digital capture can produce a legible

> 66 Light is everything. It expresses ideology, emotion, colour, depth, style. It can efface, narrate, describe. With the right lighting, the ugliest face, the most idiotic expression can radiate with beauty or intelligence."
>
> —Federico Fellini, director

image in bright or dark situations, and for many purposes, all that matters is that the subject be visible. But the practiced filmmaker wants more than legibility. The image should have pictorial impact, and for that it's vital to control the lighting. Not many actual situations would yield the delicate edge lighting or facial fill light we saw in our shot from *Inglourious Basterds* (4.1).

In artistic filmmaking, lighting is more than just illumination that permits us to see the action. Lighter and darker areas within the frame help create the overall composition of each shot and guide our attention to certain objects and actions. A brightly illuminated patch may draw our eye to a key gesture, while a shadow may conceal a detail or build up suspense about what may be present. Lighting can also articulate textures: the curve of a face, the grain of a piece of wood, the tracery of a spider's web, the sparkle of a gem.

Highlights and Shadows   Lighting shapes objects by creating *highlights* and *shadows*. A highlight is a patch of relative brightness on a surface. The man's face in **4.55** and the edge of the fingers in **4.56** display highlights. Highlights provide important cues to the texture of the surface. If the surface is smooth, like glass or chrome, the highlights tend to gleam or sparkle; a rougher surface, like a coarse stone facing, yields more diffuse highlights. Shadows likewise do the same, allowing objects to have portions of darkness (called *shading*) or to cast their shadows onto something else. Thus the fingers in 4.56 are visible partly because they are shaded, while the stark vertical shadows of 4.55 imply prison bars offscreen.

Lighting creates not only textures but also overall shape. If a ball is lit straight on from the front, it appears round. If the same ball is lit from the side, we see it as a half-circle. Hollis Frampton's short film *Lemon* consists primarily of light moving around a lemon, and the shifting shadows and shading create dramatically changing patterns of yellow and black. This film almost seems designed to prove the truth of a remark made by Josef von Sternberg: "The proper use of light can embellish and dramatize every object."

Lighting joins with setting in controlling our sense of a scene's space. In 4.55, a few shadows imply an entire prison cell. Lighting also shapes a shot's overall composition. One image from John Huston's *Asphalt Jungle* welds the gang members into a unit by the pool of light cast by a hanging lamp. At the same time, the lighting sets up a scale of importance, emphasizing the protagonist by making him the most frontal and clearly lit figure (**4.57).**

Quality   For our purposes, we can say that filmmakers exploit and explore four major aspects of lighting: its quality, direction, source, and color. Lighting *quality* refers to the relative intensity of the illumination. *Hard* lighting creates clearly defined shadows, crisp textures, and sharp edges, whereas *soft* lighting creates a diffused illumination. In nature, the noonday sun creates hard light, whereas an overcast

> 66 Every light has a point where it is brightest and a point toward which it wanders to lose itself completely. . . . The journey of rays from that central core to the outposts of blackness is the adventure and drama of light."
>
> —Josef von Sternberg

4.55

4.56

4.57

4.55–4.57 Highlights and shadows. In Cecil B. DeMille's *The Cheat,* the man's face and body display highlights (4.55), while the cast shadows suggest the unseen bars of a jail cell. In Robert Bresson's *Pickpocket,* the edge of the fingers display highlights (4.56), while the hand is subtly modeled by shading. Shadows on faces create a dramatic composition in John Huston's *Asphalt Jungle (4.57).*

4.58–4.59 Hard versus soft lighting. In Satyajit Ray's *Aparajito*, Apu's mother and the globe she holds are emphasized by hard lighting (4.58). In another shot from the same film (4.59), softer lighting blurs contours and textures and makes for more diffusion and gentler contrasts between light and shade.

4.58

4.59

4.60

4.61

4.60–4.61 Hard and soft lighting in color. The spy thriller *Skyfall* shows James Bond returning from near death to international intrigue. Hard lighting in early scenes gives his face a haggard, worn look aided by makeup (including pink-rimmed eyes). Once he's back in action in a Macau casino, Bond's face is sculpted by gentler shading and softer illumination. The difference is enhanced by the neutral, colorless lighting in 4.60 and the warmer glow in 4.61.

4.62 Frontal lighting. In Jean-Luc Godard's *La Chinoise*, frontal lighting eliminates most surface shading and makes the actress's shadow fall directly behind her, where we cannot see it.

4.63 Side lighting. In *Touch of Evil*, directed by Orson Welles, light from the left creates sharp shading of the character's nose, cheek, and lips.

4.64 Backlighting. In Godard's *Passion*, the lamp and window provide backlighting that presents the woman almost entirely in silhouette.

sky creates soft light. The terms are relative, and many lighting situations will fall between the extremes, but we can usually recognize the differences (**4.58–4.61**).

Direction   The *direction* of lighting in a shot refers to the path of light from its source or sources to the object lit. For convenience we can distinguish among frontal lighting, sidelighting, backlighting, underlighting, and top lighting.

Frontal lighting can be recognized by its tendency to eliminate shadows. In **4.62,** from Jean-Luc Godard's *La Chinoise*, the result of such frontal lighting is a fairly flat-looking image. Contrast **4.63,** in which a hard **sidelight** (also called a *crosslight*) sculpts the character's features.

Backlighting, as the name suggests, comes from behind the subject. The light can be positioned at many angles: high above the figure, at various angles off to the side, pointing straight at the camera, or from below. Used with no other sources of light, backlighting tends to create silhouettes, as in **4.64**. Combined with more frontal sources of light, the technique can create a subtle contour, as we saw with

Raine's black cowl in *Inglourious Basterds* (4.1). This use of backlighting is called *edge lighting* or *rim lighting* **(4.65).**

As its name implies, **underlighting** suggests that the light comes from below the subject. Since underlighting tends to distort features, it is often used to create dramatic horror effects, but it may also simply indicate a realistic light source, such as a fireplace, or, as in **4.66,** a flashlight. As usual, a particular technique can function differently according to context.

Top lighting is exemplified by **4.67,** where the spotlight shines down from almost directly above Marlene Dietrich's face. Here top lighting creates a glamorous image. In our earlier example from *Asphalt Jungle* (4.57), the light from above is harder, in keeping with the conventional harshness of crime films. Director Jacques Audiard chose to use top lighting with very little fill in his prison drama *A Prophet*: "It's a matter of realism—everything is not visible all the time" **(4.68).**

Source   Lighting has a quality, and it has direction. It can also be characterized by its *source*. In making a documentary, the filmmaker may be obliged to shoot with whatever light is available. Most fictional films, however, use extra light sources to obtain greater control of the image's look. Typically the table lamps and streetlights you see in a set aren't strong or varied enough to create a powerful image. Still, the filmmaker will usually create a lighting design that seems consistent with the sources in the setting. The pattern of illumination is motivated by the visible sources. (See p. 63.)

Look back at Figure 4.1, the confrontation in *Inglourious Basterds*. The pattern of light we see is roughly consistent with the source in the shot, the street lamp in the alley. But that lamp at that distance could not produce the hard light on Landa's head or the fill light that reveals his features. In **4.69,** from *The Miracle Worker,* the window in the rear and the lantern in the right foreground appear to be the sources of illumination, but many studio lights supplemented them.

Directors and cinematographers manipulating the lighting of the scene typically decide on two primary sources: a **key light** and a **fill light.** The key light is the primary source, providing the brightest illumination and casting the strongest shadows. The key light is the most directional light, and it is usually suggested by a light source in the setting. A fill is a less intense illumination that "fills in," softening or eliminating shadows cast by the key light. By combining key and fill, and by adding other sources, lighting can be controlled quite exactly.

The key lighting source may be aimed at the subject from any angle, as we've seen. In our shot from *The Sixth Sense* (4.66), underlighting may be the key source, while a softer and dimmer fill falls on the setting in the background. Lights from various directions are often combined.

4.65 Edge, or rim, lighting. Edge lighting makes the outline of each actor's body stand out from the background. This shot from *Wings* shows edge lighting on many parts of the frame, especially along the actors' faces and hair and on the edge of the porch.

4.66 Underlighting. In *The Sixth Sense*, a flashlight lights the boy's face from below, enhancing our empathy with his fright as he feels the presence of a ghost.

4.67 Top lighting for glamour. Director Josef Von Sternberg frequently used a high frontal light to bring out the cheekbones of his star, as shown here in *Shanghai Express*.

4.68 Top lighting for realism. Since actors' eyes are crucial to their performances, most filmmakers light scenes to make the eyes visible. But in the prison cells of *A Prophet,* harsh single-source lighting from above often renders the eyes as dark patches, making the characters more sinister and inscrutable.

4.69 Motivating light sources. In this shot from *The Miracle Worker,* motivated light from the window and lantern is enhanced by offscreen studio lights. If you look closely, you can see the extra sources reflected in the lantern.

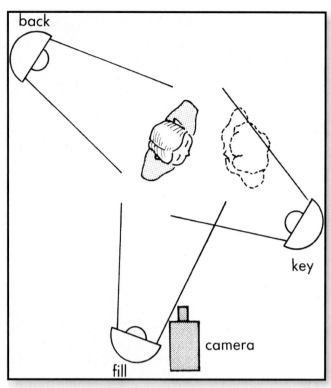

4.70 Three-point lighting, one of the basic techniques of Hollywood cinema.

CONNECT TO THE BLOG
www.davidbordwell.net/blog

We discuss a lecture on lighting by master cinematographer Steven Poster (*Donnie Darko*) in "Light is a law."

Classical Hollywood filmmaking developed the custom of using at least three light sources per shot: key light, fill light, and backlight. The most basic arrangement of **three-point lighting** on a single figure is shown in **4.70.** The *backlight* typically comes from behind and above the figure, the *key light* comes diagonally from the front, and a *fill light* comes from a position near the camera. The key will usually be closer to the figure or brighter than the fill.

In **4.71,** the title character of *Laura* is given glamorous three-point lighting. As in 4.70, the key light is off right, brightening that side of her face. A fill light from the left shades her cheek and chin while softening the shadow of her nose. This balancing of key and fill models her face to a greater degree than straight-on frontal lighting would. (Compare 4.62.)

A bright backlight from the upper rear illuminates her hat and gives a sharp edge to her shoulders. Even the left side of her hat brim is given volume and texture, thanks to shading and edge lighting. Other fill lights, called *background* or *set lighting*, fall on the setting behind her. As if this weren't enough, small lights close to the camera give her eyes a sparkle. Such *eye lights* were often used in close views.

Typically, each major character in a scene will have his or her own key light, fill light, and backlight. When characters face one another, as with the dotted figure in 4.70, the key light for one can serve as backlight for the other, and the fill light can serve as the second character's key.

A more complex arrangement is shown in **4.72,** also from *Laura*. Here the wall chandelier behind Waldo and Laura motivates two lighting patterns. On her, the key now comes from the left, the fill from the right, and backlighting from above. On Waldo, the key strikes his forehead and nose from the upper right, with the fill coming from off left, rather close to the camera, as in 4.70. Top light creates a highlight

4.71

4.72

4.71–4.72 Three-point lighting on the screen. In 4.71, light from different directions makes Laura stand out from the dim background, while enhancing the volume of her face. In 4.72, each character gets the three-point treatment. Shots like this remind us that there were many lighting units hanging from the ceiling of the Hollywood studio, each one helping to sculpt the actors' images.

on his hair, while backlighting creates a thin line of brightness along his head, ear, neck, and collar.

Three-point lighting emerged during the studio era of Hollywood filmmaking, and it is still widely used, as in **4.73.**

We've referred to key, fill, and backlight as separate sources, but in production there will often be many lighting units providing each of those. Several lamps, for instance, might be recruited to provide a strong key light. Moreover, you've probably already realized that this three-point lighting system demands that the lamps be rearranged virtually every time the camera shifts to a new framing. In spite of the great cost involved, most commercial filmmakers choose to adjust lighting for each camera position. Changing light sources this way isn't very realistic, but it does enable filmmakers to make each shot a clear and vivid composition.

Three-point lighting was particularly well suited for the high-key lighting used in classical Hollywood cinema and other filmmaking traditions. **High-key lighting** refers to an overall lighting design that uses fill light and backlight to create relatively low contrast between brighter and darker areas. Usually, the light quality is soft, making shadow areas fairly transparent. The frames from *Laura* (4.71, 4.72) and *Amélie* (4.73) exemplify high-key lighting. Hollywood directors and cinematographers have chosen this pattern for comedies and most dramas.

High-key lighting is not used simply to render a brightly lit situation, such as a dazzling ballroom or a sunny afternoon. High-key lighting is an overall approach to illumination that can suggest different lighting conditions or times of day. Consider, for example, two frames from *Back to the Future*. The first shot (**4.74**) uses high-key illumination matched to daylight and a brightly lit malt shop. The second frame (**4.75**) is from a scene set in a room at night, but it still uses the high-key approach, as can be seen from the lighting's softness, its low contrast, and its detail in shadow areas.

Low-key lighting creates stronger contrasts and sharper, darker shadows. Often the lighting is hard, and fill light is lessened or eliminated altogether. The effect is of *chiaroscuro,* or extremely dark and light regions within the image. An example is **4.76,** from *Kanal.* Here the fill light and background light are less intense than in high-key technique. As a result, shadow areas on the left third of the screen remain hard and fairly opaque. In **4.77,** a low-key shot from Leos Carax's *Mauvais sang,* the key light is hard and comes from the left side. Carax eliminates both fill and background illumination, creating very sharp shadows and a dark void around the characters.

4.73 Three-point lighting in high key. In *Amélie,* the lighthearted romantic tone is enhanced by high-key, three-point lighting. Its layout of sources is similar to that shown in 4.70.

> When taking close-ups in a colour picture, there is too much visual information in the background, which tends to draw attention away from the face. That is why the faces of the actresses in the old black and white pictures are so vividly remembered. Even now, movie fans nostalgically recall Dietrich . . . Garbo . . . Lamarr . . . Why? Filmed in black and white, those figures looked as if they were lit from within. When a face appeared on the screen overexposed—the high-key technique, which also erased imperfections—it was as if a bright object was emerging from the screen."
>
> —Nestor Almendros, cinematographer

4.74   **4.75**

4.74–4.75 High-key lighting for different times and settings. *Back to the Future*: A brightly lit malt shop in daytime (4.74) and Doc's laboratory at night (4.75) both get the high-key treatment.

4.76   **4.77**

4.76–4.77 Low-key lighting. In Andrzej Wajda's *Kanal*, low-key lighting creates a harsh highlight on one side of the woman's face, a shadow on the other (4.76). The shadow on the man's face is even darker and sharper. In *Mauvais sang*, a single key light without any fill on the actress's face leaves her expression nearly invisible (4.77).

4.78   **4.79**   **4.80**

4.78–4.80 Light, constant or changing? At the end of Fellini's *Nights of Cabiria*, the heroine moves diagonally toward us, accompanied by a band of young street musicians (4.78). As she walks, the lighting on her face does not vary, enabling us to notice slight changes in her expression (4.79). By contrast, the sword fight in *Rashomon* is intensified by the contrast between the ferocious combat and the cheerfully dappled lighting pouring into the glade (4.80).

> 66 When I started watching films in the 1940s and 1950s, Indian cinematography was completely under the influence of Hollywood aesthetics, which mostly insisted on the 'ideal light' for the face, using heavy diffusion and strong backlight. I came to resent the complete disregard of the actual source of light and the clichéd use of backlight. Using backlight all the time is like using chili powder in whatever you cook."
>
> —Subrata Mitra, cinematographer

As our examples indicate, low-key lighting is often applied to somber, threatening, or mysterious scenes. It was common in horror films of the 1930s and *films noirs* (dark films) of the 1940s and 1950s. The low-key approach was revived in the 1980s in such films as *Blade Runner* and *Rumble Fish* and continued in the 1990s in film noirs like *Se7en* and *The Usual Suspects*.

When the actors change position, the director faces another forced choice: to alter the lighting or not. Surprisingly often, directors decide to maintain a constant lighting on the actors as they walk, even though that's quite unrealistic. By overlapping several different key-lighting units, the filmmaker can maintain a constant intensity on moving actors. As a result, distracting shadows and highlights do not flit across them **(4.78, 4.79).** Alternatively, the filmmaker may prefer to have the players move through shifting patches of light and shade **(4.80).**

In today's big-budget films, there are often three or more cameras covering scenes in large settings. To avoid rearranging dozens of lamps, the cinematographer will often opt for a soft, bright, top light covering the entire scene. Wherever the cameras are placed, the lighting units will not be visible on camera. In *The Wolfman* (2010), a nighttime forest scene had many lights nested in big translucent boxes hung on cranes above the location.

Digital tools permit lighting to be adjusted in postproduction. The cinematographer and the colorist can brighten a dark shot, add highlights or shadow, and enhance faces. The filmmakers' changes will tend to respect the three-point approach and motivate light sources and intensity in the traditional way.

Color   We tend to think of film lighting as limited to two colors, the white of sunlight or the soft yellow of incandescent room lamps. In practice, filmmakers who choose to control lighting typically work with as purely white a light as they can. With filters placed in front of the light source, the filmmaker can color the onscreen illumination in any fashion.

There may be a realistic source in the scene to motivate colored light (**4.81**). Alternatively, colored light can also be unrealistic. In Eisenstein's *Ivan the Terrible,* Part 2, a blue light suddenly bursts upon the actor without any diegetic source. In the context of the scene, the abrupt lighting change expresses the character's terror and uncertainty (**4.82, 4.83**). Using lighting instead of acting to convey an emotion makes the scene more vivid and surprising.

Most film lighting is arranged as part of preparation for live-action filmmaking. But what if the settings

4.81 **Filtered lighting.** An orange filter suggests that all the light in this scene from *The Green Room* comes from candles.

and figures are created with a computer? Scanning a model or motion-capturing a figure does not record the light falling on it, and the resulting image is a neutral gray. Animators add simulated light to a scene using dedicated programs. Watch the credits for any special-effects-heavy film, and you will see long lists of names of people dealing with light and shade.

In *The Golden Compass,* the vicious combat between two armored polar bears was created entirely digitally. The fight takes place with a bright sun low in the sky, coming from off right. The icy clearing contains shadows of the surrounding crags (**4.84**). Simulated light is also used in digital animation. Pixar's *Cars* experimented with rendering the look of colored lights reflected on metal and glass (**4.85**).

4.82

We're used to ignoring the illumination of our surroundings, so film lighting is easy to take for granted. Yet the power of a shot is centrally controlled by light quality, direction, source, and color. The filmmaker can manipulate and combine these factors to shape the viewer's experience in a great many ways. No component of mise-en-scene is more important than what Sternberg called "the drama and adventure of light."

Staging: Movement and Performance

When we think of a film director, we usually think of someone directing performers. The director is the person who says, "Stand over there," "Walk toward the camera," or "Show that you're holding back tears." In such ways, the director controls a major component of mise-en-scene: the figures we see onscreen. Typically the figure is a person, but it could be an animal (Lassie the collie, Balthasar the donkey), a robot, an object (**4.86**), or even a pure shape (**4.87**). Mise-en-scene allows all these entities to express feelings and thoughts; it can also dynamize them to create kinetic patterns (**4.88, 4.89**).

Cinema gains great freedom from the fact that here expression and movement aren't restricted to human figures. The filmmaker can breathe life into two-dimensional characters, such as Shrek or Daffy Duck. Puppets may be manipulated frame by frame through the technique of *stop-action* or *stop-motion* (**4.90**). In science fiction and fantasy movies, robots and fabulous monsters created as models can be scanned and movement added via computer manipulation (1.30). Even if the figures are fantastical, however, the filmmaker is obliged to stage their actions and construct their performances.

Acting and Actuality   Although abstract shapes and animated figures can become important in the mise-en-scene, the most familiar cases of figure expression and movement involve actors performing roles. An actor's performance consists of visual elements (appearance, gestures, facial expressions) and sound

4.83

4.82–4.83 Lighting without a motivated source. In *Ivan the Terrible,* a character's fear registers on his face (4.82), and this is underscored by a blue light that bursts onto him (4.83).

CONNECT TO THE BLOG
www.davidbordwell.net/blog

Our entry on "The Cross" talks about a kind of staging largely forgotten in this era of rapid cutting and close framing. We discuss how scenic details can be integrated into staging in "You are my density."

4.84

4.85

4.84–4.85 Digitally simulated lighting. In *The Golden Compass,* stark arctic sunshine from offscreen right falls as sidelight on the snow and the fighting bears (4.84). Simulated fill light was added to the onlookers and in areas of shading on the foreground bears. *Cars* puts on a virtuoso display of computer-simulated lighting, with neon signs reflecting in shiny surfaces as the cars cruise through their small-town street (4.85).

4.86

4.87

4.86–4.87 Controlling figure movement. In *The Hudsucker Proxy,* when the mailboy Norville proposes his new toy idea, the clicking balls on his boss's desktop inexplicably stop (4.86). The abstract film *Parabola* uses lighting and a pure background to emphasize shifting sculptural forms (4.87).

4.88

4.89

4.88–4.89 Stasis and violence in figure movement. In *Seven Samurai,* the samurai have won the battle with the bandits (4.88). Virtually the only movement in the frame is the driving rain, but the slouching postures of the men leaning on their spears express their tense weariness. By contrast, in *White Heat,* explosive movements and ferocious facial expressions present an image of psychotic rage as Cody Jarrett (James Cagney) learns of his mother's death (4.89).

4.90 Stop-motion animation. Ladislav Starevich's puppet film *The Mascot* includes a conversation between a devil and a thief, with subtle facial expressions and gestures created through animation.

(voice, effects). At times, of course, an actor may contribute only visual aspects, as in silent movies. In rare cases, an actor's performance may exist only on the sound track. In *A Letter to Three Wives,* Celeste Holm's character, Addie Ross, speaks a narration over the images but never appears on the screen.

Acting is often approached as a question of realism. But concepts of realistic acting have changed over film history. Today we may think that Hilary Swank in *Boys Don't Cry* and Heath Ledger and Jake Gyllenhaal in *Brokeback Mountain* give performances that are close to natural behavior. Yet in the early 1950s, the New York Actors Studio style, as exemplified by Marlon Brando's performances in *On the Waterfront* and *A Streetcar Named Desire,* was also thought to be extremely realistic. Fine though we may still find Brando's work, today his portrayals seem deliberate, heightened, and fairly unrealistic. Going back farther, post–World War II Italian Neorealist films were hailed as almost documentary depictions of Italian life (p. 478). But many of their performances now look as polished as those in Hollywood films. Major naturalistic performances of the 1970s, such as Robert De Niro's protagonist in *Taxi Driver,* seem quite stylized. Who can say what the acting in *Boys Don't Cry, Brokeback Mountain, Frozen River, Boyhood,* and other films will look like in a few decades?

There's another reason to be cautious in appealing to realism. Not all films try to achieve it. Since the performance an actor creates is part of the overall mise-en-scene, films contain a wide variety of acting styles. Instead of assuming that acting must be realistic, we should try to understand what kind of acting style the film is aiming at. If the film is best served by a nonrealistic performance, the skillful actor will strive to deliver that.

For example, comedy seldom strives for surface realism. In *All of Me* Steve Martin portrays a man whose body is suddenly inhabited on the right side by the soul of a woman who has just died. Martin used sudden changes of voice, along with acrobatic pantomime, to suggest a split body, half-male and half-female. The performance doesn't conform to realism, since the plot situation couldn't exist in the real world. In a comedy, however, Martin's performance was completely appropriate, and hilarious.

It isn't only comedies that encourage stylized performance. Fantasy films do, too, as we see in certain parts of *The Wizard of Oz.* (How would a real Wicked Witch behave?) In melodramas and action films from Hollywood, India, Hong Kong, and other traditions, exaggerated performances are a crucial source of the audience's pleasure. Viewers do not expect narrowly realistic acting from martial-arts stars Jet Li and Jackie Chan.

Finally, when we watch any fictional film, we are to some degree aware that the performances are the result of the actors' skills and decisions. (See "A Closer Look.") When we use the phrase "larger than life" to describe an effective performance, we

 CONNECT TO THE BLOG www.davidbordwell.net/blog

How can we analyze film acting? We make some suggestions, especially about silent-film performance, in "Acting up." The entry "Faces behind Facebook" considers actors' performances in *The Social Network.*

❝ I get impatient with many Hollywood films because there's this assumption that meaning or emotion is contained in those few square inches of an actor's face and I just don't see it that way at all. I think there's a power in withholding information, revealing things gradually. Letting the audience discover things within the frame in time, in the way they stand.❞

—Alison Maclean, director, *Crush*

A CLOSER LOOK

The Film Actor's Toolkit

We might think that the most important task facing an actor is speaking dialogue in a convincing and stirring way. Certainly, voice and delivery are very important in cinema, but considered in terms of mise-en-scene, the actor is always part of the overall visual design. Many film scenes contain little or no dialogue, but at every moment onscreen, the actor must be in character. The actor and director shape the performance pictorially.

Most of the time, film actors use their faces. This was most evident before movies had sound, and theorists of the silent film were full of praise for the subtle facial acting of Charlie Chaplin, Greta Garbo, and Lillian Gish. Since some happiness, fear, anger, and other facial expressions are understood easily across cultures, silent films could become popular around the world. Today, with mainstream films using many close-ups (see p. 46), actors' faces are hugely enlarged, and the performers must control their expressions minutely.

The most expressive parts of the face are the mouth, eyebrows, and eyes. All work together to signal how the character is responding to the dramatic situation. In *Jerry Maguire,* the accountant Dorothy Boyd accidentally meets Jerry at an airport baggage conveyor. She has a crush on him, partly because she admires the courageous mission statement he has issued to the sports agency that they work for. As he starts to back off from the statement, she eagerly quotes it from memory; Renée Zellwegger's earnest smile and admiring gaze suggest that she takes the issues more seriously than Jerry does **(4.91)**. This impression is confirmed when Jerry says, "Uh-huh" and studies her skeptically, his fixed smile signaling social politeness rather than genuine pride **(4.92)**. This encounter sets up one premise of the film—that Jerry's idealistic impulses will need constant shoring up, for he might at any moment slip back into being "a shark in a suit."

The eyes hold a special place in film. In any scene, crucial story information is conveyed by the direction of a character's glance, the use of the eyelids, and the shape of the eyebrows. One of Chaplin's most heart-rending moments comes in *City Lights,* when the blind flower girl, now sighted, suddenly realizes that he's her benefactor and we must find signs of hope in his eyes **(4.93)**.

Normally, we don't stare intently at the people we talk with. We glance away about half the time to gather our thoughts, and we blink 10–12 times a minute. But actors must learn to look directly at each other, locking eyes and seldom blinking. If an actor glances away from the partner in the conversation, it suggests distraction or evasion. If an actor blinks, it suggests a reaction to what is happening in the scene (surprise, or anxiety). Actors playing forceful characters often stare fixedly. Anthony Hopkins said this of playing Hannibal Lecter: "If you don't blink you can keep the audience mesmerized." (See 8.7, 8.9.) In our *Jerry Maguire* scene, the protagonists watch each other fixedly. When Jerry closes his eyes in response to Dorothy's praise, it indicates his nervousness about confronting the issues that his mission statement raised.

Thanks to facial expressions—eyes plus eyebrows plus mouth—actors can develop their characterizations across the film. *The Social Network* centers on two college friends, Mark Zuckerberg and Eduardo Savarin, who collaborate to create Facebook. Throughout the film Jesse Eisenberg plays Mark with knitted brows, squinting eyes, and a grimly set mouth, all suggesting his fierce concentration and competitiveness **(4.94)**. By contrast Andrew Garfield portrays the more trusting Eduardo with wide eyes, raised brows, and slightly bowed head **(4.95)**. In their climactic confrontation, during a deposition for the suit that Eduardo has filed against Mark, Eduardo's facial behavior has changed to a direct, frowning challenge **(4.96)**. This causes Mark to lower his head in embarrassment, an unusual reaction for the aggressive entrepreneur we've seen so far **(4.97)**.

Actors act with their bodies as well as their faces. How a character walks, stands, or sits conveys a great deal

4.91   **4.92**

4.91–4.92 Facial expressiveness in close-ups. Perky and sincere, Dorothy pledges allegiance to Jerry Maguire's idealistic memo (4.91). Jerry smiles politely, but his sideways glance and raised brows suggest that he is a bit put off by her earnestness (4.92).

4.93 Acting with the eyes. In the climax of *City Lights,* Chaplin nervously twirls a flower, so we can't see the shape of his mouth. We must read yearning in his brows and rapt, dark gaze.

4.94

4.95

4.96

4.97

4.94–4.97 Character domination through actors' expressions. Early in *The Social Network,* Mark insists that Eduardo invest more in Facebook. The actors' expressions establish Mark as a tough, demanding leader and Eduardo as more submissive (4.94–4.95). During the climactic deposition, Eduardo fights back facially, and Mark submits (4.96–4.97).

4.98

4.99

4.100

4.98–4.100 Extroverted acting for extravagant suffering. In *Tigre Reale,* Menichelli's right hand seizes her hair, as if pulling her head back in agony; but her body still expresses defiance, thrust forward and standing firm as the left hand grips her waist (4.98). As Menichelli begins to feel shame, she retreats toward the fireplace, turning from us and slumping in a way that suggests regret (4.99). She keeps her back to the camera as she withdraws, now a pathetic figure (4.100).

about personality and attitude. In fact, during the 18th and 19th centuries, *attitude* was used to refer to the way a person stood. Stage acting gave early film a repertoire of postures that could express a character's state of mind. In the 1916 Italian film *Tigre Reale* (*The Royal Tigress*), the diva Pina Menichelli plays a countess with a shady past. At one point, she confesses this in a florid attitude that expresses noble suffering **(4.98)**. While few actors today would resort to this stylized posture, early film audiences would have accepted it as vividly expressive, like a movement in dance. Menichelli plays the rest of the scene more quietly, but she still employs expressive attitudes **(4.99, 4.100)**.

Actors who use their bodies in more naturalistic ways will still exercise firm control. *Margin Call* centers on a financial crisis in an investment firm. During a break in the negotiations, three employees take a break by going onto the building's roof. Contrasting body behavior distinguishes the cautious Peter from the more imprudent Seth, both of whom differ from their heedless, almost suicidal boss Will **(4.101, 4.102)**.

The gestures of Chaplin, Menichelli, and Quinto show that hands are important tools of the film actor. Hands are to the body what eyes are to the face: They focus our attention and evoke the character's thoughts and feelings. Actress Maureen O'Hara said of Henry Fonda, "All he had to do was wag his little finger and he could steal a scene from anybody." A good example can be seen in the doomsday thriller *Fail-Safe*. Henry Fonda plays the U.S. president, who has learned that an American warplane has been accidentally sent to bomb the Soviet Union. Fonda stands erect at the phone as he hears distressing

A CLOSER LOOK

Continued

4.101

4.102

4.101–4.102 Character contrast through body language. Peter, the analyst who has discovered the firm's overinvestment, follows Will to the edge of the rooftop but, looking down, is startled by the height. As Zachary Quinto plays the moment, Peter shies back and throws out one arm (4.101). Peter's colleague Seth (Penn Badgley) follows, and comes forward to peer over the roof edge (4.102). Throughout the plot, Seth is drawn to risk. Their superior, Will (Paul Bettany), is indifferent to danger, as he will show shortly when he climbs onto the railing far above the city.

4.103

4.104

4.105

4.106

4.103–4.106 Acting as finger exercise. In *Fail-Safe*, the president stands erect at the phone as he hears distressing news about the plane's progress, and he hangs up with his left hand (4.103). The president pauses and rubs his fingers together thoughtfully (4.104), then he taps into the intercom with his right hand (4.105). As he waits, for a brief moment his left fingers waggle anxiously, betraying his nervous concern (4.106).

news about the plane's progress, and he hangs up with his left hand **(4.103–4.106).** By keeping most of the shot still and bare, director Sidney Lumet has given Fonda's fingers the main role, letting them express the president's measured prudence but also suggesting the strain of the crisis.

CONNECT TO THE BLOG
www.davidbordwell.net/blog

For more on how actors use their hands, see "Hand jive."
For more on eyes, see "Bette Davis eyelids."

CONNECT TO THE BLOG
www.davidbordwell.net/blog

Sometimes critics concentrate on acting to the exclusion of a film's other qualities, as we complain in "Good actors spell good acting." On the conventions governing award-winning performances, see "Good actors spell good acting, 2: Oscar bait."

seem to be acknowledging the actor's craft. In analyzing a particular film, we usually must go beyond assumptions about realism and consider the purposes that the actor's craft serves. How appropriate, we can ask, is the performance to the context established by the genre, the film's narrative, and the overall mise-en-scene? A performance, realistic or not, should be examined according to its function in the film's overall formal design.

Acting: Functions and Motivation   We can consider performance along two dimensions. A performance will be more or less *individualized,* and it will be more or less *stylized*. Often we have both in mind when we think of a realistic performance: It creates a unique character, and it does not seem too exaggerated or too underplayed. Marlon Brando's portrayal of Don Vito Corleone in *The Godfather* is quite individualized. Brando gives the Godfather a complex psychology, a distinctive appearance and voice, and a string of facial expressions and gestures that make him significantly different from the standard image of a gang boss. As for stylization, Brando keeps Don Vito in the middle range. His performance is neither flat nor flamboyant. He isn't impassive, but he doesn't chew the scenery either.

Yet this middle range, which we often identify with realistic performance, isn't the only option. On the individuality scale, films may create broader, more anonymous *types*. Classical Hollywood narrative was built on ideologically stereotyped roles: the Irish cop on the beat, the black servant, the Jewish pawnbroker, the wisecracking waitress or showgirl. Through *typecasting,* actors were selected and directed to conform to what audiences expected. Often, however, skillful performers gave these conventions a freshness and vividness. The 1920s Soviet filmmakers adapted this principle, which they called *typage.* Here the actor was expected to portray a typical representative of a social class or historical movement (**4.107, 4.108**).

Whether more or less typed, the performance can also be located on a continuum of stylization. A long tradition of film acting strives for an expressive naturalness, with actors speaking their lines with slightly more clarity and emotion than we usually find in everyday life. The director and the performer may choose to enhance this streamlined naturalness by adding specific physical actions. Frequent gestures and movements by the actors add plausibility to the humor of Woody Allen's films (**4.109**).

The actor is usually obliged to express emotion, but emotions come in many colors. Some are intense and burst out violently (**4.110**). Other emotions are masked, as when jealousy and suspicion are covered by excessive politeness (**4.111**). Sometimes emotional expression is broad and sweeping, almost operatic (**4.112**). And the same film may combine different degrees of emotional stylization. *Amadeus* contrasts a grotesque, giggling performance by Tom Hulce as Mozart with Murray Abraham's suave Salieri. The two acting styles sharpen the contrast between the older composer's decorous but dull music and the young man's offensive genius. In every film, the actor needs to blend the performance with the genre, the narrative, and the overall formal patterning.

Films like *Ivan the Terrible* and *Amadeus* create stylized performances through extroversion and exaggeration. The director can also explore the possibilities of very muted performances. Compared to normal practice, highly restrained acting can seem quite stylized. Robert Bresson is noted for such restrained performances. Using nonprofessional actors and drilling them in the details of the characters' physical actions, Bresson makes his actors nearly flat by conventional standards (**4.113, 4.114**). Although these performances may upset our expectations, we soon realize that such restraint focuses our attention on details of action we never notice in most movies.

Motion and Performance Capture
Since the creation of digitally generated characters Jar Jar Binks in *Star Wars: Episode 1—The Phantom Menace* in 1999 and Gollum in *The Lord of the Rings: The Two Towers* (2002), actors have had to learn new skills. In these early films, performers in special suits covered with dots were filmed digitally to form the basis for characters' movements. Soon CGI (computer-generated imagery) programs allowed more dense arrays of dots to capture smaller details of facial movement (4.112). The addition

4.107

4.108

4.107–4.108 A range of acting styles in the same film. The opening of Eisenstein's *Strike* presents the cartoonish cliché of the top-hatted capitalist (4.107), while in contrast the workers are presented as earnest and resolute (4.108).

4.109 Expressive naturalness in acting style. In *Hannah and Her Sisters,* Mia Farrow as Hannah, Diane Wiest as her sister Holly, and Carrie Fisher as their friend April set a table, chatting about the other guests as they do so.

4.110

4.111

4.112

4.110–4.112 Stylized acting and emotion. In *Winchester 73,* James Stewart's mild manner occasionally erupts into vengeful anger, revealing him as on the brink of psychosis (4.110). The exaggerated smiles and gestures in *Trouble in Paradise* are amusing because we know that the women, competing for the same man, are only pretending to be friends (4.111). Nikolai Cherkasov's dramatically raised arm and thrown-back head are appropriate to *Ivan the Terrible,* which creates a larger-than-life portrait of its hero (4.112).

4.113

4.114

4.113–4.114 Restrained acting. Playing the heroine of *Au Hasard Balthasar,* Anna Wiazemsky looks without expression at her would-be seducer, who wants her to get in his car (4.113). She glances downward, still without registering her thoughts, before sliding in (4.114).

of tiny cameras attached to the actors' heads permitted even subtler capture of expressions.

Now a distinction is made between *motion capture,* where the whole body is filmed, and *performance capture,* which concentrates on the face **(4.115, 4.116).** Motion capture can also be used on animals. Thanks to capture dots, ordinary horses can be transformed into fantastical creatures, as with *Avatar*'s six-legged Direhorses. Animated films like *The Polar Express, The Adventures of Tintin,* and *How to Train Your Dragon 2* use performance capture for their human characters.

In predigital days, actors would play fantasy characters with heavy prosthetics and ample makeup. Motion capture and performance capture make it easier for the actor to concentrate on the performance. As James Cameron explained:

> Actors have said to me, half jokingly but a little nervously, "Are you trying to replace actors?" And of course, the answer is no, we love actors. This whole thing is about acting. It's about creating these fantasy characters through the process of acting. What we're replacing is five hours in the makeup chair, having rubber glued all over your face.

Acting in the Context of Other Techniques By examining how an actor's performance functions within the overall film, we can also notice how acting blends with other film techniques. For instance, the actor is always a graphic element in the film, but some films underline this fact. In *The Cabinet of*

4.115

4.116

4.115–4.116 Motion and performance capture. In the high-tech studio used for *Avatar,* actors wear full-body motion-capture suits (4.115). For performance capture of Sam Worthington, green dots cover the most expressive areas of the face (4.116). A miniature camera, with rows of small LED bulbs trained on his face, adds extra light as it records his shifting expressions.

4.117

4.118

4.117–4.118 The actor as graphic element. In *The Cabinet of Dr. Caligari,* Cesare's body echoes the tilted tree trunks (4.117), his arms and hands their branches and leaves. In *Breathless,* Jean Seberg's face is linked to a Renoir painting (4.118). Does she give an inexpressive performance or an enigmatic one?

Dr. Caligari, Conrad Veidt's dancelike portrayal of the somnambulist Cesare makes him blend in with the graphic elements of the setting **(4.117).** The graphic design of this scene in *Caligari* typifies the systematic distortion characteristic of German Expressionism (pp. 463–466).

In *Breathless,* director Jean-Luc Godard juxtaposes Jean Seberg's face with a print of a Renoir painting **(4.118).** We might think that Seberg is giving a bland performance here, for she simply poses in the frame and turns her head. Indeed, her acting in the entire film may seem fairly flat. Yet her face and demeanor are appropriate for her role, a capricious American woman unfathomable to her Parisian boyfriend.

A performance may be shaped by editing as well. Because a film is shot over a period of time, actors perform in bits, with separate shots recording different portions of a scene. This process can work to the filmmaker's advantage. If there are alternate takes of each shot, the editor can select the best gestures and expressions and create a composite performance better than any sustained performance is likely to be. By adding sound and other shots, the filmmaker can build up the performance still further. Sometimes a performance will be created almost wholly in postproduction. The director may simply tell an actor to stare offscreen, wide-eyed. If the next shot shows a hand with a gun, we are likely to think the actor is depicting fear effectively.

 CONNECT TO THE BLOG
www.davidbordwell.net/blog

When digital technology is involved, where does the actor's performance leave off and the special effects begin? We consider the question in "Motion-capturing an Oscar."

4.119

4.120

4.119–4.120 Performance in long shot and close-up. *The Spider's Stratagem*: In long shot, the actors' manner of walking helps characterize them (4.119). The stiff, upright way in which the heroine holds her parasol is one of the main facets of Alida Valli's performance. In a closer framing, her performance displays detailed eye and lip movements (4.120).

CONNECT TO THE BLOG
www.davidbordwell.net/blog

For more on how shot scale can affect performance, see, "Where did the two-shot go? Here."

4.121 Editing to create a performance. In *Aliens*, editing makes it seem that Jonesy is reacting angrily to something in the scene.

Camera techniques also create a controlling context for acting. Film acting, as you know, differs from theatrical acting. In a theater, we are usually at a considerable distance from the actor on the stage. We certainly can never get as close to the theater actor as the camera can put us in a film. For that reason, we're inclined to think that the film actor must always underplay—that is, act in a more restrained fashion than stage acting would require. But recall that the camera can be at *any* distance from the figure. Filmed from very far away, the actor is a dot on the screen—much smaller than an actor on stage seen from the back of the balcony. Filmed from very close, the actor's tiniest eye movement may be revealed.

Thus the film actor must behave differently than the stage actor does, but not always by being more restrained. Rather, she or he must be able to *adjust to each type of camera distance*. If the actor is far from the camera, he or she may have to gesture broadly or move around to be seen as acting at all. But if the camera and actor are inches apart, a twitch of a mouth muscle will come across clearly. Between these extremes, there is a whole range of adjustments to be made.

Often a shot will concentrate on either the actor's facial expression or on bodily movement. In most close shots, the face will be emphasized, and so the actor will have to control eyes, brows, and mouth quite precisely. But if the camera is farther back, or the actor is turned away from us, gestures and body language become the center of attention. In all, both the staging of the action and the camera's distance from the action control how we understand the performances (**4.119, 4.120**).

Matters of context are particularly important when the performers are not actors, or even human beings. Framing, editing, and other film techniques can make trained animals give appropriate performances. Jonesy, the cat in *Aliens,* seems threatening because his hissing movement has been emphasized by lighting, framing, editing, and the sound track (**4.121**).

As with every element of a film, acting offers an unlimited range of creative choices. It cannot be judged on a universal scale outside the context of the entire film's form.

Putting It All Together: Mise-en-Scene in Space and Time

Back in Chapter 2, we argued that viewers try to blend what they see and hear into a larger pattern (p. 54). This process starts at the level of the shot, when we have to assemble information into a coherent space and time. And creating that coherence requires that the filmmaker guide us to certain areas of the frame.

How do we know that viewers scan the frame for important information? The psychologist Tim Smith asked viewers to wear lightweight glasses that could track their eye movements and then showed them a scene from *There Will Be Blood.* The eye movements were recorded by computers and mapped onto the film sequence, so Smith could study how the viewers' attention shifted within the scene. There was remarkable agreement among the subjects about where to look at any moment. The primary points of attention were, as we might expect, items crucial to building up a story: faces and hand gestures (**4.122, 4.123**). The characters' dialogue was important, too; the scan-paths revealed that people tend to look at the person speaking in the shot.

Before viewers can follow the story, recognize the emotional tenor of the scene, respond with their own emotions, and reflect on possible meanings, they must notice certain things in the frame. In setting up a shot, the filmmaker makes some things more salient than others. We noticed this happening when we examined how Tarantino nudged us to watch Colonel Landa in the scene from *Inglourious Basterds.* Thinking like a filmmaker means, to a large extent, finding ways to guide the viewer's eye. In other words, directors direct attention.

4.122

4.123

4.122–4.123 Scanning the shot. Tim Smith and his colleagues tracked several subjects' eye movements during a single shot of *There Will Be Blood*. Here is one frame from the sequence, as the characters examine a map (4.122). Smith's "peekthrough heatmap" graphically indicates the areas of interest for the eight viewers watching at that moment (4.123). The black surround represents areas not watched by anyone. Areas of attention are lit up, and the hotter the color, the more viewers are looking at that spot. At this instant, most viewers were concentrating on Sunday's face and hand, with two viewers looking at the man facing front behind him. As filmmakers might expect, faces, hands, and dialogue have commanded viewers' attention.

 CONNECT TO THE BLOG
www.davidbordwell.net/blog

For more on Tim Smith's eye-tracking experiments, see "Watching you watch *There Will Be Blood.*"

CREATIVE DECISIONS

Mise-en-Scene in a Sequence from L'Avventura

To get a sense of the filmmaker's creative options in guiding our eye, let's look at another sequence. In Michelangelo Antonioni's *L'Avventura*, Sandro and Claudia are searching for Anna, who has mysteriously vanished. Anna is Claudia's friend and Sandro's lover, but during their search, they've begun to drift from their goal of finding her. They've also begun a love affair. In the town of Noto, they stand on a church rooftop near the bells, and Sandro says he regrets giving up architectural design. Claudia is encouraging him to return to his profession when he suddenly asks her to marry him.

She's startled and confused, and Sandro comes toward her. She is turned away from us. At first, only Sandro's expression is visible as he reacts grimly to her plea, "Why can't things be simpler?" **(4.124).** Claudia twists her arms around the bell rope, then turns away from him, toward us, grasping the rope and fluttering her hand. Now we can see that she's quite distraught. Sandro, a bit uneasy, turns away as she says anxiously, "I'd like to see things clearly" **(4.125).**

Brief though it is, this exchange shows how the tools of mise-en-scene—setting, costume, lighting, performance, and staging—can work together smoothly. We've considered them separately in order to examine the contribution each one makes, but in any shot, they mesh. They unfold on the screen in space and time, fulfilling several functions.

Most basically, the filmmaker has to guide the audience's attention to the important areas of the image. The filmmaker also wants to build up our interest by

> " The audience is only going to look at the most overriding thing in the frame. You must take charge of and direct their attention. It's also the principle of magic: what is the single important thing? Make it easy for them to see it, and you're doing your job."
>
> —David Mamet, director

4.124

4.125

4.124–4.125 Frontality gets attention. In *L'Avventura*, first Claudia has her back to the camera (4.124), and then Sandro does (4.125). Each shift is timed to show us a crucial facial reaction.

arousing curiosity and suspense. And the filmmaker tries to add expressive qualities, giving the shot an emotional coloration. Mise-en-scene helps the filmmaker achieve all these purposes.

How did Antonioni guide our attention in the Claudia–Sandro exchange? First, we're watching the figures, not the railing behind them. Based on the story so far, we expect Sandro and Claudia to be the objects of interest. At other points in the film, Antonioni makes them tiny figures in massive urban or seaside landscapes. Here, however, his mise-en-scene keeps their intimate interchange foremost in our minds.

Consider the first image merely as a two-dimensional picture. Both Sandro and Claudia stand out against the pale sky and the darker railing. They're also mostly curved shapes—heads and shoulders—and so they contrast with the geometrical regularity of the balcony. In the first frame, light strikes Sandro's face and suit from the right, picking him out against the rails. His dark hair is well positioned to make his head stand out against the sky. Claudia, a blonde, stands out against the railing and sky less vividly, but her polka-dot blouse creates a distinctive pattern. And considered only as a picture, the shot roughly balances the two figures, Sandro in the left half and Claudia in the right.

It's hard to think of the shot as simply two-dimensional, though. We instinctively see it as portraying a space that we could move around in. Claudia seems closer to us because her body masks things farther away, a spatial cue called *overlap*. She's also somewhat larger in the frame than Sandro, which reinforces our sense that she's closer. The rope slices across the bottom third of the frame, separating the couple (overlap again). Sandro himself overlaps the railing, which in turn overlaps the sky and the town beyond. We get a sense of distinct planes of space, layers lying closer to or farther from us. Costume, lighting, setting, and figure placement create this sense of a three-dimensional arena for the action.

Antonioni has used mise-en-scene to emphasize his characters and their interaction. But that interaction unfolds in time, and it gives him an opportunity to guide our attention while building up suspense and expressing emotion. Claudia is turned away from us when Sandro presses her to marry him, and the rope is taut between them (4.124). How will she respond?

Antonioni starts by giving Claudia a bit of business. She twists the rope around her arms and slips it over her back. This could be a hint that she's drawn to Sandro's proposal. At the same time, she hesitates. For as soon as he presses her, she turns away from him (4.125).

We know that faces give us access to characters' thoughts and emotions. Another filmmaker might have had Claudia already facing us when Sandro asked, so we'd see her response immediately. Antonioni instead makes things uncertain for a moment. He conceals Claudia's reaction and then lets her turn toward us. To make sure that we watch her and not Sandro at this moment, Antonioni has him turn away when she gestures and speaks ("I'd like to see things clearly"). Our attention is riveted on Claudia.

Soon enough, Sandro turns back toward the camera, so we can see his reaction, but already Claudia's anxiety has flashed out at us. Her mixed response to Sandro's proposal—attraction (sliding under the bell rope) and uncertainty (turning away tensely)—has been presented to us concretely.

This is only one moment in a complex scene, but it shows how various elements of mise-en-scene can cooperate to create a specific effect: the delayed revelation of a character's emotion. That revelation depended on the director's choices about what to show us at particular points. Once we've been guided to notice certain things, we can build up larger meanings and particular feelings. Let's now look at some specific options for using mise-en-scene to shape our sense of a film's space and time.

Space

Screen Space   In many respects, a film shot resembles a painting. It presents a flat array of colors and shapes. Before we even start to understand the image as a three-dimensional space, mise-en-scene offers many cues for guiding our attention and emphasizing elements in the frame.

Take something as simple as balancing the shot. Filmmakers often try to distribute various points of interest evenly around the frame. They assume that viewers will concentrate more on the upper half of the frame, probably because that's where we tend to find characters' faces. Since the film frame is a horizontal rectangle, the director usually tries to balance the right and left halves. The extreme type of such balancing is *bilateral symmetry.* In the battle scene in *Life on a String,* Chen Kaige stages one shot symmetrically **(4.126).**

More common than such near-perfect symmetry is a loose balancing of the shot's left and right regions. The simplest way to achieve compositional balance is to center the frame on the human body. Filmmakers often place a single figure at the center of the frame and minimize distracting elements at the sides, as in **4.127.** Many of our earlier illustrations display this flexible balance. Other shots may counterweight two or more elements, encouraging our eye to move back and forth, as in **4.128** and our *L'Avventura* dialogue (4.124, 4.125).

Balanced composition is the norm, but unbalanced shots can also create strong effects. In *Bicycle Thieves,* the composition emphasizes the father's new job by massing most of the figures on the right **(4.129).** A more drastic example occurs in Michelangelo Antonioni's *Il Grido* **(4.130),** where two strong elements, the hero and a tree trunk, are grouped on the right side of the shot. The shot creates a powerful urge for the audience to see the woman's hidden face.

Sometimes the filmmaker will leave the shots a little unbalanced, in order to prime our expectation that something will change position in the frame. The cinema of

4.126 Symmetrical framing. A limited palette emphasizes this symmetrical composition in *Life on a String.*

4.127

4.128

4.127–4.128 Balancing the frame. *Mars Attacks!:* centering a single character (4.127) and balancing two (4.128).

4.129–4.130 Deliberately unbalanced composition. In *Bicycle Thieves,* the men on the right don't balance the son (4.129), but he seems even more vulnerable by being such an ineffective visual counterweight. In *Il Grido,* instead of balancing the couple, the composition centers the man (4.130). If there were no tree in the frame, the shot would still be somewhat weighted to the right, but the unexpected vertical of the trunk makes that side even heavier.

4.129

4.130

4.131

4.132

4.133

4.134

4.131–4.134 Balancing and rebalancing. From quite early in cinema history, filmmakers used unbalanced compositions to prepare the viewer for new narrative developments. In Yevgenii Bauer's *The Dying Swan* (1916), the young ballerina receives a tiara from an admirer (4.131). She studies herself in a mirror, in a composition that makes the doorway more visible (4.132). As the ballerina lowers her arm, the door opens and her father appears (4.133). He comes to the front area and balances the composition (4.134).

4.135 Contrast guides attention. In V. I. Pudovkin's *Mother,* the spectator concentrates on the man's face rather than on the darkness surrounding it.

the 1910s offers intriguing examples. Very often a doorway in the back of the set allowed the director to show that new characters were entering the scene, but then figures closer to the camera had to be rearranged to permit a clear entrance. The result was a subtle unbalancing and rebalancing of the composition (**4.131–4.134**). In Chapter 6, we'll see how cutting can balance two shots containing relatively unbalanced compositions.

The filmmaker can guide our attention by use of another time-tested strategy, the principle of contrast. Our eyes are biased toward registering differences and changes. In most black-and-white films, light costumes or brightly lit faces stand out while darker areas tend to recede (**4.135**). If there are several light shapes in the frame, we'll tend to look from one to the other. But if the background is light, black elements will become prominent, as Sandro's hair does in our *L'Avventura* scene (4.124). The same principles work for color. A bright costume or bit of set-ting shown against a more subdued setting is likely to draw the eye (**4.136**). Another pertinent principle is that when lightness values are equal, warm colors in the red-orange-yellow range tend to attract attention, while cool colors like purple and green are less prominent (**4.137**).

4.136

4.137

4.136–4.137 Bright and warm colors get attention. In Jiří Menzel's *Larks on a String,* a propaganda display about happy workers stands out against the earthy grays and blacks of the junkyard (4.136). In Yilmaz Güney's *Yol,* the setting and the characters' outfits are warm in hue, but the hot pink vest of the man in the central middle ground helps make him the primary object of attention (4.137).

Color contrasts don't have to be huge, because we're sensitive to small differences. What painters call a *limited palette* involves a few colors in the same range, as in our earlier example from Fellini's *Casanova* (4.40). Peter Greenaway's *The Draughtsman's Contract* employs a limited palette from the cooler end of the spectrum **(4.138).** An extreme case of the principle is sometimes called **monochromatic color design.** Here the filmmaker emphasizes a single color, varying it only in purity or lightness. We've already seen an example of monochromatic mise-en-scene in the white décor and costumes of *THX 1138* (4.41). In a monochromatic design, even a fleck of a contrasting color will catch the viewer's attention **(4.139).**

Film has one resource that painting lacks. Our tendency to notice visual differences is strongly aroused when the image includes *movement.* In the *L'Avventura* scene, the turning of Claudia's head became a major event, but we are sensitive to far smaller motions in the frame. Normally, for instance, we ignore the movement of scratches and dust on a film. But in David Rimmer's *Watching for the Queen,* in which the first image is an absolutely static photograph **(4.140),** the jumping bits of dust on the film draw our attention. In **4.141,** from Yasujiro Ozu's *Record of a*

4.138

4.139

4.138–4.139 Limited color palettes. *The Draughtsman's Contract* uses a limited palette of green, black, and white (4.138). The color design of *Aliens* is dominated by gray and blue metallic tones, so even a dingy yellow can mark the stiltlike loader as an important prop in the narrative (4.139).

4.140

4.141

4.140–4.141 Minimal motion. *Watching for the Queen* emphasizes scratches and dust (4.140), while flapping paper catches our attention in *Record of a Tenement Gentleman* (4.141).

CONNECT TO THE BLOG
www.davidbordwell.net/blog

Whether you see *Coraline* in a 3D or a 2D version, it has some fascinating use of depth cues to differentiate the heroine's real life and the alternative life she finds behind a door in her room. We take a look at these in "Coraline, cornered."

Tenement Gentleman, many items compete for our attention. But the moment that a scrap of newspaper flaps in the wind, it immediately attracts the eye because it is the only motion in the frame.

When several moving elements appear on the screen, we are likely to shift our attention among them, according to other cues or depending on our expectations about which one is most important for the narrative. In **4.142,** from John Ford's *Young Mr. Lincoln,* Lincoln is moving much less than the dancers we see in front of him. Yet as the film's major character he is framed centrally, and the dancers pass rapidly through the frame. As a result, we are likely to concentrate on his gestures and facial expressions, however slight they might be compared to the energetic action in the foreground.

Scene Space   Looking at a film image as a two-dimensional picture helps us appreciate the artistry of filmmakers, but it requires some effort. We find it easier to immediately see the shapes on the screen as presenting a three-dimensional area, like the spaces we live in. The elements of the image that create this impression are called *depth cues.*

Depth cues are what enabled us to understand the encounter of Sandro and Claudia as taking place in a realistic space, with layers and volumes. We develop our understanding of depth cues from our experience of real locales and from our earlier experience with pictorial media. In cinema, depth cues are provided by lighting, setting, costumes, and staging—that is, by all the aspects of mise-en-scene.

Depth cues suggest that a space has both *volume* and several distinct *planes.* When we speak of an object as having volume, we mean that it is solid and occupies a three-dimensional area. A film suggests volume by shape, shading, and movement. In 4.118 and **4.143,** we don't see the actors as flat cutouts, like paper dolls. The shapes of those heads and shoulders suggest solid people. The attached shadows on the faces suggest the curves and recesses of the actors' features and give a modeling effect. We assume that if Jean Seberg in 4.118 turned her head, we would see a profile. Thus we use our knowledge of objects in the world to discern volume in filmic space.

An abstract film, because it can use shapes that are not familiar objects, can create compositions without a sense of volume. The shapes in **4.144** give us no depth cues for volume—they are unshaded, do not have a recognizable shape, and do not move in such a way as to reveal new views that suggest roundness.

Depth cues also pick out *planes* within the image. Planes are the layers of space occupied by persons or objects. Planes are described according to how close to or far away from the camera they are: foreground, middle ground, background.

Only a completely blank screen has a single plane. Whenever a shape, even an abstract one, appears, we will perceive it as being in front of a background. In 4.144, the four red S shapes are actually painted right on the frame surface, as is the

4.142 Centered framing. Central position emphasizes a background figure in *Young Mr. Lincoln.*

4.143 Volume in scene space. Shading and shape suggest volume in Dreyer's *La Passion de Jeanne d'Arc.*

4.144 Flattened space. Norman McLaren's *Begone, Dull Care,* provides no depth cues for volume.

lighter, textured area. Yet the textured area seems to lie behind the four shapes. The space here has only two planes, as in decorated wallpaper. This example, like our *L'Avventura* scene, suggests that one of the most basic depth cues is **overlap.** The curling S shapes have edges that overlap the background plane, block our vision of it, and thus seem to be closer to us.

Through overlap, a great many planes can be defined. In 4.62, from Jean-Luc Godard's *La Chinoise,* three distinct planes are displayed: the background of fashion cutouts, the woman's face that overlaps that background, and her hand, which overlaps her lower face. In the three-point lighting approach, edge lighting accentuates the overlap of planes by emphasizing the contour of the object, thus sharply distinguishing it from the background. (See again 4.65, 4.71, and 4.72.)

Color differences also create overlapping planes. Because cool or pale colors tend to recede, filmmakers commonly use them for background planes such as setting. Similarly, because warm or saturated colors tend to come forward, such hues are often employed for costumes or other foreground elements **(4.145).** (See also 4.30 and 4.38.) In *One Froggy Evening* **(4.146),** the luminous yellow of the umbrella and the frog's brilliant green skin make him stand out against the darker red curtain and the earth tones of the stage floor.

Because of the eye's sensitivity to differences, even quite muted color contrasts can suggest three-dimensional space. In *L'Argent* (4.21–4.23), Robert Bresson uses a limited, cool palette and relatively flat lighting. Yet the compositions pick out several planes by means of overlapping slightly different masses of black, tan, and light blue. Our shot from *Casanova* (4.40) articulates planes by means of slightly differing shades of red. By contrast, a filmmaker may want to minimize color differences and depth cues in order to create a flatter, more abstract composition **(4.147).**

In cinema, *movement* is one of the most important depth cues, since it strongly suggests both planes and volumes (4.142). **Aerial perspective,** or the hazing of more distant planes, is yet another depth cue. Typically, our eyes and brain assume that sharper outlines, clearer textures, and purer colors belong to foreground elements. In landscape shots, the blurring and graying of distant planes can be caused by natural atmospheric haze **(4.148).** Even when such haze is a minor factor, our vision typically assigns strong color contrasts to the foreground, as in the *Sambizanga* shot (4.145). In addition, very often lighting is manipulated in conjunction with lens focus to blur the background planes **(4.149).**

In **4.150,** the mise-en-scene provides several depth cues: overlap of edges, cast shadows, and **size diminution.** That is, figures and objects farther away from us are seen to get proportionally smaller. This reinforces our sense of seeing a deep space with considerable distances between the planes.

The same illustration dramatically displays *linear perspective.* We will consider perspective relations in more detail in the next chapter, since they derive as much from properties of the camera lens as they do from mise-en-scene. For now, we can simply note that a strong impression of depth emerges when parallel lines converge at a distant vanishing point. *Central* perspective is exemplified in 4.138 from *The Draughtsman's Contract.* *Off-center* linear perspective is illustrated in 4.150, in which the vanishing point is not the geometrical center of the frame.

All of these depth cues are *monocular,* which means that the illusion of depth requires input from only one eye. *Stereopsis* is a binocular depth cue. It results from the fact that our two eyes see the world from slightly different angles. In two-dimensional films, there is a single lens and thus no stereoptic effect. Three-dimensional

4.145

4.146

4.145–4.146 Warm color for the foreground. In Sarah Maldoror's *Sambizanga,* the heroine's dress has very warm and fairly saturated colors, making it stand out distinctly against the pale background (4.145). Brilliant colors emphasize extreme depth in Chuck Jones's *One Froggy Evening* (4.146).

4.147 Flattening space for expressive effect. Marjane Satrapi and Vincent Paronnaud's animated film *Persepolis* doesn't differentiate the schoolgirls' costumes by edge lighting or color differences. The result is a mass of black. Combined with the students' repetitive gestures, the image suggests that the school system demands conformity.

4.148 Aerial perspective through atmospheric effects. Fog emphasizes the distance between the foreground and background trees in Güney's *The Wall.*

4.149 Aerial perspective through lighting. In *The Charge of the Light Brigade,* aerial perspective is artificially created by diffused lighting of the background and a lack of clear focus behind the officer in the foreground.

4.150 Size diminution. Steep size diminution emphasizes depth in Straub and Huillet's *The Chronicle of Anna Magdalena Bach.*

cinema uses two lenses, imitating the separation of our eyes. The glasses used for viewing 3D films direct different visual information to each eye, creating a stronger illusion of depth than monocular depth cues can render. Stereopsis is a depth cue rendered by cinematography rather than mise-en-scene, so we'll talk about it more in the next chapter.

In many of the examples already given, you may have noticed that mise-en-scene serves not simply to direct our attention to foreground elements but rather to create a dynamic relation between foreground and background. In 4.62, for instance, Godard keeps our attention on the whole composition by using prominent backgrounds. Here the pictures behind the actress's head lead us to scan the various small shapes quickly.

The *La Chinoise* shot is a **shallow-space** composition. In such shots, the mise-en-scene suggests comparatively little depth, and the closest and most distant planes seem only slightly separated. The opposite tendency is **deep-space** composition, in which a significant distance seems to separate planes. Our example from *The Chronicle of Anna Magdalena Bach* (4.150) exemplifies deep-space mise-en-scene. Often a director creates a deep-space composition by making the foreground plane quite large and the background plane quite distant **(4.151).**

Shallow and deep mise-en-scene are relative concepts. Most compositions present a moderately deep space, falling between the extremes we've just considered. Sometimes a filmmaker manipulates depth cues to make a space appear deeper or shallower than it really is—creating an optical illusion **(4.152).**

4.151 Deep-space composition. Several scenes of Wajda's *Ashes and Diamonds* create large foregrounds and distant background planes.

4.152 Playing with depth cues. Leos Carax creates an optical illusion in *Boy Meets Girl* by making the painted advertisement seem to thrust out into the space inhabited by the boy.

At this point, you might want to return to shots illustrated earlier in this chapter. You'll notice that these images use depth cues of overlap, movement, cast shadows, aerial perspective, size diminution, and linear perspective to create distinctive foreground/background relations.

CREATIVE DECISIONS

Mise-en-Scene in Two Shots from Day of Wrath

The fact that our vision is sensitive to differences allows filmmakers to guide our understanding of the mise-en-scene. All the cues to story space interact with one another, working to emphasize narrative elements, direct our attention, and set up dynamic relations among areas of screen space. We can see this interaction clearly in two shots from Carl Dreyer's *Day of Wrath.*

In the first shot, the heroine, Anne, is standing before a grillwork panel **(4.153).** She isn't speaking, but since she is a major character in the film, the narrative already directs us to her. Setting, lighting, costume, and figure expression create pictorial cues that confirm our expectations. The setting yields a pattern of horizontal and vertical lines that intersect in the delicate curves of Anne's face and shoulders. The lighting yields a patch of brightness on the right half of the frame and a patch of darkness on the left, creating pictorial balance. Anne is the meeting point of these two areas. Her face is modeled by the relatively strong key lighting from the right, a little top lighting on her hair, and relatively little fill light. Anne's black dress punctuated by a white collar and her black cap edged with white further emphasize her face.

The shot is comparatively shallow, displaying two major planes with little distance between them. The background sets off the most important element, Anne. The rigid geometrical grid in the rear makes Anne's slightly sad face the most expressive element in the frame, thus encouraging our eye to pause there. In addition, the composition divides the screen space horizontally, with the grid pattern running across the top half and the dark, severe vertical of Anne's dress dominating the lower half. As is common, the upper zone is the stronger because the character's head and shoulders occupy it. Anne's figure is positioned slightly off center, but with her face turned to compensate for the vacant area on the right. (Imagine how unbalanced the shot would look if she were turned to face us squarely and the same amount of space were left empty on the right.) Thus compositional balance reinforces the shot's emphasis on Anne's expression. Without using movement, Dreyer has channeled our attention by means of lines and shapes, lights and darks, and the foreground and background relations in the mise-en-scene.

In the second example, also from *Day of Wrath,* Dreyer coaxes our attention into a to-and-fro movement **(4.154).** Again, the plot guides us, since the characters and the cart are crucial narrative elements. Sound helps, too, since Martin is at the moment explaining to Anne that the wood in the cart will fuel the witch-burning. But mise-en-scene also plays a role. Size diminution and cast shadows establish basic foreground/background relations, with Anne and Martin on the front plane and the cart of wood in the background. The space is comparatively deep (though the foreground is not as exaggeratedly close as that in *Ashes and Diamonds,* 4.151). The prominence of the couple and the cart is reinforced by line, shape, and lighting contrasts. The figures are defined by hard edges and by dark costumes within the predominantly bright setting. Unlike most shots, this puts the human figures in the lower half of the frame, which gives that zone an unusual importance. The composition thus creates a vertical balance, counterweighting the cart with the couple. Were Tim Smith to test his viewers' scanning on this shot, we'd expect eye movements glancing up and down between the two objects of our attention.

CONNECT TO THE BLOG
www.davidbordwell.net/blog

For our thoughts on some digital 3D films, see "A turning point in digital projection?"; "Bwana Beowulf"; "Do not forget to return your 3D glasses"; and "Adieu au language: $2 + 2 \times 3D$."

CONNECT TO THE BLOG
www.davidbordwell.net/blog

For a variety of staging options, in both shallow space and depth, see "Gradations of emphasis, starring Glenn Ford" and "How to watch *Fantômas,* and why." "*Dial M for Murder*: Hitchcock frets not his narrow room" analyzes how Hitchcock uses 3D to stage nearly all of a film in one apartment.

4.153

4.154

4.153–4.154 Concentrating our attention. *Day of Wrath*: Highlighting a single figure (4.153) and dividing attention between foreground and background (4.154).

4.155

4.156

4.155–4.156 Color and composition. An apparently simple shot from *An Autumn Afternoon* employs several depth cues (4.155) and harks back to the striped smokestacks seen at the beginning (4.156).

Similar processes are at work in color films. In one shot of Yasujiro Ozu's *An Autumn Afternoon* (**4.155**), our attention is concentrated on the bride in the center foreground. Many depth cues are at work. Overlap locates the two figures in two foreground planes, setting them against a series of more distant planes. Aerial perspective makes the foliage outside somewhat out of focus. Movement creates depth when the bride lowers her head. Perspective diminution makes the more distant objects smaller. The woman's face and the bright silver, red, and gold bridal costume stand out strikingly against the muted colors of the background planes. Moreover, the colors lead us to recall a red-and-silver motif that appeared in the first shot of the film (**4.156**).

In looking at a shot, we're more aware of *what* we see than *how* we see it. To think like a filmmaker, though, we need to reflect on that *how*. The filmmaker arranges shapes and colors on the two-dimensional screen. He or she also controls depth cues that suggest three dimensions. The filmmaker uses those patterns to activate what is most important at each moment. Mise-en-scene structures space in ways that guide, and sometimes dazzle, our eyes.

Time

Cinema is an art of time as well as space. So we shouldn't be surprised to find that many of our examples of two-dimensional composition and three-dimensional scenic space have unfolded over time. The director's control over mise-en-scene governs not only *what* we see but *when* we see it and for how long. In our *L'Avventura* scene between Sandro and Claudia on the rooftop (4.124, 4.125), the timing of the characters' movements—Sandro turning away just as Claudia turns toward us—contributes to the effect of a sudden, sharp revelation of her anxiety.

The director shapes the speed and direction of movement within the shot. Since our eyes are attuned to noticing changes, we can pick up the slightest cues. In **4.157,** from Chantal Akerman's *Jeanne Dielman, 23 quai du Commerce, 1080 Bruxelles,* the protagonist simply peels potatoes. This feminist film traces, in painstaking detail, the everyday routines of a Belgian housewife. The composition of this shot strongly centers Jeanne, and no competing movements distract us from her steady and efficient preparation of a meal. The same rhythm is carried throughout the film, so that when she does start to vary her habits, we are prepared to notice even the slight errors she makes under emotional pressure.

A far busier shot is **4.158,** from Busby Berkeley's *42nd Street.* This overhead view presents strongly opposed movements. The central and outer rings of dancers circle in one direction, while the second ring turns in a contrary direction. The dancers also swing strips of shiny cloth back and forth. The result is a partially abstract composition, but it's easy to grasp because the movement of the wheels within wheels has a geometrical clarity.

The dancers in *42nd Street* are synchronized to a considerable degree, but **4.159,** from Jacques Tati's *Play Time,* contains movements of differing speeds, with different visual accents. Moreover, they occur on different planes and follow contrasting trajectories. These diverse movements accord with Tati's tendency to cram his compositions with gags that compete for our attention.

As we have already seen, we scan any film frame for information. This scanning brings time sharply into play. Only a very short shot forces us to try to take in the image all at once. In most shots, we get an initial overall impression that creates formal expectations. These expectations are quickly modified as our eye roams around the frame.

As we'd expect, our scanning of the shot is strongly affected by the presence of movement. A static

4.157 Movement cues. Slow, quiet movements of the actor in *Jeanne Dielman, 23 quai du Commerce, 1080 Bruxelles* enable the audience to detect even slight changes.

4.158 Strong, synchronized movements. In *42nd Street,* the shot is busy but the movements are synchronized.

4.159 Vivid, competing movements. The competing rhythms of movement in a busy shot from *Play Time* divide the audience's attention around the frame.

composition may keep pulling our attention back to a single element, as our first shot from *Day of Wrath* does with Anne's face (4.153). In contrast, a composition emphasizing movement may use the movement's speed or direction to guide our glance. In the second image from *Day of Wrath* (4.154), Anne and Martin are turned from us and are standing still. Thus the single moving thing in the frame—the cart—catches our attention. But when Martin speaks and turns, we look back at the couple, then back at the cart, and so on, in a shuttling, dynamic shift of attention.

Our time-bound process of scanning involves not only looking to and fro across the screen but also, in a sense, looking into its depths. A deep-space composition will often use background events to create expectations about what is about to happen in the foreground. "Composing in depth isn't simply a matter of pictorial richness," British director Alexander Mackendrick has remarked. "It has value in the narrative of the action, the pacing of the scene. Within the same frame, the director can organize the action so that preparation for what will happen next is seen in the background of what is happening now."

Our example from *The Dying Swan* (4.131–4.134) illustrates Mackendrick's point. The same principle is used in **4.160–4.162,** from *Three Kings.* Here the

4.160

4.161

4.160–4.162 Movements arouse narrative expectations. In this shot from *Three Kings,* Chief Elgin comes in to tell the partying GIs that their superior is coming. Normally, when a character is looking offscreen, he or she is placed a little off center, leaving an empty space to imply the area that the person is looking at. (See the shot of Anne, 4.153.) But Elgin is decentered in a different way; here the space on the right side sits empty (4.160). That makes the tent flap behind him prominent. Without being aware of it, we're prepared for some action to develop there. Abruptly, the superior officer bursts into the background (4.161). He strides forward, which is always a powerful way to command the viewer's attention (4.162). As he comes into close-up, he ramps up the conflict, demanding to know where the men got alcohol.

4.162

frame starts off unbalanced, and the fact that it includes a background doorway prepares us for the scene's dramatic development. In addition, any movement from background to foreground is a strong attention-getter. At moments like these, the mise-en-scene is quietly setting up what will happen. By arousing our expectations, the director has engaged us with the unfolding action.

The *Dying Swan* and *Three Kings* examples also illustrate the force of *frontality.* In explaining one five-minute shot in his film *Adam's Rib,* George Cukor acknowledged this power. He remarked how the defense attorney was positioned to focus our attention on her client, who's reciting the reasons she shot her husband **(4.163)**. Katharine Hepburn "had her back to the camera almost the whole time, but that had a meaning: she indicated to the audience that they should look at Judy Holliday."

All other things being equal, the viewer expects that more story information will come from a character's face than from a character's back. The viewer's attention will thus usually pass over figures that are turned away and fasten on figures that are positioned frontally. A more distant view can exploit frontality, too. In Hou Hsiao-hsien's *City of Sadness,* depth staging centers the Japanese woman coming to visit the hospital, and a burst of bright fabric also draws attention to her **(4.164)**. Just as important, the other characters are turned away from us. It's characteristic of Hou's style to employ long shots with small changes in figure movement. The subdued, delicate effect of his scenes depends on our seeing characters' faces in relation to others' bodies and the overall setting.

Frontality can change over time to guide our attention to various parts of the shot. We've already seen alternating frontality at work in our *L'Avventura* scene, when Sandro and Claudia turn to and away from us (4.124, 4.125). When actors are in dialogue, a director may allow frontality to highlight one moment of one actor's performance and then give another performer more prominence **(4.165, 4.166)**. This device reminds us that mise-en-scene can borrow devices from theatrical staging.

4.163 Movements coordinated with other cues for attention. In *Adam's Rib,* the wife who has shot her husband is given the greatest emphasis by three-point lighting, her animated gestures, and her three-quarter frontal positioning. Daringly, the most frontal and centered character is the nurse in the background, but Cukor keeps her out of focus and unmoving so that she won't distract from Judy Holliday's performance.

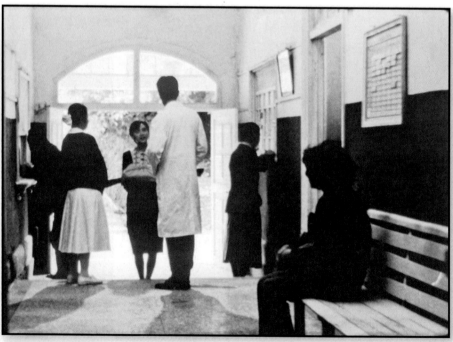

4.164 Frontality. Although she is farther from the camera than other characters, the woman visiting the hospital in *City of Sadness* draws our eye partly because she is the only one facing front. (Compare the unimportance of the front-facing nurse in 4.163.)

4.165

4.166

4.165–4.166 Fluctuating frontality. In a conversation in *The Bad and the Beautiful,* our attention fastens on the studio executive on the right because the other two characters are turned away from us (4.165). But when the producer turns to the camera, his centered position and frontal posture emphasize him (4.166).

A flash of frontality can be very powerful if it's integrated into the scene's unfolding drama. In the opening of *Rebel without a Cause,* three teenagers are being held at the police station **(4.167).** They don't know one another yet. When Jim sees that Plato is shivering, he drunkenly comes forward to offer the younger boy his sport coat **(4.168, 4.169).** Jim's frontality, forward movement, bright white shirt, and central placement emphasize his gesture. The moment foreshadows the ways in which Jim will become something of a father to Plato. Just as Plato takes the coat, Judy turns and notices Jim for the first time **(4.170).** Like Claudia's turn to the camera in our *L'Avventura* example, this sudden revelation spikes our interest. It prepares us for the tense romance that will develop between Judy and Jim in later scenes. Director Nicholas Ray has blended the scene's setting, lighting, costume, and staging in order to establish the core relationships among the three central characters.

4.167

4.168

4.169

4.170

4.167–4.170 Developing a scene over time. A long shot lays out the major characters in *Rebel without a Cause* (4.167). Jim comes forward, drawing our attention and arousing expectations of a dramatic exchange (4.168). Jim offers Plato his jacket, his action centered and his brightly lit white shirt making him the dominant player. Judy remains a secondary center of interest, segregated by the office window but highlighted by her bright red coat (4.169). Judy turns abruptly, and her face's frontal position lets us see her interest in Jim (4.170).

4.171–4.172 Frontality denied. At the height of the drama in *Naniwa Elegy,* Kenji Mizoguchi has the heroine move away from us, into depth (4.171). As she passes through patches of distant darkness, our curiosity about her emotional state intensifies (4.172). Compare the forward movement in 4.160–4.162 and 4.167–4.170.

4.171

4.172

CONNECT TO THE BLOG
www.davidbordwell.net/blog

For more on Mizoguchi's staging style, see "Mizoguchi: Secrets of the exquisite image."

The director can also achieve a strong effect by denying frontality, keeping us in suspense about what a character's face reveals. At a climactic moment in Kenji Mizoguchi's *Naniwa Elegy,* some of the usual cues for emphasis are reversed **(4.171, 4.172).** We get a long shot rather than a closer view, and the character is turned from us and moving away from the camera, through patches of darkness. Ayako is confessing to her suitor that she's been another man's mistress. Her withdrawal conveys a powerful sense of shame, and we, like her friend, have to judge her sincerity based on her posture and voice. In this and our other examples, several techniques of mise-en-scene dovetail from moment to moment in order to engage us more vividly with the action.

Narrative Functions of Mise-en-Scene in *Our Hospitality*

Throughout this chapter, most of our examples have looked at mise-en-scene techniques in isolation, studying single shots or scenes. Now we're ready to see how these techniques work together to shape a film's overall form and, consequently, our experience of it.

Like most of Buster Keaton's films, *Our Hospitality* shows that directorial choices about mise-en-scene can economically advance the narrative and create a pattern of motifs. Since the film is a comedy, the mise-en-scene also creates gags. *Our Hospitality,* then, exemplifies what we will find in our study of every film technique: An individual element almost always has *several* functions, not just one.

Consider, for example, how the settings function in the plot of *Our Hospitality.* For one thing, they help divide the film into contrasting sections. The film begins with a prologue showing how the feud between the McKays and the Canfields kills off the young Canfield and the husband of the McKay family. We are left in suspense about the fate of the baby, Willie. Willie's mother flees with her son from their southern home to the North (action narrated to us mainly by an intertitle).

The plot jumps ahead many years to begin the main action, with the grown-up Willie living in New York. There are a number of gags concerning early-19th-century life in the metropolis, contrasting sharply with the prologue scene. Soon Willie receives word that he has inherited his parents' home in the South. A series of amusing short scenes follows as he takes a primitive train back to his birthplace. During these scenes, Keaton uses real locales, but by laying out the railroad tracks in different ways, he exploits the landscapes for surprising comic effects, which we'll examine shortly.

The rest of the film deals with Willie's stay in the southern town. On the day of his arrival, he wanders around and gets into a number of comic situations. That

66 The most striking aspect of the Keaton pictures was the enormous amount of trouble lavished over every gag. Production value on such a scale requires more than a simple desire to make people laugh. It is not surprising that Keaton's childhood aim was to be a civil engineer."
—Kevin Brownlow, film historian

night he stays in the Canfield house itself. An extended chase occurs the next day, moving through the countryside and back to the Canfield house for the settling of the feud. Thus the action depends heavily on shifts of setting that establish Willie's two journeys, as baby and as man, and later his wanderings to escape his enemies' pursuit.

Along with the shifts of setting, the narration is relatively unrestricted after Willie reaches the South. It switches between him and members of the Canfield family. We usually know more about what they're doing than Willie does, and the narrative generates suspense by showing them coming toward the places where Willie is hiding.

Specific settings fulfill distinct narrative functions. The McKay estate, which Willie envisions as a mansion, turns out to be a tumbledown shack. The McKay house is contrasted with the Canfield's palatial plantation home. In narrative terms, the Canfield home gains even more functional importance when the Canfield father forbids his sons to kill Willie on the premises: "Our code of honor forbids us to shoot him while he is a guest in our house." Once Willie overhears this, he determines *never* to leave.

Ironically, the home of Willie's enemies becomes the only safe spot in town, and many scenes are organized around the Canfield brothers' attempts to lure Willie outside. At the end of the film, another setting takes on significance: the landscape of meadows, mountains, riverbanks, rapids, and waterfalls across which the Canfields pursue Willie. The feud ends back in the Canfield house itself, with Willie now welcomed as the daughter's husband.

The pattern of development is clear: from the opening shootout at the McKay house that breaks up Willie's family to the final scene in the Canfield house with Willie becoming part of a new family. In such ways, every setting becomes highly motivated by the narrative's system of causes and effects, parallels and contrasts, and overall development.

The same narrative motivation marks the film's use of costume. Willie is characterized as a city boy through his dandified suit, but the southern gentility of the elder Canfield is represented by his white planter's suit. Props become important here. Willie's suitcase and umbrella succinctly summarize his role as visitor and wanderer, and the Canfields' ever-present pistols remind us of their goal of continuing the feud. In addition, a change of costume (Willie's disguising himself as a woman) enables him to escape from the Canfield household. At the end, when the characters put aside their guns, the feud is over.

Like setting, lighting in *Our Hospitality* has both general and specific functions. The film alternates scenes in darkness with scenes in daylight. The feuding in the prologue takes place at night; Willie's trip South and wanderings through the town occur in daylight; that night Willie comes to dinner at the Canfield's and stays as a guest; the next day, the Canfields pursue him; and the film ends that night with the marriage of Willie and the Canfield daughter.

More specifically, the bulk of the film is evenly lit in the three-point method. Yet the somber action of the prologue takes place in hard sidelighting (**4.173, 4.174**). Later, the murder scene is played out in flashes of light—lightning, gunfire—that fitfully punctuate the overall darkness. Because this sporadic lighting hides part of the action from us, it helps build suspense. The gunshots themselves are seen only as flashes in the darkness, and we learn that both men have died only during a burst of lightning.

Most economically of all, virtually every bit of the acting functions to support and advance the cause-effect chain of the narrative. The way Canfield sips and savors his mint julep establishes his southern ways; his southern hospitality in turn will not allow him to shoot a guest in his house. Similarly, Willie's every move expresses his diffidence or resourcefulness.

Even more concise is the way the film uses staging in depth to present two narrative events simultaneously, obliging us to scan back and forth between them. While the engineer drives the locomotive, the other cars pass him on a parallel

4.173

4.174

4.173–4.174 Dramatic lighting changes in *Our Hospitality*. When the elder McKay flings off his hat to douse the lamp, the illumination changes from a soft blend of key, fill, and backlight (4.173) to a stark key light from the fireplace (4.174).

4.175

4.176

4.177

4.175–4.177 Deep staging and narration: How to give the audience superior knowledge. During the train journey, within the same frame (4.175) we see both cause—the engineer's cheerful ignorance—and effect—the runaway cars. Later the Canfield boys make plans to shoot Willie, who overhears them in the background (4.176). While Willie ambles along unsuspectingly toward the camera, one Canfield waits in the foreground to ambush him (4.177).

track **(4.175).** In other shots, Willie's awareness or ignorance of a situation is displayed through planes of depth **(4.176, 4.177).** Thanks to such spatial arrangements, Keaton is able to pack together two story events, resulting in a tight narrative construction and in a relatively unrestricted narration. In 4.176, we know what Willie knows, and we expect that he will probably flee now that he understands the sons' plans. But in 4.177, we're aware, as Willie is not, that danger lurks around the corner, so there's suspense as we wonder whether the Canfield boys' ambush will succeed.

Keaton has unified his film further by using mise-en-scene to create specific motifs. For one thing, there is the repeated squabble between the anonymous husband and wife. On his way to his estate, Willie passes a husband throttling his wife. Willie intervenes to protect her; the wife proceeds to thrash Willie for butting in. On Willie's way back, he passes the same couple, still fighting, but studiously avoids them. Nevertheless, the wife aims a kick at him as he passes. The repetition strengthens the film's narrative unity, but the motif functions thematically, too, as another joke on the contradictions surrounding the idea of hospitality.

Other motifs recur. Willie's first hat is too tall to wear in a jouncing railway coach. (When it gets crushed, he swaps it for the trademark flat Keaton hat.) Willie's second hat serves to distract the Canfields when Willie coaxes his dog to fetch it. There is also a pronounced water motif in the film. Rain conceals from us the murders in the prologue and later saves Willie from leaving the Canfield home after dinner. ("It would be the death of anyone to go out on a night like this!") A river functions significantly in the final chase. And a waterfall appears soon after Willie's arrival in the South **(4.178).** This waterfall initially protects Willie by hiding him **(4.179, 4.180)** but later threatens both him and the Canfield daughter as they are nearly swept over it (4.186).

4.178

4.179

4.180

4.178–4.180 The water motif. After an explosion demolishes a dam, the water spills over a cliff and creates a waterfall (4.178). The new waterfall starts to hide Willie as he sits fishing (4.179). By the time the Canfields rush into the foreground, he is invisible (4.180).

Two specific motifs of setting help tighten the narrative. First there is the recurrence of an embroidered sampler hanging on the Canfield wall: "Love Thy Neighbor." It first appears in the prologue of the film, when seeing it motivates Canfield's attempt to stop the feud. The sampler reappears at the end when Canfield, enraged that Willie has married his daughter, glances at the wall, reads the inscription, and resolves to halt the years of feuding. His change in attitude is motivated by an item of setting.

The film also uses gun racks as a motif. In the prologue, each feuder goes to his mantelpiece to get his pistol. Later, when Willie arrives in town, the Canfields hurry to their gun rack and begin to load their pistols. Near the end of the film, when the Canfields return home after failing to find Willie, one of the sons notices that the gun rack is now empty. And, in the final shot, when the Canfields accept the marriage and lay down their arms, Willie produces from all over his person a staggering assortment of pistols swiped from the Canfields' own supply.

Yet *Our Hospitality* is more than a film whose narrative system relates economically to patterns of mise-en-scene. It's a comedy, and one of the funniest. We shouldn't be surprised to find that Keaton uses mise-en-scene for gags. Indeed, so unified is the film that most of the elements that create narrative economy yield comic effects too.

The mise-en-scene bristles with many comic elements. Settings are exploited for amusement—the ramshackle McKay estate, the Broadway of 1830, the specially cut train tunnel that just fits the old-fashioned train and its smokestack (**4.181**). Costume gags also stand out. Willie's disguise as a woman is exposed by a gap in the rear of his skirt; later, Willie puts the same costume on a horse to distract the Canfields. Most strongly, comedy arises from the staging and performances. The railroad engineer's high kick unexpectedly swipes off his conductor's hat (**4.182**). The elder Canfield sharpens his carving knife with ferocious energy, just inches from Willie's head. When Willie lands at the bottom of the river, he stands there looking left and right, his hand shading his eyes, before he realizes where he is. Later, Willie scuds down the river, leaping out of the water like a fish and slithering across the rocks.

Perhaps the only aspect of mise-en-scene that competes with the comic inventiveness of the performances is the film's use of deep space for gags. Many of the shots we've already examined function to create comedy as well: The engineer stands firmly oblivious to the separation of train cars from the engine (see 4.175) just as Willie is unaware that the Canfield boy is lurking murderously in the foreground (4.177).

Even more striking, though, is the deep-space gag that follows the demolition of the dam. The Canfield boys have been searching the town for Willie. In the meantime, Willie sits on a ledge, fishing. As the water bursts from the dam and sweeps over the cliff, it completely engulfs Willie (4.179). At that very instant, the Canfield brothers step into the foreground from either side of the frame, still looking for their victim (4.180). The water's concealment of Willie reduces him to a neutral background for the movement of the Canfields. This sudden eruption of new action into the scene surprises us, rather than generating suspense, since we were not aware that the Canfield sons were so close by. Here surprise is crucial to the comedy.

However appealing the individual gags are, *Our Hospitality* organizes its comic aspects as strictly as it does its other motifs. The film's journey pattern often arranges a series of gags according to a formal principle of theme and variations. For instance, during the train trip South, a string of gags is based on the idea of people encountering the train. Several people turn out to watch it pass, a tramp rides the rods, and an old man chucks rocks at the engine. Another swift series of gags takes the train tracks themselves as its theme. The variations include a humped track, a donkey blocking the tracks, curled and rippled tracks, and finally no tracks at all.

But the most complex theme-and-variations series can be seen in the motif of "the fish on the line." Soon after Willie arrives in town, he is angling and hauls up a minuscule fish. Shortly afterward, a huge fish yanks him into the water (**4.183**). Later in the film, through a series of mishaps, Willie becomes tied by a rope to one

4.181 Setting used for comic effect. The tunnel is cut to fit the old-fashioned train.

4.182 Performance as comic surprise. As the engineer, Keaton's father, Joe, uses his famous high-kick vaudeville stunt for this gag.

4.183–4.186 Men as fish. The fish-on-the-line motif begins as Willie is jerked into the water (4.183). Later, tied to Willie, the Canfield boy falls off the cliff (4.184), and Willie braces himself to be yanked after him (4.185). Still later, Willie dangles like a fish on the end of a pole (4.186).

4.183

4.184

4.185

4.186

of the Canfield sons. Many gags arise from this umbilical-cord linkage, including one that results in Canfield's being pulled into the water as Willie was earlier.

Perhaps the single funniest shot in the film occurs when Willie realizes that since the Canfield boy has fallen off the rocks **(4.184),** so must he **(4.185).** But even after Willie gets free of Canfield, the rope remains tied around his waist. So in the film's climax, Willie is dangling from a log over the waterfall **(4.186).** Here again, one element fulfills multiple functions. The fish-on-the-line device advances the narrative, becomes a motif unifying the film, and takes its place in a pattern of parallel gags involving variations of Willie on the rope. In such ways, *Our Hospitality* becomes an outstanding example of how a filmmaker can integrate cinematic mise-en-scene with narrative form and create comedy in the process.

 SUMMARY

If we want to think like a filmmaker, we should notice mise-en-scene systematically. In any film, we can watch, first of all, for how setting, costume, lighting, and staging and performance are presented. Try tracing only one sort of element—say, setting or lighting—through a scene. How does it change, and what purposes does it fulfill?

We should also reflect on how mise-en-scene factors work together. Try pausing on a single image and scrutinizing it, as we've done throughout this chapter. How are the aspects of mise-en-scene arranged to attract our attention? Do they guide us toward key narrative elements—a face, a gesture, an object? Once we notice those elements, how are we cued to react?

Mise-en-scene can operate as part of narration, the unfolding of story information. How does it achieve this? Do the settings, lighting, costume, and staging and performance create curiosity, or suspense, or surprise? Do they become motifs that weave their ways through the entire film?

As we look more closely, we'll become aware of the vast range of possibilities offered by this area of technique. The simplest choice—where to put a light, what gesture an actor should employ—can have a powerful impact. Whether by intuition or by calculation, filmmakers have shown that mise-en-scene can engage and move viewers in an almost endless variety of ways.

5

The Shot: Cinematography

In controlling mise-en-scene, the filmmaker stages an event to be filmed. But what happens in front of the camera isn't the whole story. That event has to be captured, on a strip of film or in a digital format. The recording process opens up a new area of choice and control: cinematography.

Even if you're casually shooting a bit of video, you're making decisions about cinematography. (You might be letting the camera's automatic settings make some of them for you, but that's a decision too.) You're choosing the photographic qualities of the shot, such as exposure and frame rate. You're also choosing how to frame the shot, and whether to move the camera. And you're deciding how long the shot should run. These areas of choice are the same ones that filmmakers consider carefully. Just as nothing could be left to chance in lighting a shot like the one from *Inglourious Basterds* (4.1), so all the filmmaker's decisions about camerawork are shaped by a single concern: How will this creative choice affect the viewer?

The Photographic Image

Cinematography (literally, "writing in movement") depends to a large extent on *photography* ("writing in light"). Some filmmakers, working with 16mm or 35mm stock, have abandoned the camera to work directly on the material itself. But even the filmmaker who draws, paints, or scratches on film is creating patterns of light on celluloid. Most often, the filmmaker uses a camera to regulate how light from some object will be registered on the medium—sensitized photographic film or a video camera's computer chip. In either case, the filmmaker can select the range of tonalities, manipulate the speed of motion, and transform perspective.

The Range of Tonalities

You've probably noticed that it's rather hard to take a picture of a person lit by a sunny window. If Aunt Grace is well exposed, her garden outside the window is too bright. (The technical jargon is "blown-out.") If you expose for the garden, Aunt Grace falls into shadow. This disparity is only one example of a broader area of choice in cinematography: the control of the image's range of tones and shades. Tonality is a matter of considering how the light registers on the film. Lighting, as we've seen, is a factor in mise-en-scene, but it's intimately connected with cinematography too. In production the cinematographer is almost always the person who arranges the lighting, so he or she is in the best position to control a shot's tonality.

Contrast Let's start with one area of tonal control, the degree of contrast. **Contrast** refers to the comparative difference between the darkest and lightest

>   Both [cinematographer] Floyd [Crosby] and I wanted [*High Noon*] to look like a documentary, or a newsreel from the period of the 1880s, if film had existed at that time—which, of course, it did not. I believe that we came close to our goal by using flat lighting, a grainy texture in the printing and an unfiltered white sky."
>
> —Fred Zinnemann, director

areas of the frame. As we saw in Chapter 4, our eyes are highly sensitive to differences of color, shape, texture, and other aspects of a picture. Contrasts in the image help filmmakers to guide the viewer's eye to important parts of the frame and to give the shot an emotionally expressive quality—somber, cheerful, or whatever.

Most professional cinematography strives for a middle range of contrast: pure blacks, pure whites, and a large range in between, either grays (in black-and-white filming) or hues (in color filming). A higher-contrast image displays bright white highlights, stark black areas, and a narrow range of shades in between. A low-contrast image displays many intermediate grays or color shades with no true white or black areas **(5.1–5.6)**. High-contrast images can seem stark and dramatic, whereas low-contrast ones suggest more muted emotional states.

5.1

5.2

5.3

5.4

5.5

5.6

5.1–5.6 Tonal contrast in black-and-white and color. Most black-and-white films employ a balance of grays, blacks, and whites, as in this shot from *Casablanca* (5.1). The dream sequence early in Ingmar Bergman's *Wild Strawberries* relies on high-contrast imagery, with almost no grays (5.2). Many shots in Michelangelo Antonioni's *Red Desert* have unusually low contrast, enhanced by the flat lighting and limited palette in the color design (5.3). Some contemporary films emphasize deep, rich blacks and push toward a high-contrast look, as in *Domino* (5.4). You can see the different degrees of contrast more clearly if we drain the color out of the original shots (5.5, 5.6).

5.7   5.8   5.9

5.7–5.9 Color film and tonal range. Technicolor became famous for its sharp, saturated hues, as seen in the trolley scene of *Meet Me in St. Louis* (5.7). Soviet filmmakers used a domestically made stock that tended to lower contrast and give the image a murky greenish-blue cast. Andrei Tarkovsky stressed these qualities in the monochromatic color design of his shadowy *Stalker* (5.8). Len Lye's abstract *Rainbow Dance* exploited the English stock Gasparcolor to create pure, saturated silhouettes that split and recombine (5.9).

Many factors are used to control contrast, including lighting, filters, choice of film stock, laboratory processing, and postproduction work. Historically, photochemical filmmaking relied on photographic stocks with various degrees of sensitivity to light. Some black-and-white films gathered more light than others, and so were suited for filming news events in actual conditions. Others gave a richer, wider contrast range, and these were used for most of the studio films of the 1920s through the 1960s, where lighting could be controlled exactly. Similarly, by picking different color film stocks, cinematographers could vary the image's color contrast **(5.7–5.9)**.

Exposure   A crucial way to alter the tonalities in the image is through **exposure.** Exposure regulates how much light passes through the camera lens. Often we notice exposure only when an image seems too dark (underexposed) or too bright (overexposed). We expect that filmmakers will try for a balanced exposure. Sometimes, though, that's difficult to achieve and trade-offs must be made. Filmmakers constantly face the choice between the blown-out window and the silhouetted Aunt Grace in our amateur snapshot **(5.10, 5.11)**.

Sometimes a filmmaker wants unbalanced exposure. American film noir cinematography of the 1940s underexposed shadowy regions of the image in keeping

Why is *Who's Afraid of Virginia Woolf?* in black and white? "The words. The dialogue would have played differently in color."
—Ernest Lehman, screenwriter

5.10   5.11

5.10–5.11 Exposure levels. For *Kasba,* Indian director Kumar Shahani decided to expose for the shop interior in one scene and let the countryside behind blow out (5.10). In another scene he exposed for the background and created silhouetted window frames (5.11). The first shot displays the vibrant colors of the shop's wares, while the second emphasizes the difference between the market activities outside and the mysterious interior.

5.12

5.13

5.12–5.13 Overexposure. In *Vidas Secas*, Nelson Pereira dos Santos overexposes the windows of the prison cell to sharpen the contrast between the prisoner's confinement and the world of freedom outside (5.12). *The Lord of the Rings: The Fellowship of the Ring* used digital grading to simulate photographic overexposure in the Moria sequence. In 5.13 the overexposure of the wizard's staff makes the Fellowship a bright island threatened by countless orcs in the darkness.

> ❝ "[In digital cinematography] you start seeing lines on people's faces that aren't really there. I find myself using diffusion filters that I haven't used in 20 years just to be kinder to the faces of the people I'm photographing."
>
> —Stuart Dryburgh, cinematographer

with low-key lighting techniques. Likewise, overexposure can create expressive effects **(5.12)**. In addition, images shot with correct exposure can be overexposed or underexposed in developing, printing, or digital postproduction **(5.13)**.

Exposure can be affected by **filters**—slices of glass or gelatin put in front of the lens of the camera or printer to reduce certain frequencies of light reaching the film. Filters can alter the range of tonalities in radical ways. Hollywood cinematographers since the 1920s have sought to add glamour to close-ups, especially of women, by means of diffusion filters, along with gels or silks placed over light sources **(5.14)**. Before modern improvements in film stocks and lighting made it practical to shoot most outdoor night scenes at night, filmmakers routinely made such scenes by using blue filters in sunlight—a technique called *day for night* **(5.15)**.

Changing Tonality after Filming   Filmmakers have often manipulated the image's tonalities after filming. For instance, films could be printed on stocks that yielded different tonal values. Avant-garde directors have explored unusual ways of altering images after they came from the camera **(5.16, 5.17)**.

5.14

5.15

5.14–5.15 Filters alter tonality. Studio films like *A Farewell to Arms* often employed diffusion filters, along with soft and high-key lighting, to create romantic images of women (5.14). For *The Searchers*, this scene of the protagonists spying on an Indian camp at night was shot in sunlight using day-for-night filters (5.15).

One of the most common adjustments in the silent-film era involved adding color to black-and-white images through tinting and toning. *Tinting* is accomplished by dipping the already developed film into a bath of dye. The dark areas remain black and gray, while the lighter areas pick up the color (**5.18**). *Toning* worked in an opposite fashion. The dye was added during the developing of the positive print. As a result, darker areas are colored, while the lighter portions of the frame remain white or only faintly colored (**5.19**). More ambitious and rare was hand-coloring, which filled certain parts of the shot with an appropriate color (**5.20**). Later film-makers occasionally revived silent-film processes (**5.21**).

Many more adjustments of the image's tonality can be made in postproduction. For photochemically based filmmaking, the role of *grader* or *timer* was created to alter the color range of a print. The rise of digital filmmaking supplied even more tools to the expert now called the *colorist*. Once the film exists as a set of files, the adjustments can be very precise. For example, with analog color grading, any

5.16

5.17

5.16–5.17 Experimental manipulation after filming. Throughout *Power and Water*, Pat O'Neill creates spectacular imagery by use of optical printing, matte work, and other special effects (5.16). By scratching the emulsion, Stan Brakhage emphasizes the eye motif that runs through *Reflections on Black* (5.17).

5.18

5.19

5.20

5.21

5.18–5.21 Adding color to black and white. Tinting creates a brownish color across the entire frame in the 1914 film *The Wrath of the Gods* (5.18). The color suggests the heat of an erupting volcano. In *Cenere* ("Ashes," 1916) the deep blue of the dark areas and the nearly white patches are characteristic of toning (5.19). Night scenes like this were often colored blue. Firelight was frequently red, while interiors were commonly amber. Hand-colorists used stencils laid over each frame to create vibrant imagery, as in Albert Capellani's 1906 *Aladdin, or the Wonderful Lamp* (5.20). For her experimental film *Daisies,* Vera Chytilová employs a crimson toning (5.21).

5.22 Selective digital grading. In this close-up from *The Lord of the Rings: The Fellowship of the Ring,* the oval on the actor's face indicates the area within which the colorist wants to change the lighting or the color.

> 66 I have a hard enough time making up my mind about things without going into a DI suite; I don't think I'd ever get out of there. The process creates too many options."
>
> —Paul Thomas Anderson, director, *There Will Be Blood*

change made to a shot affected the entire frame area. But digital programs allow the colorist to target specific parts of the frame **(5.22)** and maintain that adjustment even if the parts shift during the shot. Today, some cinematographers bring a colorist to the set to make decisions during shooting.

Likewise, to get a day-for-night effect, the scene will be darkened in postproduction. For the climactic night sequence in *Winter's Bone,* two women take the heroine to a pond. Some shots were taken in bright daylight, others were taken at dusk, and the close views of the women in the boat were shot at night, with lamps providing dim illumination. Through digital grading, all the shots were blended into a uniformly dark sequence. *Julie & Julia,* a romantic comedy, used the opposite technique, adding sunlight to scenes that had been shot on overcast days.

Digital postproduction has reshaped every area of technique, from mise-en-scene and cinematography to editing and sound. (See "A Closer Look," pp. 165–166.) With more opportunities, however, come more forced decisions. One editor wonders whether digital postproduction offers too many alternatives: "I still generally feel, if you don't have it [in shooting], it wasn't meant to be. You can't manipulate everything like that or we might as well all be in animation."

Speed of Motion

A gymnast's performance seen in slow motion, ordinary action accelerated to comic speed, a tennis serve stopped in a freeze-frame—our films and videos are full of such effects. We don't often reflect on the fact that they depend on a photographic power unique to cinema: control over the speed of movement seen on the screen.

The speed of the motion presented onscreen depends on two factors: the rate at which the film was shot and the rate of projection. Both **rates** are calculated in frames per second. The standard rate for film-based shooting, established when synchronized-sound movies came in at the end of the 1920s, was 24 frames per second (fps). Today's 35mm cameras commonly offer the filmmaker a choice of anything between 8 and 64 fps, with specialized cameras offering a wider range of choice. Professional HD cameras, typically standardized at around 24, 25, and 30 fps, offer a comparable menu of frame rates.

If the movement is to look accurate on the screen, the rate of shooting should correspond to the rate of projection. This is what normally happens with modern films. The main problem comes with silent films, which are sometimes shown speeded up from their original frame rates. Before the filming rate was standardized at 24 fps, films were taken at anywhere from 16 to 22 fps, and so they look jerky when screened at 24 fps. Projected at the correct speed, silent films look as smooth as movies made today.

As the silent films show, if a film is exposed at fewer frames per second than the projection rate (say, 16 or 18 frames), the screen action will look speeded up. This is the *fast-motion* effect sometimes seen in comedies. But fast motion has long been used for other purposes. In F. W. Murnau's *Nosferatu,* the vampire's coach rushes skittishly across the landscape, suggesting his supernatural power. In

A CLOSER LOOK

FROM MONSTERS TO THE MUNDANE
Computer-Generated Imagery in The Lord of the Rings

The films adapted from J. R. R. Tolkien's trilogy *The Lord of the Rings* (*The Fellowship of the Ring, The Two Towers,* and *The Return of the King*) show how computer-generated imagery (CGI) can be used for huge battle scenes, plausible monsters, and magical events. The films also illustrate how CGI shapes less spectacular, more mundane areas of production.

CGI was used at every stage of production. In pre-production, a sort of animated storyboard (a *previs,* for "previsualization") was made, consisting of *animatics,* or rough, computer-generated versions of the scenes. Each installment's previs was about as long as the finished film and coordinated the work of the huge staff involved in both digital and physical tasks.

During production of the three films, CGI helped create the mise-en-scene. Many shots digitally stitched together disparate elements, blending full-size settings, miniature sets, and matte paintings (see 5.60). A total of 68 miniature sets were built, and computer manipulation was required in each case to make them appear real or to allow camera movements through them. Computer paint programs could generate matte paintings for the sky, clouds, distant cliffs, and forests that appeared behind the miniatures.

Rings also drew on the rapidly developing capacity of CGI to create characters. The war scenes were staged with a small number of actual actors in costumes, but CGI added vast crowds of soldiers alongside them. As happens often nowadays, the *Rings* project demanded new software programs. A crucial program was Massive (for "Multiple Agent Simulation System in Virtual Environment"). Using motion-capture on a few *agents* (costumed actors), the team could build a number of different military maneuvers, assigning all of them to the thousands of crude, digitally generated figures. By giving each figure a rudimentary artificial intelligence—such as the ability to see an approaching soldier and identify it as friend or foe—Massive could generate a scene in which figures scattered or gathered in unpredictable ways **(5.23)**.

The monsters encountered by the characters during their quest were more elaborately designed than the troops. A detailed three-dimensional model of each creature was captured with a scanning wand that could read into recesses and folds. A new software system, Character Mapper, captured motion from an actor and then adjusted body mass and muscles to imaginary skeletons. In the cave-troll sequence, the large, squat creature swings its limbs and flexes its muscles in a believable fashion.

The skeletal Gollum was created with a combination of motion-capture and CGI, but human actors didn't escape the CGI process. The main characters were given digital look-alikes who replaced stunt doubles, executing dangerous or difficult movements. The story demanded that full-size actors play three-feet-tall hobbits who interact with characters considerably taller than them. The size difference was often created during filming by using small doubles or by placing the hobbits farther from the camera in false-perspective sets.

Cinematography also depended on CGI. For the cave-troll scene, director Peter Jackson donned a virtual-reality helmet and planned camera positions by moving around a virtual set and facing a virtual troll. The camera positions were motion-captured and reproduced in the actual filming of the sequence—which has a rough, handheld style quite different from the rest of the scenes.

In postproduction, animators erased telephone poles in location shots and helicopter blades dipping into the aerial shots of the Fellowship's voyage across mountains. Specialized programs added details, such as the ripples in the water in the Mirror of Galadriel.

Perhaps most important, digital grading altered the color of shots, giving each major location a distinctive look. Rivendell's scenes are in autumnal tones, while the early scenes in the Shire were given a yellow glow that enhanced the sunshine and green fields. The grading also utilized an innovative program that permitted adjusting the color values of individual elements within a shot. When Galadriel shows Frodo her mirror, she glows bright white, contrasting with the deep blue tones of Frodo's figure and setting **(5.24)**. Thanks to digital grading, CGI techniques can do more than create crowds and creatures: They can shape the visual style of an entire film.

A CLOSER LOOK

Continued

5.23

5.24

5.23–5.24 Mise-en-scene and cinematography controlled by digital postproduction. Vast crowds of soldiers with individualized movements were generated by the Massive software program for *The Two Towers* (5.23). In *The Fellowship of the Ring*, selective digital color grading makes one figure bright white while the rest of the scene has a muted tone (5.24).

Godfrey Reggio's *Koyaanisqatsi*, delirious fast motion renders the hectic rhythms of urban life **(5.25).** More recent films have used fast motion to grab our attention and accelerate the pace, whisking us through a setting to the heart of the action.

The more frames per second shot (say, 48 or 64), the slower the screen action will appear. The resulting *slow-motion* effect is used notably in Dziga Vertov's *Man with a Movie Camera* to render sports events in detail, a function that continues to be important today. The technique can also be used for expressive purposes. In Rouben Mamoulian's *Love Me Tonight,* the members of a hunt decide to ride quietly home to avoid waking the sleeping deer; their ride is filmed in slow motion to create a comic depiction of noiseless movement.

Today slow-motion footage often functions to suggest that the action takes place in a dream or fantasy. It can also be used to convey enormous power, as in a martial-arts or superhero film. Slow motion is also used for emphasis, becoming a way of dwelling on a moment of spectacle or high drama. Slow-motion scenes of a couple walking add a lyrical rhythm to Wong Kar-wai's *In the Mood for Love,* suggesting that they are unwittingly dancing with each other.

5.25 Fast motion. Cars become blurs of light in *Koyaanisqatsi.*

To enhance expressive effects, filmmakers can change the speed of motion during a shot. Often the change of speed helps create special effects. In *Die Hard* a fireball bursts up an elevator shaft toward the camera. During the filming, the fire at the bottom of the shaft was filmed at 100 fps, slowing down its progress, and then shot at faster speeds as it erupted upward, giving the impression of an accelerating explosion.

The *Die Hard* sequence creates a realistic-looking explosion, but sometimes filmmakers choose to call our attention to changes in the speed of capturing the action. Varying the frame rate during shooting is called **ramping.** Since ramping alters exposure, lighting levels on the set have to be coordinated with the frame rate. For the fight scenes in *Sherlock Holmes,* the Phantom, a specialized digital camera used to create slow motion, was ramped from 24 fps to 800 fps and then back to 24 fps. During the passage of slow motion, a burst of light kept the exposure constant.

Ramping is sometimes used as a one-off effect to emphasize a bit of action, as in the *Die Hard* and *Sherlock Holmes* scenes. But it can also function as a motif and create parallels. In an early scene of Michael Mann's *The Insider,* researcher Jeffrey Wigand leaves the tobacco company that has just fired him. As he crosses the lobby toward a revolving door, his brisk walk suddenly slows to a dreamlike drifting. The point of this striking stylistic choice becomes apparent only in the film's last shot. Lowell Bergman, the TV producer who has helped Wigand reveal that addictive substances are added to cigarettes, has been dismissed from CBS. Bergman strides across the lobby, and as he passes through the revolving door, his movement glides into extreme slow motion. The repetition of the technique compares two men who have lost their livelihoods as a result of telling the truth: two insiders who have become outsiders.

There are more extreme forms of fast and slow motion. *Time-lapse* cinematography permits us to see the sun set in seconds or a flower sprout, bud, and bloom in a minute. For this, a very low shooting speed is required—perhaps one frame per minute, hour, or even day. For *high-speed* cinematography, such as recording a bullet shattering glass, the camera may expose hundreds or thousands of frames per second. Most cameras can be used for time-lapse shooting, but high-speed cinematography requires specially designed cameras.

After filming, the filmmaker can still control the speed of movement on the screen. Until the early 1990s, the most common tool for this was the optical printer. This device rephotographs a film, copying all or part of each original frame onto another reel of film. The optical printer can reverse the action, accelerate it by skipping frames, slow the action by reprinting frames (*stretch printing*), or freeze the action by printing the same frame over and over. Today digital postproduction permits the same manipulations that were pioneered on the optical printer.

Many experimental films have played with the possibilities of altering the speed of original footage. With the help of an optical printer, Ken Jacobs's *Tom Tom the Piper's Son* (12.11) explores the images of an early silent film by pausing the shots and enlarging portions of them. More mainstream films have also exploited the freeze-frame effect. It can underscore a piece of action or a line of dialogue,

5.26 Freeze-frame for a closing shot. In *A Moment of Innocence,* the final freeze-frame lets us contemplate what the gestures imply about the young men's attitudes toward the woman. Another example of an irresolute final freeze-frame is 3.10.

or suggest a character's memory. At the end of the film a freeze-frame can linger on a situation, imprinting it on the viewer's mind. It can also suggest that the story action hasn't quite resolved **(5.26).**

Perspective

You are standing on railroad tracks, looking toward the horizon. The tracks seem to meet in the distance, and the track ties get steadily smaller as they recede. Yet you know that the tracks are really parallel, and the ties are of uniform size. What is happening?

Your eye gathers light reflected from the scene and creates an image of space and the things in it. The objects in the scene have some regular relation to one another. The tracks converge and the ties get smaller. Your vision, in other words, shows a *perspective* view of the scene: a set of spatial relations organized around a viewing point.

The **lens** of a photographic camera does roughly what your eye does. Located at a specific point, it gathers light from the scene and transmits that light onto the flat surface of the film or video chip to form an image that represents size, depth, and other dimensions of the scene. So a camera lens also creates a perspective image.

One difference between the eye and the camera, though, is that photographic lenses may be changed, and each type of lens will render perspective in different ways. If two different lenses photograph the same scene, the perspective relations in the resulting images can be drastically different. As we'll see, a wide-angle lens could exaggerate the depth you see down the track or could make the foreground trees and buildings seem to bulge. A telephoto lens could drastically reduce the depth, making the trees seem very close together and nearly the same size.

The Lens: Focal Length Filmmakers think carefully about the perspective of an image. The main area of choice involves the **focal length** of the lens. In technical terms, the focal length is the distance from the center of the lens to the point where light rays converge to a point of focus on the film. The focal length alters the size and proportions of the things we see, as well as how much depth we perceive in the image.

We can distinguish three general sorts of lenses, based on their focal lengths and the ways they present perspective. We'll use 35mm film as our reference point, although the three types of lenses hold good for digital formats as well.

> 66 I'm standing around waiting to see where the 50mm is going to be, or what size lens they're putting on, and in that unwritten book in my brain, I said, 'Don't ever let them shoot you full face, on a wide-angle lens, you'll end up looking like Dumbo.'"
> —Tony Curtis, actor

1. *The short-focal-length* (wide-angle) *lens*

In 35mm-gauge cinematography, a lens of less than 35mm in focal length is considered a wide-angle lens. It's called that because it takes in a relatively wide field of view. But in capturing the wider field, these lenses tend to distort straight lines lying near the edges of the frame, bulging them outward **(5.27–5.29).** Less obviously, a short focal-length lens exaggerates depth, making figures in the foreground seem bigger and those in the distance seem farther away **(5.30).** As a result, when figures move toward or away from the camera, a wide-angle lens makes them seem to cover ground more rapidly.

2. *The middle-focal-length* (normal) *lens*

A common length for a medium, or normal lens, in 35mm and high-end digital cinematography, is 50mm **(5.31).** This lens seeks to avoid noticeable perspective distortion. With a medium lens, horizontal and vertical lines are rendered as straight and perpendicular. (Compare the bulging effect of the wide-angle lens.) Parallel lines should recede to distant vanishing points, as in our railroad tracks example. Foreground and background should seem neither stretched apart (as with the wide-angle lens) nor squashed together (as with the telephoto lens).

5.27

5.28

5.29

5.30

3. *The long-focal-length* (telephoto) *lens*

Wide-angle lenses stretch space along the frame edges, but longer lenses flatten the space along the camera axis. Cues for depth and volume are reduced. The planes seem squashed together, much as when you look through a telescope or binoculars (**5.32**). (For this reason, long lenses are also called telephoto lenses.) Long lenses take in a narrower angle of vision than wide-angle or normal lenses do. As you'd expect, the effect of movement with a long lens is the opposite of what happens with the wide angle. A person moving toward the camera takes more time to cover what seems to be a small distance.

Today long lenses are typically 100mm or greater in length. You'll often see them at work in televised sports events, since they magnify action at a distance. In a base-ball game, there will invariably be shots taken from almost directly behind the pitcher, using a camera located beyond the centerfield wall. You've probably noticed that such shots make the umpire, catcher, batter, and pitcher look unnaturally close to one another. In other contexts, the effect of a very long lens can be otherworldly (**5.33**).

5.31 The medium focal-length lens. A shot made with a medium lens in *His Girl Friday.* Contrast the sense of distance among the actors seen in 5.30.

5.32

5.33

5.32–5.33 Long lenses and perspective. In 5.32, from Chen Kaige's *Life on a String,* the long lens squashes the crowd members almost to a single plane. It also makes the rapids behind the men virtually a two-dimensional backdrop. In *Koyaanisqatsi,* an airport is filmed from a great distance, and an exceptionally long focal length makes the plane seem to land on a highway (5.33).

❝ In *New York, New York*, we shot only with a 32mm lens, the whole movie. We tried to equate the old style of framing, the old style meaning 1946–53."

—Martin Scorsese, director

❝ I tend to rely on only two kinds of lenses to compose my frames: very wide angle and extreme telephoto. I use the wide angle because when I want to see something, I want to see it completely, with the most detail possible. As for the telephoto, I use it for close-ups because I find it creates a real 'encounter' with the actor. If you shoot someone's face with a 200-millimeter lens, the audience will feel like the actor is really standing in front of them. It gives presence to the shot. So I like extremes. Anything in between is of no interest to me."

—John Woo, director, *A Better Tomorrow* and *Hard Boiled*

Lens length can distinctly affect the spectator's experience. For example, expressive qualities can be suggested by lenses that distort objects or characters. A decision about lens length can make a character or object blend into the setting (**5.34–5.36**) or stand out in sharp relief (**5.37**). Filmmakers may exploit the flattening effects of the long focal-length lens to create solid masses of space as in an abstract painting (**5.38**). A director can use the distortions of lens lengths for surprise effects as well (**5.39, 5.40**).

In taking snapshots you've probably used a **zoom lens** to enlarge some part of a shot. The lens changes framing, but it also changes focal length. So the zoom not only resizes what's shown; it also changes the image's perspective. With its variable focal length, the zoom combines the wide-angle, medium, and telephoto options we've already looked at.

Fixed focal-length lenses can't change perspective relations while the camera is running, but the zoom can. Zoom lenses were originally used for documentary shooting. Most filmmakers didn't try to zoom during filming, because they worried that the rapid warping or flattening of the image would be distracting. But in the late 1950s, filmmakers began zooming while shooting.

Since then, the zoom has sometimes been used to substitute for moving the camera forward or backward. During a zoom, the camera remains stationary, while the zoom shot magnifies or demagnifies the objects filmed (**5.41–5.43**). It can also create intriguing deformations of depth and scale, as we'll see when we examine *Wavelength*.

If you're not yet convinced that the choice of focal length matters, consider Ernie Gehr's abstract experimental film *Serene Velocity*. The scene is an empty corridor. Gehr shot the setting with a zoom lens, but in a very unusual way.

[I] divided the mm range of the zoom lens in half and starting from the middle I recorded changes in mm positions. . . . The camera was not moved at all. The zoom lens was not moved during recording either. Each frame was recorded individually as a still. Four frames to each position. To give an example: I shot the first four frames at 50mm. The next four frames I shot at 55mm. And then, for a certain

5.34

5.35

5.36

5.34–5.36 Long lenses and movement. In *Tootsie*, Dorothy becomes visible among the crowd at a considerable distance from the camera (5.34). After taking 20 steps, "she" seems only slightly closer (5.35). Finally, after taking 36 steps, Dorothy seems somewhat closer (5.36). The shot is held long enough for us to absorb Michael's makeover and to recognize that the masquerade is successful: He can merge into the crowd.

5.37   **5.38**

5.37–5.38 Lens length for expressive effect. In Ilya Trauberg's *China Express*, wide-angle distortion makes the man's hand more threatening (5.37). In *Eternity and a Day,* a long lens turns the beach and sea into two vertical strips behind the character (5.38).

5.39

5.40

5.39–5.40 Focal length for surprise and suspense. In Kurosawa's *Red Beard,* when the mad patient comes into the intern's room, a long focal-length lens makes her seem close and threatening (5.39). But a cut to a more perpendicular angle shows that they're actually several feet apart and that he is not yet in danger (5.40).

5.41

5.42

5.43

5.41–5.43 The zoom at work. The opening of *The Conversation* presents one of the most famous zoom shots in cinema. A long, slow zoom-in arouses considerable uncertainty about its target (5.41, 5.42), until it finally centers on a mime and our protagonist, surveillance technician Harry Caul (5.43). You can see how the varied focal lengths change perspective: In 5.41, the street tapers into the distance, but at longer lengths (5.42, 5.43), the pavement's grid doesn't recede.

5.44 Formal experiment with lens length. In *Serene Velocity,* telephoto shots of a hallway are juxtaposed to wide-angle shots taken from the same spot, creating a pulsating rhythm and an abstract play of rectangular shapes.

duration, approximately 60 feet, I went back and forth, four frames at 50mm, four frames at 55mm; four frames at 50mm, four frames at 55mm; etc. . . . for about 60 feet. Then I went to 45–60 [mm] and did the same for about 60 feet. Then to 40–65, and so on.

Onscreen, we see an image whose perspective relations pop in and out at us rhythmically—first with little difference, but gradually with greater tension between a telephoto image and a wide-angle image **(5.44)**. In *Serene Velocity* Gehr engages us sheerly through formal patterning of focal lengths.

The Lens: Depth of Field and Focus   You're well aware that a photograph or a movie scene can show some things in **focus** and let other things get fuzzy. That effect is, once more, due to the lens's focal length.

Every lens has a specific **depth of field:** a range of distances within which objects can be photographed in sharp focus, given a certain exposure setting. For example, suppose you are shooting with a 50mm lens and your subject is 10 feet away. At one common exposure level, focusing the lens at 10 feet will render everything between 8½ and 12 feet away in acceptable focus. Outside that zone, either closer to the lens or farther way, objects will blur.

All other things being equal, a wide-angle lens has a relatively greater depth of field than a telephoto lens. A 32mm lens focused at 10 feet yields an acceptable focal range of about 6 to 25 feet. The opening shot of *Simple Men* shows depth of field at work **(5.45).**

Depth of field isn't the same as deep space, discussed in Chapter 4. *Deep space* is a term for the way the filmmaker has staged the action on several different planes, *regardless of whether all of these planes are in focus.* In the case

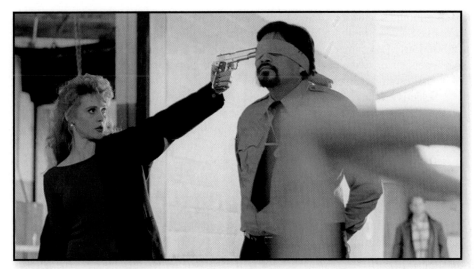

5.45 Focal length in action. The opening shot of *Simple Men* focuses on the robber and the security guard in the middle ground. The yellow railing in the foreground is out of focus. In the distant background stands the female robber's partner, who is out of focus too. The lens's depth of field picked out certain zones of space in front of the camera.

5.46

5.47

of *Our Hospitality,* those planes usually are in sharp focus, but in other films, not every plane of deep space is in focus. In the *Simple Men* shot (5.45), we can see three planes of depth, but they aren't all in focus. Deep space is a matter of mise-en-scene, involving how the scene is arranged. Depth of field depends on the camera, with the lens determining what layers of a deep-space staging are in focus.

If depth of field controls perspective relations by determining which planes will be in focus, what choices are open to the filmmaker? He or she may opt for what is usually called *selective focus*—choosing to focus on only one plane and letting the other planes blur. As the *Simple Men* example suggests, selective focus guides the viewer's eye: We tend to pay attention to what is most clearly visible. Often this involves focusing on the main character and throwing the surroundings out of focus **(5.46).** Alternatively the director may choose to put an unexpected plane in focus and let the rest blur **(5.47).**

In Hollywood during the 1940s, partly because of the influence of *Citizen Kane,* filmmakers began using lenses of shorter focal length, along with more sensitive film stock and higher light levels, to yield a greater depth of field **(5.48).** This practice came to be called **deep focus.** Combined with deep-space staging, it became a major stylistic option in the 1940s and 1950s **(5.49).** The technique was

5.46–5.47 Depth of field yields selective focus. As often happens with selective focus, the main point of interest in this shot from Agnès Varda's *Vagabond* (*Sans toi ni loi*) is kept in focus, while the background is out of focus (5.46). More unusual is Léos Carax's decision in *Boy Meets Girl* to show his protagonist in the background, fascinated by the neck of the woman in the foreground (5.47).

5.48

5.49

5.48–5.49 The golden age of deep-focus cinematography. In the famous contract-signing scene from *Citizen Kane,* the entire depth composition is in sharp focus from one plane near the lens (Bernstein's head), through several planes in the middle ground, to the wall far in the distance (5.48). A similar example of deep-space staging combined with deep-focus cinematography is Anthony Mann's *The Tall Target* (5.49).

> ❝ If I made big-budget films, I would do what the filmmakers of twenty years ago did: use 35, 40, and 50mm [lenses] with lots of light so I could have that depth of field, because it plays upon the effect of surprise. It can give you a whole series of little tricks, little hiding places, little hooks in the image where you can hang surprises, places where they can suddenly appear, just like that, within the frame itself.❞
>
> —Benoît Jacquot, director, *A Single Girl*

> On the problems of shooting in cars: "There are no new angles. They've all been done a thousand times, plus the mechanics of doing it are hideous. The camera car, the walkie-talkie, trying to keep it realistic-looking, the police motorcade that must accompany you—all of those things conspire to mar the intimacy of what you're shooting. I think they had it right in old Hollywood where they would do it in the studio with rear-screen projection."
>
> —Alexander Payne, director of *The Descendants* and *Nebraska*

even imitated in cartoons. (See 4.146.) During the 1970s and 1980s, younger directors like Steven Spielberg and Brian De Palma revived deep-focus cinematography **(5.50).** Early HD cameras had small sensors, which kept all planes in focus **(5.51).** As larger sensors were developed, cinematographers could more easily create selective, shallow-focus images.

Selective focus automatically steers our attention to a single important part of the shot. But deep focus tends to make several areas equally visible. So the filmmaker's choice of deep focus creates another set of options for guiding our eye. Those options include sound (we tend to watch who's speaking), elements of mise-en-scene, such as lighting and staging (p. 144), and aspects of framing and composition.

Just as a zoom lens lets the filmmaker change focal length while filming, focus can be altered within a shot by **racking focus,** or *pulling focus*. This is commonly used to switch our attention between foreground and background **(5.52–5.53),** making one plane blurred and another sharp.

Special Effects   The image's perspective relations can be shaped by **special effects.** The most unrealistic sort is **superimposition.** Here images are laid over one another, creating multiple perspectives within the frame. Superimpositions were originally created by double exposure either in the camera or in laboratory printing. For decades filmmakers presented dreams, visions, or memories superimposed over a character's face **(5.54).** Today, as you'd expect, superimpositions are created in digital postproduction.

Filmmakers working for American and European studios in the 1920s and 1930s devised other ways of manipulating perspective relations. Suppose you want to shoot a piece of action in the studio but persuade the viewer that it's taking place on location. The trick was to create a *composite,* in which separately photographed images are blended in a single composition.

One solution was to simply project footage of a setting onto a screen, then film actors in front of it. The whole ensemble could then be filmed from the front **(5.55).** This was called, logically enough, **rear projection** (or *process work*), and it was widely used. You'll see it in many classic Hollywood films. When people are shown inside moving vehicles, the scenery whizzes by in rear projection. To modern eyes, older forms of rear projection don't create very convincing depth cues **(5.56).**

5.50

5.51

5.50–5.51 Deep focus in film and video. In *The Untouchables,* a conversation scene is played in the foreground while setting and distant figures are also kept in focus (5.50). This shot uses a special split-focus lens that can render extreme depth, but a comparable effect is more easily achieved in digital video, where a small chip can yield extreme depth of field. If this shot, from Agnès Varda's *The Gleaners and I,* had been made on film, either Varda's hand or the truck would have been far more out of focus (5.51).

5.52

5.53

5.52–5.53 Racking focus. In this shot from *Last Tango in Paris,* Jeanne, the bench, and the wall in the distance are in focus, while Tom in the foreground is not (5.52). After the camera racks focus, Tom becomes sharp and the background is blurred (5.53).

5.54 Superimposition. In the opening of Quentin Tarantino's *Kill Bill, Vol. 1,* the Bride sees the first victim of her revenge, and her memory of a violent struggle is superimposed over a tight framing of her eyes.

A more complicated approach to composite filming, also developed in the classical studio system, was **matte work.** A *matte* is a portion of the setting photographed on a strip of film, usually with a part of the frame empty. Through laboratory printing, the matte is joined with another strip of film containing the actors. It was common to have expert artists paint an image of the setting, and the painting was then filmed, leaving a blank space in the frame. The footage was combined with footage of action, filmed to fit the blank area. Several long shots in *The Wizard of Oz* exemplify classic matte painting (2.22).

With a matte painting, the actor can't move into the painted portions of the frame without seeming to disappear. To solve this problem, filmmakers used a *traveling matte.* Here the actor was photographed against a blank, usually blue, background. In laboratory printing, a background was prepared and a moving outline of the actor was cut out of it. Then the shot of the actor was jigsawed into the moving gap in the background footage. Traveling mattes could present persuasive images of space adventure or show cartoon characters interacting with humans **(5.57, 5.58).** Like any technique, however, traveling mattes can also generate a stylized, deliberately unrealistic image **(5.59).**

Now that filmmakers have software to do compositing, it might seem that rear projection and matte work are hopelessly outdated. But today's digital techniques

5.55

5.56

5.55–5.56 Movies inside movies. Behind the scenes (5.55): Rear projection for *Boom Town* (1940). In Hitchcock's *Vertigo*, the seascape in the rear plane was shot separately and used as a back-projected setting for an embrace filmed under studio lighting (5.56). From the 1920s through the 1950s, rear projection was easier than taking cast and crew on location.

5.57

5.57–5.59 Traveling mattes. In *Star Wars: Episode IV—A New Hope*, the take-off of the *Millennium Falcon* was filmed as a model against a blue screen and matted into a shot of a building with imperial troopers firing upward (5.57). The animated figures in *Who Framed Roger Rabbit* were matted into live-action footage shot separately (5.58). For *Rumble Fish*, a black-and-white film, Francis Ford Coppola uses traveling mattes to color the fish in an aquarium—recalling early film's experiments with hand-coloring (5.59).

5.58

5.59

mimic the special effects created by analog cinematography and lab work. Rear projection is still used, although usually with digitally shot footage. Digital special effects still require that the action be shot in front of a screen, but now it's either blue or green. The backgrounds, often digital matte paintings, are added later, as in traditional compositing. Likewise, today's merging of several digital effects within a frame **(5.60)** resembles pre-digital practice. In *2001: A Space Odyssey, Blade*

5.60 Merging special effects. The digital composite from *The Fellowship of the Ring* integrates a partial but full-size set with an actor at the left, a miniature set in the middle ground, a matte painting of the background elements, and computer-animated waterfalls and falling leaves.

Runner, and other classic science fiction films, a single shot might include animated miniatures or models, traveling mattes to render their movements, and ray bursts added in superimposition—all against a matte-painted background.

Most filmmakers choose to present tonality, speed of motion, and perspective in realistic ways. Like other film techniques, though, photographic manipulations of the shot needn't be used for realism. For instance, most movie shots don't want to confuse you about the positions or sizes of the characters. But Chytilová's *Daisies* presents a comic optical illusion **(5.61).** Similarly, most CGI shots aim at a seamless integration that persuades us that we're seeing a realistic space. But in *The Mill & the Cross,* digital images of Brueghel's painting "The Way to Calvary" are stitched together with foreground scenes shot with actors **(5.62).** The result tricks our eye by combining painterly and filmic perspectives. Like mise-en-scene, visual perspective can be stylized, imaginative, and blatantly unrealistic if the filmmaker chooses that path. It all depends on how the stylistic choices function in the pattern of the overall film.

Framing

You're very aware of **framing** when you take a photo or shoot a video. You don't usually want to cut off people's heads. Like tonality, speed of motion, and perspective, framing is carefully considered by filmmakers of all sorts. It's one of the most powerful cinematographic techniques.

Framing was crucial for the first major filmmaker in history, Louis Lumière. An inventor and businessman, Lumière and his brother Auguste devised one of the first practical cinema cameras **(5.63).** The Lumière camera, the most flexible of its day, weighed only 12 pounds. This was the camera that Melies used for his cinematic trickery (p. 114), but Louis Lumière's earliest films presented simple events—workers leaving his father's factory, a game of cards, a family meal. But even at so early a stage of film history, Lumière was able to use framing to transform everyday reality into a cinematic event.

Consider one of the most famous Lumière films, *The Arrival of a Train at La Ciotat Station* (1897). Lumière might have framed the shot by setting the camera

CONNECT TO THE BLOG
www.davidbordwell.net/blog

CGI can create spectacle, and some critics claim that the special effects make the story unimportant. We argue the opposite and talk about a film historian who agrees in "Classical cinema lives! New evidence for old norms."

5.61

5.61–5.62 Playing with perspective. In *Daisies,* Vera Chytilová uses setting, character position, and deep focus to make a comic point about the two women's amused deflation of men (5.61). Lech Majewski's *The Mill and the Cross* combines the flat canvas with the real locations and figures in the foreground, inviting us into a world that is half-painting, half three-dimensional landscape (5.62).

5.62

perpendicular to the platform, letting the train enter the frame from the right. Instead, Lumière stationed the camera at an oblique angle. The result is a dynamic composition, with the train arriving from the distance on a diagonal **(5.64).** If the scene had been shot perpendicularly, we would have seen only a string of passengers' backs climbing aboard. Lumière's oblique angle lets us see people's expressions and watch the ways they walk. There is also deep space: Some figures move into the foreground and others can be glimpsed in the distance.

Simple as it is, this single-shot film, less than a minute long, shows that camera position shapes the way we perceive the filmed event. The same thing happens on a more intimate scale with another Lumière short, *Baby's Meal* (1895). A long shot would have situated the family in its garden, perhaps showing off their wealth. Instead, Lumière framed the figures at a medium distance, which emphasizes the family's gestures and facial expressions **(5.65).** The frame's sizing of the event has guided our understanding of the event itself.

5.63

5.64

5.65

5.63–5.65 Louis Lumière, early master of framing. In an era in which a camera might be the size of an office desk, the Lumière camera was portable and could be set up on a tripod quickly (5.63). For *The Arrival of a Train at La Ciotat Station,* Lumière's diagonal framing supplied a dynamic composition and considerable depth (5.64). For *Baby's Meal* (5.65), the framing is more frontal and intimate, excluding the garden in order to concentrate on the family.

A CLOSER LOOK

Virtual Perspective: 3D

Hold your index finger in front of your face. Close one eye, then open it and close the other. The finger shifts noticeably. That difference between each eye's perspective, aided by some brain work, helps you detect depth and volume in the world. But the ordinary camera lens presents a monocular—single-eyed—perspective on things. The result is a flat image, having only the dimensions of width and height. Since the beginning of cinema, some filmmakers have thought that if you could shoot scenes in ways that imitated the gap between our eyes, you could fool the viewer's brain into seeing convincing depth.

Filmmakers have created 3D imagery by shooting with two cameras, or with a single camera that has two lenses, or with a single lens that uses a beam-splitter to send the images to different cameras **(5.66).** In any case, what gets projected, as you know if you've ever peeped over your 3D glasses in the theater, is an image with two superimposed pictures. When you look through the glasses again, the two images merge.

For reasons still not fully understood, current 3D imagery typically lacks the volume and solidity of the real world. Nonetheless, we can still respond strongly to 3D moving pictures. When something thrusts out of the frame toward us, or when something glides into depth, the kinetic impact can be irresistible **(5.67).** Even movement into depth can be startling **(5.68).**

Stereoscopic filmmaking goes back to the beginnings of cinema, and it has never completely gone away. The first wave of theatrically successful 3D films came in the early 1950s, using two projectors and glasses with filters (red and green, or polarizing). Some people had trouble seeing the 3D effect and got headaches. The trend soon faded. Occasional 3D films, mostly in the exploitation

5.67

5.68

5.67–5.68 In your face and under the screen. The streaming wakes of the lightcycles float out into the auditorium in *Tron: Legacy* (5.67). At the climax of *House of Wax* (1953) the mad scientist's assistant pops up from the foreground (5.68). In 3D projection, he seems to rise up from the front row of the audience.

5.66 A 3D camera rig. James Cameron looks into a video viewfinder as he operates the camera system he helped invent for *Avatar*.

realm, were made in the years that followed. The introduction of Imax in 1985 revived the format for upscale audiences. The system used a high-resolution 70mm format, and the detail in the image helped minimize visual problems suffered by viewers. Most of the 3D Imax films were short documentaries, however, and projection utilized a complex dual-film system that commercial theaters could not afford to adopt.

The broadest resurgence of the format began in 2005, when the first digital 3D systems were installed and Disney released *Chicken Little.* Although the Imax dual-projection system could be employed for blockbuster releases like *The Dark Knight,* most theaters would need digital projection for 3D. The stereoscopic format helped studios convince theater chains to go digital. The fact that 3D screenings commanded higher ticket prices was also a persuasive factor.

Pushed by enthusiasts of the technology, notably James Cameron and DreamWorks Animation producer Jeffrey Katzenberg, thousands of 3D-capable theaters were equipped. Hollywood increased production of 3D films, usually animation and entries in the action, science fiction, and fantasy genres. More sophisticated glasses using various kinds of optical technology emerged, although exhibitors did not embrace a single standard.

The reemergence of 3D, although motivated by business concerns, created more artistic decisions for filmmakers. One option, popular at the outset, was to maximize deep focus. If all planes were clear and sharp, the 3D effect would be stronger. Maintaining such extreme depth of field was much easier in animation than in live-action filming. But uniformity of focus wasn't really necessary, and soon filmmakers returned to using shallower depth of field to guide the spectator's eye. *Coraline* experimented with soft foregrounds and shallow focus. Soon shallow focus became common in 3D films **(5.69).**

Filmmakers faced another choice. How should the depth be organized? Should 3D visuals burst out into the auditorium? Or should the frame be more like a window, inviting us into the realm beyond? Technically, the decision depends on setting the lenses' *convergence point*.

Again, if you hold your finger close to your face, your eyeballs pivot slightly inward to focus on it. Similarly, a 3D camera's lenses usually don't point directly forward along parallel lines. They are turned slightly inward, so their lines of sight converge, and like our eyes they can pivot at various angles. At the point where the lenses' fields of view converge, the two images will be perfectly aligned, with no ghostly doubling. If you take off your 3D glasses during a film, you will see objects onscreen that aren't doubled. These mark the convergence point, which defines the screen plane—essentially the "window" through which we look into the depth of the shot.

If the convergence point is set a short distance in front of the camera, say 5 feet, any action taking place beyond that distance will appear to recede into depth behind the screen. But if the cameras' lenses are set at a more distant convergence point, well into the depth of the space being filmed, that defines the screen plane as farther back. As a result, anything in front of the convergence point will seem to push out toward the viewer. The effect is sometimes called a "pop-out."

The 1950s 3D movies exploited the pop-out option. Viewers were attacked by spears, arrows, lions, and even paddle balls. This effect was perceived as tacky and clichéd, and it helped hasten the end of the cycle. Aggressive 3D was revived to camp effect in the Paul Morrissey/Andy Warhol film *Flesh for Frankenstein* (1974), in which a spear jabs Dr. Frankenstein's inner organs toward the viewer's face.

The window-view alternative proved more popular in the digital era. Cinematographer Claudio Miranda, who shot *Tron: Legacy* in 3D, describes how this approach "makes the screen appear like a box you're looking into, and keeps things from leaping out unnaturally. Additionally, we went against the 'rule' of deep-focus depth-of-field for 3D and let our backgrounds go really soft, which helps guide the eye along with depth cues." The filmmaker could accentuate the depth in the screen world by pulling back through space, letting new elements glide into the foreground.

Some films released in 3D have been shot in 2D (35mm or digital) and then converted with postproduction software. Although some viewers complained that the conversions weren't vivid enough, many directors and cinematographers felt that originating a film in 3D limited their choices. The production is time consuming, and the cameras are bulky.

Lighting raises particular problems. Sometimes the highlights on a face or object will be different for each eye. In addition, the audience sees the image as darker than it really is. "You are watching the movie through sunglasses, essentially," says one cinematographer. As a result, putting filters on the camera lens reduces the illumination even more.

3D, like other areas of cinematography, opens up opportunities, but it also forces new decisions. The filmmaker must still choose according to larger purposes, and every choice may affect the form and style of the finished film.

5.69 Out-of-focus 3D backgrounds. In *The Life of Pi,* the hero is in the foreground, in sharp focus. Behind him, a crowd of meerkats watches curiously. Compare 5.46 and 5.47.

Lumière's simple craftsmanship reminds us that the act of framing has many implications. The size and shape of the frame matter. For another, the frame defines onscreen and offscreen space. Framing also creates a vantage point, and that has a certain distance, angle, and height. And, in cinema, framing can move in relation to what it films. We'll look more closely at all these creative possibilities.

Frame Dimensions and Shape

Painters and still photographers can display images of any shape—ovals, triangles, diamond-shaped panels. Filmmakers are limited to a rectangle. But filmmakers can decide the width of that rectangle, and in some cases they can change the shape of the image inside it.

Aspect Ratios   The ratio of frame width to frame height is called the **aspect ratio.** For example, an image that is twice as wide as it is high is said to be in a 2:1 ratio. Thomas Edison, Lumière, and other early film inventors set the proportions at approximately four by three, yielding an aspect ratio of 1.33:1. In the silent era, there wasn't complete uniformity about this, and some filmmakers chose to experiment with ratios. Experiments with *widescreen* formats began quite early. Abel Gance shot and projected sequences of *Napoleon* (1927) in what he called *triptychs* **(5.70).** In contrast, the Soviet director Sergei Eisenstein argued for a square frame, which would make compositions along horizontal, vertical, and diagonal directions equally feasible. A 2014 feature, *Mommy*, put Eisenstein's idea into practice.

Synchronized sound technology in the late 1920s demanded more standardized aspect ratios. Adding the sound track to the film strip required adjusting the shape of the image. At first, some films were printed in an almost square format, usually about 1.17:1 **(5.71).** But in the early 1930s, the Hollywood Academy of Motion Picture Arts and Sciences established the so-called **Academy ratio** of 1.37:1. This modified the classic 1.33:1 format to allow room for a soundtrack **(5.72).** The Academy ratio of 1.37:1 was widely employed throughout the world until the mid-1950s, when a 1.85:1 ratio became one norm. Since then, a great many widescreen ratios have appeared in 35mm and digital filmmaking; the most common ones are reviewed in **5.73–5.77.**

The simplest way to create a widescreen image is by **masking** it at some stage in production or exhibition **(5.78).** This masking is usually called a *hard matte.* Alternatively, many contemporary films are shot full-frame (that is, between 1.37:1 and 1.17:1) in the expectation that they will be masked when the film is shown in theaters or transferred to video. Sometimes the full-frame option results in lights or sound equipment being visible on the film strip **(5.79).** Another way to create a widescreen image is by using an **anamorphic** process. Here a special lens squeezes the image horizontally, either during filming or in printing. The projectionist uses a comparable lens to unsqueeze the image during projection **(5.80, 5.81).**

CONNECT TO THE BLOG
www.davidbordwell.net/blog

Can framings create humor? We show how they can in "Funny framings." "You are my density" traces how directors can fill the frame with information.

5.70 Early widescreen. A panoramic view from *Napoleon* joins images shot with three cameras. Gance used the effect to show a single huge expanse or to put different images side by side.

5.71 Aspect ratio 1.17:1—early sound films. The frame from *Public Enemy* shows the squarish ratio of some early sound films.

5.72 Aspect ratio 1.37:1—Academy ratio. The frame from *The Rules of the Game* shows the standardized ratio used until the mid-1950s.

5.73 Aspect ratio 1.85:1—common North American ratio. The example here is from *Me and You and Everyone We Know.*

5.75 Aspect ratio 1.75:1—common European ratio. This ratio fits widescreen television monitors (16 × 9) and many digital-video formats. Shown here is *Last Tango in Paris.*

5.76 Aspect ratio 2.35:1—anamorphic widescreen. This frame from *The Valiant Ones* shows the ratio standardized in the 1950s for the CinemaScope anamorphic process.

5.77 Aspect ratio 2.2:1—70mm widescreen. *Ghostbusters* displays the ratio that was chiefly used for 70mm presentation.

 CONNECT TO THE BLOG
www.davidbordwell.net/blog

The Grand Budapest Hotel employs several aspect ratios. We consider the consequences of this for the director's style in "Wes Anderson takes the 4:3 challenge."

◀ **5.74 Aspect ratio 1.66:1—common European ratio.** Also found in digital video productions, this ratio is shown here in a frame from *Une chambre en ville.*

5.78–5.79 **Masking before and during projection.** Agnès Varda's *Vagabond* was masked during filming or printing (5.78). The full-frame image from Martin Scorsese's *Raging Bull* (5.79) includes a microphone at the top edge. This would not be seen in the theater, because the top and bottom of the frame would be masked in the projector. The colored lines in our illustration show a projection framing at 1.85:1.

5.78

5.79

5.80

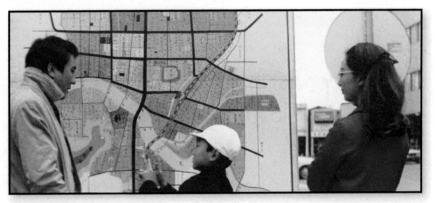

5.81

5.80–5.81 **Anamorphic widescreen.** A frame from Nagisa Oshima's anamorphic film *Boy*, as squeezed on the original film strip (5.80). The same frame, unsqueezed as it would be in projection (5.81). The anamorphic aspect ratio established by CinemaScope was 2.35:1 until the 1970s; for technical reasons, it was adjusted to 2.40:1. This is the aspect ratio of Panavision, today's most frequently used anamorphic system.

CREATIVE DECISIONS

Using Widescreen Framing

The practiced filmmaker knows that widescreen cinema, either masked or anamorphic, creates a different visual impact than the 1.37 ratio. The screen becomes a band or strip, emphasizing horizontal compositions. By offering more image area, a widescreen format offers bigger challenges about guiding attention than does the 1.37 ratio. How do you compose for it? Can you achieve the tight packing you can get in the narrower frame?

As you'd expect, filmmakers initially thought the format ideal for the sweep and spectacle of Westerns, travelogues, musicals, and historical epics. But what about ordinary dramatic conversations and more intimate encounters? A common solution today is to fill the frame with a face (p. 46). This choice will in turn require the director to cut up the scene more, as we'll see in the next chapter. For more distant shots, the director is likely to put the important information off center, so that the viewer can concentrate on that **(5.82, 5.83)**.

The wide formats challenge ambitious directors to design more screen-filling compositions. Those can't be as compact as the deep-focus compositions of the 1940s (5.48, 5.49), but they can achieve pictorial force. For example, the wide

 CONNECT TO THE BLOG
www.davidbordwell.net/blog

We trace the artistic options available in early CinemaScope in "Scoping things out: A new video lecture." For an Asian comparison, there's "Another Shaw production: Anamorphic adventures in Hong Kong."

CONNECT TO THE BLOG
www.davidbordwell.net/blog

The subtleties of emphasis that can be achieved with anamorphic widescreen framings are discussed in "Gradation of emphasis, starring Glenn Ford."

5.82–5.83 Spacing out the wide frame. Souleymare Cissé's *Yeelen* frames its hero in a slightly off-center position (5.82), a common choice in widescreen compositions. More extreme is the confrontation in John McTiernan's *Die Hard*, with the points of interest thrust to the left half of the frame (5.83). Off-center framings like these suggest action taking place offscreen, with the empty areas shaping our expectations about the next shot (see 6.19–6.20).

5.82

5.83

5.84

5.85

5.84–5.85 Widescreen for dense composition. Akira Kurosawa's *Sanjuro* uses the anamorphic process of Tohoscope, a Japanese equivalent of CinemaScope, to create a dense deep-focus composition (5.84). The busy scene from *Chunhyang* (5.85) fills the frame with bustle and glances. Director Im Kwon-Taek guides our attention around the wide frame according to who is speaking, who is facing us, and who reacts to the speaker.

format may build up significant depth, even in a confined setting **(5.84).** Or the director may multiply points of interest within the frame. This requires care in staging and timing the actors' performances **(5.85).**

Masks and Multiple Images   The rectangular frame hasn't prevented some filmmakers from embedding other image shapes in it. This has usually been done by attaching **masks** over either the camera's or the printer's lens to block the

5.86 **5.87** **5.88**

5.86–5.88 Changing compositional shape. In *La Roue,* Gance employs a variety of circular and oval masks (5.86). In one shot of Griffith's *Intolerance,* most of the frame is boldly blocked out to leave only a thin vertical slice, emphasizing the soldier's fall from the rampart (5.87). Orson Welles used an iris to close a scene in *The Magnificent Ambersons* (5.88). The old-fashioned device adds a nostalgic note to the sequence, the last moment of shared happiness among the characters.

passage of light. Masks were quite common in the silent cinema **(5.86, 5.87).** A moving circular mask that opens to reveal or closes to conceal a scene is called an **iris.** A number of directors in the sound cinema have revived the use of irises and masks **(5.88).**

We also should mention experiments with *multiple-frame,* or *split-screen,* imagery. In this process, two or more images, each with its own frame dimensions and shape, appear within the larger frame. Gance's *Napoleon* tried it on an epic scale (5.70), but it was used earlier, often to present scenes of telephone conversations. Modern filmmakers have turned to multiple-frame imagery to build suspense; we gain a godlike omniscience as we watch different story actions at exactly the same moment **(5.89).** The technique can be used subjectively as well **(5.90).**

Choices about aspect ratio and embedded imagery shape the spectator's experience in important ways. Graphic factors such as masses, edges, and movement gain their impact in relation to frame width. Just as important, frame size and shape guide the spectator's eye. The filmmaker can concentrate our attention through masking or composition, or shift our attention across the frame by creating different points of interest. The same possibilities exist with multiple-frame imagery, which must be carefully coordinated either to focus the viewer's attention or to send it ricocheting from one image to another.

Onscreen and Offscreen Space

Whatever its shape, the frame limits the image with a boundary. Our eyes have a very wide field of view, somewhat over 180 degrees, but a camera lens shows a much smaller slice of the world. Is this a disadvantage?

No. The frame shapes our experience, calling attention to what the filmmaker wants us to see. Every act of framing, as Lumière intuitively realized, creates relationships among the things we see. In Figure 5.64, the train forms a diagonal, and the people move toward us. Framing the scene differently would have created different visual patterns, different relationships between the train and the travelers. Moreover,

5.89

5.90

5.89–5.90 Multiple-frame imagery. Split-screen shots often present two or more events taking place at the same time. The opening sequence of *The Thomas Crown Affair* (1968) shows men converging to commit a robbery (5.89). In *127 Hours,* the hero is trapped in a remote canyon, and Danny Boyle uses multiple frames to convey his perceptions and imaginings (5.90).

the fact that the frame carves out only a little from the overall visual field means that filmmakers can creatively exploit the space *offscreen,* the areas not shown inside the frame.

As viewers we help the filmmaker with this task, because we know that what's in the frame is part of a continuous world. If the camera moves away from a person to show someone else, we assume that the first person is still there, outside the frame. Even in an abstract film, we can't resist the sense that the shapes and patterns that burst into the frame come from somewhere. So the filmmaker can imply the presence of things out of frame. You can have a character look or gesture at something offscreen. As we'll see in Chapter 7, sound can offer potent clues about offscreen space. And something from offscreen can come into the frame.

We're most aware of offscreen space when it creates suspense or surprise. A shadow from an unknown person outside the frame may slide across the shot and build up our expectations of a threat. Likewise, moments when a monster bursts into the frame are conventional in horror films, as we've seen in the 3D *House of Wax* (5.68). But any genre can employ incursions from offscreen. During a party scene in *Jezebel,* the heroine is the main focus of attention until a man's hand comes abruptly into the frame **(5.91–5.94).** Director William Wyler has used the selective powers of the frame to exclude something of great importance and then introduce it with startling effect. More systematically, D. W. Griffith's *Musketeers of Pig Alley* makes use of sudden intrusions into the frame as a motif developing across the whole film **(5.95, 5.96).**

These examples exploit areas lying beyond the four frame edges. There's also offscreen space behind parts of the setting, as when we see a mysterious door and hear sounds from inside it. The filmmaker can activate yet another offscreen zone, that of the camera and the area around it. In a thriller, a moving camera may represent the optical viewpoint of a stalker who isn't shown directly. The zone around the camera is used more imaginatively in Abbas Kiarostami's *Through the*

5.91–5.94 Offscreen space revealed. In *Jezebel,* the heroine, Julie, greets some friends in medium shot (5.91). Suddenly a fist holding a glass appears in the left foreground (5.92). Julie notices and comes forward flirtatiously (5.93), and the camera retreats slightly to frame her with the man who toasted her (5.94). It's an attention-getting way to introduce Julie's new suitor.

5.91

5.92

5.93

5.94

5.95

5.96

5.95–5.96 Offscreen space as motif. *The Musketeers of Pig Alley*: A gangster is trying to slip a drug into the heroine's drink. We're not aware that her friend, the Snapper Kid, is watching until a plume of his cigarette smoke wafts into the frame (5.95). At the film's end, when the Snapper Kid receives a payoff, a mysterious hand thrusts into the frame to offer him money (5.96).

5.97

5.98

5.99

5.97–5.99 The space behind the camera. In *Through the Olive Trees*, we watch as the actors redo the scene (5.97). Eventually, shots begin to show the director and his crew behind the camera (5.98). After several repetitions, the director walks in from behind the camera and tries to resolve the problem (5.99).

Olive Trees. A film crew is shooting a scene, and we watch through the lens of the camera **(5.97–5.99).** As the conflicts between two young actors spoil take after take, we watch tensely, knowing that behind the camera the crew is getting more and more frustrated. Filmmakers are well aware that we need only a few hints to start imagining things taking place outside the frame.

Camera Position: Angle, Level, Height, and Distance of Framing

When Louis Lumière decided to frame the train from an oblique angle and to present his family at breakfast in a fairly close setup (5.64, 5.65), he was doing what everyone with a camera does. He made decisions about camera position. In an animated film, there may not be an actual camera used in production, as with

5.100

5.102

5.101

5.100–5.102 Types of camera angle. A straight-on angle in *The Chronicle of Anna Magdalena Bach* (5.100). In this shot from *Family Plot* (5.101), a high-angle framing shows an investigator trailing a suspect as she leaves a funeral. A low-angle view places sailors and a machine gun against the sky in *They Were Expendable* (5.102).

drawing on film or software-based animation. Even in animation, though, the framing implies that the shot is viewed from a certain spot in space.

Angle The frame positions us at some *angle* on the subject. The filmmaker faces a huge number of choices here, but we can say roughly that the framing can present a straight-on angle, a high angle, or the low angle. You're familiar with these from taking photos and videos **(5.100–5.102).**

Level The frame can be more or less level—that is, parallel to the horizon. If the framing is tipped to one side or the other, it's said to be **canted.** Canted framing (also called a "Dutch angle") is relatively rare, although a few films make heavy use of it, such as Orson Welles's *Mr. Arkadin,* Carol Reed's *The Third Man,* and Wong Kar-wai's *Fallen Angels* **(5.103).** It can create rather disruptive effects **(5.104).**

5.103

5.104

5.103–5.104 The tipped camera. A canted framing in *Fallen Angels* (5.103). In Christopher Maclaine's *The End,* a canted framing makes a steep street in the foreground appear level and tips the houses in the background (5.104).

Height We may not think as much about camera height as we do angle and horizontal balance, but it's another area of choice for the filmmaker. Height is related to camera angle, since some angles demand that you position the camera higher or lower than the subject. But if the angle is kept straight in, crouching to take a snapshot creates a different composition than taking it from eye level. For instance, the Japanese filmmaker Yasujiro Ozu films from a low height but uses a straight-on angle (4.155, 6.142–6.145). This choice gives his shots a distinctive visual style.

Distance The framing of the image stations us relatively close to the subject or farther away. This aspect of framing is usually called *camera distance*. The terms for camera distance are approximate, and they're usually derived from the scale of human bodies in the shot. Our examples are all from *The Third Man*.

In the **extreme long shot,** the human figure is lost or tiny **(5.105).** This is the framing for landscapes, bird's-eye views of cities, and other vistas. In the **long shot,** figures are more prominent, but the background still dominates **(5.106).** Shots in which the human figure is framed from about the knees up are called **medium long shots (5.107).** These are common, since they permit a nice balance of figure and surroundings.

The **medium shot** frames the human body from the waist up **(5.108).** Gesture and expression now become more visible. The **medium close-up** frames the body from the chest up **(5.109).** The **close-up** is traditionally the shot showing just the head, hands, feet, or a small object. It emphasizes facial expression, the details of a gesture, or a significant object **(5.110).** The **extreme close-up** singles out a portion of the face or isolates and magnifies an object **(5.111).**

5.105 Extreme long shot

5.106 Long shot

5.107 Medium long shot

5.108 Medium shot

5.109 Medium close-up

5.110 Close-up

5.111 Extreme close-up

5.112 Shot scale versus camera position. In *La Passion de Jeanne d'Arc*, the framing is that of a rather long shot even though Jeanne's head is all we see of her. If the framing were simply adjusted downward, her whole body would be visible, along with much of the castle.

CONNECT TO THE BLOG
www.davidbordwell.net/blog

Even a simple framing can subtly shape the viewer's response, as we argue in "Where did the two-shot go? Here."

Note that the size of the photographed material within the frame is as important as any real camera distance. From the same camera distance, you could film a long shot of a person or a close-up of King Kong's elbow. We would not call the shot in **5.112** (from *La Passion de Jeanne d'Arc*) a close-up just because only Jeanne's head appears in the frame. In judging camera distance, the relative scale of the view determines how we label the shot.

Categories of framing are obviously matters of degree. No precise cutoff point distinguishes between a long shot and an extreme long shot. Filmmakers and film researchers find these terms useful, and they're usually clear enough for descriptive purposes.

Functions of Framing   Sometimes we're tempted to assign absolute meanings to angles, distances, and other qualities of framing. Does filming from a low angle automatically present a character as powerful? Does framing from a high angle always render the character as dwarfed and defeated? Verbal analogies are especially seductive. Does a canted frame mean that "the world is out of kilter"?

Making and watching movies would be a lot simpler if framings carried such hard-and-fast meanings. But the individual films would lose their uniqueness and richness. In fact, framings don't carry absolute or general meanings. In *some* films, angles and distance imply the meanings mentioned above, but in other films—probably most films—they don't. To rely on formulas is to forget that meaning and effect always stem from the film's overall form and the immediate context.

For instance, at many points in *Citizen Kane,* low-angle shots of Kane do suggest his looming power. Interestingly, however, the film's lowest camera positions occur at the point of Kane's most humiliating defeat—his miscarried gubernatorial campaign **(5.113)**. Here the low angle functions to isolate Kane and Leland. Similarly, the world is hardly out of kilter in the shot from Eisenstein's *October* shown in **5.114**. The canted frame dynamizes the effort of pushing the cannon. If the cliché about high-angle framings were correct, **5.115,** a shot from *North by Northwest,* would express the powerlessness of Van Damm and Leonard. In fact, the angle of Hitchcock's shot wittily prophesies how they plan to carry out a murder.

These three examples indicate that we can't reduce the richness of cinema to a few recipes. We must, as usual, look for the *functions* the technique performs in the particular *context* of the total film.

5.113

5.114

5.115

5.113–5.115 Context controls framing. In *Citizen Kane,* the protagonist is seen from below during his greatest defeat. By setting the figures against the ceiling and an abandoned campaign headquarters, the low angle suggests that Kane is increasingly isolated (5.113). A canted framing, as in Eisenstein's *October,* can create a dynamic composition and suggest a powerful force moving against gravity (5.114). In *North by Northwest,* as Van Damm reflects on pushing his mistress out of a plane, and the camera rises above him, he says, "I think that this is a matter best disposed of from a great height" (5.115).

■■■■■■■■■■ ■ ■ ■ ■ ■ ■ ■ ■ ■ ■ ■ ■ ■ ■ ■
CREATIVE DECISIONS ■■■■■■■■■■■■■■■■■■■■■■

Camera Position in a Shot from The Social Network

One of the most important matters a director decides is the placement of the camera. "There's only one right spot for the camera in each shot," the adage goes, "and it's my job to find it."

Consider a shot from *The Social Network*. Throughout the film Mark Zuckerberg has been characterized as a driven hacker. We've seen that his scowling face can seem aggressive, especially in contrast to that of his friend Eduardo (4.94–4.97). Mark's rare smiles are somewhat twisted and self-regarding. But at the moment when he has just auditioned new programmers for Facebook, he seems to wear a grin of genuine joy.

Instead of supplying a close-up of this expression, though, director David Fincher frames Mark in long shot (**5.116**). This is consistent with the narrational weight of the scene, as our range of knowledge has been restricted to Eduardo's. But the camera position also cools down any admiration we might be feeling for Mark. A closer view might have made him more sympathetic.

> ❝ I don't like close-ups unless you can get a kick out of them, unless you need them. If you can get away with attitudes and positions that show the feeling of the scene, I think you're better off using the close-up only for absolute punctuation—that's the reason you do it. And you save it—not like TV where they do everything in close-up."
> —Howard Hawks, director, *His Girl Friday*

5.116 **Camera distance and sympathy.** There are plenty of close shots of Mark elsewhere in *The Social Network*. Yet at his moment of triumph, the framing (from Eduardo's optical point of view) plays down an expression that could humanize him a bit. Perhaps the somber lighting, not shared with the background characters, even gives his smile a sinister edge.

■■■■■■■ ■ ■ ■ ■ ■ ■ ■ ■ ■ ■ ■ ■ ■ ■ ■

For filmmakers working with narrative form, camera placement is central to visual storytelling. A framing can stress a narratively important detail (**5.117, 5.118**). Camera distance specifies where characters are and how they respond to each other. Orchestrated by editing, as we'll see in the next chapter, distances and angles form patterns that guide us in building up the story.

Framing also can put us in a character's place. In Chapter 3, we saw that a film's narration may present story information with some psychological depth (p. 90). One option is perceptual subjectivity, the attempt to render what a character sees or hears. A shot's distance and angle may prompt us to take it as seen through a character's eyes, creating a *point-of-view* (*POV*) shot (**5.119, 5.120**). (See also p. 90.)

5.117–5.118 Camera distance as emphasis. The tears of Henriette in *A Day in the Country* are visible in extreme close-up (5.117). In *Day for Night,* a close framing emphasizes how carefully the film director arranges an actor's hands (5.118).

5.117

5.118

5.119–5.120 Subjective framings. In *Fury,* the hero in his jail cell is seen through the bars from a slightly low angle (5.119). The next shot, a high angle through the window toward the street outside, shows us what he sees, from his point of view (5.120).

5.119

5.120

5.121 Camera angle as a motif. In *The Maltese Falcon,* Kasper Gutman is frequently photographed from a low angle, emphasizing his obesity.

 CONNECT TO THE BLOG
www.davidbordwell.net/blog

One way to add visual interest is to shoot straight into the rear plane of the setting, as we explain in "Shot-consciousness" and "VIFF 2013 finale: The bold and the beautiful, sometimes together."

Framings may serve the narrative in yet other ways. Across an entire film, the repetitions of certain framings may associate themselves with a character or situation. That is, framings may become motifs unifying the film (**5.121**). Alternatively, certain framings in a film may stand out by virtue of their rarity. In a film composed primarily of long shots and medium shots, an extreme close-up will have considerable force. The early scenes of Ridley Scott's *Alien* present few shots depicting any character's point of view. But when Kane approaches the alien egg, we see close views of it as if through his eyes, and the creature leaps straight out at us. The POV shot provides a sudden shock and marks a major turning point in the plot.

Apart from their narrative significance, framings can add a visual interest of their own. Close-ups can give hands and feet a weight they wouldn't have if we were just attending to dialogue and facial expression (**5.122**). Long shots can permit us to explore vistas. Much of the visual delight of Westerns, of David Lynch's *The Straight Story,* and other films rendering landscapes arises from long shots that make huge spaces manifest (**5.123**). By including a range of information, the long-shot framing encourages us to search for details or discover abstract patterns (**5.124**).

In both narrative and nonnarrative films, our eye also enjoys the formal play presented by unusual angles on familiar objects (**5.125, 5.126**). "By reproducing the object from an unusual and striking angle," writes Rudolf Arnheim, "the artist forces the spectator to take a keener interest, which goes beyond mere noticing or acceptance. The object thus photographed sometimes gains in reality, and the impression it makes is livelier and more arresting."

The filmmaker may find ways to use framing for comic effect. You'll recall that in *Our Hospitality* Keaton stages many gags in depth. Now we can see that well-chosen camera angles and distances are also vital to the gags' success. If you turn back to p. 156, you'll notice that the railroad scene shown in 4.175 couldn't

5.122

5.123

5.122–5.124 Camera distance for intricacy and scope. The close shots of thieves' surreptitious gestures have a narrative function in Robert Bresson's *Pickpocket,* but they also create a dazzling ballet of fingers and wrists (5.122). Helicopter shots in *Lessons of Darkness* give the desolate burning oilfields of Kuwait an eerie, horrifying grandeur (5.123). In Hou Hsiao-hsien's *Summer at Grandpa's,* the boy from the city visits his disgraced uncle, and the neighborhood is presented as a welter of rooftops sheltering a spot of bright red (5.124).

5.124

5.125

5.126

5.125–5.126 Seeing differently. René Clair in *Entr'acte* frames a ballerina from straight below, transforming the figure into a pulsating flower (5.125). In *La Passion de Jeanne d'Arc,* the upside-down framings are not motivated as a character's point of view; they build up to the frenzy of the soldiers' massacre of the crowd witnessing Jeanne's death (5.126).

be as effective if it were filmed from the side and in extreme long shot. That way, we wouldn't clearly see that the two parts of the train are on parallel tracks. And we wouldn't see the engineer's unconcerned posture, which indicates his failure to realize what has happened. Like Lumière at the train station, Keaton chose depth staging and a diagonal camera position. The result creates a composition that highlights certain relations between things.

Similarly, offscreen space is vital to the gag shown in 4.184–4.186. Here Keaton lays out the comedy in time rather than space. Willie tugs on the rope.

5.127 Framing creates a visual joke. In *Play Time,* M. Hulot reacts with a start when he notices that a guard locking a door seems suddenly to have sprouted horns—the door handles.

CONNECT TO THE BLOG
www.davidbordwell.net/blog

We analyze subtleties of framing in films by two masters, William Wyler and Kenji Mizoguchi, in "Sleeves."

CONNECT TO THE BLOG
www.davidbordwell.net/blog

A very simple tilt can powerfully reveal a new story element, as we discuss in "Sometimes a reframing . . . "

http://www.davidbordwell.net
/blog/2015/09/01/sometimes
-a-reframing/

Then an unseen effect of that tug becomes visible as the Canfield son hurtles past and disappears. Finally, Willie reacts and is dragged down into the abyss below the frameline. Keaton could have framed this moment in a different way—say, from a low angle that showed both Willie and the Canfield boy in the same frame. But that would have sacrificed the suspense of waiting for Canfield to plummet through the shot. Throughout *Our Hospitality* our reaction to Keaton's humor depends on his careful combination of mise-en-scene and framing.

In Tati's *Play Time,* mise-en-scene and camera position cooperate to create pictorial jokes. In **5.127,** a visual pun issues from the precisely chosen camera angle and distance, as well as from the mise-en-scene: the man's stooping posture and the door handles make him look like a goat. Tati maintained the approach of silent comedy within the sound cinema. As with other filmmakers, his choice of framing was governed by imagining how it would affect the viewer.

The Mobile Frame

Cinema isn't the only visual medium that employs framing. Photographs, paintings, and comic-book panels have aspect ratios, imply things happening outside the frame, and present an implied vantage point on the scene. But there is one resource of framing that is specific to films, either photochemical or digital. In cinema, the frame can *move* with respect to what it shows us.

In cinematography, *mobile framing* allows the filmmaker to change the camera angle, level, height, or distance *during* the shot. Just as important, the movement of the frame often persuades us that we're moving too.

Types of Mobile Framing   We usually refer to the ability of the frame to be mobile as *camera movement.* In live-action filming, mobile framing is usually achieved by moving the camera physically during production. There are several kinds of camera movement, each with a specific effect onscreen.

The **pan** (short for *panorama*) movement swivels the camera on a vertical axis. The camera as a whole does not move to a new position. Onscreen, the pan scans space horizontally, as if the camera is "turning its head" right or left (**5.128, 5.129**). The **tilt** movement rotates the camera on a horizontal axis. It is as if the camera's head were swiveling up or down. Onscreen, the tilt movement yields the impression of unrolling a space from top to bottom or bottom to top (**5.130, 5.131**).

5.128

5.129

5.130

5.131

5.128–5.131 Panning and tilting the camera. During a shot in Dreyer's *Ordet*, the camera pans right to keep the figures in frame as they cross a room (5.128, 5.129). François Truffaut's *The Bride Wore Black* begins with a tilt down a church spire to the church door (5.130, 5.131).

In the **tracking** or **dolly shot,** the camera as a whole changes position, traveling in any direction along the ground—forward, backward, diagonally, in circles, or from side to side (**5.132, 5.133**). In the **crane shot,** the camera moves above ground level. Typically, it rises or descends, often thanks to a mechanical arm that lifts and lowers it. A crane shot may move vertically, like an elevator (**5.134, 5.135**), or at some angle forward or back (**5.136, 5.137**). Variations of the crane shot are helicopter and airplane shots as well as shots captured by drone aircraft.

Sometimes the camera movement we see is simulated—that is, no camera actually moved in production. The main examples are seen in animation. With cel animation, which photographs one frame at a time, the actual camera stays in one

> I realized that if I could just get to the really good scripts, I could approach it the way I approach literature—why the camera moves this way because of this motif—and then it became fascinating."
>
> —Jodie Foster, director, *Little Man Tate*

5.132

5.133

5.132–5.133 The camera moves through space. During this lateral tracking shot in Erich von Stroheim's *Greed*, the camera moves rightward along with the two characters (5.132, 5.133). Note how the figures remain in the same basic relationship to the frame as they stroll along a sidewalk, while the front of the house that they hope to buy remains visible behind them.

5.134–5.137 Craning down, craning up. In *Ivan the Terrible*, from a high-angle view of Anastasia's bier (5.134), the camera descends to end on a straight-on framing of Ivan slumped at its base (5.135). At the end of Karel Reisz's *Morgan!* the camera cranes diagonally up and back to reveal that the hero's apparently innocuous flower garden proclaims his Communist sympathies (5.136, 5.137).

5.134

5.135

5.136

5.137

5.138

5.139

5.140

5.138–5.140 Frame mobility without a moving camera. In *Peter Pan* cel animation imitates a pan shot.

> "It's a compulsion of mine to move the camera, and I now know why. It enhances three-dimensionality. It puts you in the space, and if you move the camera the audience becomes aware of the space."
>
> —George Miller, director, *The Road Warrior*

position. With computer animation, there is no camera to speak of: Its vantage point is constructed through software. Nonetheless, an animation shot can mimic a camera movement (**5.138–5.140**).

Movement and Machinery For many decades, camera movements in live-action production depended on putting the camera on a **dolly,** a heavy cart. The dolly can usually move on its own wheels, but it is often mounted on rails, hence the term *tracking* (**5.141**). Tracking shots are also made with cranes, even if the camera position doesn't rise or fall as in the usual crane shot. Suspended from a jib arm, the camera can glide over rough terrain. *The Thin Red Line* employed a 72-foot crane arm that let the camera slither over hills of tall grass during battle scenes. "The whole idea of using that crane was to not make it feel like a crane," says cinematographer John Toll. "We wanted it to look like the most continuous, smooth dolly that had ever been built."

Body-mounted camera units are common as well. These devices allow the camera operator to steer the camera while walking (see 1.21). Servo mechanisms adjust for imbalances and jerkiness, so the camera seems to glide or float. The prototype of the body-worn camera stabilizer is the Steadicam, initially used on

5.142

5.143

5.141 Tracking on rails. The camera crew must push the dolly on the tracks to capture the shot. (Compare 1.36.) The 360° tracking shot has become a common technique in modern cinema. The shot, being prepared for *The Departed,* was omitted from the final film.

5.142–5.143 Steadicam tracking shot. In Martin Scorsese's *Raging Bull,* the Steadicam follows the protagonist out of his dressing room and through a crowd up to the boxing ring.

Bound for Glory, Rocky, and *The Shining.* Now many consumer video cameras have comparable image-stabilization systems.

A body-worn camera can go places that a dolly can't. The operator can smoothly follow actors climbing stairs, riding vehicles, and walking great distances **(5.142, 5.143).** Some directors have taken advantage of the Steadicam to create lengthy shots moving through many locales, as in the opening scenes of Brian De Palma's *Bonfire of the Vanities* and Paul Thomas Anderson's *Boogie Nights.*

Sometimes the filmmaker does not want smooth camera movements and prefers a bumpy image. Commonly, this sort of shot is created by the **handheld camera.** Instead of anchoring the camera on some support like a dolly or a stabilizer, the operator simply walks with the camera braced on the shoulder. This sort of camera movement became common in the late 1950s, with the growth of the *cinéma vérité* documentary trend **(5.144, 5.145).**

5.144

5.145

5.144–5.145 The handheld camera and documentary. Don Pennebaker hand-holds the camera while filming his *Keep on Rockin'* (5.144). For the documentary *Primary,* a cameraman lifted the camera above his head and followed John F. Kennedy through a milling crowd (5.145).

5.146 **Other camera supports.** In *Leviathan*, a light GoPro camera, lashed to a pole, plunges into the sea and turns upward, yielding an eerie vision of gulls coming to feed on the netted fish.

Lightweight digital cameras allow cinematographers to create unusual camera mounts. For the race scenes of *Secretariat*, a miniature camera was attached to the end of a broomstick. GoPro cameras are usually used for sports recording, but in the poetic documentary *Leviathan* they convey unusual views of life on a commercial fishing boat. Some cameras were attached to the fishermen's helmets, while others were thrust into nets and under the sea. The result is an intimate view of the power and danger of nature **(5.146).**

The Zoom and the Mobile Frame We've already seen that a zoom lens provides a continuous range of focal lengths. When the camera operator zooms during filming, the result is a mobile framing—even though the camera stays in one spot (5.41–5.43). Some viewers have trouble distinguishing a zoom-in from a forward tracking shot, or a zoom-out from a reverse tracking shot. But filmmakers know very well that there are major differences. The choice that the director and the cinematographer make can subtly shape how the viewer responds.

The zoom lens reduces or blows up some portion of the image. Although a tracking shot and a crane shot also enlarge or reduce areas of the frame, this is not all that they do. In the genuine camera movement, static objects in different planes pass one another at different rates. We see different sides of objects, and backgrounds gain volume and depth **(5.147, 5.148).** By contrast, a zoom enlargement doesn't alter the aspects or positions of the objects we see. Our vantage point is the same at the end of the shot as at the beginning **(5.149, 5.150).** When the camera moves, we sense our own movement through the space. In a zoom, a bit of the space gets steadily magnified or demagnified.

We've pinpointed these sorts of mobile framings as isolated options. But filmmakers frequently combine them within a single shot. The camera may track

5.147

5.148

5.149

5.150

5.147–5.150 **Tracking shot versus zoom.** In Alain Resnais's *La Guerre est finie*, a tracking shot gives the objects considerable volume (5.147, 5.148). The wall has lost none of its solidity, and objects pass as if we were walking toward the sign. In Theo Angelopoulos's *Ulysses' Gaze*, a zoom shot simply blows up one area of the shot (5.149–5.150), as if we were adjusting a telescope. As the zoom occurs, the space looks flatter—the mark of a long-lens, or telephoto, framing.

and pan at the same time or crane up while zooming out. In *Vertigo,* an especially tricky combination track-*out* and zoom-*in* plastically distorts the shot's perspective and conveys the protagonist's dizziness. The device reappears in Spielberg's *Jaws,* when Sheriff Brody at the beach suddenly realizes that the shark has attacked a child. Simultaneously tracking and zooming in opposite directions has become common in modern Hollywood filmmaking to express a character's sense of confusion or astonishment (what director Sam Raimi calls the "warp-o cam"). The combinations are endless.

Frame Mobility: Functions Camera movements have held an appeal for filmmakers and audiences since the beginnings of cinema. Some of the earliest films made by Lumière cameramen were shots from trains or Venetian gondolas, and even today these films have a mesmeric power. Why?

For one thing, camera movements can increase information about the space of the image. Pan and tilt shots present new areas of the setting, and tracking shots and crane shots supply continually changing perspectives on it. As the camera shifts its point of view, objects or figures are usually revealed, so frame mobility can create a flow of new information for the viewer. Camera movement can as well make objects seem sharper and more vivid than in stationary framings. Certain camera movements give bodies greater solidity. This is apparently one reason modern directors like to circle around the action (5.141), as in the opening scene of *Reservoir Dogs.*

What's more, we tend to see camera movement as a substitute for *our* movement. When we see a forward tracking shot, we feel that we're approaching something or backing away. A crane shot that pulls away from something at ground level makes us feel a little weightless. We aren't completely fooled, of course. We never forget that we're watching a film in a theater. But camera movement provides several convincing cues for movement through space. Indeed, so powerful are these cues that filmmakers often make camera movements subjective—motivated narratively to represent what a moving character sees. Camera movement can be a powerful cue for a point-of-view shot.

When we walk through the world, our eyes see a somewhat bouncy view, but our optical system compensates for the jerkiness and creates a sense of stable motion. This sense of smooth movement can be captured by a traveling shot made with a dolly, a jib arm, or a Steadicam. Sometimes, however, handheld shots are used to suggest subjective point of view **(5.151).** Alternatively, the handheld shot can simply create a sense of anxious movement, as if the action were glimpsed on the fly **(5.152).**

5.151   5.152

5.151–5.152 Handheld impressions. In Samuel Fuller's *The Naked Kiss,* a handheld POV shot heightens the impact of a fight (5.151). As the protagonist of *julien donkey-boy* walks, we don't get a POV shot, but Harmony Korine's bouncy, mini-DV cameras follow him shuffling through his neighborhood (5.152). The handheld camera's jerky pace complements the explosions of color created by printing video up to 35mm.

5.153

5.154

5.155

5.153–5.155 **Reframing.** In *His Girl Friday,* director Howard Hawks strives to balance his compositions through reframing. When Hildy crosses from the left (5.153) to sit on the desk, the camera pans right to reframe her (5.154). This reframing is more noticeable than the next one: As Walter swivels his chair to face her, the camera reframes very slightly leftward (5.155).

> I kept wondering, 'Can people talk this much in a feature film and anybody care?' And so I had to go through every moment in those dialogue scenes and look for the little events I would treat as large events. Like the ringing of a phone or the blinds being opened. . . . I had to treat those as fairly major events and have the moves of the camera be motivated by them, so that it would be organic to the scene yet still visually interesting."
>
> —John Patrick Shanley, writer and director, *Doubt*

CONNECT TO THE BLOG
www.davidbordwell.net/blog

One common function of tracking shots is to follow actors in conversation, as we discuss in "Walk the talk."

Frame Mobility and Space   We can get a little more specific about the purposes and effects of mobile framings if we consider some functions they have—in relation to cinematic space and time, in relation to the overall form of the film.

Camera movement creates an interplay of onscreen and offscreen space. If you track the camera in, you exclude more space from the shot (5.147, 5.148). If you track back, as in our example from *Jezebel* (5.91–5.94), you reveal some space that was previously offscreen. The mobile frame also continually affects the angle, level, height, or distance of the framing. A crane-up may change the angle from a low one to a high one; a track-in may change the shot scale from long shot to close-up.

As usual, one choice leads to others. For instance, just as filmmakers must decide how to motivate story actions or whether to motivate lighting sources, they must consider whether to motivate camera movement. Should you make the frame's changing space depend on the movement in the shot? Usually, the answer is yes. A panning movement may keep a racing car centered, a tracking shot may follow a character from room to room, or a crane shot may pursue a rising balloon.

Sometimes the camera movement is quite minimal, as with **reframing.** If a character moves in relation to another character, often the frame will slightly pan or tilt to adjust to the movement **(5.153–5.155).** Because reframing movements are usually slight and motivated by the figures' movement, we seldom notice them.

The framing can move independently of the figures too. Sometimes the camera drifts away from the characters to reveal something of narrative importance; the mobile frame is motivated not by figure movement but by the demands of the narration. In Jean Renoir's *Crime of M. Lange,* the protagonist sits at his desk writing Wild West stories, but the camera pans away to show cowboy gear cluttering his room, establishing that Lange lives in a fantasy world. Similarly, an independent camera movement can point out an overlooked clue, a sign that comments on the action, or an imminent threat. The camera can thus be relatively unrestricted in its range of knowledge, as in 5.136–5.137 when it reveals Morgan's hammer-and-sickle flower bed.

Filmmakers are especially fond of solo camera movements at the beginning of a scene or the entire film. A tracking shot can establish a locale and then smoothly let the characters enter the space **(5.156–5.159).** A camera movement can even foreshadow action to come. In the opening scene of *The Milk of Sorrow,* Fausta, a woman who is terrified of the world outside her home, tends her dying mother. Cinematographer Natasha Braier describes the purpose of a tracking shot **(5.160, 5.161)** early in the film: "The whole idea of this shot was to represent

5.156

5.157

5.156–5.159 Camera movement independent of the figures. At the start of Otto Preminger's *Laura*, the camera glides through Waldo Lydecker's sitting room (5.156, 5.157), establishing him as a man of wealth and refinement, before revealing the detective McPherson (5.158). The framing then becomes motivated by figure movement, with the camera following McPherson's drift to a wall of masks (5.159).

5.158

5.159

5.160

5.161

5.160–5.161 Camera movement anticipates story action. In the opening scene of *The Milk of Sorrow,* an initial framing shows the protagonist in the room where she has spent so much time (5.160). A slow track forward nearly eliminates the window frame, framing her against the outside world that she will now have to confront (5.161).

what is going to happen in the film. At the beginning of the story, Fausta is living with her mother in a hermetic world, and now that her mother is dead, she will have to venture outside, and because of the way we frame her at the end of that shot, she actually appears to be outside."

Whether dependent on figure movement or independent of it, the mobile frame can profoundly affect how we perceive the space of the action. Different sorts of camera movements create different treatments of space. In *Last Year at Marienbad,* Resnais often tracks down corridors and through doorways, turning a fashionable resort hotel into a maze. For *Young and Innocent,* Hitchcock (a virtuoso of camera movement) devised a shot that moves from a high-angle long shot of a ballroom over the heads of the dancers to an extreme close-up of a drummer's blinking

> ❝ You really need to know why you are doing one of these moves. . . . If you pan on a long lens, it's a very different look than tracking with somebody; there's a very different feel to it.❞
>
> —Roger Deakins, cinematographer, *No Country for Old Men*

> ❝ One thing I hate in films is when the camera starts circling characters. If three people are sitting at a table talking, you'll often see the camera circling them. I can't explain why, but I find it totally fake.❞
>
> —Takeshi Kitano, director, *Sonatine*

eyes. In such films as *The Red and the White,* Miklós Jancsó specialized in lengthy camera movements that roam among groups of people moving across a plain. His shots use all of the resources of tracking, panning, craning, zooming, and racking focus to sculpt plastic, ever-changing spatial relations.

When we see any mobile framing, we can ask: What particular trajectory does the camera pursue? How does it function to reveal or conceal offscreen space? Does the frame mobility depend on figure movement or is it independent, drawing our attention to other things?

Frame Mobility and Time   Mobile framing involves time as well as space, and filmmakers have realized that our sense of duration and rhythm is affected by the mobile frame. Since a camera movement consumes time on screen, it can create an arc of expectation and fulfillment. If the camera pans quickly from an event, we may be prompted to wonder what has happened. If the camera abruptly tracks back to show us something in the foreground that we had not expected, as in our earlier *Jezebel* example (5.91–5.94), we're taken by surprise. If the camera slowly moves in on a detail, gradually enlarging it but delaying the fulfillment of our expectations, the camera movement has contributed to suspense. In the pan shot across M. Lange's study mentioned earlier, Renoir makes us wonder why the camera strays from the main character and then answers the question by revealing Lange's fascination with cowboys.

The velocity of frame mobility is important too. A zoom or a camera movement may be relatively slow or fast. Richard Lester's *A Hard Day's Night* and *Help!* started a fad in the 1960s for very fast zoom-ins and -outs. In comparison, one of the most impressive early camera movements, D. W. Griffith's monumental crane shot in Belshazzar's feast in *Intolerance,* gains majesty and suspense through its inexorably slow descent toward the immense Babylonian set (4.12).

Sometimes the speed of the mobile framing functions rhythmically, as in musical films. During the "Broadway Rhythm" number in *Singin' in the Rain,* the camera cranes quickly back from Gene Kelly several times, and the speed of the movement is timed to accentuate the lyrics.

Frame velocity can also create expressive qualities—a camera movement can be fluid, staccato, hesitant, and so forth. *Cloverfield* is presented as an amateur video record of a monster's attack on Manhattan. At many points, the operator whips the camera around to capture a shocking incident, and our anxiety is intensified by the sudden speed of the panning movement (**5.162, 5.163**). By choosing the duration and speed of camera movements, the filmmaker can pace our understanding of the plot action.

5.162

5.163

5.162–5.163 Speed of camera movement accentuates shock. In *Cloverfield* the video camera records an explosion in the street, and a whip pan to the right blurs the action (5.162). When the framing becomes stable again, we realize that the blurry movement was trying to follow the head of the Statue of Liberty rolling down the street (5.163).

Larger Patterns of Frame Mobility   While shaping time and space, mobile framings can become motifs across a film. In Carl Dreyer's *Day of Wrath,* the camera circles a shadowy chamber, surveying church officials who torture an old woman accused of being a witch. She tells her inquisitor that his death is imminent. Later in the film, her accuser lies on his deathbed, and a similar camera movement recalls her curse.

We see a more long-range motif in Hitchcock's *Psycho,* which begins and ends with a forward movement of the frame. During the film's first three shots, the camera pans right and zooms in on a nondescript building (**5.164**).

5.164

5.165

5.166

5.167

5.168

5.169

5.164–5.169 Camera movement as a motif. The opening of *Psycho*: The camera pans right and zooms in on a building in a city-scape (5.164). The camera moves toward a window to reveal the heroine and her boyfriend sharing a lunchtime tryst (5.165–5.167). The film's next-to-last shot begins at a distance from Norman (5.168) and moves in so that we see his expression as we hear his thoughts (5.169).

Camera movements carry us under a window blind and into the darkness of a cheap hotel room (**5.165–5.167**). The camera's movement inward, the penetration of an interior, is repeated throughout the film, often motivated as a subjective point of view when various characters move deeper and deeper into Norman Bates's mansion. The next-to-last shot of the film shows Norman sitting against a blank white wall, while we hear his interior monologue (**5.168**). The camera again moves forward into a close-up of his face (**5.169**). This shot is the climax of the forward movement initiated at the start of the film; the film has traced a movement into Norman's mind. Another film that relies heavily on a pattern of forward, penetrating movements is *Citizen Kane,* which depicts the same drive toward the revelation of a character's secret.

The filmmaker can develop other sorts of patterns. In Michael Snow's ←→ (usually called *Back and Forth*), the constant panning to and fro across a classroom, Ping-Pong fashion, determines the basic formal pattern of the film. It comes as a surprise when, near the very end, the movement suddenly becomes a repeated tilting up and down. As with lighting, color, and other techniques, cinematographic choices can develop in the course of the movie.

CREATIVE DECISIONS

Mobile Framing and Film Form in Grand Illusion and Wavelength

Two quite different films let us sum up ways in which the director can integrate the mobile frame into an overall form. One film uses the mobile frame in order to strengthen and support the plot's presentation of the story. The other film explores frame mobility in its own right and makes storytelling secondary—in fact, nearly nonexistent.

Jean Renoir's *Grand Illusion* is a war film in which we almost never see the war. Heroic charges and doomed battalions, the staple of the genre, are absent. World War I remains obstinately offscreen. Instead, Renoir concentrates on life in a German prisoner-of-war camp to suggest how relations between nations and social

5.170 A can used as a warning signal is sitting on a shelf.

5.171 It's pulled over, but it lands on a pillow and so makes no sound.

5.172 The camera pans left to reveal that the characters haven't noticed it.

5.170–5.172 *Grand Illusion*: Unrestricted narration.

classes are affected by war. The prisoners Maréchal and Boeldieu are both French; Rauffenstein is a German officer. Yet the aristocrat Boeldieu has more in common with Rauffenstein than with the mechanic Maréchal.

The film's plot traces the death of the Boeldieu-Rauffenstein upper class and the precarious survival of Maréchal and his pal Rosenthal. They escape the camp and take refuge in Elsa's farm, where they enjoy an interlude of peace. Eventually, however, they must flee across the border, back to France and presumably back to the war.

Within this plot, Renoir has given camera movement several functions, all directly supportive of the narrative. As we might expect, the camera will often follow the figures to keep our attention on them. The camera tracks with Maréchal and Rosenthal walking together after their escape; it tracks back when the prisoners are drawn to the window by the sound of marching Germans below. But the camera movements *independent* of character action make the film more unusual.

When the camera moves on its own in *Grand Illusion,* we are conscious of it actively interpreting the action, creating suspense or giving us information that the characters don't have. In one scene, a prisoner is digging in an escape tunnel and tugs a string signaling that he needs to be pulled out **(5.170).** An independent camera movement builds suspense by showing that the other characters have missed the signal and do not realize that he is suffocating **(5.171, 5.172).** Here camera movement creates a somewhat unrestricted narration.

The independent camera movements in *Grand Illusion* sometimes become motifs. For example, camera movements repeatedly link characters with details of their environment. Often a sequence begins with a close-up of some detail, and the camera draws back to anchor this detail in its larger context **(5.173, 5.174).** More complicated is the scene of the Christmas celebration at Elsa's that begins with a close-up of the crèche and tracks back to show, in several stages, the interplay of reactions among the characters.

Such camera movements are not simply decoration; beginning on a scenic detail before moving to the larger context makes story points economically. The opening detail not only establishes a new locale but highlights a thematic point, as with the squirrel cage. So does a track-in to a detail at the *end* of a scene, as when after Boeldieu's death, Rauffenstein cuts the geranium, the one flower in the prison **(5.175, 5.176).** Other directors would have emphasized the detail by cutting to a close-up, but Renoir keeps the film's style consistent by using a camera movement.

Characters are tied to their environment by even more ambitious moving-camera shots. These stress important narrative parallels. For example, tracking shots compare actions in two officers' bars—one French **(5.177–5.179),** one German **(5.180–5.182).** Through his camera movements, Renoir indicates a similarity between the two warring sides, blurring their national differences and stressing common desires.

5.173–5.176 Tracking shots and details of setting in *Grand Illusion* ▶

5.173 Renoir begins the scene by framing a close-up of a caged squirrel.

5.174 Creating a narrative parallel, the camera tracks back to reveal Boeldieu and Maréchal discussing their escape plans.

5.175 As Rauffenstein moves to the geranium in the window . . .

5.176 . . . Renoir tracks in to a close shot of the flower as he cuts it. Earlier Boeldieu had admired the geranium.

5.177–5.182 Parallel camera movements in *Grand Illusion* ▼

5.177 In the first scene, as Maréchal leaves the French officers' bar . . .

5.178 . . . Renoir pans and tracks left from the door to reveal pin-ups (just coming into the frame at the right) . . .

5.179 . . . and a poster.

5.180 One scene later, in the German officers' bar, a similar camera movement, this time toward the right, leaves the characters . . .

5.181 . . . and explores on its own . . .

5.182 . . . discovering some similar decorations.

5.183 One of the most elaborate camera movements in the film starts on a crucifix.

5.184 The camera tilts down to a military portrait on an altar, underlining the irony of a chapel commandeered as an officer's quarters.

5.185 The camera tracks past whips, spurs, and swords . . .

5.186 . . . to an orderly who is preparing Rauffenstein's gloves.

5.187 The orderly then walks away from the camera to close a window before returning . . .

5.188 . . . to the foreground. The camera pans left and tracks back to reveal . . .

5.189 . . . a tidy table . . .

5.190 . . . at which Rauffenstein is revealed to be sitting, ready for breakfast. For aristocratic warriors, the comforts of home aren't interrupted by war.

5.183–5.190 Prison camp: Military elegance in *Grand Illusion*.

Or consider how two moments of camera movement compare the war of the aristocrats and the war of the lower-class people. We are introduced to Rauffenstein's new position as commander of a POW camp through a lengthy tracking shot (**5.183–5.190**). During this movement, Renoir presents, wordlessly, the military mystique of grace on the battlefield that characterizes the aristocrat's war. Late in the film, however, a parallel shot criticizes this one (**5.191–5.193**). Elsa's war has none of Rauffenstein's glory, and our sense of that is conveyed chiefly through a parallel created by the repeated camera movement. Moreover, these camera movements work together with mise-en-scene, as the narrative parallel is reinforced by the subtle use of objects as motifs—the crucifixes in 5.183 and 5.193, the photographs in 5.184 and 5.191, and the tables that end both shots.

Moving the camera independently also links characters with one another. Again and again in the POW camp, the camera shifts to join one man to his comrades, spatially indicating their shared condition. As the prisoners ransack the collection of women's clothes, one man decides to dress up in them. When he appears in drag, a stillness falls over the men. Renoir tracks silently over the prisoners' faces, each one registering a reticent longing for a world they have left behind.

A more elaborate linking movement occurs in the scene of the prison vaudeville show, when the men learn that the French have recaptured a city. Renoir presents the shot as a celebration of spatial unity, with the camera moving among the men as they begin defiantly to sing the "Marseillaise" **(5.194–5.200)**. This complex camera movement circulates freely among the prisoners, suggesting their patriotic courage and unified defiance of their captors.

In Elsa's cottage as well, camera movement links characters. After feeding a cow, Maréchal enters the house, and a pan with him reveals Elsa scrubbing the floor. The culmination of the linking movements comes near the film's end, when Renoir pans from the Germans on one side of the border **(5.201)** to the distant French escapees on the other **(5.202, 5.203)**. Even on this scale, Renoir's camera refuses to honor national divisions.

The French film critic André Bazin remarked: "Jean Renoir found a way to reveal the hidden meaning of people and things without destroying the unity that is natural to them." Renoir's precisely choreographed camera movements go beyond simply enabling us to grasp the story. By providing information at a certain pace, by placing emphasis and by making comparisons, the mobile frame in *Grand Illusion* becomes as important as the mise-en-scene.

Michael Snow's experimental film *Wavelength* gives the mobile frame a different role. Instead of helping us construct a story, the camera style blocks that effort. Instead Snow asks us to concentrate our attention on how frame mobility creates patterns in its own right. Like Gehr's *Serene Velocity* (p. 172), the film becomes an experiment in cinematography.

The film begins with a long-shot framing of a loft apartment, facing one wall and window **(5.204)**. The camera zooms in abruptly a short distance and then holds that framing. It zooms in a bit more and then holds that **(5.205)**. And so it goes throughout the film's 45-minute length. By the end, a photograph of ocean waves on the distant wall fills the frame in close-up.

Wavelength is structured primarily around a single kind of frame mobility, the zoom-in. The film's progression concentrates on how changing lens lengths transforms the space of the loft. The sudden zooms create frequent abrupt shifts of perspective. In excluding parts of the room, the zoom-in also magnifies and flattens what we see; every change of focal length gives us a new set of spatial relations. As the film goes on, the zoom pushes more and more space offscreen. The sound track, for the most part, reinforces the basic formal development by emitting a single humming tone that rises consistently in pitch as the zoom magnifies the space.

Within *Wavelength*'s overall form, though, there are two contrasting patterns. The first is a series of filtered tints that play across the image as abstract fields of color. These tints often work against the depth represented in the shot of the loft. A second pattern suggests a sketchy narrative. At various intervals, characters enter the loft and talk, listen to the radio, make phone calls, and perform other ordinary actions. There's even a mysterious death: A body is glimpsed on the floor **(5.206)**. But these events remain unexplained in cause-effect terms and inconclusive (although at the film's end we do hear a sound that resembles a police siren). Furthermore, none of these actions swerves the mobile framing from its predetermined course. The jerkily shifting and halting zoom continues, even when it frames out important narrative information. *Wavelength* pulls in bits and pieces of narrative action, but they remain secondary; they're less important than the progression of the zoom.

5.191 This shot, set inside Elsa's farmhouse, also begins on an object, a photograph of her dead husband.

5.192 The camera tracks left past Elsa, who remarks, "Now the table is too large."

5.193 The camera continues, revealing the kitchen table, where her daughter sits alone. The chairs upended on the table reinforce the solitude of Elsa's life in the midst of war.

5.191–5.193 Farmhouse: War's cost in *Grand Illusion*.

5.194 As the lead "female" singer whips off his wig and requests the "Marseillaise" from the musicians . . .

5.195 . . . the camera moves right and the singer turns toward the audience.

5.196 The camera tracks farther right as others onstage sing along.

5.197 A tilt down shows two worried German guards in the foreground.

5.198 A track back to the left reveals a row of French prisoners in the audience on their feet, singing.

5.199 The camera tracks forward past them to the musicians and singer again . . .

5.200 . . . then pans quickly left to reveal the assembled prisoners again, this time declaring their patriotism directly to the camera.

5.194–5.200 *Grand Illusion*: Camera movement as prisoner solidarity.

As an experimental film, *Wavelength*'s use of frame mobility arouses, delays, and gratifies unusual expectations. The fragmentary plot briefly arouses curiosity (What are the people up to? What has led to the man's death, if he does die?) and surprise (the apparent murder). But in general, a story-centered suspense is replaced by a *stylistic* suspense. The zoom is the only sign of development, so we're curious about what it will eventually reveal.

Yet the revelation is delayed by the colored tints, the bits of plot, and the spasmodic qualities of the zoom itself. When the zoom finally reveals its target, our stylistic anticipations find fulfillment. The film's title stands revealed as a multiple pun, referring not only to the steadily rising pitch of the sound track but also to the distance that the zoom had to cross in order to reveal the photo—a "wave length."

5.201 The Germans realize that Maréchal and Rosenthal have crossed over into Switzerland.

5.202 Renoir pans to the right across the invisible border . . .

5.203 . . . to reveal the two escapees, tiny dots in the huge landscape.

5.201–5.203 Border crossing in *Grand Illusion*.

5.204

5.205

5.206

5.204–5.206 **The spasmodic space of *Wavelength*.** Early in the film, much of the apartment is visible (5.204). Near the end, the abrupt zoom-ins have made the distant wall visible (5.205). A fallen body can be glimpsed at the bottom of the frame, but the zoom-ins will soon eliminate it from the frame (5.206).

This revelation is secondary to the experience of watching the halting zoom change the space of the room, and watching a stylistic pattern curb our narrative appetite.

Grand Illusion and Wavelength illustrate, in different ways, how frame mobility can shape our perception of a film's space and time. Renoir motivated his style of frame mobility by narrative form, while Snow made the technique the principal formal concern, motivating other aspects of the film.

Duration of the Image: The Long Take

Throughout this chapter, we've seen that the decisions that filmmakers make about cinematography affect both space and time. The range of photographic tonalities, the shot's perspective relations, and the position of the camera are largely matters of space. But other possibilities, like speed of motion and mobile framing, have consequences for time too. The last area of choice and control we consider involves time in an especially intriguing way.

One popular YouTube genre is the so-called lipdub, in which a group of performers, usually students, lip-sync a pop song. Usually these videos feature lengthy camera movements within a single shot. There is a certain pride in choreographing all the "singers" with the moving camera in the two or three minutes that the song takes. Cutting would be easier, but there'd be less sense of virtuosity, less of a wow factor.

The lipdub phenomenon reflects one constant factor across the history of film art: the idea that there's something to be gained by letting a shot run long. But how

CONNECT TO THE BLOG
www.davidbordwell.net/blog

We connect the video genre of the lipdub to traditions of long-take filming in "2-4-6-8, whose lipdub do we appreciate?"

5.207

5.208

5.207–5.208 Compressing screen duration within a single shot. A shot in *The Only Son* moves from night (5.207) to morning (5.208).

CONNECT TO THE BLOG
www.davidbordwell.net/blog

We discuss artistic aspects of the long take in "Harry Potter treated with gravity" and "*Birdman*: Following Riggan's orders."

long, and why? Jean-Luc Godard asks the question explicitly. "The only great problem with cinema seems to me, more and more with each film, when and why to start a shot and when and why to end it." What guides a director in deciding how long to let a shot last?

Real Time Is . . . What?

When people talk about filming something in "real time," they often imply that the shot is recording actual duration. Usually it is. If we film a runner taking three seconds to clear a hurdle, our projected film will typically consume three seconds. But the filmmaker can choose to override real duration. As we've already seen, screen duration can be manipulated through slow or fast motion. Less obviously, narrative films don't always let us equate screen duration with story duration, even within a single shot.

As Chapter 3 pointed out (p. 80), story duration usually differs from plot duration, and both are affected by film techniques that shape screen time. You can compress story duration within a single shot. Here's an example from Yasujiro Ozu's *The Only Son*.

It is well past midnight, and we have just seen a family awake and talking. The shot shows a dim corner of the family's apartment, but eventually the light changes. By the end of the shot, morning has come (**5.207, 5.208**). This transitional shot consumes about a minute of screen time, but that plainly isn't the "real time" of the story action. The story action takes at least five hours. Thanks to cues of lighting, setting, and sound, the sustained shot has condensed a story duration of several hours into a minute or so on the screen.

Other films use tracking movements to compress longer passages of time in a continuous shot. This sort of condensation has become easier with digital postproduction (**5.209, 5.210**). The final shot of *Signs* moves away from an autumn view through a window and through a room, to reveal a winter landscape outside another window. Months of story time have passed during the tracking movement.

Functions of the Long Take

We can ask Godard's question a different way: How long should a shot last? Shot durations have varied somewhat over history. Early cinema (1895–1905) tended to rely on fairly lengthy shots, since each film often consisted of only one shot. With the emergence of continuity editing in the period 1905–1916, shots became shorter. From the late 1910s to the early 1920s, an American film would have an average shot length of about 5 seconds. After the coming of sound, the average stretched to about 10 seconds. But in the mid-1930s, directors in several countries began to experiment with very lengthy shots. The intricate camera movements in *Grand Illusion*, from 1935, are good examples. Renoir and his peers showed that unusually lengthy shots—**long takes,** as they're called—represented a powerful creative resource.

A *long take* is not the same as a *long shot,* which refers to the apparent distance between camera and object. As we saw in examining film production (pp. 22–23),

5.209

5.210

5.209–5.210 Camera movement through the seasons. In Roger Michell's *Notting Hill,* the protagonist's walk through the Portobello street market moves through autumn (5.209), then winter (5.210). Eventually the shot ends with spring.

6.128 Shot 5: . . . a cut to two-shot establishes his superior, Smith, on the scene. As Smith explains that the suspects' shotguns put them at the murder site, the camera racks focus to him, putting Exley out of focus.

6.129 Shot 6: A cutaway to White listening—again, a tight facial shot taken with a telephoto lens—reminds us of his presence. He is only an observer in this phase of the scene, but as the questioning heats up, he will burst in to attack a suspect.

6.130 Shot 7: Returning to the two-shot shows Smith demanding that Exley make the men confess.

6.131 Shot 8: A reverse angle on Exley, the first shot in the scene devoted to his face alone, underscores his determination: "Oh, I'll break them, sir."

6.132 Shot 9a: A cut back to the two-shot supplies Smith's satisfied reaction.

6.133 Shot 9 continues: Exley turns away. The lens shifts focus to catch his grim face in the foreground, preparing us for the brutality he will display.

6.134 Shot 9 continues as Exley walks out of frame, revealing with a rack-focus Vincennes's skeptical expression. The telephoto lens, supported by the rack-focus, has supplied facial views of Smith, then Exley, and then Vincennes all in a single shot.

Temporal Continuity: Order, Frequency, and Duration

As we've seen in Chapter 3, in narrative form, the plot's presentation of the story action usually involves manipulating time. Continuity editing offers the filmmaker many choices about presenting story time. Those options involve the dimensions we've already charted: order, frequency, and duration.

Order and Frequency   Continuity editing typically presents the story events in a 1-2-3 order. Spade rolls a cigarette in one shot, Effie enters in another shot, and so on. The most common violation of 1-2-3 order is a flashback, signaled by a cut or dissolve. As for frequency, classical continuity editing also often presents only *once* what happens *once* in the story. Within this tradition, it would be a gross mistake for Huston to repeat the shot of, say, Brigid sitting down (6.60). So chronological sequence and one-for-one frequency are the standard methods of handling order and frequency within the continuity style of editing. There are occasional exceptions, as we saw in our examples from *Hiroshima mon amour, The Godfather,* and *Police Story* (pp. 228–230).

Duration: Continuous or Elided   Duration offers more unusual editing possibilities. In the classical continuity system, story duration is seldom expanded by editing. Admittedly, overlapping cutting (p. 229) sometimes stretches out an action. But usually duration is presented continuously (plot time and screen time equaling story time) or is elided (story time being greater than plot time and screen time). Dialogue scenes are the most common examples; they're typically played out in their story duration.

Let's first consider *temporal continuity,* the most common possibility. Here a scene occupying, say, five minutes in the story also occupies five minutes when projected on the screen. We can pick out three ways to achieve temporal continuity, all of them present in the first scene of *The Maltese Falcon.*

First, the narrative progression of the scene has no gaps. Every movement by the characters and every line of dialogue are presented. Second, there's the sound track. Sound issuing from the story space (what is called *diegetic* sound) is a standard indicator of temporal continuity, especially when, as in this scene, the sound bleeds over each cut. Third, there's the match on action between shots 5 and 6. So powerful is the match on action that it creates both spatial *and* temporal continuity. The reason is obvious: If an action carries across the cut, we assume that the space and time are continuous from shot to shot. Continuous story action, diegetic sound overlapping the cuts, and matching on action are three primary indicators that the duration of the scene is continuous.

The filmmaker may not want complete continuity of duration. Just as a novelist sometimes condenses a scene to its high points, a filmmaker may want to skip over some less important moments. That will demand editing that creates temporal *ellipsis.* An ellipsis is something that has been omitted, and thanks to cutting a filmmaker may skip over seconds, minutes, hours, days, years, or centuries. Let's say you want to show a character getting ready for work in the morning. If you're making a classically constructed film, you might reduce this process to a few shots of the character going into the shower, putting on shoes, and frying an egg. As we saw on p. 229, the classical approach to editing may use empty frames, cutaways, or optical devices like dissolves to cover short temporal ellipses.

Elliding time offers a good example of how cinematic conventions have changed. In films made before the 1960s, dissolves, fades, or wipes were typically used to indicate an ellipsis between shots, usually the end of one scene and the beginning of the next. The Hollywood rule was that a dissolve indicates a brief time lapse and a fade indicates a much longer one.

6.135

6.136

6.137

6.135–6.137 Elliptical cuts in Wendy and Lucy. Arrested for shoplifting, Wendy is worried about having left her dog Lucy at the supermarket. As she's fingerprinted, Wendy glances up, and an eyeline match shows the clock (6.135). A cut to the next shot shows Wendy in a cell, indicating that some minutes have elapsed (6.136). The clock shot functioned as a cutaway to cover a time gap. In the cell, another cut shows Wendy in a different position (6.137). This suggests that still more time has passed. An older film would have implied the passage of time through dissolves, but here the abrupt changes of locale and character position suggest the same thing. A later shot of the clock will show that Wendy has been held for at least two hours.

Contemporary filmmakers usually employ a cut for such transitions. For example, in *2001,* Stanley Kubrick cuts directly from a bone spinning in the air to a space station orbiting the earth, one of the boldest graphic matches in narrative cinema. The cut eliminates millions of years of story time. Less drastically, most contemporary films indicate the passage of time simply by direct cuts. Changes in lighting, locale, or character position cue us that story time has passed **(6.135–6.137).**

The dissolve and fade have made a comeback in the age of digital video. For one thing, editing programs provide them, along with many varieties of wipes, so these optical effects are easy to incorporate. In addition, many online documentaries employ dissolves in the older manner, to indicate a passage of time. When the maker of a YouTube video wants to skip over the boring stretches of a cat fighting with a paper bag, a gentle dissolve may do the trick.

Montage Sequences   One form of ellipsis has persisted from the 1920s to the present. Sometimes the filmmaker wants to show a large-scale process or a lengthy period—a city waking up in the morning, a war, a child growing up. Here the filmmaker can pick another device from the menu: the **montage sequence.** (This should not be confused with the concept of *montage* in Sergei Eisenstein's film theory.) Brief portions of a process, informative titles (for example, "1865" or "San Francisco"), stereotyped images (such as the Eiffel Tower), newsreel footage, newspaper headlines, and the like can be joined by dissolves and music to create a quick, regular rhythm and to compress a lengthy series of actions into a few moments.

American studio films of the 1930s established some montage clichés—calendar pages fluttering away, newspaper presses pounding out an Extra—but in the hands of deft editors, such sequences became small virtuoso pieces. The driving pace of gangster films like *Scarface* and *The Roaring Twenties* owes a lot to dynamic montage sequences. Slavko Vorkapich, an experimental filmmaker, created somewhat abstract, almost delirious summaries of wide-ranging actions such as stock market crashes, political campaigns, and an opera singer's career **(6.138).**

Montage sequences have been a mainstay of narrative filmmaking ever since. *Jaws* employs a montage to summarize the start of tourist season through brief shots of vacationers arriving at the beach. A montage sequence in *Spider-Man* shows Peter Parker sketching his superhero costume, inspired by visions of the girl he loves **(6.139, 6.140).** All these instances remind us that because montage sequences usually lack dialogue, they tend to come wrapped in music. In *Tootsie,* a song accompanies a series of magazine covers showing the hero's rise to success as a TV star.

As with space, the filmmaker who employs the continuity style uses cinematic time primarily to advance the narrative. Like graphics, rhythm, and space, time is organized to unfold cause and effect and arouse curiosity, suspense, and surprise. In turn, we viewers who know the conventions pick up the cues and engage with the ways in which time is presented. We expect the editing to present story events in chronological order, with perhaps occasional rearrangement through flashbacks. We expect that editing will usually respect the frequency of story events. If an action is shown two or three times, it's exceptionally important. And we assume that the actions that don't matter to story causality will be dropped or trimmed by judicious ellipses. All these expectations allow the viewer to follow the story with minimal effort.

But there are many alternatives to the continuity approach, and these are worth a look.

Alternatives to Continuity Editing

Powerful and widespread as it is, the continuity tradition remains only one approach to editing. As you'd expect, some filmmakers have explored other possibilities.

6.138

6.139

6.140

6.138–6.140 Montage sequences old and new. *Maytime* uses superimpositions (here, the singer, sheet music, and a curtain rising) and rapid editing to summarize an opera singer's triumphs (6.138). *Citizen Kane* ironically refers to this passage in the montage sequences showing Susan Alexander's failures. For a montage sequence in *Spider-Man*, CGI technique creates a split image, showing both Peter's expression and a close-up of the costume he's designing (6.139). The *Spider-Man* sequence also uses a more traditional linking device, a dissolve that briefly superimposes two shots (6.140).

Graphic and Rhythmic Possibilities

Films using abstract or associational form have emphasized the graphic and rhythmic dimensions of editing. Instead of joining shot 1 to shot 2 to present a story, you could join them on the basis of purely graphic or rhythmic qualities, independent of the time and space they represent. In films such as *Anticipation of the Night, Scenes from Under Childhood,* and *Western History,* experimentalist Stan Brakhage uses purely graphic means of joining shot to shot. Continuities and contrasts of light, texture, and shape motivate the editing. Similarly, parts of Bruce Conner's *Cosmic Ray, A Movie,* and *Report* cut together newsreel footage, old film clips, film leader, and black frames on the basis of graphic patterns of movement, direction, and speed.

Many nonnarrative films have emphasized editing rhythm over the images themselves. *Single-frame films* (in which each shot is only one frame long) are the most extreme examples of this concentration on rhythm. Two famous examples are Peter Kubelka's *Schwechater* and Robert Breer's *Fist Fight* **(6.141).** Other avant-garde experiments coordinate editing rhythm with abstract graphics, as we'll see with *Ballet mécanique* in Chapter 10.

The graphic and rhythmic possibilities of editing haven't been neglected in narrative film, either. In Busby Berkeley's elaborate dance numbers in *42nd Street, Gold Diggers of 1933, Footlight Parade, Gold Diggers of 1935,* and *Dames,* the story periodically grinds to a halt, and the film presents intricate choreography that highlights geometrical configurations of dancers and background (4.158, from

6.141 **Single-frame filming.** This strip of film shows the one-frame shots in Breer's *Fist Fight*. Onscreen, they create a pulsating flicker of barely discernible images.

6.142

6.143

6.144

6.145

6.142–6.145 **Graphic matching in narrative cinema.** In *An Autumn Afternoon*, Ozu cuts from one man drinking sake (6.142) to another in a very similar costume doing the same thing (6.143). In *Ohayo*, Ozu creates a playful graphic match by cutting from a clothesline with a bright red sweater in the upper left (6.144) to an interior with a red lampshade in the same position (6.145).

42nd Street). More complex is the graphic editing of Yasujiro Ozu. Ozu's cutting is often dictated by a much more precise graphic continuity than we find in the classical continuity style. He playfully creates close graphic matches on movement, position, and color **(6.142–6.145).**

Some silent filmmakers experimented with vigorous rhythmic cutting. In such films as Abel Gance's *La Roue*, Jean Epstein's *Coeur fidèle* and *La Glace à trois faces,* and Alexandre Volkoff's *Kean,* accelerated editing renders the tempo of an onrushing train, a whirling carousel, a racing automobile, and a drunken dance. We can find strong passages of rhythmic editing in sound cinema too, from 1930s films such as Rouben Mamoulian's *Love Me Tonight* and René Clair's *Le Million* to later films like *Assault on Precinct 13* and *The Terminator.* Pulsating rhythmic editing is prominent in films influenced by music videos, such as *Moulin Rouge.*

 CONNECT TO THE BLOG
www.davidbordwell.net/blog

Early Japanese swordplay movies display some daring rhythmic editing, as we demonstrate in "Bando on the run." We find something similar in Hong Kong action films. See "Bond vs. Chan: Jackie shows how it's done" and "*Planet Hong Kong*: The dragon dances."

Spatial and Temporal Discontinuity

How might you tell a story without adhering to the continuity rules? One option is to use spatial continuity in ambiguous ways. In *Mon Oncle d'Amérique,* Alain Resnais interrupts the stories of his three main characters with shots of each character's favorite movie star, taken from French films of the 1940s. In some scenes, the cutting relies on continuity cues but uses them to create a discontinuity that arouses some uncertainty in the viewer **(6.146–6.148).**

More drastically, a filmmaker may violate or ignore the 180° system. The editing choices of filmmakers Jacques Tati and Yasujiro Ozu are based on what we might call 360° space. Instead of an axis of action that dictates that the camera be

6.146　　　　　　　　　**6.147**　　　　　　　　　**6.148**

6.146–6.148 Mixing continuity cues and discontinuity. At one point in *Mon Oncle d'Amérique*, René's pesky office mate calls to him (6.146). Resnais cuts to a shot of Jean Gabin (René's favorite star) in an older film, turning in reverse shot (6.147), as if he were replying to the man. Only then does Resnais supply a shot of René turning to meet his questioner (6.148). The film doesn't definitely present the Gabin shot as a fantasy image. We can't tell whether René imagines himself as his favorite star, or whether the film's narration draws the comparison apart from René's state of mind.

placed within an imaginary semicircle, these filmmakers work as if the action were not a line but a point at the center of a circle and as if the camera could be placed at any point on the circumference. In *Mr. Hulot's Holiday, Play Time,* and *Traffic,* Tati systematically films from almost every side; edited together, the shots present multiple spatial perspectives on a single event. Similarly, Ozu's scenes construct a 360° space that produces what the continuity style would consider grave editing errors. Ozu's films often do not yield consistent relative positions, eyeline matches, and screen directions **(6.149, 6.150).**

　　Are such cuts confusing? Defenders of the standard continuity system would say yes. But anyone who has seen films by Ozu or Tati can testify that their stories don't become unintelligible. These and other directors have found ways to keep the plot developments clear while also recalibrating our perception of space and time. Historically the continuity system offers one effective way to tell a story, but artistically, it isn't a necessity.

　　Apart from breaking or ignoring the 180° system, there are two other major tactics of discontinuity. One is the **jump cut.** This term is used in various ways but one primary meaning is this: When you cut together two shots of the same subject, if the shots differ only slightly in angle or composition, there will be a noticeable

CONNECT TO THE BLOG
www.davidbordwell.net/blog

If you have trouble spotting a jump cut, you could check our entry, "Sometimes a jump cut. . . ." The martial-arts scenes discussed there use the technique for a very different purpose from the jump cuts in 6.151–6.155.

6.149　　　　　　　　　　　　　　　　　**6.150**

6.149–6.150 Ozu's 360° editing system. One of the gravest sins in the classical continuity style is to match on action while breaking the line, yet Ozu does this comfortably in *Early Summer*. He cuts on the grandfather's gesture of drinking (6.149) to a view from the opposite side (6.150).

6.151

6.152

6.153

6.154

6.155

6.151–6.155 Jump cuts then and now. Jean-Luc Godard's *Breathless* used jump cuts freely. A cut from this shot of Patricia (6.151) to the next one (6.152), creates a jarring effect, as if some frames had been dropped. Montage sequences may use jump cuts to suggest rapid change. In *The Wolf of Wall Street*, jump-cut long shots evoke an almost magical growth of the protagonist's stock brokerage (6.153–6.155). A more gradual process is suggested by the dissolves in the montage sequences in *Maytime* and *Spider-Man* (6.138–6.140).

jump on the screen. Instead of appearing as two shots of the subject, the result looks as if some frames have been cut out of a single shot **(6.151, 6.152).** Many filmmakers believe that jump cuts can be avoided by shifting the camera at least 30 degrees from shot to shot (the so-called *30° rule*).

Even though jump cuts skip over some moments, they remain different from more common elliptical cuts. We saw an instance earlier, in the shots showing Wendy sitting in two positions on her cell bunk (6.136, 6.137). Those shots present two very different angles on the subject. A jump cut, however, shows the action from one angle or two very similar ones.

Jump cuts are quite noticeable and were long considered amateurish mistakes. But audiences eventually accepted them, although not in the doses that Godard supplied. Filmmakers now may use jump cuts in montage sequences and during moments of surprise, violence, or psychological disturbance **(6.153–6.155).**

A second sort of continuity disruption is created by the **nondiegetic insert.** Here the filmmaker cuts from the scene to a metaphorical or symbolic shot that

6.156

6.157

6.158

6.159

6.160

6.156–6.160 Nondiegetic editing. In *Lucy,* Luc Besson interrupts a scene of the title character being lured into danger (6.156) with an abstract shot of a mouse approaching a trap (6.157). A diegetic shot of Henri in *La Chinoise* (6.158) is followed by nondiegetic shots of the lion bed of King Tutankhamen (6.159) and his golden mask (6.160). Do the relics corroborate or challenge what Henri says?

doesn't belong to the space and time of the narrative **(6.156, 6.157).** In Sergei Eisenstein's *Strike,* the massacre of workers is intercut with the slaughter of a bull. In Godard's *La Chinoise,* Henri tells an anecdote about ancient Egyptians, who thought that "their language was the language of the gods." As he says this **(6.158),** Godard cuts in two close-ups of relics from the tomb of King Tutankhamen **(6.159, 6.160).** As nondiegetic inserts, coming from outside the story world, these prompt the spectator to search for implicit meanings and ask if the relics corroborate what Henri says.

There are still other alternatives to classical continuity, especially with respect to time. Although the classical approach to order and frequency of story events may seem the best option, it's only the most familiar. Story events don't have to be edited in 1-2-3 order.

Modern audiences have become accustomed to scenes that are interrupted by brief flashbacks. But some editing choices trigger greater uncertainty about exactly when something is taking place. Resnais's *La Guerre est finie* interrupts scenes cut in conventional continuity by images that may represent flashbacks, or fantasy episodes, or even future events. In Michael Haneke's *Caché* after a shot of a building, we see a boy looking out a window. This recalls the POV shots of Jeff looking at his neighbors in *Rear Window* (6.96, 6.97, 6.99–6.102). But in *Caché* the presumed chronological connection is revealed to be false **(6.161, 6.162).**

We've seen that editing can replay past scenes or Jackie Chan stunts (6.49–6.51). But filmmakers can repeat events to more disruptive effect. In *La Guerre est finie,* a future funeral is depicted in alternative ways, with the protagonist either present or absent. The escape sequence in Godard's *Pierrot le fou* not only scrambles the order of the shots but also plays with frequency by repeating one movement, Ferdinand jumping into the car (and showing it differently each time) **(6.163–6.166).** These editing choices block our normal expectations about story action and force us to concentrate on piecing together the film's narrative.

6.161

6.162

6.161–6.162 Ambiguous POV editing. *Caché* repeatedly shows a luxurious apartment building seen from across the street. After one nighttime view (6.161), there is a two-second shot of a bloodied boy watching (6.162). Later we'll learn that the editing has misled us severely.

6.163

6.164

6.165

6.166

6.163–6.166 Juggling temporal order and frequency. In *Pierrot le fou*, Ferdinand jumps into the car as Marianne pulls away (6.163), but the next shot flashes back to them fleeing their apartment (6.164). After they seem to have escaped (6.165), earlier phases of the action are repeated, including Ferdinand's jump into the car (6.166).

The editing may take liberties with story duration as well. Although complete continuity and ellipsis are the most common ways of rendering duration, expansion—stretching a moment out, making screen time greater than story time—remains a distinct possibility. François Truffaut uses such expansions in *Jules and Jim* to underscore narrative turning points, as when the heroine Catherine lifts her veil or jumps off an embankment into a river.

Filmmakers have reworked some of the most basic tenets of the continuity system. We've indicated, for example, that a match on action strongly suggests that time continues across the cut. Yet Alain Resnais creates an impossible continuity

6.167

6.168

6.167–6.168 The impossible match on action. In *Last Year at Marienbad,* small groups of guests are standing around the hotel lobby. A medium shot frames a blonde woman beginning to turn away from the camera (6.167). In the middle of her turn, there is a cut to her, still turning but in a different setting (6.168).

of motion in *Last Year at Marienbad* (**6.167, 6.168**). The smooth match on action, along with the woman's graphically matched position in the frame, implies that her head turns continuously, yet the change of setting contradicts this impression. As we'll see in Chapter 10, experimental films push ambiguous or contradictory editing even further.

Over time, audiences can become accustomed to discontinuities in narrative contexts. But with the jump cut, the nondiegetic insert, and the inconsistent match on action, temporal dislocations can push away from traditional notions of storytelling and create ambiguous relations among shots. These ambiguities needn't confuse us: they can stir our imaginations. Sergei Eisenstein's classic *October* provides many good examples.

CONNECT TO THE BLOG
www.davidbordwell.net/blog

We visit some striking editing decisions in "Some cuts I have known and loved."

■■ ■ ■■■ ■■ ■■ ■■ ■■■ ■■ ■■ ■■ ■■ ■ ■ ■
CREATIVE DECISIONS
■ ■■ ■■ ■■ ■■ ■■ ■■ ■ ■■ ■ ■

Discontinuity Editing in October

For many Soviet filmmakers of the 1920s, editing didn't simply serve the narrative progression, as in the continuity system that Kuleshov so much admired. Editing could be a tool for organizing the entire form of the film. Eisenstein's *Strike, Potemkin, October,* and *Old and New* were all built on the basis of certain editing devices—sometimes recruited to advance a plot, but at other times serving to comment on the action and suggest implicit meanings.

Eisenstein understood the continuity system quite well, but he sought to go beyond it. He believed that all sorts of clashes from shot to shot would prod the spectator to engage more actively with the film. Discontinuities of space and time could stir the spectator's senses by creating a sharp impact. They could arouse feelings, as viewers began to see the emotional connections among shots. And certain kinds of discontinuities could spur the spectator to reflect on the themes that Eisenstein sought to communicate.

No longer bound by conventional dramaturgy, Eisenstein's films roam freely through time and space. Crosscutting, eyeline cuts, and other devices of the continuity system are pushed in new directions, plunging us into a realm that could only exist on film. A short passage from *October* can illustrate how he uses editing discontinuities.

The sequence is the third one in the film (and comprises over 125 shots!). The story action is simple. The Provisional Government has taken power in Russia after the February Revolution, but instead of withdrawing from World War I, the government has kept its troops on the front. This maneuver has left the Russian people no better off than under the czar they deposed. In classical Hollywood cinema, this story might have been shown through a montage sequence of newspaper

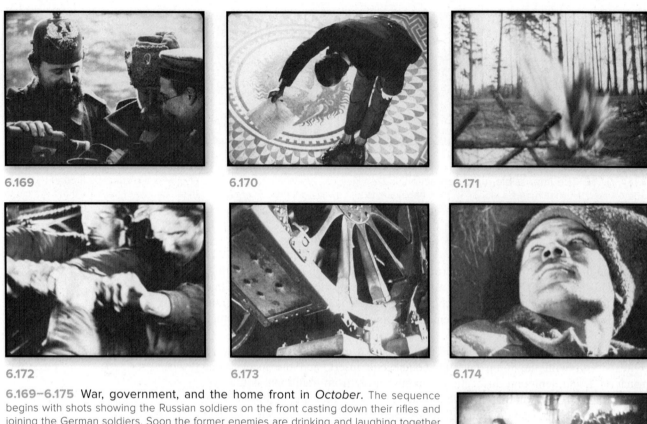

6.169 6.170 6.171

6.172 6.173 6.174

6.169–6.175 War, government, and the home front in *October.* The sequence begins with shots showing the Russian soldiers on the front casting down their rifles and joining the German soldiers. Soon the former enemies are drinking and laughing together (6.169). Eisenstein then cuts back to the Provisional Government, where a flunky extends a document to an unseen ruler (6.170); this pledges the government to continue the war. The soldiers' fraternization is suddenly disrupted by a bombardment (6.171). The soldiers run back to the trenches and huddle as dirt and bomb fragments rain down on them. Eisenstein then cuts to a cannon being lowered off an assembly line by factory workers (6.172). For a time, the narration crosscuts the descending cannon (6.173) with the soldiers (6.174). In the last section of the sequence, the shots of the cannon are crosscut with hungry women and children standing in breadlines in the snow (6.175). The sequence ends with two intertitles: "All as before . . . "/ "Hunger and war."

6.175

headlines smoothly linked to a scene showing a protagonist complaining that the Provisional Government has not solved people's problems. *October*'s protagonist, though, is not one person but the entire Russian people, and the film does not typically use dialogue scenes to present its story points. Rather, *October* seeks to go beyond a straightforward presentation of story events by making the viewer actively connect those events and reflect on their implications. So the film confronts us with a disorienting and disjunctive set of images **(6.169–6.175).**

Not only does *October* lack an individual protagonist; this sequence exploits spatial and temporal discontinuities. Although at times the 180° rule is respected (especially in the shots of women and children), never does Eisenstein introduce his situations with establishing shots. The major components of the locales are seldom shown together in one shot. On the whole, constructive editing builds up each line of action. (No surprise: Eisenstein studied under Kuleshov.)

The broader organizing principle of the sequence is crosscutting. Eisenstein alternates images of battlefield and government, factory and street. In the continuity system, crosscutting usually indicates that different actions are taking place simultaneously. But *October*'s crosscutting doesn't specify when the events are occurring. The women and children are seen at night, but it's daylight on the military front. Do the battlefield events take place before or after or during the women's vigil? We can't say. Eisenstein's crosscutting is primarily emotional

6.176 6.177 6.178

6.179 6.180 6.181

6.176–6.181 The government breaks the peace. Eisenstein cuts from a laughing German soldier facing right (6.176) to a menacing eagle statue, facing left, at the government headquarters (6.177). A static shot of rifles thrust into the snow (6.178) cuts to a long shot of a bursting shell (6.179). The impact is enhanced by a bold jump cut: The flunky is bowing (6.180), but suddenly he is standing up (6.181).

and conceptual. He's less concerned with presenting a linear story than arousing indignation at government policy and sympathy for its victims.

For example, to dramatize how the government prevents men meeting peaceably, Eisenstein shatters the friendship of the soldiers with disruptive cuts **(6.176–6.181).** The soldiers fraternize in fairly continuous duration, but the Provisional Government's behavior is given in drastic ellipses. This permits Eisenstein to identify the government as the unseen cause of the bombardment that ruptures the peace. This implication is reinforced by the way the first explosions are followed by the jump cut of the government flunky (6.180–6.181). Ellipsis takes on another role when the editing dramatizes the suffering of the women and children waiting in line. Instead of a gradual wasting away, we get abrupt decline: First we see them standing, then later lying pitiably on the ground.

Thinking like a filmmaker: How would you dramatize the idea that the government oppresses its people? Eisenstein does it daringly, by creating a visual metaphor. Once the government orders the bombardment of the front, the soldiers are huddling under the barrage. This already suggests that the government, not the German army, is the real enemy. Eisenstein takes things further by showing men crushed by the war machine. Thanks to editing, shots of the cannon slowly descending are contrasted with shots of the men crouching in the trenches (6.173, 6.174). The graphic clash of directions is reinforced by a false eyeline match. The soldier looks upward, as if he could see the lowering cannon, even though he and the cannon are in entirely separate places. By showing the factory workers lowering the cannon (6.172), the cutting links the captive soldiers to the proletariat. Finally, as the cannon hits the ground, Eisenstein crosscuts images of it with the shots of the starving families of the soldiers and the workers. They, too, are oppressed, literally pressed down, by the government machine. As the cannon wheels hit the floor ponderously, Einstein cuts to the women's feet in the snow. The machine's heaviness is linked by titles ("one pound," "half a pound") to the steady starvation of the women and children. Eisenstein's editing discontinuities encourage us to build up a political commentary on the story events.

Graphic discontinuities recur throughout *October,* especially in scenes of dynamic action, and they hit our eyes more forcefully than neatly matched shots would. To watch an Eisenstein film is to submit oneself to percussive graphic editing. But that editing also gives us powerful images—friendly soldiers, faceless bureaucrats, suffering women and children—that stir our emotions. By refusing to focus on one protagonist, Eisenstein moves masses of people to the fore.

But he did not want to stop with mere sympathy. *October* tries to show the underlying causes of the masses' suffering more directly than the traditional dramatic conflict between individualized heroes and villains could. Eisenstein's editing constructs correspondences, analogies, and contrasts that ask us to *interpret* the story events. The interpretation is not simply handed to the viewer; rather, the editing discontinuities push us to work out implicit meanings. By assembling the shots in our minds, we grasp his idea that the new government is no different from the old one and that ordinary people are sacrificed to a war machine.

No one was more aware of the multitude of creative decisions involved in editing than Eisenstein. He saw that classical continuity would not achieve his purposes. So he chose to make a film in which discontinuities of graphic elements, time, and space could prod the spectator into sympathy and thought. In the process he demonstrated that there are powerful alternatives to the principles of continuity editing.

SUMMARY

When any two shots are joined, we can ask several questions:

1. How are the shots graphically continuous or discontinuous?

2. What rhythmic relations are created?

3. Are the shots spatially continuous? If not, what creates the discontinuity? (Crosscutting? Ambiguous cues?) If the shots are spatially continuous, how does the 180° system create the continuity?

4. Are the shots temporally continuous? If so, what creates the continuity? (For example, matches on action?) If not, what creates the discontinuity? (Ellipsis? Overlapping cuts?)

More generally, we can ask the question we ask of every film technique: How does this technique *function* with respect to the film's narrative form? Does the film use editing to lay out the narrative space, time, and cause-effect chain in the manner of classical continuity? How do editing patterns emphasize facial expressions, dialogue, or setting? Do editing patterns withhold narrative information? In general, how does editing contribute to the viewer's experience of the film?

Some practical hints: You can learn to notice editing in several ways. If you are having trouble noticing cuts, try watching a film or video and tapping each time a shot changes. Once you recognize editing easily, watch any film with the sole purpose of observing one editing aspect—say, the way space is presented, or the control of graphics or time. Sensitize yourself to rhythmic editing by noting cutting rates; tapping out the tempo of the cuts can help.

Watching 1930s and 1940s American films can introduce you to classical continuity style; try to predict what shot will come next in a sequence. (You'll be surprised at how often you're right.) When you watch a film on video, try turning off the sound; editing patterns become more apparent this way. When there's a violation of continuity, ask yourself whether it is accidental or serves a purpose. When you see a film that does not obey classical continuity principles, search for its unique editing patterns. Use the slow-motion, freeze, and reverse controls on a video player to analyze a film sequence as this chapter has done. (Almost any film will do.) In such ways as these, you can considerably increase your understanding of the power of editing.

7

Sound in the Cinema

You're planning a scene that shows Jim phoning Amanda. As usual, you confront a choice.

You can show both sides of the conversation, cutting between Jim and Amanda as they exchange lines. (Many phone scenes are staged and filmed as if they were shot/reverse shot conversations.) Or you could stage it in split-screen, which would keep both Jim and Amanda visible for the whole dialogue. Either option yields unrestricted narration, which is ideal if you want to reveal both characters' behavior in the conversation.

Alternatively, you could keep the camera on one character, say Jim, for the entire scene. Instead of showing Amanda, you would simply let us hear her responses. Showing only Jim would restrict us to his range of knowledge, and that choice can add uncertainty and suspense. If we hear Amanda agree to the date, but we don't see her doing so, we might entertain some doubts about her interest or her motives. And is she alone or with someone? As often happens, restricted narration might yield some curiosity and suspense.

But there's another option still. Suppose we don't see *or* hear Amanda. We hear only Jim's side of the conversation, broken by pauses when he's listening to Amanda's replies. Our narration has grown still more restrictive: We know less than Jim knows. This option is often used for perfunctory actions, such as someone phoning to order a cab. Applied to a more significant scene, it could oblige us to listen more intently and imagine what's happening on the other end of the line **(7.1)**.

Sound Decisions

We've seen at several points that film art offers both opportunities and constraints. As a filmmaker, you face a rich array of options. But you have to choose among them, and each choice has different implications. Moreover, some decisions create a cascade of further choices. If you show only Jim and keep Amanda offscreen, you still have to decide whether to let us hear her lines or not.

Filmmakers have to consider these options, either intellectually or intuitively, because each alternative affects the audience differently. Sound, like every other technique, offers a plenitude of possibilities, but the filmmaker judges which ones to pursue, based on how they suit the film's overall form and how they shape the viewer's experience.

7.1 The telephone teaser. One way to handle a phone conversation: In *Chungking Express,* a young man dumped by his girlfriend calls up other women he's known, eventually reaching those he hasn't seen since grade school. We hear only his clumsy efforts to remind them who he is. The comic effect comes partly from imagining the puzzlement and annoyance the women must be expressing.

7.2 Sound summons up an unseen space. Orson Welles had a radio career before going to Hollywood, so he understood the power of sound to arouse the audience's imagination. At the start of this scene from *The Magnificent Ambersons*, Georgie Minafer says good-bye to his Uncle Jack, who's about to board a train. But there's no establishing shot of the station, not even a sign identifying it. We see the two men against a pillar while we hear announcements echoing in a large, hollow space. The locomotive is evoked by a whistle, a chugging engine, and blasts of steam. Welles's sound design, aided by rear projection of a roof, has conjured up an entire locale.

As we saw in Chapter 1, in the process of film production, the sound track is constructed separately from the images, and it can be manipulated independently. This makes sound as flexible and wide-ranging as other techniques. Yet sound is perhaps the hardest one to study.

It's not because we're bad at listening. Even before we're born, we can distinguish voices. We differentiate male voices from female ones, and we recognize Mother's above all. Once we've grown, we exist in a continuous bath of sound. Just as our stereoscopic vision helps us locate details in the visual world, our ears can triangulate a sound's location—particularly if it's human speech, to which our auditory system is very sensitive. At our peak of health, we can note volume differences at a range of a trillion to one. We have, auditory scientists tell us, over 400,000 distinct sounds in our memory.

Yet unless we're musicians or sound engineers, we've learned to ignore most sounds in our environment. Our primary information about the color, texture, and layout of our surroundings comes from sight, and so in ordinary life, sound is often simply a background for our visual attention. Similarly, we speak of *watching* a film and of being movie *viewers* or *spectators*—all terms implying that the sound track is a secondary factor. We're strongly inclined to think of sound as simply an accompaniment to the real basis of cinema, the moving images.

This inclination lets sound designers create a world without our noticing. On the screen we may see merely an anxious face against a cloudy sky, but we may hear a fierce wind, a police siren, and a child's cry. Suddenly we conjure up a situation of danger. A low-budget horror film with awkward acting and unconvincing special effects can stir an audience to shrieks with disgusting slurps, snaps, and gurgles. "Sound is the biggest bang for your buck of anything in the movie business," says the manager of Skywalker Sound **(7.2)**.

Fortunately, filmgoers have started to notice. *Star Wars* and other hits of the 1970s introduced the broad public to new technologies of sound recording and reproduction. Audiences came to expect Dolby noise reduction processes, expanded frequency and dynamic range, and four- and six-track theater playback. During the early 1990s, digital sound became routine for big-budget pictures, and now virtually all releases have crisp, dense sound tracks. "An older film like *Casablanca* has an empty soundtrack compared with what we do today," remarks the supervising sound editor for *Lost in Translation*. Today's romantic comedy is as densely packed with sound effects as an action picture was 20 years ago. Multiplex theaters upgraded their sound systems to meet filmmakers' challenges, and the popularity of DVDs prompted consumers to set up home theaters with ravishing sound.

Viewers' new sensitivity to sound is apparent in the custom of starting a film's sound track with dialogue or sound effects, before the images appear. You can argue that this device serves to quiet down the audience so that the opening scene gets the proper attention, but often the sonic information draws us slowly into the story. Many modern films lead us by the ear. Not since the first talkies of the late 1920s have filmgoers been so aware of what they hear.

The Powers of Sound

Sound is a powerful film technique for several reasons. For one thing, it engages a distinct sense mode. Even before recorded sound was introduced in 1926, silent films were accompanied by orchestra, organ, or piano. At a minimum, the music filled in the silence and gave the spectator a more complete experience. More significantly, the engagement of hearing opens the possibility of what the Soviet director Sergei Eisenstein called "synchronization of senses"—making a single rhythm or expressive quality bind together image and sound.

The meshing of image and sound appeals to something quite deep in human consciousness. Babies spontaneously connect sounds with what they see. For us, if a sound and image occur at the same moment, they tend to be perceived as one event, not two. Just as our minds search for patterns in a shot or for causal patterns in a narrative, we're inclined to seek out patterns that will fuse lip movements and speech. The power of musical structure to map onto visual structure is evident not only in dance but also when fans of the Pink Floyd album *The Dark Side of the Moon* play it back over *The Wizard of Oz.* Our bias toward audio-visual blending governs both our everyday activities and our experiences of arts like music, theater, and film.

Sound Shapes Our Understanding of Images

Sound is often treated as a lesser partner to the images, but we need to recognize that it can actively shape how we understand them. In one sequence of *Letter from Siberia* **(7.3–7.6),** Chris Marker demonstrates the power of sound to alter our understanding of what's onscreen. Three times Marker shows the same footage—a shot of a bus passing a car on a city street, three shots of workers paving a street. But each time the footage is accompanied by a completely different sound track. Compare the three versions tabulated alongside the sequence in Table 7.1. The first one is heavily affirmative, the second is harshly critical, and the third mixes praise and criticism. The audience will construe the same images differently, depending on the voice-over commentary.

Guiding Our Eye and Mind

The *Letter from Siberia* sequence demonstrates another advantage of film sound. It can steer our attention within the image. When the commentator describes the "blood-colored buses," we're likely to look at the buses, not the car.

Brian De Palma exploits the guiding function of sound in his conspiracy thriller *Blow-Out.* Jack Terry is a sound designer for low-budget exploitation films. While capturing environmental background noises, he records a deadly car crash. Jack takes his recording as proof that an assassin shot out the car's tire in order to kill the politician inside. A crooked detective was on the scene as well, and he shot a film of the crackup. Using still images from the detective's footage, Jack creates a mini-film he can synchronize with his recording **(7.7–7.9).** The result reveals a vital clue that was unnoticed in the published images.

What if the crucial item isn't in the shot at all? Suppose we have a shot of a man in a room. If we hear a door creaking, we anticipate that someone has entered the room, and we probably expect to see that person in the next shot. In other words, a simple sound can prod us to form expectations. Those can then be delayed, as in a horror film; in that genre, it's conventional to suggest an unseen menace but dwell on a character staring fearfully at something offscreen.

In addition, sound gives a new value to silence. A quiet passage can create almost unbearable tension, while an abrupt silence in a noisy passage can jolt us **(7.10, 7.11).** Most contemporary sound mixers drop in about a half-second of silence just before explosions and other loud noises. During the battle between Dumbledore and Voldemort in *Harry Potter and the Order of the Phoenix*, the sound team slipped in brief silences between Voldemort's attacks. The contrast made the thwacks seem abnormally loud. Just as color film turns black and white into grades of color, so sound can include all the resources of silence.

One more advantage: sound bristles with as many creative possibilities as editing. Through editing, one may join shots of any two spaces to create a meaningful relation. Similarly, the filmmaker can mix any sonic phenomena into a whole. With the introduction of sound cinema, the infinity of visual possibilities was joined by the infinity of acoustic events.

> ❝ The most exciting moment is the moment when I add the sound. . . . At this moment, I tremble."
> —Akira Kurosawa, director

TABLE 7.1 *Letter From Siberia* Footage

Images	First Commentary	Second Commentary	Third Commentary
 7.3	Yakutsk, capital of the Yakutsk Autonomous Soviet Socialist Republic, is a modern city in which comfortable buses made available to the population share the streets with powerful Zyms, the pride of the Soviet automobile industry. In the	Yakutsk is a dark city with an evil reputation. The population is crammed into blood-colored buses while the members of the privileged caste brazenly display the luxury of their Zyms—costly and uncomfortable cars at best. Bending	In Yakutsk, where modern houses are gradually replacing the dark older sections, a bus, less crowded than its London or New York equivalent at rush hour, passes a Zym, an excellent car reserved for public utilities departments on account of its scarcity.
 7.4	joyful spirit of socialist emulation, happy Soviet workers, among them this picturesque denizen	to the task like slaves, the miserable Soviet workers, among them this sinister looking Asiatic,	With courage and tenacity under extremely difficult conditions, Soviet workers, among them this Yakut
 7.5	of the Arctic reaches, apply themselves	apply themselves to the primitive labor	afflicted with an eye disorder, apply themselves to
 7.6	to making Yakutsk an even better place to live. Or else:	of grading with a drag beam. Or simply:	improving the appearance of their city, which could certainly use it.

7.7

7.8

7.9

7.7–7.9 Sound reveals a clue. In *Blow-Out*, Jack studies his DIY film made from magazine photographs (7.7). He synchronizes his tape with the image track (7.8). When the two play together, the blowout sound matches a flash from the bushes near a fence post (7.9). The flash was visible in the replayed footage, but it took the sound track to make Jack and the audience notice it.

7.10

7.11

7.10–7.11 Subjective silence. In *Babel,* when the deaf teenage girl enters the disco, the club music is about to climax (7.10). Instead, it drops out when we cut to her optical point-of-view on the boy she's following (7.11). Instead of subjective sound, we get subjective silence, and this sharply dramatizes her isolation from what is happening around her.

Fundamentals of Film Sound

Film sound can include any mixture of speech, music, and noise. Filmmakers make decisions about the types and density of sounds as well as their properties, including loudness and pitch.

Perceptual Properties

Several aspects of film sound are familiar to us from everyday experience.

Loudness   The sounds we hear result from vibrations in the air. The amplitude, or breadth, of the vibrations produces our sense of *loudness*, or volume.

Filmmakers manipulate volume constantly. A long shot of a busy street is accompanied by traffic noises, but when two people meet and start to speak, the

7.12 Manipulating volume for intelligibility. Establishing shots at the start of *Norma Rae* show the textile factory full of deafening machine noise, so that we register the harsh working conditions. As the story action starts, the noise is turned down so that the women's dialogue in the break room will be audible.

loudness of the traffic diminishes (**7.12**). A conversation between a soft-spoken character and a blustery one is characterized as much by volume as by what they say. Much of the comedy in Mel Brooks's *The Producers* comes from the contrast between the voices of booming Max Bialystock and meek accountant Leo Bloom.

Although loudness can be measured in precise acoustic terms, for the listener it's relative. A lengthy passage of high-amplitude sound may not sound as loud as a lower burst of sound after a stretch of silence. In *Capote,* a killer's confession is presented in a nearly quiet scene, with only the wind audible. That ambience makes the shotgun blast that follows seem exceptionally loud. As with mise-en-scene and the tonal qualities of the image, the sound track seizes our attention through contrast.

Loudness is also related to perceived distance. All other things being equal, the louder the sound, the closer we take it to be. This sort of assumption seems to be at work in the street traffic example already mentioned: The couple's dialogue, being closer to us, is sensed as louder, while the traffic noise recedes to the background. In addition, a film may startle the viewer by exploiting abrupt and extreme shifts in volume (usually called changes in *dynamics*), as when a quiet scene is interrupted by a very loud noise. Changes in loudness may be combined with cutting or camera movement to reinforce our sense of moving toward or away from the source of the noise (**7.13–7.15**).

Pitch   The frequency of sound vibrations affects *pitch*, or the perceived highness or lowness of the sound. Most sounds, in life and on film, are complex tones, in batches of different frequencies. Pitch helps our ear sort out the sounds.

Very low-pitched sounds suggest rumbling, whereas very high-pitched ones suggest tinkling. Pitch helps us distinguish music and speech from background noise. The filmmaker can use pitch to distinguish objects too. A thump suggests the object is hollow, but high-pitched jingle bells suggest smoother, harder objects.

Pitch can serve more specific purposes. We've already mentioned the effect of an octave leap in the song "Over the Rainbow" in *The Wizard of Oz* (p. 62). When a young boy tries to speak in a man's deep voice and fails, as in *How Green Was My Valley,* the joke is based primarily on pitch. Marlene Dietrich's vocal delivery often depends on a long upward-gliding intonation that makes a statement sound like a question. In the coronation scene of *Ivan the Terrible,* Part I, a court singer with a deep bass voice begins a song of praise to Ivan, and

7.13

7.14

7.15

7.13–7.15 Volume as a cue for distance. A hiker is trapped at the bottom of a canyon in *127 Hours*. One shot begins on a high-angle shot of him shouting for help (7.13). As the camera pulls quickly up and away from him, his cries diminish in volume (7.14), until the shot ends on an extreme-long view of the desert, with the canyon a dark line in the landscape and the hiker's voice no longer audible (7.15). Director Danny Boyle uses sound perspective, timed with drastic changes of shot scale, to dramatize how hopeless the young man's plight is.

each phrase rises dramatically in pitch **(7.16–7.18).** When Bernard Herrmann obtained the effects of shrill, birdlike shrieking in Hitchcock's *Psycho,* even many musicians could not recognize the source: violins played at extraordinarily high pitch.

Timbre The harmonic components of sound give it a certain color, or tone quality—what musicians call *timbre.* When we call someone's voice nasal or a musical tone mellow, we're referring to timbre. Timbre is actually a less fundamental acoustic parameter than amplitude or frequency, but it's indispensable in describing the texture or "feel" of a sound. In everyday life, the recognition of a familiar sound is largely a matter of various aspects of timbre.

7.16

7.17

7.18

7.16–7.18 Pitch synchronized with cutting. In *Ivan the Terrible,* Eisenstein emphasizes changes in vocal pitch by cutting from a medium-long shot (7.16) to a medium shot (7.17) to a close-up of the singer (7.18).

Filmmakers rely on timbre constantly. An actor's voice—Sean Connery's gruff Scots accent, Tom Waits's plaintive rasp—becomes distinctive, thanks to timbre. For Disney's *Beauty and the Beast*, Robbie Benson's speaking voice was mixed with tiger and lion sounds to enhance the Beast's animalistic side. Timbre, along with pitch, distinguishes musical instruments from each other, and often enhances emotion, as when sultry saxophone music comes up during a seduction scene.

More subtly, in the opening sequence of Rouben Mamoulian's *Love Me Tonight,* people starting the day on a street pass a musical rhythm from object to object—a broom, a carpet beater—and the humor of the number springs in part from the very different timbres of the objects. In preparing the sound track for Peter Weir's *Witness,* the editors drew on sounds recorded 20 or more years before, so that the less modern timbre of the older recordings would evoke the rustic seclusion of the Amish community.

Loudness, pitch, and timbre define the overall sonic texture of a film. For example, these qualities enable us to recognize different characters' voices. Both John Wayne and James Stewart speak slowly, but Wayne's voice tends to be deeper and gruffer than Stewart's querulous drawl. This difference works to great advantage in *The Man Who Shot Liberty Valance,* where their characters are sharply contrasted. In *The Wizard of Oz,* the disparity between the public image of the Wizard and the old charlatan who rigs it up is marked by the booming bass of the huge green head and the old man's higher, softer, more quavering voice. During an action sequence, the threshold for loudness is raised, so the film's sound designer may have to introduce noises of different frequencies or textures—a whining bullet during a rumbling car chase, for example—to make sure that certain details aren't drowned out.

These basic sound qualities can also shape our experience of a film as a whole. *Citizen Kane,* for example, offers a wide range of sound manipulations. Echo chambers alter timbre and volume. A motif is formed by the inability of Kane's wife, Susan, to sing pitches accurately. Moreover, in *Citizen Kane,* the plot's shifts between times and places are covered by continuing a sound thread and varying the basic acoustics. A shot of Kane applauding dissolves to a shot of a crowd applauding (a shift in volume and timbre). Leland beginning a sentence in the street cuts to Kane finishing the sentence in an auditorium, his voice magnified by loudspeakers (a shift in volume, timbre, and pitch).

Sound processes create wider ranges of frequency and volume, as well as crisper timbres than filmmakers could achieve in the studio years. Today sound editors can individualize voice or noise to a surprising degree. For *The Thin Red Line,* every character's distinctive breathing sounds were recorded for use as ambient noise. Randy Thoms, sound designer for *Cast Away,* sought to characterize different sorts of wind—breezes from the open sea, winds in a cave. Sound even announces a shift in wind direction crucial to one of the hero's plans. "We can use the wind in a very musical way," Thoms notes.

Recording, Altering, and Combining Sounds

Sound in the cinema is of three types: speech, music, and noise (usually called *sound effects*). Occasionally a sound may cross categories—Is a yell classified as speech or noise?—and filmmakers have exploited these ambiguities. In *Psycho,* when a woman screams, we expect to hear a voice but instead hear violins. Still, in most cases, the distinctions hold. Now that we have an idea of some basic acoustic properties, how are speech, music, and sound effects captured?

Recording Dialogue is usually recorded during filming, but that isn't the version we will hear in the finished film. The dialogue in the film has been dubbed, or "looped," later in a recording studio. In a process called automated

> 66 The Empire spaceship sounded a certain way as compared to the Imperial fleet; that was a deliberate style change. Everybody in the Empire had shrieking, howling, ghostlike, frightening sounds. . . . You hear it—you jump with fear. Whereas the rebel forces had more junky-sounding planes and spaceships. They weren't quite as powerful; they tended to pop and sputter more."
> —Ben Burtt, sound editor, *Star Wars*

> 66 Too many films seem essentially designed to be heard in the mixing studios. I always fight against recording every single footstep, and would rather lose the sound of people settling into armchairs, etc., and fade out a particular atmosphere sound once the emotional impact has been achieved, even at the cost of realism. You have to know how to play with silence, to treat sound like music."
> —Bernard Tavernier, director

dialogue recording (ADR), actors repeat their lines while watching the footage in "looped playback." The dialogue recorded during shooting guides the ADR process.

Music is almost never recorded during principal photography, unless the filmmaker is documenting a musical performance, as in concert films like *Stop Making Sense*, *U2 3D*, and *Year of the Horse*. Much more often, music is added in postproduction. The track might be a selection of existing pieces, such as popular songs, or it might be a score written specifically for the film. Recording a score involves the composer leading the musicians through each cue while watching the footage projected on a screen.

Like music, most sound effects are added during postproduction. A common method is the Foley process, which creates noises tailored to each scene. In a sonically clean studio, experts record people pouring drinks, splashing in mud, rubbing sandpaper, and any other actions that put human movement in contact with surfaces. Foley artists, who often collect shoes, fabrics, and car doors, also devise imaginative equivalents. Foley artist Joan Rowe used a package of liver from the supermarket to get the "liquidy and friendly" sound of the title character of *E.T.: The Extraterrestrial*.

Not all postproduction sound is generated from scratch. A great many postproduction sound effects are culled from libraries. During the studio era, Hollywood's libraries cataloged more than 100,000 distinct sounds. A "Biffs and Bangs" file, for instance, might contain an assortment of the kicks, slaps, and punches associated with fight scenes. The most famous library effect is the "Wilhelm scream," first heard in a 1951 American film when an alligator bites off a cowboy's arm. The scream was recycled in *Star Wars*, *Raiders of the Lost Ark*, *Reservoir Dogs*, *Transformers*, and over a hundred other films. (Google "Wilhelm scream" and you can hear it online.) Sound editors also build their personal collections of noises that intrigue them.

Sometimes the sound track is conceived before the image track. In a musical, the camera films singers and players who are miming to a prerecorded track. Even dancers' footwork, like taps or stomps, will already be on the playback. That track will be married to the filmed images during the editing process. Animated cartoons typically record music, dialogue, and sound effects before camera capture begins, so the action onscreen will match the sound frame by frame. For the adventures of Bugs Bunny and Daffy Duck, Carl Stalling created frantically paced jumbles of familiar tunes, weird noises, and distinctive voices.

Reworking Sound   Once the sounds are captured, the creation of the film's sound track resembles the editing of the image track. Just as you can pick the best image from several shots, you may choose what exact bit of sound will serve your purpose. And just as a shot's color or lighting may be manipulated in postproduction, a sound may be processed to change its acoustic qualities.

A common form of manipulation is blending. The noises emitted by the demonically possessed girl in *The Exorcist* consist of screams, animal thrashings, and English spoken backward. To create the roar of a Tyrannosaurus rex for *Jurassic Park*, sound engineers blended a tiger's roar, a baby elephant's trumpeting, and an alligator's growl for lower tones. To characterize a runaway train as a primal force, *Unstoppable* gave it an auditory identity derived from the sounds of beasts. After smashing another train in its path, the rogue locomotive even lets out a bellow of triumph.

Selection Guides Our Attention   As you read this, you are attending to words on the page and (to various degrees) ignoring certain stimuli that reach your ears. But if you close your eyes and listen keenly, you'll become aware of background sounds—traffic, footsteps, distant voices. You know that if you set up a

" We're always looking for things that squeak or clank or make springy, sproingy noises. If you go to a swap meet or garage sale, you're always putting your ear up to things and listening. The weirdest thing is when you listen to things in the grocery store—tap on vegetables and rustle them and crunch them a little."

—Marnie Moore, Foley artist, *Boogie Nights*, *Jarhead*

> 66 We were going for a documentary feel. We came up with a way for the loop group actors to say lines in a way we called 'nondescript dialogue.' They said lines, but they didn't say the actual words. If you put it behind people speaking, you just think it's people talking offscreen, but your ear isn't drawn to it. It would just lie there as a bed, and you can play it relatively loudly and it just fits in with the scenes."
>
> —Hugh Waddell, ADR supervisor, on *The Thin Red Line*

microphone and recorder in what seems to be a quiet environment, those normally unnoticed sounds can become obtrusive. The microphone is unselective; like the camera lens, it doesn't automatically filter out what's distracting.

It's up to the filmmaker to make what's important stand out. Normally, the sound track is clarified and simplified so that important material stands out. Dialogue, as a transmitter of story information, is usually recorded and reproduced for maximum clarity. Important lines should not have to compete with music or background noise. Sound effects are usually less important than speech. They supply an overall sense of a realistic environment and are seldom noticed; if they were missing, however, the silence would be distracting. Music is usually subordinate to dialogue as well, entering during pauses in conversation or in passages without dialogue.

All of these customs have become conventions. Christopher Nolan learned how strong those conventions are when he included muffled dialogue in *Interstellar*. "There are particular moments in the film where I decided to use dialogue as a sound effect, so sometimes it's mixed slightly underneath the other sound effects or in the other sound effects to emphasize how loud the surrounding noise is. It's not that nobody has ever done these things before, but it's a little unconventional for a Hollywood movie." Some viewers, though, assumed there was a technical problem with the screening. Nolan was asking the audience to adjust their expectations to a sound mix that didn't put dialogue at the top.

Dialogue doesn't always rank highest in importance, though. Sound effects are usually central to action sequences, while music can dominate dance scenes, transitional sequences, or emotion-laden moments without dialogue. And some filmmakers have shifted the weight conventionally assigned to each type of sound. Charlie Chaplin's *City Lights* and *Modern Times* eliminate dialogue, letting sound effects and music come to the fore. The films of Jacques Tati and Jean-Marie Straub retain dialogue but still place great emphasis on sound effects. In Robert Bresson's *A Man Escaped,* music and noise fill out a sparse dialogue track by evoking offscreen space and creating thematic associations.

By choosing only certain sounds, the filmmaker guides our perception of the action. In one scene from Jacques Tati's *Mr. Hulot's Holiday,* vacationers at a resort hotel are relaxing **(7.19)**. Early in the scene, the guests in the foreground are murmuring quietly, but Hulot's Ping-Pong game is louder; the sound cues us to watch Hulot. Later in the scene, however, the same Ping-Pong game makes no sound at all, and our attention is drawn to the muttering cardplayers in the foreground. The presence and absence of the sound of the Ping-Pong ball guides our expectations. If you start to notice how such selection of sound shapes our perception, you will also notice that filmmakers often use sound quite unrealistically, to shift our attention to what is narratively or visually important.

Our scene from *Mr. Hulot's Holiday* also points up the importance of how a chosen sound may have its acoustic qualities transformed for a particular purpose. Thanks to a manipulation of volume and timbre, the Ping-Pong game gains in vividness. When two sounds are of the same frequency or loudness, contemporary sound designers freely adjust one to make it stand out more clearly. During the jungle chase in *Indiana Jones and the Kingdom of the Crystal Skull,* the skull's thump was altered. "I changed its pitch so that it would coexist with the music," sound designer Ben Burtt explained.

Nowadays, film sound is normally reprocessed to yield exactly the qualities desired. A *dry recording* of the

7.19 Sound present, then absent. In *Mr. Hulot's Holiday,* in the foreground, guests quietly play cards while in the depth of the shot, Mr. Hulot is frantically playing Ping-Pong. Sometimes we hear the ball, sometimes not.

sound in a fairly nonreflective space will be manipulated electronically to yield the desired effect. Returning to our earlier example, if you chose to present Amanda's dialogue as heard on Jim's phone, her voice would probably have been treated with filters to make it more tinny and muffled. (In Hollywood parlance, this is called "futzing" the sound.) The almost nonstop rock-and-roll music of *American Graffiti* used two recordings of the music. A dry one was prepared for moments when the music was to dominate the scene and had to be of high quality. A more ambient one for background noise was derived from a tape recorder simply playing the tune in a backyard.

Sound Mixing   Guiding the viewer's attention, then, depends on selecting and reworking particular sounds. It also depends on **mixing,** or combining them. It is useful to think of the sound track not as a set of discrete sound bits but as an ongoing *stream* of auditory information. Each sound takes its place in a specific pattern. This pattern both links events in time and layers them at any given moment.

The auditory stream goes beyond linking one line of dialogue or bit of noise to another. It involves a constant set of decisions about how it meshes with the image track. For example, there are many fine-grained choices involved in blending the stream of sound with classical principles of continuity editing.

> 66 Spending two days on Alcatraz Island for *The Rock* brought home the eerie, lonely feel to the sound. Anyone who spent any time there and heard the soundtrack would be instantly transported to this place, which has its own unique sound signature. It is very windy, so you have lots of wind whistles setting the mood, combined with seagulls and a lighthouse electric horn, interior jail cell ambiances, and the jail door sounds. These individually common elements, when combined, became quite distinctive in this particular location."
>
> —George Watters, supervising sound editor

CREATIVE DECISIONS

Editing Dialogue: To Overlap or Not to Overlap?

If the soundtrack is a stream, the current may carry auditory elements to the surface or sink them out of awareness. One decision that faces the filmmaker involves that current: Should it be choppy or smoothly flowing?

Consider dialogue scenes. Thinking like a filmmaker, we can see that there are many choices about the timing of picture editing. You have to decide when to cut from a shot of A to a shot of B. But another choice is involved, too: How do you cut the dialogue? Editor Tom Rolfe puts it well:

> Is it better to say, "I love you," bang, then cut to the reaction? Or is it better to say, "I love you," hang on it a beat to show the emotion of the person delivering the line, then go for the reaction? It's a matter of choice. Either way, there's a different result for the audience looking at it. Are their sympathies with the guy who said the line, or the girl who said the line? Or is the audience saying, "Don't believe him, he's going to screw you over!" . . . If you find the frame to cut on at that right moment, the audience will be totally satisfied.

There's another alternative. Instead of cutting after the line or holding on the speaker for a beat, you might cut away from the speaker before the line is finished ("I love . . .") to anticipate the reaction of the listener to the final syllables (". . . you!"). Since there are plenty of shot/reverse-shot conversation scenes in movies, and a lot of cutting in those scenes, decision points like these emerge hundreds of times in making most films.

In such situations, filmmakers frequently pick the third option just mentioned, the **dialogue overlap.** In this technique, the filmmaker continues a line of dialogue across a cut, smoothing over the change of shot. During a conversation in John McTiernan's *The Hunt for Red October,* we get the following shots and dialogue:

1. (ms) Over the political officer's shoulder, favoring Captain Ramius (**7.20**)
   Officer: "Captain Tupalev's boat."
   Ramius: "You know Tupalev?"
   Officer: "I know he descends . . ."

7.20 Shot 1

7.21 Shot 2

7.20–7.22 Dialogue overlap in *The Hunt for Red October*

7.22 Shot 3

2. (ms) Reverse angle over Ramius's shoulder, favoring the officer (**7.21**)
   Officer (continuing): ". . . from aristocracy, and that he was your student. It's rumored he has a special . . ."

3. (mcu) Reverse angle on Ramius (**7.22**)
   Officer (continuing): ". . . place in his heart for you."
   Ramius: "There's little room in Tupalev's heart for anyone but Tupalev."

Here the political officer's chatter provides an auditory continuity that distracts from the shot changes. Moreover, by cutting to a closer view of the listener before a sentence is finished, the sound and editing concentrate our attention on Ramius's response. The principle of dialogue overlap can be used with noise as well. In the *Hunt for Red October* scene, sounds of a spoon clinking in a tea cup and of papers being riffled also carry over certain cuts, providing a continuous stream of sonic information.

Sometimes the filmmaker wants to introduce more tension. In Fritz Lang's *M,* the city is on edge because a child murderer is at large. An unprepossessing little man urges a little girl to go home, but onlookers suspect him of being the killer. One comes up to him challengingly.

1. (ls) The little man is accosted by a huge one, who asks, "What's it to you where she lives?"

   The first man turns (**7.23**).

2. (ms) High-angle POV on the little man (**7.24**)

   Little man: "I?" Although intimidated, he starts to speak.

3. (ms): Low angle POV on the big man (**7.25**)

   Little man (offscreen): "Excuse me?"

   Big man: "What do you want with that kid?" (pause)

4. (ms) as 2 (**7.26**)

   Little man (pause): "Absolutely nothing!"

7.23 Shot 1

7.24 Shot 2

7.23–7.26 Cuts emphasize pauses in dialogue in *M*.

7.25 Shot 3

7.26 Shot 4

Here the cuts accentuate the suspense evoked by the pauses. In shot 2, the little man takes time to register the danger he's in. When he finally summons up a feeble self-defense ("Excuse me?"), it is heard offscreen. Lang forces us to wait for the ominous question from the thug, which is uttered in full. In shot 4, the little man gets to assert himself fully. After another pause, he defends himself, and his line isn't interrupted by a cut. The pattern of cutting has given his denial a greater weight because we didn't see him speak during shot 3, and shot 4 plays out his entire line.

Lang was perfectly capable of overlapping sound across his cuts. *M* does it throughout; in fact, the next line the little man speaks initiates a dialogue overlap. By aligning certain cuts with dramatic pauses in the dialogue, Lang gives special weight to the lines spoken by the thug in shot 3 and his innocent target in shot 4. As usual, different stylistic choices produce different effects onscreen.

Layers and Contrasts The sounds flow not only in streams but also in layers. We have already seen that in production, combining sounds is usually done after shooting, in the mixing process. The mixer can precisely control the volume, duration, and tone quality of each sound, weaving them in and out, making them momentarily clear or pushing them out of hearing. For example, in *Jurassic Park,* Steven Spielberg manipulates volume unrealistically for purposes of narrative clarity. After a live cow has been lowered into the velociraptors' pen, the South African hunter gives important information about the habits of these predators, and his

7.27 Selective sound volume. In *Jurassic Park*, Hammond and Ellie are closer to the camera than is anything else in the shot, but their dialogue is an unintelligible murmur. In the background, the hunter supplies important information about velociraptors, and that is clearly audible.

CONNECT TO THE BLOG
www.davidbordwell.net/blog

We've been fortunate enough to sit in on some mixing sessions and learn from people who mix sound. See "Christian Bale picks up a rail," "What does a Water Horse sound like?" and "The Boy in the Black Hole."

66 For the last few years—since *Blue Velvet,* I think—I have tried to do most of the music before the shoot. I discuss the story with my composer, Angelo Badalamenti, and record all sorts of music that I listen to as I'm shooting the film, either on headphones during dialogue scenes or on loudspeakers, so that the whole crew gets in the right mood. It's a great tool. It's like a compass helping you find the right direction."

—David Lynch, director

voice comes through louder than those of characters closer to the camera **(7.27).**

In modern filmmaking, a dozen or more separate tracks may be layered at any moment. The mix can be quite dense. An airport scene may combine the babble of voices, footsteps, luggage trolleys, Muzak, and plane engines. Or the mix can be very sparse, with an occasional sound emerging against a background of total silence. That's what happens in the *M* scene (7.23–7.26), where no ambient sound distracts from the confrontation of the two men. Most cases will fall somewhere between a thick mix and a thin one. In our *Hunt for Red October* scene (7.20–7.22), a distant throbbing engine and slight brushings of fabric form a muted background to the conversation.

The filmmaker may create a mix in which each sound blends smoothly with the others. This is commonly the case when music and effects are mixed with speech. In classical Hollywood cinema of the 1930s, the musical score may become prominent in moments in which there is no dialogue, and then it's likely to fade unnoticeably down just as the characters begin to talk. (In studio parlance, this is called *sneaking in* and *sneaking out.*) This sort of smooth rising and falling pattern provides a clearer, simpler sound world than we encounter in everyday life. The legendary sound designer Walter Murch carefully limits the amount of sound information he provides viewers. "There is a rule of thumb I use, which is never to give the audience more than two-and-a-half things to think about aurally at any one moment." In Murch's mix for *The English Patient,* when the nurse feeds the patient a plum, a distant church bell rings. The clean auditory background makes the bell an evocative overtone, suggesting that the hospital is a calm refuge from the war.

Alternatively, the acoustic stream may contain much more abrupt contrasts. In *The Godfather,* just as Michael Corleone is steeling himself to shoot the rival gangster Sollozzo, we hear a loud, metallic screech, presumably from a nearby elevated train. The sound suggests impending danger, both for the victim and for Michael: After the murder, Michael's life will change irrevocably **(7.28).** Hollywood films often exploit the dynamic range of Dolby technology to fill chase sequences with startling shifts between low, rumbling engines and whining sirens or squealing tires.

Yet another alternative is explored in Alexander Sokurov's *Alexandra.* A soldier's grandmother visits him at his camp and wanders freely among the men preparing for war. The sound track includes naturalistic dialogue and effects. But these conventional elements are wrapped in soft voices, orchestral chords, and snatches of rising and falling soprano singing. The murmuring auditory collage suggests a collective dimension to the old lady's stay, as if she is visiting on behalf of the unseen families of all the men, perhaps all soldiers' families throughout history.

A Dramatic Sound Stream: *Seven Samurai*   Akira Kurosawa was well aware of how sounds can combine to create a stream of information, as we can see from the final battle sequence of his *Seven Samurai.* In a heavy rain, marauding bandits charge into a village defended by the villagers and the samurai. Kurosawa chooses to keep the torrent and wind as a constant background noise. Before the battle, he punctuates the conversation of the waiting men, the tread of footsteps, and the sound of swords being drawn with long pauses in which we hear only the drumming rain. Like the defenders, we're uncertain about when and how the attack will come.

Suddenly distant horses' hooves are heard offscreen. This triggers the expectation that we will soon see the attackers. Kurosawa cuts to a long shot of the bandits; their horses' hooves become abruptly louder. (The scene employs vivid **sound perspective:** The closer the camera is to a source, the louder the sound.) When the bandits burst into the village, yet another sound element appears—the bandits' harsh war cries, which increase steadily in volume as they approach.

The battle begins. The rhythmic cutting and the muddy, storm-swept mise-en-scene gain impact from the way in which the incessant rain and splashing are explosively interrupted by brief noises—the howls of the wounded, the splintering of a fence one bandit crashes through, the whinnies of horses, the twang of a samurai's bowstring, the gurgle of a speared bandit, the screams of women when the bandit chieftain breaks into their hiding place. The sudden intrusion of certain sounds marks abrupt developments in the battle, standing out against the pounding rain. Such frequent surprises heighten our tension, as the narration rapidly snaps us from one line of action to another.

7.28 Harsh sound contrasts: *The Godfather.* As Michael sits opposite Sollozzo, the sudden rumble and whine of an offscreen train sound all the more harsh when compared with the calm expression on Michael's face.

The scene climaxes after the main battle has ended. Offscreen the pounding of horses' hooves is cut short by the sharp crack of a bandit's rifle shot, which fells one samurai. A long pause, in which we hear only the rain, emphasizes the moment. The samurai furiously flings his sword in the direction of the shot and falls dead into the mud. Another samurai splashes toward the bandit chieftain, who has the rifle; another shot cracks out and he falls back, wounded; another pause, in which only the relentless rain is heard. The wounded samurai kills the chieftain. The other samurai gather. At the scene's end, the sobs of a young samurai, the distant whinnies and hoof beats of riderless horses, and the rain all fade slowly out.

Kurosawa's relatively dense mix gradually introduces sounds that turn our attention to new narrative elements (hooves, battle cries) and then modulates these sounds into a harmonious stream. This stream is then punctuated by abrupt sounds of unusual volume or pitch associated with crucial narrative actions (hooves, archery, women's screams, gunshots). Overall, the combination of sounds enhances the unrestricted, objective narration of this sequence, which shows us what happens in various parts of the village rather than confining us to the experience of a single participant.

Sound and Film Form   By choosing and combining sound materials, the filmmaker can create engaging patterns that run through the whole film. The process is most evident in a film's musical score.

Sometimes the filmmaker picks preexisting pieces of music to accompany the images. Directors like Stanley Kubrick and Terrence Malick are known for their bold choices of classical music, whereas others, like Wes Anderson or Quentin Tarantino, select older pop songs to give their films a hipster cachet.

In other cases, music is composed for the film, and here the filmmaker and the composer make several choices. The rhythm, melody, harmony, tempo, volume, and instrumentation of the music can strongly affect a viewer's emotional reactions. We've already seen how the commentary track of *Letter from Siberia* created different impressions of the footage. The same thing can happen with music alone. A close-up of an actor with a neutral expression may seem happy, excited, melancholy, or disturbed, depending on the kind of music that accompanies the image. Near the end of *Queen Christina*, the heroine renounces her throne in order to marry the Spanish envoy she loves. After he dies in a duel, Christina sails from Sweden to live in his homeland. Director Rouben Mamoulian told star Greta Garbo to maintain a neutral expression in the final shot as the camera tracks into a tight close-up of her on the ship's deck. We might expect to hear

> " It's a lot like writing an opera. There's a lot of form and structure. We're very conscious that LOTR is one story that has been broken into three parts. My score is a complex piece that has to be structured carefully, musically and thematically, so that all the parts relate to one another."
>
> —Howard Shore, composer, *The Lord of the Rings*

mournful music, but instead a triumphant melody suggests Christina's courage and determination.

A melody or musical phrase can be associated with a particular character, setting, situation, or idea. The ominous, two-note motif played in the lower strings in *Jaws* (1975) becomes a musical signal of the shark's movement toward his victims. The brassy fanfare for *Star Wars* (1977) captures Luke Skywalker's bravery and impetuousness.

As in opera and musical comedy, themes can intertwine. *Local Hero,* a film about a confused young executive who leaves Texas to close a business deal in a remote Scottish village, uses two major musical themes. A rockabilly tune is heard in the urban Southwest, whereas a slower, more poignantly folkish melody is associated with the seaside village. In the final scenes, after the young man has returned to Houston, he recalls Scotland with affection, and the film plays the two themes simultaneously.

In contrast, a single musical theme can change its quality when associated with different situations. In *Raising Arizona,* the hapless hero has a terrifying dream in which he envisions a homicidal biker pursuing him, and the accompanying music is appropriately ominous. But at the film's end, the hero dreams of raising dozens of children, and now the same melody, reorchestrated and played at a calm tempo, conveys a sense of peace and comfort.

Musical Motifs in *Breakfast at Tiffany's*

Musical motifs can subtly compare scenes, trace patterns of development, and suggest implicit meanings. Henry Mancini's score for Blake Edwards' *Breakfast at Tiffany's* (1961) mixes jazz and pop elements to reflect vibrant, cosmopolitan New York City. At the same time, the film employs musical themes to suggest traits of character and situation.

The film's main musical theme, "Moon River," hints at Holly Golightly's rural past. Mancini claimed that the concept of the score grew out of the lonesome, melancholy timbre of the harmonica, an instrument associated with American folk music. The theme first appears over the film's opening shots of Holly exiting a cab near Fifth Avenue. She walks over to the display windows of Tiffany's jewelry store **(7.29).** Later, the visuals echo the film's title by showing Holly munching a croissant and drinking coffee, but the music tells a somewhat different story. The guitar and harmonica sounds seem an odd choice to accompany shots of New York City. Yet the orchestration reflects character traits rather than setting. The harmonica in "Moon River" expresses Holly's pervasive sense of wistful longing. Its rural association foreshadows the later revelation that she was once Lulamae Barnes, a child bride living in Tulip, Texas, married to a widowed veterinarian.

Repetitions of "Moon River" help to develop the storyline of Holly's past. When Holly beds down next to Paul early in the film, "Moon River" plays over vibraphone chords, its wavering vibrato adding a pensive tone as Holly talks in her sleep **(7.30).** "Moon River" returns in the bus-station scene in which Holly bids a tearful adieu to Doc Golightly, her former husband **(7.31).** This arrangement places the theme in the high register of the violins, a musical technique that often indicates strong passions and emotional conflict. Mancini's arrangement captures Holly's feelings by expressing her sadness at abandoning a man she loves, but whose life she cannot share.

At the film's climax, "Moon River" underscores the search for Cat, who Holly capriciously turns loose in an alley during a rainstorm. Holly's gesture demonstrates both her complete independence and her desire to escape the limelight of scandal-infested New York. Holly's emotional resolve softens, though, after

7.29

7.30

7.31

7.32

7.33

7.29–7.33 Music suggests narrative development. Henry Mancini's "Moon River" is introduced during the film's opening credits (7.29), but reappears later in the film to recall Holly's past as a "wild thing." Scenes show Holly talking in her sleep (7.30), bidding good-bye to Doc Golightly (7.31), and searching for Cat (7.32). A final variant of the theme enters for the couple's embrace (7.33).

Paul rebukes her for failing to let anyone penetrate her brittle shell. Regretting her impetuous decision, Holly joins Paul as they search the alley **(7.32).** Here the "Moon River" melody plays in a minor key over the lurching rhythm of dissonant piano chords. When Holly finds Cat hiding in a cardboard box, the melody returns to a major key and a slow, simple waltz tempo.

Holly and Paul's reconciliation is emphasized by a lush arrangement of the theme for orchestra and chorus that signals a happy ending **(7.33).** By tailoring each cue's harmony, orchestration, and meter to the needs of each scene, Mancini makes "Moon River" not only dramatically appropriate but a reminder of the rural motif that runs through the film.

A CLOSER LOOK

Orchestrating Romance in *Jules and Jim*

Breakfast at Tiffany's adapts its major melody to the drama of Holly's New York life. Francois Truffaut's *Jules and Jim* ties three musical motifs to different aspects of a character. In the process, it traces how a love triangle passes from light-hearted friendship to melancholy and revenge.

Overall, Georges Delerue's score evokes the Paris of 1912–1933, the years during which the action takes place. Many of the melodies resemble works by Claude Debussy and Erik Satie, two prominent composers of the period. But Delerue constrains himself by limiting nearly the whole score to melodies in 3/4 meter. Many of the tunes are in waltz time, and all the main themes are in keys related to A major. The choice of rhythm and tempo fits the characters' carefree youth, as if they are dancing an endless waltz, while the changes in harmony express the more somber turn that the action will take.

Jules and Jim compete for Catherine's favors, and she enjoys flitting between them. Her view of life is conveyed by her "Tourbillon" ("Whirlwind") song, which says that life consists of constantly changing romantic partners. But as the trio's relationship becomes more strained over the years, the score reflects this in the development of major motifs.

A lyrical melody is first heard when Jules, Jim, and Catherine visit the countryside and bicycle to the beach **(7.34)**. This "idyll" tune will recur at many points when the characters reunite, but as the years pass, it will become slower in tempo and more somber in instrumentation, and will shift from a major to a minor mode.

Another motif that reappears in different guises is a "dangerous love" theme associated with Jim and Catherine. This grave, shimmering waltz is first heard when he visits her apartment and watches her pour a bottle of sulphuric acid down the sink **(7.35)**. (The acid, she says, is "for lying eyes.") Afterward, this harmonically unstable theme, which resembles one of Satie's *Gymnopédies* for piano, is used to underscore Jim and Catherine's stormy love affair. At times it accompanies scenes of passion, but at other times it accompanies their growing disillusionment and despair.

The most varied theme is a mysterious phrase first heard on the flute when Jules and Jim encounter a striking ancient statue **(7.36)**. Later they meet Catherine and discover that she has the statue's face; a repetition of the musical motif confirms the comparison. Throughout the film, this brief motif is associated with the enigmatic side of Catherine.

In the film's later scenes, this motif is developed in an intriguing way. The bass line (played on harpsichord or strings) that softly accompanied the woodwind tune now comes to the fore, creating a relentless, often harsh, pulsation. This "menace" waltz underscores Catherine's fling with Albert and accompanies her final revenge on Jim: driving her car, with him as passenger, off a broken bridge and into the river.

7.34

7.35

7.36

7.34–7.36 *Jules and Jim*: Three musical motifs. An idyllic bicycle ride in the country introduces the main musical theme associated with the three characters' relations (7.34). Catherine pours out the acid, which she has said is "for lying eyes, accompanied by the 'dangerous love' theme." (7.35). The camera slowly arcs around the statue as a new musical motif is introduced (7.36).

Once musical motifs have been selected, they can be combined to evoke associations. During Jim and Catherine's first intimate talk after the war, the bass-line-dominated version of the enigma waltz is followed by the love theme, as if the latter could drown out the menacing side of Catherine's character. The love theme accompanies long tracking shots of Jim and Catherine strolling through the woods. But at the scene's end, as Jim bids Catherine farewell, the original woodwind version of her theme recalls her mystery and the risk he is running by falling in love with her.

Similarly, when Jim and Catherine lie in bed, facing the end of their affair, the voice-over narrator says, "It was as if they were already dead" as the dangerous-love theme plays. This sequence associates death with their romance and foreshadows their fate at the film's end.

A similar sort of blending can be found in the film's final scene. Catherine and Jim have drowned, and Jules is overseeing the cremation of their bodies. As shots of the coffins dissolve into detailed shots of the cremation process, the enigma motif segues into its sinister variant, the menace motif. But as Jules leaves the cemetery and the narrator comments that Catherine had wanted her ashes to be cast to the winds, the string instruments glide into a sweeping version of the whirlwind waltz **(7.37).** The film's musical score concludes by recalling the three sides of Catherine that attracted the men to her: her mystery,

> " So, given this mood-altering potential of music, it becomes a great source of fun, as well as a chance to make a scene that works OK work a whole lot better—to bring out the point of a scene that you haven't captured in the shooting of it, to excite the audience, to create the impression that something is happening when something isn't, and also to create little emotional touchstones which you can draw upon as the story changes—so that the music that seemed so innocent and sweet earlier, in new circumstances brings on a whole other set of feelings."
> —Jonathan Demme, director

7.37 Combining the motifs. The sadness of the ending is undercut by the lilting whirlwind waltz.

her menace, and her vivacious openness to experience. In such ways, a musical score can create, develop, and associate motifs that enter into the film's overall form.

Dimensions of Film Sound

We've seen what sounds consist of and how the filmmaker can select among the different kinds of sounds available. We've also seen how sound can guide the viewer's attention and create patterns across the film. But filmmakers have still more choices when they consider how to connect sounds to images.

First, sound unfolds over time, so it has a *rhythm.* Second, a sound can relate to its perceived source with greater or lesser *fidelity.* Third, sound suggests something about the *spatial* conditions in which it occurs. And fourth, the sound relates to visual events that take place at particular points in time, and this relationship gives sound a *temporal* dimension. These dimensions offer the filmmaker a great many areas of control and choice.

Rhythm

Rhythm works on us at deep levels. Our body maintains its own biorhythm, the most basic of which is the heartbeat. Psychologists have shown that music in a film triggers changes in heartbeat and other physical responses. Rhythmic audio stimuli can provoke visual attention, as when a chugging rhythm in the music prompts us to see that a train is approaching.

Rhythm involves, minimally, a *beat,* or pulse; a *tempo,* or pace; and a pattern of *accents,* or stronger and weaker beats. In the realm of sound, all of these features are naturally most recognizable in film music, since there beat, tempo, and accent are basic compositional features. In our examples from *Jules and Jim,* the motifs can be characterized as having a 3/4 metrical pulse, putting an accent on the first beat, and displaying variable tempo—sometimes slow, sometimes fast.

We can find rhythmic qualities in sound effects as well. The plodding hooves of a farm horse differ from a cavalry mount galloping at full speed. The reverberating tone of a gong may offer a slowly decaying accent, while a sudden sneeze provides a brief one. In a gangster film, a machine gun's fire creates a regular, rapid beat, while the sporadic reports of pistols may come at irregular intervals.

Speech also has rhythm. People can be identified by voice prints that show not only characteristic frequencies and amplitudes but also distinct patterns of pacing and syllabic stress. In *His Girl Friday,* our impression is of very rapid dialogue, but the scenes actually are rhythmically subtler than that. In the start of each scene, the pace is comparatively slow, but as the action develops, characters talk at a steadily accelerating rate. As the scene winds down, the conversational pace does as well. This rise-and-fall rhythm matches the arc of each scene, giving us a bit of a rest before launching the next comic complication.

Rhythm in Sound and Image: Coordination   A filmmaker who wants to exploit sonic rhythm faces the fact that the movements in the images have a rhythm as well, distinguished by the same principles of beat, tempo, and accent. In addition, the editing has a rhythm. As we have seen, a succession of short shots helps create a rapid tempo, whereas shots held longer tend to slow down the pace.

In most cases, the rhythms of editing, of movement within the image, and of sound all cooperate. Possibly the most common tendency is for the filmmaker to match visual and sonic rhythms to each other. In a dance sequence in a musical, the figures move about at a rhythm determined by the music. But variation is always possible. In the "Waltz in Swing Time" number in *Swing Time,* the dancing of Fred Astaire and Ginger Rogers moves quickly in time to the music. Yet no fast cutting accompanies this scene. Indeed, the scene consists of a single long take from a long-shot distance.

Animated films often closely coordinate visible movement and sound. In Walt Disney films of the 1930s, the characters often move in exact synchronization with the music, even when they aren't dancing. (As we've seen, such exactness was possible because the sound track was recorded before the drawings were made.) Tightly matching movement to music came to be known as *Mickey-Mousing.*

The credit sequence of Quentin Tarantino's *Reservoir Dogs* shows how a director can coordinate the different rhythms of music, editing, and figure movement **(7.38, 7.39)**. Although the gang of thieves is striding in slow motion, the music has a very fast tempo, close to 190 beats per minute. The editing rhythm is somewhat slower, as each cut comes at five-second intervals to match the phrase structure of the song. The rhythm of movement and gesture is even slower: The slow-motion image stretches out the characters' movements.

A tight correspondence between musical and visual rhythms can yield a powerful dramatic climax. Michael Mann's *The Last of the Mohicans* culminates in a chase and a fight along a mountain ridge. Alice has been captured by the renegade Magua, and Hawkeye, Uncas, and Chingachgook race up the trail to rescue her. We might expect, then, the standard thunderous action score, but what we hear is a quick, grave Scottish dance, initially played on fiddle, mandolin, and harpsichord. The tune was heard in an earlier dance scene at the fort, so it functions to recall the two couples' romances, but here it gives the scene a propulsive energy. Hand-to-hand struggles stand out against the throbbing music. Eventually, the theme swells to the full orchestra, but the same implacable beat governs the action. When Alice hovers on the cliff edge, about to jump off, somber chords repeat a seesaw pulse, as if time is standing still.

At the scene's climax, Chingachgook sprints into the fray, and faster musical figures played by stringed instruments recall the early dance tune. Chingachgook's attack on Magua consists of four precise blows from his battle-axe; each blow

CONNECT TO THE BLOG
www.davidbordwell.net/blog

We survey Lea Jacobs's theories about cinematic rhythm in "The getting of rhythm: Room at the bottom."

7.38

7.39

7.38–7.39 Rhythmic contrast in *Reservoir Dogs.* As the credits start, the opening bass line of the George Baker Selection's "Little Green Bag" begins as well. When the drums join in, Tarantino cuts to a lateral tracking shot of the gang, many dressed in black suits, as they walk in slow motion (7.38). When the verse of the song starts, we cut to a medium shot of Mr. White. Harvey Keitel's credit is superimposed over this shot to link the actor and the character (7.39). Each of the principal cast members is introduced in a similar fashion, with each cut coordinated with the start of a new musical phrase.

coincides with the third beat in a series of musical measures. In the final moment of combat, the two warriors stand frozen opposite each other. The shot lasts three beats. On the fourth beat, Chingachgook launches the fatal blow. As Magua topples over, the music's pulse is replaced by a sustained string chord. *The Last of the Mohicans* synchronizes dance music with visual rhythms, but the result doesn't feel like Mickey-Mousing. The throbbing 4/4 meter, the accented beats, and the leaping melody give the heroes' precise movements a choreographic grace.

Rhythm in Sound and Image: Disparities The filmmaker may also choose to create a disparity among the rhythms of sound, editing, and image. One of the most common options is to edit dialogue scenes in ways that cut against natural speech rhythms. In our example of dialogue overlap from *The Hunt for Red October* (7.20–7.22), the editing doesn't coincide with accented beats, cadences, or pauses in the officer's speech. Thus, the editing smoothes over the changes of shot and emphasizes the words and facial expressions of Captain Ramius. If a filmmaker wants to emphasize the speaker and the speech, the cuts usually come at pauses or natural stopping points in the line, as in our example from *M* (7.23–7.26).

The filmmaker may contrast the rhythm of sound and picture in more noticeable ways. For instance, if the source of sound is primarily offscreen, the filmmaker can utilize the behavior of onscreen figures to create an expressive counterrhythm. Toward the end of John Ford's *She Wore a Yellow Ribbon,* the aging cavalry captain, Nathan Brittles, watches his troops ride out of the fort just after he has retired. He regrets leaving the service and longs to go with the patrol. The sound of the scene consists of two elements: the cheerful title song sung by the departing riders, and the quick hoof beats of their horses. Yet only a few of the shots show the horses and singers, who ride at a rhythm matched to the sound. Instead, the scene concentrates our attention on Brittles, standing almost motionless by his horse. The contrast of brisk musical rhythm and the static images of the solitary Brittles expresses his regret at having to stay behind for the first time in many years.

Sometimes the musical accompaniment might even seem rhythmically inappropriate to the images. At intervals in *Four Nights of a Dreamer,* Robert Bresson presents shots of a large, floating nightclub cruising the Seine. The boat's movement is slow and smooth, yet the sound track consists of lively calypso music. (Not until a later scene do we discover that the music comes from a band aboard the boat.) The strange combination of fast sound tempo with the slow passage of the boat creates a languid, mysterious effect.

In Chris Marker's *La Jetée,* the contrast between image and sound rhythms dominates the entire film. *La Jetée* is made up almost entirely of still shots; except for one tiny gesture, all movement within the images is eliminated. Yet the film utilizes voice-over narration, music, and sound effects of a generally rapid, constantly accented rhythm. Despite the absence of movement, the film doesn't seem uncinematic, partly because it offers a dynamic interplay of audio-visual rhythms.

Most films don't follow just one strategy in combining the rhythms of pictures and sounds. A filmmaker may change rhythms in order to reset our expectations. In the famous battle on the ice in *Alexander Nevsky,* Sergei Eisenstein develops the sound from slow tempos to fast and back to slow. The first 12 shots of the scene show the Russian army anticipating the attack of the German knights. The shots are of moderate length, and they contain very little movement. The music is comparably slow, consisting of short, distinctly separated chords. Then, as the German army rides into sight over the horizon, both the visual movement and the tempo of the music increase quickly, and the battle begins. At the end of the battle, Eisenstein creates another contrast: A long passage of slow, lamenting music accompanies majestic tracking shots with little figure movement.

Fidelity

By *fidelity,* we don't mean the quality of recording. In our sense, fidelity refers to the extent to which the sound is faithful to the source as we conceive it. If a film shows us a barking dog and we hear a barking noise, that sound is faithful to its source; the sound maintains fidelity. But if the image of the barking dog is accompanied by the sound of a cat meowing, there enters a disparity between sound and image—a lack of fidelity.

From the filmmaker's standpoint, fidelity has nothing to do with what originally made the sound in production. Even if our dog emits a bark onscreen, perhaps in production the bark came from a different dog or was electronically synthesized. We do not know what light sabers really sound like, but we accept the whang they make in *Return of the Jedi* as plausible. (In production, their sound was made by hammering guy wires that anchored a radio tower.) You can make a dog meow as easily as making it bark. If the viewer takes the sound to be coming from its source in the diegetic world of the film, then it is faithful, regardless of its actual source in production. Fidelity is thus purely a matter of expectation.

When we're led to notice that a sound is unfaithful to its source, that awareness is usually used for comic effect, as with our meowing dog. In Jacques Tati's *Mr. Hulot's Holiday,* much humor arises from the opening and closing of a dining room door. Instead of recording a real door, Tati inserts a twanging sound like a plucked cello string each time the door swings. Aside from being amusing in itself, this sound functions to emphasize the rhythmic patterns created by waiters and diners passing through the door. Because many gags in Tati films are based on quirkily unrealistic noises, his films are good specimens for the study of fidelity.

Lack of fidelity yields both humor and subjectivity in Jerry Lewis's *The Nutty Professor* (1963). After a night of binge drinking, Professor Kelp returns to the classroom with a severe hangover. He's sensitive to every noise. When he closes the door,

7.40 Fun with fidelity. After several exaggerated noises indicating Kelp's hangover, drops in a test tube are heard as a reverberating snare drum played over fragmentary sounds of ocean waves.

it slams behind him with a hollow boom, sounding more like a metal drum. When he bumps into his desk and a book falls over, the noise echoes for several seconds and finishes with an electronic shimmering. There follows a string of closely miked, highly reverbed noises: the squeak of a chalk on the blackboard, the wet crackle of gum being chewed, and a blast from a student blowing her nose. The most flagrant manipulation of fidelity comes as drops from an eyedropper trickle into a test tube **(7.40).** Throughout, the comic manipulation of fidelity is motivated by Kelp's state of mind.

Still, not every play with fidelity is comic. In Alfred Hitchcock's *The Thirty-Nine Steps*, a landlady discovers a corpse in an apartment. We see her scream but hear a train whistle; then the scene shifts to action on a train. The whistle isn't faithful to its apparent source, but it provides a swift, vivid transition.

Space

Sound has a spatial dimension because it comes from a *source*. Our beliefs about that source have a powerful effect on how we understand the sound.

Diegetic Versus Nondiegetic Sound   When we considered narrative form back in Chapter 3, we described events taking place in the story world as *diegetic* (p. 76). Accordingly, **diegetic sound** is sound that has a source in the story world. The words spoken by the characters, sounds made by objects in the story, and music represented as coming from instruments in the story space are all diegetic sound.

Diegetic sound is often hard to notice as such. It may seem to come naturally from the world of the film. But as we saw when the Ping-Pong game in *Mr. Hulot's Holiday* becomes abruptly quiet to allow us to hear action in the foreground, the filmmaker may manipulate diegetic sound in ways that aren't at all realistic.

Alternatively, there is **nondiegetic sound,** which is represented as coming from a source outside the story world. Music added to enhance the film's action is the most common type of nondiegetic sound. When Roger Thornhill is climbing Mount Rushmore in *North by Northwest* and tense music comes up, we don't expect to see an orchestra perched on the side of the mountain. Viewers understand that movie music is a convention and does not issue from the world of the story. The same holds true for the so-called omniscient narrator, the disembodied voice that gives us information but doesn't belong to any of the characters in the film. An example is *The Magnificent Ambersons,* in which the director, Orson Welles, speaks the nondiegetic narration.

> ❝ [Sound] doesn't have to be in-your-face, traditional, big sound effects. You can especially say a lot about the film with ambiences—the sounds for things you don't see. You can say a lot about where they are geographically, what time of day it is, what part of the city they're in, what kind of country they're in, the season it is. If you're going to choose a cricket, you can choose a cricket not for strictly geographic reasons. If there's a certain cricket that has a beat and a rhythm to it, it adds to the tension of a scene."
>
> —Gary Rydstrom, sound editor, *Toy Story*

7.41 Nondiegetic sound effects. As characters in *Le Million* toss the coat around, director René Clair fades in the sounds of a football game. Because the maneuvers of the chase do look like a scrimmage, this enhances the comedy of the sequence by creating a sort of audio-visual pun.

Nondiegetic sound effects are also possible. In *Le Million,* various characters pursue an old coat with a winning lottery ticket in the pocket. The chase converges backstage at the opera, where the characters race and dodge around one another, tossing the coat to their accomplices. What we hear, however, are the sounds of a football game, including a cheering crowd and a referee's whistle **(7.41).**

Nondiegetic sound effects have become common in contemporary Hollywood. Whooshing sounds are synchronized with rapid camera movements. In Tony Scott's remake of *The Taking of Pelham 123*, after the ransom has been gathered at the Brooklyn Federal Reserve, a nondiegetic whoosh accompanies a rapid zoom out to a satellite view showing the money's destination in midtown Manhattan. Similarly, nondiegetic "needle scratches," imitating a phonograph needle scraping across an LP record, are used for comic effect. Whooshes and needle scratches have become so common that online sound effects libraries offer them to aspiring filmmakers. A film's soundtrack can be completely nondiegetic. Bruce Conner's *A Movie,* Kenneth Anger's *Scorpio Rising,* and Derek Jarman's *War Requiem* use only nondiegetic music. Similarly, many compilation documentaries include no diegetic sound; instead, omniscient voice-over commentary and orchestral music guide our response to the images.

As with fidelity, the distinction between diegetic and nondiegetic sound reflects the conventions of film viewing. Viewers understand that certain sounds seem to come from the story world, while others come from outside the space of the story events. We've learned these conventions so thoroughly that we usually don't have to think about which type of sound we're hearing at any moment. At many times, though, a film's narration deliberately blurs boundaries between different spatial categories. A play with the conventions can be used to puzzle or surprise the audience, to create humor or ambiguity, or to suggest thematic implications. We'll give some examples shortly.

Resources of Diegetic Sound: Offscreen Sound We know that the space of the narrative action isn't limited to what we can see onscreen at any one moment. The same thing holds true for sound. In the last shot of our *The Hunt for Red October* scene, we hear the officer speaking while we see a shot of just Captain Ramius, listening (7.22). Early in the attack on the village in *The Seven Samurai,* we, along with the samurai, hear the hoof beats of the bandits' horses before we see a shot of them. These instances remind us that diegetic sound can be either *onscreen* or *offscreen,* depending on whether its source is inside the frame or outside the frame.

Offscreen sound is crucial to our experience of a film, and filmmakers know that it can save time and money. A shot may show only a couple sitting together in airplane seats, but if we hear a throbbing engine, other passengers chatting, and the creak of a beverage cart, we'll conjure up a plane in flight. Offscreen sound can create the illusion of a bigger space than we actually see, as in the cavernous prison sequences of *The Silence of the Lambs.* As with our creaking-door example (p. 265), offscreen sounds can shape our expectations of how a scene will develop **(7.42–7.44).**

7.42

7.43   7.44

7.42–7.44 Offscreen sound implies space. In *His Girl Friday,* Hildy goes into the pressroom to write her final story. As she chats with the other reporters, a loud clunk comes from an offscreen source, and they glance to the left (7.42). Hildy and another reporter walk to the window (7.43) and see a gallows being prepared for a hanging (7.44).

A CLOSER LOOK

Offscreen Sound and Optical Point of View

The Money Exchange in Jackie Brown

Optical point-of-view cutting can be very powerful, as we saw in examining *Rear Window* (p. 241). Now we're in a position to see—and hear—how it can be coordinated with onscreen and offscreen sound. Quentin Tarantino's *Jackie Brown* offers an illuminating example because, like our sequence from *Letter from Siberia* (pp. 265–266), it runs the same sequence of actions three times, with varying sound tracks. Unlike Chris Marker's film, however, *Jackie Brown* presents the scene as different characters experience it.

Jackie is supposed to deliver over half a million dollars in cash to the dangerous arms dealer Ordell. Ordell has sent his girlfriend, Melanie, and his partner, Louis, to pick up the money from a fitting room in a dress shop. Jackie, however, is playing her own game. She's agreed to help federal agents arrest Ordell, but she has also recruited the bail bondsman Max Cherry to help her switch shopping bags and leave Ordell empty-handed.

This story action is presented three times in the plot, each time adding a layer to our understanding of what's really happening. It would be worthwhile to study the careful auditory touches in these three sequences, such as the replay of the shop's Muzak and the delicate Foley work on footsteps, fabric, and other noises. Here we'll concentrate on optical subjectivity and offscreen sound, because these techniques are crucial in making the triple play clear to the audience. They also serve to contrast Ordell's squabbling, inept partners and the self-possessed Jackie and Max.

The first run-through confines us to Jackie's range of knowledge. She tries on a pantsuit, and the saleswoman says, "Wow, you look really cool!" **(7.45).** Jackie goes

back to the fitting rooms and waits for Melanie. We hear Melanie arrive offscreen, and Tarantino shows us her shoes from Jackie's viewpoint. After Melanie has left, Jackie repacks the money in a shopping bag she leaves in the cubicle and hurries out. She hastily pays the sales clerk, who calls after her, "Wait, your change!" and waves her bills **(7.46).** Jackie rushes out to the mall and summons the federal agents, shouting that Melanie stole the bag from her.

Tarantino flashes back to an earlier phase of the action, with Louis and Melanie arriving at the shop. As the camera follows them **(7.47, 7.48),** we hear the saleswoman say from offscreen, "Wow, you look really cool!" The camera pans to Jackie and the clerk **(7.49).** The offscreen sound has motivated showing this dialogue again, and its unnatural loudness assures that we understand that we're entering the scene at a point we've already witnessed. Louis and Melanie try to look inconspicuous. When Melanie teases Louis about his nervousness, he angrily twists her arm, and she blurts out, "Hey, would you let go!" **(7.50).**

Tarantino now uses offscreen sound to test Louis's dull wits. Louis looks down at the shirts he's riffling through **(7.51),** and we hear an offscreen phone ring. Louis doesn't look up, but we are given a shot of the clerk answering **(7.52).** What does get Louis's attention is Melanie, who abruptly departs for the fitting rooms. Looking uneasily this way and that, Louis sees Max, whom he dimly recognizes, and the two men exchange glances in shot/reverse shot. Then Melanie hustles out of the fitting rooms, and Louis catches up with her. They leave quarreling about who should carry the bag.

7.45 The sales clerk tells Jackie, "Wow, you look really cool!"

7.45–7.46 *Jackie Brown*: The first run-through

7.46 After Jackie has left the money in the fitting room, she hurries away, pretending to be distraught. The clerk calls after her, "Wait, your change!"

A CLOSER LOOK

Continued

7.47 As Melanie and Louis head toward the shop, the camera tracks rightward with them, passing Max Cherry in the foreground.

7.48 As Melanie and Louis approach, we hear, "Wow, you look really cool!" fairly softly.

7.49 The camera pans to pick up Jackie and the clerk, as Jackie says she'll buy the outfit. Sound perspective makes the dialogue louder and clearer, emphasizing that this is a repetition of the scene we've just witnessed. (Compare 7.45.)

7.50 Quarreling at the garment racks, Louis grabs Melanie's arm and she snaps, "Hey, would you let go!"

7.51 Louis browses through shirts. At the end of the shot, a telephone rings offscreen.

7.47–7.52 **The second version**

7.52 The clerk answers the phone, but this isn't Louis's point of view; it's close to what he might have seen if he *had* looked up.

The scene runs a third time, now attaching us to Max's range of knowledge. The second version hinted at his presence early, when the tracking shot following Melanie and Louis glided past him in the foreground (7.47, 7.48). We see him enter and browse, waiting calmly for the scam to begin. Once more Jackie comes out wearing the outfit, and the sales clerk says, "Wow, you look really cool!" But now the exchange is observed from Max's point of view **(7.53, 7.54).** The sound track fades out the dialogue between the clerk and Jackie and fades up the quarrel between Melanie and Louis. Max turns his attention to them and then back to Jackie and the clerk. Here the sound mixing is quite subjective, conveying Max's shifting attention between the two conversations.

While Max is watching the action at the counter, we hear Louis and Melanie quarreling, and this motivates another switch in Max's attention, in time for him to observe her exclaiming, "Hey, would you let go!" **(7.55, 7.56).** The ringing phone drives his eyes back to the clerk **(7.57, 7.58),** but he keeps Melanie in mind too. A little before Louis notices, Max sees Melanie set off on her mission. Louis clumsily scans the shop, but Max is calm and purposeful. Each offscreen sound snaps his attention to what is crucial to the plan. After Melanie and Louis leave, it's through Max's eyes that we see Jackie's departure, with the shop woman calling, "Wait, your change!" **(7.59).** Max pauses, then heads for the fitting room to retrieve the shopping bag and the fortune.

By repeating key actions, noises, and lines of dialogue, the replays lay out the mechanics of the exchange cogently. The variations between the second and third sequences allow Tarantino to characterize the thieves. Max is more alert than Louis and Melanie, and offscreen sounds prompt him to shift his attention precisely. Moreover, each version of story events is nested neatly inside the next one: Jackie and the clerk, then Jackie and the clerk watched by Melanie and Louis, then all the others watched by Max, who completes the money exchange. Sound and image work together to peel back each layer and expand our appreciation of Jackie's intricate double-cross.

7.53 Pretending to be killing time in the shop, Max turns his attention to Jackie . . .

7.54 . . . just as the clerk exclaims, "Wow, you look really cool!" The repeated line anchors us in action we remember. The framing from Max's optical point of view varies what we saw in 7.45 and 7.49.

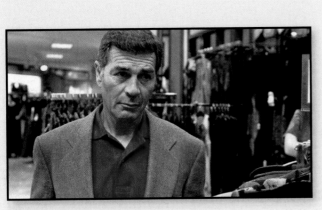

7.55 After Jackie leaves for the changing room, Max shifts his attention to Melanie and Louis, in time to hear her say, "Hey, would you let go!"

A CLOSER LOOK

Continued

7.56 His switch in attention is conveyed through a point-of-view shot. Compare 7.50.

7.57 Max has been studying the couple, but the sound of a ringing phone offscreen makes him shift his glance. Unlike Louis, he notices.

7.58 The clerk answers the phone. (Compare 7.52.) This diversion impels Melanie to seize the moment and stride into the changing room, watched by Max and, eventually, Louis.

7.53–7.59 The third run-through

7.59 After the bogus switch has been made, Jackie comes out and hurries to the counter. Max watches the transaction, and from his point of view we see Jackie rush off, with the clerk calling after, "Wait, your change!" (Compare 7.46.) Now Max walks to the counter. His approach will be presented, in keeping with the rest of the sequence, as his optical point-of-view.

Offscreen sound can fill in information very economically. In *Zodiac,* we see the alcoholic reporter Avery wake up after sleeping in his car. As he abruptly sits up, we hear the clink of bottles on the floor. The sound confirms our suspicion that he has spent another night drinking.

Used with optical point-of-view shots, offscreen sound can create restricted narration, guiding us toward what a character is noticing. In *No Country for Old Men,* Llewelyn Moss is holed up in a hotel room with a bag of cash, hiding from his implacable pursuer Anton Chigurh. When he realizes that a tracking device has been hidden among the bills, the narration is limited solely to what Moss sees and hears. He tries calling the downstairs desk. We dimly hear the distant phone ringing unanswered, so like him we infer that Chigurh has killed the clerk.

The sonic texture is very detailed, highlighting the slight noises of Moss shifting on the bed and switching off the lamp. Then, against a muted background of wind, we hear steadily approaching footsteps in the hall, accompanied by rapid pinging on a homing device. Moss's optical point-of-view confirms Chigurh's arrival: We see the shadows of his feet in the crack under the door. Moss cocks his shotgun, creating a click that seems abnormally loud and close. The shadows move away, and we hear the slight creaking of a light bulb being unscrewed in the hall, eliminating the streak of illumination under the door. The auditory climax of the scene is the metallic burst of the door lock rocketing into the room. *No Country*'s narration has created suspense by restricting both vision and sound to Moss's range of knowledge. For another instance of sound controlled by narration, see "A Closer Look."

Resources of Diegetic Sound: Subjectivity   Diegetic sound harbors other possibilities. It can give us perceptual subjectivity, in a way parallel to an optical POV shot (p. 241). In *The King's Speech,* a therapist treats a man with a bad stammer. He directs the patient to read a text into a microphone while listening to music on headphones **(7.60).** But we hear only the music that the patient hears. The therapist says the reading went well, while the patient believes he did badly. Who's right? We can't know until a later scene, when the patient's recorded reading is presented. The sound track here creates a restricted range of knowledge, building up suspense until we hear the recording.

Just as dreams, memories, and fantasies can be shown on the image track, mental subjectivity (p. 91) can be presented on the sound track too. We may hear a character's thoughts even though the character's lips don't move; presumably, other characters cannot hear these thoughts. Here the narration uses sound to achieve subjectivity, giving us information about the mental state of the character. Such spoken thoughts are comparable to mental images on the visual track. A character may also remember words, snatches of music, or events as represented by sound effects. In this case, the technique is comparable to a visual flashback.

Again, we can set out some of the choices a filmmaker faces. Does the sound have a physical source in the scene? It's diegetic, so let's call this **external diegetic sound.** Does the sound come from inside the mind of the character? That is also diegetic, but rather **internal diegetic sound.** Our example of the dripping sound during the Nutty Professor's hangover is an example. More explicitly, Laurence Olivier's version of *Hamlet* presents Hamlet's famous soliloquies as inner monologues. Hamlet is the source of the thoughts we hear represented as speech, but the words are only in his mind, not in his objective surroundings. Gus Van Sant employs a similar tactic in *Paranoid Park.* A teenage boy fleeing from a horrific accident is plagued by inner voices, some of them auditory flashbacks. By having snatches of dialogue burst in from different stereo channels and with different degrees of clarity, Van Sant presents the boy as engulfed by confusion about what to do next.

A filmmaker may cross the internal/external border for expressive purposes. *The Snake Pit* begins with close views of Virginia on a bench. We hear voices questioning her, and she makes replies, looking left and right **(7.61).** We also hear Virginia's inner monologue wondering why people keep asking these things. We might take the voices to be offscreen, particularly since their sound quality differs from the texture of her thoughts. Eventually, though, the camera pulls back to reveal that no one is around her. Everything except her spoken replies has been internal. But the filmmakers have subtly adjusted the timbre and volume of the questions to distinguish them from her thoughts. This choice suggests that they are real to Virginia—a woman institutionalized with hallucinations.

7.60 In this shot from *The King's Speech,* we don't see the patient's optical POV. In fact, we are viewing him from the opposite side of the microphone. We expect to hear his voice as he reads. The only sound, however, is subjective—the music coming through the headphones. We hear what the patient does, and only the therapist hears the voice reading.

7.61 Internal or external? In *The Snake Pit,* Virginia replies to one of her questioners. Differences in timbre and volume differentiate her speech from two layers of internal sound: her private thoughts and her hallucinations of people's voices questioning her.

Multiple-channel theater sound has reshaped the conventions of internal diegetic sound even more. *The Iron Lady* presents an aged Margaret Thatcher hallucinating that her dead husband is still alive and talking with her. Some scenes present close framings on her face, as in *The Snake Pit,* with the husband's voice offscreen. We might expect that his subjective dialogue should come from the center channel, where Mrs. Thatcher's head is. But in those moments, director Phyllida Lloyd chooses to let his voice issue only from the left or right channel. By suggesting that he hovers just outside the frame, the sound captures Mrs. Thatcher's sense that he solidly exists in offscreen space.

More drastically, in today's films an inner monologue may not be signaled by close shots of a character who's thinking, as in *Hamlet* and *The Snake Pit.* Wong Kar-wai and Terrence Malick will sometimes inject a character's voiced thoughts into scenes in which the character isn't prominent, or even visible. When the voice of a paid killer reflects on his job in Wong's *Fallen Angels,* we see distant shots of him mixed with several shots of the woman who arranges his contracts. In Malick's *The Thin Red Line* and *The New World,* characters are heard musing during lengthy montage sequences in which they don't even appear. These floating monologues come to resemble a more traditional voice-over narration. This impression is reinforced when the inner monologue uses the past tense, as if the action we're seeing onscreen is being recalled from a later time.

A different sort of internal diegetic sound occurs in Wim Wenders's *Wings of Desire.* Dozens of people are reading in a large public library **(7.62).** Incidentally, this sequence also constitutes an interesting exception to the general rule that one character cannot hear another's internal diegetic sound. The film's premise is that Berlin is patrolled by invisible angels who *can* tune in to humans' thoughts. This is a good example of how the conventions of a genre (here, the fantasy film) and the film's specific narrative context can modify a traditional device.

To summarize: Sound may be diegetic (in the story world) or nondiegetic (outside the story world). If it's diegetic, it may be internal (subjective) or external (objective). If it's external, it may be onscreen or offscreen.

Playing with the Diegetic/Nondiegetic Distinction In most sequences, the sources of the sounds are clearly diegetic or nondiegetic. But some films blur the distinction. Since we're used to identifying a sound's source easily, a film may try to cheat our expectations.

In Mel Brooks's *Blazing Saddles,* we hear what we think is nondiegetic musical accompaniment for a cowboy's ride across the prairie—until he rides

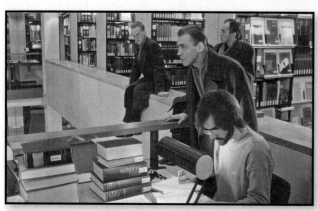

7.62 Angels overhearing. As the camera tracks past the readers in *Wings of Desire,* we hear their thoughts as a throbbing murmur of many voices in many languages.

past Count Basie and his orchestra **(7.63, 7.64).** This joke depends on a reversal of our expectations about the convention of nondiegetic music. A more elaborate example is the 1986 musical version of *Little Shop of Horrors.* There a trio of female singers strolls through many scenes, providing musical commentary on the action without any of the characters noticing them. To complicate matters, the three singers also appear in minor diegetic roles, and then they do interact with the main characters.

In one scene of John Ford's *Stagecoach,* a diegetic sound slowly emerges out of a nondiegetic score. The stagecoach is desperately fleeing from a band of Indians. The ammunition is running out, and all seems lost until a troop of cavalry suddenly arrives. But instead of showing the cavalry riding to the rescue, the film's narration confines us to what happens inside the coach. First,

7.63

7.64

7.63–7.64 Nondiegetic sound becomes diegetic: Comedy. The hero of *Blazing Saddles* rides jauntily through the desert accompanied by apparently nondiegetic music (7.63) until he passes Count Basie's orchestra, which makes the music (implausibly) diegetic (7.64).

offscreen sound shows one passenger killed, but then a bugle call signals that the coach is being rescued **(7.65–7.69).**

More complicated is a moment in *The Magnificent Ambersons* when Orson Welles creates an unusual interplay between the diegetic and nondiegetic sounds. A prologue to the film outlines the background of the Amberson family and the birth of the son, George. A nondiegetic narrator, who isn't a character in the story, explains the Amberson family history. At one point, a woman replies to the narrator's comment **(7.70–7.72).** Welles playfully departs from conventional usage to emphasize the arrival of the story's main character and the hostility of the townspeople to him.

This passage from *The Magnificent Ambersons* juxtaposes diegetic and nondiegetic sounds in a disconcerting way. In other films, a single sound may be ambiguous because it could fall into either category. In *Vicki Cristina Barcelona* (2008), Vicki becomes quite moved by a Spanish guitar performance to which Juan Antonio takes her. This same music returns in the next scene when Juan Antonio seduces Vicki and later when they bump into each other at a social gathering. The recurring guitar music might be taken as nondiegetic, a recurring musical motif like "Moon River" in *Breakfast at Tiffany's*. But since it isn't changed in rhythm or instrumentation, it might represent the characters' shared memory of the performance.

Similarly, at a major point in Paul Thomas Anderson's *Magnolia,* several characters are shown in different locations, each singing softly along to the Aimee Mann

7.65

7.66

7.67

7.68

7.69

7.65–7.69 Nondiegetic sound becomes diegetic: Drama. In *Stagecoach,* Ford shows a medium close-up of one of the passengers, Hatfield, who has just discovered that he is down to his last bullet (7.65). He glances off right and raises his pistol (7.66). The camera pans right to Lucy, praying. During all this, orchestral music, including bugles, plays nondiegetically. Unseen by Lucy, the gun comes into the frame from the left as Hatfield prepares to shoot her to prevent her from being captured by the Indians (7.67). But before he shoots, an offscreen gunshot is heard, and Hatfield's hand and gun drop down out of the frame (7.68). Then bugle music becomes somewhat more prominent. Lucy's expression changes as she says, "Can you hear it? Can you hear it? It's a bugle. They're blowing the charge" (7.69). Only then does Ford cut to the cavalry itself racing toward the coach.

7.70

7.71

7.72

7.70–7.72 A character replies to the narrator. We see a group of townswomen gossiping about the marriage of Isabel Amberson, and one predicts that she will have "the worst spoiled lot of children this town will ever see" (7.70). The nondiegetic narrator resumes his description of the family history: "The prophetess proved to be mistaken in a single detail merely; Wilbur and Isabel did not have *children.* They had only one." But at this point, over the shot of the street, we hear the gossiper's voice again: "Only one! But I'd like to know if he isn't spoiled enough for a whole carload" (7.71). The narrator goes on, "Again, she found none to challenge her. George Amberson Minafer, the Major's one grandchild, was a princely terror." While they're talking, a pony cart comes up the street, and we see George for the first time (7.72). In this exchange, the woman seems to reply to the narrator, even though we must assume that she can't hear what he says. (After all, she's a character in the story and he isn't.)

> ❝ I like to think that I not only record a sound but the space between me and the sound: The subject that generates the sound is merely what causes the surrounding space to resonate."
>
> —Walter Murch, sound designer, *American Graffiti* and *Apocalypse Now*

song "Wise Up." When the sequence begins in Claudia's apartment, the song might be taken as diegetic and offscreen, since she has been listening to Aimee Mann tunes in an earlier scene. But then Anderson cuts to other characters elsewhere singing along, even though they cannot be hearing the music in Claudia's apartment. It would seem that the sound is now nondiegetic, with the characters accompanying it as they might do in a musical. The sequence underlines the parallels among several suffering characters and conveys an eerie sense of disparate people for once on the same emotional wavelength. The sound also works with the crosscutting to pull the characters together before the climax, when many will meet face to face.

A more disturbing uncertainty about whether a sound is diegetic often crops up in the films of Jean-Luc Godard. He narrates some of his films in nondiegetic voice-over, but in other films, such as *2 or 3 Things I Know About Her,* he seems also to be in the story space, whispering questions or comments whose sound perspective makes them seem close to the camera. Godard does not claim to be a character in the action, yet the characters onscreen sometimes behave as though they hear him. This uncertainty as to diegetic or nondiegetic sound sources enables Godard to stress the conventionality of traditional sound usage.

Sound Perspective

Throughout this chapter we've referred to sound perspective—the way a film suggests the placement of the sound in the story world. Sound perspective operates in a way similar to the cues for depth that we get with visual perspective.

Our earlier examples have shown that sound perspective is often indicated by volume. Volume varied with distance in the canyon scene of *127 Hours* (p. 269), and increasing loudness signaled the approach of the bandits in *The Seven Samurai* (pp. 276–277). Timbre helps create sound perspective too. If you combine directly recorded sounds with sounds reflected from the environment, you'll create reverberations suggesting a particular distance. Timbre is most evident with echoes. In *The Magnificent Ambersons,* the conversations that take place on the baroque staircase have a distinct echo, giving the impression of huge, empty spaces around the characters. A small room wouldn't yield the same timbre.

Sound perspective is important in cinematic narration because it can ease us from one point of view to another, as we saw in the *Jackie Brown* example (pp. 287–290). A similar shift occurs in Robert Altman's *Gosford Park.* A music-hall star performs a song for guests at a country estate. At the start, the sound perspective places us in the drawing room, where guests gossip and play bridge. When Altman cuts to two servants listening in another room, the song's softer volume and a touch of reverberation indicate greater distance from the performance.

Point of View and Expressiveness

As the camera follows a character, the filmmaker may use changes in sound perspective to suggest the character's movement through space, a sort of sonic point of view. But many uses of sound perspective don't try to be realistic. In a long shot, a character's voice will usually be clearer than if we were the same distance from her or him in reality, and when we cut to a close-up, that character's voice will not be significantly louder or crisper. In a conversation with sound overlaps, like the one in *The Hunt for Red October* (pp. 273–274), the speaker's voice doesn't change perspective when the camera shifts to show the listener.

In our hypothetical example presenting Jim and Amanda talking on the phone, one option would involve sound perspective. If we stayed with Jim and only heard Amanda's replies, her voice would be given a different perspective. Generally, when the person on camera is speaking, the lines are clear and enhanced by natural ambient sounds. A voice heard over the receiver is usually more coarsely rendered and more reverberant, carrying lower pitches and providing little ambient sound. Sound editors call this disparity the *telephone split.* It represents the fact that the listener is hearing a voice on the line, but it seldom matches what a phone call sounds like in reality.

Like all conventions, the telephone split can be adjusted for expressive possibilities. In *Phone Booth,* a publicist is trapped in a booth, pinned down by an unseen sniper who keeps him talking on the phone. Here the telephone split takes an unusual form. The publicist is heard normally, with ambient sound, but we don't hear the sniper as a crackling telephone voice. Instead, we hear soft, closely miked speech in a dry sound envelope. It does not change when the camera moves toward or away from the booth. The voice has a slight electronic twang, so it doesn't sound as neutral as a narrator's voice-over, but it remains closer to our perspective than to the protagonist's. Whispering, laughing, making rude remarks about what's happening around the booth, the sniper's voice hovers in a realm somewhere between us and the street. It enhances the sense that the protagonist is being watched by a distant, somewhat ghostly threat.

Sound Perspective in the Theater Space

In daily life, a sound reaches one ear a few thousandths of a second before it reaches the other. Slight as the difference is, the proportion of direct and reflected sound gives us information about where the source is. Thanks to multichannel playback, modern theater design can mimic these disparities with great accuracy.

In the typical Dolby 5.1 setup (p. 45), the three speakers behind the screen transmit most dialogue, effects, and music. These channels can suggest regions of sound within the frame, as in *Lawrence of Arabia* when airplanes bombing a camp swoop overhead and the rumble of their engines slides from channel to channel. The front channels can evoke space offscreen as well. In farcical comedies such as *The Naked Gun,* left or right channels can suggest collisions and falls just outside the frame. During the climactic scene of *The Fugitive,* Richard Kimble is sneaking up on the friend who has betrayed him, and he reaches down past the lower frame line. As he slides his arm to the right, a rolling clank in the center channel tells us that there is an iron pipe at his feet.

With use of surround channels, a remarkably immersive sound environment can be created in the theater. The *Star Wars* series uses multiple-channel sound to suggest space vehicles whizzing all around the audience. As one sound designer puts it, surround effects allow the filmmaker to "hang" noises in the auditorium much as an interior designer might hang draperies on a wall. We've mentioned one example of the process in a scene from *Brave* (p. 45).

CONNECT TO THE BLOG
www.davidbordwell.net/blog

We consider how minutely filmmakers can adjust the telephone split in "Little things mean a lot: Micro-stylistics."

> ❝ She first hears the music at a bit of a distance, coming from the house, and as she walks in—the music is getting closer, step-by-step—she goes from the entrance way up the stairs—the music is still growing—and she finally passes by a guitarist on the stairs."
> —Tony Volante, re-recording mixer, *Rachel Getting Married*

> "At the climax when the two snipers see each in their scopes, we focused on water drips only. The German's drip was a drum-like rhythm on the window where he's hiding, and then the metallic drip where the American is hiding. We cut to that drip, then that drip, in this case following the visuals. You don't always have to, because you can choose what you hear. Think like a director or DP, staging a scene with equivalent techniques like depth of field, and choose what the audience's ears are focused on."
>
> —Gary Rydstrom on shifting aural perspective in *Saving Private Ryan*

Like other techniques, sound localization in the theater needn't be used for realistic purposes. Most dialogue is placed in the center channel speakers, but as we've seen, *Paranoid Park* and *The Iron Lady* spread imaginary conversations to subsidiary channels (pp. 291, 292). In Terry Gilliam's *12 Monkeys*, James Cole is a convict volunteer sent from the future to discover the cause of a viral outbreak. The dialogue of onscreen characters comes from the front channels, but when the doctors from the future attempt to communicate with Cole, we hear their voices coming from every channel around the audience. Their disembodied quality evokes Cole's sound perspective and raises the possibility that he may be a delusional schizophrenic who "hears voices" and imagines being part of a future world.

Time

Sound also permits the filmmaker to represent time in various ways. Just as the sources we hear need not be in the space we see, the time represented on the sound track need not coincide with the time that the image presents. To capture all the choices the filmmaker faces, we'll need to make some distinctions that require a little patience.

Most often, the filmmaker decides to hear the sound at the same time as we see what makes it. Characters move their lips, and we hear the appropriate words. A gun fires and we hear a blast. These are instances of **synchronous sound.**

When the sound does go out of synchronization, through a mechanical error, the result is quite distracting. Would a filmmaker ever want to put such **asynchronous,** or out-of-sync, **sound** into the film itself? Yes, sometimes. It can spoof poorly dubbed films in other languages. *Wayne's World 2* features asynchronous sound in a fight scene between Wayne and his girlfriend's father, Mr. Wong.

More systematically, *Singin' in the Rain* creates gags based on asynchronous sound. In the early days of sound filming, a pair of silent screen actors have just made their first talking picture, *The Dueling Cavalier.* Their film company previews the film for an audience, but the technology fails and the picture gets out of synchronization. All the sounds come several seconds before their sources are seen in the image. A line of dialogue begins and *then* the actor's lips move. A woman's voice is heard when a man moves his lips, and vice versa. The humor of this disastrous preview in *Singin' in the Rain* depends on our realization that a film's synchronization of sound and image is simply a mechanical illusion.

A lengthier play with our expectations about synchronization comes in Woody Allen's *What's Up Tiger Lily?* Allen dubbed a new sound track on an Asian spy film, but the English-language dialogue isn't a translation of the original. Instead, it creates a new story. The movie's one-liners and non sequiturs are enhanced by our constant awareness that the words are barely synchronized with the actors' lips. Allen has turned the usual problems of the dubbing of foreign films into the basis of his comedy.

Matters of synchronization are fairly easy to spot. They relate to screen duration, or *viewing* time. As we saw in Chapter 3, though, narrative films can also present *story* and *plot* time. Story time consists of the order, duration, and frequency of all the events pertinent to the narrative, whether they are shown to us or not. Plot time consists of the order, duration, and frequency of the events actually represented in the film. Plot time shows us selected story events but skips over others.

Filmmakers have realized that sound can manipulate story and plot time in two basic ways. Does the sound take place at the same time as the image, in terms of the story events? If so, we can call it **simultaneous sound.** This is overwhelmingly the most common usage. We see and hear two characters speaking, or we see a truck driving down the street and hear the truck's sounds. The plot isn't manipulating the order of sound events.

But filmmakers also realize that the sound we hear can occur earlier or later in the story than the events we see in the image. This manipulation of story order involves **nonsimultaneous sound.** The most common example of this is the sonic flashback. For instance, we might see characters chatting in the present but hear another character's voice from an earlier scene. Or, instead of hearing the truck's engine, we hear gunshots from an earlier scene. By means of nonsimultaneous sound, the film can present earlier story events without showing them.

So filmmakers have a wide range of options about sound and story time. To help to distinguish them, Table 7.2 sums up the possible temporal and spatial relationships that image and sound can display.

Diegetic Sound   The first and third of these possibilities are rare, so let's start with the second and most common option:

1. *Sound simultaneous in story with image.* As we just mentioned, this is by far the most common temporal relation that sound displays in fiction films. Noise, music, or speech that comes from the space of the story almost invariably occurs at the same time as the image.

    Like any other sort of diegetic sound, simultaneous sound can be either external (objective) or internal (subjective). So instead of a character speaking, we might hear an inner monologue, with the character talking to oneself. But that monologue is still presumably simultaneous with the image onscreen.

2. *Sound earlier in story than image.* Here the sound comes from an earlier point in the story than the action we're seeing onscreen. A sonic flashback is one example.

    Usually sonic flashbacks are subjective, representing character memory. Recalling Obi-wan Kenobi's words, Luke Skywalker decides to trust the Force and turn off his ship's targeting computer. Many contemporary films use these mental "replays."

    On rare occasions, the sonic flashback isn't subjective. Sound from earlier in the story action may simply be laid over the current scene for emphasis. Joseph Losey's *Accident* opens with sound indicating an offscreen car crash (**7.73**). The plot goes on to present a long flashback tracing what led up to the accident. Back in the present, the film ends with a parallel image, accompanied by the noise of the fatal crash (**7.74**). There isn't another crash taking place nearby, and there's no evidence that the professor is remembering the original

Today's films often replay scenes in order to give us new story information, but sometimes a film does this just on the auditory level. We look at two examples of sound from the story past rerun in the present in "Play it again, Joan."

TABLE 7.2	Temporal Relations of Sound in Cinema	
	Space of Source	
Time	**Diegetic (Story Space)**	**Nondiegetic (Nonstory Space)**
1. Nonsimultaneous; sound from *earlier* in story than image	Sound flashback; image flashforward with sound continuing in present; sound bridge	Sound marked as past put over images (e.g., sound of John Kennedy speech put over images of United States today)
2. Sound simultaneous in story with image	*External:* dialogue, effects, music *Internal:* thoughts of character heard	Sound marked as simultaneous with images put over images (e.g., narrator describing events in present tense)
3. Nonsimultaneous; sound from *later* in story than image	Sound of flashforward; image flashback with sound continuing in present; character narrates earlier events; sound bridge	Sound marked as later put over images (e.g., reminiscing narrator of *The Magnificent Ambersons*)

7.73–7.74 Sound from earlier in the story. *Accident* begins on a long shot of a house and driveway at night. As the camera tracks forward, offscreen traffic noises give way to the sound of screeching tires and a crash. We see a figure, later to be identified as an Oxford professor, come to the doorway (7.73) and hurry to the crash site. At the end of the film, we see a similar image of the home in daylight, after the main action of the plot has concluded. As the camera tracks back, the professor and his sons go into the house (7.74). Offscreen traffic sounds increase in volume, and again we hear the initial crash.

7.73

7.74

7.75

7.76

7.75–7.76 A sound bridge between scenes. One scene of *The Silence of the Lambs* ends with Clarice Starling on the telephone, as she mentions a location called the "Your Self Storage facility . . ." (7.75). Her voice continues, ". . . right outside central Baltimore" over the first shot of the next scene, the sign for the Your Self warehouse (7.76).

incident. Instead, an unrestricted narration inserts this auditory flashback. Along with the repeated camera position, the sound reminds us of the opening situation and may imply that the tragedy will haunt the family's life.

Sound may belong to an earlier time than the image in another way. The sound from the previous scene may linger briefly while the image is already presenting the next scene. This common device is called a **sound bridge.** Sound bridges of this sort may create smooth transitions by setting up expectations that are quickly confirmed **(7.75, 7.76).**

Sound bridges can sometimes make our expectations more uncertain. In Tim Hunter's *The River's Edge,* three high school boys are standing outside school, and one of them confesses to having killed his girlfriend. When his pals scoff, he says, "They don't believe me." There is a cut to the dead girl lying in the grass by the river, while on the sound track we hear one of his friends call it a crazy story that no one will believe. There's a brief uncertainty. Is a new scene starting, with the friend's response an offscreen one? Or are we are seeing a cutaway to the corpse, which could be followed by a shot returning to the three boys at school? The shot dwells on the dead girl, and after a pause, we hear, with a different sound ambience, "If you brought us . . ." Then there is a cut to a shot of the three youths walking through the woods to the river, as the same character continues, ". . . all the way out here for nothing. . . ." The friend's remark about the crazy story belongs to an earlier, somewhat indeterminate time than the shot of the corpse, and it becomes an unsettling sound bridge to the new scene.

3. *Sound later in story than image.* Sound may also occur at a time later than that depicted by the images. Here we usually tend to take the images as occurring in the past and the sound as occurring in the present or future.

    A simple prototype occurs in many trial dramas. The testimony of a witness in the present is heard on the sound track, while the image presents a flashback to an earlier event. The same effect occurs when the film employs a reminiscing narrator, as in John Ford's *How Green Was My Valley.* Aside from a glimpse at the beginning, we don't see the protagonist Huw as a man, only as a boy, but his grown-up voice-over accompanies the bulk of the plot, which is set in the distant past. Huw's present-time voice on the sound track creates a strong sense of nostalgia for the past and constantly reminds us of the pathetic decline that the characters will eventually suffer.

    Since the late 1960s, it has become somewhat common for the sound from the next scene to begin while the images of the last one are still on the screen. Like the instances in which the next scene begins when we're hearing sound from the previous one, this transitional device is called a *sound bridge.* In Wim Wenders's *American Friend,* a nighttime shot of a little boy riding in the back seat of a car is accompanied by a harsh clacking. There is a cut to a railroad station, where the timetable board flips through its metal cards listing times and destinations. Since the sound over the shot of the boy comes from the later scene, this portion is nonsimultaneous.

    In principle, one could also have a sound *flashforward.* The filmmaker could, say, use the sounds that belong with scene 5 to accompany the images in scene 2. In practice, such a technique is almost unknown. In Godard's *Contempt,* a husband and wife quarrel, and the scene ends with her swimming out to sea while he sits quietly on a rock formation. On the sound track, we hear her voice, closely miked, reciting a letter in which she tells him she has driven back to Rome with another man. Since the husband has not yet received the letter, and perhaps the wife has not yet written it, the letter and its recitation presumably come from a later point in the story. Here the sound flashforward sets up strong expectations that a later scene confirms: We see the wife and the husband's rival stopping for gas on the road to Rome. In fact, we never see a scene in which the husband receives the letter.

Nondiegetic Sound   Most nondiegetic sound has no relevant temporal relationship to the story. When mood music comes up over a tense scene, it would be irrelevant to ask if it is happening at the same time as the images, since the music has no existence in the world of the action. But occasionally, the filmmaker uses a type of nondiegetic sound that does have a defined temporal relationship to the story. Welles's narration in *The Magnificent Ambersons,* for instance, speaks of the action as having happened in a long-vanished era of American history.

An Abundance of Choices   As viewers watch a film, they don't mentally slot sounds into each of these spatial and temporal categories. We offer them here as a way of looking systematically at creative decisions filmmakers have made. Once we've done that, we can use the distinctions to help understand our viewing experience. Tracing out the choices explicitly offers us ways of noticing important aspects of films—especially films that play with our expectations about sounds. By

CONNECT TO THE BLOG
www.davidbordwell.net/blog

Some films include voice-over narrators talking to us. Sometimes the narrator is a character in the story, sometimes he or she is an external voice of authority. But what do we do with the character narrator who happens to be dead? Posthumous voice-over has become a common convention in films, television, and graphic novels. We look at some early examples in "Dead man talking."

http://www.davidbordwell.net
/blog/2015/08/24/dead-man
-talking/

becoming aware of the rich range of possibilities, we're less likely to take a film's sound track for granted and more sensitive to unusual sound strategies.

Conversation Piece

Francis Ford Coppola's *The Conversation* makes fluent use of many of the options we've surveyed in this chapter—particularly the ways in which sound works in space and time. But instead of using sound to help us follow the action, the film's sound track creates ambiguities about the action, and eventually it helps us reflect on how we can *mis*understand what we thought we heard.

The plot centers on Harry Caul, a sound engineer specializing in surveillance. Harry is hired by a shadowy corporate executive to tape a conversation between a young man and woman in a noisy park. Harry cleans up the garbled tape, but he starts to suspect foul play and refuses to give the tape to his client. Harry obsessively replays, refilters, and remixes all his tapes of the conversation. Finally, Harry arrives at a good dub, and we hear the man say something extremely damaging.

The overall situation is quite mysterious. Harry does not know who the young couple is. (Is the woman his client's wife or daughter?) Still, he suspects that they are in danger from the executive. When the executive's hirelings steal Harry's tapes, he feels he is involved in a criminal plot. After a highly ambiguous series of events, including an overheard act of violence, Harry realizes that the basic situation was not as he had thought.

From the very start, *The Conversation* suggests that we can't trust what we hear. The problems are initially about space: What is the source of the sound on the track? As described in Chapter 5, the film begins with a long, slow zoom in on a bustling city square at lunchtime (5.41–5.43). Initially we hear a Dixieland combo playing "Bill Bailey," gradually increasing in volume as the camera enlarges the view. Almost immediately, the music starts to warp and distort. Is the interference part of the sound track? Is it a glitch in the theater's sound system?

The distortion returns periodically during the band's next number, "When the Red, Red Robin (Comes Bob, Bob, Bobbin' Along)." Eventually, the film's first cut reveals a man on a rooftop. He aims a shotgun microphone at the young couple who are the target of Caul's surveillance (**7.77, 7.78**). The sound we've been hearing is not that heard by the people on Union Square, but rather the audio picked up by this microphone. Our initial impression was that these sounds were external and objective. Now, however, we realize that at least some of them were the input to the unknown technician's headphones. This apparently objective, external sound is colored by subjectivity.

After an extreme long shot of the city square with the camera closer to ground level, a cut back to the musicians brings with it a jump in the volume of the music.

7.77

7.78

7.77–7.78 Blurring the boundaries between objective and subjective sounds. After the opening shot of the conversation, we're shown a man on a rooftop overlooking Union Square (7.77). He is aiming a microphone toward a strolling couple (7.78). The revelation suggests that the sounds heard in the first shot were transmitted to his headphones and hence subjective to a degree.

This implies a shift to a more objective narration, particularly as the camera picks up passersby as they cross the frame. Eventually, though, the scene's action returns to the couple, following them as they talk. The harsh distortion returns, suggesting that all this, too, has been audio picked up by a microphone.

We start to realize that Harry has other sound recordists planted in the square. One shadows the couple's movements, while another sits in a van monitoring all the audio inputs. Any of the sounds we've been hearing could be what one of these spies' microphones have picked up. This creates a continual play between offscreen and onscreen sound. Once we're shown that the surveillance team surrounds the couple, we often hear their conversation over shots in which they aren't present. Throughout the opening scene, the sound sources don't mesh comfortably with the images.

Coppola's spatial manipulation of sound departs from convention in other ways. As the scene develops, the couple walks toward a group of drummers playing in the park. The music's volume swells as they approach, creating a massive "foreground plane" of sound **(7.79).** When the man leans in to tell the woman something, his line is buried under the hammering of the drums. This is the line that Harry will devote himself to revealing.

As *The Conversation* develops from this opening, the play with sound space is accompanied by an indeterminate use of time. The narration tightly restricts our knowledge to Harry's. We are with him in nearly every scene, and we sometimes enter his mind. We see a haunting, apparently prophetic dream at one point, but at other moments the narration doesn't signal when it moves to subjectivity—when, that is, the sound is in Harry's head.

At a crucial point Harry employs equalizers and filters to uncover what the man said in the drumming scene. To some extent, his task is like that of Jack Terry in *Blow-Out*: reconstructing an event that isn't what it seems (p. 265). But Jack has access to photographic evidence he can sync up with his recording, whereas Harry has only the sounds. Here is where Coppola and sound designer Walter Murch start to manipulate auditory time.

As Harry obsessively replays his tapes, Coppola could have only shown shots of him working with his gear. Instead, the film's imagery returns us to the pivotal moment in the conversation **(7.80, 7.81).** We get a visual flashback, with the plot repeating action shown earlier in the story. Is it Harry's memory? Unlikely, since he didn't see this part of the conversation. Most likely, this passage is simply the narration's repetition of the moments in the city square. As an objective flashback to what occurred, it seems to be like those rearrangements of story chronology we find in *Pulp Fiction* (p. 80). Thanks to the repetition of actions and camera positions we saw earlier, *The Conversation*'s flashback to the first scene seems reliable.

That impression, however, is undercut by noise and hiss on the tape recording. If the image is supposedly in the past, then the sound is in the present, as Harry patiently cleans it up. There is a temporal split between image and sound. Still, both channels seem compatible. We're cued to assume that the present-time sound replays are, like the images, accurate and reliable— what others would hear if they were at Harry's workstation. And when Harry's tweaking makes the man's line intelligible, the sound seems to fit what we see. Later, however, we will find that the reconstruction we hear is open to misunderstanding.

The disjunctions between past and present, onscreen and offscreen sounds, and external and internal sounds run through the film. Although the opening has warned us to be on our guard, Coppola trusts that our habits will lead us to keep misinterpreting what we see and hear. The film's surprise climax and its lingering mysteries rely on sonic ambiguities operating in space and time.

7.79 Sound mixing as creative choice. As the couple approaches the drummers in the foreground, the music drowns out what they're saying. Normally dialogue takes precedence on the sound track, and music and ambient sounds soften to accommodate it (see 7.12). Coppola, however, uses a realistic soundscape to limit our access to the couple's talk. The man's key line of dialogue will be inaudible to us.

7.80   **7.81**

7.80–7.81 Blurring the boundaries between past and present. The recording process splits the time periods represented in the images and the sounds. Shots of the couple belong to the past, but what the man is apparently saying is played back on tape in the present. The imperfections in the recording force Harry, and the audience, to fill in what the conversation really means.

The Conversation shows that distinguishing different types of sound can help us analyze filmmakers' creative choices. The film, like the examples we've analyzed in this chapter, also suggests that our categories correspond pretty well to how viewers understand what they hear. We unconsciously distinguish between diegetic and nondiegetic, internal and external, simultaneous and nonsimultaneous sound. That's not surprising. Filmmakers have worked for nearly a century to establish those conventions.

Coppola, like other filmmakers we've considered, plays with those conventions. But he still counts on our knowing them. By surveying options for creating the sound track, we can make explicit what audiences and filmmakers take for granted. We can also analyze how more experimental films appeal to our assumptions about sound. By considering both the conventions and the ways they may be manipulated, we gain an understanding of how sound shapes our experience of a film.

 SUMMARY

As usual, both wide viewing and focused attention will sharpen your awareness of this technique. You can get comfortable with the analytical tools we have suggested by asking several questions about a film's sound:

1. What sounds are present—music, speech, noise? How are loudness, pitch, and timbre used? Is the mixture sparse or dense? Modulated or abruptly changing?

2. Is the sound related rhythmically to the image? If so, how?

3. Is the sound faithful or unfaithful to its perceived source?

4. *Where* is the sound coming from? In the story's space or outside it? Onscreen or offscreen? If off-screen, how is it shaping your response to what you're seeing?

5. *When* is the sound occurring? Simultaneously with the onscreen story action? Before? After?

6. How are the various sorts of sounds organized across a sequence or the entire film? What patterns are formed, and how do they reinforce aspects of the film's overall form?

7. For each of questions 1–6, what *purposes* are fulfilled and what *effects* are achieved by the sonic manipulations?

Practice at answering such questions will familiarize you with the basic uses of film sound.

As always, it isn't enough to name and classify. These categories and terms are most useful when we take the next step and examine how the types of sound chosen by the filmmakers *function* in the total film.

8

Summary: Style and Film Form

I n Part Two, we considered how the parts of a film create its overall *form* and how that form engages the viewer. In this, the third part of the book, we've explored the techniques of the film medium. Just as narrative filmmakers decide how to construct a plot that will shape the viewer's experience, they make choices within each of the areas of technique we've examined—mise-en-scene, cinematography, editing, and sound—and then organize those choices. The distinctive patterns of technique we find in a film constitute its **style.**

The Concept of Style

From the start of this book, when we examined Michael Mann's production of *Collateral*, we've seen how artistic decisions govern a film's distinctive style.

The earlier chapters in this part showed how a film's style is coordinated with its overall form. Buster Keaton's use of deep space reinforces the comedy of *Our Hospitality*'s plot, and Jean Renoir's long takes and camera movements create connections and parallels among characters in *Grand Illusion*. John Huston's choices about continuity editing emphasize certain aspects of the opening of *The Maltese Falcon*, while Sergei Eisenstein's discontinuity editing provides thematic commentary on the action of *October*. We've also analyzed how the opening sequence of *The Conversation* establishes story action and creates ambiguities about who is hearing what. Our smaller examples have pointed to the same conclusion: Patterns of techniques work within the film's overall form, shaping the effects the movie has on its viewer.

As a start, then, we use the term "style" to talk about particular films. Sometimes, though, critics talk about style in several films by the same filmmaker. We examined how *Our Hospitality* organizes its comic mise-en-scene around long shots; this is part of Buster Keaton's style in other films, too. It's not surprising that we extend the term to talk about a filmmaker's distinctive style across several films. Everyone builds up certain habits in ordinary life, a particular way of dressing or talking or behaving with others, and we often call that his or her personal style.

In art, as in ordinary life, this styling may be done deliberately or without much thought. Either way, it comes down to decisions. Recall a quotation from Chapter 2: "At the point of making the movie," says Ethan Coen, "it's just about making individual choices," and his brother Joel adds: "You make specific choices that you think are appropriate or compelling or interesting for that particular scene. Then, at the end of the day, you put it all together and somebody looks at it and, if there's some consistency to it, they say, 'Well, that's their style.'"

CONNECT TO THE BLOG
www.davidbordwell.net/blog

Two radically different film styles are considered in "Tony and Theo." For an example of a filmmaker's distinctive style, see "Alexander Payne's vividly shot reality."

" The choices you make push you in a certain direction, and that becomes what people call style."
—Chris Doyle, cinematographer, *Chungking Express*

CONNECT TO THE BLOG
www.davidbordwell.net/blog

A screenwriter-director explains his choices in "David Koepp: Making the world movie-sized."

The term "style" has still other meanings. Sometimes we speak of a *group style*—the consistent use of techniques across the work of several filmmakers. We can speak of a German Expressionist style or a Soviet montage style. In Part Six, we consider some significant group styles that have emerged in film history.

CREATIVE DECISIONS

Style and the Filmmaker

Throughout this book we've suggested that considering a filmmaker's creative options can make you a keener viewer. When it comes to style, as with form, creative choices aren't infinite. The filmmaker is always choosing within limits.

What can limit the choices? For one thing, technology. Before 1928, directors didn't have the option of using synchronized dialogue, and making films in lifelike color was very difficult and expensive. Even today, when the range of technical choices seems far broader, there are limits. Contemporary filmmakers can't use the orthochromatic film stock of the silent era, although in some respects it was superior to today's stocks. As digital grading improved, filmmakers had to abandon the advantages of photochemical grading.

It isn't only technology that constrains creative choices. So do tastes, fashion, dominant trends, and stylistic norms. D. W. Griffith is acclaimed as a great director, but directors today would be reluctant to let their performers display the sort of acting we find in *Intolerance*. Few directors have the power to make a black-and-white film today, since it's widely believed that audiences will spurn films that aren't in full color. Changes in viewers' tastes eliminate certain options.

Some constraints, as we saw in Chapter 1, stem from the mode of production in which the filmmaker works. The studio mode of production developed a standardized menu of options, such as continuity editing, partly because that makes planning, shooting, and postproduction more efficient. Filmmakers working independently have more freedom to make daring choices about form and style, as is seen in limit cases like Michael Snow's *Wavelength* but also in unusual films like *Memento* and *Run Lola Run.*

Filmmakers know that making one decision doesn't end the matter. One choice leads to further choices—and constraints. If you shoot a conversation in the intensified continuity technique, giving each speaker a tight single shot, you'll probably have to cut more often. You need to remind the audience of the other characters who are present, even if they don't speak. If you choose to play a scene in a long take, your actors' performances must be more carefully timed and executed than if you build the scene out of lots of cuts. Choosing to shoot in 3D enforces a new set of constraints. With a distant convergence point (p. 180), a character in the foreground can't be partly cut off by the left or right frameline, because then the audience sees a bisected body floating out at them. Every choice creates new problems to be solved.

As a result of pressures like these, a filmmaker tends to rely on similar techniques across the film. After certain choices have been made in one scene, it's easier to replicate them in another. But there are more positive reasons why directors embrace certain possibilities and rule out others. Most directors feel comfortable with a particular stylistic option because it suits the stories they're telling. Antonioni's complex staging techniques in *L'Avventura* are appropriate for characters whose feelings fluctuate unpredictably from moment to moment (4.124, 4.125). The filmmaker's personality plays a role too. Some directors prefer straightforward, efficient technique, while others, like Alfred Hitchcock and James Cameron, enjoy setting themselves technical problems. And some filmmakers want to find new possibilities in the techniques that appeal to them. Eisenstein plunged into editing because he believed he could force it to do things it had never done before.

Decision Making: Techniques Working Together

Because one choice creates further choices later, filmmakers tend to think out their decisions fairly carefully. Many, for instance, watch for ways to create parallels among situations and characters. Piotr Sobociński, cinematographer for Krzysztof Kieślowski, says that in *Three Colors: Red,* a crane shot down to a fashion show was designed to recall an earlier camera movement, when the camera craned down as a book fell into the street. Similarly, in filming *Viva Zapata!* Elia Kazan tracked in on Zapata, who is ignoring the fact that a crowd of peasants is marching with him. "We had to go close on that shot and dolly [i.e., track] because what I wanted to show was his expression or lack of expression. We later contrasted that with a similar dolly shot on the police chief beginning to notice what was happening. The point was to contrast those two attitudes."

Films setting up narrative or thematic contrasts may recruit several techniques to reinforce them. Jacques Tati's *Mon Oncle* opposes the charm and community spirit of old Parisian neighborhoods to the sterile, enclosed homes that replace them. M. Hulot lives in a ramshackle apartment building on a quiet little square. The Arpel family—Hulot's sister, brother-in-law, and nephew—have just moved into an ultramodern house full of high-tech gadgets and chic but uncomfortable furniture. Scenes in Hulot's neighborhood tend to be accompanied by jaunty music. In this locale, the camera stays outside his apartment, stressing the interactions of the many people living and working around the square **(8.1).** By contrast, the Arpel scenes contain no music. Instead, we hear the tapping of shoes on stone floors and the clicks and whirs of the absurd appliances. There are frequent shots inside the house, and the street is almost invisible behind the family's security wall **(8.2).**

Many filmmakers let stylistic elements cooperate to differentiate locales or story lines. In *Inception,* a complicated science fiction plot takes its characters into four layers of dreams within dreams. Each dream level involves a distinct fantasy world, and about midway through the film, the action starts shifting abruptly among these levels. Yet settings, costumes, lighting, color schemes, weather, and other aspects of the mise-en-scene allow us to keep track of which level each shot occurs in **(8.3–8.6).** Cinematographer Wally Pfister said of the different levels, "We wanted to have the color palette change quite a bit when we go from one location to another. . . . You immediately know where you are, even if we cut to a tighter shot or to something that is slightly out of context. It's a choice that helps tell the story." Steven Soderbergh's *Traffic* uses color contrasts to help spectators follow the three plotlines as he crosscuts them. There are washed-out, yellow images for the scenes in Mexico, blue-cast scenes for the story of a newly appointed drug czar and his addicted daughter, and a more conventional range of colors for scenes involving the wealthy wife of an arrested drug smuggler.

When we see techniques lining up and working together this way, it's likely that the patterning has been created more or less consciously by the filmmaker. Perhaps it wasn't done through elaborate storyboarding or deep thought. Often, as the Coens' remarks suggest, a director may shoot one scene fairly spontaneously, then realize that another scene could parallel it through lighting or music or some other technique. That is, the filmmaker may discover significant patterns while making the film. The task then becomes to find ways to enhance those patterns in ways that will give the audience a particular experience.

CONNECT TO THE BLOG
www.davidbordwell.net/blog

We trace the stylistic and formal development of a major contemporary filmmaker in "The sarcastic laments of Béla Tarr." On the styles of two art film directors of the previous generation, see "Bergman, Antonioni, and the stubborn stylists."

8.1

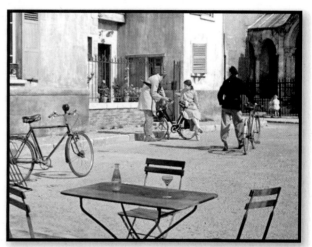

8.2

8.1–8.2 Old style community, modern domestic fortress.
In *Mon Oncle*, Mr. Hulot chats with a neighbor while others pass (8.1). The Arpels' inconveniently laid-out garden has a metal security door that blots out their view of the street (8.2).

8.3

8.4

8.5

8.6

8.3–8.6 Differentiating dreams. *Inception*'s first dream level takes place mostly outdoors in a city, with a white, gray, and black color scheme tinged with blue. In this dream, it's raining (8.3). The second dream's action occurs inside a hotel. The characters wear business clothes, and the corridors and bathrooms have warm brown and orange tones (8.4). The next level involves a large gray fortress and white costumes, set against a snowy mountain landscape (8.5). Finally, "Limbo" places the characters in deserted cities and bare seascapes, where high-contrast sunshine creates both glare and deep shadows (8.6).

Watching and Listening: Style and the Viewer

During a film, the filmmakers' stylistic choices register on us at every moment. We don't take them in passively; we're alert to them, even though we may not be aware of how sensitive we are.

For example, we tend to have expectations about style. If we see two characters in a long shot, we expect a cut-in to a closer view. If the actor seems about to leave the frame, we expect the camera to pan or track to keep the person in the shot. If a character speaks, we expect to hear diegetic sound that is faithful to its source. Like other kinds of expectations, stylistic ones derive from both our experience of the world generally (people talk; they don't chirp) and our experience of film and other media. The specific film's style can confirm our expectations, or modify them or challenge them.

The conventions of the classical Hollywood cinema and of specific genres provide a firm basis for reinforcing our prior assumptions. But other films ask us to revise our expectations somewhat. *Our Hospitality* accustoms us to deep-space manipulations of figures and objects, while *Grand Illusion* makes us expect that camera movements will link characters. Still other films make highly unusual technical choices, and to follow them we must construct new stylistic expectations. The editing discontinuities in *October* and the distorted sound track in *The Conversation* in effect teach us how to understand the film's distinctive style.

In other words, a director directs not only the cast and crew. A director also directs us, directs our attention, and thus shapes our reaction. The filmmaker's technical decisions affect what we perceive and how we respond.

Analyzing Style

In watching a narrative film, we usually don't notice style; we're too busy following the story. Suppose, though, we want to notice stylistic patterning—to enhance our appreciation, or to understand how we might also create films. How can we study style?

One suggestion is apparent: *Look and listen carefully*. But what should we watch and listen for? The last four chapters have made plenty of suggestions. We've also urged you: *Think like a filmmaker*. That mindset can coax you into considering the functions of what you're seeing and hearing. In addition, you can try picking a single scene and concentrating on how techniques blend to create particular effects. We'll do that shortly.

First let's consider four general questions we can ask in trying to understand a film's style.

1. What Is the Film's Overall Form?

A good starting point is to think about how the film is put together as a whole. If it's a narrative film, it will draw on all the principles discussed in Chapter 3. (Not all films tell stories. We'll discuss other types of form in Chapter 10.) Typically, we'll confront a plot that cues us to construct a story. The film will manipulate causality, time, and space. It will probably give characters some goals, motives, thoughts, and feelings, all of which need to be conveyed to the viewer through form and style. The film will use its opening (abrupt or gradual) to introduce a situation. It will have a distinct pattern of development—a search, a journey, an escalating conflict. Characters will change, situations will become emotionally weighted, and parallels will emerge. The film's narration will manipulate what we know and how and when we learn of it, to guide us toward specific responses. And it may play games with conventions by rearranging scenes in time, manipulating degrees of subjectivity, or otherwise challenging us to create a story out of the plot's presentation. Whatever the film's overall form, once you have a grasp on it, you'll find it easier to understand how style works, and works on us.

2. What Are the Main Techniques Being Used?

Here your analysis can draw on our survey of technical possibilities in Chapters 4–7. You can look for things like color, lighting, framing, cutting, and sound. Once you notice them, you can identify them as creative options: not just music, but nondiegetic music; not just framing, but low-angle framing.

Noting and naming are only the beginning. You should try to identify *salient* techniques. What techniques does the film most rely on? The jerky forward zoom in *Wavelength* and the rapid, discontinuous editing of *October* stand out because they play a central role in the overall effect of each film.

In addition, what is salient depends partly on your interests. If a film's style strikes you as typical of a broader approach to filmmaking, you may focus on how the technique conforms to stylistic expectations. The 180-degree editing of *The Maltese Falcon* isn't obvious or emphasized, but adherence to rules of classical continuity is one characteristic of the film's style. Our purpose in Chapter 6 was to show that the film is typical in this respect.

If you want to explore more unusual stylistic devices, you can concentrate on more original, even puzzling choices. Eisenstein's editing in *October* is unusual, representing choices that few filmmakers would make. It was the originality of these options that we chose to stress in Chapter 6. From the standpoint of originality, costume in *October* isn't as salient a stylistic feature as editing because it isn't as original. Your decision about what techniques are salient will be influenced partly by what the film emphasizes, and partly by what you're interested in knowing more about.

3. What Patterns Are Formed by the Techniques?

Once you've identified salient techniques, you can notice how they are organized. Techniques will be repeated and varied, developed and paralleled, across the whole film or within a single segment. Chapters 4–7 have shown how this occurs in some films.

You can zero in on stylistic patterns in two ways. One way is to reflect on your responses. If a scene begins with a track-in, do you expect that it will end with

CONNECT TO THE BLOG
www.davidbordwell.net/blog

We discuss *Indiana Jones and the Kingdom of the Crystal Skull* and some aspects of Steven Spielberg's editing and use of light in "Reflections in a crystal eye."

CONNECT TO THE BLOG
www.davidbordwell.net/blog

Some unusual examples of sound/image patterning are analyzed in "Play it again, Joan."

8.7–8.10 Patterns of camera distance and angle. During the initial conversation in *The Silence of the Lambs,* shooting in depth emphasizes the distance between Clarice and Lecter, and each one looks slightly to the right or left (8.7, 8.8). As their conversations become more intense and intimate, the camera positions move closer to each character and shift subtly toward the axis of action until each person is looking directly into the lens (8.9, 8.10).

8.7

8.8

8.9

8.10

CONNECT TO THE BLOG
www.davidbordwell.net/blog

In "Alignment, allegiance, and murder," we consider how staging, camera position, and cutting blend to create a play of point-of-view in a scene.

a track-out? If you see a character looking left, do you assume that someone or something is offscreen and will be revealed in the next shot? If you feel a mounting excitement in an action scene, is that traceable to a quickening tempo in the music or to accelerating editing?

A second strategy is to look for stylistic patterns that reinforce the unfolding narrative. As we've seen throughout this part of the book, filmmakers often deliberately design the film's style to create parallels or underscore developments in the drama. Shifting color schemes reflect three stages of the plot's development in *Women in Love* (4.42–4.44). A repetition of a key line of dialogue in *The Conversation* creates mystery and leads to conflicting interpretations (p. 301).

Even within a shorter span, style can create a subtle sense of narrative progression. A scene usually has a dramatic pattern of encounter, conflict, and outcome, and the style often reflects this, with the cutting becoming more marked and the shots coming closer to the characters as the scene progresses. We saw this happening in our *Maltese Falcon* scene (6.54–6.74). In *The Silence of the Lambs,* for example, the scenes between Clarice Starling and Hannibal Lecter tend to begin with conventional shot/reverse-shot conversations but become more intimate and psychologically revealing **(8.7–8.10).** In a later chapter, we'll see how style can also reinforce the organization of nonnarrative films.

Occasionally, stylistic patterning doesn't accord neatly with the overall structure of the film. Style can claim our attention in its own right. We saw this happen in such experimental films as *Serene Velocity* and *Wavelength.* It can happen in more straightforward narratives, too. In 6.144 and 6.145, a cut from a washline to a living room acts as a transition between scenes. But the cut is of interest for other reasons, too, since we don't expect a narrative film to treat objects as flat patches of color to be matched across shots. This sort of attention to graphic play is more common in abstract form.

In this passage from Ozu's *Ohayo,* a stylistic choice becomes salient because it goes beyond its narrative function. Even here, though, stylistic patterns continue to call on the viewer's expectations and to draw the spectator into a dynamic process. Anyone who notices the graphic match on red objects in *Ohayo* will most likely be intrigued at such an unconventional way of editing. And, if stylistic patterns do swerve off on their own, we still need a sense of the film's narrative organization to show how and when that happens.

4. What Functions Do the Techniques and Patterns Fulfill?

Now we look for the role that style plays in the film's overall form. Does the use of music or noise alter our attitude toward a character? Does the composition of the shot tend to make us concentrate on a particular detail (4.153, the shot of Anne's face in *Day of Wrath*)? Does the use of camera movement hold off story information to create suspense, as in the opening of *Touch of Evil* (pp. 213–215)? Does the use of discontinuous editing cue us to create thematic comparisons, as in the sequence we analyzed in *October* (pp. 259–262)?

A direct route to noticing function is to notice the *effects* of the film on our viewing experience. Style may enhance *emotional* aspects of the film. Rapid cutting in *The Birds* triggers shock, while the solo piano score in *The Conversation* underlines Harry's melancholy and loneliness. The sadness of Elsa's life with her daughter in *Grand Illusion* is conveyed by the tracking shot to the table that is "too large," especially when we compare that shot with Rauffenstein's conscription of a chapel for his quarters (5.183–5.193). Style is intimately tied to the emotions that the film expresses and that it can engender in the viewer.

Style also shapes *meaning*. Eisenstein clearly wants us to take away a message from the *October* sequence: The Provisional Government is dictatorial, oppressing both the families at home and the soldiers on the front. We should, however, avoid reading isolated elements atomistically, taking them out of context. As we noted on p. 190, a high angle does not automatically mean "defeat," just as a low angle does not automatically mean "power." Thematic interpretation can be sensitive to contexts—the particular scene, the whole film, the patterns of techniques, and the overall effects.

Meaning is only one type of effect, and there is no reason to expect that every stylistic feature will yield thematic significance. One part of a director's job is to direct our attention, and so style will often function simply *perceptually*—to get us to notice things, to emphasize one thing over another, to clarify, intensify, or complicate our understanding of the action. One shot in *Red Beard* makes the woman patient seem close to the young doctor, but another corrects that impression (5.39, 5.40). Here, as often happens, film style is readjusting the story information we're getting, guiding our uptake moment by moment.

One way to sharpen our sense of the functions of specific techniques is to *imagine alternatives* and reflect on what differences would result. Suppose the director had made a different technical choice. How would this create a different effect?

Our Hospitality creates its gags by putting two elements into the same shot and letting us observe the comic juxtaposition. Suppose Keaton had instead isolated each element in a single shot and then linked the two elements by editing. The basic information might be the same, but our response would be different. Instead of a simultaneous presentation that lets our attention shuttle to and fro, we would have a more step-by-step pattern of building up the gags and paying them off. Or, suppose that John Huston had handled the opening scene of *The Maltese Falcon* as a single take with camera movement. How would he then have drawn our attention to Brigid O'Shaughnessy's and Sam Spade's facial reactions, and how would this have affected our expectations? By focusing on effects and imagining alternatives to the technical choices that were made, the analyst can gain a sharp sense of the particular functions of style in the given film.

The rest of this chapter provides three illustrations of how we can analyze film style. First we concentrate on a single scene, from Alfred Hitchcock's *Shadow of a Doubt*. (See "A Closer Look.") This will show you how all the techniques we've surveyed can work together to create a specific attitude toward a character and a phase of story action. Even though we focus on one scene, our analysis has to take other scenes, and the film's overall narrative form, into account.

CONNECT TO THE BLOG
www.davidbordwell.net/blog

For a discussion of how various techniques of film style can function to call our attention to items of narrative importance, see "Gradation of emphasis, starring Glenn Ford."

" There's no scene in any movie that 50 different directors couldn't have done 50 different ways."
—Paul Mazursky, director

CONNECT TO THE BLOG
www.davidbordwell.net/blog

Subtle stylistic echoes enrich *The Prestige*, as we show in "Niceties: How classical filmmaking can be at once simple and precise."

CONNECT TO THE BLOG
www.davidbordwell.net/blog

For another example of Hitchcock's style, see "Sir Alfred simply must have his set pieces."

A CLOSER LOOK

Stylistic Synthesis in *Shadow of a Doubt*

Uncle Charlie has come to visit his sister's family in Santa Rosa, California. Charlie is a suave, sophisticated man who flashes money around freely. His sister Emmy adores him and has even named her daughter Charlie in his honor. But as Uncle Charlie lingers in town, Young Charlie begins to suspect that he's a serial killer who preys on rich widows. She can't prove it—she has only the shadow of a doubt—but she now sees his menacing side. In many scenes, Hitchcock organizes film style to link our perception and understanding of events to those of Young Charlie.

A decisive moment in this progression comes in a scene of the family having dinner. Uncle Charlie praises small-town living. Towns like Santa Rosa, he says, keep their women busy, while cities let them sink into self-indulgence. He slips into a venomous monologue:

> And what do the wives do, these useless women? You see them in the hotels, the best hotels, every day by the thousands. Drinking the money, eating the money, losing the money at bridge, playing all day and all night. Smelling of money. Proud of their jewelry but nothing else. Horrible . . . fat, faded, greedy women.

Reacting to this, Young Charlie blurts out, "But they're alive! They're human beings!" Uncle Charlie replies, "Are they? Are they, Charlie? Are they human or are they fat, wheezing animals?" As if realizing he's gone too far, Uncle Charlie smiles and switches back to his ingratiating manner.

This powerful scene depends on many stylistic decisions about how to affect the audience. The dialogue constitutes a step in the process of strengthening Young Charlie's suspicions that her uncle is a murderer. The scene nudges us closer to the same belief. The scene also suggests that Uncle Charlie is slightly mad; his killing proceeds not only from lust for money but also from a deep-seated hatred of women. His harangue gives us

a better understanding of his personality. Our response has an emotional dimension, too, since his description of the women dehumanizes them to chilling effect.

Within the context of the film, this scene serves several functions. The development of the story depends on Uncle Charlie's visit to his family and Young Charlie's growing suspicions about his murderous instincts. She can't tell anyone the truth, though, since doing so would devastate her mother. This creates a powerful conflict, not only between Young Charlie and her uncle but also within her mind. Similarly, as she learns the truth, her attitude changes. Initially, she worships her uncle, but eventually, she becomes bitterly aware of his real nature, and her trust in the world starts to crack. The dinner scene, then, contributes to a growth in Young Charlie's character.

Even the fact that the scene occurs at dinner is important. More cheerful scenes have taken place at the same table. At one point, Uncle Charlie gives Emmy restored photographs of their parents, which seems to convey his sincere love for her and their family. Young Charlie is exuberant **(8.11)**. In these early scenes, we're told of a special rapport that uncle and niece share, and he even presents her with an elegant ring **(8.12)**. The ring plays an important role in the plot, since Young Charlie discovers an inscription on it (a clue that it came from one of her uncle's victims). So Uncle Charlie's hate-filled monologue fits into a pattern of other moments we've already seen.

Hitchcock firmly believed in using the medium to arouse the viewer's mind and feelings. So, as Uncle Charlie launches into his monologue, Hitchcock presents us with an establishing shot of the entire table **(8.13)**. We've seen similar shots in earlier scenes, and it orients us to the positions of the scene's major characters. At the same time, Hitchcock stages the scene so that Uncle Charlie rather than Emmy's husband sits at the head of

8.11 In *Shadow of a Doubt,* Young Charlie is delighted when Uncle Charlie presents pictures of her grandparents.

8.12 In an eerie parallel to a lovers' engagement, Uncle Charlie presents his niece with a ring.

8.13 A general shot shows the family at table, with the two Charlies most visible.

the table. His domination of the household is presented visually. As Charlie starts to talk, after a shot of Emmy we get a brief shot of Young Charlie, eying him anxiously **(8.14).** When he begins to denounce the "useless women," we see a close view of him as he continues his attack **(8.15).**

Joseph Cotten's performance is very important here. He seethes with resentment of the "fat, faded, greedy women." He delivers the speech without blinking, as if musing to himself rather than talking to others. Hitchcock magnifies the effect of Cotten's performance with a tracking shot that eliminates everyone else at the table. The camera comes steadily forward, filling the frame with Uncle Charlie's face as his monologue increases in anger and intensity **(8.16).**

Hitchcock could have used other techniques. He could have filmed Uncle Charlie from the rear, concealing his face but showing us the reactions of others at the table. He could have interrupted shots of Uncle Charlie with the reactions of Emmy, her husband, and her children. But Hitchcock achieves a very different effect by the slow, riveting movement toward Uncle Charlie's face as his hatred for women surfaces. Even though he's speaking the lines aloud, the relentless forward tracking movement suggests that we're getting a glimpse into his mind.

When Young Charlie objects, "But they're alive! They're human beings!" most directors would have cut to a shot of her. But Hitchcock keeps her outburst off-screen. Then he adds an unexpected and eerie touch. As the tracking shot ends on an extremely tight close-up, Uncle Charlie turns slightly and looks into the camera as he replies, "Are they, Charlie?" **(8.17).**

Suddenly, we're put in the young woman's place, seeing the full force of her uncle's hatred. (We've just seen Jonathan Demme employing a comparable technique in filming Hannibal Lecter in *The Silence of the Lambs,* 8.7–8.10.) Like Young Charlie, we begin to realize that he's a sociopath, made all the more frightening by his steady gaze and controlled speech. Hitchcock's decisions about staging, framing, sound, and editing have intensely engaged our minds and emotions in the story.

Hitchcock's style here is related to technical choices in the movie as a whole. For one thing, the shot of Uncle Charlie is the closest we ever come to him, so this tight framing gives the scene particular force. More generally, Hitchcock employs techniques that put us in the position of the characters. Throughout the film, he uses optical point of view, most often allowing us to share Young Charlie's vantage point **(8.18, 8.19).**

This pattern of stylistic choices is sustained throughout the dinner table monologue. The brief shot of Young Charlie reminds us of her position beside her uncle (8.14). But rather than have Uncle Charlie start his monologue

8.14 After a shot of Emmy, Hitchcock cuts to Young Charlie looking uneasily at her uncle.

8.15 Uncle Charlie begins his monologue about useless women.

8.16 The camera moves closer to him . . .

8.17 . . . and is very close when he turns and replies to Young Charlie's protests that these women are human. "Are they, Charlie?"

8.18 Earlier in the film, when Young Charlie has begun to suspect her uncle, she pauses on the front doorstep.

8.19 Hitchcock then gives us an optical point-of-view shot of what makes her hesitate: Uncle Charlie holding her mother spellbound.

A CLOSER LOOK

Continued

by glancing at her, Hitchcock lets him speak to the others at the table, or perhaps merely to himself (8.15, 8.16). Only after Young Charlie's offscreen outburst does Uncle Charlie turn to her—and us (8.17). Hitchcock has saved the most startling point-of-view moment for the end of the shot.

The style of this scene enhances the film's pattern of restricted narration. After Uncle Charlie arrives in Santa Rosa, we get some private glimpses into his activities, but the scenes concentrate largely on Emmy's family and particularly on Young Charlie. We know a bit more than she knows about her uncle. For example, from the start, we suspect that he's being sought by the police, but we don't know what they're investigating. Later

we learn that Uncle Charlie has torn a story out of the newspaper, but not until Young Charlie finds it do we discover what he was trying to conceal. Slowly, along with Young Charlie, we discover that the Merry Widow Murderer is at large and that Uncle Charlie is a prime suspect.

The overall form of the plot and the stylistic presentation in each scene work to put us close to Young Charlie. We know roughly what she knows, and we learn some key information when she does. In the dinner table scene, the developing storyline and Hitchcock's style combine to tie us even more tightly to Young Charlie. The moment when Uncle Charlie turns challengingly to the camera becomes a high point of this pattern.

Our second example is *Citizen Kane*. Chapter 3 discussed the film's narrative organization, and we'll refer back to that to ground our comments. (You may want to return to reread it as preparation for what follows.) Our analysis will concentrate on identifying some salient techniques, locating stylistic patterns, and proposing some functions for the patterns we detect. At the end of this chapter, as our third example, we consider how *Gravity* creates stylistic patterns using digital tools to enhance traditional technique.

Style in *Citizen Kane*

Orson Welles didn't make *Citizen Kane* alone. He had at his disposal a major Hollywood studio, RKO, and he assembled exceptionally gifted collaborators. Just as the film's narrative organization owes a good deal to the screenplay that Welles wrote with Joseph Mankiewicz, its style is the result of thousands of decisions made by director, cast, and crew.

Several of Welles' actors had worked with him in theater and radio, so he knew what they could bring to the project. Among other talents were cinematographer Gregg Toland, composer Bernard Herrmann, and special-effects supervisor Vernon Walker. All three had distinguished careers before and after *Kane*. Walker created dazzling special effects for 1930s musicals and comedies. Toland's style helped popularize the deep-focus look during the 1940s, while Herrmann worked frequently with Hitchcock, notably on *Psycho*.

Welles had unusual directorial control over the project, so he could ask his colleagues to execute his ideas. At the same time, he could encourage their suggestions. For instance, *Kane* allowed Toland to push further his experiments in deep-focus cinematography. Ultimately, it was Welles' responsibility to decide how to blend all these contributions into the film that became *Citizen Kane*. The result harmonizes the various techniques in ways that sometimes brashly, sometimes subtly, shape our experience as viewers.

Mystery and the Penetration of Space

In analyzing *Citizen Kane*'s narrative, we discovered that the film is organized as a search (p. 100). A detective-like figure, the reporter Thompson, tries to find the significance of Kane's last word, "Rosebud." But even before Thompson appears as a character, the film's narration invites us to ask questions about Kane and to seek the answers.

The very beginning of the film sets up a mystery. After a fade-in reveals a "No Trespassing" sign, in a series of craning movements upward, the camera travels over a set of fences, all matched graphically in the slow dissolves that link the shots. There follows a series of shots of a huge estate, always with the great house in the distance **(8.20)**. The gloomy lighting, the deserted setting, and the ominous music give the opening of the film the eerie uncertainty that we associate with tales of mystery and horror. These opening shots are connected by dissolves, making the camera seem to draw closer to the house although there is no forward camera movement. From shot to shot, the foreground changes, yet the lighted window remains in almost exactly the same position on the screen. Graphically matching the window from shot to shot already focuses our attention on it; we assume that whatever is in that room will be important in initiating the story.

At several points later in the film, the camera moves toward things that might reveal the secrets of Kane's character. One instance is in the spectacular crane up the side of a nightclub to a skylight as Thompson goes to interview Susan Alexander **(8.21–8.24)**. As the camera reaches the skylight, a dissolve and a crack of lightning shift the scene inside to another craning movement down to Susan's table.

8.20 The opening of *Citizen Kane*. At the film's start, dissolving views bring us closer to Xanadu. This sequence depends largely on special effects. The house itself is a series of paintings, combined through matte work with three-dimensional miniatures in the foreground.

8.21

8.22

8.23

8.24

8.21–8.24 Exploring the mystery, advancing into space. As this scene begins, the camera frames a poster of Susan Alexander on an outside wall of the nightclub (8.21). The camera cranes up the wall toward the roof (8.22). The camera continues its advance through the "El Rancho" sign (8.23) and over to the skylight (8.24). Some of these camera movements were created through laboratory special effects.

8.25

8.26

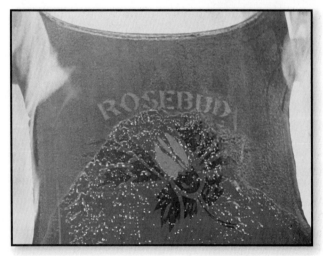

8.27

8.25–8.27 The final camera movement. A crane shot near the end (8.25) moves down to center on Kane's sled (8.26). Another forward camera movement brings the sled into close-up (8.27). Interestingly, the original program booklet for *Kane* included a section called "Star Orson Welles Makes Fluid Camera the Star of 'Citizen Kane'."

The opening scene and the introduction to El Rancho have some striking similarities. Each begins with a sign ("No Trespassing" and the publicity poster), and each moves us into a building to reveal a new character. The first scene uses a series of shots, whereas the second depends more on camera movement, but these different techniques are working to create a consistent pattern of penetration that becomes part of the film's style. Later, Thompson's second visit to Susan at the club repeats the crane shots of the first. The second flashback of Jed Leland's story begins with yet another movement into a scene. The camera is initially pointed at wet cobblestones. Then it tilts up and tracks in toward Susan coming out of a drugstore. Only then does the camera pan right to reveal Kane standing, splashed with mud, on the curb. This pattern of gradual movement into the story space not only suits the narrative's search pattern but also creates curiosity and suspense.

Films' endings often contain variations of their beginnings. Toward the end of *Citizen Kane,* Thompson gives up his search for Rosebud. But after the reporters leave the huge storeroom of Xanadu, the camera begins to move over the great expanse of Kane's collections. It cranes forward high above the crates and piles of objects (**8.25**), then moves down to center on the sled from Kane's childhood (**8.26**). After a cut to the furnace, the camera again moves in on the sled as it is tossed into the fire. At last we are able to read the word "Rosebud" on the sled (**8.27**). The ending continues the pattern set up at the beginning; the film techniques create a penetration into the story space, probing the mystery of the central character.

After our glimpse of the sled, however, the film reverses the pattern. A series of shots linked by dissolves leads us back outside Xanadu, the camera travels down to the "No Trespassing" sign again, and we are left to wonder whether this discovery really provides a resolution to the mystery about Kane's character. Now the beginning and the ending explicitly echo each other.

Style and Narration: Restriction and Objectivity

Our study of *Citizen Kane*'s organization (pp. 108–109) showed that Thompson's search is presented through a fairly complex narrational strategy. At one level, our knowledge is restricted principally to what Kane's acquaintances know about him. Within the flashbacks, the style avoids crosscutting or other techniques that would move toward a more unrestricted range of knowledge. Many of the flashback scenes are shot in fairly static long takes, strictly confining us to what participants could know. When the youthful Kane confronts Thatcher during the *Inquirer* crusade, Welles could have cut away to the reporter in Cuba sending Kane a telegram or could have shown a montage sequence of a day in the life of the paper. Instead, because this is Thatcher's tale, Welles handles the scene in a long take showing Kane and Thatcher in a face-to-face standoff, which is then capped by a close-up of Kane's cocky response.

8.28

8.29

8.30

8.31

8.28–8.31 Deep-focus for objectivity and simultaneous action. The principal shot in *Citizen Kane*'s childhood scene begins as a long shot of the young Kane at play in the snow (8.28). This becomes an interior view as the camera reveals a window, with Kane's mother appearing at the left and calling to him (8.29). The camera tracks back with Mrs. Kane (8.30) and keeps the boy in extreme long shot throughout the rest of the scene (8.31). Although the cabin interior is rendered in photographic deep focus, the image of the boy Charles is a rear projection, creating another layer of depth.

We've also seen that *Kane*'s narration requires us to take each narrator's version as objective within his or her limited knowledge. Welles reinforces this by avoiding shots that suggest optical or mental subjectivity. As usual, once a filmmaker commits to one creative option, this excludes other possibilities. By contrast, Hitchcock favors POV cutting in *The Birds* and *Rear Window* (pp. 222–223 and 241–242), which militate against the long-take option Welles pursues.

Welles' commitment to an external perspective on the action is also evident in his choice of deep-focus cinematography. The shot in which Kane's mother signs her son over to Thatcher is a good example. After some shots showing him playing in the snow, we get what at first seems a simple long shot of the boy (**8.28**). Soon, however, the camera is tracking back and following the adults to a table (**8.29, 8.30**), where they settle the guardianship. Mrs. Kane and Thatcher sit at a table in the foreground to sign the papers, while Kane's father remains standing farther away at the left, and the boy plays in the distance (**8.31**).

By eliminating cutting here, Welles captures a complex, developing stretch of the drama, like the opening of *Touch of Evil* discussed on pp. 213–215. Most Hollywood directors would have handled this scene in shot/reverse shot, but Welles keeps all the implications of the action before us throughout. The boy, who is the subject of the discussion, remains framed in the distant window through the whole scene, unaware of what the adults are doing.

The tensions between the father and the mother are conveyed straightforwardly: Mrs. Kane excludes him from the discussion at the table. The sound plays a while as well. Mr. Kane's objections to signing his son away mix in with the dialogue in the foreground, and even the boy's shouts (ironically, "The Union Forever!") can be heard in the distance. The framing also emphasizes the mother in much of the scene. This is her only appearance in the film. Her severity and clamped-down emotions help motivate the many events that follow from her action here. We have had little introduction to the family before this scene, but the combination of sound, cinematography, and mise-en-scene conveys the complicated action with an overall objectivity.

8.32 Depth and centering. Although Susan is much larger than Kane in this shot, his placement in frame center, as well as his frontal position, assure that we will look at him. The main purpose of the shot seems to be to emphasize that the vast spaces of Xanadu reflect their emotional distance from one another.

Every director directs our attention, but Welles does so in unusual ways. *Citizen Kane* offers a good example of how a director can choose between stylistic alternatives. In the scenes that avoid cutting, Welles cues our attention by using deep-space mise-en-scene (figure behavior, lighting, placement in space) and sound. We can watch expressions because the actors play frontally (8.27). In addition, the framing emphasizes certain figures by putting them in the foreground or in the center **(8.32)**. And, of course, our attention shifts from one character to another as they speak lines, as Tim Smith's eye-tracking study shows (p. 140). Avoiding the classical Hollywood shot/reverse shot, Welles uses other techniques to prompt us to build up the story.

Style and Narration: Omniscience

Citizen Kane's narration also embeds the narrators' objective but restricted versions of events within broader contexts. Thompson's investigation links the various tales, so we learn substantially what he learns. Yet he must not become the protagonist of the film, for that would remove Kane from the center of interest. Welles makes a crucial stylistic choice here. By the use of low-key selective lighting and patterns of staging and framing, Thompson is made virtually unidentifiable. His back is to us, he's tucked into the corner of the frame, and he's usually in darkness. The stylistic handling makes him the neutral investigator, less a character than a channel for information.

More broadly still, we have seen that the film encloses Thompson's search and each narrator's recollection within a more omniscient narration. Our discussion of the opening shots of Xanadu is relevant here. In the gradual approach to Xanadu, film style is used to convey a high degree of knowledge that no character has. When we enter Kane's death chamber, the style suggests even more—that the narration can plumb characters' minds. We see shots of snow covering the frame (for example, **8.33**), which hint at a subjective vision. Later in the film, the camera movements occasionally remind us of the broader range of narrational knowledge, as in the first version of Susan's opera premiere, shown during Leland's story in segment 6. There the camera moves to reveal something neither Leland nor Susan could know about **(8.34–8.36).** The final sequence, which at least partially solves the mystery of "Rosebud," also uses a vast camera movement to give us an omniscient perspective. The camera cranes over objects from Kane's collection, moving forward in space but backward through Kane's life to concentrate on his earliest memento, the sled. Again a salient technique conforms to pattern by giving us knowledge no character will ever possess.

Narrative Parallels: Settings

In looking at the development of the film's narrative (pp.108–109), we saw that Kane changes from an idealistic young man to a friendless recluse. The film contrasts Kane's early life as a newspaper publisher and his later withdrawal from public life. This contrast is most readily apparent in the settings. The *Inquirer* office is initially an efficient but cluttered place. When Kane takes over, he creates a casual atmosphere by moving in his furniture and living in the office. The low camera angles tend to emphasize the office's thin pillars and low ceilings, which are white and evenly, brightly lit. Xanadu, in contrast, is huge and sparsely furnished (8.32). The ceilings are too high to be seen in most shots, and the few furnishings stand far apart. The lighting often strikes figures strongly from the back or side, creating a few patches of hard light in the midst of general darkness. The expanded collection of antiquities and mementos now is housed in colossal storerooms.

The contrast between the *Inquirer* office and Xanadu is also created by the sound techniques associated with each locale. Several scenes at the newspaper office (Kane's initial arrival and his return from Europe) involve a dense sound mix with a babble of overlapping voices. Yet the cramped space is suggested by the relative lack of resonance in timbre. In Xanadu, however, the conversations sound very different. Kane and Susan speak to each other slowly, with pauses between. Moreover, their voices have a booming echo effect that combines with the setting and lighting to suggest huge, empty space.

This transition from Kane's newspaper days to his eventual seclusion at Xanadu is suggested by changes in the mise-en-scene at the *Inquirer*. While Kane is in Europe, the paintings and statues he sends back begin to fill up his small office. The new clutter hints at Kane's growing ambitions and declining interest in working personally on his newspaper. This change culminates in the last scene in the *Inquirer* office—Leland's confrontation with Kane. The office is being used as a campaign headquarters. With the desks pushed aside and the employees gone, the room looks larger and emptier than it had before. Welles emphasizes this by placing the camera at floor level and shooting from a low angle (5.113). The Chicago *Inquirer* office, with its deep, shadowy spaces, pushes this pattern further **(8.37)**, as do later conversation scenes in the caverns of Xanadu (8.32).

Contrast these scenes with one near the end of the film. The reporters invade Kane's museum-like storeroom at Xanadu **(8.38).** Although the echoes remind us of the estate's vastness, the reporters transform the setting briefly by the same sort of dense, overlapping dialogue that characterized the early *Inquirer* scenes and the scene after the newsreel. By bringing together these reporters and Kane's final surroundings, the film creates another parallel emphasizing the changes in the protagonist.

Parallels: Other Techniques

Parallels are important throughout *Citizen Kane,* and most of the techniques chosen by Welles, Toland, and their colleagues help create them. For example, deep focus and deep space can pack many characters into the frame in order to summon up similarities and contrasts. Late in Thatcher's account (segment 4), a scene presents Kane's financial losses in the Depression. He is forced to sign over his newspaper to Thatcher's bank. In a single take, a turning point in the plot is created by the arrangement of the figures and the image's depth of field **(8.39, 8.40).** The lowering of the contract recalls the previous scene, when Thatcher puts down the newspaper that has concealed him **(8.41, 8.42).** There Thatcher had been annoyed, but Kane could defy him. Years later in the story, Thatcher has gained control and Kane paces restlessly, still defiant but stripped of his power over the *Inquirer* chain.

Editing patterns can also suggest similarities between scenes, as when Welles compares two moments in which Kane seems to win public support. In the first scene, Kane is running for governor and makes a speech at a mammoth rally. This scene is principally organized around an editing pattern that shows one or two shots of Kane speaking, then one or two close shots of small groups of characters in the audience (Emily and their son, Leland, Bernstein, Gettys), then another shot of Kane. The cutting establishes the characters who are important for their views of Kane. Boss Gettys is the last to be shown in the scene, and we expect him to retaliate against Kane's denunciation.

After his defeat, Kane sets out to make Susan a successful singer, not because she wants it but because she will be an extension of him. "We're going to be a great opera star," he promises a reporter. In Susan's debut, the organization of shots follows the pattern of the campaign rally. Again the figure on the stage, Susan,

8.33

8.34

8.35

8.36

8.33–8.36 Wide-ranging narration at work. The snowstorm paperweight is itself bathed in fluttering snowflakes, suggesting a mental vision (8.33). In the film's first opera scene, the camera cranes up from the stage (8.34) and through the rigging above (8.35) to reveal a stagehand indicating that Susan's singing stinks (8.36).

8.37

8.38

8.37–8.38 Depth and cavernous spaces. In *Citizen Kane,* rear projection exaggerates the depth of the *Inquirer* office. Welles as Kane performed at the foreground typewriter, while wide-angle, deep-focus footage of Joseph Cotten (Leland) and Everett Sloane (Bernstein) was projected behind him (8.37). Extreme deep focus, also possibly enhanced by back projection, is employed in the final scene in Xanadu's warehouse, which is enlivened by rapid dialogue (8.38).

serves as a pivot for the editing, with shots of her alternating with shots of the listeners (Bernstein, Leland, the singing teacher, and above all Kane) **(8.43, 8.44).** The general narrative parallels are sharpened by specific stylistic techniques. Together they articulate two stages of Kane's power quest: first his own attempt and then with Susan as his proxy.

Parallels can be brought out by music as well. Susan's singing is causally central to the narrative, for it propels her to the limelight with Kane as her backer;

8.39–8.42 Parallel gestures underscored by deep space. The contract scene opens with a close-up of Kane's manager, Bernstein, reading the contract (8.39). He lowers the paper to reveal Thatcher, now much older, seated opposite him. We hear Kane's voice offscreen, and Bernstein moves his head slightly, the camera reframing a little. Now we see Kane pacing beyond them in a huge office or boardroom (8.40). This shot echoes the composition of an earlier scene (8.41), which dramatizes our first real look at Kane as an adult (8.42). Here he is a far more commanding figure; in 8.40, after losing his newspaper empire, he has shrunken.

8.39

8.40

8.41

8.42

her failure becomes another phase of his failure. Musically, Susan's elaborate aria in *Salammbo* contrasts sharply with the other main diegetic music, the party song about "Charlie Kane." But both relate to Kane's ambitions. The lyrics of the "Charlie Kane" ditty show that Kane intends it as his signature song, and it does turn up later as campaign music. In addition, the chorus girls who sing the song wear costumes with boots and Rough Rider hats (**8.45**). Kane's desire for war with Spain has shown up even in this apparently simple farewell party for his departure to Europe. When Kane's political ambitions are dashed, he tries to create a career for his wife instead, but her voice falters in singing grand opera. The songs cooperate with other techniques in creating parallels between phases of Kane's career.

8.43

A Convincing Newsreel

The "News on the March" sequence is crucial to the film. It fills us in about Kane's background, and it provides a map of the upcoming plot events (pp. 103–104). Also, we need to believe that this is a real newsreel in order to motivate Thompson's search for the key to Kane's life. A plausible-looking newsreel sequence also helps establish Kane's power and wealth, which will be the basis of much of the upcoming action.

Welles sets off this sequence by techniques that don't appear elsewhere in *Citizen Kane*. These techniques imitate the look and sound of documentary footage of the period. The music and the voice-over commentary recall actual newsreels, and the insert titles, outmoded in fictional films, were still a convention of documentaries. Welles uses several different film stocks to make it appear that the shots have been assembled from widely different sources. Some shots copy the jerkiness of silent film run at sound speed. Welles also scratched and faded this footage to give it the look of old, worn film. This distressing of the footage, combined with the makeup work, creates a remarkable impression that Kane was a historical figure. We see him with major political leaders (**8.46**), and glimpse him wheeled around his estate (**8.47**). The visual conventions are enhanced by the use of a narrator whose booming voice mimics (and mocks) the commentary typical in newsreels of the day.

8.44

8.43–8.44 Editing parallels opera and politics. Susan's opera debut repeats the editing pattern of Kane's campaign rally. Shots of Susan onstage (8.43) are followed by shots of listeners, most notably her brooding and domineering puppet master (8.44).

Plot Time through Editing

One of *Citizen Kane*'s outstanding formal features is the way its plot manipulates story time (pp. 101–102). This process is motivated by Thompson's inquiry and the order in which he interviews Kane's acquaintances (p. 104). Welles and his collaborators selected a variety of techniques to signal shifts from scene to scene, creating both ellipses and rearrangements of story chronology.

8.45

8.46   **8.47**

8.45–8.47 Kane in history. The chorus girls, bearing hats modeled on Teddy Roosevelt's Rough Riders, clap them on the partying journalists' heads (8.45). In "News on the March," simulated newsreel footage shows Kane visiting world leaders like Hitler (8.46). After Kane becomes a recluse, the handheld camera, the barriers, and the ill-composed framing imitate covertly shot footage (8.47).

8.48 Editing for shock. After Raymond says, "Like the time his wife left him," a quick dissolve is underscored by a cockatoo's shriek and an abrupt close-up, starting the scene at a high dramatic and auditory pitch.

Perhaps the most startling transitional device for 1941 audiences was the *shock cut*. A shock cut creates a jarring juxtaposition, usually by means of a sudden shift to a higher sound volume and a considerable graphic discontinuity. *Citizen Kane* offers several instances: the abrupt beginning of the newsreel after the lingering deathbed image, the leap from the quiet conversation in the newsreel projection room to the lightning and thunder outside El Rancho, and the sudden appearance of a screeching cockatoo in the foreground as Raymond's flashback begins **(8.48).** The shock cuts create surprise and sharply mark off certain scenes. Somewhat milder shock cuts occur within scenes as well, creating tension and edginess. The newsreel comes to an abrupt, skidding halt and during the scene in which Susan berates Kane for sending Leland a $25,000 check, her shrill demands, "What?" "What is it?" are accentuated by abrupt sound cuts and brief shots.

Some transitions that skip over or drastically compress time are less abrupt than the harsh sound and image cuts. Kane's sled is covered by snow through a languid series of dissolves. More extensively, the breakfast table montage (segment 6) shows, with big ellipses, the decline of Kane's first marriage. It starts with the loving couple at their early wedding breakfast, rendered in a track-in and a shot/reverse-shot series. Then the sequence moves through several brief episodes, consisting of shot/reverse-shot exchanges linked by superimpositions of lighted windows whizzing by. (The effect resembles the transitional device of the **whip pan,** a fast panning movement.) In each episode, Kane and Emily become more sharply hostile. The segment ends by tracking away to show the surprising distance between them at the table, using spatial distance to indicate emotional distance in the way that will be developed in scenes with Kane's second wife Susan (8.32).

Composer Bernard Herrmann also guided our experience of the breakfast-table montage. The romantic breakfast is accompanied by a lilting waltz. At each shift, the music changes. A comic variation of the waltz follows, and then a tense one; then horns and trumpets restate the Kane theme. The payoff of the sequence shows the couple eating in stony silence, with Emily ostentatiously reading a rival newspaper. That passage is accompanied by a slow, eerie variation on the initial theme. The dissolution of the marriage is stressed by this theme-and-variations accompaniment. A similar sort of temporal compression and sonic elaboration can be found in the montage of Susan's opera career (segment 7).

Our brief examination of *Citizen Kane*'s style has pointed out only a few of the major patterns in the film. You can find others. There's the musical motif associated with Kane's power; the "K" motif appearing in Kane's costumes and in Xanadu's settings; the way the childish decor of Susan's room in Xanadu reveals Kane's attitude toward her; the changes in the actors' performances as the characters age in the course of the story; and the striking photographic devices, such as the photos that become animated or the many superimpositions during montage sequences.

Critics have argued that the film's stylistic richness, along with its complex narrative structure, works somewhat against our feeling much for its protagonist. Kane, seen mostly from the outside by those who knew him, is an object of admiration or dislike, but never real sympathy. (For a more intensely emotional film, we must go to Welles' next film, *The Magnificent Ambersons.*) Is *Citizen Kane* then a cold intellectual exercise? Our analysis of the film's form and style suggests that an emotional distance on Kane is exactly what Welles and his collaborators were aiming at. Through the flashback structure and the omniscient but detached narration, we're asked to judge him from the outside—or rather, given the revelation of the Rosebud sled, to suspend final judgment on a figure we can't fully understand. "I don't think any word can explain a man's life," says Thompson.

Yet one implication of the revelation of Rosebud is that old age leaves one reflecting on what might have been. Bernstein talks of recalling a girl in a white dress, and Leland remembers Kane's first wife Emily from dancing school. The snowstorm paperweight that Kane drops as he dies is a motif recalling not only the Kane family cabin and the boy's games in the snow but also his failure to find new happiness with Susan **(8.49, 8.50).** The film's formal and stylistic dynamics grant some sympathy for an arrogant, self-centered man. Even so forbidding a figure as Charles Foster Kane can cherish a fleeting memory of a moment in childhood just before his world changed forever.

8.49

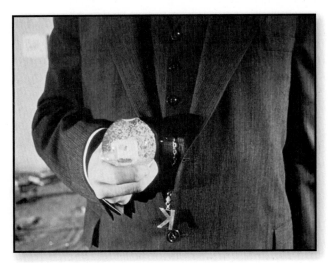

8.50

8.49–8.50 Pieces in a puzzle. The snowstorm paperweight on Susan's dressing table, the night Kane meets her (8.49). The globe is center left, just in front of the girl's picture. Note that Welles doesn't cut in to a close-up emphasizing this; many viewers probably don't notice it, or the picture of Susan as a child behind the paperweight. In addition, when Susan says that her mother wanted her to become a singer, she says softly, "You know how mothers are." Years later Susan leaves Kane, and after he has wrecked her room in a fury, he picks up the glass ball and sorrowfully murmurs, "Rosebud" (8.50). The word evokes not only her departure and the sled we see at the film's end but the whole cluster of childhood imagery that is presented in Thatcher's flashback. At this point, it seems, Kane has lost everything and his retreat from the world becomes complete.

A CLOSER LOOK

Gravity: Film Style in the Digital Age

We've seen throughout this part that traditional film techniques survive in digital cinema. Mise-en-scene, cinematography, editing, and sound remain central to filmmaking. Digital tools have allowed filmmakers to expand these techniques. Now roaring monsters and flying superheroes seem more convincing than ever. Going beyond fantasy special effects, however, digital technology can help a film achieve a distinctive style.

Gravity's story could easily have been conceived in the predigital age. A space walk involving three astronauts turns disastrous when hurtling space debris slams into them. One man is killed, and the protagonist, Dr. Ryan Stone, is sent spinning into space. Matt Kowalski, a veteran astronaut, rescues her. His jet-pack allows the two to travel short distances.

Their goal is to get back to earth, and the bulk of the plot shows the setbacks they encounter in their search for a re-entry vehicle. First they head toward their space shuttle, but they find it irreparably damaged. They must go on to the International Space Station (ISS). Although Kowalski dies in the attempt, Stone makes it to the ISS. She finds its escape pod incapable of landing, though she can use it to fly to another vessel. Stone, a scientist with little flight experience, must continue on to a Chinese space station and use its escape pod to reach the earth.

Alongside the suspense generated through its characters' harrowing predicament, *Gravity* concentrates on Stone's psychological journey. At first she goes about her work listlessly, and she becomes terrified when set adrift in space. As she and Kowalski travel to the space shuttle, she confesses that she has been devastated by the death of her daughter. On earth she has spent her evenings driving around aimlessly, and in her grief the silence of space calms her. At the climax in the Chinese station, when her situation seems hopeless, she is about to accept a passive death. In a vision Kowalski returns and gives her a new will to live.

The filmmakers use traditional strategies to make us empathize with Stone. The narration is highly restrictive, since our knowledge is almost entirely limited to hers. For instance, we never see a cutaway to the Houston space agency. We hear only a man's voice conversing with Stone and Kowalski through their helmet radios. Similarly, we stay with her rather than her rescuer, Kowalski, when she is hurled off into the void. Sometimes the camera takes her optical POV, as when she floats weightlessly through the Chinese space station.

What, then, does digital technology add to traditional technique? For one thing, greater realism. The filmmakers sought to make *Gravity* look and sound as if it had actually been made 600 kilometers above the earth. The biggest challenge was representing weightlessness.

The filmmakers found that suspending the actors by wires that would be digitally erased didn't look authentic (though wire-work was used in some scenes within the ISS). Director Alfonso Cuarón decided to create most of the mise-en-scene with CGI. Cameras photographed actors' faces, the interiors of escape pods, and the final scene on earth, but the costumes and most settings were digitally constructed. The visors were given dust, scratches, fingerprints, and mist forming on the interior as the characters breathe **(8.51).** Props were made and scanned to be added to the images through animation.

The cinematography used new tools to convey the effect of weightlessness. When Kowalski and Stone are in danger or bouncing along the exterior of a space station, they are often swinging and spinning. The actors could not move so freely in a set, so they were placed in a "tilt rig," a conical basket that rotated. A camera was mounted on a flexible crane run by computer. The crane could circle the actors from all sides to create the effect of them spinning freely.

As often happens, one artistic choice triggers further choices. Once the characters were spinning and drifting, what to do about lighting? The light coming from the sun and reflected from the earth had to constantly change on the faces and bodies. Conventional film lamps could not move around the actors fast enough, and adding the light via digital animation would have been very time consuming. Moreover, in most films with digital special effects, the lighting added via computer to the effects elements seldom matches the lighting on the live-action parts of the shot. The result is a vague sense in the viewer that the image is not quite real.

Cinematographer Emmanuel Lubezki, inspired by the programmable walls of LED lights used at rock concerts, created a large Light Box within which the actors performed. The LED walls of the box projected onto the actors' faces the animated images of sun, earth, stars, and the spaceships that would eventually be added to the scene digitally. Even when the characters were tumbling in space, the light and colors changed in synchronization with the Light Box images. The effects and the live-action footage could be joined with no disparity that would mar the realism of the scene.

Apart from heightened realism, the filmmakers sought to extend our attachment to Stone through greater illusions of immersion. The staging of shots, putting us close to the characters or between them, enhances this sense. But the major factor in creating immersion was the decision to shoot in 3D, which expands the usual staging options. Actors glide toward the camera or reach out to retrieve a tool drifting toward us. Inside the space vehicles, chess pieces and Post-Its float freely. The sense of being

A CLOSER LOOK *Continued*

absorbed in the film's visual world became even stronger for those viewers who saw the film in the vast Imax format.

Weightlessness and immersion work together in the film's camerawork and editing. The film has only 206 shots total, while most modern Hollywood films have 1,800 or more. As a result, there are many long takes—most dramatically, the opening shot, which runs 13 minutes. Cuarón points out that NASA video shots have shown people what the earth really looks like from space and have set up a new visual convention: "When you see all those documentaries of space exploration, they are one single shot." NASA cooperated extensively in providing images and information to the filmmakers.

Sometimes the long takes keep us oriented in relation to the characters, often with the camera hovering around or between them. Even so, there is some disorientation, as the astronauts are seen upside down or sideways **(8.52).** During this scene, the tether provides an axis of action, but most of the time the axis changes too rapidly to provide orientation. At other moments, the rotating framing denies us a sense of ground underneath us. One shot of Stone flung far away from the shuttle shows the earth whizzing repeatedly through the background (8.51). Again the effect is immersion, as we feel that the earth is spinning around us as well. With the characters gliding in all directions and the camera at times gyrating on its own, the long take serves as our best guide to the action. Conventional analytical editing could have been very confusing. There is only one passage of conventional shot/reverse shot, when Stone tries to convince Kowalski not to unhook himself from her and drift away to his death.

As you'd expect, the sound track is designed to intensify realism and the immersive effect. The film's opening title explains that above the earth's atmosphere, "There is nothing to carry sound." Accordingly, the filmmakers avoid all voices and effects in exteriors. Some scenes are dead silent, as at the very beginning, when the camera drifts above the earth and the shuttle has not yet

appeared. To compensate for lack of noises, the filmmakers created a musical score that includes noises similar to sound effects. Scenes of destruction or threat in the vacuum of space are accompanied by music evoking grinding metal or squealing radio distortion. The viewer may get the impression of hearing debris hitting the ISS, but that barrage is part of the nondiegetic sound track.

The sound track also reinforces our attachment to the characters. Apart from hearing their radio communication, we hear distorted vibrations coming through their suits from the things they seize and bump against. When Stone struggles to activate her experimental equipment, the rasps of bolts and sliding metal are muffled, as though they were recorded under water.

At moments, when the audience is as spatially disoriented as the characters, *Gravity* recalls experimental films like *Leviathan* (p. 198). As we've seen, though, the development of a film's plot may be accompanied by a changing stylistic pattern. As Stone settles into one space vehicle after another, more conventional creative choices gradually appear. Often the camera pans between her and a control board, with stable framing providing us a firm orientation. The long take is now used to present her hallucination of Kowalski returning to guide her, and this near-miracle reminds us that from the start he has been associated with the angel of his favorite country and western song. Motifs of spirituality in each ship's setting (a Christian icon in the Russian space station, a Buddha figurine in the Chinese vessel) suggest that Stone's decision to risk everything for survival could release her from despair over her daughter's death. When Stone joyfully manages to launch the Chinese escape pod earthward, we get rapid cutting, camerawork more jittery than before, and a traditional orchestral score dramatizing the danger and exhilaration of her fiery descent. While providing its audience a suspenseful and emotional adventure, *Gravity* shows how digital tools can extend and even transform techniques familiar from the age of film.

8.51 Digital decoration. A digital space suit and visor were added to Sandra Bullock's face. The fogging effect of her breath condensing in the helmet and the earth repeatedly spinning past behind her were also digital creations. The washed-out illumination on the astronauts' white suits simulates sunlight in an airless environment.

8.52 Digital disorientation. Many shots present no cues for directions of up and down, as when Kowalski and Stone, tethered together, move slowly above the earth's surface toward the International Space Station.

▶ SUMMARY

This concludes our introduction of the basic cinematic techniques. In this chapter we've suggested ways to analyze stylistic functions in the overall form of individual films. We offer additional examples of analysis in Part Five.

Before that, however, there's one more factor that filmmakers take into account as a way of shaping our experience. Nearly every film we see belongs to a larger category of films. Filmmakers declare their plans to make a thriller or a musical or an experimental film. An audience member may decide to watch a horror film or a documentary. These groupings play a central role in filmmaking and film viewing. In Part Four we offer you some ways to think about them.

PART 4

We launched our study of film as art by asking how the films we see are shaped by filmmakers' creative decisions and how these decisions affect production, distribution, and exhibition (Chapter 1). Then we considered how those decisions affect a film's overall form, particularly narrative form (Chapters 2–3). We went on to examine how the techniques of the film medium—mise-en-scene, cinematography, editing, and sound—give the filmmaker a wide range of artistic choices (Chapters 4–8). In the next two chapters, we consider how filmmakers and audiences share certain expectations about the kinds of films that can be made and seen.

In online video services like Netflix, films are filed under different headings—by star, by period ("Silent Movies"), occasionally by director (Alfred Hitchcock, Woody Allen), by place of origin ("Foreign Films"). To understand how films work and how we experience them, we need to gain a sense of some significant ways audiences and filmmakers sort films into groups.

Types of Films

One popular way of grouping fiction films is by *genre,* such as action films, romantic comedies, science fiction, and so on. Critics and viewers use genre labels like these in talking about films, and filmmakers are guided by them in planning projects. In Chapter 9, we examine the idea of genre. We look briefly at four widely recognized genres: the Western, the horror film, the musical, and the sports film.

Another way we group films is based on ideas about how they were made and what effects they attempt to achieve. In Chapter 10, we discuss three major types of filmmaking: documentary, experimental, and animation.

Documentary films, as their name implies, record some aspect of the real world. They are distinguished from fiction films because we assume they're making factual claims. In effect, they're saying, "This actually happened, and what I'm telling you is true." Another particular kind of filmmaking is termed *experimental.* Such films play with film form and conventions in ways that challenge audience expectations and provide unusual emotional and intellectual experiences. Finally, *animated* films are defined by the way they are made. Drawings, models, or other subjects are presented frame by frame to create illusory movements that never existed in front of the camera. Although we often think of animated films as being for children, we'll see that virtually any type of film can be made using animation.

9

Film Genres

In Chapter 2 (p. 50), we offered you a choice about how to begin a film. Do you start with an abrupt plunge into action? Or do you try to draw the viewer in slowly? But we didn't say much about what kind of film you were making. If you're making a horror film like *Jurassic Park,* maybe you want an initial scare to galvanize your audience. If you're making more of a science fiction adventure like *Close Encounters of the Third Kind,* hints at a time-traveling mystery may work better as an opening.

At the start of Chapter 3, we speculated on how you might tell a love-and-marriage story by arranging the events in various patterns. Our purpose was to get you thinking about how the same basic story could be presented in different plots (p. 74). We reflected that starting with an impending wedding and then flashing back to the partners' initial meeting could make the viewer curious about how the people fell in love, or how the couple's first quarrels were smoothed over.

In all these cases, we were assuming that some creative choices about film form depended on the *kind* of film you were making. Take the romantic comedy we asked you to design. To fill out our plot, the two main characters have to meet for the first time. How? One convention of romantic comedy is the "Cute Meet." The characters should first encounter each other in a way that is amusing, perhaps embarrassing. In *Trouble in Paradise,* two sophisticated thieves go on a date, and at one point they realize that they've robbed each other. A man and a woman in *Love Actually* meet when they are both performing in a pornographic film.

Similarly, you need to create some obstacles to the lovers' union. One convention is sometimes called the Big Misunderstanding. In *The Wedding Singer,* the heroine tries on a wedding dress while imagining she's marrying the hero. But when he glimpses her trying it on, he assumes she's preparing to marry someone else. An extreme example is *Tootsie,* in which Michael is disguised as a woman, so that he is forced to lie to Julie about his feelings. The Big Misunderstanding can be multiplied, as it is in *Tootsie,* when men become attracted to Michael-as-Dorothy.

Another way to create an obstacle is to separate the couple physically, either by decision or accident **(9.1).** To pile on the obstacles to true love, we could add rivals, unreliable friends (handy for bungled messages), advice-giving confidants, or authority figures such as parents and bosses. In plotting the rest of the movie, we'd try to come up with particular scenes that touch some familiar bases **(9.2).**

But if the film touched every base, it could sink into stale repetition. So we might try to tweak romantic-comedy formulas. Nora Ephron's *Sleepless in Seattle* delays the Cute Meet until very late in the story. The Big Misunderstanding that divides the couple in *50 First Dates* involves amnesia, so the woman never recognizes the man from one day to the next. *Love Actually* innovates by intertwining many

9.1

9.2

9.1–9.2 Romantic comedy conventions. Accidents of timing, with lovers just missing appointments, are frequent in romantic comedies. In *Serendipity,* a fluke of timing and a mischievous kid in an elevator keep Jonathan and Sara from reuniting (9.1). *(500) Days of Summer* uses another convention, the montage sequence with a pop song conveying a lover's mood. The film innovates by treating the hero's daffy elation as contagious, leading to a dance number in a park and a touch of fantasy with the animated blue bird (9.2).

romances, some of which go nowhere. *Bridesmaids* innovates by incorporating elements of male-centered comedy into romantic plotlines centering on women.

In short, in planning our film we would remember that it falls into a *genre* and that the genre has specific conventions. If we were ambitious, we'd also be trying to come up with some original ways to handle those conventions.

Understanding Genre

The word *genre* is originally French, and it simply means "kind" or "type." It's related to another word, *genus,* which is used in the biological sciences to classify groups of plants and animals. When we speak of film genres, we're indicating certain types of movies. The science fiction film, the action picture, the comedy, the musical, the Western—these are some genres of fictional storytelling cinema.

Scientists can usually place plants or animals within a single genus with confidence, but film genres lack that sort of scientific precision. Instead, genres are convenient terms that develop informally. Filmmakers, industry decision makers, critics, and viewers all share the sense that certain films resemble one another in significant ways. Genres also change over time, as filmmakers invent new twists on old formulas. Although we have solid intuitions about what genre a film falls into, defining the precise boundaries between genres can be tricky, as we'll see.

When we think about genre, the examples that come to mind are usually those of fictional live-action films. We'll see in the next chapter that there can be genres of other basic sorts of cinema. There are genres of documentary, such as the compilation film and the concert movie. Experimental films and animated films contain genres as well.

Defining a Genre

Popular, mass-market cinema rests on genre filmmaking. Most countries have versions of romance stories, action sagas, supernatural tales, and comedies. Some genres are more local in flavor. Germany has its *Heimatfilm,* the tale of small-town life. The Hindi cinema of India has produced *devotionals,* films centering on the lives of saints and religious figures, as well as *mythologicals,* derived from legend and literary classics. Mexican filmmakers developed the *cabaretera,* a type of melodrama centering on prostitutes.

Sometimes reviewers dismiss genre films as shallow and trivial, assuming them to be simply formulaic: It's only a Western; it's just a horror film. Undoubtedly, many films in all genres are cheaply and unimaginatively made. Yet, because genres are central to most filmmaking, a genre picture can be excellent. *Singin' in the Rain* is a musical, as well as one of the best American films. *Grand Illusion* is a war film. *Psycho* is a thriller. *The Godfather* is a gangster film. On the whole, genre is a category best used to describe and analyze films, not to evaluate them.

Audiences know the genres of their culture very well—so well that genres may structure people's ways of seeing the world. Children may grow up pretending to be superheroes or fairy-tale princesses. Patton Oswalt reports that his high school friends categorized themselves along genre lines: They were Zombies (fans of Goth culture and metal rock), Spaceships (high-tech gadgets, futuristic utopias), or Wastelands (punk rock, apocalyptic fiction). Since the Internet allows everyone to learn as much as they want about anything in popular culture, everyone can be a genre connoisseur, a passionate and knowledgeable fan.

> " I've got news for you—pop culture *is* nerd culture."
>
> —Patton Oswalt, comedian and actor

What Makes a Genre? Everyone seems reasonably agreed on what genres exist and what films fall into them, but it's not clear how we arrive at that consensus. What makes us think that dozens or hundreds of films belong to the same category?

Most scholars agree that no genre can be defined in a single hard-and-fast way. In some genres the films share subjects or themes. A gangster film centers on urban organized crime. A science fiction film features a technology beyond the reach of contemporary science. A fantasy film typically involves magical powers and supernatural creatures.

Subject matter or theme isn't so central to defining other genres. Musicals are recognizable chiefly by their manner of presentation: singing, dancing, or both. The detective film is partly defined by the plot pattern of an investigation. And some genres are defined by the distinctive emotional effect they aim for: amusement in comedies, tension in suspense films.

Even when we have a firm sense of what a particular genre is, we may find films that fit the category to different degrees. Typically, we think of a genre as consisting of clear cases and fuzzier examples. *Singin' in the Rain* is a prime example of a musical, but David Byrne's *True Stories,* with its ironic presentation of musical numbers, is more of a borderline case. And an audience's sense of the core cases can change over history. For modern audiences, a core example of the thriller would be *The Girl with the Dragon Tattoo,* whereas for audiences of the 1950s, a prime example would have been something less gory, like Hitchcock's *North by Northwest.*

Sometimes a film seems to straddle two genres. Is *Groundhog Day* a romantic comedy or a fantasy? Is *Psycho* a slasher film or a mystery thriller? Steven Spielberg's

War of the Worlds combines horror, science fiction, and family melodrama. As we'll see, mixing genres is one important source of change in film history.

Subgenres You've probably noticed that some genre labels are very broad. The comedy category includes slapstick comedies such as *Animal House,* romantic comedies such as *The Proposal,* parodies such as the Austin Powers series, and raunchy male-oriented comedies such as *The Hangover.* Similarly, melodrama, as thought of today, encompasses stories of crises in marriage (*In the Bedroom*), dysfunctional families (*Magnolia*), and doomed love affairs (*The Fault in Our Stars*).

For this reason, it's useful to have the idea of *subgenres* to refer to distinct and fairly long-lasting types within a genre. There are science fiction films involving interplanetary travel (sometimes mockingly called "space opera"), alien invasions of earth, biological experiments (like *Rise of the Planet of the Apes*), or future societies, like the worlds of *Elysium* and *THX-1138.* These subgenres will have distinct conventions of their own and perhaps appeal to different viewers. Again, sometimes critics call our attention to subgenres. Reviewers have popularized terms like "dystopias" for bleak science fiction futures and "buddy films" for action movies like *21 Jump Street* that display male bonding.

The Usefulness of Genre Categories Everyone who comes into contact with cinema relies on ideas of genre. Genre concepts help producers decide what films to make. When science fiction and fantasy films are popular, executives are likelier to green-light projects in those genres. The massive success of young-adult fantasy fiction, crystallized in the Harry Potter franchise, led many studios to finance costly but unprofitable ventures into the same territory (*Inkheart, The Golden Compass*). During the 1960s studios backed *The Sound of Music* and other big-budget musicals because they attracted a wide audience. Such lavish projects are risky today, and many have failed, even when they were based on acclaimed Broadway shows (such as *The Phantom of the Opera* and *Rent*). Contemporary musicals tend to be lower-budget items such as *Mamma Mia!* and the *Step Up* series.

Advertising tends to pinpoint a film's genre. The poster for *Twilight: Eclipse* proclaims: "Vampires. Werewolves. Humans. It's time to choose a side." Coming-attractions trailers and the film's poster design usually leave no doubt about what genre the film is in, the better to target fans. Critics and entertainment reporters play a role in this promotional process. To call *(500) Days of Summer* "a romantic comedy that remembers that the best romances have a touch of the bittersweet" not only announces what genre the film belongs to but also expresses an evaluation of how well it fulfills certain conventions.

For viewers, genre categories are a part of their tastes. Every moviegoer likes some genres, tolerates others, and loathes others. Fans may try to see everything in a genre they love and to learn as much as possible about their favorites. They may exchange information via magazines, websites, or conventions. Peter Jackson and Guillermo del Toro started out as passionate genre geeks, and their intimate knowledge of horror and fantasy traditions pervades the films they direct.

Analyzing a Genre

Both filmmakers and film viewers, then, share some general notions about the types of films that compete for our attention. We largely agree on the genre's conventions, the kinds of recurring elements we picked out in romantic comedies. For the filmmaker, the conventions are materials they work with. For the viewer, conventions shape our expectations about what we're likely to see and hear.

Conventions of Story and Style Genre conventions often center on plot patterns. We anticipate an investigation in a mystery film; revenge plotlines are common in Westerns; a musical finds ways to provide song-and-dance situations.

9.3

9.4

9.3–9.4 Genre-specific techniques. An aggressive depth composition would usually be out of place in a musical or romantic comedy, but it suits the tension developing in a police interrogation in *The Secret in Their Eyes* (9.3). In *The Exorcist,* a single streetlight picks out the priest as he arrives at night, while light streams from the room where the possessed girl is confined (9.4).

9.5 Hollywood conventions elsewhere. Hineer Saleem's *My Sweet Pepper Land* shows a Kurdish lawman trying to bring peace to a war-torn border town. The film draws on classic Western iconography—threatening outlaws on horses, the hero poised to draw his pistol—to depict a showdown.

The gangster film usually centers on the gangster's rise and fall as he struggles against police and rival gangs. We expect a biographical film ("biopic") such as *Lincoln* or *The Theory of Everything* to trace significant episodes in an actual person's life. In a cop thriller, certain characters are conventional: the shifty informer, the comic sidekick, the exasperated captain who despairs of getting the squad to follow procedure.

Other genre conventions are more thematic, involving broad meanings that are summoned again and again. The Hong Kong martial-arts film commonly celebrates loyalty and obedience to one's teacher. A standard theme of the gangster film has been the price of criminal success, with the gangster's rise to power portrayed as a hardening into egotism and brutality. The screwball comedy traditionally sets up a thematic opposition between a stiff, snobbish social milieu and characters' urges for freedom and innocent zaniness. A melodrama such as *One Day* suggests the cost of failing to recognize your true love.

Still other genre conventions involve stylistic patterns. Techniques that would be jarring in one genre may become common in another (**9.3**). Low-key and high-contrast lighting is rare in a musical or romantic comedy but it's standard in the horror film and the thriller (**9.4**). In an action picture, we expect rapid cutting and slow-motion violence. In the melodrama, an emotional twist may be underscored by a sudden burst of poignant music. That sort of music would be out of place in a horror film, which might instead offer us a grating burst of sound effects.

Genre Iconography As a visual medium, cinema can also define genres through conventional *iconography*. A genre's iconography consists of recurring symbolic images that carry meaning from film to film.

Objects and settings often furnish iconography for a genre. A close-up of a tommy gun lifted out of a 1920s Ford would probably be enough to identify a scene as being from a gangster movie, while a shot of a long, curved sword hanging from a kimono would place us in the world of the samurai. The war film takes place in battle-scarred landscapes, the backstage musical in theaters and clubs, the space-travel film in starships and on distant planets.

Film industries outside America can draw on Hollywood iconography (**9.5**). Certain film stars can become iconographic as well—Judy Garland and Barbra Streisand for the musical, John Wayne and Clint Eastwood for the Western, Arnold Schwarzenegger for the action picture, Steve Carell and Seth Rogen for comedy, Amy Adams and Sandra Bullock for romantic drama and comedy.

By knowing conventions, viewers have a clear pathway into the film. Our expectations are set, and the film can communicate information economically. When we meet the weak sheriff, we strongly suspect that he will not stand up to the outlaw gang. We can then focus attention on the cowboy hero as he is slowly drawn into helping the townspeople defend themselves.

Audiences expect the genre film to offer something familiar, but they demand something new as well. So a film can revise or even reject the conventions associated with its genre. *Bugsy Malone* is a gangster musical in which children play all the traditional adult roles. *2001: A Space Odyssey* violated several conventions of the science fiction genre: beginning with a lengthy sequence set in prehistoric times, synchronizing classical music to outer-space action, and ending with an enigmatically symbolic fetus drifting through space. Some reviewers objected to the Tesla machine in *The Prestige,* claiming that it violated the conventions of a historical mystery film. But what one critic called "a sudden, desperate leap into fantasy" can be seen as an effort to update traditional backstage conflicts for an audience fascinated by fantasy and science fiction.

By blending or varying or even rejecting genre conventions, filmmakers force viewers to reset their expectations and engage with the film in fresh ways. (See "Creative Decisions in a Contemporary Genre.") The interplay of convention and innovation, familiarity and novelty, is central to the genre film.

> 66 Fixed forms can yield infinite, ingenious variations."
> —Joyce Carol Oates, novelist

Genre History

Because filmmakers frequently play with conventions, genres change constantly. A comedy from the 1920s is likely to be very different from one in the 1960s. Across history, the conventions of genres and subgenres get recast, and by mixing conventions from different genres, filmmakers create new possibilities surprisingly often.

Origins Many film genres begin by borrowing conventions from other media. The melodrama has clear antecedents in stage plays and novels such as *Uncle Tom's Cabin.* Types of comedy can be traced back to stage farces or comic novels. Musicals draw on both musical comedies and variety shows.

Yet the film medium always reshapes an adopted genre. For example, Western novels were already popular in the 19th century when cinema was invented. Yet Westerns did not become a film genre until after 1908. Why the delay? Westerns need outdoor landscapes. As films got longer (up to roughly 15 minutes) and studios hired actors on contract, filmmakers may have been encouraged to shoot more on location. Using rural American landscapes in turn fostered stories involving the frontier, and the Western quickly became a tremendously popular genre. It was also a uniquely American genre, giving U.S. films a way to compete in the growing international market. In such ways film genres acquire their own history, combining borrowings from other arts and distinctive innovations.

One important pressure on genres is technology. The musical film crystallized with the arrival of synchronized sound. Fantasy and science fiction became popular partly because filmmakers had digital tools that could conjure up unreal creatures and imaginary landscapes. Digital special effects have also enabled filmmakers to build photorealistic worlds for comic-book superheroes (1.33, 1.34).

Genres and Cycles Once a genre and its subgenres are launched, there seems to be no predictable trajectory. We might expect that the earliest films in the genre are the purest instances, with genre mixing coming at a late stage. But genre mixing can take place very soon. *Whoopee!* (1930), a musical from the beginning of talking pictures, is also a Western. *Just Imagine* (1930), one of the first sound science fiction films, contains a comic song. Some historians have also speculated that a genre inevitably passes from a phase of maturity to one of parody, when it begins to mock its own conventions. Yet an early Western, *The Great K & A Train Robbery* (1926), is an all-out parody of its own genre. Early slapstick comedies often take moviemaking as their subject and ruthlessly poke fun at comic conventions, as in Charlie Chaplin's farcical *His New Job* (1915).

Over history, genres rise and fall in prestige and popularity. The result is the phenomenon known as *cycles.* A cycle is a batch of related genre films that enjoys intense popularity and influence over a fairly brief period.

A CLOSER LOOK

Creative Decisions in a Contemporary Genre
The Crime Thriller as Subgenre

The thriller, like the comedy, is a very broad category, with many subgenres. There are supernatural thrillers (*The Sixth Sense*), political thrillers (*Munich*), and spy thrillers (*The Bourne Ultimatum*). Many others revolve around crime—planned, committed, or thwarted.

Using few special effects and set in contemporary urban locations, crime thrillers can be comparatively cheap to produce. They offer showy roles to actors, and they allow writers and directors to display their ingenuity in playing with the audience's expectations. Although the genre has fuzzy edges, we can chart some core cases by considering the ways in which filmmakers have exploited narrative conventions of the genre.

Four Character Roles   A crime is at the center of the thriller plot, and usually four sorts of characters are involved. There are the victims, the more or less innocent bystanders, the forces of justice, and the lawbreakers. Typically, the filmmaker decides to organize the film's narration around one or two of these character roles.

In *Double Jeopardy*, a husband disappears and his wife is found guilty of his murder. In prison, she discovers that he is alive and hiding out with his mistress. Released on parole, she sets out to find her son, but she is pursued by her hard-bitten parole officer. Suspense arises from the double chase and the cat-and-mouse game played by the desperate husband and his embittered "widow," who can now murder him with impunity. The plot action and narration are organized around the victimized wife. Her vengeful pursuit propels the action forward, and the narration favors her, restricting us largely to what she believes and eventually learns.

Double Jeopardy concentrates on an innocent person who is the target of the crime, and this is one common pattern in the person-in-peril subgenre. At some point, the victim usually realizes that he or she cannot react passively and must fight back, as in *Duel, The Fugitive, Breakdown,* and *Panic Room* **(9.6).** In *Ransom,* the father of a kidnapped boy refuses to pay the ransom, offering it as a bounty on the gang holding his son.

Alternatively, the filmmaker can center the plot on an innocent bystander dropped into a struggle between the criminal, the victims, and the forces of justice. In *Die Hard,* an off-duty detective is accidentally trapped in a hostage crisis, so he must fight both police and thieves to rescue the hostages. *The Ghost Writer* thrusts a freelance biographer into a murderous political conspiracy. In *Cellular,* through an accidental phone call, a beach idler must locate a woman who's been kidnapped.

Thematically, this innocent-bystander plot pattern often emphasizes characters discovering resources within themselves—courage, cleverness, even a capacity for violence. *Collateral* centers on a taxi driver forced to chauffeur a paid killer from target to target. In the course of the night, Max must abandon his fantasy of a desert island and face the sordid reality of the city he lives in (p. 5).

Instead of spotlighting the victim or an innocent bystander, the filmmaker may build the plot around the forces of justice. The action then typically becomes an investigation, in which police or private detectives seek to capture the criminal or prevent a crime. A classic example is *The Big Heat,* in which a rogue cop seeks to avenge the death of his wife by capturing the mobsters responsible. *The Bodyguard, In the Line of Fire,* and *Non-Stop* present protagonists seeking to forestall a threatened murder. The contemporary serial-killer plot tends to emphasize police pursuit, offering only glimpses of the criminal. *Se7en* follows two policemen in their efforts to untangle a string of murders emblematic of the seven deadly sins. When a plot highlights the investigators, themes of the fallibility of justice tend to come to the fore. In *L.A. Confidential,* three ill-matched detectives join forces to reveal how official corruption has led to the murders of prostitutes.

Alternatively, the plot of a crime thriller can put the criminal center stage. Perhaps the protagonist is a mild-mannered murderer, as in *The Suspect,* or a paid killer, as in Jean-Pierre Melville's *Le Samourai.* Another variant is the heist or caper film, showcasing a tightly orchestrated robbery. This subgenre became a mainstay in the 1950s, with *The Asphalt Jungle, Bob Le Flambeur,* and *Rififi,* and it made a comeback in recent years with the *Ocean's Eleven* series. There is also the avenging outlaw, as in *Payback* and *Drive,* but there's also the dishonor-among-thieves variant, in which criminals betray one another. *A Simple Plan* portrays nervous amateur thieves, whereas *Jackie Brown* traces an expanding web of double-crosses.

Sometimes the filmmaker will devote equal time to the police and the criminal, a strategy which can build up thematic parallels. In John Woo's *The Killer,* a hit man tries to quit the business, aided by his weak mentor. At the same time, we follow the investigation conducted by a police detective, who's also under the sway of an older colleague. Michael Mann's *Heat* creates strong parallels between cop and robber, each having problems with the women in their lives. In both *The Killer* and *Heat,* the opposing characters recognize their kinship. In contrast, *Fargo* plays on the sharp differences between the sunny common sense of the policewoman and an almost pitiably blundering kidnapper.

Narration's Effects   Thrillers obviously aim to thrill us—that is, to startle, shock, and maintain suspense. How do we distinguish them from horror films, which seek similar effects? Horror aims to disgust as well. The central character of a horror film is a monster that is both fearsome and repellent. By contrast, a thriller need not involve disgust. The villain may be quite attractive (the suave men in *Red Eye* and *Primal Fear,* the enticing women in *Red Rock West* and *Gone Girl*). While suspense and surprise are important in all cinematic storytelling, these responses dominate the crime thriller. The plots highlight clever plans, still more clever blocking moves, and sudden coincidences that upset carefully timed schemes. Tracing out a plan or following an investigation can yield suspense (Will the criminal succeed? How?), while unexpected twists trigger surprise, forcing us to reconsider the odds of the criminal's success.

More specifically, the thriller's effects depend on which characters are highlighted by the plot and narration. If the protagonist is a victim or a bystander, the suspense we feel comes from the likelihood that he or she will be harmed. If the hero is a figure of justice, we become concerned that she or he will not be able to protect the innocents. When the investigator doesn't have the police force as backup, anxiety can intensify: the unauthorized detectives of *The Girl with the Dragon Tattoo* must fight on their own.

When the narration centers on the criminal, how can the filmmaker arouse the viewer's sympathy for him or her? One way is to rank the lawbreakers on a scale of immorality. The most sympathetic criminals will be ones who are trying to give up their crime career (*The Killer*) or ones who oppose even more immoral figures. The heroes of *Out of Sight* are easy-going, good-humored thieves ripping off a white-collar embezzler and a band of crazed killers. Sometimes criminal protagonists can stretch our sympathies in challenging directions to frighten. We might admire the bravado of the *Ocean's Eleven* gang, but we aren't so comfortable with the ingratiating psychopath of *The Talented Mr. Ripley.* In *A Simple Plan,* basically good people turn crooked after a momentary weakness. Even though they have done wrong, we may find ourselves hoping that they succeed in their crime. As Dostoevsky showed in *Crime and Punishment,* a crime tale can make us think about what forces drive people to murder **(9.7).**

Innovations in the Thriller Like any genre or subgenre, the crime thriller can mix with others. It blends with the horror film in *From Dusk Till Dawn* and with

9.6

9.7

9.6, 9.7 Crime thriller: Victims and victimizer. Innocents in jeopardy: an unusual camera position for a classic thriller situation in *Panic Room* (9.6). In *A History of Violence,* Tom Stall, quiet owner of a small-town diner, is revealed to have a killer's instincts (9.7).

science fiction in *Blade Runner* and *Minority Report*. *Rush Hour* and *The Other Guys* push the police investigation toward farce, while *Lock, Stock, and Two Smoking Barrels* piles up absurd coincidences around a quartet of petty crooks who steal ganja and money from a cutthroat gang.

The thriller's emphasis on suspense and surprise encourages the filmmaker to mislead the audience, and this invites experiments with narrative form. Hitchcock pioneered this tendency by suddenly switching protagonists in *Psycho* and by letting two couples' lives intertwine in *Family Plot*. Many films whose plots play with story time (see pp. 82–84) are crime thrillers. A crime in the story may be replayed in the plot, showing different clues each time (*Snake Eyes*) or presenting different points of view (*The Killing, Jackie Brown*; see pp. 287–290). *Memento* tells its investigation story in reverse order. *The Usual Suspects* creates an unreliable flashback narration, at the end turning a minor character into a major player. *Bound* consists largely of flashbacks launched from a cryptic present-time situation—a woman tied and gagged in a closet. As the crime story is revealed, we have reason to suspect that at some phase the robbery scheme she and her partner have devised will fail.

Independent filmmakers have found that audiences will accept storytelling experiments when packaged in a crime thriller. For other independents, the subgenre offers a structure on which they can hang their personal concerns. David Mamet's interest in how people conceal their true motives surfaces in *House of Games* and *The Spanish Prisoner*. Joel and Ethan Coen set *Blood Simple* and *The Man Who Wasn't There* in bleak, small-town locales populated with losers lusting for one big chance. David Lynch uses the conventions of suspense and surprise to summon up a dread-filled atmosphere that may never receive rational explanation. In *Blue Velvet, Lost Highway,* and *Mulholland Drive,* the crimes are ominous but obscure, the criminals nightmarish grotesques, and the innocents not wholly innocent.

Because crime thrillers can be shot fairly cheaply, the subgenre has offered Hollywood's rivals a path to international distribution. Hong Kong has exported many such items, notably *Infernal Affairs* (the source for *The Departed*) and more experimental entries such as *The Mission* and *PTU*. Comparable films have come from France (*La Femme Nikita, Polisse*), Germany (*Dreileben*), Britain (*Snatch, Sexy Beast*), Spain (*Live Flesh*), Japan (*Sonatine*), Argentina (*The Secret in Their Eyes*), Korea (*Nowhere to Hide, Chaser*), and Thailand (*Bangkok Dangerous*). Audiences worldwide share similar expectations about thrillers, and filmmakers can innovate by injecting local cultural traditions into the narrative and thematic conventions. Two of our sample analyses, of *Breathless* (pp. 418–422) and of *Chungking Express* (pp. 428–432), focus on non-Hollywood films that imaginatively shift the expectations we bring to the crime thriller.

Cycles typically occur when a successful film triggers a burst of imitations. *The Godfather* unleashed a brief spate of gangster movies. During the 1970s, there was a cycle of disaster movies (*Earthquake, The Poseidon Adventure*). A cycle of fantasy adventures including the *Lord of the Rings* trilogy, the *Harry Potter* series, and the *Chronicles of Narnia* franchise, emerged in the early 2000s. Later there developed a cycle of romantic vampire films spearheaded by *Twilight* (2008), then another cycle of dystopian fantasies like *The Hunger Games* and *Divergent*.

Often what seems a short-term cycle has persisted so long that it becomes a well-entrenched subgenre. Few observers would have predicted that the horror cycle that emerged with *Halloween* and *A Nightmare on Elm Street* would have lasted past the 1980s, but it earned the label of "slasher film" and was frequently revived, notably in the *Scream* series. Action movies centering on comic-book superheroes formed a small cycle in the 1980s but became a flourishing subgenre in the 2000s with *Batman Begins, Spider-Man, Iron Man,* the X-Men series, and many other entries.

Because cycles and subgenres can emerge at any time, we should expect that no genre ever really dies. A genre may pass out of fashion for a time, only to return in updated garb. The sword-and-sandal epic set in ancient times was popular in the 1950s and 1960s. It virtually disappeared until Ridley Scott revived it to considerable acclaim in 2000 with *Gladiator,* inspiring a cycle that included *Troy, Alexander,* and *300*.

Genre Mixing   A genre may also change by mixing its conventions with those of another genre. In 1979, *Alien* proved innovative because it fused science fiction conventions with those of the contemporary horror film, centering on a monster stalking its victims one by one. The rusting spaceship became the futuristic equivalent of the old dark house full of unseen dangers. By the 2000s, the science fiction/horror blend had become conventional, as in *Pitch Black* and *Doom*.

9.8 Drama plus comedy. The serious drama at the core of *Barbershop*—whether a son should sustain his father's business for the good of the community—is lightened by sight gags, inventive insults, and scabrous monologues, like Eddie's rants about Rosa Parks and other African-American icons.

The musical blends easily with other genres. There have been musical melodramas, such as *Yentl* and two versions of *A Star Is Born*. The *Rocky Horror Picture Show* created the musical horror movie. During the 1930s and 1940s, singing cowboys such as Gene Autry were popular, and the Western musical was revived in the 1960s with *Cat Ballou*. Likewise, comedy can merge with any other genre. Mel Brooks and Woody Allen have created comedies out of the conventions of science fiction (*Spaceballs, Sleeper*), Westerns (*Blazing Saddles*), outlaw films (*Take the Money and Run*), thrillers and detective stories (*High Anxiety, Manhattan Murder Mystery*), even historical epics (*History of the World Part I, Love and Death*). Comic touches can lighten dramas, and if the proportions are somewhat equal, we have what some call a "dramedy" or a "seriocomedy" **(9.8)**. The combinations seem almost limitless. In *O Brother, Where Art Thou?*, bumbling escaped prisoners accidentally become country singing stars, and the result is at once an outlaw movie, a social protest film, a slapstick comedy, and a musical.

Filmmakers understand that mixing genres is a good way to innovate. The romantic comedy is typically associated with female audiences, but in the late 2000s some producers believed that adding some elements of raunchy comedy would attract men. The result was such films as *The Wedding Crashers* and *Knocked Up*. According to one producer: "Fundamentally, they're romantic comedies, but the concepts are very male-appropriate." *Guardians of the Galaxy* found success by treating save-the-universe space opera as a comic premise.

> 66 So it's kind of a psychic political thriller comedy with a heart." "With a heart. And not unlike *Ghost* meets *Manchurian Candidate*."
>
> —Producer and screenwriter in the opening scene of Robert Altman's *The Player*

Filmmakers may borrow from other cultures too. The Japanese swordplay film, based on virtuoso combat and themes of honor and revenge, has blended well with the Western. Sergio Leone based his Italian Western *For a Fistful of Dollars* loosely on the plot of Akira Kurosawa's *Yojimbo*, and the same Japanese director's *Seven Samurai* provided the basis for the Hollywood Western *The Magnificent Seven*. Similarly, widespread fan interest in Hong Kong movies during the 1980s and 1990s led the Wachowski brothers to mix high-tech science fiction effects with martial-arts choreography in *The Matrix*.

The fact that genres can intermingle doesn't mean that there are no distinctions among them. *The Matrix* is a hybrid, but we can still differentiate standard Hong Kong martial-arts films from standard Hollywood science fiction tales. Although we can't pin down a single description of a genre that will apply for all time, we can recognize that at any moment in film history, filmmakers, critics, and audiences agree closely on the genres in play. Again, there are usually core examples, ones that makers and viewers agree are clear-cut instances, as well as more peripheral or mixed cases.

The Social Functions of Genres

The fact that every genre has fluctuated in popularity reminds us that genres are tightly bound to cultural factors. Why do audiences enjoy seeing the same conventions over and over?

Rituals and Ambivalence Many film scholars believe that genres are ritualized dramas resembling holiday celebrations—ceremonies that are satisfying because they reaffirm cultural values in a predictable way. At the end of *Saving Private Ryan* or *You've Got Mail,* who can resist a surge of reassuring satisfaction that cherished values—self-sacrificing heroism, the desirability of romantic love— have been validated? And just as one can see these ceremonies as helping us forget the more disturbing aspects of the world, the familiar characters and plots of genres may also serve to distract the audience from real social problems.

Some scholars would argue that genres go further and actually exploit ambivalent social values and attitudes. The gangster film, for instance, makes it possible for audiences to relish the mobster's swagger while still feeling satisfied when he receives his punishment. Seen from this standpoint, genre conventions arouse emotion by touching on deep social uncertainties but then channel those emotions into approved attitudes.

Because genre films promise something new based on something familiar, they may also respond quickly to broad social trends. During the economic depression of the 1930s, for instance, the Warner Bros. musical films introduced social commentary into stage numbers. In *Gold Diggers of 1933,* a singer asks the Depression-era audience to remember "my forgotten man," the unemployed war veteran. More recently, Hollywood producers have tried to suit romantic comedies to the tastes of career women with the *Sex and the City* films and Sandra Bullock vehicles such as *The Proposal* and *Two Weeks Notice.* In Chapter 11, we consider how another musical, *Meet Me in St. Louis,* seems tailored to the home-front audience of World War II.

Genres as Social Reflection It's one thing to suggest that filmmakers deliberately address their films to current concerns or tastes. But some scholars suggest that at different points in history, the stories, themes, values, or imagery of the genre harmonize with public attitudes in a more involuntary fashion. For instance, don't the science fiction films of the 1950s, with hydrogen bombs creating Godzilla and other monsters, reveal fears of nuclear technology run amok? Even if the filmmakers didn't knowingly put such messages in their work, perhaps the success of the films reflected what the audiences felt. The hypothesis is that genre conventions, repeated from film to film, reflected the audience's pervasive doubts or anxieties. Many film scholars would argue that this approach helps explain why genres vary in popularity. As the public anxieties change, new genres will reflect more up-to-date concerns.

Social processes can be reflected in genre innovations as well. Ripley, the female protagonist of *Aliens,* is a courageous, even aggressive, warrior who also has a warm, maternal side **(9.9, 9.10).** This was something of a novelty in the science fiction genre. Many commentators saw Ripley as a product of attitudes derived from the women's movement of the 1970s. Feminist groups argued that women could be seen as active and competent without losing positive qualities associated with feminine behavior, such as gentleness and sympathy. As these ideas spread through mainstream media and social opinion, films such as *Aliens* could turn traditionally masculine roles over to female characters. Perhaps the filmmakers didn't intend to send this message, but the attitudes in the films could be seen as harmonizing with new conceptions of gender roles.

Such ways of looking at genre are usually called *reflectionist,* because they assume that genres reflect social attitudes, as if in a mirror. Some critics would object that reflectionist readings can become oversimplified. If we look closely at a genre film, we usually discover complexities that nuance a reflectionist account. For instance, if we look beyond Ripley, the protagonist of *Aliens,* we find that all the characters lie along a continuum running between "masculine" and "feminine" values, and the survivors of the adventure, male or female, seem to blend the best of

9.9

9.10

9.9–9.10 Genre and gender roles: Warrior and mother. In *Aliens,* Ripley learns how to use a weapon (9.9), but she can also comfort the orphaned girl the soldiers find (9.10).

both gender identities. Moreover, often what seems to be social reflection is simply the film industry's effort to exploit the day's headlines. A genre film may reflect not the audience's hopes and fears but the filmmakers' guess about what might sell.

Four Genres

Whether we study a genre's history, its cultural functions, or its representations of social trends, conventions remain our best point of departure. To illustrate how we might analyze conventions and their change across history, we look at four significant genres of American filmmaking.

The Western

The Western is one of the earliest film genres, having become established in the 1910s. It is partly based on historical reality, since in the American West there were cowboys, outlaws, settlers, and tribes of Native Americans. Films also derived their portrayal of the frontier from songs, popular fiction, and Wild West shows. Early actors sometimes mirrored this blend of realism and myth: Cowboy star Tom Mix had been a Texas Ranger, a Wild West performer, and a champion rodeo rider.

Quite early, the central theme of the genre became the conflict between civilized order and the lawless frontier. From the East and the city come the settlers who want to raise families, the schoolteachers who aim to spread learning, and the bankers and government officials. In the vast natural spaces, by contrast, people outside Eastern civilization thrive—not only the Native Americans but also outlaws, trappers and traders, and greedy cattle barons.

Iconography reinforces this basic duality. The covered wagon and the railroad are set against the horse and canoe; the schoolhouse and church contrast with the lonely campfire in the hills. As in most genres, costume is iconographically significant too. The settlers' starched dresses and Sunday suits stand out against American Indians' tribal garb and the cowboys' jeans and Stetsons.

Interestingly, the typical Western hero stands between the two thematic poles. At home in the wilderness but naturally inclined toward justice and kindness, the cowboy is often poised between savagery and civilization. William S. Hart, one of the most popular early Western stars, crystallized the character of the "good bad man" as a common protagonist. In *Hell's Hinges* (1916), a minister's sister tries to reform him; one shot represents the pull between two ways of life (**9.11**).

9.11–9.12 Hero in between. The "good bad" hero of *Hell's Hinges* reads the Bible, a bottle of whiskey at his elbow (9.11). In *Straight Shooting*, the hero stands framed in the farmhouse doorway, halfway between the lure of civilization and the call of the wilderness (9.12).

9.11

9.12

" I knew Wyatt Earp. In the very early silent days, a couple of times a year he would come up to visit pals, cowboys he knew in Tombstone; a lot of them were in my company. I think I was an assistant prop boy then and I used to give him a chair and a cup of coffee, and he told me about the fight at the O.K. Corral. So in *My Darling Clementine,* we did it exactly the way it had been. They didn't just walk up the street and start banging away at each other; it was a clever military manoeuvre."

—John Ford, director, *Stagecoach*

The in-between position of the hero affects common Western plots. The protagonist may start out on the side of the lawless, or he may simply stand apart from the conflict. In either case, he becomes uneasily attracted to the life offered by the newcomers to the frontier. Eventually, the hero decides to join the forces of order, helping them fight hired gunmen, bandits, or whatever the film presents as a threat to stability and progress.

As the genre developed, a social ideology governed its conventions. White populations' progress westward was considered a historic mission, while the conquered indigenous cultures were usually treated as primitive and savage. Western films are full of racist stereotypes of Native Americans and Hispanics. On a few occasions, filmmakers treated Native American characters as tragic figures, ennobled by their closeness to nature but facing the extinction of their way of life. The best early example is probably *The Last of the Mohicans* (1920).

Nor was the genre always optimistic about taming the wilderness. The hero's eventual commitment to civilization's values was often tinged with regret for his loss of freedom. In John Ford's *Straight Shooting* (1917), Cheyenne Harry (played by Harry Carey) is hired by a villainous rancher to evict a farmer, but he falls in love with the farmer's daughter and vows to reform. Rallying the farmers, Harry helps defeat the rancher. Still, he is reluctant to settle down with Molly **(9.12)**.

Within this set of values, a great many conventional scenes became standardized— the Indians' attack on forts or wagon trains, the shy courting of a woman by the rough-hewn hero, the hero's discovery of a burned settler's shack, the outlaws' robbery of a bank or stagecoach, the climactic gunfight on dusty town streets. Writers and directors could distinguish their films by novel handlings of these elements. In Sergio Leone's flamboyant Italian Westerns, conventions are stretched out in minute detail and amplified to a huge scale **(9.13).**

9.13 Showdown in an arena. The three-way shootout at the climax of *The Good, the Bad, and the Ugly* (1966) is filmed to resemble a bullfight.

9.14

9.15

9.14–9.15 **The solitary hero.** During the closing shot of *The Searchers* (9.14), John Wayne repeats Harry Carey's characteristic gripping of his forearm in *Straight Shooting* (9.15).

There were narrative and thematic innovations as well. After such liberal Westerns of the 1950s as *Broken Arrow* (1950), indigenous cultures began to be treated with more respect. In *Little Big Man* (1970) and *Soldier Blue* (1970), the conventional thematic values were reversed, depicting Indian life as civilized and white society as marauding. Some films played up the hero's uncivilized side, showing him perilously out of control (*Winchester 73,* 1950), or even psychopathic (*The Left-Handed Gun,* 1958). The heroes of *The Wild Bunch* (1969) would have been considered unvarnished villains in early Westerns.

The new complexity of the protagonist is evident in John Ford's *The Searchers* (1956). After a Comanche raid on his brother's homestead, Ethan Edwards sets out to find his kidnapped niece Debbie. He is driven primarily by family loyalty but also by his secret love for his brother's wife, who has been raped and killed by the raiders. Ethan's sidekick, a young man who is part Cherokee, realizes that Ethan plans not to rescue Debbie but to kill her for becoming a Comanche wife. Ethan's fierce racism and raging vengeance culminate in a raid on the Comanche village. At the film's close, Ethan returns to civilization but pauses on the cabin's threshold before turning back to the desert **(9.14)**.

The shot eerily recalls the doorway compositions of Ford's *Straight Shooting* (9.12); John Wayne even repeats Harry Carey's characteristic gripping of his forearm **(9.15)**. Now, however, it seems that the drifting cowboy is condemned to live outside civilization because he cannot tame his grief and hatred. More savage than citizen, he seems condemned, as he says of the souls of dead Comanches, "to wander forever between the winds." This bitter treatment of a perennial theme illustrates how drastically a genre's conventions can change across history.

The Horror Film

Whereas the Western is most clearly defined by subject, theme, and iconography, the horror genre is most recognizable by the emotional effect it tries to arouse. The horror film aims to shock, disgust, repel—in short, to horrify. This impulse is what shapes the genre's other conventions.

What can horrify us? Typically, a monster. In the horror film, the monster is a dangerous breach of nature, a violation of our normal sense of what's possible. The monster might be unnaturally large, as King Kong is. The monster might violate the boundary between the dead and the living, as ghosts, vampires, and zombies do. The monster might be an ordinary human who is transformed, as when Dr. Jekyll drinks his potion and becomes the evil Mr. Hyde. Or the monster might be something wholly unknown to science, as with the creature in the *Alien* films.

9.16

9.16–9.17 Horror implied, not shown. A shadow and a character's reaction suggest an offscreen menace in *Cat People* (9.16). Video surveillance in *Paranormal Activity*: The readout indicates that the heroine, who has mysteriously risen from her sleep, stands transfixed for nearly two hours (9.17).

2:29:45 AM

9.17

CONNECT TO THE BLOG
www.davidbordwell.net/blog

We analyze the *Paranormal Activity* series in "Return to paranormalcy."

CONNECT TO THE BLOG
www.davidbordwell.net/blog

Director Joe Dante specializes in comic horror films. We discuss his work in "Dante's cheerful purgatorio."

The genre's horrifying emotional effect, then, is usually created by a character convention: a menacing, unnatural monster.

Other conventions follow from this one. Our reaction to the monster may be guided by other characters who react to it in the properly horrified way. In *Cat People* (1942), a mysterious woman can, apparently, turn into a panther. Our revulsion and fear are confirmed by the reaction of the woman's husband and his coworker **(9.16).** By contrast, we know that *E.T.* is not a horror film because, although the alien is unnatural, he isn't threatening, and the children don't react to him as if he is.

The horror plot will often start with the monster's attack on normal life. In response, the other characters must discover that the monster is at large and try to destroy it. This plot can be developed in various ways: by having the monster launch a series of attacks, by having people in authority resist believing that the monster exists, or by blocking the characters' efforts to destroy it. In *The Exorcist,* the characters only gradually discover that Regan is possessed; after they realize this, they still must struggle to drive the demon out.

The genre's characteristic themes also stem from the response the filmmakers aim to arouse. If the monster horrifies us because it violates the laws of nature that we know, the genre is well suited to suggest the limits of human knowledge. It's probably significant that the skeptical authorities who must be convinced of the monster's existence are often scientists. In other cases, the scientists themselves unintentionally unleash monsters through their risky experiments. A common convention of this type of plot has the characters concluding that there are some things that humans are not meant to know. Another thematic pattern of the horror film plays on fears about the environment, as when nuclear accidents and other human-made disasters create mutant monsters like the giant ants in *Them!*

Not surprisingly, the iconography of the horror film includes settings where monsters might lurk. The old dark house in which a group of potential victims gather was popularized by *The Cat and the Canary* in 1927 and was reused for *The Haunting* (1999) and *The Others* (2001). A more modern version of the haunted house is seen in *Paranormal Activity* (2008; **9.17**). Cemeteries can yield the walking dead; scientists' laboratories, an artificial human (as in *Frankenstein*). Filmmakers have played off these conventions cleverly, as when Hitchcock juxtaposed a mundane motel with a decaying mansion in *Psycho,* or when George Romero set humans battling zombies in a shopping mall in *Dawn of the Dead.* The slasher subgenre has made superhuman killers invade everyday settings such as summer camps and suburban neighborhoods.

Heavy makeup is very prominent in the iconography of horror. A furry face and hands can signal transformation into a werewolf, while shriveled skin indicates a mummy. Some actors have specialized in transforming themselves into frightening figures. Lon Chaney, who played the original Phantom in *The Phantom of the Opera* (1925), was known as "the man of a thousand faces." Boris Karloff's makeup as Frankenstein's monster in *Frankenstein* (1930) rendered him so unrecognizable that the credits of his next film informed viewers that it featured the same actor. More recently, computer special effects and motion capture have supplemented makeup in transforming actors into beastly creatures.

Like the Western, the horror film emerged in the era of silent moviemaking. Some of the most important early works in the genre were German, notably *The Cabinet of Dr. Caligari* (1920) and *Nosferatu* (1922), the first adaptation of the novel *Dracula*. The angular performances, heavy makeup, and distorted settings characteristic of German Expressionist cinema conveyed an ominous, supernatural atmosphere (**9.18**).

9.18 German Expressionist horror. In *Nosferatu*, Max Schreck's makeup and acting make his Count Orlok eerily resemble a rat or a bat.

Because a horror film can create its emotional impact with grisly makeup and other low-technology special effects, the horror genre has been favored by filmmakers on tight budgets. During the 1930s, a second-rank Hollywood studio, Universal, launched a cycle of horror films. The popularity of *Dracula* (1931), *Frankenstein* (1931), and *The Mummy* (1932; **9.19**) helped the studio become a major company. A decade later, RKO's B-picture unit under Val Lewton produced a cycle of literate, somber films on minuscule budgets. Lewton's directors proceeded by hints, keeping the monster offscreen and cloaking the sets in darkness. In *Cat People,* for instance, we never see the heroine transform herself into a panther, and we only glimpse the creature in certain scenes. The film achieves its effects through shadows, offscreen sound, and character reaction (9.16).

> 66 Our formula is simple. A love story, three scenes of suggested horror and one of actual violence. Fade-out. It's all over in less than 70 minutes."
>
> —Val Lewton, producer, *Cat People*

In later decades, horror became a staple of 1960s low-budget independent production, with many American entries targeted at the youth market. George Romero's *Night of the Living Dead* (1968) was budgeted at only $114,000, but it found wide success on college campuses. At the other end of the budgetary scale, the genre acquired a new respectability, chiefly because of the prestige of *Rosemary's Baby* (1968) and *The Exorcist* (1973). These films innovated by presenting violent and disgusting actions with unprecedented explicitness. When the possessed Regan vomited in the face of the priest bending over her, a new standard for horrific imagery was set. Decades later, the *Saw* series raised the gore quotient even higher.

The horror film entered into a period of popularity that has not yet ended. Many major Hollywood directors have worked in the genre, and several horror films—from *Jaws* (1975) and *Carrie* (1976) to installments in the *Twilight* saga (2008 on)—have become huge hits. Low-budget horror has flourished as well. *The Blair Witch Project* (1999), shot for a reputed $35,000, found a huge audience internationally. A decade later, *Paranormal Activity,* shot for $11,000, earned a spectacular $200 million at worldwide box offices.

More broadly, the genre's iconography pervades contemporary culture, decorating lunch boxes and theme park rides. Horror novels by Stephen King and Stephenie Meyer have been adapted for films and TV series, while genre classics such as *The Mummy* and *Frankenstein* have been remade for

9.19 Subtle horror on a low budget. A tiny gleam reflected in Boris Karloff's eye signals the moment when the monster revives in *The Mummy.*

modern audiences. The interest in producing horror films is global, with Europe and Asia adding to the repertory with *Anatomy* (Germany), *28 Days Later* (UK), *Nightwatch* (Russia), *The Host* (South Korea), *The Ring* (Japan), *The Devil's Backbone* (Spain), *Let the Right One In* (Sweden), and many more titles.

The centrality of horror to modern American cinema has set scholars looking for cultural explanations. Many critics suggest that the 1970s subgenre of family horror films, such as *The Exorcist* and *Poltergeist,* reflects social concerns about the breakup of American families. Others propose that the genre's questioning of traditional categories of normality is in tune with both the post-Vietnam and the post–Cold War eras: Viewers may be uncertain of their fundamental beliefs about the world and their identity. Fans are also drawn by the imaginative special effects and makeup, so filmmakers compete to show ever gorier and more grotesque imagery. For all these reasons, horror-film conventions grew so familiar that parodies such as the *Scary Movie* franchise and *Shaun of the Dead* became as popular as the films they mocked. Through genre mixing and the give-and-take between audience tastes and filmmakers' ambitions, the horror film has displayed the interplay of convention and innovation that's basic to any genre.

The Musical

The Western is largely based on the subject matter of the American frontier, and the horror film is characterized by the emotional effect it wants to arouse. By contrast, the musical came into being in response to a technological innovation. Although there had been attempts to synchronize music and song with moving images during the silent era, the notion of basing a feature-length film on a series of musical numbers did not emerge until the late 1920s with the successful introduction of recorded sound tracks. One of the earliest features to include the human voice extensively was *The Jazz Singer* (1927), which contained almost no recorded dialogue but had several songs.

At first, many musicals were *revues,* programs of numbers with little or no narrative linkage between them. Such revue musicals aided in selling these early sound films in foreign-language markets, where spectators could enjoy the performances even if they could not understand the dialogue and lyrics. When subtitles and dubbing solved the problem of the language barrier, musicals featured more complicated storylines. Filmmakers devised plots that could motivate the introduction of musical numbers.

Two major subgenres of the musical emerged during the 1930s and are still with us. One of these was the *backstage musical,* with the action centering on singers and dancers who perform for an audience within the story world. Warner Bros. successful early musical, *42nd Street* (1933), set the classic pattern for backstage musicals by casting dancer Ruby Keeler as the understudy for a star who breaks her leg just before the big opening. The director tells Keeler, "You're going out a youngster, but you've *got* to come back a star!" and indeed she wins the audience's cheers **(9.20).** During the decade, Warner's elaborately choreographed Busby Berkeley musicals, MGM's pairing of the youthful Judy Garland and Mickey Rooney in a series of "Let's put on a show!" plots, and RKO's elegant cycle of films starring the dance team of Fred Astaire and Ginger Rogers established the conventions of the backstage musical. Later examples included musicals in which the characters are film performers, as in *Singin' in the Rain* (1952). More recent backstage musicals are *The Commitments, Music and Lyrics, Jersey Boys,* and *Dreamgirls.* In some cases, dance competitions become the equivalent of stage shows, as in *You Got Served* and *Stomp the Yard.*

Not all musicals take place in a show-business situation, however. There is also the *straight musical,* where people may sing and dance in situations of everyday life. Even in backstage musicals, the characters occasionally break into song in an everyday setting. Straight musicals tend to be romantic comedies as well, so that

> " [Producer Arthur Freed] came to me and said, 'What are you going to do with it?' I said, 'Well, Arthur, I don't know yet. But I do know I've gotta be singing and it's gotta be raining.' There was no rain in that picture up to then."
>
> —Gene Kelly, actor/choreographer, on *Singin' in the Rain*

9.20

9.21

9.20–9.21 Backstage musical vs. straight musical. Ruby Keeler hoofs her way to stardom in *42nd Street*'s title number (9.20). The citizens of a whole town are drawn into the dance in Jaques Demy's *Young Girls of Rochefort* (9.21).

songs and dances express the characters' fears, longings, and joys. We analyze one straight musical, *Meet Me in St. Louis,* in Chapter 11. In 1968, *The Young Girls of Rochefort* took the romantic musical to extremes by having its characters sing most of the dialogue in the film, with dozens of passersby joining in dance numbers in the town's streets **(9.21).** Straight musicals are rare today, but Julie Taymor made an effort to revive the subgenre in *Across the Universe,* basing the score entirely on Beatles songs and adding social commentary in the spirit of the 1960s **(9.22).**

In both backstage and straight musicals, the numbers often reflect a couple's courtship. Often the hero and heroine realize that they are an ideal couple because they perform beautifully together. In *Top Hat* the Ginger Rogers character sheds her original annoyance with Fred Astaire during the "Isn't It a Wonderful Day" number, and by the end, they have clearly fallen in love. This plot device has remained a staple of the genre. Astaire again charms his reluctant partner, this time Cyd Charisse, in the "Dancing in the Dark" number in *The Band Wagon* (1953), and John Travolta meets his romantic match on the disco dance floor in *Saturday Night Fever* (1977). In *Moulin Rouge!* the lovers serenade each other, both onstage and off, with classic pop and rock songs **(9.23),** and the dance interludes in the *House Party* and *Step Up* films become courtship rituals.

Musicals have long been associated with children's stories, from *The Wizard of Oz* to *Frozen.* Many animated features contain musical numbers, a practice going back to Disney's *Snow White and the Seven Dwarfs.* But adult-oriented

9.22 A musical evoking 1960s counterculture. In *Across the Universe,* a young man taking his army draft physical is greeted by the Beatles song "I Want You." The film was released at the height of the U.S. occupation of Iraq.

9.23 Performance as courtship. A flamboyant onstage musical number in *Moulin Rouge!* centers on the rapturous lovers.

CONNECT TO THE BLOG
www.davidbordwell.net/blog

Big musicals may be rare these days, but small ones thrive online as mash-ups and lipdubs. See our "2-4-6-8, whose lipdub do we appreciate?"

musicals have taken on more serious material. *West Side Story* portrays a romance that tragically crosses ethnic lines, and *Pennies from Heaven* evokes the bleak atmosphere of the Depression through characters who lip-synch to recordings from that era. Biopics of troubled performers, such as *Control, Get on Up,* and *Walk the Line,* become somber backstage musicals.

Still, while the Western and the horror film may explore the darker side of human nature, Hollywood musicals tend to accentuate the positive. High ambitions are rewarded when the show is a hit, and lovers are united in song and dance. In *The Pajama Game,* a strike is averted when the leaders of the union and management become a romantic couple. Some of these conventions persist today. *The School of Rock* and today's hip-hop and stepping musicals rework the backstage musical's theme that talent and hard work will eventually win out. Even the grittier *8 Mile* follows the traditional plot pattern of showing a gifted young performer overcoming disadvantages and finding success.

The range of subject matter in musicals is so broad that it may be hard to pin down specific iconography associated with the genre. The backstage musical has its characteristic settings: the dressing rooms and wings of a theater, the flats and backdrops of the stage (as in 9.20), and the nightclub with orchestra and dance floor. Similarly, performers in these musicals are often recognizable by their distinctive stage costumes. During the 1930s, Fred Astaire wore the most famous top hat in the cinema, a hat so closely associated with his musicals that the beginning of *The Band Wagon*—where Astaire plays a washed-up movie actor—could make a joke about it. Similarly, Travolta's white suit in *Saturday Night Fever* became an icon of the disco era. Opportunities for novelty have always been present in the musical, however, as the musical numbers set in a factory (*The Pajama Game*) or on the prairie (*Oklahoma!*) indicate.

The characteristic techniques of the musical are similarly diverse. Musicals tend to be brightly lit, to set off the cheerful costumes and sets and to keep the choreography of the dance numbers clearly visible. For similar reasons, color film stock was applied quite early to musicals, including Eddie Cantor's *Whoopee!* and, as we saw in Chapter 2, *The Wizard of Oz*. While classic musicals tend to rely on long takes, contemporary musicals tend to be cut very quickly, partly because of the influence of MTV videos. Still, to show off the patterns formed by the dancers in musical numbers, crane shots and high angles remain common **(9.24).** One technique widely used in the musical is not usually evident to viewers: lip-synching to prerecorded songs. On the set, performers move their lips in synchronization to a playback of the recording. This technique allows the singers to move about freely and to concentrate on their acting.

9.24 Genre motivation for stylistic choices. Swooping crane shots emphasize the geometry and coordination of an ensemble in *Stomp the Yard.*

The 1935 RKO Astaire–Rogers musical *Swing Time* is one of the exemplary backstage musicals. Early in the film, the hero, a gambler and tap dancer nicknamed Lucky, is trying to quit his stage act and get married. At once, we sense that his fiancée is not right for him. She isn't a dancer, and she isn't even seen during the early scenes in which his colleagues try to trick him into missing the wedding. The opening scenes take place in the conventional settings of the stage, wings, and dressing room of a theater. Later, when Lucky goes to the city and meets the heroine, Penny (a name that echoes Lucky's precious lucky quarter), she quickly takes a strong dislike to him. An amusing scene in the dance school where she works shows Lucky pretending to be hopelessly clumsy. Yet when the school's owner fires Penny, Lucky saves her job by suddenly launching into a graceful, unrehearsed dance with her. By the end, her animosity has disappeared, and the school owner arranges for the couple to audition at a fashionable club.

Obstacles ensue, primarily in the form of a romantic rivalry between Lucky and the orchestra leader at the club. Further complications result from the sort of Big Misunderstanding characteristic of romantic comedies: Penny thinks that Lucky intends to return to his fiancée. Near the end, Penny seems ready to marry the conductor. She and Lucky meet, apparently for the last time, and their talk at cross-purposes reveals the link between performance and romance:

PENNY: "Does she dance very beautifully?"

LUCKY: "Who?"

PENNY: "The girl you're in love with?"

LUCKY: "Yes—very."

PENNY: "The girl you're going to marry."

LUCKY: "Oh, I don't know. I've danced with you. I'm never going to dance again."

That Fred Astaire will never dance again is the ultimate threat, and his song "Never Gonna Dance" leads into a duet that reconfirms that they are meant for each other. In the end, Lucky and Penny reconcile.

The film calls on the newly established conventions of the genre. Lucky wears Astaire's classic top hat and formal clothes **(9.25).** Astaire and Rogers dance in the Art Deco–style sets that were typical of musical design in the 1930s **(9.26).** The film departs from convention, however, in a remarkable number, "Bojangles of Harlem," where Astaire pays tribute to the great

9.25

9.26

9.25–9.26 *Swing Time* as musical. After losing his suit in a card game, Lucky still wears Astaire's signature top hat (9.25). Penny and Lucky dance in the Art Deco nightclub set (9.26).

CONNECT TO THE BLOG
www.davidbordwell.net/blog

We discuss other genres on our blog. For the relationship between fantasy and sci-fi films in recent years, see "Swords vs. lightsabers," and for movies based on superhero comic books, see "Superheroes for sale." We analyze spy-thriller conventions in "*Tinker Tailor Soldier Spy*: A guide for the perplexed" and our entries on the *Bourne* franchise. We consider as well how *Safe Haven*, *Side Effects*, and *Gone Girl* draw on strategies of narration typical of the domestic thriller.

African-American dancers who had influenced him during his New York stage career in the 1920s. When he appears in blackface here, it is not to exploit a demeaning stereotype but to impersonate Bill "Bojangles" Robinson, the most famous black tap dancer of the era. (The tribute is all the more unusual because Robinson was then costarring in Shirley Temple musicals for a rival studio, Twentieth Century Fox.)

Despite its backstage settings and show business plot, *Swing Time* sets some numbers in an everyday environment. When Lucky visits Penny's apartment, he sings "The Way You Look Tonight" as she shampoos her hair—using a convenient piano in her apartment to accompany himself (though a nondiegetic orchestra plays along as well). When the couple visits the snowy countryside and sings "A Fine Romance," there is no diegetic accompaniment at all, only an unseen orchestra. The world of the musical makes it possible for people, at any time and in any place, to express their feelings through song and dance.

The Sports Film

You could argue that sports movies don't form a genre in the way Westerns, horror films, and musicals do. Perhaps basketball, baseball, prizefighting, and other sports are simply subject matter for more traditional genres—dramas like *Friday Night Lights*, romantic comedies like *Wimbledon*. But sports films have been a staple of film history since boxing matches drew audiences to Edison Kinetoscope parlors. And just as there are fans of science fiction movies and gross-out comedies, there is a distinct audience for sports films.

Sports films display their own plot patterns, iconography, and themes. Competition and tournaments provide conflict, while a climactic win-or-lose big game can resolve the action and provide closure. Suspense and surprise are built into sporting events. Just as important, films about sports can raise larger ideological issues. Succeeding in amateur sports can emphasize either individual achievement or group accomplishment. Professional sports give athletes access to money and power, and so the genre can develop themes of social mobility. And to a surprising extent, sports films explore themes of racial and gender roles.

One common plot pattern is the Cinderella story, showing how an underdog overcomes long odds to make it in the big leagues or to compete for a championship. The film may have a central protagonist, as in *Rocky* and *The Rookie*. Or the plot may focus on a group, usually a ragtag bunch that learns to overcome personal differences and work as a team. This plot pattern shapes *The Bad News Bears* (1976), *Major League,* and *Dodgeball: A True Underdog Story*. Other Cinderella plots, such as those in *Slap Shot* and *Any Given Sunday*, match grizzled veterans with rising young stars in ways that highlight their differences in age, expertise, values, and styles of play.

Critics may call the Cinderella pattern a cliché, but any sport contains real-life examples of underdogs beating the odds. Actual success stories were the basis of *Miracle* (2004), about the 1980 United States Olympic hockey team, and *The World's Fastest Indian* (**9.27**). Cinderella stories appeal to the audience because the hero or heroes are unlikely to succeed, and we sympathize with characters who risk everything for a dream.

A second plot type in sports movies depicts athletes in the prime of their careers who are felled by disease or injury. Examples are *Pride of the Yankees*, *Bang the Drum Slowly*, and *Million Dollar Baby*. These movies show how easily the conventions of sports films can mix with other genres, such as the medical drama or the melodrama. In *Eight Men Out* and *The Hurricane* (1999), the athlete's career is cut short by social factors, such as scandal or a biased judicial system. Like the Cinderella story, the prime-of-life storyline is made more plausible by being based on actual events.

9.27 Underdog stories. Burt Munro, an elderly New Zealander, seems an especially unlikely racing champion in *The World's Fastest Indian*. At age 67, though, Munro set land speed records at Utah's Bonneville salt flats on a self-modified 1920 Indian motorcycle. Director Roger Donaldson had already filmed Munro's story in a short documentary, *Burt Munro: Offerings to the God of Speed.*

Then there are films like *Fear Strikes Out*, *The Color of Money*, and *Seabiscuit*. Their plots resemble the Cinderella story in depicting battles against big odds, and they depend on the interrupted-career situation. But these films center on the athlete's comeback, a return to glory after battling personal demons. Comeback stories present the sport as a meritocracy: You can overcome almost any mistake if you have powerful skills and enduring passion.

Along with these plot types come character conventions: the tough coach, the dedicated but flawed athlete, the unscrupulous adversary, and the mate—male or female—who resents the partner's obsession with winning at all costs. A few films focus on figures more peripheral to the actual sporting event. *The Scout* and *Million Dollar Arm* dramatize efforts to nurture raw baseball talent. In *Jerry McGuire*, a cocky sports agent tries to build a company around the career of a temperamental wide receiver. *Moneyball* and *Draft Day* concentrate on maverick general managers who take risks to field a contender.

Some sports films deviate sharply from these conventions of plot and character. Normally we are emotionally invested in the athlete's quest for a championship, but *Raging Bull* complicates our sympathy. Its hero, Jake La Motta, seems fueled by an almost pathological jealousy and by his acceptance of boxing as a brutal bloodsport. (For more on *Raging Bull*, see Chapter 11.)

Similarly, in *Cobb*, a warts-and-all biography of Detroit Tiger great Ty Cobb, writer-director Ron Shelton probes the dark side of the baseball legend. Cobb was a fierce competitor, willing to hurt an opponent if he could gain an edge. He was an expert base stealer, who slid into the bag "spikes up," hoping to use his cleats to gash any player in his path. Off the field, Cobb was a racist, a woman-hater, and a bully. Instead of presenting an admirable athlete, *Cobb* reminds us that some competitors channel their personal demons into their performance.

In another departure from sports film conventions, a few movies concentrate on fans. *Fever Pitch* tells the story of Ben, whose obsessive passion for the Red Sox impedes his romance with his girlfriend, Lindsay. Initially, Lindsay treats Ben's fixation as an amusing personality quirk. But Lindsay realizes that Ben is unwilling to consider their future together; he won't even make vacation plans without consulting the Sox's schedule.

In making Ben a Red Sox fan, directors Peter and Bobby Farrelly shrewdly capitalized on the folklore surrounding the "lovable losers" of the baseball world. The Red Sox had not won a world championship since 1918, but in 2004 they wound up winning the world series. By sheer luck, the Sox's championship season gave the Farrellys an unexpected ending that combined the Cinderella story and the comeback story (**9.28**).

9.28 Sports movies about fans. After the unlikely Red Sox World Series victory in 2004, the Farrellys took advantage of the moment to surreptitiously film *Fever Pitch*'s Ben and Lindsay celebrating the team's clinching victory on the field of Busch Stadium in St. Louis.

The Iranian film *Offside* adds a fresh thematic twist to sports film conventions. Using the 2005 match between Bahrain and Iran as a backdrop, *Offside* focuses on a group of female fans of the Iranian team who disguise themselves as men and try to sneak into Azadi Stadium. The plot of *Offside* initially centers on a girl paying her first surreptitious visit to a game. (We later learn that the girl's scheme is a tribute to her friend, a die-hard soccer fan killed in riots after the 2005 Iran-Japan World Cup match.) Security policemen see through the girl's disguise and take her to an improvised detention area. The bulk of the film's plot takes place around this holding pen. As we come to know the other female fans held there, we hear the match's progress offscreen; like the women, we will never see the actual game.

By keeping the main event out of sight, *Offside* highlights the religious, cultural, and gender issues that affect an entire community. As the match progresses, the soldiers and the girls gradually develop trust with one another. Yet their friendly relations are sometimes overshadowed by social taboos on women's roles. The situation leads to somewhat absurd complications. Only men are allowed in Azadi Stadium, so there are no women's restrooms. When one of the detainees needs to use the toilet, the soldier accompanying her takes several steps to preserve her virtue. First, the soldier makes the girl wait as he shoos men out of the lavatory. Then, when the soldier sees graffiti written on the restroom's walls, he instructs the girl to wear a poster over her face to shield her eyes **(9.29)**.

9.29 Gender and religious taboo in *Offside*. Because the makeshift mask obstructs her vision, the woman must grope her way to a toilet stall, a situation that provides a comic and poignant comment on how traditions make even ordinary activities difficult.

9.30 Sports and social bonding in *Offside*. The female soccer fans join the crowds celebrating Iran's victory over Bahrain. The girl shown at the start of the film waves seven sparklers, one for each of the victims killed in the riots that occurred after the Iran-Japan match.

In scenes like this, director Jafar Panahi blends implicit commentary on social ideology with a concern for flesh-and-blood individuals. *Offside* is filled with small vignettes showing soldiers and detainees' growing awareness that they are mutually constrained by Iran's larger social structures. The soldiers must confront the fact that women can have deep love and knowledge of this apparently men's-only sport. Similarly, the female fans resent being shut out, but they come to understand that the soldiers are doing their duty as defined by Islamic law.

In the film's final scenes, the bus carrying the soldiers and detainees gets stuck in traffic. Masses of people have taken to the streets in hope of Iran's victory over the Bahrain team. While the men go to get snacks, the camera stays with the women on the bus. A shop window shows them a TV broadcast of the final seconds. Iran wins, the crowd goes wild, and the soldiers are swept up in the street celebration. With no one to guard them, the women join the cheering, singing, and dancing crowds. The final image is a long tracking shot that follows these female fans parading through the streets of Tehran **(9.30)**. An Iranian national anthem plays nondiegetically over this final shot, showing that women are not only loyal fans but loyal citizens.

Like many genre films, *Offside* ritualistically resolves the drama's social problems. The conclusion dissolves the gender differences under Islamic law and absorbs everyone into the larger community. On this triumphant night, sports becomes the glue that holds the nation together.

Although the sports film might seem to be a masculine genre, women's concerns also surface in *A League of Their Own* and *Bend It Like Beckham*. Other films, like *Remember the Titans*, *Glory Road*, and *42*, explore cultural attitudes toward race. *Offside* has used the genre to present a modest and sympathetic portrait of female fans as a cross section of Iranian society. In this respect, it reminds us that the sports film can merge a concern for social issues with engaging dramas of suspenseful competition.

In studying film, we often need to make explicit some things we ordinarily take for granted—those assumptions so fundamental that we no longer even notice them. Genres are examples of such taken-for-granted categories. At the back of our minds whenever we watch a film, these categories govern what we expect to see and hear. They guide our reactions. They press us to make sense of a movie in certain ways. Shared by filmmakers and viewers alike, genre categories shape film art as we most often experience it.

Still other kinds of categories guide our assumptions about the films we see. If we look beyond live-action fictional features, we find alternative modes of filmmaking. These depend on ways in which the films are made and the intentions of the filmmakers, and they often have distinctive approaches to form and style. The most common modes are documentary, experimental, and animated cinema. We examine these in the next chapter.

SUMMARY

One of the most common ways in which we approach films is by type, or genre. Genres are categories that are largely shared across society, by filmmakers, critics, and viewers. Films are most commonly grouped into genres by virtue of similar plot patterns, similar thematic implications, characteristic filmic techniques, and recognizable iconography.

When trying to characterize a film genre, you can ask such questions as these:

1. Before you saw the film, did you know what genre or subgenre it belonged to? What factors in advance publicity or conversation gave you hints?

2. What conventions in the film signal its genre? How do those conventions function? Do they allow storytelling to be more rapid and economical? Do they aim to arouse strong emotional responses?

3. What genre innovations can you find in the film? A good way to determine these is to ask if your expectations were thrown off at certain points.

4. Does this film seem to be combining conventions from more than one genre? If so, how does it make the genre elements compatible? Do innovative aspects of the film depend on the genre mixing, and if so, how?

10

Documentary, Experimental, and Animated Films

Studying genres shows that categories shape our experience of films. Our sense of genre guides our expectations: We anticipate one sort of thing from a comedy, something quite different from a horror film. Our knowledge of the genre's conventions shapes what we think is likely to happen from moment to moment.

There are still other ways to categorize films. Viewers and filmmakers distinguish documentary from fiction, experimental films from mainstream fare, and animation from live-action filming. Each of these types of film leads us to different sorts of expectations about form, style, and theme.

In a way, these types are more basic categories than genres. Most of our familiar genres are fiction films; it would be odd to call a documentary about witchcraft a horror movie. A cartoon can be a musical or a comedy, but more basically it's an animated movie. Chapter 3, on narrative form, drew its examples principally from fictional, live-action, nonexperimental cinema. Now we explore these other important types of films.

Documentary

Before we see a film, we nearly always have some sense whether it is a documentary or a piece of fiction. Moviegoers entering theaters to view *March of the Penguins* expected to see real birds in nature, not the wisecracking penguins of *Madagascar*. A filmmaker launching a project will keep in mind the fiction/nonfiction distinction, although sometimes the project will change directions. Errol Morris began what became the documentary *Vernon, Florida* as a fictional film set in that city. And the same incident can be treated in the two modes. Werner Herzog remade his documentary on a Vietnam-era fighter pilot, *Little Dieter Needs to Fly,* as a fiction film, *Rescue Dawn.*

What Is a Documentary?

What justifies viewers assuming that this or that film is a documentary? With two films titled *Spellbound,* how do we know that one is a Hitchcock thriller and the other is about children's spelling contests? For one thing, a documentary typically comes labeled as such. The filmmakers tell us through publicity, and press coverage reinforces the message. (The *New York Times* review of *Spellbound* called it a documentary in the first paragraph.) In turn, the documentary label leads us to expect that the persons, places, and events shown to us exist or have existed. We'd feel cheated if the kids in *Spellbound,* struggling to spell "logorrhea," were in fact actors. A documentary claims to present factual information about the world.

This information can be presented in a variety of ways. In some cases, the filmmakers are able to record events as they actually occur **(10.1).** This is what happened in *Spellbound,* with filmmaker Jeff Blitz filming the 1999 National Spelling Bee. In making *Primary,* an account of John Kennedy and Hubert Humphrey campaigning for the 1960 Democratic presidential nomination, the camera operator and sound recordist were able to closely follow the candidates through crowds at rallies (5.145).

But a documentary may also convey information without photographing events as they're occurring. The filmmaker might present charts, maps, or other visual aids **(10.2),** even using animation. In addition, the filmmaker might stage certain events for the camera to record.

Staging Events for the Camera   It's worth pausing on that last point. Some viewers suspect that a documentary is unreliable if it manipulates the events that are filmed. It is true that, very often, the documentary filmmaker records an event without scripting or staging it. For example, in interviewing an eyewitness, the documentarist typically controls where the camera is placed, what is in focus, and so on. The filmmaker likewise controls the final editing of the images. But the filmmaker doesn't tell the witness what to say or how to act. The filmmaker may also have no choice about setting or lighting.

Still, viewers and filmmakers regard some staging as legitimate in a documentary if the staging serves the larger purpose of presenting accurate information. Suppose you are filming a farmer's daily routines. You might ask him or her to walk toward a field in order to frame a shot showing the whole farm. After all, walking into the field is something the farmer does when the camera isn't there. The title performer in Dziga Vertov's documentary *Man with a Movie Camera* is clearly performing for Vertov's camera, but he's not doing things he wouldn't do ordinarily **(10.3).**

Some documentaries make extensive use of staging. For *Man on Wire,* director James Marsh had very little footage of acrobat Philippe Petit's astounding wire-walking between New York's World Trade Center towers. To clarify how Petit and his associates sneaked into the buildings and set up the stunt, Marsh assigned actors to reenact their tactics. In some cases, staging may intensify the documentary value of the film. Humphrey Jennings made *Fires Were Started* during the German bombardment of London in World War II. Unable to film during the air raids, Jennings found a group of bombed-out buildings and set them afire. He then filmed the fire patrol battling the blaze **(10.4).** Similarly, after Allied troops liberated the Auschwitz concentration camp near the end of World War II, a newsreel cameraman assembled a group of children and had them roll up their sleeves to display the prisoner numbers tattooed on their arms. This staging of the action arguably enhanced the film's reliability.

Documentary restaging is at the center of *The Act of Killing*, which centers on Indonesian death squads of the 1960s. After the army took power, gangsters were hired to kill anyone labeled as a communist. In a single year, over a million men,

10.1

10.2

10.1–10.2 On the scene or after the fact. For *The War Tapes,* lightweight digital video equipment allowed National Guard fighters to present their perspective on their tours of duty in Iraq. Here a U.S. serviceman, filming from a military vehicle, captures the explosion of a roadside bomb (10.1). But some things can't be directly filmed, so *Inside Job* includes animated charts to illustrate causes of the 2007–2008 financial collapse (10.2).

> ❝ There are lots of in-between stages from shooting to public projection—developing, printing, editing, commentary, sound effects, music. At each stage the effect of the shot can be changed but the basic content must be in the shot to begin with."
>
> —Joris Ivens, documentary filmmaker

10.3

10.4

10.3–10.4 Staging in documentary. Although the central figure of *Man with a Movie Camera* is an actual cinematographer, his actions were staged (10.3). Blazes like this in *Fires Were Started* were staged, but the firefighters judged the film to be an accurate depiction of their challenges under real bombing (10.4).

women, and children were massacred. Joshua Oppenheimer, a strong critic of the regime, follows the killers today as they bully and extort money, and he shows rallies in which government officials praise them as national heroes.

After the killers boast of their crimes, they accept Oppenheimer's invitation to make a film displaying their methods of torture and murder **(10.5).** As a result, *The Act of Killing* makes assertions about both the past and the present. The killers demonstrate what they did in 1965, and nearly all their comments and brutal reenactments show that today they feel no guilt. Both the participants and the filmmaker ask us to take the staged scenes as trustworthy depictions of horrific historical events.

Truth and Opinion in Documentary   As a type of film, documentaries present themselves as factually trustworthy, but across film history many documentaries have been challenged as inaccurate. *An Inconvenient Truth,* Vice-President Al Gore's film about global warming, was accused in some quarters of presenting weak arguments and skewed data. Even if its claims proved false, however, *An Inconvenient Truth* would not then turn into a fiction film. An unreliable documentary is still a documentary. Just as there are inaccurate or misleading news stories, so there are inaccurate or misleading documentaries.

A documentary may take a stand, state an opinion, or advocate a solution to a problem. As we'll see shortly, documentaries often use rhetoric to persuade an audience. But simply mounting an argument does not turn the documentary into fiction. To persuade us, the filmmaker marshals evidence, and this evidence is put forth as being factual and reliable. A documentary may be strongly partisan in its viewpoint, but as a documentary, it presents itself as providing trustworthy information about its subject.

The Boundaries between Documentary and Fiction

Fictional Films and Actuality   Shown a fictional film, we assume that it presents imaginary beings, places, or events. We take it for granted that Don Vito Corleone and his family never existed, and that their activities, as depicted in *The Godfather,* never took place. Yet just because a film is fictional, that doesn't mean that it's completely unrelated to actuality.

For one thing, not everything shown or implied by a fiction film need be imaginary. *The Godfather* alludes to World War II and the building of Las Vegas, both historical events; it takes place in New York City and in Sicily, both real locales. Nonetheless, the characters and their activities remain fictional, with history and geography providing a context for the made-up elements.

Fictional films are tied to actuality in another way. They often comment on the real world. *Dave,* about an imaginary U.S. president and his corrupt administration, criticizes contemporary political conduct. In 1943, some viewers took Carl Dreyer's *Day of Wrath,* a film about witch-hunts and prejudice in 17th-century Denmark, as a covert protest against the Nazis currently occupying the country. Through theme, subject, characterization, and other means, a fictional film can directly or obliquely present ideas about the world outside the film.

Sometimes our response to a fictional film is shaped by our assumptions about how it was made. The typical fictional film stages all or nearly all its events; they are designed, planned, rehearsed, filmed, and refilmed. The studio mode of production is well suited to creating fiction films, since it allows stories to be scripted and action to be staged until what

10.5 Reenacting murder. Indonesian gangsters stage their strangulation method for their film. They adopt a film noir style in tribute to the Hollywood movies they claim inspired them.

is captured on film satisfies the decision makers. As a result, in a fictional film, the characters are portrayed by actors. The camera films not Vito Corleone but Marlon Brando portraying the Don.

This assumption about how the film was made typically comes into play when we consider historical films or biographies. *Apollo 13, Schindler's List,* and *Margin Call* base themselves on actual events, while *Malcolm X, Walk the Line, Milk, The Iron Lady, Selma, The Imitation Game,* and other *biopics* trace episodes in the lives of people who really existed. Should we call these documentaries or fictional films?

In practice, most such films add purely make-believe characters, speeches, or actions. (Because of copyright restrictions *Selma's* writers even changed the wording of Martin Luther King's speeches.) But even if the films didn't tamper with the record at all, they would remain fictional according to our assumptions about how they were produced. The events we see aren't taking place at the time of the actual events. More important, the films don't present themselves as documentaries. They come to us labeled as historical re-creations or reenactments that take liberties with actual events.

10.6 Signaling manipulation. Carefully composed shots such as this from *The Thin Blue Line* emphasize the fact that some events have been reenacted. Several of these staged sequences dramatize witnesses' alternative versions of the crime.

Blurring the Boundaries   As you might expect, filmmakers have sometimes tried to test our ability to distinguish documentary from fiction. A notorious example is Mitchell Block's *No Lies,* which purports to present an interview with a woman who has been raped. Audiences are usually disturbed by the woman's emotional account and by the callousness of the offscreen filmmaker questioning her. A final title, however, reveals that the film was scripted and that the woman was an actor. Part of Block's purpose was to show how presenting a film as a documentary can induce viewers to believe in the reality of what they see.

Most fake documentaries, or "mockumentaries," are not this serious. Often mock documentaries imitate documentary conventions but don't pretend to portray actual people or events. This strategy turns the film into fiction. A classic case is Rob Reiner's *This Is Spinal Tap,* which uses documentary conventions to satirize rock bands and their followers.

A filmmaker may fuse documentary and fiction in other ways. For *JFK,* Oliver Stone inserted documentary footage into scenes in which actors played historical figures such as Lee Harvey Oswald. Stone also staged and filmed the assassination of Kennedy in a pseudo-documentary manner. Errol Morris's *The Thin Blue Line,* a documentary investigation into a murder, mixes interviews and archival material with episodes performed by actors. The sequences, far from being the jittery reenactments of television true-crime shows, are shot with smooth camera work, dramatic lighting, and vibrant color **(10.6).** The result is a film that not only seeks to identify the real killer but also raises questions about how fact and fiction may mingle (see pp. 436–441).

Genres of Documentary

As with fiction films, the documentary filmmaker faces choices about genre. One common documentary genre is the *compilation* film, produced by assembling images from archival sources. *The Atomic Cafe* compiles newsreel footage and instructional films to suggest how 1950s American culture reacted to the proliferation of nuclear weapons **(10.7).** The *interview,* or *talking-heads,* documentary records testimony about events or social movements. *Word Is Out* consists largely of interviews with lesbians and gay men discussing their lives.

The *direct-cinema* documentary characteristically records an ongoing event as it happens, with minimal interference by the filmmaker. Direct cinema emerged in the 1950s and 1960s, when portable camera and sound equipment became available and allowed films such as *Primary* to follow an event as it unfolds. For this reason, such documentaries are also known as *cinéma-vérité,* French for "cinema-truth." *Hoop Dreams* traces two aspiring basketball players moving through high school and into college, while *Citizen Four* records several days in the life of Edward Snowden, on the run for exposing classified security information. The deceptiveness of *No Lies* owed something to its being shot in the style of *cinéma-vérité.*

CONNECT TO THE BLOG
www.davidbordwell.net/blog

Portrait of Jason, a classic of direct-cinema documentary, is examined in "I'll never tell: Jason reborn."

10.7

10.8

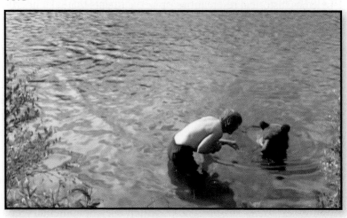

10.9

10.7–10.9 Documentary genres: Compilation, portraiture, and synthesis. Old footage of protective radiation gear was incorporated into *The Atomic Café* (10.7). *Searching for Sugar Man* portrays a little-known singer who became a cult figure in the 1970s and then disappeared (10.8). Ten days before his death, the protagonist of *Grizzly Man* displays his intimacy with the bears he loves (10.9).

CONNECT TO THE BLOG
www.davidbordwell.net/blog

Documentary films often explore unusual formal and stylistic options. We look at films by Wim Wenders and Ben Rivers that mix the two modes in "Ponds and performers: Two experimental documentaries."

Another common type is the *nature* documentary such as *Winged Migration,* which used in-flight cameras to soar and float along with birds. A *portrait* documentary centers on aspects of the life of a compelling person. Terry Zwigoff's *Crumb* captures the eccentricities of underground cartoonist Robert Crumb and his family. *Searching for Sugar Man* presents many sides of the career of a mysterious blues singer **(10.8).**

Very often a documentary pursues several of these genre options at once. A film may mix archival footage, interviews, and material shot on the fly, as do *Fahrenheit 9/11, The Fog of War,* and *An Unreasonable Man,* a portrait documentary centering on Ralph Nader. *Wordplay,* a study of crossword-puzzle fans, interweaves portraits of makers and solvers along with the drama of the annual American crossword competition. This *synthetic* documentary format is also common in television journalism.

Werner Herzog makes memorable use of the synthetic approach in the portrait film *Grizzly Man.* An adventurous young man, Timothy Treadwell, became convinced that he had made friends with the bears in a national park. But he was wrong: He and his girlfriend were killed and partially eaten by a bear. Herzog combines his own present-day inquiry into Treadwell's life, consisting of interviews and explorations of the park sites, with still photos and letters that cover Treadwell's efforts to protect the bears. Most vivid are the extracts from Treadwell's own video footage showing his encounters with grizzlies **(10.9).**

Form in Documentary Films

Back in Chapter 3, we mentioned that stories offer a major lens through which people understand their world and their lives. So we shouldn't be surprised that many documentarists organize their films as narratives, just as makers of fiction films do. William Wyler's World War II–era *Memphis Belle* follows the course of a single raid over Germany, seen largely from inside a B-17 bomber. Eugene Jarecki's *Why We Fight* traces how what President Eisenhower called "the military-industrial complex" achieved greater power over U.S. policies after the 9/11 attacks. On a more intimate level, the portrait documentary *Rivers and Tides* explains how an artist makes his unique natural-landscape sculptures (**10.10**).

The filmmaker can choose to employ *non*narrative types of form as well. The film might be designed to convey categorized information, so we can call this formal patterning **categorical form.** Or the filmmaker may want to make an argument that will convince the spectator of something. In this case, the film draws on **rhetorical form.** Given the attractiveness of stories, narrative principles sometimes mix with these other sorts of form. One section of a categorical or rhetorical documentary may tell a story, thus following principles of chronology and cause-and-effect. In these other types, however, the narrative sections fulfill the larger purpose of exploring a category or building an argument.

10.10 Narrative documentary. In Nova Scotia, environmental artist Andy Goldsworthy creates a delicate sculpture out of stones and icicles. It will eventually be carried away by the tides.

As we consider each formal option, we'll analyze one film as a prime example. To get a sense of each film's overall form, we'll break it into segments, as we did with *Citizen Kane* in Chapter 3. Along the way, we'll discuss how particular stylistic choices support the film's large-scale development.

> **"** To deprive the audience entirely of narrative in a long film is a real risk."
> —Pat O'Neill, experimental filmmaker

Categorical Form: Introduction

Categories are groupings that individuals or societies create to organize their knowledge of the world. Some categories are based on scientific research, and these often attempt to account exhaustively for all the data in question. For example, scientists have developed an elaborate system to classify every known animal and plant into genus and species.

Most of the categories we use in our daily life are less strict, less neat, and less exhaustive. Ordinarily, for example, we do not sort animals we see by genus and species. We use rough categories such as "pets," "wild animals," "farm animals," and "zoo animals." Such groupings are not clear-cut; at one time or another, some animals might fit into most or all of these categories. Yet they suffice for our usual purposes. Similarly, we may employ ideologically based categories such as distinctions between "primitive" and "advanced" societies. These are groupings that have been developed out of clusters of beliefs, and they may not stand up to scrutiny.

If you're a documentary filmmaker and you want to convey some information about the world to audiences, you can organize the movie around categories. Suppose the Discovery cable television channel hires you to make a film about butterflies. You might organize it according to scientific classification, showing one type of butterfly and giving information about its habits, then showing another, with more information, and so on. Alternatively, a travelogue about Switzerland might offer a sampling of local sights and customs, using more commonsensical categories (mountains, chocolates) that your audience can easily recognize.

Leni Riefenstahl's *Olympia,* Part 2, was made in 1936 as a record of the Berlin Olympics. Its basic category is the Games as an event, which Riefenstahl had to condense and arrange into two feature-length films. Within these films, the games are broken down into subcategories—sailing events, sprinting events, and so on. Beyond this, Riefenstahl creates an overall tone, stressing the games' grandeur and the international cooperation implicit in the gathering.

A categorical film often begins by identifying its subject. Our clichéd travelogue might start with a map of Switzerland. Riefenstahl begins *Olympia*'s second part with athletes jogging and then fraternizing in their clubhouse. They aren't identified by the sport each specializes in but are presented simply as participants in the Olympics. Later the individual sequences assign the athletes to various events.

CREATIVE DECISIONS

Engaging Viewers Using Categorical Form

The filmmaker using categorical form tends to use simple patterns of development. The film might move from small to large, local to national, personal to public, and so on. Your film on butterflies, for example, might begin with smaller species and work up to large ones, or it might go from drab to colorful types.

Because categorical form tends to develop in fairly simple ways, it risks boring the spectator. If the progression from segment to segment depends too much on repetition ("And here's another example . . ."), our expectations are too easily satisfied. If you were to make a categorical film, you'd be challenged to introduce variations and make us adjust our expectations.

For example, you might choose a category that is exciting or unusual enough to present many ways of stirring the viewer's interest. Riefenstahl realized that the Olympics have an innate drama based on competition and a potential for beauty in the display of physical grace. In *Cinemania,* a portrait documentary, we meet five passionate New York City film lovers who schedule their lives around screenings, sometimes four or five each day. But the film maintains our interest by contrasting its subjects in age, gender, and tastes. What might seem an obsessive lifestyle becomes a small community that accommodates people with varying personalities.

You might also engage a viewer by showing how the category and subcategories connect to broader matters. What designers think about a typeface might seem of pretty narrow interest, but Gary Hustwit made *Helvetica* into an engrossing film. He showed that those who love or hate Helvetica often belong to different generations and hold contrasting views about modern life. For the film that provides our main example, *Gap-Toothed Women,* Les Blank chose an offbeat category that turns out to be broad enough to encompass many sorts of women. As a result, the film's interviews cover a range of varying viewpoints.

Another way in which the filmmaker can maintain our interest across a categorical film is through patterned use of film techniques. Your film about butterflies might concentrate on conveying information about species, but it could also exploit colors and shapes to add abstract visual interest. The diving sequence at the end of *Olympia* is famous for its dazzling succession of images of divers filmed from many angles **(10.11),** while *Helvetica* seeks out varieties of the typeface in public places, suggesting that it's a pervasive part of the modern city **(10.12).**

Finally, the categorical film can maintain interest by mixing in other kinds of form. Although overall a film might be organized around categories, it can include small-scale narratives. At one point, *Olympia* singles out track-and-field athlete Glenn Morris and follows him through the stages of his event, because he unexpectedly won the decathlon. Similarly, a filmmaker might try to make an ideological point about the category, injecting a bit of rhetorical form into the film. We'll see that Les Blank hints that treating gapped teeth as a flaw reflects a society's bias about what constitutes beauty.

Categorical form is simple in principle, but it can create surprising effects. In *The Sweetest Sound,* Alan Berliner surveys the category of people's names. He investigates the origins of his name, tracks down other Alan Berliners, and asks strangers how they feel about their names. His compilation of newsreel footage, home movies, interviews, voice-over narration, and sound bites yields some diverting gags ("Every Tom, Dick, and Harry is called John") and neurotic reflections on identity ("Are they better Alan Berliners than I am?").

10.11

10.12

10.11–10.12 Striking visual values in categorical form. Filmed against the sky, the divers at the end of *Olympia,* Part 2 become soaring shapes rather than individual competitors (10.11), while *Helvetica* often presents examples of the typeface straight-on, as if a building were a page in a book (10.12).

❝ The whole history of movie making has been to portray extraordinary things, and no one has felt that much confidence in looking at life itself and finding the extraordinary in the ordinary."

—Albert Maysles, documentary filmmaker

An Example of Categorical Form:
Gap-Toothed Women

Les Blank made modest personal documentaries from the 1960s to his death in 2013. His *Garlic Is as Good as Ten Mothers* captures different people's attitudes toward the popular condiment. Blank employed categorical organization in original ways, showing that this formal approach can be entertaining and thought provoking.

Gap-Toothed Women was conceived, directed, and filmed by Blank, in collaboration with Maureen Gosling (editor), Chris Simon (associate producer), and Susan Kell (assistant director). The film consists largely of brief interviews with women who have spaces between their front teeth. Why make a film on this unusual, maybe inconsequential subject?

The film's organization suggests a larger theme: Sometimes society has rather narrow notions of what counts as beauty. After introducing the category, the film examines social attitudes, both positive and negative, toward gap-toothed women. If gapped teeth seem to be flaws at the beginning of the film, by the end, being gap-toothed is identified with attractiveness, energy, and creativity.

We can break *Gap-Toothed Women* into these segments:

1. A pretitle sequence introducing a few gap-toothed women.
2. A title segment with a quotation from Chaucer.
3. Some genetic and cultural explanations for gaps.
4. Ways American culture stigmatizes gapped teeth, and efforts to correct or adjust to them.
5. Careers and creativity.
6. An epilogue: gaps and life.
C. Credits.

These segments are punctuated with songs, as well as with still images from magazine covers and photographs that comment on the subject matter of the interviews.

The Opening The first image is a startlingly close view of a woman's mouth (**10.13**) as she recalls baby-sitting for her brothers. Somehow her parents knew when she had stolen bites from forbidden sweets. She has a wide gap between her teeth, and Blank cuts to a close view of an apple, the clue that tipped off her parents (**10.14**). Blank sets up the film's category humorously, making the tooth gap a wry mark of a woman's individuality. A quick series of closer views of six smiling gap-toothed mouths follows, culminating in a shot of a woman's entire head. All are accompanied by folksy harp music that enhances the cheerful tone.

While quickly establishing the category governing the film, this sequence also sets up a recurring stylistic choice. Usually, documentary talking heads are framed in medium shots or medium close-ups, but Blank also includes many close-ups centering on the subjects' mouths, as in the opening view of gapped teeth (10.13). Blank zooms in on the woman's mouth, and presents the face against a neutral background; both choices reappear often in the film. Once we've learned to notice tooth gaps, we'll concentrate on the speaker's mouth even in the more normally composed head shots (**10.15**). Later Blank (in one of his few offscreen comments) coaxes an elderly woman to grin more broadly to show off her gap (**10.16**). As we start to notice the gaps, we register their differences. Some are wide, some narrow, and we're invited to compare them. By a certain point, the speakers no longer mention them, and the filmmakers seem confident that by then we'll pay attention to them as a visual motif.

10.13

10.14

10.13–10.14 The opening. In *Gap-Toothed Women*, a close view of a woman's mouth with a large gap (10.13) leads to the telltale apple—"My signature, which was my teeth marks" (10.14).

10.15

10.16

10.15–10.16 Emphasizing the gaps. "My father has a gap, about as wide as mine is; my mom has a gap that's a little smaller" (10.15). Later, we strain to see a woman's gap as she smiles at the camera (10.16).

The second segment switches to slower shots of a woman playing a harp in a garden. The pleasant tone of this opening is echoed at the end by another, more buoyant, musical performance. In between, the film explores its subjects' attitudes toward being gap toothed.

During the harpist's performance, the film's title appears in white longhand **(10.17)**. This writing recalls the initial woman's reference to her gap-teeth as "my signature." The title leads to a superimposed epigraph: "'The Wife of Bath knew much about wandering by the way. She was gap-toothed, to tell the truth.'—Geoffrey Chaucer, The Canterbury Tales, 1386 A.D." This epigraph suggests that the film's central category originated long ago. Moreover, Chaucer's Wife of Bath is traditionally associated with erotic playfulness, and this element becomes a motif in the film as a whole.

Gaps: Truth and Myth   The film's third segment deals with where gaps come from and what they are thought to mean. In a cluster of brief interviews, three women mention that other members of their family had gap-teeth as well, so we infer that this feature might be inherited genetically. All three women speak in a neutral way about gapped teeth, but the first, mentioning that her mother had worn braces, drops the hint that some people take gapped teeth to be undesirable.

This segment then shifts its focus to consider how various cultures—specifically, non-white societies—have interpreted gap-teeth. A young Asian woman with a gap speculates on a "stupid" myth that gap toothed women "are supposed to be sexier." Blank then cuts to a brief clip from the fiction film *Swann in Love,* with the protagonist making love to a beautiful gap-toothed woman in a carriage. Does this confirm the myth? Or only suggest that the myth has been applied to gap-toothed women in general, since the actress is not Asian? This clip from another film introduces Blank's tactic of intercutting images from art and popular culture with the interview footage. This other material tests the comments and reminds us of how pervasive the image of the gap-toothed woman is.

The erotic motif brings back the Wife of Bath, now in an engraving showing her riding at the head of a group of pilgrims **(10.18)**. A scholarly male voice-over explains that in medieval times being gap toothed was associated with a love of travel and an amorous nature. There follows a string of interviews developing positive interpretations of the motif. A gap-toothed woman explains, in sign language, that she dreamed of kissing her instructor and having their gaps interlock. An African-American woman describes how, in places like Senegal, gaps are seen as lucky or beautiful **(10.19)**. An Indian woman asserts that in her culture gaps are so normal as not to require comment. Abruptly, Blank cuts to a modern copy of a sphinx, and we hear a woman's voice claiming that ancient Egyptian women

10.17

10.18

10.19

10.17–10.19 Gaps and femininity. The film's title is superimposed on a garden scene (10.17). The image of the Wife of Bath stands out incongruously from the dignified group, with her low-cut dress and broad grin (10.18). Blank follows this with imagery from cultures in which gaps are valued (10.19).

believed that gaps were associated with beautiful singing. Overall, the segment shows that most cultures don't consider gap-teeth to be flaws, and many treat them as signs of beauty.

Segment 4 tries to show that, in contrast to these cultures, modern Western society stigmatizes gaps. Several more interviews, intercut with other material, show that women have felt that their own teeth were unattractive. One tells of a dentist who tried to convince her to fix her gap (mocked in a song about "filling your mouth with wires, your head with lies"). But the idea that gapped teeth are ugly is immediately counterbalanced by vigorous editing. Two magazine images of models without gaps are followed by a pretty little African-American girl with a gap; then a photo of Madonna, a gap-toothed glamour icon; and then a *Vogue* cover (**10.20**). As if in reply to these images, a woman says she's worried about her height and weight, as well as her teeth, although she herself is conventionally attractive (**10.21**). Her comment is then countered by other opinions, as one woman talks about how in magazines "you never see a person with gapped teeth," and a mother with a gap-toothed toddler recalls that she had hated her own teeth until Lauren Hutton became a successful model. By intercutting the woman's comments with illustrations of what she mentions (**10.22–10.25**), Blank achieves an intellectual comparison somewhat akin to Sergei Eisenstein's intellectual montage (pp. 259–262). Overall, the editing drives home conflicting attitudes toward what is beautiful.

These interviews have been less playful than the opening sequence, but now the film lightens again. In an amusing sequence, Lauren Hutton herself roams through city streets in a vain attempt to find gap-toothed people to interview (**10.26**). Hutton is then interviewed in her home, saying that if a person finds herself attractive on the inside, she can be satisfied with her appearance.

The same playfulness is sustained in another musical interlude, folk singer Claudia Schmidt's "I'm a Little Cookie," a song accompanied by 10 photos of gap-toothed girls and teenagers, all smiling. This segues into a series of testimonies

10.20

10.21

10.22

10.23

10.24

10.25

10.20–10.25 Western attitudes toward gaps. Images from popular culture reveal attitudes: Les Blank shows Lauren Hutton, the first major gap-toothed fashion model (10.20). By contrast, a beautiful woman worries that her gap makes her unattractive (10.21). Another young woman recalls being teased and compared to Howdy Doody (10.22–10.23). This comparison is followed by a shot of the woman praising Lauren Hutton (10.24), which leads to a glamorous cover photo of Hutton revealing her gap (10.25; compare 10.20).

10.26

10.27

10.26–10.27 Satirizing the media. In an echo of traditional documentary, Blank uses a TV-style handheld camera to follow Lauren Hutton's search for gap-toothed women (10.26). Later Blank includes a fake commercial demonstrating a device designed to fill in gaps (10.27).

about how women have tried to correct their teeth with homemade devices, followed by a mock commercial for an actual device designed to fill in gaps (**10.27**). This segment of the film ends with the interview with the elderly woman who is proud to still have her own teeth, gap and all (10.16).

Women Glorying in the Gap Segment 5, which we've labeled "Careers and Creativity," begins with another Schmidt song about gaps. As we see images of more gap-toothed women, including Whoopi Goldberg, the song reintroduces the Wife of Bath motif ("old Chaucer knew where the score was at") and leads into an interview with Schmidt herself. She recalls that she used to be defiant about having a gap and extolled "gap power." There follows an interview with the cartoonist Dori Seda, standing beside a poster for the film we're watching and explaining that recognizing her gap helped her link herself to a tradition of unusual women (**10.28**). The film is moving toward associating gapped teeth with pride, comradeship, and creativity.

The next string of interviews reinforces this theme—oddly, by not mentioning gapped teeth at all. The emphasis now falls on women's activities (**10.29**). The Indian woman seen earlier draws rice-paint patterns on her threshold; a Hispanic woman trucker describes a long, difficult trip through a storm. The editing contrasts these stories with one, told by Catherine de Santis, about Arab women who remove body hair with a hot-wax concoction. This tale recalls the theme that it can be dangerous to conform to external standards of beauty.

More positive instances follow, as a heavy-metal singer explains that she quit her band because of its violent messages, and a gap-toothed woman displays the symbols for "woman" and "peace" painted on her face. A sudden sound bridge plays a dual role here. Over the woman's face, we hear a chorus singing, "They'll be marching, marching, marching when the Army comes to town," as if referring to her antiwar slogans. A cut to a new sequence reveals the music to be diegetic, played by a Salvation Army band before a speech is given by Sandra Day O'Connor (**10.30**).

Why is this Supreme Court Justice in the movie? For one thing, she's gap toothed. For another, her speech emphasizes "creativity, work, and love" as things that make life worthwhile. Since we've just seen several working and creative women, the thematic connection becomes stronger.

The Epilogue O'Connor also says that when creativity is gone, "the will to live seems to go with it." Her remark leads to the final summarizing segment of the film. In a tight shot, a woman's midriff gyrates in a belly dance. We glimpse other costumed women looking on and musicians accompanying the dancer. The dancer's voice-over commentary explains that she is in remission from acute cancer. A cut moves us to a quiet interview with her, identified as Sharlyn Sawyer,

10.28

10.29

10.30

10.28–10.30 Gaps and creative energy. Cartoonist Dori Seda discusses active women (10.28). A sculptor talks of how her work helps communities (10.29). Sandra Day O'Connor extols "creativity, work, and love" (10.30).

in everyday clothes against a simple board fence. After facing death, she explains, physical flaws no longer bother her. "You get stepped on by a horse, fine, you know, you've got a scar on your leg. Oh, well, you know, you've got a gap between your teeth, hey, no problem!" To underscore the comment, the film freezes on her cheerful face (**10.31**). Sawyer's spontaneity and commonsense acceptance of physical flaws and aging help put the anxieties of some of the earlier women in perspective.

10.31

Another sound bridge—this time, applause that seems to approve of what Sawyer has said—takes us back to the Middle Eastern dance class, where Sawyer performs another lively dance (**10.32**). The credits begin to roll, revealing a very close photo of a smiling gap-toothed mouth, an image that echoes the first shot. A final acknowledgment maintains the film's exuberant tone: "Many thanks to all the wonderful Gap-Toothed women who made this film possible!"

Categorical Form and Interpretation *Gap-Toothed Women* shows that category-based form need not be a dry recitation of similarities and differences. A filmmaker choosing this method of organizing can take a stance on a subject, play off contrasting attitudes, and entertain an audience. By choosing an unusual category and using simple but vivid film techniques, Blank and his collaborators have created a light film with a serious point.

10.32

10.31–10.32 Putting gaps in perspective. The frame freezes on a leukemia survivor's gap-toothed smile, underscoring the fact that in the larger scheme of things, gaps are insignificant (10.31). Soon she is leaping and spinning to great applause (10.32).

The filmmakers also show that categorical form can operate on the four levels of meaning that we described in Chapter 2 (pp. 58–61). On the referential level, *Gap-Toothed Women* presents a series of gap-toothed women from different races and different cultural and class backgrounds. We may know some of their faces and names from previous experience (Madonna and Whoopi Goldberg most obviously, Claudia Schmidt and Dori Seda to fans of folk music and underground comics). We also know that *Vogue* is a fashion magazine and assume that the magazines with Russian or other foreign writing are those countries' equivalents of *Vogue*.

Moving to the level of explicit meaning, the interviewees display a range of reactions to gapped teeth. Some are obviously proud, some embarrassed, others more ambivalent. Some express quite directly the idea that mass media often stigmatize people with gaps, while others reveal that gaps are admired in some cultures. At one point, the sculptor compares the lack of gap-toothed models in magazines to the notion of black people seeing only white faces in media images. This explicitly links stereotyped attitudes about feminine beauty to racism. In most cases, the filmmakers' voices are not heard; they let their interviewees make these points.

The film's form is not organized as an explicit argument in favor of gap-teeth being a natural, even attractive, trait. Yet on the level of implicit meaning, the music and photographs of smiling, gap-toothed women tend to suggest that. The choice of beautiful women who are worried about their gaps cues us to interpret their fears as unnecessary. Certain women's comments signal the ideas that the filmmakers wish to convey. Dori Seda's discussion of how important it is for women to do things helps define the film's segment on careers and creativity, and the cancer survivor's speech at the end makes anxieties about gapped teeth trivial in relation to the potential joys of life.

Beyond these three levels of meaning, we can also discern symptomatic meanings. Blank began making films in the 1960s, when a counterculture based on distrust of authority emerged. More specifically, it was an era of women's liberation, with its demands for gender equality and the breaking down of feminine stereotypes. By 1987, when Blank's film appeared, the counterculture of the 1960s and 1970s had waned, but many people preserved its ideals. Several of the women interviewed in Blank's film share this sensibility. Moreover, one legacy of the counterculture has been widespread attention paid to society's pressures on women to conform to limiting ideals of beauty. *Gap-Toothed Women* could be interpreted as an example of how radical attitudes of the 1960s slipped into the mainstream—a situation that persists and makes Blank's 1987 film still relevant today.

Rhetorical Form: Introduction

Another type of documentary film uses *rhetorical* form, in which the filmmaker presents a persuasive argument. The goal in such a film is to persuade the audience to adopt an opinion about the subject matter and perhaps to act on that opinion. This type of film goes beyond the categorical type in that it tries to make an explicit argument.

Rhetorical form is common in all the media, most obviously in televised political speeches. We encounter rhetoric in daily life too, whenever people try to persuade each other. Salespeople try to get you to buy something, and over lunch you may try to convince a skeptical friend of the virtues of a band or athlete you like. Television bombards us with one of the most pervasive uses of rhetorical form in film—commercials, which try to compel viewers to buy products or vote for candidates.

Factors in Rhetorical Form We can define rhetorical form in film by four basic attributes. First, it addresses the viewer openly, trying to move him or her to a new intellectual conviction, to a new emotional attitude, or to action.

Second, the subject of the film is usually not an issue of scientific truth but a matter of opinion, an issue you can take many plausible attitudes toward. The filmmaker tries to make the particular position convincing by presenting different types of arguments and evidence. Because rhetorical films deal with beliefs and arguments, they involve the expression of ideology; indeed, perhaps no type of film form centers so consistently on explicit meaning and ideological implications.

A third aspect of rhetorical form follows from the emphasis on opinion. If the conclusion cannot be proved beyond question, the filmmaker often appeals to our emotions, rather than presenting only factual evidence. And fourth, the film often attempts to persuade the viewer to make a choice. That may be big or small, but rhetorical form asks you to take a side, and perhaps take action. Which shampoo to buy? What candidate to vote for? Should my country go to war?

Types of Rhetorical Argument Filmmakers can use all sorts of arguments to shape our choices. Often, however, they don't present these arguments *as* arguments. A rhetorical film frequently presents arguments as if they were simply observations or factual conclusions. Nor does the film tend to point out other opinions. The filmmaker using rhetorical form tries to get the audience to accept debatable arguments as plausible on their face. The arguments we encounter may relate to the source, to the subject, and to the viewer.

Arguments from Source Some of the film's arguments will rely on what are taken to be reliable sources of information. The film may present firsthand accounts of events, expert testimony at a hearing, or interviews with people assumed to be knowledgeable. Most political documentaries include talking-head footage of investigators, scholars, or insiders. At the same time, the filmmakers will try to show that they themselves are well informed and trustworthy. They may insert themselves into the interview situation, as Michael Moore does in his documentaries, or they may use a voice-over narrator speaking in tones of crisp conviction.

Subject-Centered Arguments The film also employs arguments about its subject matter. Sometimes the film appeals to beliefs common at the time in a given culture. For example, many contemporary Americans suspect that most politicians are cynical and corrupt. Accordingly, a candidate may invoke that belief and tell potential voters that he or she will bring a new honesty to government.

Typically, a subject-centered approach relies on *evidence* to support the film's argument. Evidence could consist of statistics, research findings, poll results, eyewitness testimony, expert judgment, and the like—the sort of evidence you would use in a research paper. But often the documentarist will select vivid examples that stand in for a body of data. Instead of a poll chart showing citizens' resistance to going to war, you the filmmaker might supply shots of a demonstration, with placards and footage of speakers. This footage is more vivid than a chart, but it may suggest that the demonstrators' position is widely held, even if it's a minority view. In other words, evidence may be more or less strong, and dramatic examples may not be typical of wider trends.

Further, filmmakers can back up an argument by exploiting familiar, easily accepted argumentative patterns. Students of rhetoric call such patterns *enthymemes,* arguments that rely on widespread opinion and usually conceal some crucial assumptions. "He must favor low taxes. After all, he's a millionaire" is a common political claim. The implicit argument runs: *He's a millionaire; all millionaires favor low taxes; he must favor low taxes.* But the middle premise is questionable. There are many millionaires and billionaires who claim that out of a sense of social obligation they would support raising tax rates.

Enthymemes allow an easy but slippery movement from problems to a solution. Suppose you're making a film about your city's problem with graffiti. You find that in some cities, after strict vandalism laws were enacted, the incidents of tagging dropped. So you could argue that stiffer punishment is the best solution for your town. This sort of inference is so familiar that we tend to accept it as reasonable. But in this case you'd be assuming that your town is like the other cities in respects that are relevant to graffiti. That might not be true. In some cities, tagging is a casual pastime that could be cut by stronger penalties. In other cities, it's a strong tradition among youth gangs and artistic subcultures and resists policing. At the same time, the stiffer-punishment solution that your film proposes might overlook other solutions, such as providing approved areas for graffiti. (In some cities graffiti zones have become tourist attractions.)

Often the problem-then-solution enthymeme isn't as well justified as we'd like to think. Solutions to human problems are hard, and sometimes we're not sure why certain policies have succeeded or failed. It's easy to assume that solutions fit problems perfectly. Shortly, we'll see taken-for-granted enthymematic patterns at work in *The River.*

Viewer-Centered Arguments   Beyond appeals to authority and subject-centered appeals like enthymemes, the film may make an argument that taps into the emotions of the viewer. Politicians seek out photo ops that show them with flag, family, and ordinary folks. Appeals to patriotism, family sentiments, and other emotions are common in rhetorical films. Sometimes emotional appeals can disguise the weakness of other arguments of the film.

A viewer-centered appeal need not be heavy handed. *Darwin's Nightmare* argues that Lake Victoria in Tanzania exemplifies basic problems facing Africa as a whole. The area has been colonized by an industry that impoverishes the locals, and it is a prime drop-off point for armaments that fuel civil wars. But the film's point is not introduced explicitly. Instead, we get vignettes showing a wasp being swatted, mysterious men getting off planes and carousing with local women, looming shots of giant fish, images of desolate poverty, and scenes of street musicians and brawling youths. This opening relies on unusual viewer-centered appeals. It arouses curiosity about how all these disparate elements will coalesce into an overall argument. The problem at the core of *Darwin's Nightmare* emerges gradually from the evidence that the filmmaker accumulates after whetting our interest with vivid, perplexing scenes.

If you were to make a rhetorical documentary about a problem, you could organize the types of argumentative appeals in various ways. You could start by introducing the problem explicitly, perhaps dramatizing it with strong emotion. Then you could review some supporting evidence before proposing a solution. You might end your film with a scene that bathes the solution in an affirmative tone. *The River*, our main example of rhetorical form, adheres to this pattern.

An Example of Rhetorical Form: *The River*

Pare Lorentz made *The River* for the U.S. government's Farm Security Administration. In 1937, the country was making progress toward pulling out of the Great Depression. Under the administration of Franklin Delano Roosevelt, the federal government used its powers to create public works programs. These programs sought to provide jobs for thousands of unemployed workers, as well as to correct various social problems. Although many people tend now to think of Roosevelt's policies as the right ones and to credit him with bringing America out of the Depression, he faced strong political opposition at the time.

The River hails the Tennessee Valley Authority (TVA) as the solution to the region's problems of flooding, agricultural depletion, and non-electrification. The argument had a definite ideological slant: It sought to promote Roosevelt's controversial policies. Let's look at how this film sets out to persuade its audience that the TVA is a good program.

The River can be broken into 11 segments.

C. Credits.

1. A prologue title setting forth the subject of the film.

2. A description of the rivers that flow into the Mississippi and then into the Gulf of Mexico.

3. A history of the early agricultural use of the river.

4. The problems caused in the South by the Civil War.

5. A section on lumbering and steel mills in the North, and the building of urban areas.

6. The floods caused by careless exploitation of the land.

7. The current effects of these cumulative problems on people: poverty and ignorance.

8. A map and description of the TVA project.

9. The dams of the TVA and the benefits they bring.

E. An end title.

At first the film seems merely to be giving us information about the Mississippi. It proceeds for quite a while before its argument becomes apparent. Slowly, by careful repetition, variation, and development, Lorentz builds up a case that depends on all the segments working together.

Prelude and Premises   The opening credits of the film appear over an old-fashioned picture of steamboats on the Mississippi and then over a map of the United States **(10.33).** The film immediately suggests to the audience that its makers are reliable and knowledgeable and that it is based on historical and geographical facts. The same map returns under the prologue in the brief opening segment, which states: "This is the story of a river." Such a statement disguises the rhetorical purpose of the film, implying that the film will be an objectively told story, drawing on narrative form.

Segment 2 continues the introduction with shots of the sky, mountains, and rivers. This motif of the majestic beauty of the Mississippi valley will be repeated at the start of later sections and then contrasted with the bleak landscapes that dominate the middle parts of the film. As we see the beauty of the river **(10.34),** a resonant male voice tells us how water flows into the Mississippi from as far away as Idaho and Pennsylvania. The narrator's rich voice accords with conventional

10.33

10.34

10.33–10.34 Winning the viewer's trust. While we hear a resonant, assuring voice-over narrator, *The River* shows the Mississippi River and its tributaries exaggerated in size (10.33). Soon we have an idyllic image of nature (10.34).

notions of a trustworthy person. The narrator, Thomas Chalmers, was an opera baritone whose voice resonates with calm assurance.

Lorentz uses the sound track to arouse emotion. While we see rivers swelling as they join, the narrator's commentary avoids the dry, factual tone of most documentaries. The sentences rush in an urgent rhythm: "Down the Yellowstone, the Milk, the White, and Cheyenne . . . the Cannonball, the Musselshell, the James, and the Sioux." This famous roll call of the rivers, recalling the teeming catalogues of Walt Whitman's poetry, evokes the power and the grandeur of the Mississippi valley. No less emotional is the spacious folk-song score composed by Virgil Thomson. The film identifies itself with American tradition, appealing to the viewer's patriotic sentiments and implying that the whole country should face up to a regional problem.

The River in History   Segment 2 has established an idyllic situation, with its beautiful images of mountain and river landscapes. The overall development of the film is toward a restoration of this beauty, but with a difference. Segment 3 begins to fit the Mississippi into one version of American history.

The new section begins much as segment 2 did, with a view of clouds. But now, instead of the mountains we saw earlier, we see mule teams and drivers. Again the narrator launches a list: "New Orleans to Baton Rouge . . . Baton Rouge to Natchez . . . Natchez to Vicksburg." The narrator tells of the dikes built along the Mississippi to control flooding in pre–Civil War days. The facts and dates he provides present him as a credible source, trustworthy and knowledgeable. We see cotton bales loaded onto steamboats, giving a sense of the country's early strength as an exporter of goods. The brisk cutting here, as elsewhere in the film, evokes American enterprise and energy. Graphic discontinuities suggest both change and continuity **(10.35, 10.36).** Dynamic compositions suggest the exhilaration of a growing nation **(10.37).**

In segments 1–3, Lorentz has seemed simply to be telling a story of the river. But in segment 4, the film begins to introduce the problems that the TVA will eventually solve. Bleak images show the results of the Civil War: destroyed houses, the land worn out by the cultivation of cotton, and people forced to move west. The tone of concern becomes apparent, and it appeals to emotion. Over images of impoverished people, somber music plays. It is based on a familiar folk tune, "Go Tell Aunt Rhody," which, with its line "The old gray goose is dead," underscores the farmers' losses. The narrator's voice expresses compassion as he speaks of the South's "tragedy of land impoverished." This attitude of sympathy may incline us to accept as true other things that the film tells us. The narrator also refers to the

10.35   10.36   10.37

10.35–10.37 Dynamic visuals present energetic growth. Lorentz uses graphic contrast in cutting from a mud-filled sledge (10.35) to a plow thrusting in the opposite direction (10.36). The clashing movements suggest a shift in technology, but their similarities suggest a connection between building a dike and farming cotton. Later, a canted framing shows workers loading cotton bales onto a steamboat (10.37). The composition, accompanied by sprightly banjo music, makes the bales seem to roll downhill almost effortlessly.

10.38

10.39

10.38–10.39 Before and after. *The River* returns to the motifs of pines and clouds seen in the beginning (10.38), but soon the pines become stumps, the clouds an ominous fog (10.39).

people of the period as "we": "We mined the soil for cotton until it would yield no more." Here the film's persuasive intent becomes evident. It was not literally *we*—you and I and the narrator—who grew this cotton. The use of *we* is a rhetorical strategy to make us feel that all Americans share a responsibility for this problem and for finding a solution.

The narrator resumes his story, moving outside the impoverished South to arouse our pride in the growth of other regions. In segment 5, poetically repetitious narration describes the lumber industry's growth after the Civil War, listing "black spruce and Norway pine" and other trees. In the images, we see evergreens against the sky, echoing the cloud motif that opened segments 2 and 3 **(10.38)**. This creates a parallel between the riches of the agricultural areas and the industrial ones. A sprightly sequence of logging, accompanied by music based on the tune "Hot Time in the Old Town Tonight," again gives us a sense of America's vigor. A section on coal mining and steel mills follows, enhancing this impression. This segment ends with references to the growing urban centers: "We built a hundred cities and a thousand towns," and a roll call invokes many of their names.

Up to this point, we have seen the strengths of America associated with the river valley, with just a hint of problems that growth has sparked. But segment 6 switches tactics and creates a lengthy series of contrasts to the earlier parts. It begins with the same list of trees—"black spruce and Norway pine"—but now, instead of seeing trees against clouds, we see stumps against fog **(10.39)**. Another line returns, but with a new phrase added: "We built a hundred cities and a thousand towns . . . but at what a cost." Beginning with the barren hilltops, we are shown how melting ice runs off, and how the runoff gradually erodes hillsides and swells rivers into torrential floods. Once more we hear the list of rivers from segment 2, but now the music is somber and the rivers are no longer idyllic. Again we get a parallel, this time between the soil erosion here and the soil depletion in the South after the Civil War.

Style Arousing Emotion

It's worth pausing to comment on Lorentz's use of film style, because he reinforces the film's argument through techniques that arouse the audience's emotions. The contrast of segment 6 with the lively logging segment that precedes it could hardly be stronger. The sequence begins with lingering shots of the fog-shrouded stumps (10.39). There is little movement. The music consists of threatening, pulsing chords. The narrator speaks more deliberately. Dissolves, rather than straight cuts, connect the shots. The segment slowly builds up tension. One shot shows a stump draped with icicles, and an abrupt cut-in emphasizes the steady drip from them **(10.40)**. A sudden, highly dissonant chord signals us to expect danger.

Then, in a series of close-ups of the earth, water gathers, first in trickles, then in streams washing the soil away. By now the music presents soft, tom-tom-like beats punctuating a plaintive and rising orchestral melody. As the narrator intones dates, we see streams turning into creeks, and creeks into waterfalls, and eventually rivers overflowing their banks **(10.41–10.43)**. Lorentz uses rhythmic editing and music to sweep us along with the mounting tragedy.

As the flooding intensifies, brief shots of lightning bolts are intercut with shots of raging water. The dramatic musical score is overwhelmed by sirens and whistles. From a situation of natural beauty, the film has taken us to a disaster for which humans were responsible. Lorentz's stylistic choices have blended to convey a sense of rising tension, convincing us of the flood's menace. The film's overall argument becomes more compelling because we're made to grasp that threat emotionally as well as factually. Throughout *The River*, voice, music, editing, and movement within the shot combine to create a rhythm for such rhetorical purposes.

By this point, we understand the problems of flooding and erosion that the film is presenting. Still, the film withholds the solution and presents the effects

10.40

10.41

10.42

10.43

10.40–10.43 Editing and music create a flood. In *The River*, shots of icicles dripping lead to a segment on erosion (10.40). Streams form, and as they grow out of control, the narrator begins supplying dates, each time more urgently insistent: "Nineteen-seven" (10.41), "Nineteen-thirteen" (10.42), "Nineteen-sixteen" (10.43), and on up to 1937.

of the floods on people's lives in contemporary America. Segment 7 describes government aid to flood victims in 1937 but points out that the basic problem remains. The narrator employs a striking enthymeme here: "And poor land makes poor people—poor people make poor land." This sounds reasonable on the surface, but how did the poor people deplete the land? Didn't the southern plantation owners whose ruined mansions we saw in segment 4 have a lot to do with the impoverishment of the soil? Such statements are employed more for their poetic neatness and emotional appeal than for any rigorous reasoning they may contain. Scenes of tenant farmer families appeal directly to our emotional response to such poverty **(10.44)**. This segment picks up on motifs introduced in segment 4, on the Civil War. Now, the film tells us, these people cannot go west, because there is no more open land there.

Solving the Problem   The core problem has been introduced and discussed, and emotional appeals have prepared the audience to accept a solution. Segment 8 presents that solution and begins the part of the film devoted to the proofs that this solution is an effective one.

In segment 8, the map of the opening titles returns, and the narrator becomes analytical. "There is no such thing as an ideal river in nature, but the Mississippi River is out of joint." Here we have another example of an enthymeme—an inference assumed to be logically valid and factually accurate. The Mississippi may be "out of joint" for certain uses, but would it be out of joint for the animals and plants in its ecosystem? This statement assumes that an "ideal" river would be one perfectly suited to *our* needs and purposes. The narrator goes on to give the film's most clear-cut statement of its argument: "The old River *can* be controlled. We had the power to take the Valley apart. We have the power to put it together again."

10.44 The human cost. After delineating the environmental dangers, Lorentz gives them a human face.

10.45

10.46

10.45–10.46 Problem solved. The idyllic imagery of the beginning returns, but now the lakes are human-made (10.45). The new economy of the Valley allows men to work again, heroically framed in low angle against the sky (10.46).

Now we can see why the film's form has been organized as it has. In early segments, especially 3 and 5, we saw how America developed great agricultural and industrial strength. At the time, we might have taken these events as simple facts of history. But now they turn out to be crucial to the film's argument. We have seen that the American people have the power to build and to destroy; therefore, they have the power to build again.

The narrator continues: "In 1933 we started . . . ," going on to describe how Congress formed the Tennessee Valley Authority, an agency tasked with restoring the region. This segment presents the TVA as an already settled solution to the problem and offers no alternative solutions. Although the TVA was very controversial, it's presented as a matter of straightforward implementation. Nor does *The River* show the dislocations caused by the building of the dams. There is no mention of the 15,000 people who had to leave their homes and be resettled elsewhere. Nor does the film attempt to rebut the alternative proposals that arose at the time. In all, the solution that was adopted is assumed to be the inevitable one, without risks or drawbacks.

Segment 9 introduces features that recall several earlier parts, but with an emphasis on the future rather than the past. It begins with a list of dams, which we see in progress or finished. This echoes the lists of rivers, trees, towns, and so on that we have heard at intervals. The serene shots of the artificial lakes that follow link the ending to the beginning, recalling the lyrical river shots of segment 2 (**10.45**). The flooded-out and unemployed people from segment 6 seem now to be happily marching to work (**10.46**), building planned model towns on government loans. Electricity generated by the dams links these rural communities to those "hundred cities and thousand towns" we heard about earlier, bringing to the countryside "the advantages of urban life." Many motifs planted in a simple fashion are now picked up and woven together to act as proofs of the TVA's benefits.

Nature and Humans in Harmony   The ending shows life as being parallel to the way it was in the beginning—beautiful nature, productive people—but enhanced by modern government planning. The film's middle segments have denied us the picturesque views of mountains and sky we saw at the beginning. But after the introduction of the TVA, such shots return (**10.47, 10.48**). Tying the ending back to the beginning, the imagery shows a return to idyllic nature, under the auspices of government planning.

An upswell of music and a series of images of the dams and rushing water create a brief epilogue summarizing the force that has wrought the change—the TVA. Under the ending titles and credits, we see the U.S. map again. A list tells us

10.47

10.48

10.47–10.48 Nature regained. The hillsides celebrated in the beginning now shelter modern, model towns.

the names of the various government agencies that sponsored the film or assisted in its making. These again seem to lend authority to the source of the arguments in the film.

The River achieved its purpose. Favorable initial response led a major American studio, Paramount, to agree to distribute the film to theaters, a rare opportunity for a government-sponsored short documentary at that time. Reviewers and public alike greeted the film enthusiastically. A contemporary critic's review testifies to the power of the film's rhetorical form. After describing the early portions, Gilbert Seldes wrote: "And so, without you knowing it, you arrive at the Tennessee Valley—and if this is propaganda, make the most of it, because it is masterly. It is as if the pictures which Mr. Lorentz took arranged themselves in such an order that they supplied their own argument, not as if an argument conceived in advance dictated the order of the pictures."

President Roosevelt was pleased with *The River*. He helped get congressional support to start a separate government agency, the U.S. Film Service, to make other documentaries like it. But not everyone was in favor of Roosevelt's policies or believed that the government should set itself up to make films that espoused the views of the current administration. By 1940, the Congress had taken away the U.S. Film Service's funding, and documentary films were once again made only within other government agencies. In such ways, rhetorical form can lead both to direct action and to controversy.

Experimental Film

Another basic type of filmmaking is willfully nonconformist. Some filmmakers challenge normal notions of what a movie can show and how it can show it. These filmmakers work independently of commercial production, distribution, and exhibition, and often they work alone. Their films are hard to classify, but usually they are called *experimental* or *avant-garde*.

Experimental films are made for many reasons. The filmmaker may wish to express personal experiences or viewpoints in ways that would seem eccentric in a mainstream context. In *Mass for the Dakota Sioux,* Bruce Baillie suggests his despair at the failure of America's optimistic vision of history. Su Friedrich's *Damned If You Don't,* a story of a nun who discovers her sexuality, presents the theme of release from religious commitment. Alternatively, the filmmaker may seek to convey a mood or a physical quality (**10.49, 10.50**).

The filmmaker may also wish to explore some possibilities of the medium itself. Experimental filmmakers have tinkered with cinema in myriad ways. They have presented cosmic allegories, such as Stan Brakhage's *Dog Star Man,* and highly private japes, as in Ken Jacobs's *Little Stabs at Happiness.* Robert Breer's *Fist Fight* experiments with shots only one or two frames long (6.141); by contrast, the shots in Andy Warhol's *Eat* last until the camera runs out of film. You can make an experimental film through improvisation, or a mathematical plan, or just letting nature take its course. For *Eiga-zuke (Pickled Film),* Japanese-American Sean Morijiro Sunada O'Gara applied pickling agents to negative film and then handprinted the blotchy abstractions onto positive stock.

The experimental filmmaker may tell no story, creating poetic reveries (**10.51**) or pulsating visual collages such as *Ballet mécanique,* which serves as one of our main examples here. Alternatively, the filmmaker may create a fictional story, but it's likely to challenge the viewer. Yvonne Rainer's *Film About a Woman Who . . .* presents its narrative partly through a series of slides that a group of men and women are watching. At the same time, on the sound track, we hear anonymous voices carrying on a conversation, but we cannot confidently assign any voice to an individual onscreen. Rainer thus forces us to weigh everything we see and hear on its own terms, apart from any involvement with characters (**10.52**).

> " One of the things that goes on in *Critical Mass* (this is also true of much of the rest of my work and of the work by others I admire) is a process of training the spectator to watch the film."
>
> —Hollis Frampton, experimental filmmaker

10.49

10.50

10.49–10.50 Kinetic grace in the experimental film. Maya Deren's *Choreography for Camera* shows a dancer lifting his leg in a forest (10.49) and bringing it down in a studio (10.50). The match on action yields smooth movement across different times and places.

10.51

10.52

10.51–10.52 Nonnarrative and narrative form in experimental film. In Willard Maas's *Geography of the Body,* an ear creates an abstract, lyrical composition (10.51). Thanks to Rainer's combination of images, sounds, and captions in *Film About a Woman Who . . . ,* the viewer is encouraged to imagine several possible stories (10.52).

10.53

10.54

10.53–10.54 The found-footage film. *A Movie* cuts from a low-angle shot of a stagecoach (10.53) to a similar one of a hurtling tank (10.54), mixing staged footage and newsreel footage to create a graphic match.

A Range of Technical Choices

Any sort of footage may be used for an avant-garde film. Images that a documentarist might take as fragments of actuality can be mobilized for quite different purposes. For the aptly titled *A Movie,* Bruce Conner pulls footage from Hollywood Westerns, travelogues, and newsreels to create a sweeping image of the destruction of civilization **(10.53–10.54).** Within the experimental mode, such scavenged works are often called *found-footage films.* Found-footage films rely on editing, but experimentalists have also expressed distinct feelings or ideas through staging **(10.55, 10.56).** There is avant-garde animation as well, as we'll see later in this chapter.

The freedom available to experimental film is on flamboyant display in Kenneth Anger's *Scorpio Rising.* Anger takes as his subject the motorcycle culture of the 1960s, and he includes scenes of bikers working on their machines, dressing, partying, and racing. Alongside footage of bikers glimpsed on the streets or in parties, there are many staged incidents—chiefly around Scorpio, a James Dean–like figure. Anger also cuts in still photos, comic strips, found footage from old movies, and Nazi posters. In addition, each segment is accompanied by a rock-and-roll song that adds an ironic or ominous tone to the images **(10.57).** Throughout the film, Anger links biking to a death wish. *Scorpio Rising* creates elusive but powerful associations, suggesting homoerotic aspects of bike culture, comparing its rituals to fascism and Christianity, and evoking the possibility that people often model their behavior on images supplied by mass media.

10.55

10.56

10.55–10.56 Staging in experimental film. James Broughton's *Mother's Day* offers carefully composed arrays of adults playing children's games (10.55). By superimposing different phases of a kitchen scene, Ivan Galeta's *Two Times in One Space* creates cycles of people splitting or drifting like phantoms (10.56). Mysteriously, the action on the distant balcony unfolds in normal duration.

Impossible to capture in a neat formula, avant-garde cinema is recognizable by its efforts at self-expression or experimentation outside mainstream cinema. Yet the boundary lines can be breached. Techniques associated with the avant-garde have been deployed in music videos by Michel Gondry and Chris Cunningham. In fact, Conner, Anger, Derek Jarman, and other experimentalists were early pioneers of music video. Meanwhile, mainstream features have been continually drawing on the avant-garde for ideas and techniques, just as experimentalists have plundered mainstream films for ideas to push in unexpected directions.

Types of Form in Experimental Films

Like documentaries, experimental films sometimes use narrative form. James Sibley Watson, Jr., and Melville Webber's 1928 film *The Fall of the House of Usher* evokes the atmosphere of the Edgar Allan Poe story through expressionistic sets and lighting. Occasionally, we find an experimental film organized by categories. Peter Greenaway's *The Falls* traces, in alphabetical order, information about an imaginary group of people with the surname Fall. Christian Marclay's 24-hour *The Clock* is organized by times of day, as illustrated in shots from fiction films.

Two other types of form are characteristic of experimental films: abstract form and associational form.

Abstract Form: Introduction

When we watch a film that tells a story, or surveys categories, or makes an argument, we usually pay little attention to the sheer pictorial qualities of the shots. Yet it's possible to organize an entire film around colors, shapes, sizes, and movements in the images.

How could you do this? Consider *Railroad Turnbridge,* by the sculptor Richard Serra. A turnbridge allows a section of railroad tracks to swivel on a central column, clearing space for tall boats passing along a river. Serra set up a camera at the center of a turnbridge and filmed the bridge's movement. The result onscreen is surprising. The bridge is swiveling, but because the camera is anchored to it, the crossed girders and powerful uprights seem monumentally static, and the landscape rotates majestically **(10.58).** There is no argument here, no survey of categories. A narrative film might have used the bridge for an exciting chase or fight, but Serra invites us to contemplate the bridge as a geometrical sculpture, all grids and angles, in relation to the curves and sweeps of nature beyond. Serra asks us to notice and enjoy the slowly changing pictorial qualities of line, shape, tonalities, and movement.

Of course, all films contain pictorial qualities like these; we noticed them when we studied mise-en-scene, frame composition, and editing. In this chapter, we've seen how the lyrical beauty of the river and lake shots in *The River* functions to create parallels, and the rhythm of its musical score enhances our emotional involvement in the argument being made. But in *The River,* an abstract pattern becomes a means to an end, always furthering Lorentz's rhetorical purposes. *The River* isn't organized around abstract qualities but rather emphasizes such qualities only occasionally. In **abstract form,** the *whole* film's patterning will be determined by such qualities.

10.57 *Scorpio Rising.* As a young man fetishistically tunes up his bike, the figure of death looms above him. On the soundtrack we hear, "My boyfriend's back . . . and he's coming after you."

CONNECT TO THE BLOG
www.davidbordwell.net/blog

Christian Marclay's *The Clock* is both an epic experimental film and a clock itself, because the times shown onscreen correspond to the time that the audience is living. See our entry "Time piece."

10.58 Abstracting a real object. The slowly changing background emphasizes the symmetrical geometry of the bridge's design in *Railroad Turnbridge.*

▪▪
CREATIVE DECISIONS

Designing Form in an Abstract Film

How can you organize a film based on visual qualities? A common option is a pattern of *theme and variations.* This term usually applies to music, where a melody or other type of motif is introduced, and then a series of different versions of that same melody follows—often with such extreme differences of key and rhythm that the original melody becomes difficult to recognize.

You can design an abstract film's form in a similar fashion. An introductory section typically shows us the kinds of relationships the film used as its basic material. Then other segments go on to present similar kinds of relationships but with changes. The changes may be slight, but soon they will differ sharply from the introductory material. Bigger contrasts emerge, and sudden variations can help us to sense when a new segment has started. If the film's formal organization has been created with care, the similarities and differences won't be random. There will be some underlying principle that runs through the film.

The theme-and-variations principle is clearly evident in J. J. Murphy's *Print Generation*. Murphy selected 60 shots from home movies, then rephotographed them over and over on a contact printer. Each succeeding duplication lost photographic quality, until the final images became unrecognizable. *Print Generation* presents the footage 25 times, starting with the most abstract images and moving to the most recognizable ones. Then the process is reversed, and the images gradually move back toward abstraction **(10.59, 10.60).** On the sound track, the progression is exactly the opposite. Murphy rerecorded the sound 25 times, but the film begins with the most clearly audible version. As the image clarifies, the sound deteriorates; as the image slips back into abstraction, the sound clarifies. Part of the fascination of this experimental film derives from seeing blobs and sparkles of abstract color become slowly defined as people and landscapes before passing back into abstraction. The film also teases us to discover its overall formal pattern.

As *Railroad Turnbridge* and *Print Generation* indicate, by calling a film's form abstract, we don't mean that the film has no recognizable objects in it. True, you could make an abstract film out of pure shapes and colors, created by painting, drawing, cutting out pieces of colored paper, or playing with computer-generated shapes. But you could also film real objects in such a way that their abstract qualities come forward. After all, every abstract quality you might explore exists both in nature and in human-made objects. Bird songs, cloud formations, the markings on fur or feathers—natural phenomena like these attract us because they seem beautiful or unusual. They are some of the same qualities that we look for in artworks. Moreover, even those objects that we create for very practical uses may have pleasing contours or textures. Chairs are made to sit on, but we will usually try to furnish our home with chairs that also look attractive to us.

So experimental filmmakers often start by photographing real objects. But the filmmakers then juxtapose the images to emphasize relations of shape, color, movement, and so on. As a result, the film is still using abstract organization in spite of the fact that we can recognize the object as a bird, a face, or a spoon.

The result often pushes us to use our senses in an unusual way. Normally, there's a practical purpose in noticing abstract qualities. Driving a car, we use colors and shapes to spot traffic signs and signals. Picking out a new shirt or dress, we often ask whether it makes us look fashionable or will cost too much. In watching an abstract film, though, we don't need to use our eyes for practical purposes. The abstract side of the world becomes interesting for its own sake.

> *Thematic interpretation comes from literature: it's been carried over to conventional narrative films, but it shouldn't be grafted onto experimental films, which are often a reaction against such conventions."*
>
> —J. J. Murphy, experimental filmmaker

10.59–10.60 Theme and variations in *Print Generation.* In early portions of the film, each one-second shot is more or less identifiable (10.59). After many generations of reprinting, the same image becomes abstract, with hot highlights remaining (10.60). The color is biased toward red because that is the last layer of the emulsion to fade in rephotography.

10.59

10.60

This "impractical" interest has led some critics and viewers to think of abstract films as frivolous. Critics may call them "art for art's sake," since all they seem to do is present us with a series of interesting patterns. Yet these films make us more aware of such patterns. No one who has watched *Railroad Turnbridge* can see bridges in quite the same way afterward. In talking about abstract films, we might amend the phrase to "art for life's sake," because such films can enhance our lives as much as do films of other formal types.

■■■

An Example of Abstract Form: *Ballet Mécanique*

Ballet mécanique ("*Mechanical Ballet*"), one of the earliest abstract films, was also one of the most influential. It remains a highly enjoyable avant-garde film and a classic example of how mundane objects can be transformed when their abstract qualities become the basis for a film's form.

Two filmmakers collaborated on *Ballet mécanique* during 1923–1924. They were Dudley Murphy, a young American journalist, and Fernand Léger, a major French painter. Léger had developed his own version of Cubism in his paintings, often using stylized machine parts. His interest in machines contributed to the central formal principles of *Ballet mécanique.*

This title suggests a paradox. We expect a ballet to be flowing, with human dancers performing it. Here, however, we have a mechanical dance. Few of the many objects in the film are actually machines; we see hats, faces, bottles, kitchen utensils, and the like. But the context trains us to see even a woman's moving eyes and mouth as being like machine parts.

Film style plays a crucial role in most films using abstract form. In keeping with its overall formal design, *Ballet mécanique* uses film techniques to stress the geometric qualities of ordinary things. Close framing, masks, unusual camera angles, and neutral backgrounds isolate objects' shapes and textures **(10.61).** Through overall form and selected techniques, Léger and Murphy reverse our normal expectations about the nature of movement, making objects dance and turning human action into machine motion.

We can't segment *Ballet mécanique* by tracing its arguments or dividing it into scenes of narrative action. Instead, we must look for changes in abstract qualities occurring at different points in the film. Going by this principle, we can find nine segments in *Ballet mécanique:*

C. A credits sequence with a stylized, animated figure of Charlie Chaplin ("Charlot" in France) introducing the film's title.

1. The introduction of the film's rhythmic elements.

2. A treatment of objects viewed through prisms.

3. Rhythmic movements.

4. A comparison of people and machines.

5. Rhythmic movements of intertitles and pictures.

6. More rhythmic movements, mostly of circular objects.

7. Quick dances of objects.

8. A return to Charlot and the opening elements.

Ballet mécanique uses the theme-and-variations approach in a complex way. Léger and Murphy introduce many individual motifs in rapid succession, then bring them back at intervals and in different combinations. Each new segment picks up on a limited number of the abstract qualities from the previous one and plays with these for a while. The final segments use precise elements from early in the film once again, so that the ending strongly echoes the opening.

10.61 Abstracting ordinary objects. A horse collar in *Ballet mécanique.*

10.62

10.63

10.62–10.63 **Humans become puppets.** The figure of Charlie Chaplin is highly abstract—recognizably human but also made up of simple shapes that move in a jerky fashion (10.62). A more realistic figure, a woman swinging and looking this way and that, becomes a puppet too (10.63).

10.64

10.65

10.64–10.65 **Film technique makes real objects abstract.** The woman now swings upside down (10.64), and a prismatic shot makes a pot lid into a disc, its shape picking up that of both the ball and the hat of the previous segment (10.65).

10.66 **Stressing pure shape.** Just as the upside-down shot turned the swinging woman into mass and motion, masking makes facial expression a play of lines and textures.

Preparing Us to Notice Abstract Qualities The introductory portion of an abstract film usually gives us strong cues as to what we can expect to see developed later. *Ballet mécanique*'s animated Chaplin begins this sort of process **(10.62).** Already the human figure becomes an object. Segment 1 might seem to contradict this: Instead of a doll we see a woman swinging in a garden **(10.63).** Yet she seems unnatural: She repeatedly lifts her eyes and head and then lowers them, a fixed smile on her face. Coming after the Chaplin image, this shot cues us to notice the regular rhythm of her swinging. As we'd expect, the opening makes abstract qualities especially prominent.

Suddenly, a burst of images appears. We glimpse a hat, bottles, an abstract white triangle, and other objects. A woman's mouth appears, smiling, then not smiling, then smiling again. The hat returns, then the smiling mouth again, then some spinning gears; then a shiny ball circles close to the camera. The woman in the swing returns, but upside down **(10.64).** This segment ends with a shiny ball swinging back and forth directly toward the camera, and we are invited to compare its movement with that of the woman in the swing. The formal development confirms our expectation that she is not a character in a story but an object, like the bottle or the ball. The same is true of that smiling mouth, which does not suggest an emotion as much as a regularly changing shape. In the sequences to come, shapes of objects (such as the round hat and the vertical bottles), direction of movement (the swing, the shiny ball), textures (the shininess of both the ball and the bottles), and the rhythms of the objects' movements will be the qualities that draw our attention.

New Motifs With these expectations set up in the short introductory section, the film goes on to vary its imagery. Segment 2 sticks fairly closely to the elements just introduced by beginning with another view of the shiny ball, now seen through a prism. There follow other shots of household objects, also shiny and prismatic **(10.65).** Here is a good example of how a mundane object can be taken out of its everyday context and made abstract.

In the middle of the series of prism images, we see a rapid burst of shots, alternating a white circle with a white triangle. This is yet another motif that will return at intervals, with variations. These shapes invite us to make comparisons: The pot lid is also round, while the prismatic facets are somewhat triangular. During the rest of segment 2, we see more prism shots, interspersed with another rapid series of circles and triangles, followed by views of a woman's eyes opening and closing, a woman's eyes partially masked off by dark shapes **(10.66),** and finally the smiling/unsmiling mouth from segment 1.

Segment 2 has further confirmed our expectations that the film will compare shapes, rhythms, or textures. We also begin to see a pattern in which bursts of brief shots interrupt the segment. In segment 1, interruptions were created by shots alternating objects and a single triangle. Now we have twice seen a circle and triangle alternate. In creating abstract relationships, the rhythm of editing becomes as important as the rhythmic movement within individual shots.

Ballet mécanique provides a good example of how filmmakers may work outside the continuity editing system and create intriguing patterns of shots. One of the film's funniest moments in segment 2 depends on a precise graphic match **(10.67–10.69)**. Once again, aspects of the human face are reduced to moving geometry. Amusing touches like this make *Ballet mécanique* as enjoyable to watch today as it must have been when it was first shown 80 years ago.

Now that our expectations about the film are more or less established, the film plays with them by introducing new elements. Segment 3 begins with shots of rows of platelike discs, alternating with spinning shapes reminiscent of a fairground game wheel. Will round shapes and movements provide the main principle of development in this segment? Suddenly, the camera plunges down a twisting fairground slide. We see marching feet, cars hurtling over the camera, and rapid shots of a carnival ride's cars spinning past. Here different rhythms succeed one another, and common shape seems less important. Many of the objects shown are new to the film. Yet, after the carnival cars, we see a relatively lengthy shot of a spinning, shiny object—not in a prism view but at least recalling the image of the kitchen utensils seen earlier. The segment ends with the familiar rapid alternation of circle and triangle.

Variations at a New Level   Segment 4 is quite different from earlier ones, but it does bring back motifs: The prism recurs briefly (from segment 2), spinning shiny objects recall those of segment 3, and the woman's eyes and mouth (segments 1 and 2) return, having been absent from segment 3. Above all, in this segment Léger and Murphy give us the film's most explicit comparison of humans and machines.

We first see a carnival slide from above, picking up on an element from segment 3. The slide stretches across the screen, and in quick succession, a man's silhouette whizzes along it four times **(10.70)**. Next we see a machine part, strongly vertical on the screen **(10.71)**, with a piston moving up and down rhythmically. Again we see similarities—a tubelike object with another object moving along it—and differences—the compositions use opposing directions. More shots compare the slide and machine parts, ending with one machine seen through a prism. After more of the alternating circle and triangle, and more spinning shiny objects and machine parts, the film brings back the motif of the woman's masked eye (as in 10.66). Now the motions of the eye are compared to machine parts.

10.67

10.68

10.69

10.67–10.69 Those eyes . . . We see an extreme close-up of a woman's wide-open eyes (10.67). She closes them, leaving her eyeliner and brows as dark crescents against her white skin (10.68). A nearly unnoticeable cut presents us with a very similar composition (10.68). When the eyes pop open (10.69), we're surprised to find that the face is now upside down.

10.70

10.71

10.70, 10.71 Geometrical clashes. The fairground slide's horizontal layout (10.70) clashes with the vertical piston (10.71).

10.72

10.73

10.72–10.73 Repetitive machine, repetitive shot. A throbbing machine part gives way to many repetitions of the same shot of the laundry woman.

Segment 4 closes with one of *Ballet mécanique*'s most famous and daring moments. After a shot of a rotating machine part, we see 7 identically repeated shots of a laundry woman climbing a stair and gesturing (**10.72, 10.73**). After more glimpses of the smiling mouth, we get 11 more repetitions of the same shot of the laundry woman, then a shot of a large piston, and 5 more repetitions of the laundry woman shot. Instead of the woman on the swing, who moves to a rhythm she creates, the film endows the laundry woman with rhythm by repeating the same shot again and again. Again, even though she is a real woman in a real place, we must notice her movements' rhythms.

Word and Number Machines   Segment 4 has been the culmination of the film's comparison of mechanical objects with people. Although some motifs, such as the masked eye, reappear in segment 5, this portion of the film will introduce a new set of elements. The clue is given at the opening. Unlike other segments, this one begins with a black screen, which is gradually revealed to be a dark card on which a white zero is painted.

Unexpectedly, an intertitle appears: "ON A VOLÉ UN COLLIER DE PERLES DE 5 MILLIONS" ("A pearl necklace worth 5 million has been stolen"). In a narrative film, this might give us story information, but the filmmakers are now starting to use printed language as one more visual motif for rhythmic variation. We're now peppered with quick shots showing large zeros, sometimes one, sometimes three, appearing and disappearing, shrinking and growing. Parts of the intertitle appear in isolation (*on a vol*é), participating in this dance of letters. The film plays with an ambiguity: Is the zero really an "O," the first letter of the sentence? Or is it part of the number 5,000,000? Or is it a geometric representation of the pearl necklace itself? Beyond this sort of play with a visual pun, the zero recalls and varies the circle motif that has been so prominent in the film.

More punning occurs as the zero gives way to a picture of a horse collar—which resembles the zero visually but also refers to the word *collier* (which in French can mean either "necklace" or "collar"). Editing makes the collar execute a hopping dance (10.61). The collar images alternate with moving zeros and parts of the intertitle sentence, sometimes printed backward—to emphasize their graphic, rather than informative, function.

Returning to the Beginning   After its efforts to mechanize words and numbers, the film moves toward variations that are closer to the opening segments. Segment 6 shows us rhythmic movements involving mostly circular shapes (**10.74, 10.75**). Once again we're asked to compare persons and objects. An abstract circular shape grows. A woman's face appears in a prismed view; she passes a piece of cardboard with holes cut in it before her face, with her expression continually changing in a mechanical fashion. We see the circles and triangles alternate again, but this time in four different sizes. There follows a quick series of shots of rows of shiny kitchen utensils (**10.76**), with short bursts of black film interspersed. This blackness picks up and varies the dark backgrounds of the intertitles in segment 5, and the shiny pots and other utensils reintroduce a motif that has appeared in every segment *except* 5. The motif of rows of objects had come in segment 3, while the swinging motion of the utensils in many of these shots echoes the swinging of the woman and the shiny ball from segment 1.

Segment 7 continues the turn back to the beginning. It begins with a shot of a display window dominated by a corkscrew shape (**10.77**). The circle motif returns, leading into a set of dances that vary key motifs. Very rapid editing makes a pair of mannequin legs dance (**10.78**); then the legs start to spin within the shots. The shiny ball motif returns, but now two balls spin in opposite directions. Then a hat and a shoe alternate quickly (**10.79**), and the editing creates a startlingly abstract effect. At first, we see the different shapes distinctly, but as the brief shots continue to alternate, we notice variations. The hat changes position, and sometimes the shoe

10.74

10.75

10.76

10.77

10.74–10.77 Circles. A new series of circular shapes begins with a woman's head, eyes closed (10.74). She turns, and then a statue swings toward and away from the camera (10.75). Soon there are circular kitchen utensils (10.76). In a shop window, spiral shapes seem to freeze the gyrating motions that have made up so much of the film (10.77).

points in one direction, sometimes the other. The cutting rhythm accelerates, and the shots become so short that we see only a single white object pulsating, morphing from circle to lozenge and back again. The filmmakers use the graphic contrasts they've created to make us aware of apparent motion, our tendency to see movement in a series of slightly different still pictures. This is one process that makes cinema itself possible (see Chapter 1).

After the shoe-and-hat duet, more shots of the woman follow, again making her face execute artificial shifts **(10.80).** Finally, quick shots of bottles make them seem to change position in a dancelike rhythm. Here, where the mechanical ballet becomes most explicit, the film draws together elements from its beginning and from the previous segment, where the recapitulation of the earlier segments had begun. Segment 7 avoids motifs from the center of the film—segments 3–5—and thus gives us a sense both that the film is continuing to develop and that it is coming full circle.

The final segment makes this return more obvious by showing us the Chaplin figure again. Now its movements are even less human, and at the end, most of its parts seem to fall away, leaving the head alone on the screen. The spinning head may remind us of the woman's profile (10.74) seen earlier. But the film is not quite over. Its last shot brings back the woman from the swing in segment 1, now standing in the same garden smelling a flower and looking casually around her **(10.81).**

Seen in another context, the woman's gestures might seem ordinary to us. But as Hollis Frampton puts it (p. 369), *Ballet mécanique* has taught us to look at this image in the light of everything that has come before it. By now we're so accustomed to seeing rhythmic, mechanical movement that we're invited to see her smiles and head gestures as *un*natural, like other motifs we have seen in the film.

10.79

10.78   **10.80**

10.78–10.80 Artificial motion. The mannequin legs seem to move when they're presented in short shots (10.78). At silent film speed, the three-frame shot in the center would flash by in less than a third of a second. (Recall the short shots we described in *The Birds,* pp. 222–224.) Similarly, rapidly alternating shots make a hat seem to squash into a shoe (10.79), and a woman seem to nod her head (10.80).

Léger and Murphy end their abstract film by emphasizing how much they have altered our perception of ordinary objects and people.

Abstract form isn't only a matter of older cinema. Apart from earlier examples in this chapter, we could point to *Tape Generations* (p. 43), a recent film that creates geometric patterns out of ordinary transparent tape. Abstract form will always be attractive to filmmakers who want us to see the world around us with fresh, sharpened vision.

Associational Form: Introduction

Abstract form, then, is one option for the experimental filmmaker. Another is **associational form.** Associational form suggests ideas and emotions to the viewer by assembling images and sounds that may not have any logical connection. But the very fact that the images and sounds are put together prods us to look for some connection—an *association* that binds them together.

Bruce Conner's compilation *A Movie* is a vivid example of associational form. The 12-minute film pulls together shots of widely different things—blimps and stagecoaches, auto races and undersea exploration. Early on, shots of stagecoaches and cavalry from old Westerns are followed by shots of a charging elephant and locomotive wheels. The shots ask us to build up associations. Galloping horses are like rampaging elephants and locomotives, and all evoke motion across a landscape. Soon that association will embrace armored tanks and race cars. Eventually we'll see car crashes and vehicles hurtling off cliffs, as if the frantic race that started with cowboys has led to mass suicide.

A Movie doesn't tell a story in the manner of narrative filmmaking. It offers no characters, no specific causal connections, and no temporal order among the scenes. The film suggests that humans enjoy dangerous excitement and that films encourage that (hence the title *A Movie*). But it doesn't try to persuade us that humans are by nature reckless; Connor doesn't offer reasons or evidence. There is no voice-over narrator as in *The River* to define problems, assemble evidence, and point to a conclusion. Nor does the film explore a clear-cut set of categories. And yet *A Movie* is not purely a pictorial exercise either, in the manner of abstract form. It employs patterns of imagery and music (Respighi's classical piece *The Pines of Rome*) in order to conjure up ideas and emotions.

Poetic Film We can think of associational form as working somewhat as poetry does. When Robert Burns says, "My love is like a red, red rose," we don't assume that his love is prickly to the touch, glowing red, or vulnerable to aphids. Rather, we look for the possible associations: Her beauty is the most likely reason for the comparison. A similar process goes on in associational films. Here the metaphorical implications that poetry conveys through language are presented in images and sounds. A director could film a woman he loved in a garden and suggest that she is like the flowers that surround her. (This might be an implicit meaning that viewers could assign to *Ballet mécanique*'s last shot, if it were taken out of context.)

Associational form offers the filmmaker a rich array of choices. You could pick very conventional images or more original ones, and you can create both simple and complicated linkages. Again, poetry offers examples. In "America the Beautiful," the images of "spacious skies," "purple mountains' majesty," and "fruited plain" add up to suggest the patriotic fervor expressed in the chorus, "God shed his grace on thee." Another poem might be more elusive in its effect, giving us less explicit statements of the associative qualities of its imagery. The Japanese poetic form called *haiku* usually juxtaposes two images in a brief three-line form, in order to express a mood. Here is a haiku by the Japanese poet Kakei:

> The eleventh moon—
>
> Storks listlessly
>
> Standing in a row

Kakei's images are very sparse, but if we fill them in with our imaginations, we can feel a mood of autumnal stillness, with perhaps a little melancholy. This tone isn't present in the moon or the storks alone but emerges from the juxtaposition of the two images—something akin to the Kuleshov effect in film (pp. 225–226).

10.81 Back to normal? The final shot of *Ballet mécanique,* with ordinary human movement now seeming a little mechanical.

Basic Principles of Associational Form

An entire film can be made along associational lines. But imaginative links are unpredictable, so it's impossible to generalize about this formal pattern as clearly as we can with narrative or rhetorical patterns. Still, if you were to make an associational film, you would probably follow some basic principles.

First, you would probably gather your images into distinct sections. This principle of grouping is also seen in abstract form, as our *Ballet mécanique* analysis shows. Second, your film would likely create variations from part to part. Many filmmakers achieve this by changing tempo, following a fast section by a slow one. In one section of *A Movie,* disasters result from the frantic chase we've already mentioned; later in the film, the disasters are shown in much less energetic imagery, such as acrobats balancing above a city street. Third, as with other types of form, you would probably use repeated motifs to reinforce associations. *A Movie* constantly invokes images of catastrophe, created by man or nature. Finally, associational form strongly invites interpretation, the assigning of general meanings to the film. Watching *A Movie,* we're tempted to conclude that Conner is suggesting that if a society keeps overstimulating itself, it will collapse.

Associational form tends to shy away from explicit statement, however. Very often the filmmaker won't necessarily give us obvious cues to the appropriate expressive qualities or concepts. He or she may simply create a series of unusual and striking combinations and let our imaginations tease out their relations. Kenneth Anger's *Scorpio Rising,* for instance, strongly associates motorcycle gangs with traditional religious groups and with Nazi violence, while implying that gang regalia and rituals have homoerotic aspects.

Because associational form can be demanding for an audience, it's often confined to shorter films like *A Movie* and *Scorpio Rising,* as well as music videos like Björk's *Joga.* David Byrne's feature-length *True Stories* includes some song sequences, notably "Puzzling Evidence," that work by association. Making a lengthy film based on these principles is more of a challenge, but it can be done, as the feature-length *Koyaanisqatsi* shows.

> ❝ That shot [of a puppy in *Winter*] is preceded by a series of car headlights. So then with the dog's two black eyes, which are like negative headlights, there's something interesting to me there. . . . The nature of the human mind is such that it tries to build concepts out of each moment, and so, therefore, if I think the concept it can build is interesting and poignant, then I'll stick with it."
>
> —Nathaniel Dorsky, experimental filmmaker

An Example of Associational Form: *Koyaanisqatsi*

With its breathtaking desert vistas and vast cityscapes, *Koyaanisqatsi* might seem a ripe example of a *National Geographic* documentary aiming to explore different environments, perhaps through a trip taken by a friendly narrator. It might also seem ready-made for rhetorical form, perhaps pressing an argument about the problems of urban sprawl and mechanized lifestyles. Yet Godfrey Reggio, the principal filmmaker behind *Koyaanisqatsi,* has claimed something quite different. The film, he says, is "meant to provoke, to offer an experience rather than an idea or information or a story about a knowable or fictional subject."

The experience Reggio refers to, we think, stems from associational form. Because of its worldwide success as a theatrical feature, *Koyaanisqatsi* is probably the most famous example of the associational strategy. The film does suggest some ideas about technology and modern life, but it does so without appeal to narrative or rhetoric. Both large-scale parts and shot-by-shot connections are linked by principles of analogy, metaphor, and implication, the sort of principles we find in poetry. Reggio and his collaborators guide us to follow certain motifs, to make comparisons, and to register the sheer impact of images combined with expressive music. The result focuses on the differences between a natural environment and a human-made one.

The appeal to our imagination starts at the title, which will be unintelligible to most audience members. The subtitle given in some versions is "Life out of Balance," but not until the end of the film will we learn that this phrase is one of several possible translations of *koyaanisqatsi,* a word from the Hopi Native-American language. Reggio could have called the film *Life out of Balance,* but the unfamiliar word creates an aura of mystery, along with echoes of a society very different from that of the modern America on display in much of the film.

Koyaanisqatsi can be segmented into 10 distinct parts, signaled by changes in both imagery and Philip Glass's virtually nonstop musical score. Our titles are less precise than the ones we've seen in earlier segmentations in this chapter, as you might expect in a film based on imaginative associations. We'll try to specify them more as we move through the film.

1. Prologue.
2. Drifting.
3. Flowing.
4. Taming the Land.
5. Man-Made Majesty.
6. Collapse.
7. Inhabitants.
8. The Frenzy of Daily Life.
9. Dirge.
10. Epilogue.

The film is framed by a Prologue (Part 1) and an Epilogue (Part 10), both of which center on humanlike figures painted on stone. The film doesn't tell us that these pictographs were created hundreds of years ago by Native Americans in Horseshoe Canyon in Utah's Canyonlands National Park. As with the title, this lack of explanation encourages us to build our own associations (**10.82**).

Primal Beginnings In the Prologue, the pictographs dissolve to blazing shots of a NASA rocket being launched, the fire from the blast eventually wiping across the screen. More associations accrue. The painted figures resemble rockets, and the juxtaposition of an ancient culture with a modern one marks a strong contrast between eternal calm and furious mechanical movement. On liftoff, the rocket emits a blizzard of metal fragments, a bursting motif we'll

10.82

10.83

10.82–10.83 *Koyaanisqatsi:* From ancient to modern. The age and simplicity of the drawings evoke an ancient culture, while the figures convey a certain mystery (10.82). The fact that they're painted on stone may indicate an enduring authority lacking in the modern culture we see almost immediately, in the exploding rocket (10.83).

see later in the film **(10.83)**. The effect is to suggest that the drawings have been incinerated.

To a large extent, the Prologue gives us the film in miniature form, because many upcoming segments will end with explosions that seem to demolish natural surroundings or the human-built environment. Likewise, the Prologue establishes the power of the film's score, a central factor in guiding us to make certain associations. The pictographs are accompanied by thunderous organ chords and a male chorus chanting, "Koyaanisqatsi." The effect is of primal, monumental solemnity, as if the figures on the wall are chanting and the organ is providing a cavernous echo. Throughout, Glass's rhythmic and repetitive score provides a firm base for the imagery, with changes in instrumentation often signaling a shift within a section.

Drifting and Flowing   The next two sequences give us much more placid imagery, returning to the sense of serenity summoned up by the canyon drawings. Prolonged aerial shots drift over desert buttes and huge wrinkles of rock winding to the horizon. Droning chords on the sound track suggest that time is suspended. Soon things get more energetic, when the camera shows steaming and smoking craters. There follows a passage of associations based on wind **(10.84, 10.85)**. There is plenty of movement, underlined by a fast tempo in the score, but the movement is gentler and less mechanical than what we saw in the rocket launch. A final shot of this "Drifting" part includes smoke, dripping water, and the natural movement of birds and insects **(10.86)**. This is organic, free movement, very different from the harshness of the rocket launch.

The third sequence, which we call "Flowing," accentuates the quality of organic movement. The camera yields fast-motion shots of clouds racing through the frame. Soon they are intercut with rushing water, inviting us to associate streams

10.84

10.85

10.86

10.87

10.84–10.87 Wind and water. An analogical link among shots: The drifting smoke (10.84) leads to blowing sand (10.85), then the shifting shadows of clouds (10.86). As if to confirm the likeness between different aspects of nature, the film gives us a "cloud waterfall" (10.87).

10.88 Webs of metal. In the Epilogue, a title will cite a Hopi prophecy that "there will be cobwebs spun back and forth in the sky," but this metaphor is already suggested in the electric pylons standing like giants.

and rivers with clouds as another form of water (which, after all, they are; **10.87**). The movement of flowing is intensified when aerial shots race along the landscape, sort of a "cloud POV shot" as the music becomes livelier.

The unity of water, air, and land is now evident, but the terrain has changed. Instead of the desert vistas of Part 2, we have lush landscapes teeming with crops. Have the clouds and water of the early images fertilized the desert? This new blend of the elements is affirmed by a majestic aerial shot moving toward a butte surrounded by sky and water. Suddenly organic harmony is shattered by quick shots of explosions, as if the butte were under assault.

Machines Invade and Build   A shift in the musical score announces Part 4, which we call "Taming the Land." To ominously pulsing chords, trucks arrive wrapped in black smoke, contrasting with the white and gray clouds we've seen in earlier sections. We glimpse some humans, but they're swallowed up by the haze and the vast machines they manipulate. (We won't be able to identify individuals until later in the film.) Colossal pipelines cut across the landscape, and geometrical forms like wheels and grids are laid across more organic shapes **(10.88)**. A fast-paced passage of mining the earth leads quickly to a string of fires and explosions, culminating in a nearly 60-second shot of an atomic bomb test. The rush of imagery suggests that taming nature has led to a cataclysm. This implication will again be tied down in the Epilogue, with a prophecy: "If we dig precious things from the land, we will invite disaster."

10.89

10.90

10.89–10.90 Artificial nature. Skyscrapers seem to become windows onto the sky (10.89), and thanks to a telephoto lens jet planes emit heat ripples that recall streams of clouds and water (10.90).

"Man-Made Majesty," our title for Part 5, begins with an image of a power plant looming over a beach where people sunbathe. Early portions of this sequence suggest that humans have created a vast environment on a scale like the buttes and canyons of the desert. The score, a warbling chorus, has a quality of awe, while the cinematography suggests a new, human-made harmony of elements **(10.89, 10.90)**. The same sort of achievement is seen in traffic, with aerial angles showing highways forming beautiful spirals and the bubbling pulse of the music suggesting elation at this splendid human accomplishment.

But technology again turns destructive. The natural flowing we saw in Part 3 is evoked, but negatively, when military images emerge. Fighter jets whoosh over the desert and missiles are launched. Again the atomic bomb is evoked, and we get another montage of explosions—this time not related to construction and mining, but wartime bombardment. The imagery reinforces the implication of the nuclear blast at the end of Part 4: The technology that built this awe-inspiring world can destroy it.

Collapse and Survivors   Part 6 probes the built environment more closely, suggesting that it is vulnerable to decay, or what we'll dub "Collapse." The sequence starts with shining buildings, as the shadows of clouds wipe across them in the manner of the desert vistas of Parts 2 and 3. Likewise, the streets are filmed to resemble canyons **(10.91)**. So far, so successful: Humans have created their own massive landscape to live in. Yet it's an eerie place, with the sound of wind rising and fretful string chords in the score.

10.91

10.92

10.91–10.92 Monuments built and destroyed. City canyons echo the rugged desert landscapes (10.91). The destruction of failed housing projects (10.92) parallels the slowly floating debris seen in the opening rocket launch (10.83).

Gradually the cityscape becomes desolate. To the accompaniment of slowly rising and falling musical phrases, the camera takes us to decaying neighborhoods, hollowed-out buildings, and glimpses of misery. Instead of the springs and rivers seen earlier, water now sprays out of a fire hydrant. Now the wind no longer blows across sand dunes but instead ruffles dead grass and flaps a strip of canvas in a wrecked building.

After swooping aerial shots of massive housing blocks, as bare of human presence as the buttes of Monument Valley, the sequence ends in more explosions. This time the assault stems from humans' recognition that they have failed to create a new world. To the sound of frantically wailing choruses, we see housing projects, sky-scrapers, derricks, and bridges blasted apart, melting back to earth, and the sequence ends with floating debris choking the frame (**10.92**).

The ending of "Collapse" is bleak enough, but the next part, which we call "Inhabitants," heightens this quality with a view of lowering clouds and thunderstorms striking a city. What follows is our first extended view of human-scale life in this built world. In contrast to the extreme wide-angle imagery that surveyed the desert vistas, urban spaces here and in other sections are shot with very long lenses (**10.93**). Fast- and slow-motion imagery, reinforced by plod-ding, electronically tinged music, offer glimpses of people (**10.94**). Are they enjoying their lives? Are they unhappy? We're allowed to come to our own conclusions, as a few seem quite cheerful, while others—notably the fighter pilot toward whom the camera tracks—are severe and impassive.

Life at Warp Speed Most of the film's parts have run seven or eight minutes, but the one we call "The Frenzy of Daily Life" lasts over 20 minutes. It's hypnotic and exhaust-ing. The pace of the cutting and the action in the shot (given in hyper-fast motion) rises relentlessly with the dizzying pace of multiple rhythms in Glass's score. The sequence is tied together by the images of work and play, transporta-tion and recreation. In this respect, the sequence recalls "city symphonies" like Vertov's *Man with a Movie Camera* (pp. 432–436).

10.93

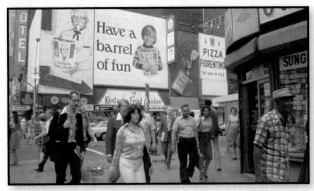

10.94

10.93–10.94 The new world. Shadows sweep in fast motion across skyscrapers (10.86), as they had moved across the buttes (10.86). Meanwhile, citizens walk the streets, captured against ironic signs (10.94).

10.95

10.96

10.95–10.96 **Electrical flows.** In Part 4, water was shown captured (10.95); now traffic, flowing in fast motion, creates similar patterns of channeled energy (10.96).

CONNECT TO THE BLOG
www.davidbordwell.net/blog

In "Solomonic judgments," we examine the work of Phil Solomon, whose films blend abstract and associational formal principles.

At first things are calm enough. Long, static shots show skyscrapers at dusk. Earlier we've seen clouds reflected in buildings, and now we see the sun set in reflection; it's as if such natural occurrences can no longer be seen directly, only through our artificial environment. The pace picks up, and night traffic streams in accelerated motion (**10.95, 10.96**). The music becomes exhilarating and the city seems to pulse with energy. People rush down escalators and bustle through the streets.

As the film starts to mix daytime shots with night ones, fast-motion filming makes all human activity part of a gigantic machine. People process meat, sort letters, sew jeans, assemble TV sets. In the film's most famous sequence, frankfurters pumped out of machines are compared to the flow of traffic and people hurtling up escalators (**10.97, 10.98**). This might be the moment of the film's most explicit meaning: Mechanization has ground humans into identical sausages. These images of production are followed by shots of consumption: video games, bowling, film viewing, and above all eating (**10.99, 10.100**). Still building the pace, the sequence shows people leaving work, commuting home, and reveling in consumption (**10.101, 10.102**). The sequence climaxes in a flurry of TV images, with talking heads and commercials bombarding us. A reprise of people stalking to the camera as in the "Portraits" section seems to remind us that the frantic robots we've seen are really human, but this passage is interrupted by another string of explosions. Now it's TV sets that are blown up, suggesting that the new built environment includes the media world, and it, too, is self-destructive.

We call Part 9 "Dirge" because it changes tempo drastically from the furious movement of its predecessor. Slow, nearly silent shots gliding over the city suggest a weary giant at rest. Urban grids are now compared to the patches on a microprocessor (**10.103, 10.104**), as if the city were no longer a machine but a repository of information.

The bits, we might think, are the people, and immediately we see them in a rather different way than we do in "Inhabitants." To plaintive organ chords and an almost funereal chorus, people haunt the streets. A woman can't light her cigarette; a policeman lifts a man off the sidewalk. Most faces are blank, puzzled, or suspicious (**10.105**). These wraiths might be the exhausted survivors of all the hectic rush of the previous section. Are they zombies or ghosts (**10.106**)? Abruptly, a rocket is launched, and (as in *Ballet mécanique*) the film starts to circle back to its opening imagery.

Several sections of *Koyaanisqatsi* have included extremely lengthy shots. The image of the passenger jet nosing its way through traffic runs about two and a half minutes. Arguably, however, the nearly four-minute slow-motion shot of the rocket rising and exploding and falling to earth forms the climax of the film (**10.107**).

10.97

10.98

10.99

10.100

10.101

10.102

10.97–10.102 People as products. Juxtaposing commuters and frankfurters, both shoved through rigid pathways, implies that mechanization has turned people into standardized units (10.97, 10.98). Fast food becomes very fast food in this rapid footage of mass-produced snacks and people eating identical items (10.99, 10.100). A shot hurtling through the streets (10.101) is followed by a Twinkie's-eye view (10.102), as if the people hurrying home had become another assembly-line product.

A briefer shot shows the rocket as it continues to spin endlessly in its descent, and Glass's repetitive score, replaying the hollow chanting of the title that we heard at the start, gives no hint about when the rocket will hit the earth. The image fuses many motifs: air and fire and smoke, as well as the bright particles that have showered other scenes. More broadly, the rocket that was launched in the Prologue has now apparently self-destructed, and along with it the overambitious hopes of man-made technology.

The Epilogue, a very brief sequence, returns to the canyon pictures and zooms back to a fuller view before the shot fades out. Appended titles give the word *koyaanisqatsi* several definitions, including "a state of life that calls for another way of living." A film using rhetorical form would have spelled out that new way, but

10.103

10.104

10.103–10.104 **Grids.** The city as microchip.

10.105

10.106

10.105–10.106 **Faces of the city.** Glimpses of life on the street (10.105). On the Stock Exchange, ghosts trade shares (10.106).

this film doesn't do that. Indeed, by opening out the title onto a range of meanings, Reggio encourages us to create various interpretations of the film we have seen.

All these associations point toward some implicit meanings. We might say, for instance, that the film implies that technological progress is too often pursued without thinking about its consequences for both nature and human beings. This theme would tie together a lot of what we've seen, especially the final contrast between the rocket's death spiral and the solemn humanoids on the walls. We have already quoted two of the three closing Hopi prophecies that sum up certain motifs, and the third one recalls the plummeting rocket: "A container of ashes might one day be thrown from the sky, which could burn the land and boil the oceans."

Like other associational films, *Koyaanisqatsi* invites us to tease out implications from its combination of images and sounds. That invitation doesn't end with the epilogue. There is no spoken language in the film until now, but as the final credits roll, we hear a babble of voices. It's a mix of TV commercials, newscasts, and stock-market reports. This sound montage reenacts the associational patterning we've seen onscreen throughout the film, but it also reminds us of the overwhelming media environment in which we live. Having exercised our eyes and ears and imaginations, this final sequence suggests, we might return to our everyday world more sensitive to the costs of the modern American way of life.

10.107 **Epilogue.** The final piece of debris: The exploded rocket spins endlessly.

The Animated Film

Most fiction and documentary films photograph people and objects in full-sized, three-dimensional spaces. As we have seen, the standard shooting speed for such *live-action* film-making is usually 24 or 25 frames per second.

Animated films are distinguished from live-action ones by the kinds of work done at the production stage. Instead of continuously filming an ongoing action in real time, animators create a series of images by shooting one frame at a time. Between the exposure of each frame, the animator changes the subject being photographed. Daffy Duck isn't a tangible creature you can film, but you can film a series of slightly different images of Daffy as single frames. When projected, the images create illusory motion comparable to that of live-action filmmaking. Anything in the world can be animated by means of two-dimensional drawings, three-dimensional objects, or information stored in software. As we shall see, digitally created films usually imitate the various traditional methods of animation.

10.108 **The animated documentary.** A recurring memory image in *Waltz with Bashir* shows soldiers wading toward an eerily beautiful bombardment.

Because animation is the counterpart to live action, any sort of film that can be shot live can be made using animation. We're most familiar with animated fiction films, both short and featurelength. There are animated documentaries too, usually instructional ones. Animation provides a convenient way of showing things that are normally not visible, such as the internal workings of machines or the extremely slow changes of geological formations. We've already seen animation used for charts and graphs in documentaries such as *Inside Job* (10.2). More daringly, after interviewing Israeli army veterans, Ari Folman sought to represent their lives and recollections in hallucinatory animated imagery **(10.108)**.

With its potential for stylized imagery, animation lends itself readily to experimental filmmaking as well. Many classic experimental animated films employ either abstract or associational form. For example, both Oskar Fischinger and Norman McLaren made films by choosing a piece of music and arranging abstract shapes to move in rhythm to the sound track.

> "Animation is not a genre, it's a medium. And it can express any genre. I think people often sell it short. But 'because it's animated, it must be for kids.' You can't name another medium where people do."
>
> —Brad Bird, director, *The Incredibles*

CONNECT TO THE BLOG
www.davidbordwell.net/blog

For a discussion of how animation can be used in documentaries, see "Showing what can't be filmed."

Types of Traditional Animation

The oldest type of animated film is *drawn* animation. From almost the start of cinema, animators drew and photographed long series of cartoon images. At first, they drew on paper, but copying the entire image, including the setting, over and over proved too time consuming. During the 1910s, animators started using clear rectangular sheets of celluloid, nicknamed **cels.** Characters and objects could be drawn on different cels, and these could then be layered like a sandwich on top of an opaque painted setting. The whole stack of cels would then be photographed. New cels showing the characters and objects in slightly different positions could then be placed over the same background, creating the illusion of movement **(10.109).**

The cel process allowed animators to save time and to split up the labor among assembly lines of people doing drawing, coloring, photography, and other jobs. The most famous cartoon shorts made during the 1930s to the 1950s were made with cels. Warner Bros. created characters such as Bugs Bunny, Daffy Duck, and Tweety Bird; Paramount had Betty Boop and Popeye; Disney made both short films (starring Mickey Mouse, Pluto, Goofy) and, beginning with *Snow White and the Seven Dwarfs* in 1937, feature-length cartoons.

Cel animation continued well into the 1990s, with big-budget studio cartoons employing *full* animation. This approach renders figures in fine detail and supplies them with tiny, nonrepetitive movements. (See 4.146, as well as 5.138–5.140.) Cheaper productions use *limited* animation, with only small sections of the image

10.109

10.110

10.109–10.110 Cel animation.
Two layered cels from a Road Runner
cartoon, with Wile E. Coyote on one
cel and the patches of flying dust on
another (10.109). Limited animation in
Silent Möbius creates fairly static images
recalling comic-book panels (10.110).

          You don't very often see
model animation which is well
lit, do you? For me, that's part of
the comedy of it; I love the idea
that you're making a thriller and
it all looks authentic, but the lead
character is in fact a Plasticine
penguin."

—Nick Park, director and animator,
The Wrong Trousers

moving from frame to frame. Limited animation is mainly used on television, although Japanese theatrical features also exploit it **(10.110).**

    Cels and drawings are photographed, but you can create animation without a camera. You might draw directly on the film, scratch on it, even attach flat objects to it. Stan Brakhage taped moths' wings to film stock in order to create *Mothlight*. The innovative animator Norman McLaren made *Blinkety Blank* by engraving the images frame by frame, using knives, needles, and razor blades **(10.111).**

    Another type of traditional animation working with two-dimensional images involves *cut-outs*. Sometimes filmmakers make flat puppets with movable joints **(10.112).** Animators can also manipulate cut-out images frame by frame to create moving collage **(10.113).** A very simple form of cut-out animation involves combining flat shapes of paper or other materials to create pictures or patterns. *South Park: Bigger, Longer & Uncut* employs computer animation to mimic the rudimentary shapes and unshaded colors of crude cut-out animation.

    Three-dimensional objects can also be manipulated frame by frame to create apparent movement. Animation of objects falls into three closely related categories: clay, model, and pixillation. *Clay animation,* often termed *claymation,* sometimes actually does involve modeling clay. But more often, flexible Plasticine is used, since it is cleaner to work with and is available in a wider range of colors. Sculptors create objects and characters of Plasticine, and the animator then bends, twists, or stretches them slightly between exposures.

    Although clay animation has been used occasionally since the early years of the 20th century, it has grown in popularity since the mid-1970s. Nick Park's *Creature Comforts* parodies the talking-heads documentary by creating droll interviews with the inhabitants of a zoo. His "Wallace and Gromit" series (including *The Wrong Trousers* and *A Close Shave*) and *Chicken Run* (codirected with Peter Lord; **10.114**) contain complex lighting and camera movement.

    Model or *puppet animation* is often similar to clay animation. As the name implies, it employs figures with bendable wires or joints. Historically, the master of this form of animation was Ladislav Starevich, who as early as 1910 baffled Russian audiences with realistic insect models acting out human dramas and comedies **(10.115).** Starevich's puppets display intricate movements and detailed facial expressions (4.90). Some of the main characters in his films had up to 150 separate interchangeable faces to render different expressions. Perhaps the most famous animated puppet was the star of the original 1933 version of *King Kong,* a small, flexible doll. If you watch *King Kong* closely, you can see his fur rippling—the traces of the animator's touch as he shifted the puppet between exposures. Recent feature-length puppet films include *The Nightmare Before Christmas, Coraline,* and *Fantastic Mr. Fox* **(10.116).**

    Pixillation is a term applied to frame-by-frame manipulation of people and ordinary objects **(10.117).** Although actors ordinarily move freely and are filmed

10.111

10.112

10.113

10.111–10.113 Varieties of animation. A nearly abstract but recognizable bird is etched directly into the black emulsion in *Blinkety Blank* (10.111). Lotte Reiniger specialized in lighting her cut-outs in silhouette to create delicate, intricate fairy tales, as in *The Adventures of Prince Achmed* (10.112). Released in 1926, it was the first feature-length animated film. Frank Mouris's exuberant *Frank Film* presents a flickering dance of popular-culture imagery (10.113).

10.114

10.115

10.116

10.117

10.114–10.117 Animating objects. A flock of Plasticine hens in *Chicken Run* receives Hollywood-style lighting (10.114). In 1912, *A Cameraman's Revenge* used realistic insect puppets to enact a comic melodrama of infidelity, jealousy, and revenge (10.115). In *Fantastic Mr. Fox,* the hero endangers his family and neighbors when he can't resist his urge to steal from local farmers (10.116). In 1908, Arthur Melbourne-Cooper animated toys in a miniature set to create dense layers of movement in *Dreams of Toyland* (10.117), an early example of pixillation.

in real time, occasionally an animator pixillates them. That is, the actor freezes in a pose for the exposure of one frame, then moves slightly and freezes again for another frame, and so on. The result is a jerky, unnatural motion quite different from ordinary performance. The innovative animator Norman McLaren uses this approach to tell the story of a feud in *Neighbours* and to show a man struggling to tame a rebellious piece of furniture in *A Chairy Tale.*

Traditional animation has sometimes been mixed with live-action filming. Walt Disney's earliest success came with a 1920s series, "Alice in Cartoonland," which embedded an actress in a black-and-white drawn world. Gene Kelly entered a world of cels to dance with Jerry the Mouse in *Anchors Aweigh.* Perhaps the most elaborate combination of cel animation and live action has been *Who Framed Roger Rabbit* (5.58).

Types of Computer Animation

Computer imaging has revolutionized animation. Software can quickly generate the thousands of slightly altered images that will supply the illusion of movement. On a creative level, software can be devised that enables filmmakers to create images of things that could not be filmed in the real world.

CGI (computer-generated imagery) was used occasionally for special effects scenes in the 1970s and 1980s. In the next decade, George Lucas's Industrial Light & Magic, Steve Jobs's Pixar Animation, and other firms developed powerful computers and complex programs for creating animated imagery. Images generated in computers were transferred to film either by filming directly off a high-resolution monitor or by using a laser to imprint individual pixels onto each frame. In 1995, Pixar's *Toy Story,* the first animated feature created entirely via computer, was released through Disney. It presented a compelling three-dimensional world peopled by figures that resembled Plasticine models **(10.118).** Pixar's programs steadily improved the rendition of fur (*Monsters, Inc.*), water (*Finding Nemo*), reflective metal (*Cars*), and other surface textures.

Toy Story's illusion of solid, sculptural cartoon figures helped establish the conventions of **3D computer animation.** (The term "3D" is also applied to movies giving a stereoscopic impression of depth when viewed through special glasses, as indicated in Chapter 5. Things get confusing when some animated films are released in stereoscopic 3D, so we can have "3D animation" that isn't presented in 3D projection. Usually only the context indicates which type of 3D is being referred to.) By contrast, **2D computer animation** uses digital imaging to simulate the look of traditional cel animation, as in *The Prince of Egypt* and *My Dog Tulip.*

"Computer animation" doesn't mean that the filmmaker just makes a few mouse clicks and the computer generates a movie. The software can work only with what the filmmaker puts into it. If you were to make a computer-animated film, your input might be a scanned image **(10.119)** or a three-dimensional model. You might draw on a digital tablet **(10.120, 10.121)** or build up a wire-frame image and

10.118

10.119

10.120

10.121

10.118–10.121 Computer animation. *Toy Story*'s computer-generated world (10.118). Nina Paley created all the images for her feature *Sita Sings the Blues* herself. Here she combines scans from printed images in a collage fashion, placing a scanned silhouette in the foreground, and placing a computer-generated sunburst shape as a background (10.119). Compare her image with *Frank Film,* 10.113. Paul and Sandra Fierlinger worked on their own to draw and color the 2D images for *My Dog Tulip.* Here Paul draws on a digital tablet (10.120). The result resembles traditional cel animation (10.121).

10.122

10.123

10.122–10.123 Digital animation mimics traditional animation. The digital characters in *Rango* resemble puppets (10.122). Ben Hibon designed digital silhouettes for the three-minute animated segment of *Harry Potter and the Deathly Hallows: Part 1* (10.123). Hibon, a fan of Lotte Reiniger, deliberately recalled the effects she achieved with paper cut-outs (10.112).

then render a surface onto it. Increasingly, visual material is fed into the computer using motion capture, as we saw in Chapter 4 (pp. 137–140). Once the basic visual material is digitized, you would create the most important bits of the figures' movements (called "keyframing"). The software fills in the frames between those poses, saving you the effort of creating every frame yourself. Other programs add color, texture, and lighting.

The kinds of films made with computer animation are similar to the traditional ones we surveyed above. 3D animation frequently resembles puppet films. In *Rango*, a Western parody featuring a chameleon as a reluctant sheriff, solid shapes and detailed textures suggest elaborate three-dimensional creatures (**10.122**). Similarly, the short segment, "The Tale of the Three Brothers," an animated scene in *Harry Potter and the Deathly Hallows: Part 1*, imitated the look of a traditional silhouette film (**10.123**).

Some animators, most famously Hiyao Miyazaki, combine analog and digital imaging (**10.124**). They may draw the pictures but use a paint program to add the color. Or a complicated camera movement may be rendered using computer animation, while the rest of the film is hand-drawn. This tactic was also used in *The Illusionist*, where a shot flying over a cityscape was created via computer while the other shots used traditional cel drawings.

Traditional animation was so labor intensive that for decades only the extensive Disney studio could regularly turn out full-length animated features. The lower cost of computer animation has led to an explosion of feature-length cartoons. Moreover,

CONNECT TO THE BLOG
www.davidbordwell.net/blog

For more on Ben Hibon's animated segment of *Harry Potter and the Deathly Hallows: Part 1,* see "Three minutes of 'Three Brothers.'"

CONNECT TO THE BLOG
www.davidbordwell.net/blog

We comment on the Oscar-nominated animated shorts for 2007 in "Do sell us shorts," and the ones for 2008 in "Do sell us shorts, the sequel." The rise of computer animation led to an expansion of the Best Animated feature Oscar category. We discuss the trend in "The other expanded Oscar category."

10.124 Merging cel and computer animation. In *Princess Mononoke,* five portions of the image (the grass and forest, the path and motion lines, the body of the Demon God, the shading of the Demon God, and Ashitaka riding away) were joined by computer. That yielded smoother, more complex motions than regular cel animation could achieve.

> ❝ As the six-year-old boy protested when I was introduced to him as the man who draws Bugs Bunny, 'He does not! He draws pictures of Bugs Bunny.'"
>
> —Chuck Jones, animator

> ❝ Animators have only one thing in common. We are all control freaks. And what is more controllable than the inanimate? You can control every frame, but at a cost. The cost is the chunks of your life that the time consuming process devours. It is as if the objects suck your time and energy away to feed their own life."
>
> —Simon Pummell, animator

as Nina Paley's *Sita Sings the Blues* and Paul and Sandra Fierlinger's *My Dog Tulip* show, an individual or small team can make professional-level features that play in theaters and at festivals. Thanks to digital technology, animation has moved into the mainstream of commercial filmmaking.

An Example of Traditional Animation: *Duck Amuck*

During the golden age of Hollywood short cartoons, from the 1930s to the 1950s, Disney and Warner Bros. were rivals. Disney animators had far greater resources at their disposal, and their animation was more elaborate and detailed than the simpler Warner product. Warner cartoonists fought back by exploiting the comic fantasy possible in animated films and playing with the medium in imaginative ways.

Warner Bros. cartoons reveled in fast, violent action. In *Rabbit Seasoning,* shotgun blasts keep rearranging Daffy Duck's features. The Warner team exploited an impudent tone as well, making Daffy and Bugs Bunny wisecracking cynics far removed from the sweet altruism of Mickey Mouse. Warner's comedy was often surreal, letting characters speak to the audience or mock studio executives. The unit's producer Leon Schlesinger appeared in *You Ought to Be in Pictures,* letting Porky Pig out of his contract so that he could move up to live-action features.

Of the many Warner experiments, none went further than *Duck Amuck,* directed by Charles M. (Chuck) Jones in 1953. It is now recognized as one of the masterpieces of American animation. Although it was made within the Hollywood system and uses narrative form, it has an experimental feel because it invites the audience to take part in an exploration of techniques of cel animation.

As the film begins, it seems to be a swashbuckler of the sort Daffy Duck had appeared in before, such as *The Scarlet Pumpernickel* (1950), itself a parody of one of Errol Flynn's most famous Warner Bros. films. When Daffy is first seen, he is a dueling musketeer. But when he moves to the left, he passes the edge of the painted background **(10.125)**. He's baffled, calls for scenery, and exits. A giant animated brush appears from outside the frame and paints in a barnyard **(10.126).** When Daffy enters, still in musketeer costume, he is annoyed but changes into a farmer's outfit. Such quick switches continue throughout the film, with the paintbrush and a pencil eraser adding and removing scenery, costumes, props, and even Daffy himself, with dizzying illogic. At times the sound cuts out, or the film seems to slip in the projector, so that we see the frame line in the middle of the screen **(10.127).**

10.125   **10.126**   **10.127**

10.125–10.127 The breakdown of cartoon space. Early in *Duck Amuck,* the background tapers off into white blankness (10.125). An inappropriate background for a swashbuckler appears in the blank space (10.126). In *Duck Amuck,* as the image apparently slips in the projector, Daffy splits in two and converses with himself (10.127).

All these tricks result in a peculiar narrative. Daffy repeatedly tries to get a plot, any plot, going, and the unseen animator constantly thwarts him. As a result, the film's principles of narrative progression are unusual. We begin to realize that the film is creating comedy by frankly acknowledging various techniques of animation: painted backgrounds, sound effects, framing, music, and so on. Meanwhile, the outrages perpetrated against Daffy escalate, and his frustration builds accordingly. Soon a mystery surfaces. Who is this perverse animator? Why is he tormenting Daffy?

At the end, the mystery is solved when the animator blasts Daffy with a bomb and then closes a door in his face **(10.128).** The next shot moves us to the animation desk itself, where we see Bugs Bunny, who has been the animator all along. He grins at us: "Ain't I a stinker?" **(10.129).** To a spectator who has never seen a Warner Bros. cartoon before, this ending would be puzzling. The narrative logic of *Duck Amuck* depends largely on knowing that Bugs and Daffy often costarred in other cartoons. Invariably the calm, ruthless Bugs would get the better of the manic, dim-witted Daffy.

Duck Amuck's use of animation techniques is just as unconventional as its narrative form. Because the action moves so quickly, we might fail on first viewing to note that aside from the credit title and the familiar "That's All, Folks!" logo, the film contains only four separate shots, three of which come in quick succession at the end. The bulk of the cartoon consists of a single lengthy and continuous shot—animation's equivalent of a long take. Yet the settings and situations change quickly as the paintbrush and pencil re-create the image, and Daffy moves in and out of the frame. Often he appears against a stark white background. Such moments emphasize the fact that in cel animation, the figures and background are layers that can be photographed separately. In *Duck Amuck,* the only certain space is that of the frame itself—a quality quite different from the clearly established settings provided in more conventional cartoons.

Similarly, the time frame becomes warped as Daffy moves into and out of diegetic situations, launching into one possible plotline only to find it cut short by the mystery animator. Daffy keeps assuming that the cartoon is just beginning, but time is flowing inexorably by in the outer cartoon, *Duck Amuck* itself. (Traditionally, cartoons were around seven minutes long to fit into the shorts section of movie theater programs.) At one point more than halfway through, Daffy shouts, "All right! Let's get this picture started!" Immediately a "The End" title appears, but Daffy pushes it aside and tries to take charge: "Ladies and gentlemen, there will be no further delays, so I shall attempt to entertain you in my own inimitable fashion," going into a soft-shoe routine against the blank background.

Duck Amuck also plays with onscreen and offscreen space. Many of the startling transformations we witness come from outside the limits of the frame. Most

10.128

10.129

10.128–10.129 Who's in charge here? A pencil protruding into the frame finally begins to reveal *Duck Amuck's* fiendish animator (10.128). As in many other Warner Bros. cartoons, Bugs turns and speaks to the audience after he triumphs over Daffy (10.129).

10.130   **10.131**

10.130–10.131 Daffy beseiged. Daffy is trapped without background or sound track (10.130). Daffy struggles to preserve his personal space as the frame collapses on him like syrup (10.131).

important, the unknown animator is in the space from which the camera photographs the scene, with the brush and pencil sliding in from under the camera. Daffy enters and exits frequently, and the frame often moves to reveal or conceal new portions of the scenery. When the sound cuts out entirely, Daffy asks to get it back **(10.130),** and then we hear a scratchy sound, as if from a phonograph playing a worn record. This unseen phonograph provides inappropriate noises—a machine gun when Daffy strums the guitar, a donkey's bray when he breaks it—an elaborate joke on the fact that in animated films, the sound is never really produced by the characters and objects we see on the screen.

The most spectacular gag involving the space outside the edges of the image comes when the top of the frame sags, dripping down onto Daffy **(10.131).** For a moment, what we can't see—the areas outside the frame—invade what goes on inside it.

The inventiveness of *Duck Amuck* sets it apart from typical Hollywood animated films. Yet Chuck Jones also motivates its play with the medium by using narrative form, situating it in the genre of comedy, and presenting familiar characters (Bugs mistreating Daffy, as usual). It's possible to go further, however. Other filmmakers have created experimental animation more surprising and disturbing than the antics of the Warner Bros. stars.

An Example of Experimental Animation: *Dimensions of Dialogue*

Jan Švankmajer, a Czech animator, is probably best known for the feature-length narrative films *Alice* and *Faust*. But he has also explored several daring formal options. His short film *Game of Stones* utilizes abstract form in the manner of *Ballet mécanique*. Another short, *Historia Naturae, Suita,* is organized by ancient biological categories (Reptiles, Birds, Sea-dwelling, and others) and whimsically correlates each one with a different musical form (tango, minuet, and so on). This film, incidentally, reminds us that categorical form isn't found only in documentaries.

Short or long, Švankmajer's films display a striking individual style. Most of his work relies on pixillation, which creates movement by shifting the positions of humans or objects frame by frame. His shots often look like still-life paintings, but they are seldom still. Stones, skulls, stuffed animals, and slabs of meat scuttle around Švankmajer's frames. In giving life to our everyday tools and furnishings, Švankmajer reawakens the sense of magic that we find in the earliest pixillated films.

But his approach to pixillation is sinister. Švankmajer's world is on the verge of decay or annihilation. Everything seems to crumble, collapse, or be crushed. Thanks to fast editing and high-key lighting, close-ups of familiar objects being

CONNECT TO THE BLOG
www.davidbordwell.net/blog

We look at a very creepy version of *Alice in Wonderland* made by Švankmajer in "That reminds me . . ."

❝ We have been seeking the feeling of emotional security in touch from the day we were born, in our tactile experiences with our own mother. This was our first contact with the world, before we could see it, smell it, hear it, or taste it."

—Jan Švankmajer, animator

10.132 10.133 10.134

10.132–10.134 "Factual Dialogue." Food profile meets Utensil profile in *Dimensions of Dialogue* (10.132). Office-Supply profile spits out Utensil profile (10.133). Throughout the film, the minced items are heaped together or whipped into a sludge that condenses into smooth heads (10.134).

maimed or pulled apart yield an almost horrifying effect. We expect to flinch from a decaying zombie, but why should we feel repelled when we see vegetables hammered to pulp, or scissors snipping apart a peach? Švankmajer's films arouse the sense of touch by dwelling on images that a child would call icky and that a grownup might find disgusting.

Dimensions of Dialogue displays the aggressive alchemy that is Švankmajer's hallmark. Its overall structure depends on an odd trio of categories: "Factual Dialogue," "Passionate Dialogue," and "Exhausting Dialogue." The titles are important clues to interpretation, but initially they serve to mark off three narrative encounters between vaguely human characters made of clay or assembled out of house-hold objects.

Dialogue as Aggression   The first episode is populated by vaguely human profiles. One is made out of common food items, another out of kitchen utensils, a third out of office supplies. The action consists of a simple theme-and-variations pattern. Two of the profiles lumber along and meet **(10.132)**. In each "dialogue," one profile devours the other, chops and mashes its components mercilessly, and spews out the bits **(10.133)**. After several such ravenous encounters, the profiles are reduced to mush, metal shards, and paper scraps. Finally the profiles emulsify into smooth rounded heads **(10.134)**. This shift into identical heads is puzzling but becomes coherent in retrospect. The process of reducing differences among the "speakers" will conclude later parts.

"Passionate Dialogue" gives us a more familiar story. Human figures made of smooth clay, reminiscent of the busts at the end of "Factual Dialogue," face each other across a table. One is male, the other female. They share a kiss, and this leads to a complete merger of their forms, an analogy to copulation **(10.135)**. Once they have split apart, a lump of clay is left over. It tries to get their attention, but both mistreat it. When the man tries to mash the "baby" into the woman's face, she scratches his face, and soon they are tearing each other apart. In the end both dribble into a mass of clay.

The final episode, "Exhausting Dialogue," revives motifs from the first two parts. Two clay busts of men's heads echo the end of Part 2 (10.134), though these middle-aged fellows aren't identical, as the heads were earlier. The heads spring up from a mass of clay and rest on a table, recalling the end of the second part. As in the first part, household objects are brought into play in a cycle of turn-taking that resembles conversation. Each man sticks out his tongue and reveals an object resting on it **(10.136)**. Returning to a theme-and-variations structure that sets up clear expectations, this "Exhausting Dialogue" is also an exhaustive one, running through humorous but also disturbing combinations of familiar things.

10.135 "Passionate Dialogue." Male and female figures kiss and merge into one another.

10.136

10.137

10.138

10.136–10.138 "Exhausting Dialogue." Butter knife and bread meet in the third section (10.136). The opening passage suggests cooperation, with each man's object appropriate to his partner's. In the second round of exchanges, however, the objects don't suit one another, and the encounters turn violent (10.137). The dialogue ends with deflated heads (10.138).

In the first round, each man's proffered object complements the other man's. One offers a toothbrush, the other toothpaste. One offers bread, the other butter. After four turns in which each pair of objects harmonizes, the men switch positions. Now the process breaks down crazily. Toothpaste is spread on bread, butter drips onto a pencil, and a pencil sharpener grinds away at a toothpaste tube. Every possible mismatch is tried, always with disastrous results **(10.137)**.

The heads, now starting to crack, swap places again. Each man's tongue offers his counterpart an identical object—shoe to shoe, laces to laces, and so on. But this apparent harmony is actually undercut because the objects always start fighting. Slices of bread become jaws; shoelaces wrestle one another. When all of the possibilities have been exhausted, the heads sag like fallen soufflés **(10.138)**.

Formal Patterning: Theme and Variations The simplicity of each episode highlights some subtle variations. Part 1's profiles are flat, whereas figures in the following sections are three dimensional. Švankmajer has filmed each set of conversationalists differently, with Part 2 introducing head-on views and shot/reverse shot angles. The couple in Part 2 have blank eyes, but the men in Part 3 have realistic and expressive eyes of different colors. Parts 1 and 3 assemble kitchen and office implements. The profile figures are collaged from familiar tools, while the tongue sequence brings mismatched objects into harsh conflict. Švankmajer was affiliated with the Czech branch of the Surrealist movement, reminding us that artists in this vein often used bizarre juxtapositions to evoke the mystery and irrationality of life. (See pp. 468–470.)

The force of these juxtapositions is greater because the objects have vivid textures. The smooth clay figures in Part 2 eventually become a mass of smudges, while the poor offspring of the mating ceremony gets mashed against the table and its parents. The brutal chopping and shredding of items in Part 1 are shown in high-key lighting more appropriate to food photography, while Part 3's punishing tongue close-ups could make any viewer squirm **(10.139, 10.140)**. The film would be much less harsh without all the glimpses of unassuming objects pulped and shredded, accompanied by whacks and crunches on the sound track.

Each episode features violent confrontation. Part 2's erotic encounter gives conflict an eerie human face, and the other sections are just as disquieting. We're not used to seeing tools and vegetables maiming each other, or tongues flexing like fists. Although the assaults have a dark humor, the imagery and abrupt, grating noises suggest a mechanized massacre **(10.141, 10.142)**. In making us feel the pain of these inanimate objects, Švankmajer has made a shocking, violent movie without gore.

10.139

10.140

10.141

10.142

10.139–10.142 Tabletop Armageddon. In Part 1, an envelope viciously crushes thimbles (10.139). In Part 3 a pencil sharpener peels slivers of the butter knife onto the tongue (10.140). An apple is strangled in Part 1 (10.141), and pencils collide like jousting lances in the last segment (10.142).

Conversation as Annihilation In about 11 minutes, *Dimensions of Dialogue* surveys different sorts of interactions, and it cries out for thematic interpretation. Here, instead of being a civil exchange of ideas and opinions, dialogue consists of unbridled attack and retaliation. In the "Factual Dialogue," even before views are exchanged, one head minces another. But nobody wins: Eventually all three speakers are reduced to rubbish and then identical busts. Is the film suggesting that inducing someone to agree with you eventually creates a bland uniformity?

Švankmajer made the film during a period of severe political repression in Czechoslovakia, and some critics see the first episode as an implied protest against state-imposed conformity. From this perspective, the "factual" side of the conversation wouldn't be a matter of arguing about facts but rather recognizing the basic fact that under tyranny dialogue is nonexistent. Opinions get crushed, and everyone winds up looking and thinking the same. Significantly, the film was banned by the Communist government.

Part 2 doesn't start with the violence that opens the first dialogue. Here the couple's mutual attraction seems to hold out the possibility of harmony. But soon they attack their offspring and eventually one another. Again, the individuals are reduced to uniformity, a heap of clay, but this time in a family setting.

Harmony and cooperation are again seen at the start of Part 3. When butter meets bread and laces wind their way onto shoes, both parties seem to be in agreement. Yet the tongue game spirals into an exchange of mismatched objects, as if the two heads are talking past one another, and violence is the result. During the third round of Part 3, the heads thrust out identical objects, in effect "saying the same thing." Yet even the identical objects attack one another. This might imply that each person isn't really responding to the other, that dialogue has become two

CONNECT TO THE BLOG
www.davidbordwell.net/blog

We profile another great experimental animator in "Len Lye, Renaissance Kiwi."

monologues. In the end, both partners have collapsed, becoming, like the characters at the end of the previous parts, indistinguishable.

Throughout the film, face-to-face interactions are brutally aggressive and self-destructive, and they usually end in exhaustion. This is a fairly bleak view of human relationships, but delivered with arresting imagery and black humor.

Like *Duck Amuck, Dimensions of Dialogue* summons up bizarre transformations and creates comedy by violating our expectations. But Daffy's dislocated adventures are eventually explained by Bugs's prankishness. The Švankmajer flavor is more elusive. Setting a trio of narratives within the frame of categorical form, he takes us through sharply etched formal variations. These present motifs that are more disturbing, even queasy, than the slapstick offered by Chuck Jones. The very different experiences provided by the two films illustrate the range of expressive choices available to the film animator.

SUMMARY

In most situations, when we watch a film, we have some idea of what type it will be, and this shapes our expectations. If we're seeing a documentary, we expect to learn something, perhaps in a way that will entertain or move us in the process. An experimental film, however, will probably challenge us, rather like a game, to figure out its patterns and strategies. Animated films that we encounter in theaters will most likely amuse and entertain us.

In watching a documentary film, we can ask ourselves what it claims to be true about the world. Does it present one or more categories of things? If so, how are these organized? Is the filmmaker trying to convey an attitude about the topic? Are there abstract or narrative portions that lend interest to its subject? Or is the topic organized as an argument? If so, is the argument convincing?

As we have seen, experimental films often employ abstract or associational formal patterns. From moment to moment, we can try to understand the connections among shots or small-scale segments. Is there a similarity in shapes on the screen, in directions of movement, or in colors? If so, the film probably uses abstract form. But if you detect linkages that shift in evocative ways as the film progresses, associational form is probably at work.

Animated films can present narratives, convey documentary information, or experiment with the medium. In most cases, however, you should be able to detect generally what techniques were used in making the film. Is the movement on the screen based on drawings or on moving puppets, clay figures, flat cut-outs, or computer-generated images? If you're attentive to how these techniques are employed, you should be able to enjoy the freedom from reality that animation offers the filmmaker.

The Classical Narrative Cinema
His Girl Friday

1940. Columbia. Directed by Howard Hawks. Script by Charles Lederer from the play *The Front Page* by Ben Hecht and Charles MacArthur. Photographed by Joseph Walker. Edited by Gene Havlick. Music by Morris W. Stoloff. With Cary Grant, Rosalind Russell, Ralph Bellamy, Gene Lockhart, Porter Hall.

His Girl Friday is often said to be the fastest sound comedy ever made, largely because most of the dialogue is delivered at a machine-gun pace. It resembles *The Social Network,* another movie driven by quick thinkers and fast talkers. To speed up the dialogue, director Howard Hawks encouraged his actors to allow few pauses and to start talking before the previous actor had finished. In *His Girl Friday,* however, dialogue isn't the only factor creating a sense of speed. Conventions of classical narrative form, along with particular film techniques, play important parts in this whirlwind experience.

> " If you'll ever listen to some people who are talking, especially in a scene of any excitement, they all talk at the same time. All it needs is a little extra work on the dialogue. You put a few words in front of somebody's speech and put a few words at the end, and they can overlap it. It gives you a sense of speed that actually doesn't exist. And you can make the people talk a little faster."
> —Howard Hawks, director

Lines of Action and Character Goals Classical Hollywood narrative is well suited to give the impression of speed. Its tradition of concise exposition and tightly woven plotting can carry us along swiftly. For example, *His Girl Friday* contains only 13 major scenes, so the filmmakers haven't chosen to create the pace through a series of very brief sequences. Moreover, the action takes place in only a handful of settings, so there's a sense of greater pressure as people rush in and out of the same locale and new groups of characters collide with one another in pursuit of their own purposes.

Those purposes fit into broader patterns of development. As we saw in Chapter 3 (pp. 85–86), classical Hollywood cinema often centers stories on characters with definite traits who want to achieve specific goals. These characters' contrasting traits and conflicting goals propel *His Girl Friday*'s plot forward along two primary lines of action.

1. *The romance.* Hildy Johnson wants to quit newspaper reporting and settle down with Bruce Baldwin. But Hildy's editor and ex-husband, Walter Burns, has a different goal: He wants her to continue as his reporter and to remarry him. Given these two goals, the characters enter into a conflict in several stages. First, Walter lures Hildy by promising a nest egg for the couple in exchange for her writing one last story. But Walter also arranges to have Bruce robbed. Learning of Walter's scheme, Hildy tears up her story. Walter continues to delay Bruce, however, and eventually wins Hildy through her renewed interest in reporting. She changes her mind about marrying Bruce and stays with Walter.

2. *Crime and politics.* Earl Williams is to be hanged for shooting a policeman. The city's political bosses are relying on the execution to ensure their reelection. This is the goal shared by the mayor and the sheriff. But Walter's goal is to induce the governor to reprieve Williams and thus unseat the mayor's party at the polls. Through the sheriff's stupidity, Williams escapes and is concealed by Hildy and Walter. In the meantime, a reprieve does arrive from the governor; the mayor bribes the messenger into leaving. Williams is discovered, but the messenger returns with the reprieve in time to save Williams from death and Walter and Hildy from jail. Presumably, the mayor's political allies will be defeated at the election.

The crime-and-politics line of action is tied tightly to the romance line. Walter uses the Williams case to lure Hildy back to him, Hildy chases the Williams story instead of returning to Bruce, Bruce's mother reveals to the police that Walter has concealed Williams, and so on. More specifically, the interplay of the two lines of action alters the characters' goals. By inducing Hildy to write the story, Walter fulfills his goals of embarrassing the politicos and of tempting Hildy back into his life. Hildy's goals are more significantly changed. After she destroys her article, her abrupt decision to report on Earl Williams's jailbreak marks her acceptance of Walter's scheme. Her later willingness to hide Williams and her indifference to Bruce's pleas firmly establish her goals as linked to Walter's.

As the two goal-oriented plotlines interconnect, the actions start to multiply and expand. For example, Walter's delaying tactics (involving his confederates Duffy, Louie, and Angie) set up short-term bursts of cause and effect. At the same time, Bruce is shouldered out of the romance plot as he is shuttled in and out of precinct jails. Earl Williams undergoes a parallel experience as he is manipulated by Hildy, the sheriff, the psychologist, and Walter. Swiftly, the tangle of romance and politics pulls in secondary characters, such as Mollie Malloy (Williams's sweetheart), Bruce's mother, the other reporters, and Pettibone, the delightful emissary from the governor. All these characters aren't simply pawns of the larger plotlines, however. They can affect those plotlines by their actions, as when Earl Williams escapes or Mrs. Baldwin bursts in to denounce Walter as a kidnapper. With so many characters pulled in, swerving the action this way or that, the plot twists can become rapid and unpredictable.

Picking up the Pace: Time Pressures   Classical narrative not only tries to tie all the characters to a broader momentum; it also ties one scene to another. In *His Girl Friday,* an event at the end of one scene becomes a cause leading to an effect—the event that begins the next scene. For example, at the end of the first scene, Walter offers to take Bruce and Hildy to lunch; scene 2 starts with the three of them arriving at the restaurant. In *His Girl Friday,* this linear pattern helps keep the plot action hurtling, setting up each new scene quickly at the end of the previous one.

One of the most common ways in which Hollywood storytelling dials up the pace involves setting a deadline for the action. The deadline is a convention of the newspaper genre, adding a built-in suspense factor. But in *His Girl Friday,* each line of action has its own deadlines. The mayor and the sheriff face an obvious deadline: Earl Williams must be hanged before the governor can reprieve him. In his political strategizing, Walter Burns faces the same deadline: He wants Williams reprieved.

The romance plot has deadlines as well. Bruce and Hildy are set to leave on a train bound for Albany and marriage at four o'clock that very day. Walter's machinations keep forcing the couple to postpone their departure. Add to this the fact that when Bruce comes to confront Hildy and Walter, he exits with the defiant ultimatum "I'm leaving on the nine o'clock train!" (Hildy misses that train as well.) The film's sense of mounting tension depends on the tight deadlines. If Earl Williams were to be hanged next month, or if the election were two years off, or if Bruce and Hildy were planning a marriage at some distant future date, the sense of dramatic pressure would be lacking. The piled-up deadlines squeeze together all the lines of action and sustain the breathless pace of the film.

His Girl Friday finds another, more unusual way to drive that pace. The plot presents events in straightforward chronological order, but it takes remarkable liberties with story duration. Of course, since the primary story action consumes about nine hours (from around 12:30 P.M. to around 9:30 P.M.), we expect that certain portions of time *between* scenes will be eliminated. What's unusual is that the time *within* scenes has been accelerated as well.

At the start of the very first scene, for example, the clock in the *Post* office reads 12:36; after 12 minutes of screen time have passed, the same clock reads 12:57. Yet there have been no editing ellipses in the scene; the story duration has simply been compressed. If you time the film's longest scene (33 minutes!), you will find even more remarkable acceleration. People leave on long trips and return less than 10 minutes later. Again, the editing presents continuity of duration: It's story time that goes faster than screen time. This temporal compression combines with everything we've surveyed so far—tight causal connections, unexpected entrances and exits, and frenetically rushed dialogue—to create the film's breakneck pace.

With so much talk and turmoil, you might expect that the cutting would be quick. But actually the film's editing rhythm is much slower than we'd find in today's intensified continuity approach. The average shot in the film runs 15 seconds, four to five times slower than what we'd get in a comedy now. Instead, by sustaining the shot, Hawks can let the dialogue move more quickly, without distracting cuts, and can shift his actors around the frame in expressive patterns. Many shots let staging and the actors' performances define the comedy (**11.1, 11.2**). And for simultaneous dialogue, it's preferable to keep the actors in the same shot rather than trying to cut between them (**11.3**).

When Hawks does cut, he often uses continuity tactics to anticipate or underline a dramatic point. He will smoothly match on action during a comic climax (**11.4, 11.5**). Virtually every scene, especially the early restaurant lunch and the dizzying final scene in the courthouse pressroom, offers many subtle examples of classical editing. Hawks's aim is clearly to enhance the dialogue and the plot twists.

The film increases the tension of these rapid scenes through one device that involves both sound and mise-en-scene. We'd expect that newspapermen in 1939 use telephones, but *His Girl Friday* makes the phone integral to the narrative. Walter's subterfuges demand phones. At the restaurant, he pretends to be summoned away to a call; he makes and breaks promises to Hildy via phones; he directs Duffy and other minions by phone. More generally, the pressroom is equipped with a veritable flotilla of phones, enabling the reporters to contact their editors. And, of course, Bruce keeps calling Hildy from the various police stations in which he continually finds himself. The telephones become a communications network that relays story action from point to point.

CONNECT TO THE BLOG
www.davidbordwell.net/blog

How did *His Girl Friday* go from obscurity to being hailed as a masterpiece? See "Creating a classic, with a little help from your pirate friends."

11.1

11.2

11.3

11.4

11.5

11.1–11.5 Long takes and cutting for comic flow. In *His Girl Friday,* Walter and Hildy pace in a complete circuit around the desk (11.1). Cutting would distract from Walter's dynamic and comic postures (11.2). Several long takes employ deep-space staging and deep-focus cinematography (11.3). In the opening scene, Hildy's action of throwing her purse at Walter (11.4) is matched at the cut to a more distant framing (11.5). The mismatch in his arm positions goes unnoticed in projection, probably because we tend to focus on Hildy's broader gestures.

Given the prominence of phones, Hawks visually and sonically orchestrates the characters' use of them. There are many variations. One person may be talking on the phone, or several may be talking in turn on different phones, or several may be talking at once on different phones, or a phone conversation may take place during a conversation elsewhere in the room. When several reporters race in to phone their editors, the cutting accentuates single lines or words. Later, while Hildy frantically phones hospitals, Walter hollers into another phone (11.3). When Bruce returns for Hildy, a confused din arises that eventually sorts itself into three sonic lines: Bruce begging Hildy to listen, Hildy obsessively typing her story, and Walter yelling into the phone for Duffy to clear page one ("No, no, leave the rooster story! That's human interest!"). (See 5.31.) Like much in *His Girl Friday,* the telephones are pulled into the unfolding action in ways that boost the rapid tempo.

North by Northwest

1959. MGM. Directed by Alfred Hitchcock. Script by Ernest Lehman. Photographed by Robert Burks. Edited by George Tomasini. Music composed by Bernard Herrmann. With Cary Grant, Eva Marie Saint, James Mason, Leo G. Carroll, Jessie Royce Landis.

Hitchcock long insisted that he made thrillers, not mystery films. For him, creating a puzzle was less important than generating suspense and surprise. While there are mystery elements in films such as *Notorious, Stage Fright,* and *Psycho, North by Northwest* shows that the mystery element can serve as merely a pretext for intriguing the audience. The film's tight causal unity enables Hitchcock to create an engrossing plot that fulfills the norms of classical filmmaking. This plot is presented through a narration that continually emphasizes suspense and surprise. (For more on thrillers, see pp. 332–334.)

Plot and Counterplot   Like most spy films, *North by Northwest* has a complex plot. There are two main lines of action. In one, a gang of spies mistakes advertising agency executive Roger Thornhill for a secret agent, George Kaplan. Although the spies fail to kill Thornhill, he becomes the chief suspect in a murder that the gang commits. He must flee the police while trying to track down the real George Kaplan. Unfortunately, Kaplan does not exist; he is merely a decoy invented by the United States Intelligence Agency (USIA). Thornhill's pursuit of Kaplan leads to the second line of action: his meeting and falling in love with Eve Kendall, who is the mistress of Philip Van Damm, the spies' leader. The spy-chase line and the romance line further connect when Thornhill learns that Eve is actually a double agent, secretly working for the USIA. He must then rescue her from Van Damm, who has discovered her identity and has resolved to kill her. In the course of all this, Thornhill also discovers that the spies are smuggling government secrets out of the country in pieces of sculpture.

From even so bare an outline, it should be evident that the film's plot presents many conventional patterns to the viewer. There's the search pattern, seen when Thornhill sets out to find Kaplan. There's also a journey pattern: Thornhill and his pursuers travel from New York to Chicago and then to Rapid City, South Dakota, with side excursions as well. In addition, the last two-thirds of the plot is organized around the romance between Thornhill and Eve. Moreover, each pattern develops markedly in the course of the film. In the course of his search, Thornhill must sometimes assume the identity of Kaplan, the man he is trailing. The journey pattern gets varied by all the vehicles Thornhill uses—cabs, train, pickup truck, police car, bus, ambulance, and airplane.

Most subtly, the romance line of action is constantly modified by Thornhill's changing awareness of the situation. Believing that Eve wants to help him, he falls in love with her. But then he learns that she sent him to the murderous appointment

CONNECT TO THE BLOG
www.davidbordwell.net/blog

We have several entries on Hitchcock's unique approach to storytelling. See *"Dial M for Murder:* Hitchcock frets not at his narrow room" and "Sir Alfred simply must have his set pieces: *The Man Who Knew Too Much* (1934)." Our series on his idea of suspense and surprise starts with "Hitchcock, Lessing, and the bomb under the table."

" He (Hitchcock) was fairly universal, he made people shiver everywhere. And he made thrillers that are also equivalent to works of literature."

—Jean-Luc Godard, director, *Breathless*

at Prairie Stop, and he becomes cold and suspicious. When he discovers her at the auction with Van Damm, his anger and bitterness impel him to humiliate her and make Van Damm doubt her loyalty. Only after the USIA chief, the "Professor," tells him that Eve is really an agent does Thornhill realize that he has misjudged and endangered her. Each step in his growing awareness alters his romantic relation to Eve.

This intricate plot is unified and made comprehensible by other strategies of classical Hollywood storytelling. *North by Northwest* has a strict time scheme, comprising four days and nights (followed by a brief epilogue on a later night). The first day and a half take place in New York; the second night on the train to Chicago; the third day in Chicago and at Prairie Stop; and the fourth day at Mount Rushmore. The timetable is neatly established early in the film. Van Damm, having abducted Roger as Kaplan, announces: "In two days you're due at the Ambassador East in Chicago, and then at the Sheraton-Johnson Hotel in Rapid City, South Dakota." This itinerary prepares the spectator for the shifts in action that will occur in the rest of the film.

Apart from the time scheme, the film also gives Thornhill specific traits of character. He's initially presented as a resourceful liar when he grabs a cab from another pedestrian. Later, he will have to lie in many circumstances to evade capture. Similarly, Roger is established as a heavy drinker, and his ability to hold his liquor will enable him to survive Van Damm's attempt to force him to kill himself when driving while drunk.

A great many motifs are repeated and help make the film cohere. Roger is constantly in danger from heights: his car hangs over a cliff; he must sneak out on the ledge of a hospital; he has to clamber up Van Damm's modernistic cliff-top house; and he and Eve wind up dangling from the faces on Mount Rushmore. Thornhill's constant changing of vehicles also constitutes a motif that Hitchcock varies. A subtler example is the motif that conveys Thornhill's growing suspicion of Eve (**11.6, 11.7**).

11.6

11.7

11.6–11.7 Gesture motifs for psychological revelation. On the train, when Thornhill and Eve kiss, his hands close tenderly around her hair (11.6). But later, when he believes she has sent him to be murdered, his hands freeze in place, as if he fears touching her (11.7).

Narration and Knowledge, Suspense and Surprise   Still, narrative unity alone can't explain the film's strong emotional appeal. In Chapter 3's discussion of narration, we used *North by Northwest* as an example of a hierarchy of knowledge (p. 88). We suggested that as the film progresses, sometimes we're restricted to what Roger knows, but at other times, we know significantly more than he does. At still other moments, our range of knowledge, while greater than Roger's, is not as great as that of other characters. Now we're in a position to see how Hitchcock's decision to create this pattern of narration helps create suspense and surprise across the whole film.

The most straightforward way in which the film's narration controls our knowledge is through the many optical point-of-view (POV) shots Hitchcock employs. This device yields a degree of subjective depth: We see what a character sees more or less as she or he sees it. More important here, the optical POV shot restricts us to what that character learns at that moment. Hitchcock gives almost every major character a shot of this sort. The very first optical POV we see in the film is taken from the position of the two spies who are watching Roger apparently respond to the paging of George Kaplan. Later, we view events through the eyes of Eve, of Van Damm, of his henchman Leonard, and even of a clerk at a ticket counter.

By far the greatest number of POV shots are attached to Thornhill. Through his eyes, we see his approach to the Townsend mansion, the mail he finds in the library, his drunken drive along the cliff, and the airplane that is "crop dusting where there ain't no crops." Some of the most extreme uses of optical POV give us Roger's experience directly, as when he's punched by a state trooper or caught in the path of a fuel truck.

Thornhill's optical POV shots function within a narration that is often restricted not only to what he *sees* but also to what he *knows*. The plane attack at Prairie Stop, for example, is confined wholly to Roger's range of knowledge. Hitchcock could have cut away from Roger waiting by the road in order to show us the villains spotting him from their plane, but he doesn't. Similarly, when Roger is searching for George Kaplan's room and gets a phone call from the two henchmen, Hitchcock could have used crosscutting to show the villains phoning from the lobby. (Telephone calls, as we mention on p. 263, are always notable decision points for directors.) Instead, we learn that the thugs are in the hotel when Roger does. And when Thornhill and his mother hurry out of the room, Hitchcock does not use crosscutting to show the villains in pursuit. This makes it more startling when Roger and his mother get on the elevator and discover the two men there already. In scenes like these, confining us to Thornhill's range of knowledge sharpens the effect of surprise.

Sometimes the same effect comes from the film's restricting us to Roger's range of knowledge and then giving us information that he does not at the moment have. On p. 88, we suggested that this sort of surprise occurs when the plot shifts us from Roger's escape from the United Nations murder to the scene at the USIA office, where the staff discusses the case. At this point, we learn that there is no George Kaplan—something that Roger won't discover for many more scenes to come.

The abrupt shifts from Roger's range of knowledge yield a similar effect during the train trip from New York to Chicago. During several scenes, Eve Kendall helps Thornhill evade the police. Finally, they are alone and relatively safe in her compartment. At this point, the narration shifts the range of knowledge. We see a message delivered to another compartment. Hands unfold a note: "What do I do with him in the morning?" The camera tracks back to show us Leonard and Van Damm reading the message. We realize that Eve is not merely a sympathetic stranger but someone working for the spy ring. Again, Roger will learn this much later.

Such moments evoke surprise, but we have already noted that Hitchcock claimed in general to prefer to generate suspense (p. 89). Suspense is created by giving the spectator *more* information than the character has. In the scenes we've just mentioned, once the short-term surprise has been achieved, the narration can use our superior knowledge to build suspense across several sequences. After the audience learns that there is no George Kaplan, every attempt by Thornhill to find him builds up suspense about whether he will discover the truth. Once we learn that Eve is working for Van Damm, her message to Roger on behalf of Kaplan will make us worry that Roger will fall into the trap.

In these examples, suspense arises across a series of scenes. Hitchcock also uses unrestricted narration to build up suspense within a single scene. The sequence in Chicago's Union Station employs both cutting and camera movement to widen our knowledge and create suspense. Crosscutting moves us from Roger shaving in the men's room to Eve talking on the phone. A lateral tracking shot reveals that she is talking to Leonard, who's giving her orders from an adjacent phone booth. We are now certain that the message she will give Roger will endanger him, and the suspense is ratcheted up. Note, though, that the narration doesn't reveal the conversation itself. As often happens, Hitchcock conceals some information for the sake of further surprises.

The Climax on Mount Rushmore Thornhill's knowledge expands as the lines of action develop. On the third day, he discovers that Eve is Van Damm's mistress, that she is a double agent, and that Kaplan doesn't exist. He agrees to help the Professor in a scheme to clear Eve of any suspicion in Van Damm's eyes. When the scheme (a faked shooting in the Mount Rushmore restaurant) succeeds, Roger believes that Eve will leave Van Damm. Once more, however, he has been duped (as we have). The Professor insists that she must go off to Europe that night on Van

11.8

11.9

11.10

11.11

11.8–11.11 Embedded POV patterns. In *North by Northwest,* Thornhill watches in dismay as Leonard betrays Eve to Van Damm (11.8, 11.9). When Van Damm reacts by punching Leonard, he is seen from Leonard's POV (11.10). Then Leonard is seen from his POV (11.11). This POV exchange is enclosed within a broader pattern presenting the entire scene through Thornhill's range of knowledge.

Damm's private flight. Roger resists, but he is knocked out and held captive in a hospital. His escape leads to the final major sequence of the film.

Here the plot resolves all its lines of action, and the narration continues to expand and contract our knowledge for the sake of suspense and surprise. This climactic sequence comprises almost 300 shots and runs for several minutes, but we can conveniently divide it into three sections.

In the first section, Roger arrives at Van Damm's house and reconnoiters. He clambers up to the window and learns from a conversation between Leonard and Van Damm that the piece of sculpture they bought at the auction contains microfilm. More important, he watches Leonard inform Van Damm that Eve is an American agent. This action is conveyed largely through optical POV (**11.8, 11.9;** also 3.20–3.22). At two moments, as Leonard and Van Damm face each other, the narration gives us optical POV shots from each man's standpoint (**11.10, 11.11**), but these are enclosed within Roger's ongoing witnessing of the situation. For the first time in the film, Roger has more knowledge of the situation than any other character. He knows how the smuggling has been done, and he discovers that the villains intend to murder Eve.

The second phase of the sequence begins when Roger enters Eve's bedroom. She has gone back downstairs and is sitting on a couch. Again, Hitchcock emphasizes the restriction to Thornhill's knowledge through optical POV shots (**11.12, 11.13**). This time, however, he doesn't show us what the other character sees and instead only suggests Eve's reaction (**11.14**). Roger's range of knowledge remains the broadest, and his optical POV encloses another character's experience. On a pretext, Eve returns to her room, and Roger warns her not to get on the plane.

As the spies make their way to the landing field outside, Roger starts to follow. Now Hitchcock's narration shifts again to show Van Damm's housekeeper spotting Roger's reflection in a television set. As earlier in the film, we know more than Roger does, and this generates suspense when she walks out . . . and returns with a pistol aimed at him.

The third section of the climax is an extended chase that shifts between restricted and unrestricted narration. As Eve is about to get on the plane, she hears shots from the house. Has the housekeeper shot Roger? No. When he arrives to rescue her, he reminds her that Leonard's gun had blanks. With the statuette the couple start to flee across the presidents' faces on Mount Rushmore. There's some crosscutting here, but mostly we are restricted to what Roger and Eve know.

11.12   **11.13**   **11.14**

11.12–11.14 **Suppressing characters' POVs.** To warn Eve, Roger uses his ROT monogrammed matchbook (a motif set up on the train as a joke). He tosses the matchbook down toward her (11.12, 11.13). This initiates suspense when Leonard sees it, but he unconcernedly puts it in an ashtray on the coffee table. Earlier Hitchcock shifted optical POV to present the face-off between Van Damm and Leonard (11.10, 11.11). Now he does not show us Eve's face or what she sees. Instead, through Roger's eyes, we see her back stiffen; we *infer* that she has noticed the matchbook (11.14).

> ❝ In *North by Northwest* during the scene on Mount Rushmore I wanted Cary Grant to hide in Lincoln's nostril and have a fit of sneezing. The Parks Commission of the Department of Interior was rather upset at this thought. I argued until one of their number asked me how I would like it if they had Lincoln play the scene in Cary Grant's nose. I saw their point at once.❞
>
> —Alfred Hitchcock, director

At the climax, Eve is dangling over the edge while she clings to Roger's hand and Leonard grinds his shoe into Roger's other hand. A rifle shot cracks out and Leonard falls unexpectedly; now the narration reveals that he was targeted by a marksman under the Professor's direction. Throughout this sequence, periods of suspense are interrupted by momentary surprises, as we recognize that there was something important we didn't know.

The same effect gets magnified at the very end. In a series of optical POV shots, Roger pulls Eve up from the cliff edge. But this gesture is made continuous, in both sound and image, with that of him pulling her up to a train bunk. The narration ignores the details of their rescue in order to cut short the suspense of Eve's plight. Such a self-conscious transition isn't completely out of place in a film that has taken time for offhand jokes. (During the opening credits, Hitchcock himself is shown being shut out of a bus. As Roger strides into the Plaza Hotel, about to be plunged into his adventure, the Muzak is playing "It's a Most Unusual Day.") This final twist shows once again that Hitchcock's moment-by-moment manipulation of our knowledge yields a constantly shifting play between the probable and the unexpected, between suspense and surprise.

Do The Right Thing

> 1989. Forty Acres and a Mule Filmworks (distributed by Universal). Directed and scripted by Spike Lee. Photographed by Ernest Dickerson. Edited by Barry Alexander Brown. Music by Bill Lee et al. With Danny Aiello, Ossie Davis, Ruby Dee, Giancarlo Esposito, Spike Lee, Bill Nunn, John Turturro, Rosie Perez.

At first viewing, Spike Lee's *Do The Right Thing,* with its many brief, disconnected scenes, restlessly wandering camera, and large number of characters without goals might not seem a classical narrative film. And, indeed, in some ways, it does depart from classical usage. Yet it has the redundantly clear action and strong forward impetus that we associate with classical filmmaking. It also fits into a familiar genre of American cinema—the social problem film. Moreover, closer analysis reveals that Lee has also drawn on many traits of classicism to give an underlying unity to this apparently loosely constructed plot.

A Day in the Life of a Community   *Do The Right Thing* takes place in the predominantly African-American Bedford–Stuyvesant section of Brooklyn during a heat wave. Sexual and racial tensions rise as Mookie, a pizza delivery man, tries to get along with his Puerto Rican girlfriend, Tina, and with his Italian-American boss, Sal. An elderly drunk, Da Mayor, sets out to ingratiate himself with his sharp-tongued neighbor, Mother Sister. An escalating quarrel between Sal and two customers, Buggin' Out and Radio Raheem, leads to a fight in which Radio Raheem is killed by police. A riot ensues, and Sal's pizzeria is burned.

Do The Right Thing has many more individual sequences than *His Girl Friday* or *North by Northwest*. Even if we lump together some of the very briefest scenes, there are at least 42 segments. Laying out a detailed segmentation of *Do The Right Thing* might be useful for another analysis, but here we want to concentrate on how Lee weaves his many scenes into a whole.

Setting helps hold the characters and their actions together. The entire narrative is played out on one block in Bedford–Stuyvesant. Sal's Famous Pizzeria and the Korean market lie at one end of the block, where much of the action takes place. Other scenes take place in or in front of the brownstone buildings that line the rest of the street.

In accord with the limited setting, the action consumes a short time span, running from one morning to the next. Structuring a film around a brief stretch in the lives of several major characters isn't unknown in American filmmaking, as with *Street Scene, Dead End, American Graffiti, Car Wash, Nashville,* and *Magnolia.*

The radio DJ Mister Señor Love Daddy provides a running motif that binds the film's events together. He appears in close-up in the first shot of the opening scene, and this initial broadcast provides important information about the setting and the weather, a heat wave that ratchets up the characters' tensions and contributes to the final burst of violence. As the DJ speaks, the camera tracks slowly out and cranes up to reveal the street, still empty in the early morning. At intervals throughout the film, Mister Señor Love Daddy provides commentary on the action, as when he tells a group of characters spewing racist diatribes to "chill out." The music he plays creates sound bridges between otherwise unconnected scenes, since the radios in different locations are often tuned to his station. The end of the film echoes the beginning, as the camera tracks with Mookie in the street and we hear the DJ's voice giving a spiel similar to the one on the previous morning, then dedicating the final song to the dead Radio Raheem.

As the setting and the neighborhood radio station suggest, *Do The Right Thing* centers more on the community as a whole than on a few central characters. The need to respect community, it seems, is a central theme of the film. On the one hand, there are older traditions that are worth preserving, represented by the elderly characters: the moral strength of the matriarch Mother Sister, the decency and courage of Da Mayor, the wit and common sense of the three chatting men, M. L., Sweet Dick Willie, and Coconut Sid. On the other hand, the younger people need to create a new community spirit by overcoming sexual and racial conflict. The women are portrayed as trying to make the angry young African-American men more responsible. Tina pressures Mookie to pay more attention to her and to their son; Jade lectures both her brother Mookie and the excitable Buggin' Out, telling the latter he should direct his energies toward doing "something positive in the community." The emphasis on community is underscored by the fact that most of the characters address one another by their nicknames.

One of the main conflicts in the film arises when Sal refuses to add some pictures of African-American heroes to his "Hall of Fame" photo gallery of Italian Americans. Sal might have become a sort of elder statesman in the community, where he has run his pizzeria for 25 years. He seems to like the kids who eat his pizza, but he also views the restaurant as entirely his domain, emphatically declaring that he's the boss. He reveals his lack of real integration into the community and ends by goading the more hot-headed elements into attacking him.

In creating its community, *Do The Right Thing* includes an unusually large number of characters for a classical film. Eight of them provide the main causal action: Mookie, Tina, Sal, Sal's son Pino, Mother Sister, Da Mayor, Buggin' Out, and Radio Raheem. The others, intriguing or amusing as they may be, are more peripheral, mainly reacting to the action set in motion by these characters' conflicts and goals. (Some modern American screenwriting manuals recommend seven to eight important characters as the maximum for a clearly comprehensible film, so Lee is not departing from tradition here.) Moreover, the main causal action falls into two related lines, as in *His Girl Friday* and other traditional Hollywood films. One line of action involves the community's relations to Sal and his sons; the other deals with Mookie's personal life. Mookie becomes the pivotal figure, linking the two lines of action.

Revising Classical Conventions   *Do The Right Thing* also departs from classical narrative conventions in some ways. Consider the characters' goals. Usually, the main characters of a film formulate clear-cut, long-range goals that bring them into conflict with one another. In *Do The Right Thing,* most of the eight main characters create goals only sporadically; the goals are sometimes introduced fairly late in the film, and some are vague.

Buggin' Out, for example, demands that Sal put up pictures of some black heroes on the pizzeria wall. When Sal refuses and throws him out, Buggin' Out shouts to the customers to boycott Sal's. Yet a little while later, when he tries to persuade his neighbors to participate in the boycott, they all refuse, and his project seems to sputter out. Then, later in the film, Radio Raheem and the mentally disabled Smiley agree to join him. Their visit to the pizzeria to threaten Sal then precipitates the climactic action. Ironically, Buggin' Out's goal is briefly achieved when Smiley puts a photograph of Malcolm X and Martin Luther King Jr. on the wall of the burning pizzeria—but by that point, Buggin' Out is on his way to jail.

Mookie's goal is hinted at when we first see him. He is counting money, and he constantly emphasizes that he just wants to work and get paid. His repeated reference to the fact that he is due to be paid in the evening creates the film's only appointment, helping to emphasize the compressed time scheme. Yet his purpose remains unclear. Does he simply want the money so that he can move out of his sister's apartment, as she demands? Or does he also plan to help Tina care for their son?

Some characters have goals, but they are vague and long-range. Da Mayor tells Mother Sister that someday she will be nice to him. After he persistently acts courteously and bravely, she does in fact relent and become his friend. Sal's goal is similarly open ended. He wants simply to keep operating his pizzeria in the face of rising tensions. This puts him in conflict with his son Pino, who has the long-range goal of convincing Sal to sell the pizzeria and leave the neighborhood. Perhaps he will get his desire at the end, although the narrative leaves open the question of whether Sal will rebuild.

In traditional classical films, clear-cut goals generate conflict, since the characters' desires often clash. Lee neatly reverses this pattern by making character goals less sharply defined, but creating a community that is full of conflict from the very beginning of the film. Racial and sexual arguments break out frequently, and insults fly. Such conflict is tied to the fact that *Do The Right Thing* is a social-problem film. Its didactic message gives it much of its overall unity. Everything that happens relates to a central question: With the community torn with such tensions, what can be done to heal it?

The characters' goals and actions suggest some of the possible ways of reacting to the situation. Some of the characters desire simply to avoid or escape this tense atmosphere—Pino by leaving the neighborhood, Da Mayor by overcoming Mother Sister's animosity. Mookie attempts to stay out of trouble by not siding with either Sal or his black friends in their escalating quarrel. Only the death of Radio Raheem drives him to join in, and indeed initiate, the attack on Sal's pizzeria.

Other characters attempt to solve their problems. One central goal is Tina's desire to induce Mookie to behave like a responsible father and spend time with her and with their child. There is a suggestion at the end that she may be succeeding to

> ❝ It's funny how the script is evolving into a film about race relations. This is America's biggest problem, always has been (since we got off the boat), always will be. I've touched upon it in my earlier works, but I haven't yet dealt with it head on as a primary subject."
>
> —Spike Lee, from the production journal of *Do The Right Thing*

some extent. Mookie gets his pay from Sal and says that he will get another job and that he's going to see his son. The last shot shows him walking down the now-quiet street, hinting that he may become a better father.

The central question in the film, however, is not whether any one character will achieve his or her goals. It is whether the pervasive conflicts can be resolved peacefully or violently. As the DJ says on the morning after the riot, "Are we gonna live together—together are we gonna live?"

Do The Right Thing leaves questions unanswered at the end. Will Sal rebuild? Is Mookie really going back to see his son? Most important, though the conflict that flared up has died down, the tension is still present in the community, waiting to resurface. The old problem of how to tame it remains, and so the film does not achieve complete closure. Indeed, such an ending is typical of the social-problem genre. While the immediate conflict may be resolved, the underlying dilemma that caused it remains.

That's also why there is a deliberate ambiguity at the end. Just as we are left at the end of *Citizen Kane* to wonder whether the revelation of the meaning of "Rosebud" explains Kane's character, in *Do The Right Thing* we are left to ponder what "the right thing" is. The film continues after the final story action, with two nondiegetic quotations from Martin Luther King, Jr., and Malcolm X. The King passage advocates a nonviolent approach to the struggle for civil rights, whereas Malcolm X condones violence in self-defense.

Do The Right Thing refuses to suggest which leader is right—although the overall action and use of the phrase "by any means necessary" at the end of the credits seem to weight the film's position in favor of Malcolm X. Still, the juxtaposition of the two quotations, in combination with the open-ended narrative, also seems calculated to spur debate. Perhaps the implication is that each position is viable under certain circumstances. The line of action involving Sal's pizzeria ends in violence; yet at the same time, Da Mayor is able to win Mother Sister's friendship through kindness.

Lee's Technical Choices Like its narrative structure, the style of *Do The Right Thing* stretches the traditional techniques of classical filmmaking. The film begins with a credits sequence during which Rosie Perez performs a vigorous dance to the rap song "Fight the Power." The editing here is strongly discontinuous; sometimes she wears a red dress, sometimes a boxer's outfit, and sometimes a jacket and pants. This brief sequence, which is not part of the narrative, employs the flashy style made familiar by MTV and by television commercials. But stylization during a credits sequence is itself a convention of classical Hollywood film, as we've already seen in Chapter 3 (pp. 94–95).

Throughout *Do The Right Thing,* Lee employs the continuity system. As we saw in Chapter 6, he is adept at handling complicated scenes without breaking the axis of action (6.81–6.86, from *She's Gotta Have It,* pp. 238–239). Most scenes use standard shot/reverse shots and eyeline matching **(11.15, 11.16),** but other moments are marked by different handling. The lengthy conversation in which Pino asks Sal to sell the pizzeria is rendered in one solemn, somewhat suspenseful long take **(11.17–11.19).** At two moments, Lee cuts together two takes of the same action, so that the plot presents a single important story event twice: when Mookie first kisses Tina and when the garbage can hits Sal's window. These instants of discontinuity gain special emphasis, highlighting Mookie's genuine love for Tina and the decisive moment when he turns on Sal, the employer he's defended in earlier scenes.

Just as continuous is the sound track, which gives us the flavor of the neighborhood in a smooth sound stream. As Mookie walks past a row of houses, we hear radios tuned to different stations fade up and down, giving us audio perspective but also reminding us that the neighborhood's ethnic groups have differing tastes in music. The DJ's radio show helps pull the brief scenes together, with the same song carrying over various exchanges of dialogue.

11.15

11.16

11.15–11.16 Classical cutting and camera movement. *Do The Right Thing* often employs classic shot/reverse-shot editing, as in this conversation between Jade and Buggin' Out (11.15–11.16).

11.17

11.18

11.19

11.17–11.19 Classical cutting and camera movement. At another point Lee uses an exceptionally long take to give weight to the serious father-son exchange at the window (11.17). When Smiley appears, the forward tracking movement accumulates suspense (11.18). His interruption of their talk seems to prove Pino's point about the neighborhood, and Pino goes out to chase Smiley away while Sal slumps despondently (11.19).

11.20

11.21

11.22

11.20–11.22 Camera movement ties together lines of action. On the morning after the riot, Da Mayor wakes up in Mother Sister's apartment. Da Mayor and Mother Sister talk and then move out into her front room, the camera tracking with them (11.20). The camera moves backward through the window as they reach it and starts to crane down (11.21). The camera movement ends on a close view of Mookie, on his way to the pizzeria (11.22).

At certain points, Lee's choices of form and style emphasize the community as a whole. The narration is largely unrestricted, flitting from one batch of characters to another, seldom lingering with any individual. Similarly, complex camera movements follow characters through the street, catching glimpses of other activities going on in the background. As in *Grand Illusion* (pp. 203–208), camera movements link characters to one another **(11.20–11.22)**. Stylistic patterning also stresses the underlying problems in the community **(11.23, 11.24)**.

The vagueness about goals, the treatment of the community as the central protagonist, and the moments of unusual style exemplify how Lee, like other contemporary filmmakers, has reshaped some conventions of classical filmmaking. (See pp. 482–488.) Overall, however, *Do The Right Thing* adheres to the formal

11.23

11.24

11.23–11.24 Style emphasizing community problems. Radio Raheem's threatening demeanor is emphasized in some scenes by his direct address into a wide-angle lens (11.23). Mookie's self-absorption is suggested in a visual motif of high-angle views showing him stepping unheedingly on a cheerful chalk picture of a house that a little girl is drawing on the pavement (11.24).

and stylistic traditions of Hollywood cinema. Its multiple-threaded plot builds to a climax that is causally motivated by what went before, and our responses to the characters are built out of a concise, clear narration. Lee's approach to storytelling helps his film fulfill one convention of the social-problem genre: to raise questions and to stir debate.

Moonrise Kingdom

2012. Indian Paintbrush and American Empirical Pictures (distributed by Focus Features). Directed by Wes Anderson. Scripted by Anderson and Roman Coppola. Photographed by Robert D. Yeoman. Edited by Andrew Weisblum. Music by Alexandre Desplat. With Jared Gilman, Kara Hayward, Bruce Willis, Edward Norton, Bill Murray, Frances McDormand, Tilda Swinton, Jason Schwartzman, and Bob Balaban.

Moonrise Kingdom presents a common story pattern: Young love overcomes adult opposition. But this romance is presented in a very unusual fashion. The plot juggles time frames and ranges of knowledge, posing mysteries and twisting our expectations. Sometimes the narration shifts from the young couple, Sam and Suzy, to dwell on secondary characters. Most strikingly, the story world is that of a modern fairy tale.

The action is set in 1965, so it includes references to the popular culture of that year. But *Moonrise Kingdom* doesn't try to recreate the era in the manner of movies like *American Graffiti*. It presents an enclosed, highly stylized setting: the fictitious East Coast island of New Penzance, a place with its own history, geography, and daily routines. Big-budget films like *Star Wars* and *Avatar* have created parallel universes, but *Moonrise Kingdom* is one of the few independent films that makes the same attempt.

CONNECT TO THE BLOG
www.davidbordwell.net/blog

For a more extensive analysis of the film, see "*Moonrise Kingdom*: Wes in Wonderland."

Overseen by an elflike narrator, New Penzance seems an enchanted realm. Director Wes Anderson has transferred the cartoony look of his stop-motion animated film *Fantastic Mr. Fox* to live-action storytelling. He gives us imaginary young-adult books and a make-believe version of the Boy Scouts. Normality seems suspended **(11.25–11.27)**. As in a fairy story, an unhappy princess in a tower waits for her hero to rescue her, while he braves the wilderness. Not only are the protagonists very young, not only does the plot make the adults seem somewhat infantile, but the characters may look as flat as paper dolls, and their homes often resemble dollhouses. This fairy-tale ambience is created by both the plotting and some unusual stylistic choices.

Four Days at Summer's End   *Moonrise Kingdom* presents a simple cycle of action. Sam and Suzy run off together, get caught, and are torn apart. Then they escape again, are rescued, and stay together. Within these cycles, our goal-oriented protagonists clash with other characters—not only Suzy's parents but the Khaki Scouts sent to retrieve Sam. At the climax, when a huge storm rises, they face a conflict with nature as well. Parallel subplots run alongside the central romance. The devotion of Sam and Suzy contrasts with the ennui of Suzy's parents and the shy courtship of Scoutmaster Ward and the telephone operator Becky. Suzy likens herself to the heroines of the adventure books she reads, while Sam parallels the melancholy Sheriff Sharp, who is conducting a furtive affair with Suzy's mother.

This action, spread across four days, could have been rendered in simple chronology. But Anderson's plot plays with story order to intrigue us and build sympathy for his young couple. On the first day, we're introduced to Suzy, who's constantly scanning the landscape with her binoculars. We're immediately attached to her, and at different points we'll learn story information through POV surveillance shots. Yet when she receives a mysterious letter, we don't learn its contents, and her secret creates a mystery that leads us forward.

11.25

11.26

11.27

11.25–11.27 **A make-believe world.** The Khaki Scouts' treehouse is built impossibly high (11.25). A toylike landscape on New Penzance, with a lighthouse suggesting a candy cane (11.26). When Sam starts to kiss Suzy, they share a burst of electricity, the result of Sam's being struck by lightning earlier (11.27).

Many filmmakers would have followed the letter scene by showing Sam sneaking out of Camp Ivanhoe. Instead, Anderson sustains the mystery. The plot shows Scoutmaster Ward assembling his cadets, discovering Sam's escape, and alerting Sheriff Sharp. This portion of the film introduces the characters whose lives the young teens' romance will affect: Mr. and Mrs. Bishop, Sharp, and Ward and his troop. These scenes also establish Sam's background. He is an orphan, he has been ostracized by the other scouts, and his foster parents don't want him returned. Even before we meet him, he has a measure of our sympathy.

The first day ends with Ward glumly admitting that his search has failed. Then the plot skips back to the day's start and finally introduces our second protagonist, Sam. After his escape in a canoe, he meets Suzy in a meadow. A further flashback shows the reason for their rendezvous: The previous summer they met at *Noye's Fludde*, Britten's church pageant about Noah's ark (a scene that foreshadows the climactic storm). Now we realize that Sam's mysterious letter to Suzy has clinched this rendezvous.

Sam and Suzy spend the first day hiking, camping, fishing, and getting to know one another. These scenes offer a sharp contrast to the ongoing search for them. While the runaways try to be serious adventurers, the scouts hope for a violent clash, and the adults are short tempered, confused, and abrasive. As darkness falls, the Bishops discover Suzy's disappearance, and they find the letters revealing her romance with Sam. Through a quick string of flashbacks, with Sam and Suzy's voice-over, we see him bullied in the foster home and her lashing out at her parents and her classmates. These glimpses of backstory build up still more sympathy for them.

After the double-decker presentation of Day 1, the second day is presented in a more linear fashion. Brief scenes show the search party and a skirmish in which Sam and Suzy drive off the scouts. Then the adults learn from the Narrator where Sam is likely to have gone. The plot spends the rest of the day tracing the growing love between Sam and Suzy, shadowed by our knowledge that the adults are coming to break up their idyll. The couple swim, Suzy poses for Sam's paintings, he pierces her ears, and they end up dancing and embracing. The second day ends with Suzy reading aloud to Sam at their campfire. Anderson adds another playful touch: We're about halfway through the film when Suzy reads, "Part Two."

Early on the third day the adults arrive, furious to discover Suzy and Sam asleep together. The lovers are separated. Scoutmaster Ward and Sheriff Sharp learn that Sam will probably be sent to an orphanage. While Suzy, bitter and unhappy, spends the night at home with her parents, Sam has supper with Sharp, who serves as an inarticulate father figure. But late that night the Khaki Scouts intervene and help Sam and Suzy escape to another island.

The final day merges all the storylines through crosscutting. At Fort Lebanon, a casually corrupt scoutmaster presides over the couple's mock marriage and readies them for jobs on a crab-fishing boat. As the storm hits, Ward rescues the head scoutmaster from his burning headquarters. The whole community takes shelter in the local church.

With the eloped couple still missing, the Bishops, Ward, and Sharp quarrel with one another and with the agent from Social Services. Meanwhile, Sam and Suzy make their way to the church rooftop in the driving rain, planning to jump—either to safety or to their deaths. Sheriff Sharp rescues them and extracts a promise from Social Services that he can become Sam's guardian.

The film ends more or less happily ever after. The adults' melancholy lives have improved a little. Mr. and Mrs. Bishop seem to have come to an understanding. Ward has been proven a hero and now has Becky as a romantic partner. Lonely Sheriff Sharp has gained a surrogate son. The aftermath of the storm, the Narrator informs us, has led to a lush crop yield on the island.

What of the central couple? *Moonrise Kingdom* began with a prologue touring the Bishop household. The shots introduced the family and usually ended with Suzy peering out at us through her binoculars. What was she looking for? Now we know it was Sam. In a symmetrical epilogue, the camera revisits the rooms we saw at the start, only now Sam is in the house, working on a painting while Suzy reads. Sam slips out a window with the promise he will be back tomorrow. Blowing a kiss, Suzy uses her binoculars to watch Sam drive away with Sharp. Although their magical summer has ended, the princess in the tower has found her prince.

Playing with Form   The film's flashbacks and character comparisons are reinforced by playful narration. The most apparent mark of this is the Narrator. Is he a character in the film's fictional world? At first, he seems an external commentator, like the Stage Manager in the play *Our Town*. As if introducing a documentary, he explains the geography and history of New Penzance **(11.28).** Yet he also knows the future, announcing that a 1965 storm will take place "in three days' time." His prediction sets up a deadline for the plot. Is he outside the film's story world? Not entirely, because he materializes in one scene to tell the adults that Sam has probably taken Suzy to the Mile 3.25 Tidal Inlet. At the film's very end he reappears to explain how things turned out. In supplementary material online (at http://insidemovies .ew.com/2012/06/07/moonrise-kingdom-animation) he is said to be the town librarian, but that doesn't explain how he could know the future.

The Narrator's fussy, comic omniscience is matched by Anderson's habit of inserting written texts. Several letters pop up, with voice-over recitation by the writer. More oddly, when Sam seems doomed to go to a youth facility, we cut directly to a news article about an orphanage's Christmas celebration—the sort of wry link we might find in a film with associative form. Later Anderson interrupts a Khaki Scout's instructions with a shot of a "supply list"

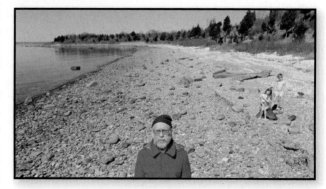

11.28 A gnomish narrator. The Narrator introduces the island, in a shot that looks forward to Sam and Suzy's campsite.

11.29 Kids' games. Resembling a comic-book frame or a child's stick-on label, the inserted scissors image treats the Scouts' skirmish with Suzy and Sam as play rather than an act of violence.

CONNECT TO THE BLOG
www.davidbordwell.net/blog

Anderson is not alone in his choices about framing and staging. We consider this "planimetric" approach more generally in "Shot-consciousness." Our entry, "*The Grand Budapest Hotel*: Wes Anderson takes the 4:3 challenge," considers how Anderson adapts his style to different aspect ratios.

“ Usually when I'm making a movie, what I have in mind, first, for the visuals, is how we can stage the scenes to bring them more to life in the most interesting way, and then how we can make a world for the story that the audience hasn't quite been in before."

—Wes Anderson

11.30 Dollhouse sets. In the opening sequence, the camera films the Bishops' household as if it were a cutaway scale model, with Suzy often revealed watching us through binoculars.

enumerating what they'll need to rescue Sam and Suzy. The extreme formality of this printed-out list, which was probably never actually created by the characters, gently mocks the quasi-military solemnity of the mission.

Probably the most startling interruption occurs when Sam and Suzy are attacked by the aggressive scout Redford. We don't see the actual fight, just some very rapid shots of an arrow in flight and of abstract images of scissors (**11.29**). Later we'll learn that Suzy has used her scissors to stab Redford. The sequence is presented as a fantasy re-creation of an actual tussle.

Rules for Style   In choosing techniques, Anderson sets up rules that are stricter than those most filmmakers follow. He shoots rooms in straight-on views with central vanishing-point perspective (**11.30**). Sometimes the characters stand in profile, at 90 degrees to the camera. More often, figures stand facing us, like the Narrator (11.28), even when they are talking to others. They move straight toward or away from the camera, or at right angles to it. In other films, such as *The Royal Tenenbaums* and *The Grand Budapest Hotel*, Anderson has employed a similar style, but here it reinforces the fantasy aspect of the action. The characters might be figures in a simple comic strip or a *South Park* episode.

The limited options in staging and framing push Anderson toward other stylistic choices. To retain his right-angled treatment of space, he's obliged to use tracking and panning movements that are severely horizontal or vertical. Likewise, to accommodate his frontal staging, he treats the 180-degree system in an unusual way. He puts the camera directly on the axis of action, which enables him to cut between characters at opposite ends of it (**11.31, 11.32**). The film's distinctive style depends on choosing some rare options from the classical film-making menu.

Nearly all the dialogue scenes in the film are treated in this rigid, compass-point fashion. But there's one important exception: The development of Sam and Suzy's romance in the wilds is echoed by a gradual shift in the stylistic pattern (**11.33–11.38**). In a film that avoids the most common form of shot/reverse shot, Anderson uses it to give Sam and Suzy's encounter an intimacy that is denied the other characters.

The film's score is somewhat rule governed as well. It employs several Benjamin Britten pieces associated with youth. There is Britten's "Simple Symphony," based on tunes he wrote as a teenager, as well as *Noye's Fludde* and children's songs. Britten's *Young Person's Guide to the Orchestra* is heard at several points. It served as a model for Desplat's score, which is organized around seven variations on a theme, entitled "The Heroic Weather Conditions." Over the closing credits, this theme deliberately mimics *The Young Person's Guide* as Sam's voice introduces the instruments used in Desplat's orchestration.

Anderson saves one surprise for the end of the plot. During the afternoon at Mile 3.25 Tidal Inlet, Suzy reveals she doesn't like the place's name. Sam agrees and suggests they come up with another. We don't learn what name that is until the last shot. Sam's painting in Suzy's parlor is revealed to be a landscape of the inlet. The storm has filled it in, so it no longer exists, except in Sam's picture. He has painted the words "Moonrise Kingdom" on the beach. The title, recalling Suzy's fantasy novels, is a suitable name for a magical summer interlude that removed its characters, and its audience, from the everyday world.

11.31–11.32 Camera on the axis. Anderson's version of shot/reverse-shot cutting puts the camera directly on the axis of action, so that characters look straight out at us. This doesn't violate the continuity system, but it's more typical of optical POV passages like those in *Rear Window* (pp. 241–242).

11.33

11.34

11.35

11.36

11.37

11.38

11.33–11.38 More and more normal. When Sam and Suzy first meet at *Noye's Fludde*, and when they reunite in the meadow, they are shot in Anderson's standard way. We get profile or head-on views (for example, 11.33, 11.34). As they get to know one another, the angles become more like the ¾ views we see in most films (11.35, 11.36). (Compare p. 237.) When they declare their love for each other, they are shown in conventional over-the-shoulder angles (11.37, 11.38). The stylistic development echoes Sam and Suzy's growing intimacy.

Narrative Alternatives to Classical Filmmaking

Breathless (À bout de souffle)

1960. Les Films Georges de Beauregard, Impéria Films and Société Nouvelle de Cinéma. Directed by Jean-Luc Godard. Story outline by François Truffaut, dialogue by Godard. Photographed by Raoul Coutard. Edited by Cécile Decugis. Music by Martial Solal. With Jean-Paul Belmondo, Jean Seberg, Daniel Boulanger, Henri-Jacques Huet, Van Doude, Jean-Pierre Melville.

In some ways, *Breathless* imitates a 1940s Hollywood staple, the **film noir,** or "dark film." Such films dealt with hard-boiled detectives, gangsters, or ordinary people tempted into crime. Often a seductive femme fatale would lure the protagonist into a dangerous scheme (for example, *The Maltese Falcon*). *Breathless*'s plot links it to a common noir vehicle: the outlaw movie involving young criminals on the run, such as *They Live by Night* and *Gun Crazy*.

An Outlaw Couple? The bare-bones story could serve as the basis of a Hollywood script. A car thief, Michel, kills a motorcycle cop and flees to Paris to get money to escape to Italy. He also tries to convince Patricia, an American art student writer with whom he had a brief affair, to leave with him. After equivocating for nearly two days, she agrees. Just as Michel is about to receive the cash he needs, Patricia calls the police, and they kill him.

Yet Godard's presentation of this story could never pass for a polished studio product. For one thing, Michel's behavior is presented as driven *by* the very movies that *Breathless* imitates. He rubs his thumb across his lips in imitation of his idol Humphrey Bogart. But he is a petty thief whose life spins out of control. He can only fantasize himself as a Hollywood tough guy.

The film's ambivalent attitude toward classical American cinema also pervades form and technique. As we've seen, the norms of classical style and storytelling promote narrative clarity and unity. In contrast, *Breathless* appears awkward and casual, almost amateurish. It makes character motivations ambiguous and lingers over incidental dialogue. Its editing jumps about frenetically. And, whereas film noirs were made largely in the studio, where selective lighting could swathe the characters in a brooding atmosphere, *Breathless* utilizes location shooting with available lighting.

These strategies make Michel's story quirky, uncertain, and deglamorized. They also ask the audience to enjoy the film's rough-edged reworking of Hollywood formulas. An opening title dedicates the film to Monogram Pictures, a Poverty Row studio that churned out B-movies. The title seems to announce a film that is indebted to Hollywood but not wholly bound by its norms.

Goals, Delays, and Puzzles Like many protagonists in classical Hollywood films, Michel has two main goals. To leave France, he must search for his friend Antonio, the only one who can cash a check for him. Michel also hopes to persuade Patricia to go with him. As the plot progresses, it becomes apparent that, despite his flippant attitude, Michel's attraction to her outweighs his desire to escape.

In a classical film, these goals would drive the action along fairly steadily. Yet in *Breathless,* the plot moves in fits and starts. Brief scenes, some largely unconnected to the goals, alternate with long stretches of seemingly irrelevant dialogue. Most of *Breathless*'s 22 separate segments run four minutes or less. One 43-second scene consists simply of Michel pausing in front of a theater and looking at a picture of Bogart.

Scenes containing crucial action are sometimes brief and confusing. The murder of the traffic cop, the crucial event that makes Michel a hunted man, is handled in a very elliptical fashion. In long shot, we see the officer approaching Michel's car, parked in a side road. In medium long shot, Michel reaches into the car for the gun. After that, the action becomes fragmentary **(11.39–11.42).** So much has been left out that we can barely comprehend what is happening, let alone judge whether Michel shot deliberately or by accident.

In contrast to the whirlwind presentation of this key action, a lengthy conversation in the middle of the film brings the narrative progression almost to a standstill. For nearly 25 minutes, Michel and Patricia chat in her bedroom. At some points, Michel attempts to further his goals, trying to phone Antonio and to persuade Patricia to come to Rome. Patricia suggests that she will not run off with him, because she does not know if she loves him. Michel: "When will you know?" Patricia: "Soon." Michel: "What does that mean—soon? In a month, in a year?" Patricia: "Soon means soon." So although the pair make love, by the end of the long scene (which occupies nearly a third of this 89-minute film), we still do not have a definite step forward or backward in Michel's courting of Patricia, and he has made no progress toward escaping. Such scenes make him seem more like a wandering, easily distracted delinquent than the desperate, driven hero of a film noir.

You could argue that the bedroom scene functions not to advance the plot but to characterize the couple. Yet here too, nothing definite emerges. Most of the conversation is trivial, as when Michel criticizes the way Patricia puts on lipstick or when she asks whether he prefers records or the radio. The pair try to outstare each other, and they discuss Patricia's new poster. So rambling is their exchange that some critics have assumed that the dialogue was improvised (although Godard attests that it was all scripted). Sam and Suzy, the runaway kids in *Moonrise Kingdom*, are far more focused in their desire to be together, and their conversations fill in their character traits to a degree we don't find in the pillow talk of Michel and Patricia.

It's not until the scene outside the *Tribune* office that another decisive action occurs. A passerby (played by Godard) recognizes Michel and tells

11.39

11.40

11.41

11.42

11.39–11.42 Temporal discontinuity for a murder scene. In *Breathless,* Michel's shooting of the cop is fractured by abrupt cuts and camera movements. We see a close shot of his head, as the cop's voice is heard saying, "Don't move or I'll drill you" (11.39). Two very brief close-ups pan along Michel's arm and along the gun (11.40, 11.41), accompanied by the sound of a gunshot (though the pistol doesn't seem to be firing). We then get a glimpse of the cop falling into some underbrush (11.42), followed by an extreme long shot of Michel, running far across a field.

the police. This triggers a chain of events that lead to Michel's death. Yet now the plot meanders once more. In the next scene, Patricia participates in a news conference with a famous novelist, a character unrelated to the main action. Most of the questions asked by the reporters deal with the differences between men and women, but the novelist's responses seem more playful than meaningful. Finally, Patricia asks him his greatest ambition, and he replies enigmatically: "To become immortal and then to die." Patricia's puzzled glance into the camera at the close of the scene prepares us for the ambiguity that will linger at the film's end.

After Detective Vital questions Patricia at the *Tribune* office, she and Michel realize that the police are on his trail. Now *Breathless* begins to progress in a somewhat more conventional way. In the next scene, Patricia says that she loves Michel "enormously," and they steal a car. Here Michel seems to reach his romantic goal, as Patricia commits herself to fleeing with him. When Antonio agrees to bring the cash the next morning, Michel moves toward his second goal. We might anticipate possible outcomes: The pair will escape, or one or both will be killed in the attempt. The next morning, however, Patricia confounds our expectations by betraying Michel to Vital. Even then Michel has a last chance. Antonio arrives just before the police, with money and a getaway car—yet Michel cannot bring himself to leave Patricia.

More Questions   The ending is particularly enigmatic. As Michel lies bleeding to death, Patricia looks down at him. He slowly makes the same playful faces at her that he had made during their bedroom conversation. Muttering, "That's really disgusting" (*"C'est vraiment dégueulasse"*), he dies. Patricia asks Detective Vital what he said, and Vital misreports Michel's last words: "He said, 'You are really a bitch'" (*"Il a dit, 'Vous êtes vraiment une dégueulasse'"*). We are left to ponder what Michel thought was disgusting—Patricia's betrayal, his own last-minute failure to flee, or simply his death. In the final shot, Patricia looks out at the camera, asks what *dégueulasse* means, rubs her lips with the Bogart-inspired gesture that Michel has used throughout the film (**11.43**), and abruptly turns her back on us as the image fades out.

Breathless achieves a degree of closure: Michel fails to achieve his goals. But we are left with many questions. Although Michel and Patricia talk constantly about themselves, we learn remarkably little about why they act as they do. Unlike characters in classical films, they do not have a set of clearly defined traits. The film begins with Michel saying, "All in all, I'm a dumb bastard," and in a way, his actions bear this out. Yet we never learn background information that would explain his decisions.

Patricia's traits and goals are even more uncertain. When Michel first finds her selling newspapers on the Champs Elysées, she is far from welcoming. Yet at the scene's end, she runs back to give him a kiss. She keeps saying she wants to get a job as a *Tribune* reporter and to write a novel, yet she seems to throw these ambitions away when she thinks she loves Michel. Patricia also tells Michel she is pregnant by him, but she has not received the final test results, and she never raises this as a reason she should stay in Paris. Her speech about why she informed on Michel seems not really to explain her abrupt change of heart. Just as Michel is ill suited to be a tough guy, Patricia is too naive and indecisive to play the role of the classic femme fatale.

In the outlaw film noir, the characters are intensely committed to each other, but Michel and Patricia seem to have few strong feelings about what they do. When the treacherous woman deceives the noir hero, he often becomes bitterly disillusioned; but Michel apparently does not blame Patricia for betraying him. It is as if these ambivalent, diffident, confused characters are unable to play out the desperately passionate roles that the Hollywood tradition has assigned to them.

11.43 Gesture as motif. Patricia's enigmatic gesture at the end of *Breathless* mimics the way Michel copies Humphrey Bogart.

Breaking with Tradition   *Breathless*'s elliptical, occasionally opaque narrative is presented through techniques that are equally unconventional. As we have seen, Hollywood films use a three-point system of key light, fill light, and backlight, carefully controlled in a film studio (pp. 128–129). *Breathless* was shot entirely on location, even the interiors. Godard and cinematographer Raoul Coutard often decided not to add any artificial light in the settings. As a result, the characters' faces sometimes fall into shadow **(11.44).**

11.44

Filming on location, especially in small apartments, would ordinarily make it difficult to obtain a variety of camera angles and movements. But taking advantage of new portable equipment, Coutard was able to film while hand-holding the camera. Several lengthy tracking shots follow the characters **(11.45).** Coutard apparently rode in a wheelchair to film this shot, as well as more elaborate movements that follow the characters in interiors **(11.46).** Such shots recall the location shooting of many film noirs, such as the final airport scenes of Stanley Kubrick's *The Killing,* but the low camera position and the passersby who turn to look at the actors (as with the man at the right in 11.45) call attention to the technique in a way that departs from Hollywood usage.

11.45

Even more striking than the mise-en-scene is Godard's editing. Again he sometimes follows tradition, but at other points, he breaks away. Standard shot/reverse-shot cutting organizes several scenes **(11.47, 11.48).** Similarly, when Michel spots the man examining the telltale photo in the newspaper, Godard supplies correctly matched glances. Since this is a turning point in the plot, it's important that the audience understand that the man may recognize Michel, and so Godard adheres to the 180° line.

Yet the film also violates continuity editing, and in ways that are still jolting today. In the opening scene, as Michel's accomplice points out a car he wants to steal, the eyelines are quite unclear, and we get little sense of where the two are in relation to each other. Nor does Godard feel an obligation to respect screen direction **(11.49, 11.50).** Most original of all are his jump cuts. During the classic studio years, Hollywood editors avoided the jump cut, in which a segment of time is eliminated without the camera being moved to a new vantage point (p. 255–256). By contrast, *Breathless* employs the technique throughout. In an early scene, when Michel visits an old girlfriend, jump cuts shift their positions abruptly **(11.51, 11.52).**

11.46

11.44–11.46 Available lighting and flexible camerawork. When Patricia sits against a window and lights a cigarette, the natural light of the scene illuminates her only from behind (11.44). Michel's first meeting with Patricia as she strolls along the Champs Elysées selling papers occurs in a three-minute take (11.45). Later, when Michel visits a travel agent trying to claim his check, the framing glides with ease as he moves through offices and corridors (11.46).

Even when Godard shifts the camera position between cuts, he may drop out a bit of time or mismatch the actors' positions. At many cuts, the action seems to jerk forward. One effect of this jumpy editing is to enliven the rhythm. At times, as during the murder of the police officer, we have to be very alert to follow the action. The elliptical editing also makes other scenes stand out by contrast, particularly the single-take scenes with moving camera and the rambling 25-minute conversation in Patricia's apartment.

The film's sound often reinforces these editing discontinuities. When the characters' dialogue and other diegetic sounds continue over the jump cuts, we are forced to notice the contradiction: Time drops out of the visual track but not the sound track. The location shooting also creates situations in which ambient noises intrude on the dialogue. A passing siren outside Patricia's apartment nearly overwhelms her conversation with Michel during the long central scene. Later the press conference with Parvulesco inexplicably takes place on an airport observation platform, where the whines of nearby planes drown out the dialogue. Such scenes lack the balance of volumes of the well-mixed Hollywood sound track.

Godard's avoidance of the rules of smooth sound and picture steers *Breathless* away from the glamorous portrayals seen in the Hollywood crime film. The stylistic awkwardness suits the pseudo-documentary roughness of filming in an actual, hectic Paris. The discontinuities are also consistent with other nontraditional techniques, like the motif of the characters' mysterious glances into the camera. In addition, the jolts in picture and sound create a self-conscious narration that makes

      On *À Bout de souffle,* he'd [Godard] ask the script-girl what kind of shot was required next to fulfill the requirements of traditional continuity. She'd tell him, and then he'd do the exact opposite."

—Raoul Coutard, cinematographer

11.47

11.48

11.49

11.50

11.47–11.50 Editing, normal and disruptive. When Michel pauses in front of a movie theater and looks at a photo on display (11.47), Bogart seems to look back at him in reverse shot (11.48). At other times, Godard breaks the 180° rule. In the first shot, Patricia moves from left to right (11.49), but in the next, she is walking right to left (11.50). This cut flagrantly violates conventional screen direction.

the viewer aware of its stylistic choices. In making the director's hand more apparent, the film presents itself as a deliberately unpolished revision of tradition.

Godard did not set out to criticize Hollywood films. Instead, he took genre conventions identified with 1940s America and gave them a contemporary Parisian setting and a modern, self-conscious treatment. In the process he created a new type of hero and heroine. Aimless, somewhat banal lovers on the run became central to later outlaw movies such as *Bonnie and Clyde, Badlands,* and *True Romance.* More broadly, Godard's film became a model for directors who wished to create exuberantly offhand homages to, and reworkings of, Hollywood tradition. This attitude would be central to the stylistic movement that *Breathless* helped launch, the French New Wave. (See Chapter 12, pp. 479–482.)

11.51–11.52 The jump cut. During Michel's visit to an old girlfriend, we get several jump cuts. Compare the last frame of one shot (11.51) with the first of the next shot (11.52). We've seen another example earlier, when jump cuts show Patricia riding in a car (6.151, 6.152, again the last and first frames of adjacent shots).

11.51

11.52

Tokyo Story (Tokyo Monogatari)

1953. Shochiku/Ofuna, Japan. Directed by Yasujiro Ozu. Script by Ozu and Kogo
Noda. Photographed by Yuharu Atsuta. With Chishu Ryu, Chieko Higashiyama,
So Yamamura, Haruko Sugimura, Setsuko Hara.

 CONNECT TO THE BLOG
www.davidbordwell.net/blog

Ozu is one of our favorite directors. Apart from the book *Ozu and
the Poetics of Cinema* (an e-book
linked on our site), you can read
about him in "A modest extrava-
gance: Four looks at Ozu" and
"Watch again! Look well! Look!
(For Ozu)."

We've seen that the classical Hollywood approach to filmmaking tends to let story
action dominate. The plot is constructed to encourage us to build the story in our
minds in a certain way. What do you show and when do you show it? The answer
to these questions is usually based on how the filmmaker wants us to experience
the story's action.

With so much emphasis on the story, we seldom pay particular attention to the
space in which it occurs. The setting, and the manner of showing it to us, functions
chiefly as an arena for character conflict and change. Spade's office in *The Maltese
Falcon* (pp. 233–237) isn't explored as a locale, it's merely a nondescript area for
initiating the mystery plot. *North by Northwest* doesn't want us to study Mount
Rushmore as a piece of mammoth sculpture; it's rather a dramatic backdrop for a
chase and cliff-hanging.

What, however, if a filmmaker wanted to change the way we thought about
the space around a story? You wouldn't have to go as far as Michael Snow in
Wavelength and almost obliterate a story altogether (pp. 207–209). You might try
to tell a story, in fact a rather emotional one, but allow the locales in which the
story takes place to gain more prominence, to claim our attention in their own right.
Patterns of space could enrich the story while at the same time having a certain
independence.

This all sounds a little abstract, so let's look at a famous example. The Japanese
director Yasujiro Ozu has sought to tell gripping stories while also making narrative
space more than a container for action. We've given you a preview of Ozu's unique
style of exploring space through graphic matching (6.142–6.145) and using an area
of space to condense story time (5.207, 5.208). Through such choices, Ozu created
a systematic alternative to classical continuity filming (p. 254). Our analysis here
tries to show how his strategies operate across an entire film.

Oblique Storytelling   *Tokyo Story,* Ozu's first film to make an impression on
Western audiences, presents a simple narrative. An elderly provincial couple visit
their grown children in Tokyo, only to be treated as nuisances. As the couple return
home, the wife falls ill, and she dies after reaching their house. Now the children
come to visit the parents, and though some are sorrowful, others continue to be
emotionally distant. The plot lacks the goals, conflicts, crises, and climaxes that
we associate with Hollywood cinema. In outline, it seems merely a sad anecdote.

What makes this tale more complex, and our responses more nuanced, is
Ozu's handling. *Tokyo Story*'s narration is, by classical standards, rather oblique.
Sometimes we learn of important narrative events only after they have occurred.
For example, although the grandparents are the film's central characters, we do not
see the grandmother falling ill. We hear about it only when her son and daughter
get telegrams with the news. Similarly, the grandmother's death occurs between
scenes. In one scene, her children are gathered by her bedside; in the next scene,
they are mourning her.

Yet these ellipses are not evidence of a fast-paced film such as *His Girl Friday,*
which tries to cover a lot of narrative ground in a hurry. On the contrary, the
sequences of *Tokyo Story* often linger over details: the melancholy conversation
between the grandfather and his friends in a bar as they discuss their disappoint-
ment in their children, or the grandmother's walk on a Sunday with her grandchild.
The result is a shift in narrative balance. Big narrative events are played down by
means of ellipses, whereas narrative events that we do see in the plot are ones that
would be considered minor.

Transitional Spaces As Ozu shifts our attention away from the most dramatic events, he often steers us away from dramatically significant space. Scenes don't begin and end with shots showing the most important elements in the mise-en-scene. Instead of the usual transitional devices, such as dissolves and fades, Ozu typically employs a series of separate transitional shots linked by cuts. A landscape or object becomes the pivot to a new scene. In effect, Ozu makes bits of setting fill in the time gaps between scenes. This already gives greater weight to the space around the story action.

Moreover, these transitional shots often show spaces not directly connected with the action of the scene; the spaces are usually *near* where that action will take place. The opening of the film, for example, has five shots of the port town of Onomichi—the bay, schoolchildren, a passing train—before the sixth shot reveals the grandparents packing for their trip to Tokyo. Although a couple of important motifs make their first appearances in these first five shots, no narrative causes occur to get the action underway. (Compare the openings of *His Girl Friday* and *North by Northwest*.)

These transitions have only a minimal function as establishing shots. In fact, sometimes they mislead us about what's coming next. At a crucial moment in the drama, the narration moves from the daughter-in-law Noriko to the clinic of the eldest son, yet Ozu can extend the transition with shots of a construction site (**11.53–11.56**). The shots of the building under construction aren't necessary to the action, and we get no hint of where the building is. We might assume that it is outside Noriko's office, but the riveting sound we hear in the transitional shots isn't audible in the interior shots before and after.

> 66 I don't think the film has a grammar. I don't think film has but one form. If a good film results, then that film has created its own grammar."
>
> —Yasujiro Ozu, director

11.53

11.54

11.55

11.56

11.53–11.56 Ambivalent transitions in *Tokyo Story*. After the daughter-in-law, Noriko, gets a phone call at work telling her of the grandmother's illness, the scene ends in a medium shot of her sitting pensively at her desk. The only diegetic sound is the loud clack of typewriters (11.53). A nondiegetic musical transition comes up in this shot. Then there is a cut to a low-angle long shot of a building under construction (11.54). Riveting noises replace the typewriters, with the music continuing. The next shot is another low angle of the construction site (11.55). A cut changes the locale to the clinic belonging to the eldest son, Dr. Hirayama. The sister, Shige, is present. The music ends and the new scene begins (11.56).

What are the functions of these stylistic patterns? It's hard to assign them explicit or implicit meanings. For example, someone might propose that the transitional shots symbolize the new Tokyo that is alien to the visiting grandparents from a village reminiscent of the old Japan. But often the transitional spaces don't present outdoor locales, and some shots are within the characters' homes. Moreover, why insert these shots here rather than anywhere else in the film, where the same thematic opposition would be just as appropriate? And finally, if the shots reiterate the old/new theme, they would be quite redundant, because the contrast between the grandparents' tradition and their children's urban lives is already stressed in the story action.

A more systematic function, we suggest, is narrational, having to do with the flow of story information. Ozu's narration alternates between scenes of story action and inserted portions that lead us to or away from them. As we watch the film, we start to form expectations about these wedged-in shots. Ozu emphasizes stylistic patterning by creating anticipation about when a transition will come and what it will show. The patterning may delay our expectations and even create some surprises.

For example, early in the film, Mrs. Hirayama, the doctor's wife, argues with her son, Minoru, over where to move his desk to make room for the grandparents. This issue is dropped, and there follows a scene of the grandparents' arrival. This ends on a conversation in an upstairs room. Transitional music comes up over the end of the scene. The next shot frames an empty hallway downstairs that contains Minoru's school desk, but no one is in the shot. There follows an exterior long shot of children running along a ridge near the house; these children are not characters in the action. Finally, a cut back inside reveals Minoru at his father's desk in the clinic portion of the house, studying.

Here the editing creates a very indirect route between two scenes, going first to a place where we expect a character to be (at his own desk) but isn't. Then the scene moves completely away from the action, outdoors. Not until the third shot does a character reappear and the action continue. Likewise, after we leave Noriko at her typewriter (11.53) and see the building under construction, we might expect to move to another office building. Instead, the next shot takes us to the family's suburban home. The construction site is neither fully urban (the building is unfinished), nor rural either. In its in-between status we can see it, in retrospect, as a conceptual link between Noriko and the clinic. In these transitional passages, a kind of game emerges. Ozu asks us to form expectations not only about story action but about editing and setting. Just as Ozu's plotting is unpredictable, leaving major actions offscreen and elevating minor ones, so too is his film's movement through space and time.

The Space around the Characters

Ozu finds another way to activate the space his characters inhabit. We mentioned in Chapter 6 (p. 255) that he creates a 360° space for many of his scenes. He will cut across the 180° line to frame the scene's space from the opposite direction. This, of course, violates rules of screen direction, since characters or objects on the right in the first shot will appear on the left in the second, and vice versa. He's not doing this occasionally, as Ford does in our *Stagecoach* example (6.94, 6.95), but consistently. The editing in Shige's beauty salon exemplifies Ozu's typical approach to framing and editing a scene **(11.57–11.59)**.

When we look closely, we find that Ozu has his own rules for staging, shooting, and cutting, and these revise the continuity guidelines. He relies on eyeline cuts, but these are often "wrong" by Hollywood standards, since both characters are looking in the same direction **(11.60, 11.61)**. He matches on action but shifts back and forth across the axis of action, as when Noriko and her grandmother walk toward the door of Noriko's apartment **(11.62, 11.63)**. Instead of restricting his camera

11.57

11.58

11.59

11.57–11.59 **360° editing space.** At the beginning of a scene in Shige's beauty salon, the initial interior medium shot frames Shige from opposite the front door (11.57). A 180° cut reveals a medium long shot of a woman under a hair dryer; the camera now faces the rear of the salon (11.58). Another 180° cut presents a new long shot of the room, again oriented toward the door, and the grandparents come into the salon (11.59).

positions to one side of the axis of action, Ozu cuts in a full circle around the action, usually in segments of 90° or 180°. This means that backgrounds change drastically, as in our examples. In a Hollywood film, the camera rarely crosses the axis of action to look at the fourth wall. Because surroundings change more frequently in *Tokyo Story,* they become more prominent in relation to the action; the viewer must pay attention to setting or become confused.

This 360° space works together with the transitional shots that prolong or thwart the viewer's expectations. One of the most famous scenes in the film shows the grandparents visiting a spa at Atami, sent there because they inconvenience their offspring. Even though they enjoy looking at the sea, their nights are disturbed by partyers around them. Ozu introduces us to their unhappiness gradually and without sentimental pathos. For seven shots, the film slowly explores the space of

11.60–11.63 **360° space breaks the axis of action.** The grandfather and his old friend converse, but they look in the same direction (11.60–11.61). Adherents of classical continuity would say that this cut implies that the two men are looking off at something else, yet we aren't confused by it. Similarly, Noriko and her grandmother advance to the camera, then away from it (11.62–11.63). The women's movements are closely matched, and normally head-on and tail-on shots of action can cut together. (See 6.89–6.93.) But here the similar framings make the characters seem to bump into themselves. Their screen positions, left and right, are also abruptly reversed, something that is usually considered an error in the continuity style.

11.60

11.61

11.62

11.63

the scene, gradually letting us discover the situation **(11.64–11.71).** The presence of the couple's slippers in the second shot (11.65) is almost unnoticeable. It hints that the grandparents are there, but the revelation of their whereabouts is then put off for several more shots as the shots sidle through other rooms in the spa. The unpredictability of the scene's unfolding is created through the transitional shots and the 360° shifts.

In these ways, Ozu draws our attention away from the strictly causal functions of space and makes space important in its own right. He does the same with the flat space of the screen by cutting to highlight graphic configurations. Now we can see that his strategy of 360° cutting also functions to create strong graphic matches between shots. (Look back at 11.60 and 11.61, and you'll see the same sort of graphic matching we pointed out in 6.142–6.145.) The stylistic device is

11.64 **11.65** **11.66** **11.67** **11.68** **11.69** **11.70** **11.71**

11.64–11.71 Sidling into a scene. The Atami spa scene begins with a long shot along a hallway (11.64). Latin-style dance music plays offscreen, and several people walk through the hall. The next shot (11.65) is a long shot of another hallway upstairs, with a maid carrying a tray; two pairs of slippers are just visible by a doorway at the lower left. But instead of taking us into the room with the grandparents, Ozu takes us to a hallway (11.66) and then a mah-jongg game nearby (11.67). Ozu cuts 180° across the axis, framing another mah-jongg table (11.68). The first table is now in the background, viewed from the opposite side. So will the scene's action take place here among the mah-jongg players? The next cut returns to the medium long shot along the courtyard hallway (11.69). Finally, there is a medium shot of the two pairs of slippers by the door in the upper hallway (11.70), suggesting that this is the grandparents' room. A medium shot of the Hirayamas in bed, trying to sleep through the noise, finally reveals the narrative situation (11.71). Only now do the Hirayamas start to talk.

characteristic of Ozu, who seldom uses the graphic match for any narrative purpose. In this respect, Ozu's style owes something to abstract form (see Chapter 10, pp. 371–378). It's as if he sought to make a narrative film that would make graphic similarities as evident as they are in an abstract film like *Ballet mécanique.*

Ozu's narration may not seem as suspenseful as Hitchcock's or as eccentric as Godard's. His dwelling on the spaces around the characters may seem less economical than Spike Lee's concise creation of a city block in *Do The Right Thing.*

His style resembles the frontal staging and cutting we see in Wes Anderson's *Moonrise Kingdom.* It's possible that Anderson was influenced by Ozu. But Ozu's framing and cutting show us more angles on his characters. Anderson also seems more interested in the spaces behind his characters, while Ozu emphasizes the areas around them. In other words, Ozu suggests that around his characters, behind them, alongside them, exist places and people that have their own integrity and interest. Moreover, by asking us to form expectations about what areas of the setting we will see next, he draws us into an experience that involves more than building up the story. Just as when we read a novel we can appreciate a lyrical paragraph of description as well as a conflict among characters, Ozu takes us beyond the immediate action and shows that patterns of cinematic space can be enjoyed in their own right.

Chungking Express (Chung Hing sam lam)

1994. Jet Tone, Hong Kong. Directed by Wong Kar-wai. Script by Wong Kar-wai. Photographed by Andrew Lau Wai-keung and Christopher Doyle. With Brigitte Lin Ching-hsia, Takeshi Kaneshiro, Tony Leung Chiu-wai, Faye Wong Jingwen.

Filmmakers in many countries have sometimes explored what has been called the *web-of-life plot* or the *network narrative.* Instead of two primary lines of action, as in *His Girl Friday* or *North by Northwest,* some recent films weave together a large number of plotlines, often involving many characters. American precedents for this can be found in *Grand Hotel* (1932) and *Nashville* (1976), but in the 1990s, such films as *Short Cuts, Pulp Fiction, Magnolia, Traffic, Babel,* and *Love Actually* made this sort of plotting more common. Unlike the characters of *Do The Right Thing,* who all live in the same neighborhood, the characters in a web-of-life plot start out unknown to one another. Eventually, however, they are likely to converge, revealing unexpected causal connections. In *Magnolia,* disparate as the characters are, they are connected either to the television producer Earl Partridge or through chance encounters, as when the police patrolman meets Partridge's unhappy daughter.

The audience expects a network narrative to reveal unforeseen relations among the disparate characters. Seen from this standpoint, *Chungking Express* constitutes an intriguing experiment in nonclassical form. It is broken into two distinct stories, each organized around a different batch of characters. The two stories aren't cross-cut but simply set side by side. What has director Wong Kar-wai accomplished by putting these two stories in the same film?

Two Sad Policemen   In the first tale, Officer 223 (for ease of recall, we'll call him Officer 1) has just broken up with his girlfriend and lives in hope that she'll take him back before May 1, his 25th birthday. Wandering the city at night, he runs into a mysterious woman in dark glasses and a blonde wig. He doesn't know that she is part of a drug-smuggling outfit. She has hired some Indian down-and-outs to carry bags of cocaine out of the country, but they have defected with the drugs. She must recover the shipment or face the wrath of her boss, who runs a bar. Officer 1 meets her in a bar and takes her to a cheap hotel, where she sleeps off her drinking and he eats snacks. In the morning, he leaves her. She posts an affectionate message on his pager before returning to the bar and shooting her boss dead.

The second and longer tale introduces Officer 633 (Officer 2), who is happy with his girlfriend, a flight attendant. But one day she leaves him. He is still trying

> " [Financiers in Asia] always ask, 'Is it a cop story or a gangster story?' So you have to choose. One or the other. . . . So with *Chungking Express,* I said it is a cop and a gangster story. We have gangsters, and we have cops. But it is not a gangster/cop story. It's just about their lives, and that's it."
> —Wong Kar-wai, director

to get over their affair when Faye, a counterwoman at his favorite fast-food spot, the Midnight Express, takes an interest in him. The flight attendant leaves Officer 2's keys at the Midnight Express snack bar for him to retrieve, and Faye uses them to explore his apartment while he's out. She tidies it up and redecorates it, leaving fresh soap and towels and filling his aquarium with fish. After catching her in the apartment, he realizes she's flirting with him. They make a date. But she stands him up, leaving for California—the place she had always hoped to visit. A year later, Officer 2 has bought the Midnight Express and is renovating it when Faye returns. Now *she's* a flight attendant, and there is a hint that their romance might finally begin.

11.72 Passing unawares. In *Chungking Express,* while the mysterious blonde woman lounges outside a shop, Faye (whom we do not meet until part two) leaves with a stuffed toy (perhaps destined for Officer 2's apartment). Each of the three main characters of part two is glimpsed during the first story.

What links the two parts? Both employ handheld camera work, moody music, and voice-over commentaries drifting in and out. But common stylistic choices aren't normally enough to justify putting two stories together. Since both protagonists are policemen, we might expect them to encounter one another, but they never do; the first is a plainclothes detective, while the second pounds a beat. Nor does the mysterious blonde's drug smuggling ever impinge on the cops' activities. Officer 1 is ignorant of her racket, and Officer 2 doesn't investigate the murder of the bar owner, as he might in another kind of plot. The two strands do share one locale: Both Officer 1 and Officer 2 hang out at the Midnight Express. Nonetheless, this doesn't connect the parts causally, since Officer 1 meets Faye only once, and he never becomes a rival for her affections. As if to tease sharp-eyed repeat viewers, Wong inserts into the first part a brief, distant shot of each main character who will appear in the *second* part—Officer 2, the flight attendant, and Faye **(11.72).** But they are unknown to us the first time we see the film, and they aren't presented as shaping the story action in the first part.

It is as if Wong has juxtaposed the two stories in such a way to demand that we find our own connections between them. By analyzing narrative form and style, we can bring to light some intriguing similarities and differences, which in turn point to a set of themes that unify the film.

Two Times, Two Places   In broad narrative terms, the two parts stand in sharp contrast. The first takes place on the Kowloon peninsula of Hong Kong, in and around Chungking Mansions, a decaying block of cheap guest quarters, shops, and Indian restaurants. (The Cantonese title of the film translates as "Chungking Jungle," and it may tease the local viewer into believing that eventually the second story will return to this neighborhood.) The second part takes place on Hong Kong Island, across the bay from Kowloon, in the vicinity of the Midnight Express. The Kowloon of part one teems with crime; Officer 1 chases suspects down at gunpoint, while the blonde works for a drug cartel. Part two presents a far less threatening world, where romance can blossom and the cop on the beat drops in for snacks. The English-language title of the film fuses the basic locales of each part, balancing Chungking Mansions with Midnight Express in a single phrase.

The two parts offer very different time schemes as well. The first part takes place over a short span, about four days, and the action labors under deadlines. Officer 1 has given May, his ex-girlfriend, the month of April to come back to him. The blonde's deadline for the smuggling operation has been set by her boss, and she meets it by shooting him and escaping from Hong Kong on May 1. The second part has a much looser time frame and no strong deadlines. Over a period of weeks, Officer 2's girlfriend leaves him, Faye invades his apartment, he transfers his beat, and after a series of casual encounters they finally make a date. Faye stands up Officer 2 and, like the blonde woman, departs. The action concludes a year later when she flies back to Hong Kong.

CONNECT TO THE BLOG
www.davidbordwell.net/blog

For an analysis of a Wong Kar-wai martial-arts movie, see "*The Grandmaster*: Moving forward, turning back."

11.73

11.74

11.73–11.74 **Policemen wounded by romance.** Wong uses parallel images to show Officer 1 and Officer 2 moping in their apartments.

Yet within these broad contrasts, some echoes do emerge. Each man is coming out of a love affair; each meets a woman by chance; quickly or slowly, the man becomes attached to her; the woman abruptly departs. The characters' goals are also revealing. Officer 1 seeks a new woman to love, and although Officer 2 is content to drift, Faye seems to try to ease his bruised heart. These goals are presented more vaguely and pursued more erratically than in a Hollywood film, but the parallels suggest that *Chungking Express* revolves around romance. The more closely we look at cause-effect chains, motifs, and visual style, the more evidence we find that the film is comparing ways in which people try to find love.

The two policemen's romantic problems shape their attitudes toward time. Neither man realizes that love affairs must adjust to change. In part one, ruled by fast pace and deadlines, Officer 1 has been pining for a month and now wants to find a new girlfriend immediately. Officer 2, suddenly dumped by his flight-attendant girlfriend, can't summon up the energy to restart his love life. Both men fill their stretches of waiting with cycles of repetitive behavior. Officer 1 badgers May's family and then calls old girlfriends to ask for a date. Officer 2 repeatedly visits the Midnight Express, first to pick up snacks for himself and his girlfriend, then simply to brood. Although one wants a sudden adventure and the other falls back on routine, both are caught in spirals of inactivity. Wong emphasizes this through parallel images of each man moping in his apartment (**11.73, 11.74**).

Food and Flight The two cops need a change—according to the film's most pervasive motif, a change of menu. Food is central to both stories, announced at the start in the headlong tracking shots through Chungking Mansions, where the snack stalls are filled with eaters. May loved pineapple, so Officer 1 measures the time he waits for her in pineapple cans, each day buying one with a May 1 expiration date. On the last day, when she hasn't returned to him, he gorges himself on the 30 cans he has saved. When he meets the blonde, he asks if she likes pineapple. Similarly, Officer 2 always orders chef's salads at the Midnight Express.

The men stick with one food, but the women crave varied menus. As the blonde studies Officer 1 in the bar, her voice-over commentary remarks, "Knowing someone doesn't mean keeping them. People change. A person may like pineapple today and something else tomorrow." When Officer 2 brings home pizza and fish and chips, his girlfriend leaves him. He muses that she realized that she had a choice of lovers as well as dinners.

The food motif goes on to define the men's attitudes toward change. While the blonde sleeps in a Chungking Mansions hotel room, Officer 1 stuffs himself with hamburgers, salads, and fries. Once outside, he thinks that she has forgotten him, but her pager message ("Happy birthday") leads him to wish that the expiration date on his memory of her will last forever. No longer treating a girlfriend as a fast-food snack, Officer 1's sense of time has expanded. Instead of seeking a new future, he treasures a moment in the past (**11.75**).

As the counter girl Faye invades Officer 2's life, she replaces his cheap tinned fish with another brand, spikes his water jug to help him sleep, and pushes him out of his self-pity (in which he imagines his towel crying and his soap wasting away). When she skips their date, she leaves him a fake boarding pass she inks

11.75

11.76

11.75–11.76 Messages in the rain. After his morning run, Officer 1 gets the pager message wishing him a happy birthday (11.75). Officer 2 had discarded the mock boarding pass Faye left him. Now, in a comparable framing to 11.75, he waits for it to dry so he can read it (11.76).

onto a napkin. At first he discards it, but then, in a composition paralleling that of Officer 1's meditation on his pager message, he dries it in a snack-shop rotisserie **(11.76)**. A year later, Officer 2 has embraced a varied menu. He has bought the Midnight Express, and when Faye returns, he persuades her to write him a new boarding pass. Before he had been reluctant to travel with her, but now, when she asks where he wants to fly, he replies, "Wherever you want to take me." He has broken out of routine and is ready for a change.

This last scene sums up another motif, airplane flight, that runs through both parts and marks parallels. Air travel is associated with the women's desire for change. In the first part, the blonde prepares her drug mules for a trip, and she flees her crime by taking an early plane out. In the second part, Officer 2's air hostess is replaced by Faye **(11.77)**. Musical motifs also signal the importance of change. The repeated reggae song in the first part states, "It's not every day that's gonna be the same way, there must be a change somehow." The second part highlights the song "What a Difference a Day Makes" and the Mamas and Papas' "California Dreamin'," which expresses a wish to leave for sunnier surroundings. Several pictorial motifs parallel the two main women, including their shoes, their dark glasses, and their habit of slipping into reverie **(11.78, 11.79)**.

Crime Thriller or Romantic Drama or Both? If the film's primary theme is the need to accept change as part of love, then the two parts are cunningly designed to lead us toward it indirectly. The first part opens with the blonde hurrying through Chungking Mansions, then shows Officer 1 racing after a criminal and colliding with her before moving on. Her femme fatale disguise and the drug deal suggest that this is the start of a crime thriller (see pp. 332–334). But soon the smuggling situation is overwhelmed by Officer 1's romantic yearnings. The blonde woman's abrupt shooting of her boss ends the crime line of action. The second tale begins, and Officer 2's placid routine and personal problems take over. The thriller elements have served largely as bait, luring us to study the characters before the plot switches genres and becomes an open-ended romantic drama.

Wong signals the genre shift through a stylistic parallel. At the start of the film, as Officer 1 collides with the blonde, the frame freezes, and in voice-over he says, "Fifty-seven hours later I fell in love with this woman." At the end of the first part

11.77 Replacement women. When Faye first meets the woman who dumped Officer 2, she secretly measures herself against her. At the end of the film, Faye will become a flight attendant herself.

11.78

11.79

11.78–11.79 Musing women. The blonde woman of part one (11.78) strikes a posture similar to that of Faye in part two (11.79).

11.80

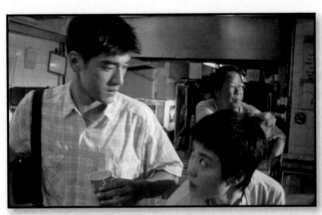

11.81

11.80–11.81 Freeze-frames and voice-overs. Part one of *Chungking Express* ends with Officer 1 bumping into Faye at the Midnight Express (11.80). Part two begins with Officer 2 approaching the Midnight Express; he will replace Officer 1 as the film's male protagonist (11.81). Both parallels are marked by Officer 1's voice-over commentary.

Officer 1 revisits the Midnight Express, and he bumps into Faye **(11.80).** His commentary remarks, "Six hours later . . ." The image fades out and fades in on Officer 2 approaching the snack bar **(11.81),** and we hear Officer 1 continue, ". . . She fell in love with another man." We will never see Officer 1 again. These voice-over remarks (highly implausible on grounds of realism—how could Officer 1 know that Faye falls in love with Officer 2?) mark the film's romantic parallels explicitly.

Since the plotlines in the two parts aren't linked causally, the film may at first disappoint the viewer's expectations. Why don't the couples meet? Wong did entertain the possibility of having all four main characters converge at the airport, but he decided to give us something a little more challenging. By keeping the two stories separate, he forces us to seek thematic connections. The parallel situations point to the idea that change is as necessary to love as variety is to diet. The thematic implications are reinforced by mise-en-scene, cinematography, music, and voice-over commentary. Yet *Chungking Express* isn't heavy-handed, partly because it slides cleverly from crime movie to stop-and-start romance, and partly because it invites us to appreciate its playful artifice.

Documentary Form and Style

Man with a Movie Camera (Chelovek s kinoapparatom)

Made 1928, released 1929. VUFKU, Union of Soviet Socialist Republics. Directed by Dziga Vertov. Photographed by Mikhail Kaufman. Edited by Elizaveta Svilova.

Man with a Movie Camera might seem to be a straight reportorial documentary; it surveys a day in the life of Russian society. The day-in-the-life documentary format has been a sturdy one, right up to *One Day on Earth* (2011). But Dziga Vertov's approach is more experimental. His film is as much a celebration of cinema as it is a portrait of his country's life. Vertov will try to show that documentary film goes beyond simply recording its subjects. Thanks to editing and cinematography, along with associational form, a multitude of tiny scenes from everyday reality becomes an exploration of the power of moviemaking.

A City Symphony   *Man with a Movie Camera* belongs to a genre of documentaries that became important during the 1920s: the *city symphony*. There are many ways of making a film about a city, of course. One might use categorical form to lay out its geography or scenic attractions, as in a travelogue. Rhetorical form could make arguments about problems in city planning or government policies that need changing. A narrative might stress a city as the backdrop for many characters' actions, as in Rossellini's *Rome Open City* or Jules Dassin's semidocumentary crime drama *The Naked City*. Early city symphonies, however, established the convention of taking candid (or occasionally staged) scenes of city life and linking them, usually without commentary, through associations to suggest emotions or concepts. Associational form is evident in such early examples of the genre as Alberto Cavalcanti's *Rien que les heures* (1926) and Walter Ruttmann's *Berlin, Symphony of a Great City* (1927). Godfrey Reggio's *Koyaanisqatsi* (1983) use of associational principles to create moods and evoke concepts about contemporary urban life ties it to the city-symphony tradition. (See pp. 379–386.)

In *Man with a Movie Camera*'s opening, we see a camera operator filming, then passing between the curtains of an empty movie theater and moving toward the screen. Then we see the theater opening, the spectators filing in, and the orchestra preparing to play. The screening starts. The film that we and the audience watch seems at first to be a city symphony laying out a typical day in the life of a town (as Ruttmann's *Berlin* does). We see a woman asleep, mannequins in closed shops, and empty streets. Soon a few people appear, and the city wakes up. Indeed, much of *Man with a Movie Camera* follows a rough principle of development that progresses from early morning through work time to leisure time.

But early in the waking-up portion, we also see the cameraman again, setting out with his equipment, as if starting his workday. This action creates the first of many deliberate inconsistencies. The cameraman now appears in his own film, and Vertov emphasizes this by cutting back immediately to the sleeping woman who had been the first thing we saw. From the start, this city symphony announces it will also be a cinema-symphony, a film dedicated to the process of creating a film.

Cinematographer as Hero   The very title *Man with a Movie Camera* emphasizes the fact of filmmaking. Vertov was a keen advocate of editing; in Chapter 6 (p. 225), we quoted a passage in which he equated the filmmaker with an eye, gathering shots from many places and linking them creatively for the spectator. Vertov's theoretical writings also compare the eye to the lens of the camera, in a concept he termed the "kino eye." (*Kino* is the Russian word for "cinema," and one of his earlier films is called *Kino-Glaz, or Cinema-Eye.*)

Man with a Movie Camera takes this idea—the equation of the filmmaker's eye with the lens of the camera—as the basis for associational form. The film becomes a demonstration of cinema's power to control our perception of reality through editing and special effects. The opening image shows a camera in close-up. Through a double-exposure effect, we see the cameraman of the film's title suddenly climb, in extreme long shot, onto the top of the giant camera **(11.82)**. He sets up his own camera on a tripod and films for a bit and then climbs down again. This play on shot scale within a single image emphasizes at once the power the cinema has to alter reality in a seemingly magical way.

Cinematographic special effects of this sort appear as a motif throughout the film. These are not intended to be unnoticeable, as in a science fiction film. Instead, they flaunt the fact that the camera can alter everyday reality **(11.83)**.

11.82

11.83

11.82–11.83 The hero and his superpowers. Vertov's regular cinematographer, Mikhail Kaufman, played the cameraman in *Man with a Movie Camera* (11.82). Kaufman alters an ordinary street scene by exposing each side of the image separately, with the camera canted in opposite directions (11.83).

11.84

11.85

11.86

11.84–11.86 Surpassing reality through special effects. Thanks to pixillation, a crayfish dances (11.84). Vertov conveys the sound of a radio by superimposing images of a dancer and of a hand playing a piano against a black background (11.85). *Man with a Movie Camera* ends with an eye superimposed over the camera lens, staring out challengingly (11.86).

11.87

11.88

11.87–11.88 Camera as all-powerful machine. The animated camera crawls out of its box, climbs onto the tripod, and demonstrates how its various parts work (11.87). A climactic shot uses an extraordinary deep-focus composition to show the camera scanning the city (11.88).

Later Vertov uses pixillation to animate objects and superimpositions to evoke sound **(11.84, 11.85)**. The virtuosic special effects culminate in the famous final shot **(11.86)**. Cinema's powers make the filmmaker something of a superhero.

At several points in the film, the camera is also personified, associated by editing with the actions of human beings. One brief segment shows the camera lens focusing, followed by a blurry shot of flowers coming into sharp focus. This is followed immediately by a comic juxtaposition rapidly intercutting two elements: a woman's fluttering eyelids as she dries her face with a towel and a set of venetian blinds opening and closing. Finally, another shot shows the camera lens with a diaphragm closing and opening. A human eye is like venetian blinds, just as the lens is like an eye—all can admit or block out light. Later, pixillation allows the camera to move by itself **(11.87)** and finally then to walk off on three legs. The machine has become human, and the human has become a machine.

The opening has laid out the whole process of documentary filmmaking, from shooting through editing to projection in a theater. Throughout *Man with a Movie Camera,* we see an action being filmed, then edited, then viewed by the onscreen audience, though not always in this neat order. Later Vertov intercuts shots of the cameraman filming from a motorcycle with shots of the audience in the theater watching the footage. In the final portions of the film, motifs from earlier parts of the day return, many now in fast motion. The chronological order of the ordinary city symphony is broken and jumbled. Vertov creates an impossible time scheme, once more emphasizing the extraordinary manipulative powers of the cinema.

The film also refuses to show only one city, instead mixing footage filmed in Moscow, Kiev, and Odessa, as if the cameraman hero can move effortlessly across the USSR during this "day" of filming. Vertov's view of the cinema's relation to the cityscape is well conveyed in one shot that makes the camera loom over distant buildings **(11.88)**. The camera conquers all. *Man with a Movie Camera* is a city symphony, but it goes beyond the genre as well.

Social Criticism and Self-Advertisement   Apart from its exuberant celebration of the powers of cinema, Vertov's film contains many explicit and implicit meanings. Explicitly, the film seeks both to praise and to criticize aspects of Soviet society a decade after the Revolution.

Many of the film's juxtapositions involve machines and human labor. Under Stalin, the USSR was beginning a major push toward industrialization, and the mechanized factories are portrayed as fascinating places full of bustling movement **(11.89)**. The camera operator scales a huge factory smokestack or swings suspended over a dam to capture a new society being built. Workers are presented as participating cheerfully in the country's growth, as when one young woman laughs and chats as she folds cigarette boxes on an assembly line.

Vertov also points out weak spots in contemporary life, such as lingering class inequalities. Shots in a beauty shop suggest that some bourgeois values have survived the Revolution, and the leisure-time sequence near the end contrasts workers involved in outdoors sports with chubby women exercising in a weight-loss gym.

Vertov also takes pains to criticize drunkenness, a major social problem in the USSR. One of the first shots within the inner film shows a derelict sleeping outdoors, juxtaposed with a huge bottle advertising a café. A shop front that we repeatedly see advertises wine and vodka, and later there is a scene where the cameraman visits this bar. When he leaves, we see shots of workers' clubs, converted from former churches. Associational crosscutting contrasts these two places where workers can spend their leisure time: A woman shooting at targets in one of the clubs seems to be shooting away bottles of beer that, thanks to stop-motion, disappear from a crate in the bar.

11.89 The glamor of the machine. Framing and lighting enhance the dynamism of throbbing, gleaming machine parts.

During the 1920s, government officials sought to steer Soviet citizens away from taverns and churches and toward film theaters and workers' clubs. (Since the government's biggest source of income came from its monopoly on vodka sales, the policy also aimed at making film a major alternative source of revenue.) *Man with a Movie Camera* seems to be subtly promoting this policy by using playful camera techniques to make both movie houses and clubs seem attractive.

Implicitly, *Man with a Movie Camera* can be seen as an argument for Vertov's approach to filmmaking. He opposed narrative form and the use of professional actors, preferring that films use camera technique and editing to create their effects on the audience. He was not, however, entirely against controlling the mise-en-scene, and several scenes, particularly the woman waking up and washing, clearly were staged. On the whole, the film is a sort of demonstration of what path Vertov thought cinema should take.

Vertov strengthens his case by associating making a film with other sorts of productive labor. The camera operator goes to his job in the morning, like other workers. Like them, he uses a machine; editing compares the camera's crank with the crank on a cash register and with moving parts on factory equipment. And the filmmaker is dedicated. He accepts dangerous missions, climbing up a huge smokestack, crouching on the tracks to film an oncoming train, riding a motorcycle one-handed as he cranks the camera to capture a race. Even when other workers are relaxing at the beach or at sporting events, the cameraman is on the job.

As the cameraman's work is compared with running factory machines or taking on hazardous missions, editing is seen as a patient craft. The editor whom we see cutting the footage is Elizaveta Svilova, Vertov's wife and the actual editor of *Man with a Movie Camera.* Her gestures of scraping the film and dabbing cement to make a splice are crosscut with shots of a manicure in a beauty parlor. More generally, across the film we see the same shots in different contexts: on our screen, on the screen within the movie theater, in fast-motion, or in freeze frame. We see shots filmed, snipped apart, spliced together. We must therefore view these images not only as moments of recorded reality but also as pieces of a whole put together through the painstaking efforts of film workers like Svilova. The film becomes a sort of machine to be assembled and tuned to perfection by expert hands. Filmmaking is a job, not an elite-oriented art, and it has a useful role in building the new society.

Judging from the delighted reactions of the audience we see in the theater, Vertov hoped that the Soviet public would find his celebration of filmmaking educational and entertaining. This hope went unfulfilled. During the late 1920s, Soviet authorities wanted films that would be easily understandable and would convey propagandistic messages to a far-flung, often illiterate, populace. Policy makers were increasingly critical of filmmakers such as Sergei Eisenstein and Vertov, whose films, though celebrating revolutionary ideology, were extremely complex. In Chapter 6, we saw how Eisenstein adopted a dense, discontinuous style of editing. While Vertov disagreed with Eisenstein, particularly over the latter's reliance on narrative form, both belonged to a larger stylistic movement called Soviet Montage, whose history we examine in Chapter 12 (pp. 470–473). Both filmmakers used very complex editing that they hoped viewers would learn to enjoy.

With its contradictory time scheme and rapid editing (it contains over 1,700 shots, more than twice what most Hollywood films of the same period had), *Man with a Movie Camera* is a difficult film, especially for an audience unaccustomed to the conventions of Montage filmmaking. Over the next few years, Soviet authorities increasingly criticized Vertov and his colleagues, limiting their ability to experiment with concepts like the kino-eye. Vertov was constrained in his later projects, but *Man with a Movie Camera* eventually came to be recognized around the world as a sophisticated documentary, a classic experiment in associational form, and an uninhibited display of the power of cinematic technique.

The Thin Blue Line

1988. An American Playhouse production (PBS). Directed by Errol Morris. Photographed by Stefan Czapsky, Robert Chappell. Edited by Paul Barnes. Music by Philip Glass.

On a west Dallas highway one night in 1976, a police officer named Robert Wood was fatally shot by a driver he had pulled over. Wood's partner, officer Teresa Turko, saw the killer drive off, but it took months of investigation for the police to discover that the car had been stolen by David Harris. Harris, a 16-year-old from the small town of Vidor, admitted to being in the car but said that the killer was Randall Adams, a man with whom he had hung around that day. Adams was tried for murder, found guilty, and sentenced to death. Eventually, through an appeal process, his sentence was commuted to life imprisonment. Harris, because of his age and his cooperation with the police, was given a suspended sentence.

In 1985, documentary filmmaker Errol Morris met Randall Adams while he was researching another project. Morris became convinced that Adams had been unjustly convicted, and over the next three years, he prepared a film based on his investigation of the case.

The Thin Blue Line employs narrative form, telling the story of events leading up to and following the murder of Officer Wood. Yet the film's narration enriches that basic story. By juggling time, inserting many details, developing the reenactments of the killing into a powerful pattern, and subtly engaging our sympathy for Randall Adams, Morris not only takes us through a criminal case but also suggests how difficult the search for truth can be.

Parts and Wholes The overall plot guides us through the story events, but not in a wholly linear way. For this reason, it's useful to draw up a segmentation of the film. We can find 31 fairly distinct sequences, although many contain brief flashbacks to the interrogation and the crime. Some also contain fairly lengthy reenactments, which are signaled here by italics.

   C. Opening credits
   1. Dallas, Randall Adams, and David Harris are introduced.
   2. Officer Wood is shot. *First shooting reenactment*
   3. Adams is arrested and interrogated. *First interrogation reenactment*
   4. Police describe the interrogation and the beginning of the investigation. *Second interrogation reenactment*
   5. Police describe the two officers' states of mind. *Second shooting reenactment*
   6. Police search for the car, even using hypnotism. *Third shooting reenactment*

7. Big break: David Harris is discovered in Vidor, Texas.
8. Harris accuses Randall Adams of the shooting.
9. Adams responds to Harris's charge.
10. Adams is interrogated. *Third interrogation reenactment*
11. Police explain the mistaken auto identification.
12. Adams's two lawyers are introduced and describe their inquiry into Harris's hometown.
13. Adams's lawyers discuss Harris as a criminal; the judge describes his attitude toward police.
14. Adams recounts Harris's version of events. *Fourth shooting reenactment*
15. Adams explains his alibi.
16. Trial: Officer Turko testifies, implicating Adams. *Fifth shooting reenactment*
17. Trial: New witnesses emerge. Mr. and Mrs. Miller claim to have seen Adams shoot Wood. *Sixth shooting reenactment*
18. Adams's lawyers and Mrs. Carr rebut the Miller couple's testimony.
19. Trial: Third new witness, Michael Randell, claims to have seen Adams shoot Wood. *Seventh shooting reenactment*
20. Trial: Jury declares Adams guilty.
21. Trial: Judge sentences Adams to death.
22. Adams reacts to the death sentence.
23. Adams's lawyers petition for a retrial and lose.
24. Adams's appeal is supported by the U.S. Supreme Court; his sentence is commuted to life in prison.
25. Vidor detective explains: Harris is arrested again.
26. Rethinking the case: Witnesses reflect, and Harris hints that he has lied. *Eighth shooting reenactment*
27. Vidor detective explains: Harris has committed a murder in town.
28. Adams: "The kid scares me"; he reflects on the mistake of letting Harris go free.
29. Harris, now on death row, reflects on his childhood.
30. Final interview on audiotape: Harris calls Adams a "scapegoat" and virtually confesses.
31. Title: Current situation of the two men.
E. Closing credits.

Segments 1–3 form a prologue, introducing the essential information and arousing our curiosity and concern. The opening sequence presents the city of Dallas; the two main characters, Randall Adams and David Harris; and their current situation: both men are in jail. What has brought them there? They tell of meeting each other and spending the day drinking, smoking marijuana, and going to a drive-in movie. Segment 2 is the first of many shocking reenactments of the shooting of Officer Wood at the dark roadside. Here, as in all the others, actors play the participants, and the framing often conceals their faces, concentrating instead on details of action or setting. The third sequence depicts Adams's arrest and interrogation **(11.90)**.

Then the film's plot flashes back to explain events leading up to Adams's arrest, concentrating on the police investigation (segments 4–11). In the course of this, David Harris names Randall Adams as the killer (8), and Adams is arrested and interrogated (10). Eventually, the confusion about the make of the car is cleared up, though Morris hints that the police investigation was muddled (11). These sequences are interrupted by two more reenactments of Adams's questioning and two reenactments of the death of Officer Wood.

11.90 Staging in documentary. *The Thin Blue Line:* The questioning of Randall Adams, staged so that it is clearly a reenactment.

The longest stretch of the film (segments 12–24) centers on Randall Adams's confrontation with the courts. After his lawyers and the judge are introduced (12–13), we're given two conflicting versions of events—Adams's and Harris's (14–15). Three surprise witnesses identify Adams as the shooter (16–19), although some of the testimony is undercut by a woman who claims that two witnesses bragged to her about trying to earn a reward (18). Again, at certain moments the crime is reenacted to illustrate witnesses' testimony. The jury finds Adams guilty (20), and he's sentenced to death (21–22). The legal maneuvers that follow put Adams in prison for life without parole (23–24).

The film has answered one question posed at the outset. Now we know how Randall Adams got to prison. But what of David Harris, who is also serving time? The final stretch of the film continues the story after the trial, concentrating on Harris's criminal career. Harris is arrested for other crimes (25), and Morris inserts a sequence (26) designed to suggest his guilt in the Wood case. The surprise eye-witnesses are shown to be unreliable and confused, and as having things to hide. Most tellingly, Harris explains, "Of course I picked out Randall Adams." In the next sequence, a detective in Harris's hometown of Vidor explains how Harris invaded a man's home, violently abducted his girlfriend, and fatally shot the man (27). Harris, now revealed as a polite, easygoing sociopath, reflects on his childhood, when his brother drowned and his father seemed to become more distant (29). But whatever sympathy he might arouse is undercut by his final acknowledgment, captured by Morris on audiotape, that Randall Adams is innocent (30). A title explains that Adams is still serving his life sentence, while Harris is on death row (31).

Complicating the Plot   In outline, then, this is a straightforward tale of crime and injustice. The film's explicit meaning was compelling enough to trigger a new inquiry into the case, and Adams was freed in 1989. But Morris's film is more than a brief for the defense. It demands a great deal of the viewer; it does not spell out its message in the manner of most documentaries. We tend to side with Randall Adams and to distrust the police, prosecutors, and "eyewitnesses" aligned against him, but Morris does not explicitly favor Adams and criticize the others. The film's form and style shape our sympathies rather subtly. At another level, the film denies the viewer many of the usual aids for determining what happened on that night in 1976. Instead, it asks us to heighten our attention, to concentrate on details, and to weigh the incompatible information we are given. Morris's detective story asks us to reflect on the obstacles to arriving at the truth about any crime.

The film's materials are for the most part the stuff of any true-crime report. Morris uses talking-head interviews, newspaper headlines, maps, archival photos, and other documents to present information about the crime. He also includes reenactments of key events, signaled as such. Nonetheless, other documentary conventions are missing. There is no voice-over narrator explaining the situation, and no captions identify the speakers or provide dates. The reenactments don't carry the "Dramatization" caption seen in television documentaries. As a result, we're forced to evaluate what we see and hear without help. This extra responsibility is intensified by a framing that is rare in most documentary interviews: Several of the speakers look straight out at the camera, a tactic that forces us to weigh the testimony we hear **(11.91).**

Moreover, the use of paper documents is fairly cryptic: The film doesn't always specify their source, and the extreme close-ups often show only fragments of text. (One shot of a news article frames these partial phrases: ". . . ved to be a 1973 . . . earing Texas licens . . . with the letters H . . .") Likewise, Philip Glass's repetitive score is hardly conventional documentary music, especially for a true-crime story. With its mournful, unresolved harmonies and nervously oscillating figures, the music arouses tension, but it also creates an eerie distance from the action: It throbs on, unchanged whether it accompanies an empty city landscape or a violent murder.

Other formal and stylistic qualities complicate the plot. For example, when an interviewee mentions a particular place, Morris tends to insert a quick shot of that

CONNECT TO THE BLOG
www.davidbordwell.net/blog

Real-life mysteries come in many forms. The magicians Penn and Teller track a man who tried to penetrate a great painter's secrets. We consider the result in "I am a camera, sometimes: *Tim's Vermeer.*"

11.91 Address to the viewer. A police detective gives his version of Adams's interrogation in a somewhat unnerving direct address.

locale (**11.92**). So many abrupt interruptions wouldn't appear in a normal documentary, since they don't really give us much extra information. It's as if Morris wants to suggest the vast number of tiny pieces of information that an investigator must process. Similarly, during most of the reenactments, people's faces aren't shown. Instead, the scenes are built out of many close-ups: fingers resting on a steering wheel, a milkshake flying through the air in slow motion, a popcorn machine (**11.93**). Again, Morris stresses the apparently trivial details that can affect our sense of what really happened on the highway.

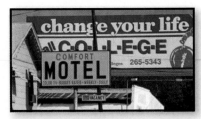

11.92

By amplifying apparently minor details he also invites us to see some of these shots metaphorically. Carefully composed and lit in high-key, the details become evocative motifs. Some inserts comment ironically on the situation (11.92). Others, such as the ever-present clocks and watches, indicate the ominous passing of time. Even the slowly shattering flashlight and the milkshake dribbling onto the pavement suggest the life pumping out of the fatally wounded officer Wood.

11.93

Reenactments and Revelations

Morris subtly orchestrates our attitudes toward the people presented in the film. By and large, the plot is shaped to create sympathy for Randall Adams. He is the first person we see, and Morris immediately makes him appealing by letting him explain that he was grateful to find a good job soon after coming to Dallas. "It's as if I was meant to be here." Morris presents him as a decent, hardworking man railroaded by the justice system. The interrogation of Adams is associated with filled ashtrays, making him seem nervous and vulnerable (**11.94**), as do the repeated close-ups of newspaper photos of his frightened eyes. When the accusers state their case, Morris keeps us on Adams's side by letting him rebut them. In segment 9, Adams replies to Harris's charge that he was the shooter; in segment 15, Adams presents his alibi in reply to Harris's claims about the time frame of events. By the end, Adams becomes the authoritative commentator. In segment 28, after Harris has committed another murder, Adams reminds us that a life could have been saved if the Dallas police hadn't released Harris. At this point, our sympathies for Adams are strong, and we understand why he reverses his initial judgment on Dallas: It's now "hell on earth."

11.94

11.92–11.94 Minor details as motifs. Morris cuts away to the motel where Adams stayed; in light of Adams's fate, the billboard in the background becomes ironic (11.92). A popcorn machine at the drive-in ominously fills the foreground, while the clock serves as the basis for David Harris's testimony (11.93). While Harris the teenager is associated with popcorn, Adams the panicked victim is associated with an ashtray full of cigarettes (11.94).

Our acceptance of Adams's account is subtly reinforced by the many reenactments of the murder. They are clearly set off as reconstructions by their use of techniques more closely associated with the fiction film, particularly film noir (**11.95**; also 4.63). They also distinguish themselves from the restagings shown on true-crime television shows, which tend to include the faces of actors and which are usually shot in a loose, handheld style suggesting that we are witnessing the real event.

The reenactments present different versions of the crime in accord with different witnesses' recollections. By presenting contradictory versions of what happened that night, Morris may seem to be suggesting that everyone involved saw things from his or her own perspective, and so there is no final fact of the matter. But the overall progression of the film leads us to a likely conclusion: that David Harris, on his own, killed Wood. Rather than suggesting that truth is relative, the incompatible reconstructions dramatize the conflicting testimony. Like jurors or courtroom spectators, we have to decide on the most plausible version, and the plot develops the reenactments in a strongly suggestive pattern.

In the segments devoted to the police investigation, the restagings emphasize matters of procedure. Did Officer Turko identify the car correctly? No, the police detectives eventually decide; but both before and after they arrive at this conclusion, Morris shows us two different cars, making the uncertainty visually concrete. Another question is just as important: Did Turko back up Officer Wood according to procedure, or did she remain in the car? Morris dramatizes both possibilities, but he leads us to infer that she probably was inside the car drinking her milkshake, since in the crime scene sketch, spilled chocolate liquid was found near the car. It is a matter of probabilities, and we can never be certain; but on the evidence we are given, we infer that she probably did not back up Wood.

11.95 An echo of film noir. In a reenactment, Officer Wood is shown approaching the car.

CONNECT TO THE BLOG
www.davidbordwell.net/blog

For more on Errol Morris's
approach to documentary, see the
entry "Errol Morris, boy detective."

The reenactments of Officer Wood's murder in the investigation section con-centrate on police procedure, but during the trial section, the reenactments suggest different versions of what was happening in the killer's car. Was David Harris duck-ing down in the front seat? Was Adams's bushy silhouette mistaken for a fur-lined coat collar? When the surprise witnesses are introduced, Morris shows reenact-ments that present their cars passing the murder scene. Again, the reconstructions present the alternatives neutrally, but some become more plausible than others, especially once the eyewitnesses are rebutted by other testimony or betrayed by their own evasive answers.

The last reenactment, presented in the section devoted to David Harris, shows how Harris could have committed the murder, and significantly, it is accompanied by his voice virtually confessing to it. Now, after many other reenactments, this one is presented as most worthy of our belief. Morris carefully refrains from say-ing explicitly that Harris was the killer. But the development of the reconstructions, eliminating the most questionable versions and focusing more and more on the identity of the driver, pushes us toward accepting this as the likeliest account.

Digressions and Motifs   As in any narrative film, then, the manner of story-telling, the play with narration and knowledge, shapes our attitudes toward the characters. By letting Adams comment on other characters, and by arranging the reenactments so as to point eventually toward David Harris's guilt, the film aligns us with Randall Adams, the innocent victim. Correspondingly, Morris uses other stylistic devices to make us mistrust the forces set against Adams. The film doesn't present the Dallas law officers as brutal villains, though. All are soft-spoken and articulate, and Judge Metcalfe comes across as calm and patient. But Morris's edit-ing decisions give prominence to Adams's account and allow him to answer their charges, so we're inclined to appraise their words cautiously.

Morris comes closest to criticizing the authorities at two points. Both are semi-comic digressions relying on the sort of associational form exploited by *Koyaanisqatsi* (pp. 379–386). Judge Metcalfe reminisces about the death of John Dillinger **(11.96, 11.97)** and supplies background trivia about the woman who betrayed Dillinger. When he says she was sent back to her native Romania, Morris cuts to a map of Bucharest, as if that were as relevant to Adams's case as the Texas maps used elsewhere in the film. A similar bit of mocking humor appears when one eyewitness says that she always imagined herself as a girl detective in 1950s TV shows. Morris lets her voice-over commentary run during a clip from a B-film in which a young woman helps a detective capture a crook. These sequences suggest that Adams's adversaries hold a conception of crime fighting derived from popular movies.

11.96   **11.97**

11.96–11.97 Romanticizing the war on crime. Judge Metcalfe recalls that he grew up with a great respect for law and order because his father was present when FBI agents shot the gangster John Dillinger (11.96). Morris cuts to a scene from a Hollywood crime movie that presents Dillinger's death, an ancestor of the reenactments in *The Thin Blue Line* (11.97).

The color motifs that evoke police authority and duplicity are subtler. A motif of redness links Dallas and the police as forces aligned against Adams, and it suggests an explanation for why in the opening title credit, the word *Blue* is lettered in red (**11.98–11.100**). The film's title is taken from Judge Metcalfe's reference to the prosecutor's summation, in which he called the police the "thin blue line" between civilization and anarchy. By changing the color of the word, Morris not only evokes bloodshed, but he links the police blue to the ominous blinking red lights of the opening.

11.98

The motif expands further into Judge Metcalfe's account of the death of Dillinger, who was betrayed by the notorious "woman in red." Metcalfe claims that in fact she wasn't actually wearing red; her orange dress merely looked red in a certain light. David Harris, throughout his interviews in the film, is shown wearing an orange prison uniform, suggesting that he is another figure of betrayal and perhaps hinting at his relationship to the red of the police-car light. As a documentarist, Morris probably didn't dictate what outfit Harris wore, but he did create other images that emphasize the color motif, and he did decide to retain Metcalfe's irrelevant remarks about the woman in red. Like many documentarists, Morris highlights certain aspects of his footage to bring out thematic implications.

11.99

The story of Randall Adams's unjust imprisonment is presented as an intersection of several people's lives. Instead of simplifying the case for the sake of clarity, Morris treats it as a point where many stories crisscross—the private lives of the eyewitnesses, the professional rivalries among lawyers, the Dillinger tale, TV crime dramas, scenes from the drive-in movie that Adams and Harris attended. Any crime, the film suggests, will be a tangle of threads. Any crime will seem buried in an avalanche of details (license numbers, car makes, spilled milkshakes, TV schedules), and it will engender many alternative scenarios about what really happened. *The Thin Blue Line* builds the complications and dead ends inherent in an investigation into its very structure and style. The narration grants each version of the shooting some time onscreen, but Morris finally guides us to eliminate the implausible ones. He dwells on trivial details, but finally discards certain ones as less important. And he shows that a crime's complex mass of testimony and evidence can be sorted out. The film presents itself as both an account of what really happened on that Texas highway and a meditation on how persistent inquirers can eventually arrive at truth.

11.100

11.98–11.100 The motif of redness. The first few shots of the film show skyscrapers and other structures, each with a single blinking red light (11.98). After a cut to Randall Adams beginning his tale, the screen goes dark, and we see the rotating red light of a police car, an image that will recur elsewhere in the film (11.99). The film's title, with a crucial word colored red (11.100).

Form, Style, and Ideology

Meet Me in St. Louis

1944. MGM. Directed by Vincente Minnelli. Script by Irving Brecher and Fred F. Finklehoffe, from the book by Sally Benson. Photographed by George Folsey. Edited by Albert Akst. Music by Hugh Martin and Ralph Blane. With Judy Garland, Margaret O'Brien, Mary Astor, Lucille Bremer, Leon Ames, Tom Drake.

❝ I don't shoot elegant pictures. Mr. Vincente Minnelli, *he* shot elegant pictures."

—Billy Wilder, director, *Sunset Blvd.*

Just over halfway through *Meet Me in St. Louis,* Alonzo Smith announces to his assembled family that he has been transferred to a new job in New York City. "I've got the future to think about—the future for all of us. I've got to worry about where the money's coming from," he tells the dismayed group. These ideas of family and future, central to the form and style of the film, also create an ideological framework within which the film gains impact.

All the films we've analyzed could be examined for their ideological standpoints. Any film combines formal and stylistic elements in such a way as to create an ideological stance, whether overtly stated or tacit. We've chosen to stress the ideology of *Meet Me in St. Louis* because it provides a clear example of a film that doesn't seek to change people's ways of thinking. Instead, it tends to reinforce certain aspects of a dominant social ideology. In this case, *Meet Me in St. Louis,* like most Hollywood films, seeks to uphold what are conceived as characteristically American values of family unity and home life.

No Place Like Home *Meet Me in St. Louis* is set during the preparations for the Louisiana Purchase Exposition in St. Louis, with the fair itself becoming the culmination of the action. The film displays its form in a straightforward way, with a title card identifying each of its four sections with a different season **(11.101).** In this way, the film simultaneously suggests two aspects of time: the movement toward the spring 1904 fair, which will bring the fruits of progress to St. Louis, and the unchanging cycle of the seasons. The seasonal structure allows the film to show the Smiths at the traditional times of family unity, the holidays; we see them celebrating Halloween and Christmas. At the end, the fair becomes a new sort of holiday, the celebration of the Smiths' decision to remain in St. Louis.

The opening of the film quickly introduces the idea of St. Louis as a city on the boundary between tradition and progress. The fancy candy-box title card for summer forms a vignette of white and red flowers around an old-fashioned black-and-white photo of the Smiths' house. As the camera moves in, color fades into the photo, and it comes to life **(11.102).** Slow, subdued chords over the title card give way to a bouncy tune more in keeping with the onscreen movement. Horse-drawn beer wagons and carriages move along the road, but an early-model automobile (a bright red, which draws our eye) passes them. Already the motif of progress and inventions becomes prominent; it will develop quickly into the emphasis on the upcoming fair.

As Lon Smith, the son, arrives home by bicycle, a dissolve inside to the kitchen launches the exposition. The Smiths are a large, close-knit family, and we're introduced to each character as they go through a round of household activities and pass the song "Meet Me in St. Louis" from one to another. Thanks to close matches on action, the image track yields a flow of movement that presents the house as full of bustle and music **(11.103).** When Grandpa hears offscreen voices singing the same song, he moves to a window, and Esther's arrival brings the sequence full circle back to the street outside the house **(11.104).**

The house remains the main image of family unity throughout most of the film. Most of the film's plot takes place in or near the Smith house. Although Mr. Smith's job provides the reason to move to New York, we never see him at his office. In the opening sequence, the family members return home one by one, until they all gather around the dinner table. Every seasonal section of the film begins with a similar candy-box title card and a move in toward the house. In the film's ideology, the home appears to be a self-sufficient place; other social institutions become peripheral, even threatening.

At the center of this idealized household stand the women. The narration is organized around Mrs. Smith, the oldest daughter Rose, the youngest daughter Tootie, and in particular Esther. Moreover, women are portrayed as the agents of stability. The action in the story constantly returns to the kitchen, where Mrs. Smith

11.101

11.102

11.101–11.102 Family life and the cycle of seasons. The opening title card, "Summer 1903," in *Meet Me in St. Louis* (11.101). The candy-box image becomes the Smith household as we enter the world of 1903 St. Louis (11.102).

and the maid, Katie, work calmly in the midst of small crises. By contrast, the men threaten the family's unity. Mr. Smith wants to take the family to New York, thereby destroying its ties with the past. Lon goes away to the East, to college at Princeton. Only Grandpa, as representative of the older generation, sides with the women in their desire to stay in St. Louis. In general, the narrative's causality makes any departure from the home problematic—an example of how a narrative's pattern of development can generate an ideological premise.

Within the family, there are minor disagreements, but the members cooperate. The two older sisters, Rose and Esther, help each other in their flirtations. Esther is in love with the boy next door, John Truitt, and marriage to him poses no threat to family unity. Several times in the film, she gazes across at his house without having to leave her own home. First, she and Rose go out onto the porch to try to attract his attention; then she sits in the window to sing "The Boy Next Door" **(11.105).** Finally, much later, she sits in a darkened bedroom upstairs and sees John pull his shade just after they have become engaged. That the girls might want to travel, or to educate themselves beyond high school, is never considered. By concentrating on the round of small incidents in the household and neighborhood, the film blocks consideration of any alternative way of living—except the dreaded move to New York.

Family Life through Mise-en-Scene and Music
Many stylistic devices build up a picture of a happy family life. The Technicolor design contributes greatly to the lushness of the mise-en-scene, making the costumes, the surroundings, and the characters' hair color stand out richly. In general, color contrasts are used to emphasize the Smith daughters. In 5.7, a shot from the trolley scene, Esther is conspicuous because she is the only woman in black amidst the generally bright-colored dresses. Esther and Rose wear red and green to the Christmas dance **(11.106),** and this makes the sisters easy to pick out in the swirling crowd of pastel-clad dancers. At the same time, these costumes strengthen the association of the family unity with holidays.

Meet Me in St. Louis is a musical, and music plays a large part in the family's life. Songs come at moments of romance or gathering. Rose and Esther sing "Meet Me in St. Louis" in the parlor before dinner. When Mr. Smith interrupts them on returning from work—"For heaven's sake, stop that screeching!"—he's immediately characterized as opposed to the singing and to the fair. Esther's other songs show that her romance with John Truitt is a safe and reasonable one. A woman does not have to leave home to find a husband: She can find him in her own neighborhood ("The Boy Next Door") or by riding the trolley ("The Trolley Song"). Other songs accompany the two parties, and Esther sings "Have Yourself a Merry Little Christmas" to Tootie, the youngest sister, after the Christmas dance. Here she tries to reassure Tootie that life in New York will be all right if the family can remain together.

But already there is a sense that such unity is in danger. Esther sings, "Someday soon we all will be together, if the Fates allow / Until then we'll have to muddle through somehow." We know already that Esther has achieved her romantic goal and become engaged to John Truitt. If the Smiths do move to New York, she will have to decide between him and her family. By this point, the plot has reached an impasse; whichever way she decides, the old way of life will be destroyed. The narrative needs a resolution, and Tootie's hysterical crying in reaction to the song leads Mr. Smith to reconsider his decision.

Tootie's destruction of the snow people after Esther's song is a striking image of the threat to family unity posed by the move to New York. As the winter season section opened, the children were building the snow people (and a bear cub) in the yard. In effect, they had created a parallel to their own family **(11.107).** At first these snow people were part of the comic scene in which Esther and Katie persuade Lon and Rose to go to the Christmas dance together. But when Tootie becomes

11.103

11.104

11.103–11.104 The passed-along song. The camera follows the second youngest daughter, Agnes, as she goes upstairs singing "Meet Me in St. Louis" (11.103), and soon Grandpa will pick up the tune. A high-angle shot from over his shoulder shows the second oldest sister Esther stepping out of a buggy after completing the song (11.104).

11.105 The importance of the family house. Esther sings her yearning for "The Boy Next Door." (Compare 11.104.)

11.106 Brilliant color contrasts. Highly saturated Christmas party gowns fit into the film's holiday motif.

11.107

11.108

11.107–11.108 The model family. Snow people of various sexes and sizes parallel the family (11.107). Tootie's attack on the snow people (11.108).

11.109 Comfort food as motif. A framing in depth stresses the family as a group, with a plate of cake prominent on the piano in the foreground.

hysterical at the prospect of leaving St. Louis, she runs down in her nightgown to smash the snow people. The scene is almost shocking, since Tootie seems to be killing the doubles of her own family (**11.108**). In terms of plot motivation, this moment has to be emotional because it must trigger the father's change of mind. He realizes that his desire to move to New York threatens the family's harmony. This realization leads to his decision to stay in St. Louis.

Two other elements of the mise-en-scene create motifs that stress the family's comfortable life. The Smiths live surrounded by food. In the initial scene, the women are making ketchup, which is shortly served at the family dinner. After the scene in which Rose's boyfriend fails to propose to her by phone, the tensions are reconciled, and the maid serves large slices of corned beef.

In the Halloween scene, the connection between plentiful food and family unity becomes even more explicit. At first, the children gather around to eat cake and ice cream, but the father arrives home and makes his announcement about moving to New York. The family members depart without touching their food. Only when they hear the mother and father singing at the piano do they gradually drift back to eat (**11.109**). The words of the song—"Time may pass, but we'll be together"—accompany them. The use of food as a motif associates the family's life in the house with abundance and with the individual's place as part of a group. At the fair in the last sequence, the family decide to visit a restaurant together. The food motif returns at the moment of their reaffirmation of their life together in St. Louis.

Light and Family Life   Another motif of family unity involves light. The house is ablaze much of the time. As the family sits together at dinner, the low evening sun sends bright yellow rays through the white curtains. Later, one of the loveliest scenes involves Esther's request that John accompany her through the downstairs to help her turn out the lights (**11.110**). As the rooms darken and the couple moves out to the hall, the camera cranes down to a height level with their faces. The shot contains a remarkable shift of tone. It begins with Esther's comically contrived excuse ("I'm afraid of mice") to keep John with her and develops gradually toward a genuinely romantic mood.

The Halloween sequence takes place entirely at night and makes light a central motif. The camera initially moves in toward the house's glowing yellow windows. Tense, slightly eerie music makes the house seem an island of safety in the darkness. As Tootie and Agnes go out to join the other children in playing tricks, they are silhouetted against the flames of the bonfire the group has gathered around. At first the fire seems threatening, contradicting the earlier associations of light with safety and unity, but this scene actually harmonizes with the previous uses of light. Tootie is excluded from the group activities because she is "too little." After she proves herself worthy, she is allowed to help feed the flames along with the others. In the long track-back as Tootie leaves the fire to play her trick, the fire appears as a haven she has left behind (**11.111**). Indeed, the first sequence of the Halloween section of the film becomes a sort of miniature working out of the entire narrative structure. Tootie's position as a part of the group is abandoned as she moves away from the fire and then triumphantly affirmed as she returns to it.

Similarly, light plays an important part in the resolution of the threat to the family's unity. Late on Christmas Eve, Esther finds Tootie awake. They look out the window at the snow people standing in the yard below. A strip of yellow light falls across the snow, suggesting the warmth and safety of the house they plan to leave (11.108). Tootie's hysterical crying, however, leads Mr. Smith to reconsider his decision. As he sits thinking, he holds the match, with which he was about to light his cigar, unnoticed in his hand until it burns his fingers. Combined with the slow playing of the "Meet Me in St. Louis" theme, the flame serves to emphasize his distraction and his gradual change of mind.

As he calls his family down to announce his decision not to move, he turns up all the lights. The dim, bleak halls full of packing boxes become again the scene of busy activity as the family gathers. The lamps' glass shades are red and green, identifying the house with the appropriate Christmas colors and recalling Esther's and Rose's party dresses. The announcement of the decision leads directly to the opening of the presents, as if to emphasize that staying in St. Louis will not create any financial hardship for the family.

11.110

A trip to the fair provides a reassuring epilogue. Earlier Alonzo had dismissed the fair as an annoyance and praised New York as the future. After realizing that family unity outweighed his job opportunity, he's enjoying the event. He affirms his leadership of the family by guiding them to a French restaurant. (No need to go East for exotic cuisine.) The motif of light, earlier associated with safety and comfort, is restated in the shot of the blazing exhibition halls **(11.112)**. The Smiths can remain together and still benefit from progress. The film closes with this dialogue:

MOTHER: There's never been anything like it in the whole world.

ROSE: We don't have to come here in a train or stay in a hotel. It's right in our own hometown.

TOOTIE: Grandpa, they'll never tear it down, will they?

GRANDPA: Well, they'd better not.

ESTHER: I can't believe it. Right here where we live. Right here in St. Louis **(11.113)**.

11.111

These lines do not *create* the film's ideology, which has been present in the narrative and stylistic devices throughout. The dialogue puts into words what has been presented through narrative and stylistic patterning all along.

Ideology and Broader Meanings

Understanding a film's ideology typically involves analyzing how form and style create meaning. As Chapter 2 suggested, meaning can be of four general types: referential, explicit, implicit, and symptomatic. Our analysis of *Meet Me in St. Louis* has shown how all four types work to reinforce a social ideology—in this case, the values of tradition, home life, and family unity. The referential aspects of the film presuppose that the audience can grasp the difference between St. Louis and New York, and that it knows about international expositions, American family customs, national holidays, and so on. These address the film to a specifically American audience. The explicit meaning of the film is formulated by the final exchange we have just considered, in which the small city is discussed as the perfect fusion of progress and tradition.

11.112

11.110–11.112 Light as motif. As Esther and John turn out the downstairs lights one by one, a long-take crane shot follows the characters from room to room (11.110). At each pause, the chandelier is framed in the upper portion of the screen. During the Halloween sequence, a terrified Tootie moves into the darkness to play her trick (11.111). The motif of light culminates in the revelation of the fairgrounds (11.112).

We have also traced out one major implicit meaning: the family and home as creating a "haven in a heartless world," the central reference point for the individual's life. What, then, of symptomatic meanings?

Chapter 2 mentioned that systems of values and beliefs may seem unquestionable to the social groups that hold them. One way that groups maintain such systems is to assume that certain things are beyond human choice or control, that they are simply natural. Historically, this habit of thought has often been used to justify oppression and injustice, as when women, minority groups, or the poor are thought to be naturally inferior. *Meet Me in St. Louis* participates in this general tendency, not only in its characterization of the Smith women (Esther and Rose are simply presumed to want husbands) but also in the very choice of a white, upper-middle-class household as an emblem of American life. More subtly, the natural cycle of the seasons is harmonized with the family's life, and the conclusion of the plot takes place in the spring, the time of renewal.

11.113 Resolution through the couple. The film's final shot, with Esther's dazzled reaction to the fair.

We can also consider more historically specific symptomatic meanings. The film opened in November 1944 (just in time for Christmas). World War II was still raging, although some countries had already been liberated from the

Nazis. The audience for this film would have consisted largely of women and children whose male relatives had been absent for extended periods, often overseas. Families were often forced apart, and the people who remained behind had to make considerable sacrifices for the war effort. In a time when women were required to work in defense plants, factories, and offices (and many were enjoying the experience), there appeared a film that restricted the range of women's experiences to home and family, and yearned for a simpler time when they ruled only the kitchen.

Meet Me in St. Louis can thus be seen as a symptom of a nostalgia for a distant America. In a 1944 audience, parents of young fighting men would remember the 1903–1904 period as part of their own childhoods. All of the formal and stylistic choices—narrative construction, seasonal segmentation, songs, color, and visual motifs—can be seen as reassuring the viewers. If the women and others left at home can be strong and hold their families together, domestic harmony will eventually return. From this perspective, *Meet Me in St. Louis* upholds dominant conceptions of American life and may even propose an ideal of family unity for the postwar future.

Raging Bull

> 1980. United Artists. Directed by Martin Scorsese. Script by Paul Schrader and Mardik Martin. From the book *Raging Bull* by Jake La Motta, with Joseph Carter and Peter Savage. Photographed by Michael Chapman. Edited by Thelma Schoonmaker. With Robert De Niro, Cathy Moriarty, Joe Pesci, Frank Vincent, Nicholas Colasanto, Theresa Saldana.

In analyzing *Meet Me in St. Louis,* we argued that the film upholds a characteristically American ideology. It's also possible for a film made in Hollywood to take a more ambivalent attitude toward ideological issues. Martin Scorsese's *Raging Bull* does so by making violence its central theme.

Violence is widespread in American cinema, often serving as the basis for entertainment. Extreme violence has become central to many genres, from crime films to science fiction and horror films. Such genres often make their violence very stylized, usually thanks to special effects, and thus not fundamentally disturbing. *Raging Bull* uses a different tactic, drawing on conventions of cinematic realism to make violence visceral. Not only the brutal boxing matches but also the harsh quarrels in everyday life bring brutality to the fore.

Scorsese's film is loosely based on the career of boxer Jake La Motta, who became the world middleweight champion in 1949. *Raging Bull* treats the scenes based on actual prizefights as emblematic of the violence that pervades Jake's life. He seems incapable of dealing with people without picking quarrels, making threats, or exploding in fury. His marriages, especially his second one to Vickie, are full of bickering and domestic abuse. Although his closest relationship is apparently with his brother Joey, who initially manages his career, Jake eventually thrashes Joey in a jealous rage and permanently alienates him. Moreover, while Jake's actions hurt others, he also wreaks havoc on himself. He drives away everyone he loves and ends up as an overweight stand-up comic, then as an actor reciting speeches from famous plays and films.

How are we to understand the ideology of a film that makes such a vicious bully its hero? We might be tempted to posit either/or interpretations. Either the film celebrates Jake's murderous rage, or it condemns him as a pathological case. Yet in settling on one of these simple notions, we would fail to confront the film's uneasy balance of sympathy for and revulsion toward its central character. We suggest that *Raging Bull* uses a variety of strategies, both of narrative and style, to make Jake a case study in the role of violence in American life. By balancing repulsion with a degree of compassion, Scorsese thus creates a complex context within which Jake's actions must be judged.

Narrative Progression   As usual, it helps to start an analysis by mapping the film's formal structure. If we were to segment *Raging Bull,* we would come up with about 46 distinct scenes, including the opening credits and the closing quotation title. To make things manageable, we group them into 12 major parts:

1. The opening credits, shown over a lengthy shot of Jake warming up alone in a boxing ring.

2. Backstage in a nightclub, 1964. Jake practices a poem he will recite.

   Flashback begins:

3. 1941. Expository scenes of Jake losing a match, fighting with his wife, seeing Vickie, and having his first date with her.

4. 1943. Two matches with Sugar Ray Robinson, separated by a love scene between Jake and Vickie.

5. A montage sequence alternating a series of fights, 1944 to 1947, and home movies of Jake's private life.

6. A lengthy series of scenes in 1947, including three in the Copacabana nightclub, establishing Jake's jealousy over Vickie and hatred of the mob. He ends by throwing a fight for them.

7. 1949. An argument with Vickie, followed by Jake's winning the middleweight champion bout.

8. 1950. Jake beats up Vickie and his brother Joey in an unjustified jealous rage. He defends his title and fights Robinson again.

9. 1956. Jake retires and buys a nightclub in which he does comedy routines. Vickie leaves him, and he is arrested on a morals charge.

10. 1958. Jake does his comedy act in a cheap strip joint; he fails to persuade Joey to reconcile with him.

    Flashback ends.

11. 1964. Jake prepares to go onstage to perform his recital.

12. A black title with a biblical quotation and the film's dedication.

The beginning and ending of the film are vital in shaping our attitude toward Jake's career. The first image shows him warming up in the ring before an unspecified fight **(11.114).** Several filmic devices create our initial impressions of the protagonist. He bounces up and down in place, in slow motion. This slow tempo is accompanied by languid classical music, suggesting that his boxing warm-up is like a dance. The deep-space staging places the ring's ropes prominently in the foreground and makes the ring seem huge, emphasizing Jake's solitude. This long take continues through the main credits, establishing boxing as both a beautiful and a lonely sport. The image remains abstract and remote: it is the only scene in the narrative that does not take place in a year specified by a superimposed title.

A straight cut to segment 2 shows Jake, suddenly fat and old. He's practicing, but now it's rehearsal for a one-man show of readings and recitations. He tries out a poem he has written about himself: "So give me a stage / Where this bull here can rage / And though I can fight / I'd much rather recite—That's entertainment!" The opening image has given him a bare stage, but the comedown from his glory days is apparent. This backstage episode takes place quite late in the story chronology, after the long struggles of his boxing career. Not until segment 11 will the plot return to this moment, with Jake continuing to rehearse his lines. In segment 11, as the manager summons him onstage, he executes some warm-up punches to build his confidence, muttering rapidly over and over, "I'm the boss, I'm the boss."

By framing most of the story action as a flashback, Scorsese links violence with entertainment, in the ring or in a nightclub. Jake's gesture of spreading his

11.114 The isolated fighter. The slow-motion opening shot of *Raging Bull.* Unspecified in time and place, it presents a lyrical, idealized image of prizefighting very different from the bouts we'll see.

11.115

11.116

11.115–11.116 Contrast for realistic impact. A graphic match cuts straight from a medium close-up of Jake at the end of segment 2, in 1964 (11.115), to a similar framing of him in the ring in 1941 (11.116).

arms as he says, "That's entertainment!" in segment 2 resembles the triumphant raising of his glove-clad hands whenever he wins a fight in the lengthy central flashback. Correspondingly, *Raging Bull* ignores Jake's early life and concentrates on two periods: his boxing career and his turn to stand-up comedy and literary performances. Both periods present him as trying to control his life and the people around him. "I'm the boss," the last line spoken in the film, sums up Jake's attitude in every phase.

The plot structure we've outlined also traces a rise-and-fall pattern of development. After segment 7, Jake's high point, his life runs downhill, and his violence appears more and more savagely self-destructive. In addition, certain motifs highlight the role of violence in his life and the lives of those around him. During a rest period in his first bout (segment 3), a fistfight breaks out in the stands, suggesting from the start that violence spills beyond the ring. Domestic relations are expressed through aggression, as in the tough-guy shoving between Jake and Joey and in Joey's disciplining his son by threatening to stab him.

Most vividly, violence is turned against women. Both Jake and Joey insult and threaten their wives, and Jake's beating of both his wives forms a grim counterpoint to his battles in the ring. During the first scene at the Copacabana, women emerge as targets of abuse. Jake accuses Vickie of flirting with other men; he insults a boxer and a mob member by suggesting that both are like women; and even the comedian onstage mocks women in the audience. Scene by scene, the organization of incidents and motifs suggests that male aggression pervades American life.

Violence: Realism and Stylization   The film's presentation of violence draws on particular conventions of realism. A series of superimposed titles identify each boxing match by date, locale, and participants. This narrational tactic yields a quasi-documentary quality. The most important factor creating realism, however, is probably the acting. Aside from Robert De Niro, the cast was chosen from virtually unknown actors or nonactors. As a result, they did not bring glamorous star associations to the film. De Niro was known mainly for his grittily realistic performances in Scorsese's *Mean Streets* and *Taxi Driver,* as well as Michael Cimino's *The Deer Hunter.* In *Raging Bull,* the actors speak with thick Bronx accents, repeat or mumble many of their lines, and make no attempt to create likable characters. In the publicity surrounding the film, much was also made of the fact that De Niro gained 60 pounds in order to play Jake as an older man. The film emphasizes De Niro's transformation at various points (**11.115, 11.116**). Such realism in the acting and other techniques makes it difficult for us to accept the film's violence casually, as we might in a conventional horror or crime film.

Film techniques also make violence disturbing. Outside the ring, domestic violence is presented harshly, but usually in long shots and without extravagant sound effects. More aggressive stylistically are the prizefight scenes, which arouse visceral shock in the viewer. Many of the fights are filmed with the camera on a Steadicam brace, which yields ominous tracking movements or close shots of grimaces. Backlighting, motivated by the spotlights around the ring, highlight droplets of sweat or blood that spray off the boxers (**11.117**). Punches are intensified with loud, stinging cracks on the sound track and rapid editing, often with abrupt ellipses from shot to shot. Special makeup shows facial blood vessels spurting grotesquely.

Through its narrative structure and its use of the stylistic conventions of realism, the film offers a criticism of violence in American life, both in the ring and in the home. Yet the film doesn't permit us to condemn Jake as merely a raging bull. It also presents violence as fascinating and ambiguous. Although the fight scenes favor brutal realism, aspects of them are distorted in mesmerizing ways. The sounds of punches assault our ears with shuddering impact. The sound mix for the fights blended animal cries, airplane motors, whizzing arrows, and even music, but the sources are unrecognizable because they are slowed down or played backward. For

11.117 Visceral impact. Realistic violence in the boxing scenes.

all their bloodiness, the fight scenes have their own beauty, partly thanks to slow-motion shooting and stylized lighting.

Narrational Restriction and Masculine Aggression

Violence is made disturbingly attractive even in the scenes outside the ring. This is partly because the narration concentrates far more on the perpetrators of the violence than on the victims. In particular, the three important female characters—Jake's first wife, Joey's wife Lenore, and Vickie—have little to do in the action except take abuse or rail ineffectually against it. We never learn why they are initially attracted to the violent men they marry or why they stay with them so long. At first Vickie seems to admire Jake for his fame and his flashy car, but her willingness to sustain their marriage for so long is not explained. Indeed, her sudden decision to leave him after 11 years has no specific motivation.

The victims of Jake's violence serve chiefly to provoke him to respond. One portion of the action focuses on his pummeling of a "pretty" fighter to whom he thinks Vickie is attracted. Another deals with Jake's violent reaction to his irrational belief that Joey and Vickie have had an affair. It is notable that after this crisis, when Jake beats Joey up, Joey becomes as peripheral a figure as Vickie. We glimpse him briefly watching Jake's bloody title defeat and then see a short scene of him resisting Jake's offer of reconciliation. The film thus offers no positive counterweight to Jake's excesses.

The film's restriction to a male perspective is even more apparent when the narration shifts into subjective presentation. Several scenes show events from Jake's point of view, using slow motion to suggest that we are seeing not just what he sees but how he responds to it. This technique becomes especially vivid when Jake notices Vickie with other men and becomes jealous. Similarly, in the final fight with Robinson, Jake's vision of his opponent is shown via a markedly subjective point-of-view framing. The POV imagery also incorporates a combined track-forward and zoom-out to make the ring seem to stretch far into the distance, while a decrease in the frontal light makes Robinson appear even more menacing **(11.118)**. Other deviations from realism, such as the thunderous throbbing on the sound track during Jake's major victory bout, also suggest that we're entering Jake's mind.

11.118

Moments of perceptual and mental subjectivity don't necessarily make us forgive Jake's brutality, but they do make us understand him better. Along similar lines, Scorsese includes scenes that suggest that Jake can at moments tame his aggressiveness. However much he hurts other people, he injures himself too. He sometimes regrets having hurt people, as several parallel scenes show. In segment 3, Jake has a vicious argument with his first wife in which he threatens to kill her but then immediately says, "Come on, honey, let's be— let's be friends. Truce, all right?" Later, after he has beaten Vickie up for her imagined infidelities, he apologizes and persuades her to stay with him. These domestic reconciliations are echoed in the big title fight where he defeats the current champion, Marcel Cerdan, then walks to his opponent's corner and magnanimously embraces him.

A degree of compassion for Jake is reinforced by other means. *Raging Bull* suggests that he is strongly masochistic, inducing others to inflict pain on him. This notion is emphasized in the love scene in segment 4, when he childishly asks Vickie to caress and kiss the wounds from his triumph over Sugar Ray Robinson **(11.119)**. Soon Jake denies himself sexual gratification by pouring ice water into his shorts. The scene then leads directly into a fight in which Robinson defeats Jake. This defeat is paralleled in segment 8, another boxing scene, when Jake simply stands and goads Robinson into beating him to a pulp. The motif of masochism comes to a climax in segment 9, when Jake is thrown into solitary confinement in a Dade County jail. A long, disturbing take has Jake beating his head and fists against the prison wall, as he asserts that he is not an animal and berates himself as stupid.

11.119

11.118–11.119 Violence as entertainment and as psychological drive. Jake's point of view during a fight (11.118). At home, a close-up links violence and sexuality as Jake asks Vickie to kiss his bruises (11.119).

More implicitly, the film suggests that some of Jake's aggressiveness can be traced to repressed homosexuality. His embrace of the defeated opponent, Cerdan, in his title fight, as well as his urging of Robinson to attack him in his final bout, suggest such an interpretation. In segment 6, when Jake sits down at a nightclub table and jokes about how pretty his upcoming opponent is, he tauntingly offers him as a sex partner to a mobster he suspects of being in love with Vickie. In segment 8, one scene begins with an erotically suggestive slow-motion shot of seconds' hands massaging Jake's torso. There are hints that Jake's fascination with boxing and his refusal to deal with his domestic life stem from an unacknowledged homosexual urge. Such an implication goes against the usual ideology of Hollywood, which assumes that a heterosexual romance is the basis for most narratives.

Ultimately, the ideological stance that *Raging Bull* offers is far from being as straightforward as that of *Meet Me in St. Louis.* Instead of displaying an idealized image of American society, the film criticizes one pervasive aspect of that society: its penchant for violence, as public entertainment and private conduct. Yet it also displays a considerable fascination with that violence, acknowledging its visceral force and considerable beauty. Similarly, Jake is admirable as a dedicated gladiator, but he's also a brute. The film doesn't make us like Jake or even sympathize with him, but it does suggest ways of understanding him—with even a degree of compassion. A man who does not know why he does what he does, who slams his head against the wall shouting that he's not an animal, is perhaps more to be pitied than despised.

> **"** I was fascinated by the self-destructive side of Jake La Motta's character, by his very basic emotions. What could be more basic than making a living by hitting another person on the head until one of you falls or stops? . . . I put everything I knew and felt into that film, and I thought it would be the end of my career. It was what I call a kamikaze way of making movies: pour everything in, then forget about it and go find another way of life."
>
> —Martin Scorsese, director

Closing on an Uncertain Note   The film's ambiguity intensifies at the end. In segment 12, a biblical quotation appears: "So, for the second time, [the Pharisees] summoned the man who had been blind and said: 'Speak the truth before God. We know this fellow is a sinner.' 'Whether or not he is a sinner, I do not know,' the man replied. 'All I know is this: once I was blind and now I can see.'"

As this quotation emerges line by line, we are cued to relate it to the protagonist. Has Jake achieved some sort of enlightenment through his experiences? Several factors suggest not. Despite being a poor actor, he continues to perform literary recitals, trying to regain his public ("I'm the boss"). Furthermore, the speech he practices at the end is the famous "I could have been a contender" passage from *On the Waterfront.* In that film, a failed boxer blamed his brother for his lack of a chance to succeed. Is Jake now blaming Joey or someone else for his decline? Or is it possible that he has become aware enough of his faults to ironically recall a film in which the hero admits his mistakes?

After the biblical quotation, there appears Scorsese's dedication of the film: "Remembering Haig R. Manoogian, teacher, May 23, 1916–May 26, 1980, with love and resolution, Marty." Now the biblical quotation may apply to Scorsese, also from the tough Italian neighborhoods of New York. Were it not for people like this teacher, he might have ended up somewhat like Jake. And perhaps the film professor, who helped him "to see," enabled Scorsese to present Jake with a mixture of detachment and sympathy. Like the two taglines at the close of *Do The Right Thing,* these final inscriptions invite us to weigh alternative interpretations of the action we've seen.

As a cinema student, Scorsese was well aware of innovative foreign films such as *Breathless* and *Tokyo Story,* so it's not surprising that his own work invites a range of interpretations. The film's ending places *Raging Bull* in a tradition of Hollywood films, such as *Citizen Kane,* that keep us at some distance from their protagonist so that we can judge him objectively. Like *Kane,* Scorsese's film avoids complete closure and opts for a degree of ambiguity, a denial of either/or answers. This ambiguity can render the film's ideology equivocal, generating contrasting and even conflicting implicit meanings.

PART 6

Film Art and Film History

Investigating film history can take you in many different directions. You might study the business, asking how a studio worked or how exhibitors promoted a particular film. You could study major individuals—a star, a director, a mogul, a cinematographer, a composer. You could research movie audiences and the ways in which social and cultural forces have shaped tastes at different times. In keeping with the focus of this book, this final chapter offers another perspective. Here we ask you to think about how film form and style have changed across history.

General interest in the history of film art has probably never been higher. Classics are rereleased on video. The anniversaries of *Casablanca* and *The Godfather* bring forth theatrical showings. Newly restored silent films such as *Metropolis* and *Napoléon* are screened accompanied by orchestras. The success of *Hugo* and *The Artist* suggests that a great many people enjoy getting glimpses into film history.

Studying how the art of film has changed across time is fascinating. It's intrinsically interesting to learn that our ways of making movies aren't the only ways. An Eisenstein or a Renoir had rather different conceptions of filmic storytelling than most directors have today. Just as important, by examining the development of the medium, we realize that this week's blockbuster or buzzed-about indie hit is already part of history. Every new film carries within it conventions and choices that reach far back into the past. If we're tuned to the right frequency, we can feel film history pulsing through every movie made now. We can better appreciate the accomplishments of our filmmakers if we realize that they're working creatively with, and sometimes against, traditions that are part of a long legacy.

12

Historical Changes in Film Art: Conventions and Choices, Tradition and Trends

Throughout this book, we've urged you to think like a filmmaker. We believe that it's a good way to enhance your appreciation of how films work. We've tried to aid that appreciation by setting out the range of options filmmakers face when they shape their film's overall form (Chapters 1–3), when they employ techniques of the medium (Chapters 4–8), and when they position the film within genres or other categories (Chapters 9–10). The book has surveyed a very big menu of artistic choices.

As we've also suggested, filmmakers are obliged to make creative decisions at every stage of the process. But actually all the options we've scanned aren't available to any one filmmaker at any particular period. In different times and places, filmmakers have had narrower menus of options.

We can understand the art of film better if we're aware of those options, of the constraints and opportunities available to earlier film creators. Just as important, when we understand the choices the filmmakers could make, we can have richer experiences of the films. For instance, it wouldn't be reasonable to say that because Buster Keaton couldn't make *Our Hospitality* with sound we couldn't enjoy the movie. Once we notice how Keaton uses deep space, theme-and-variations gags, and other resources of visual storytelling, the film offers us a delightful experience (pp. 154–158). Similarly, some people won't watch black-and-white films, but if we understand that most filmmakers before the 1960s could not afford the costs of color filming, we're in a good position to notice how this constraint could be exploited to make lighting, set design, and costumes vivid in black and white.

In this chapter we consider some options and opportunities available to film-makers at certain points in history. Sometimes the options seem limited, but surprisingly, they can also nourish creative moviemaking. If you willingly cut down your choices, you can concentrate on working *within* them. For example, if you've embraced intensified continuity (pp. 246–250) as your editing paradigm, you will still face all manner of choices, but they're more focused and specific.

At the same time, limits can be challenges, provoking filmmakers to seek alternatives. Again and again we'll see that filmmakers who found the classical Hollywood model too confining have sought other, equally effective ways to make movies. But even when filmmakers refuse tradition, that tradition has shaped their creative thinking. And often rebellion against one tradition will draw upon other traditions. We'll see, for instance, that young Soviet filmmakers, refusing the meticulously staged melodramas of the older generation, drew inspiration from the emerging tradition of Hollywood. Studying film history reminds us that, one way or another, filmmakers are always indebted to other filmmakers—their contemporaries, or those who have come before.

CREATIVE DECISIONS

Film Form and Style across History

Why do older movies feel different from those we see today? It's not that their makers were less smart or sophisticated than we are. We can appreciate films from earlier times better if we think in terms we've discussed throughout this book.

Perhaps the biggest obstacle to understanding older films is the fact that they operate according to different *conventions*. Across most of film history, for instance, censorship blocked filmmakers from directly presenting intimate sexual situations. That forced screenwriters and directors to hint that two people were erotically attracted or were having an affair. By contrast, many of today's movies present nudity, intercourse, and other sexual displays. That convention of our time doesn't make our films better, just different—although some historians will argue when filmmakers were forced to be indirect, their films became more slyly unpredictable than ours are **(12.1).**

Because audiences of earlier times knew the conventions, they came in with different *expectations* than we do today. For instance, an audience for silent films expected the acting to be visually expressive. That doesn't mean that silent-film acting was broad or overdone; in fact, we find plenty of subtle performances in the period. (See p. 134.) It's just that viewers of the 1910s and 1920s expected actors to use their whole bodies to communicate emotion pictorially. Our actors are more likely to rely on their facial expressions and line readings.

Most basically, filmmakers of earlier eras had different formal and stylistic options to choose from. Since we're used to thinking that we enjoy a wider range of creative choices than they did, their films might seem limited.

There were certainly technological constraints. Before 1930 or so, most directors couldn't make a film with sound, and before 1960 or thereabouts, most producers couldn't afford to make a film in color. Zoom lenses weren't practical until the 1950s, and digital effects had to wait for faster chips, bigger storage space, and more sophisticated programs.

Less obviously, some storytelling options just weren't thinkable at certain points. Today we routinely see complicated flashback plots in such ordinary movies as *The Hangover,* but we seldom see them in films of the silent era. The discontinuity editing Eisenstein exploited in *October* (1927) wasn't on the menu five years earlier. Nobody thought of it. Likewise, filmmakers could have employed slow motion in fiction features in the 1930s and 1940s, but it was almost unknown. Today it's common.

Do all these factors mean that formal and stylistic options have expanded? Does today's filmmaker have a greater range of choice than in earlier times? To some extent, yes; innovations have accumulated, providing the filmmaker a big toolkit. But some older options aren't live ones for every filmmaker.

12.1 Images say what dialogue can't. Shadows prophesy the outcome of a flirtation in Ernst Lubitsch's *Trouble in Paradise* (1932).

12.2

12.3

12.2–12.3 Widescreen staging. The anamorphic 2.55 ratio widescreen of early CinemaScope (p. 182) encouraged filmmakers to use broad, distant staging in long takes, as in *The Robe* (1953; 12.2). Director Henry Koster uses several characters' eyelines to call attention to Marcellus, the figure on the near left. This stylistic choice is rare in contemporary Hollywood. Yet some recent filmmakers in other countries have found distant staging a fruitful technique. In *Dust in the Wind* (1986; 12.3) Hou Hsiao-hsien also uses characters' eyelines to direct our attention to the significant action, the father on his deathbed. In addition, Hou's set blocks off the right portion of the frame and minimizes other characters through shadow and aspects of setting. A chair conceals the face of the kneeling daughter, so that her face won't distract us from the father.

For example, directors working with the CinemaScope widescreen process in the early 1950s felt obliged to stage the action fairly far from the camera and to spread the action out across the frame **(12.2).** Fairly soon, improvements in lenses and other equipment enabled them to use more medium shots and close-ups. By the mid-1960s, broad and distant staging became rare, and today a Hollywood filmmaker who decided to revisit that approach would risk looking old-fashioned. The contemporary approach is to frame actors tightly, even in widescreen formats (1.52, 6.119–6.134). Yet this distant, lateral staging was by no means a dead end creatively. Directors in other countries have refined techniques that are similar to what we see in early 'Scope films **(12.3).**

Or go back to the example of a telephone conversation (p. 263). Suppose you want to show both Jim and Amanda as they talk. Today most directors would simply cut from one to the other. In the 1910s, however, there was another option: a split screen **(12.4).** It was striking but a bit complicated to shoot, so it was eventually dropped in favor of cutting. But during the 1960s it was occasionally revived for

12.4

12.5

12.6

12.4–12.6 Techniques revived. Split-screen presentation of phone conversations was not unusual in the period of *Suspense* (1913; 12.4). For decades afterward it was almost never used, but it was revived in the 1960s occasionally for suspense or comedy, as in the musical *Bye Bye Birdie* (1963; 12.5). It was also a handy way to fill up the wide screen. The 2003 retro comedy *Down with Love* refers back to the 1960s convention (12.6).

comedies **(12.5).** Today a director might call on it for comic effect, or to hark back to its 1960s usage **(12.6).**

The art historian Heinrich Wölfflin summed up this situation in a famous line: "Not everything is possible at all times." At any moment in film history, there are forces—technology, budget, political censorship, prevailing tastes, clashes within the production team—working to limit artistic choices. The limits on today's filmmakers aren't as visible to us, but they are there. In watching an older film, we should try to understand the options that filmmakers had to work with at the time. That will sensitize us not only to the range of possibilities but also to the ways in which some filmmakers, in a quest to try something different, came up with innovations that later creators could use.

Traditions and Movements in Film History

We've presented artistic decision making in film as a matter of individual choice. That's accurate, up to a point. But most filmmakers work in groups, as we saw back in Chapter 1. Members of the group contribute to decisions about the project. Moreover, the team members have learned their craft from other filmmakers. The community that shapes a filmmaker's choice includes many who have gone before, who have laid down best practices and solid solutions to recurring problems.

In other words, filmmakers belong to *traditions*. They pass ideas about moviemaking from peer to peer, from expert to novice. And many of those ideas are suggestions about what choices you should make. Screenwriters learn to write using three-act structure; cinematographers learn favored ways of lighting faces;

 CONNECT TO THE BLOG
www.davidbordwell.net/blog

Some modern filmmakers have tried to imitate older films' look and feel. Does it work? On *The Good German,* see "Not back to the future, but ahead to the past." On *Casino Royale,* see "Can they make 'em like they used to? Continued."

CONNECT TO THE BLOG
www.davidbordwell.net/blog

"What's left to discover today? Plenty" considers the ways that our knowledge of filmmaking traditions changes as forgotten films come to light.

actors learn what counts as a good performance. A tradition, in effect, favors certain creative choices over others.

One of the best examples of a filmmaking tradition is American studio cinema, so at various points in the chapter we'll examine how that tradition emerged and changed. In many respects, the Hollywood tradition influenced filmmaking around the world. A more limited tradition is that of Hong Kong action cinema of the 1980s and 1990s. That too, as we'll see, proved quite influential.

Traditions nudge a filmmaker toward certain choices and away from others. But sometimes filmmakers want to explore those others. In instances like these, we get the shorter-lived trends we call *movements*. In a movement, filmmakers typically operate within a common production structure and share certain assumptions about filmmaking. Above all, they favor a common approach to form, style, and theme that sets them somewhat apart from the usual practices. They innovate. Movements, then, are *un*traditional in some ways. They press filmmakers to make unusual formal and stylistic choices.

Sometimes the filmmakers in a movement know one another well and respond to one another's projects. This situation occurred with the Soviet Montage filmmakers of the 1920s, the Surrealists of the period, and the French New Wave of the 1950s–1960s. Here we find young people cooperating and competing because they wanted to explore some new ideas about what cinema could be. To clarify those ideas, they often wrote books and articles. Other movements are more diffuse, with unconnected filmmakers gravitating toward a common approach to form and style.

Most movements don't last more than a few years, but they can exercise a far-reaching effect. Some movements of the silent and early sound era have affected filmmaking for decades afterward. As we'll see, many movements have been selectively absorbed into broader traditions, particularly Hollywood's. The films of our time reenact creative decisions made by filmmakers in the past.

You should already have a sense of this process, because our examples from both recent films and older ones show that today's films often accept or rework choices that were made in much earlier work. In several sections that follow, we mention how some contemporary filmmakers have found inspiration in the choices favored by film movements.

Because we're exploring historical contexts, we'll go beyond noting stylistic and formal qualities. For each tradition and movement, we'll point to relevant factors that affect the filmmakers' options—factors such as the state of the industry, artistic theories held by the filmmakers themselves, technological features, and cultural and economic forces. These factors help explain how a particular trend began and developed. This material will also provide a context for particular films we've already discussed. For example, we introduced you to Georges Méliès in Chapter 4 and Louis Lumière in Chapter 5. In the previous chapter, we analyzed a Soviet Montage film (*Man with a Movie Camera*) and a French New Wave one (*Breathless*). Now you have a chance to see this work in a broader context.

In the sections that follow, we haven't tried to characterize other important traditions, such as that of Japanese cinema, or other movements, such as Brazil's Cinema Nôvo of the early 1960s. Readers interested in knowing more can consult our *Film History: An Introduction*. Here we simply trace how certain possibilities of film form and style were explored in a few typical and well-known historical traditions and movements. The first section sets the stage for them by examining the origins of cinema itself.

Early Cinema (1893–1903)

In Chapter 1, we saw that film is a technology-driven medium. To create the illusion of movement, still pictures must appear in rapid succession. To prepare those images and display them at the right rate, certain technologies are necessary.

Photography and Cinema

Most basically, there must be a way of recording a long series of images on some sort of support. In principle, one could simply draw a string of images on a strip of paper or a disc. But photography offered the cheapest and most efficient way to generate the thousands of images needed for a reasonably lengthy show. Thus the invention of photography in 1826 launched a series of discoveries that made cinema possible.

Early photographs required lengthy exposures (initially hours, later minutes) for a single image; this made photographed motion pictures, which need 12 or more frames per second, impossible. Faster exposures, of about 1/25th of a second, became possible by the 1870s, but only on glass plates. Glass plates weren't usable for motion pictures since there was no practical way to move them through a camera or projector. In 1878, Eadweard Muybridge, an American photographer, did make a series of photographs of a running horse by using a series of cameras with glass plate film and fast exposure, but he was primarily interested in freezing phases of an action, not re-creating the movement by projecting the images in succession.

In 1882, another scientist interested in analyzing animal movement, the Frenchman Étienne-Jules Marey, invented a camera that recorded 12 separate images on the edge of a revolving disc of film on glass. This constituted a step toward the motion picture camera. In 1888, Marey built the first camera to use a strip of flexible film, this time on paper. Again, the purpose was only to break down movement into a series of stills, and the movements photographed lasted a second or less. In 1889, George Eastman introduced a crude flexible film base, celluloid. After this base was improved and camera mechanisms had been devised to draw the film past the lens and expose it to light, the creation of long strips of frames became possible.

Projectors had existed for many years and had been used to show slides and shadow entertainments. These magic lanterns were modified by the addition of shutters, cranks, and other devices to become early motion picture projectors.

One final device was needed if films were to be projected. Since the film stops briefly while the light shines through each individual frame, there had to be a mechanism to create an *intermittent* motion of the film. Marey used a Maltese cross gear on his 1888 camera, and this became a standard part of early cameras and projectors.

A flexible and transparent film base, a fast exposure time, a mechanism to pull the film through the camera, an intermittent device to stop the film, and a shutter to block off light—all these innovations had been achieved by the early 1890s. After several years, inventors working independently in many countries had developed film cameras and projection devices. The two most important firms were the Edison Manufacturing Company in America, owned by inventor Thomas A. Edison, and Lumière Frères in France, the family firm of Louis and Auguste Lumière.

Edison vs. Lumière

By 1893, Thomas A. Edison's assistant, W. K. L. Dickson, had developed a camera that made short 35mm films. Interested in exploiting these films as a novelty, Edison hoped to combine them with his phonograph to show sound movies. He had Dickson develop a peep-show machine, the *Kinetoscope* **(12.7),** to display these films to individual viewers.

But Edison believed that movies were a passing fad, so he didn't develop a system to project films onto a screen. This task was left to the Lumière brothers. They invented their own camera independently; it exposed a short roll of 35mm film and also served as a projector **(12.8).** On December 28, 1895, the Lumière brothers presented motion pictures on a screen, at the Grand Café in Paris.

There had been several earlier public screenings, but the Lumières found the most practical method for projecting films, and their format largely determined the direction in which the new medium developed. Edison was obliged to follow their example, abandoning the Kinetoscope and creating his own production company to make films for public projection.

CONNECT TO THE BLOG
www.davidbordwell.net/blog

Early cinema was influenced by other media of its day, including narrative painting. We suggest some similarities in "Professor sees more parallels between things, other things."

12.7–12.9 Alternative approaches to early filmmaking. Edison's Kinetoscope threaded film in a continuous loop around a series of bobbins (12.7). The film was watched by one viewer at a time. The Lumière brothers aimed for public screenings, so they put a magic-lantern projector behind their camera so the images could be displayed to several viewers (12.8). In Edison's rotating film studio, the Black Maria, a hinged central portion of the roof swung open for filming (12.9).

12.7

12.8

12.9

> **❝** In conjuring you work under the attentive gaze of the public, who never fail to spot a suspicious movement. You are alone, their eyes never leave you. Failure would not be tolerated. . . . While in the cinema . . . you can do your confecting quietly, far from those profane gazes, and you can do things thirty-six times if necessary until they are right. This allows you to travel further in the domain of the marvellous."
>
> —George Méliès, magician and filmmaker

Early Form and Style

The first films typically consisted of a single shot framing an action, usually at long-shot distance. In the first film studio, Edison's Black Maria (**12.9,** vaudeville entertainers, famous sports figures, and celebrities such as Annie Oakley performed for the camera. A hinged portion of the roof opened to admit a patch of sunlight, and the entire building turned on a circular rail (visible in 12.9) to follow the sun's motion. The Lumières, however, took their cameras out to parks, gardens, beaches, and other public places to film everyday activities or news events, as in their *Arrival of a Train at La Ciotat Station* (5.64).

Until about 1903, most films showed scenic places or noteworthy events, so these can be considered early documentaries. The Lumières sent camera operators all over the world to photograph important events and exotic locales.

Staged narratives, brief skits or gags, were also popular. Edison's staff played out comic scenes, such as one copyrighted 1893 in which a drunken man struggles briefly with a policeman. The Lumières made a popular short, *L'Arroseur arrosé* (*The Waterer Watered,* 1895), also a comic scene, in which a boy tricks a gardener into squirting himself with a hose (4.8).

The earliest films may look crude to us today. This is partly because we seldom see good copies. In properly preserved prints, shown at the right projection speed, the films have a photographic richness that has seldom been equaled. But because they were so short—before 1905, running only a few minutes—the first films couldn't develop complex stories or rhetorical arguments. Relying on unusual events, cute animals, and other brief attractions, they look forward to the amateur videos that show up on YouTube today (12.10). Early films have inspired avant-garde filmmakers to explore movement and abstract photographic qualities (12.11).

12.10

12.11

12.10–12.11 Early film and later interests. A Lumière film from 1900, *La petite fille et son chat (The Little Girl and Her Cat),* centers on a perennial attraction of today's online videos (12.10). In *Tom, Tom the Piper's Son* (1969), avant-garde filmmaker Ken Jacobs uses an optical printer to dissect and stylize a 1905 film of the same name, creating what Jacobs calls "a dream within a dream" (12.11).

Méliès, Magic, and Fictional Narrative

In 1896, Georges Méliès built his own camera, based on a projector he had bought. His first films resembled the Lumières' shots of everyday activities. But as we have seen (pp. 113–114), Méliès was a stage magician, and he discovered the possibilities of special effects. In 1897, Méliès built his own studio, filled with flats and trapdoors. These allowed him to control his effects very precisely (12.12).

Méliès built elaborate settings to create fantasy worlds within which his magical transformations could occur. As we've already seen, this care in manipulating setting, lighting, costume, and staging made Méliès the first master of mise-en-scène (4.3–4.6). He was also an important innovator in editing. For one thing, he found that he could create magical transformations by stopping the camera, adjusting elements in the scene, and then resuming filming. Inspecting the original material, historians have found that Méliès trimmed a few frames at each special effect. Stopping and restarting the camera created light bursts on the first few frames, and these had to be snipped out.

Méliès progressed to longer narratives, with each scene played out in a single camera position, and he used cuts to link them. The most famous of these was *A Trip to the Moon* (1902). Méliès's Star Film company was associated with magic tricks and fairy stories, but it turned out an astonishing variety of films, including scenes from the Bible and a series based on the Dreyfus case. The dazzling special effects, the impressive settings and costumes, and the expansive fantasies and historical narratives made Méliès's films popular and widely imitated. They still exercise a powerful hold, having been painstakingly collected and restored, released on DVD, and given a central role in Martin Scorsese's *Hugo* (2011), which pays homage to Méliès by restaging some of the films.

The work of Lumière, Méliès, and other early filmmakers gained worldwide fame because films circulated freely from country to country. The French phonograph company Pathé Frères moved into filmmaking in 1901, establishing production and distribution branches in many countries. Until 1914, Pathé was the largest film concern in the world. In England, several entrepreneurs managed to invent or obtain equipment and made scenics, narratives, and trick films from 1895 into the early years of the 20th century. Members of the Brighton School (primarily G. Albert Smith and James Williamson), as well as others such as Cecil Hepworth, shot their films on location or in simple open-air studios (as in 12.13). Their innovative films circulated abroad and influenced other filmmakers. Pioneers in other countries invented or bought equipment and were soon making their own films of everyday scenes or fantasy transformations.

As films became longer, narrative form became the most prominent type of filmmaking in the commercial industry, and the popularity of cinema continued to grow. French, Italian, and American films ruled world markets. Later, World War I was to restrict the international flow of films, and Hollywood emerged as

CONNECT TO THE BLOG
www.davidbordwell.net/blog

In the first years, filmmaking sprang up in small towns all across America. The films are still being rediscovered, as we found in "You can go home again, and maybe find an old movie."

12.12

12.13

12.12–12.13 Early studio shooting. Unlike Edison's Black Maria, Méliès's studio was glass-sided, like a greenhouse, and admitted sunlight from many directions (12.12). G. Albert Smith's *Santa Claus* (1898) was filmed in the open air, with a false backdrop (12.13). It displays typical traits of the first fictional narratives: distant camera position, flat lighting, and a rear wall placed perpendicular to the camera lens.

CONNECT TO THE BLOG
www.davidbordwell.net/blog

For an international survey of the important year 1913, see "Lucky '13," and for a look at alternatives to continuity editing, see "Looking different today?" We examine the work of two early French masters in "Capellani trionfante" and "How to watch *Fantômas*, and why."

" The cinema knows so well how to tell a story that perhaps there is an impression that it has always known how."
—André Gaudreault, film historian

the dominant industrial force in film production. In some countries, filmmakers responded by creating movements that differed sharply from the look and feel of the American product.

The Development of the Classical Hollywood Cinema (1908–1927)

Edison, determined to make money from his invention, brought patent-violation suits against competing moviemaking firms. When he failed to stamp out his rivals, he allied with several of them in 1908 to establish the Motion Picture Patents Company (MPPC). Edison and the American Mutoscope and Biograph company were the only stockholders and patent owners. They licensed other members to make, distribute, and exhibit films, and they standardized film lengths at one reel (running about 15 minutes). But this move didn't eliminate the other production companies, who sprang up quickly. In 1912 the U.S. government sued the MPPC, and three years later it was declared a monopoly and forced to break up.

Hollywood and the Studio System of Production

At the same period, both MPPC companies and independents began to relocate from New York and Chicago to California. Los Angeles offered a climate that permitted shooting year-round, and a great variety of locations—mountains, ocean, desert, city. Soon Hollywood and other small towns on the outskirts of Los Angeles hosted film production.

Through the 1910s and 1920s, the smaller firms merged to form the large film corporations that still exist today. Famous Players joined with Jesse L. Lasky and then formed a distribution wing, Paramount. By the late 1920s, most of the major companies—MGM (a merger of Metro, Goldwyn, and Mayer), Fox Film Corporation (merged with 20th Century in 1935), Warner Bros., Universal, and Paramount—had been created. Though in competition with one another, the companies cooperated to some degree, because they realized that the demand for films was so great that no one firm could satisfy the market.

By the early 1920s, the American industry had created a structure that would continue for decades. A few large firms with individual artists under contract were supplemented by small independent producing companies. Within a company, filmmaking tasks were carefully divided among specialists, and each project was overseen by a producer, who kept an eye on budget and schedule. Thomas Ince, a major producer, pioneered the use of detailed shooting scripts and time sheets so that the shooting could be cost-efficient. The stages of production we surveyed in Chapter 1 (pp. 17–29) were systematized by the Hollywood companies of the late 1910s. This business model came to be known as the studio system. Aiming to turn out films in large quantities, the American cinema became oriented toward narrative form.

Narrative Continuity: Early Prototypes

One of Edison's directors, Edwin S. Porter, made some of the first films to use narrative continuity and development. Among these was *The Life of an American Fireman* (1903), which showed the race of the firefighters to rescue a mother and a child from a burning house. Although this film used several striking narrative elements (a fireman's premonition of the disaster, a series of shots of the horse-drawn engine racing to the house), the cutting presents an odd time scheme. We see the rescue of a mother and her child twice, from both inside and outside the house. Porter had not realized the possibility of intercutting the two locales to sustain simultaneous action.

In 1903, Porter made *The Great Train Robbery,* in some ways a prototype for the classical American film. Here the action develops with a linear time, space, and cause-effect logic. We follow each stage of the robbery **(12.14),** the pursuit, and the final defeat of the robbers. In 1905, Porter also created a simple parallel narrative in *The Kleptomaniac,* contrasting the fates of a rich woman and a starving woman who are both caught stealing.

British filmmakers were working along similar lines. Indeed, many historians now believe that Porter derived some of his editing techniques from films such as James Williamson's *Fire!* (1901) and G. A. Smith's *Mary Jane's Mishap* (1903). The most famous British film of this era was Lewin Fitzhamon's 1905 film *Rescued by Rover* (produced by a major British firm, Cecil Hepworth), which treated a kidnapping in a linear fashion similar to that of *The Great Train Robbery.* After the kidnapping, we see each stage of Rover's journey to find the child, his return to fetch the child's father, and their retracing of the route to the kidnapper's lair. All the shots make the geography of the action completely intelligible **(12.15, 12.16).**

In 1908, D. W. Griffith began his directing career. Over the next five years, he would make hundreds of one- and two-reelers (running about 15 and 30 minutes, respectively). These films created relatively complex plots in short spans. Griffith certainly didn't invent all the devices with which he has been credited, but he did give many techniques strong narrative motivation. For example, a few other filmmakers had used simple last-minute rescues with crosscutting between the rescuers and victims, but Griffith developed and popularized this technique (6.111–6.114). By the time he made *The Birth of a Nation* (1915) and *Intolerance* (1916), Griffith was creating lengthy sequences by cutting among several different locales.

Griffith made another creative choice that was unusual for the early 1910s: He concentrated on subtle changes in facial expression (4.33). To catch such nuances, he set up his camera closer to the action than did many of his contemporaries, framing his actors in medium long shot or medium shot.

Griffith's films were widely influential. In addition, his dynamic, rapid editing in the final chase scenes of *Intolerance* was to have a considerable impact on the Soviet Montage style of the 1920s. But he wasn't alone in refining technique. Supervising production at his company, Thomas Ince demanded tight narratives, with no digressions or loose ends, and his request for detailed shooting scripts favored breaking scenes up into several camera positions. Films made under Ince's control, such as *Civilization* (1915), *The Italian* (1915),

12.14 An early effort at narrative continuity. The robbers in the telegraph office in *The Great Train Robbery,* preparing to board the train seen through the window. The train portion of the image is an early matte shot.

12.15

12.16

12.15–12.16 Matching screen direction. In *Rescued by Rover,* the heroic dog leads his master along a street from the right rear moving toward the left foreground (12.15). The pair is moving from right to left as they reach their destination (12.16).

CONNECT TO THE BLOG
www.davidbordwell.net/blog

A Spanish filmmaking student created a revealing video analyzing a 1912 Griffith Biograph short. We talk about the analysis and link to it in "A variation on a sunbeam."

12.17

12.18

12.17–12.18 Narrative coherence. The opening scene of *The Cheat* introduces the branding motif (12.17). It returns later when the villain brands the heroine as another item of property (12.18). Both use the "Rembrandt lighting" that made De Mille famous.

CONNECT TO THE BLOG
www.davidbordwell.net/blog

On two of the most important filmmakers of the early classical period, see our entries on William S. Hart in "Rio Jim, in discrete fragments," and Douglas Fairbanks in "His Majesty the American."

and the Westerns of William S. Hart (p. 337), helped stabilize the emerging continuity conventions.

Cecil B. De Mille, a director who was to have a much longer career than Griffith and Ince, made several feature-length dramas and comedies. His *The Cheat* (1915) reflects important changes occurring in the studio style between 1914 and 1917. During that period, the glass-roofed studios using daylight for illumination gave way to studios dependent on artificial lighting. *The Cheat* used spectacular effects of chiaroscuro, with only one or two bright sources of light and no fill light. According to legend, De Mille justified this effect to nervous exhibitors by calling it "Rembrandt lighting." This north lighting was to become part of the classical repertoire of lighting techniques.

Like many American films of the teens, *The Cheat* uses a linear pattern of narrative. The first scene **(12.17)** quickly establishes the Japanese businessman as a ruthless collector of objects; we see him burning his brand onto a small statue. The initial action motivates a later scene in which the businessman brands the heroine, who has fallen into his power by borrowing money from him **(12.18)**. *The Cheat* was one of several 1915 films that showed that Hollywood films were moving toward greater complexity in their storytelling.

The 180° system of staging, shooting, and editing (pp. 231–233) was developing as well. Eyeline matches became more common from 1910 on, and the match on action was in common use by 1916. Shot/reverse-shot cutting became widespread as well, as seen in *The Cheat* (1915), Hart's Western *The Narrow Trail* (1917), and Griffith's *A Romance of Happy Valley* (1919).

Classical Form and Style in Place

By the early 1920s, the continuity system had become a standardized style that directors in the Hollywood studios used to create coherent, gripping storytelling. Screen direction was usually respected. A match on action could provide a cut to a closer view in a scene **(12.19, 12.20)**. A conversation around a table would no longer be handled in a single frontal shot **(12.21–12.25)**. When an awkward match might have resulted from the joining of two shots, the filmmakers could cover it by inserting a dialogue title.

Filmmakers conceived ways to handle large-scale narrative form as well. By 1923, Buster Keaton could construct a perfectly balanced plot for *Our Hospitality*. As we saw in Chapter 4, the action develops logically from the death of Willie McKay's father to Willie's final resolution of the feud. Along the way, motifs like the railroad tracks, water, and pistols are carefully motivated and ingeniously varied.

❝ That evening I tried to increase my knowledge of motion-picture technique by going to the movies. I sat with a stop watch and notebook and tried to estimate the number of cuts or scenes in a thousand-foot reel, the length of individual scenes, the distance of the subject from the camera, and various other technical details."

—King Vidor, director, recalling the night before he began directing his first film, c. 1912

12.19

12.20

12.19–12.20 Smooth action matching in the early 1920s. In Fred Niblo's *The Three Musketeers* (1921), a long shot of the group (12.19) leads to a cut-in to the central character, played by Douglas Fairbanks (12.20).

12.21

12.22

12.23

12.24

12.25

12.21–12.25 Consistent eyelines around a table. In an establishing shot from *Are Parents People?* (Malcolm St. Clair, 1925), the daughter sits down at the table (12.21). In the medium shot she looks leftward toward her father (12.22). He responds to her by looking rightward in the reverse shot (12.23). The daughter then turns to look to the right at her mother (12.24). Her mother returns her gaze in reverse shot (12.25).

In only a decade or so, Hollywood cinema had developed into a sophisticated cinematic tradition. As we've indicated (p. 230), classical continuity became a kind of universal language of fictional moviemaking that's still in force today. Yet no sooner had the tradition crystallized than alternatives began to appear. Filmmakers in other countries pushed in directions that American cinema had not explored. After examining these alternative movements, in the silent era, we'll return to consider the classical Hollywood cinema after the coming of sound.

CONNECT TO THE BLOG
www.davidbordwell.net/blog

For more on the emergence of Hollywood film style in the late 1910s, see "Happy birthday, classical cinema!" We also have a video lecture, "How Motion Pictures Became the Movies, 1908–1920" that considers this period.

German Expressionism (1919–1926)

The worldwide success of American films in the late 1910s and through the 1920s confronted filmmakers abroad with a harsh choice. Should they try to imitate Hollywood? The big budgets of the American studios were hard to match in the aftermath of a war that had devastated the European continent. Or should they try to offer a type of cinema markedly different from the Hollywood standard? Most

12.26 The UFA historical epic.
Madame Dubarry: A crowd scene in the Tribunal of the French Revolution.

66 Everything is composition; any image whatsoever could be stopped on the screen and would be a marvellously balanced painting of forms and lights. Also, it is one of the films which leaves in our memories the clearest visions—precise and of a slightly static beauty. But even more than painting, it is animated architecture."

—François Berge, French critic, on Fritz Lang's *The Nibelungen*

filmmakers took the first option and adopted American techniques of lighting, staging, and editing. (Principles of story construction took longer to be adopted.) But a few filmmakers sought to be more original, and some of them formed movements that had an enduring effect on world cinema.

In 1914, although some impressive pictures had been made in Germany, the industry's output was relatively small. The nation's 2,000 movie theaters were playing mostly French, American, Italian, and Danish films. When the war began, America and France banned German films from their screens immediately, but Germany couldn't afford to ban French and American films, for then the theaters would have had little to show.

To combat imported competition, as well as to create its own propaganda films, the German government began to support the film industry. In 1916, film imports were banned except from neutral Denmark. Production increased rapidly; from a dozen small companies in 1911, the number grew to 131 by 1918. But government policy encouraged these companies to band together into cartels.

In late 1917, the government, the Deutsche Bank, and large industrial concerns combined several small film firms to create the large company UFA (short for Universum Film Aktiengesellschaft). Backed by these conservative interests, UFA was a move toward control of the German market and, its backers hoped, the postwar international market as well. With this huge financial backing, UFA was able to gather superb technicians and build the best-equipped studios in Europe.

One tactic UFA tried was making big-budget spectacle films that could rival Hollywood's effort. This proved successful. Ernst Lubitsch's *Madame Dubarry* (1919; **12.26**), a historical epic of the French Revolution, broke down international opposition to German films. Although the French authorities treated it as propaganda, it proved extremely popular elsewhere and helped reopen the world market for local films. Other Lubitsch historical films were soon exported, and in 1923, he became the first German director to be hired by Hollywood.

A more unusual strategy of differentiation emerged at the same time. Despite UFA's expansion, some small companies remained independent. Among these was Erich Pommer's Decla (later Decla-Bioscop). In 1919, the firm undertook to produce an unconventional script by two unknowns, Carl Mayer and Hans Janowitz. These young writers wanted their story to be told in an unusually stylized way. The three designers assigned to the film—Hermann Warm, Walter Reimann, and Walter Röhrig—suggested that it be done in an Expressionist style. As an avant-garde movement, Expressionism had first been important in painting (starting about 1910) and had been quickly taken up in theater, then in literature and architecture. Pommer consented to try it in the cinema, apparently believing that this might be a selling point in the international market. This belief was vindicated in 1920 when Decla's low-budget *The Cabinet of Dr. Caligari* (1920) created a sensation in Berlin and then in the United States, France, and other countries.

Thanks to the success of *Caligari*, UFA, along with smaller companies, invested in Expressionist films because these could compete with Hollywood.

The first film of the movement, *Caligari*, is a powerful example of the Expressionist style. One of its designers, Warm, claimed, "The film image must become graphic art." With its extreme stylization, *Caligari* was like a moving Expressionist painting or woodcut print. In contrast to French Impressionism, which based its style primarily on cinematography and editing, German Expressionism depended heavily on mise-en-scene. Shapes are distorted and exaggerated to suggest emotional states. Actors often wear heavy makeup and move in jerky or slow,

12.27 **12.28** **12.29**

12.27–12.29 Actors as part of setting. In Robert Wiene's *Genuine,* the bedroom is flamboyantly Expressionist. As the heroine leans backwards, she blends in with the curved, spiky shapes behind her (12.27). *The Cabinet of Dr. Caligari:* Dr. Caligari totters along a corridor that suggests a madman's vision of the world (12.28). When the hero arrives at Caligari's asylum, he steps into the center of a pattern of black-and-white lines that radiate across the floor and up the walls (12.29).

sinuous patterns. Most important, all of the elements of the mise-en-scene interact graphically to create an overall composition. We have already seen an example of this in 4.117, where the character Cesare collapses in a stylized forest, his body and outstretched arms echoing the shapes of the trees' trunks and branches. Characters do not simply exist within a setting but rather form visual elements that *merge with* the setting **(12.27).**

Such a departure from realism demands motivation, which *Caligari* provides through mental subjectivity. We see the world as the mad hero imagines it to be **(12.28).** This narrative function of the settings becomes explicit at one point, when the hero enters an asylum in his pursuit of Caligari. As he pauses to look around, the world of the film is literally a projection of the hero's mind **(12.29).**

Later, as Expressionism became an accepted style, filmmakers didn't motivate the style as the subjective state of mad characters. Instead, genre conventions were invoked. Expressionist design could create stylized imagery for fantasy and horror stories, as with *Waxworks* (1924) and *Nosferatu* (1922; see 9.18). *The Nibelungen* (1923–1924) showed that abstract patterning of costume, sets, and crowds could be applied to historical epics as well.

By the mid-1920s, German films were regarded as among the best in the world. UFA's rich studio facilities attracted foreign filmmakers, including the young Alfred Hitchcock. During the 1920s, Germany coproduced many films with companies in other countries, thus spreading its stylistic influence abroad. The rampant inflation of the early 1920s actually favored Expressionist filmmaking, partly by making it easy for exporters to sell German films cheaply overseas. Inflation discouraged imports as well, because the tumbling exchange rate of the mark made foreign purchases too expensive.

In 1924, the U.S. Dawes Plan helped to stabilize the German economy, and foreign films came in more frequently, offering a degree of competition unknown in Germany for nearly a decade. Expressionist film budgets, meanwhile, were climbing. The last major films of the movement, F. W. Murnau's *Faust* (1926) and Fritz Lang's *Metropolis* (1927; see **12.30**), were costly epics that drove UFA deeper into financial difficulty. Erich Pommer quit and tried his luck briefly in America. Other personnel were lured away to Hollywood as well. Trying to counter the stiffer competition, the Germans began to imitate the American product. The resulting films, though sometimes impressive, diluted the unique qualities of the Expressionist style.

CONNECT TO THE BLOG
www.davidbordwell.net/blog

For many years, incomplete versions of *Metropolis* circulated. In 2008 nearly all the long-lost footage was finally discovered. We tell the story and assess how the new scenes changed the film in "*Metropolis* unbound."

12.30

12.31

12.30–12.31 Lang sustains Expressionism. *Metropolis* contained many large, Expressionistic sets, including this garden, with pillars that appear to be made of melting clay (12.30). In *M*, reflections and a display of knives in a shop window create a semi-abstract composition that mirrors the murderer's obsession (12.31).

12.32 Expressionism for horror-comedy. The Afterlife as portrayed by *Beetlejuice* recalls the contorted décor of *Caligari* (12.28).

By 1927, Expressionism as a movement had died out. But as Georges Sadoul has pointed out, an expressionist (spelled with a lowercase "e" to distinguish it from the Expressionist movement proper) tradition lingered on in many of the German films of the late 1920s and even into such 1930s films as Fritz Lang's *M* (1930; see **12.31**) and *Testament of Dr. Mabuse* (1932). Some set designers came to the United States and applied techniques there. Hollywood horror and crime films sometimes displayed expressionist tendencies in their settings and lighting. Although the movement lasted only about seven years, expressionism has never entirely died out as one approach to film style, and even today directors may refer to the original German version of it **(12.32).**

French Impressionism and Surrealism (1918–1930)

During the silent era, a number of film movements in France posed major alternatives to the emerging Hollywood tradition. Some of these alternatives, such as abstract cinema and Dada filmmaking, weren't specifically French and constituted instead a part of the growing international avant-garde. But two alternatives to the American mode remained quite localized.

Impressionism was an avant-garde style that operated largely within the film industry. Most of the Impressionist filmmakers started out working for major French companies, and some of their avant-garde works proved financially successful. In the mid-1920s, most formed their own independent companies but remained within the mainstream commercial industry by renting studio facilities and releasing their films through established firms. The other alternative movement, Surrealism, lay largely outside the film industry. Allied with the Surrealist movement in other arts,

CONNECT TO THE BLOG
www.davidbordwell.net/blog

We discuss some major Impressionist films on DVD in "Albatros soars."

these filmmakers relied on their own means and private patronage. France in the 1920s offers a striking instance of how different film movements may flourish in the same time and place.

Impressionism

World War I struck a serious blow to the French film industry. Personnel were conscripted, studios were shifted to wartime uses, and much export was halted. The two major firms, Pathé Frères and Léon Gaumont, also controlled circuits of theaters and they needed to fill vacant screens. As a result, in 1915 American films began to flood into France. Represented by De Mille's *The Cheat* and films featuring Douglas Fairbanks, Charlie Chaplin, William S. Hart, and other popular stars, the Hollywood cinema dominated the market by the end of 1917. After the war, French filmmaking never fully recovered. The industry tried in several ways to recapture the audience, mostly through imitation of Hollywood production methods and genres. Alternatively, there emerged a movement consisting of younger directors: Abel Gance, Louis Delluc, Germaine Dulac, Marcel L'Herbier, and Jean Epstein.

> 66 Another period arrived, that of the psychological and impressionist film. It would seem stupid to place a character in a given situation without penetrating into the secret realm of his inner life, and the actor's performance is explained by the play of thoughts and of visualized sensations."
> —Germaine Dulac, director

Films and Feelings   The previous generation had regarded filmmaking as a commercial craft, but the younger filmmakers wrote essays proclaiming cinema to be an art comparable to poetry, painting, and music. Astonished by the verve and energy of the American cinema, the young theorists compared Chaplin to a ballet dancer and the films of Hart to *The Song of Roland.* Cinema should, the young filmmakers argued, be what other arts were: a vehicle for feelings. Gance, Delluc, Dulac, L'Herbier, Epstein, and other members of the movement sought to put this idea into practice as filmmakers. Between 1918 and 1928, the younger directors experimented with cinema in ways that posed an alternative to the emerging Hollywood tradition.

The movement gained the name "Impressionist" because filmmakers wanted to give their narration subjective depth, to capture the momentary impressions that flit through a character's mind. Believing that cinema should project heightened and subtle emotional states, the directors concentrated on intimate psychological stories. They favored situations with a small number of characters, often caught up in a love triangle, as in Gance's *La Dixième symphonie* (1918), Delluc's *L'Inondation* (1924), and Epstein's *Coeur fidèle* (1923) and *La Belle nivernaise* (1923). These charged situations created fleeting moods and shifting sensations.

An Impressionist film replaces external action with an exploration of the characters' inner life. Flashbacks depict memories; sometimes the bulk of a film will be one flashback or a series of them. The films register characters' dreams, fantasies, and mental states. Dulac's *The Smiling Mme. Beudet* (1923) consists almost entirely of the main character's imaginary escape from a dull marriage. Despite its epic length (over five hours), Gance's *La Roue* (1922) rests essentially on the erotic relations among only four people, and the director seeks to trace the development of each character's feelings in great detail.

12.33

12.34

12.33–12.34 Cinematography for subjectivity. In *Coeur fidèle,* the barmaid looks out a window, and a superimposition of the flotsam of the waterfront conveys her dejection at working in a dockside tavern (12.33). In *El Dorado,* a man's tipsiness in a cabaret is conveyed by means of a curved mirror that stretches his body sideways (12.34).

Subjective Style   The movement earned its name as well for its distinctive film style. *The Cabinet of Dr. Caligari* had evoked its protagonist's mental states through mise-en-scene, but the French relied more on cinematography and editing. In Impressionist films, optical effects such as superimpositions imply characters' thoughts and moods **(12.33).** In *La Roue,* the image of Norma is laid over the smoke from a locomotive, representing the fantasy of the engine driver, who is in love with her. Going beyond mental subjectivity, the filmmakers try to register characters' optical impressions as well. POV cutting is common, and so are shots suggesting altered states of perception. When a character in an Impressionist film gets drunk or dizzy, that experience is rendered in vertiginous camera movements, or slow motion, or distorted or filtered shots **(12.34).**

CONNECT TO THE BLOG
www.davidbordwell.net/blog

We consider the heritage of Expressionism and Impressionism in the work of Martin Scorsese, including *Taxi Driver* and *Shutter Island,* in "Scorsese, 'pressionist."

The Impressionists also experimented with pronounced rhythmic editing to suggest the pace of an experience as a character feels it, moment by moment. During scenes of violence or emotional turmoil, the rhythm accelerates—the shots get shorter and shorter, building to a climax, sometimes with images only a few frames long. In *Coeur fidèle,* lovers at a fair ride in whirling swings, and Epstein presents their giddiness in a series of shots 4 frames, then 2 frames, long. In *La Roue,* a train crash is presented in accelerating shots ranging from 13 frames down to 2, and a man's last thoughts before he falls from a cliff are rendered in a hail of single-frame shots. We've seen this pattern of accelerated editing in *The Birds* (p. 222), but these passages from *La Roue* are the first known instances of it.

Impressionist form and style put demands on film technology. Abel Gance, the boldest innovator in this respect, used his epic *Napoléon* (1927) as a chance to try new lenses (even a 275mm telephoto), multiple-frame images (called Polyvision), and widescreen ratio (the celebrated triptychs; see 5.70). Impressionists were especially interested in frame mobility. After all, if the camera was to represent a character's eyes, it should be able to move with the ease of a person. Impressionists strapped their cameras to cars, carousels, and locomotives. For Gance's *Napoléon,* the camera manufacturer Debrie perfected a handheld model that let the operator move on roller skates. Gance lashed the machine to wheels, cables, pendulums, and bobsleds. In *L'Argent* (1928), L'Herbier sent his camera gliding through huge rooms and plummeting down from the dome of the Paris stock exchange **(12.35).**

Such innovations had given French filmmakers the hope that their films could be as popular as Hollywood's product. Some Impressionist films did appeal to the French public, but foreign audiences weren't attracted. Two behemoth productions of the decade, *Napoléon* and *L'Argent,* failed and were reedited by the producers; they were among the last Impressionist films released. With the arrival of the sound film, the French film industry tightened its belt and had no money to risk on experiments.

Impressionism as a distinct movement may be said to have ceased by 1929. But the filmmakers' explorations of psychological narrative and subjective style became a legacy to future generations. These innovations continued in the work of Alfred Hitchcock and Maya Deren, in Hollywood montage sequences, and in certain American genres and styles (the horror film, film noir). Even today, when a director wants to convey what a character is sensing or feeling in some abnormal state of mind, Impressionist techniques of camerawork and editing—blurred imagery, superimposition, slow motion, accelerating cutting—prove to be common choices **(12.36**; see also 3.42, from *The Road Warrior*).

Surrealism

The French Impressionist filmmakers worked within the commercial film industry, but Surrealist filmmakers relied on private patronage and screened their work in small artists' gatherings. Not surprisingly, Surrealist cinema was a more radical movement, producing films that would perplex and shock ordinary audiences.

Surrealist cinema was directly linked to Surrealism in literature and painting. According to its leader, André Breton, "Surrealism [is] based on the belief in the superior reality of certain forms of association, heretofore neglected, in the omnipotence of dreams, in the undirected play of thought." The Impressionist filmmakers sought to catch the flow of consciousness as a tumble of sensations and memories. But Surrealist art, influenced by Freudian psychology, wanted to go deeper. Surrealists wanted to plumb the hidden currents of the unconscious.

Automatic writing and painting, the search for bizarre or evocative imagery, the deliberate avoidance of rationally explicable form or style: These became

12.35 The dizzying crane shot. In *L'Argent,* the camera drops toward the floor of the stock exchange in an effort to convey the traders's frenzied excitement.

12.36 Camerawork for hallucination. Impressionists would probably have admired the opening of *Apocalypse Now* (1979). Superimpositions, striking compositions, and the mixing of sounds and images of battle with the whirring of the overhead fan—all take us into Willard's mind.

features of Surrealism as it developed in the period 1924–1929. From the start, the Surrealists were attracted to the cinema, especially films that presented untamed desire or the fantastic and marvelous. They admired slapstick comedies, *Nosferatu*, and serials about mysterious super-criminals. In due time, painters such as Man Ray and Salvador Dalí and writers such as Antonin Artaud began dabbling in cinema, while the young Spaniard Luis Buñuel, drawn to Surrealism, became its most famous filmmaker.

Hollywood filmmakers, the Expressionists, and the Impressionists were all committed to storytelling, even if their methods differed. But Surrealist cinema was anti-narrative, attacking causality and coherence. If rationality is to be fought, connections among events must be dissolved, as in *The Seashell and the Clergyman* (1928—scripted by Artaud, filmed by the Impressionist Germaine Dulac; **12.37**) In Dalí and Buñuel's *Un Chien andalou* (*An Andalusian Dog,* 1928), the hero drags two pianos, stuffed with dead donkeys, across a parlor. In Buñuel's *L'Age d'or* (1930), a woman begins obsessively sucking the toes of a statue.

But even while banishing causality, many Surrealist films tease us to find it. It becomes as evasive as in a dream. Instead, we find events juxtaposed for their disturbing effect. The hero gratuitously shoots a child (*L'Age d'or*), a woman closes her eyes only to reveal eyes painted on her eyelids (Ray's *Emak Bakia*, 1927), and—most horrifying of all—a man strops a razor and deliberately slits the eyeball of an unprotesting woman (**12.38**). An Impressionist film would motivate such events as a character's dreams or hallucinations, but in these films, character psychology can't be determined. Sexual desire, violence, blasphemy, and bizarre humor take the place of conventional narrative. The hope was that the free form of the film would arouse the deepest impulses of the viewer, even if those impulses were unsavory. Buñuel called *Un Chien andalou* "a passionate call to murder."

The style of Surrealist cinema is eclectic. Mise-en-scene is often influenced by Surrealist painting. The ants in *Un Chien andalou* come from Dalí's pictures; the pillars and city squares of *The Seashell and the Clergyman* hark back to the Italian painter Giorgio de Chirico. Surrealist editing is an amalgam of some Impressionist devices (many dissolves and superimpositions) and some devices of the dominant cinema. The shocking eyeball-slitting at the start of *Un Chien andalou* relies on continuity editing as well as the Kuleshov effect (p. 226). However, discontinuous editing is also commonly used to fracture space and time. In *Un Chien andalou*, a

12.37

12.38

12.37–12.38 Surrealists' irrational imagery. *The Seashell and the Clergyman*: the clergyman's distorted view of a threatening military officer, inexplicably dressed in baby's clothes (12.37). A shocking eye-slitting scene opens *Un Chien andalou* (12.38).

12.39 Surrealism's heritage. The mysterious ear, discolored and covered with ants, discovered at the opening of *Blue Velvet* (1986) recalls *Un Chien andalou.*

woman locks a man out of a room only to turn and find him inexplicably behind her. On the whole, Surrealist film style refused to define itself by any particular techniques, since that would order and rationalize what had to be an "undirected play of thought."

The fortunes of Surrealist cinema shifted with changes in the art movement as a whole. By late 1929, when Breton joined the Communist Party, Surrealists were embroiled in internal dissension about whether communism was a political equivalent of Surrealism. Buñuel left France for a brief stay in Hollywood and then returned to Spain. The chief patron of Surrealist filmmaking, the Vicomte de Noailles, supported Jean Vigo's *Zéro de Conduite* (1933), a film of Surrealist ambitions, but then stopped sponsoring the avant-garde. As a unified movement, French Surrealism was no longer viable after 1930.

Individual Surrealists continued their efforts, however. The most famous was Buñuel, who continued to work in his own brand of the Surrealist style for 50 years, in films such as *Belle de Jour* (1967) and *The Discreet Charm of the Bourgeoisie* (1972). He was followed by other filmmakers, including the avant-gardist Kenneth Anger. Similarly, David Lynch's *Blue Velvet, Lost Highway,* and *Mulholland Dr.* owe a good deal to Breton's demand to plumb the unconscious mind "in the absence of any control exercised by reason, and beyond any aesthetic and moral preoccupation" **(12.39).**

Soviet Montage (1924–1930)

Few artists were as determined to shake up filmmaking as the men and women who came of age during the Russian Revolution of October 1917. In all the arts, the call went out for a new way of seeing, and the creation of an art that would reflect Communist social ideals. The film world was galvanized by young people who scorned the current customs. They wanted to forge a cinema that would be revolutionary in subject, theme, form, and style. They wanted to provide filmmakers with brand-new tools.

Most Russian films made before the revolution were somber, slow-paced melodramas featuring bravura performances by popular stars **(12.40).** The dominant style favored long takes and intricate staging. One master of the period was Yevgenii Bauer, who brought pictorial elegance to tales of flirtation and betrayal among the upper classes. (See 4.131–4.134.) The young filmmakers, fascinated by continuity editing and the extroverted, athletic performance style in Westerns and comedies, saw the Hollywood style as the cutting-edge approach. But the aspiring directors didn't simply copy the American methods. They pushed them to the limit, in the process creating a new and distinctive set of filmmaking tools.

Artists and the State

The government aimed to remake all sectors of life. At first, policy makers tried to nationalize all private property. In response, film companies simply refused to supply films to theaters operating under the government control. In July 1918, the State Commission of Education put strict controls on the existing supplies of raw film stock. As a result, producers began hoarding their stock; the largest firms took all the equipment they could and fled to other countries. Some companies made films commissioned by the government, while hoping that the Reds would lose the Civil War and that things would return to pre-Revolutionary conditions.

CONNECT TO THE BLOG
www.davidbordwell.net/blog

We analyze Bauer's masterful staging in his upper-class melodramas in "Watching movies very, very slowly" and "What's left to discover today? Plenty."

12.40 The tsarist style. In Yakov Protazanov's 1916 *The Queen of Spades,* the gambling-addicted hero, played by the popular Ivan Mozhukin, imagines himself winning at cards, with his vision superimposed at the right.

Like other Soviet industries, film production and distribution took years to build up a substantial output. To fill the void in theaters, American films, particularly those of D. W. Griffith, Douglas Fairbanks, and Mary Pickford, circulated for years. They became a tremendous influence on young filmmakers.

Faced with little equipment and difficult living conditions, a few young film-makers made tentative moves that would result in the development of a national cinema movement. Dziga Vertov shot documentary footage of the war; at age 20, he was placed in charge of all newsreels. Lev Kuleshov, in his early 20s, was teaching in the newly founded State School on Cinema Art. There he built up a series of experiments by assembling footage, some that he shot, some from existing films, into short segments that created an impression of continuity (pp. 225–226). Kuleshov, perhaps the most conservative of the young Soviet filmmakers, tried to systematize principles of editing based on the emerging Hollywood style. Even before they were able to make films, Kuleshov and his young pupils were working at the first film school in the world and writing theoretical essays on the new art form. This grounding in theory would be the basis of the Montage style.

Other young people moved into cinema, often from scientific backgrounds. The engineer Sergei Eisenstein began directing plays in a workers' theater in Moscow. For one 1923 production he made a short film, and soon he was directing a feature. Vsevolod Pudovkin, trained in chemistry, made his acting debut in a play presented by Kuleshov's State Film School. He had been inspired to go into filmmaking by seeing Griffith's *Intolerance,* and he would make his first feature a few years later. Some tsarist-era directors, Protozanov, for example, would continue to work under the Soviet regime, but the breakthroughs came from newcomers.

NEP Cinema

Circumstances favored their rise. By 1921, the country was facing tremendous problems, not least a widespread famine. To facilitate the production and distribution of goods, Lenin instituted the New Economic Policy (NEP), which for several years permitted private management of business and a measure of free enterprise. For film, the NEP meant a sudden reappearance of film stock and equipment. Slowly, Soviet production began to grow as private firms made more films.

"Of all the arts, for us the cinema is the most important," Lenin stated in 1922. Since Lenin saw film as a powerful tool for education, the first films encouraged by the government were documentaries such as Vertov's newsreel series *Kino-Pravda.* Soviet fictional films were being made from 1917 on, but it was not until 1923 that a Georgian feature, *Red Imps,* became the first Soviet film to compete successfully with the foreign films dominating local screens. And not until 1927 did the industry's income from its own films top that of the films it imported.

The NEP brought forth a burst of fresh, daring films from the young-sters. From Kuleshov's class at the State Film School came *The Extraordinary Adventures of Mr. West in the Land of the Bolsheviks* (1924; **12.41**). This satiric comedy, along with Kuleshov's next project, *The Death Ray* (1925), were stunningly different from the tsarist cinema—fast-paced, full of stunts, chases, and fights, and cut with the freedom of an American film. Kuleshov showed that a Soviet film could be as entertaining as the Hollywood product. Eisenstein's first feature, *Strike* (1925) mixed cartoonish satire with violent action, including a workers' massacre intercut with the slaughter of a bull. Although it wasn't seen outside the USSR until decades later, historians now consider it the first full-blown exercise in the Montage style. Eisenstein's next film, *The Battleship Potemkin* (1925), came to epitomize the new movement. Stupendously successful abroad, it was praised as a masterpiece. Over the next few years, as silent cinema was coming to an end, Eisenstein, Pudovkin, Vertov, Alexander Dovzhenko, and other directors created films that became classics.

> " Everyone who has had in his hands a piece of film to be edited knows by experience how neutral it remains, even though a part of a planned sequence, until it is joined with another piece, when it suddenly acquires and conveys a sharper and quite different meaning than that planned for it at the time of filming."
>
> —Sergei Eisenstein, director

12.41 Soviet satire. *The Extraordinary Adventures of Mr. West in the Land of the Bolsheviks:* A gang of thieves terrifies the naive American, Mr. West, by presenting him with clichéd caricatures of fierce Soviet revolutionaries.

The Priority of Editing

What was the basis of the Montage movement? In their writings and films, these directors championed editing over all other film techniques. This was a clear attack on the long-take style that had dominated earlier Russian film. Inspired by viewings of American and French Impressionist films, the young Soviet directors declared that a film's power arose not from the delicate performances of expert actors, but from the combination of shots. Through editing, they maintained, two shots give birth to a feeling or idea not present in either one. This is the insight behind Kuleshov's experiments. If you intercut different images with impassive shots of a man's face, or show a couple looking offscreen and then a shot of a building, the editing is what endows the performance with meaning. Here the Soviets went beyond their Hollywood peers, who counted on star actors to help carry the story.

"Montage," the Russian word for cutting, seemed to show the way forward for modern cinema. But not all of the young theoreticians agreed on exactly what the Montage approach to editing should be. Pudovkin, for example, believed that shots were like bricks, to be joined together to build a sequence. Eisenstein disagreed, saying that the maximum effect would be gained if the shots did not fit together perfectly, if they created a jolt for the spectator. Many filmmakers tried out discontinuities of this sort (**12.42**). Eisenstein also favored juxtaposing shots to create an abstract theme, as we've already seen with his use of conceptual editing in *October* (pp. 259–262). Vertov disagreed with both theorists. He disapproved of the fiction film altogether and promoted montage-based documentary cinema, as in *Man with a Movie Camera* (pp. 432–436).

However the filmmakers might have disagreed in debate, they often converged in practice. Pudovkin's *Storm over Asia* makes use of conceptual editing similar to that of Eisenstein's *October.* Shots of a military officer and his wife being dressed in their accessories are intercut with shots of the preparation at the temple. Pudovkin's parallel montage points up the absurdity of both rituals (**12.43–12.46**). Elsewhere *Storm over Asia* employs many jump cuts, breaking spatial and temporal coherence for the sake of stirring the spectator's senses. American continuity style taught the Montagists the power of editing, but once they learned the lesson, they pushed the technique in radical directions that would have shocked Hollywood filmmakers.

The Montage movement went even farther beyond Hollywood in their approach to narrative. Soviet films tended to downplay character psychology as a trigger for plots; instead, social forces provided the major causes. Characters were interesting not as individuals but as examples of how large-scale processes affected people's lives. As a result, Soviet Montage films didn't always have a single protagonist. Social groups could form a collective hero, as in Eisenstein's early films. In the *October* sequence (pp. 260–262), his editing shows how social groups, such as the soldiers at the front or the women and children on the breadlines, are victimized by brutal government policies.

In keeping with this downplaying of individual personalities, Soviet filmmakers often preferred to cast non-actors. This practice was called **typage,** since the filmmakers would often choose an individual whose appearance seemed directly to convey the type of character in the role. Except for the hero, Pudovkin used non-actors to play all the Mongols in *Storm over Asia.*

The Movement Ends

By the late 1920s, each of the major directors of this movement had made about four important films. The decline of the movement was not caused primarily by industrial and economic factors, as in Germany and France. Instead, the Communist government came to disapprove of the Montage style. Vertov,

CONNECT TO THE BLOG
www.davidbordwell.net/blog

For more on Eisenstein's approach to editing, see "Seed-beds of style."

12.42 Discontinuity for shock. In *House on Trubnoi Square,* Montage director Boris Barnet uses a jump cut to convey the heroine's sudden realization that a streetcar is headed straight for her.

12.43

12.44

12.45

12.46

12.43–12.46 Crosscutting for thematic parallels. In *Storm over Asia*, Pudovkin shows a medium close-up of an elaborate piece of jewelry being lowered over the head of a priest (12.43). Cut to a close-up of a servant placing a necklace around the neck of the officer's wife (12.44). Cut back to a large headdress being positioned on a priest's head (12.45). Cut to a close-up of a tiara being set on the wife's head (12.46).

Eisenstein, and Dovzhenko were criticized for their excessively formal and esoteric approaches. In 1929, Eisenstein went to Hollywood to study the new technique of sound; by the time he returned in 1932, the attitude of the film industry had changed. While he was away, a few filmmakers carried their Montage experiments into sound cinema. But the Soviet authorities, under Stalin's direction, encouraged filmmakers to create simple films that would be readily understandable to all audiences. Stylistic experimentation and nonrealistic subject matter were condemned.

This trend culminated in 1934, when the government instituted a new artistic policy called Socialist Realism. This policy dictated that all artworks must depict revolutionary development while being firmly grounded in realism. The Montage theories of the 1920s had to be discarded or modified. Eisenstein continued experimenting with editing and occasionally incurred the wrath of the authorities until his death in 1948. As a movement, the Soviet Montage style can be said to have ended by 1933, with the release of such films as Vertov's *Enthusiasm* (1931) and Pudovkin's *Deserter* (1933).

Yet like other silent film movements, its legacy proved enormous. As Kuleshov and his pupils imitated American films, Hollywood borrowed Soviet strategies by creating the "montage sequences" (p. 252) that became common in the 1930s and are still used today. American filmmakers have paid homage to *The Battleship Potemkin* in movies as different as *Bananas* and *The Untouchables*. The films of Resnais, especially *Hiroshima mon amour, Muriel,* and *La Guerre est finie,* rework Soviet Montage principles. Even more pervasive were Montage influences on avant-garde filmmaking. Makers of found-footage films such as *A Movie* owe a good deal to Vertov's Kino-Eye, and Eisenstein's idea that discontinuity in editing was one creative option underwrote many modern experiments **(12.47)**. The writings of the Montage directors, with their passionate call for breaking with the past, have inspired young filmmakers to make daring creative choices.

12.47 Discontinuity multiplied. Panels from old comic books, panned over jerkily and cut together disjunctively, are glimpsed in Lewis Klahr's *Two Minutes to Zero Trilogy* (2003–2004). In a test of Soviet Montage theories, we're invited to assemble the fragmentary shots into an ominous story of crime and panic.

The Classical Hollywood Cinema after the Coming of Sound (1926–1950)

The arrival of synchronized sound filming in the late 1920s dramatically shows how technological change can widen a filmmaker's creative choices. Before that, nearly all music heard in cinema was played on the spot, provided by a piano, organ, or an orchestra. Sound effects might be added; some organs could mimic pistol shots. But there would be no spoken dialogue. The silent cinema had written language in its intertitles, but not speech.

You can argue that film form and style would have been very different if cinema could have recorded spoken dialogue when movies began. Wouldn't the line of least resistance have been to simply photograph stage performances? If cinema had not been condemned to silence, would actors like Chaplin and Fairbanks have developed such a visually expressive performance style? Would Griffith and other directors have developed crosscutting and continuity editing? Would the Impressionists have tried to render the fluidity of thought, or the Soviet Montagists sought to make conceptual points through their cutting patterns? More likely, as many writers thought at the time, cinema would have become primarily a recording medium, and films would have been canned theater, like television situation comedy.

From this perspective, the absence of recorded speech was a great gift. It drastically constrained filmmakers' choices. It pushed them to find ways of telling stories visually, and the results yielded a new art form.

With the advent of synchronized sound, filmmakers faced perhaps the most important decision point in film history. Should they give up all the resources of film form and style developed over 30 years of silent moviemaking? Should they simply turn movies into photographed stage plays? Or should filmmakers try to integrate spoken language, along with music and effects, into the sophisticated visual storytelling of the late silent era? Or were there still other options? The decision would shape the future of a medium that was already still very young compared to the other arts.

Converting to Sound

Like many media technologies, synchronized sound was born from a business decision. During the mid-1920s, Warner Bros. was expanding its facilities and holdings. One of these expansions was the investment in a sound system using records in synchronization with film images. By releasing *Don Juan* (1926) with orchestral accompaniment and sound effects on disc, along with a series of vaudeville shorts with singing and talking, Warner Bros. began to popularize the idea of sound films. In 1927, *The Jazz Singer* (a part-talkie with some scenes accompanied only by music) was a tremendous success, and the Warner Bros. investment began to pay off.

The success of *Don Juan, The Jazz Singer,* and the shorts convinced other studios that sound contributed to profitable filmmaking. Unlike the era of the Motion Picture Patents Company, there was now no fierce competition within the industry. Firms realized that whatever sound system the studios finally adopted, it would have to be compatible with the projection machinery of any theater. Eventually, the sound-on-disc system was rejected and a sound-on-film one became the standard up to the present. As we saw in Chapter 1, the sound track was printed on the strip of film alongside the image. By 1930, most theaters in America were wired for sound. The question for filmmakers was: What to do with this new technology?

Problems and Solutions

It seemed for a few years that much of the visual storytelling of the silent era would be lost. Camera positions were more limited, because the camera had to be put inside a soundproof booth so that its motor noise would not be picked up by the

66 You know, when talkies first came in they were fascinated by sound—they had frying eggs and they had this and that—and then people became infatuated with the movement of the camera; I believe, the big thing right now is to move a handheld camera. I think the director and his camerawork should not intrude on the story."

—George Cukor, director

microphone (**12.48**). The camera operator could hear only through his earphones, and the camera could not move except for short pans to reframe. The bulky microphone, on the table at the right in 12.48, also did not move. Complicated staging was ruled out because the actors had to stay close to the microphone. Often several cameras in their booths were filming from different angles, so lighting had to be rather broad and flat; it could not be tailored to a particular shot. Such restrictions seemed to confirm critics and filmmakers' worst fears: Movies would now be static and stagey.

Still, from the very beginning of sound filming, problems were solved. When several cameras recorded the scene from different angles, the footage could be cut together to provide continuity editing patterns, complete with close-ups. A booth might be mounted on wheels to create camera movements, or a scene might be shot silent and a sound track added later. Early sound films such as Rouben Mamoulian's *Applause* (1929) showed that the camera could regain considerable flexibility of movement. Later, equipment manufacturers came up with smaller enclosures that replaced the cumbersome booths. These *blimps* (**12.49**) permitted cinematographers to place the camera on movable supports. Similarly, microphones mounted on booms and hanging over the heads of the actors could also follow moving action and maintain recording quality.

It became clear that instead of wiping out all the options of classical Hollywood form and style, recorded sound would be integrated into that system. Once cutting, camera movement, and fluid staging were restored, filmmakers returned to many of the stylistic characteristics developed in Hollywood during the silent period. Diegetic sound provided a powerful addition to the system of continuity editing. A line of dialogue could continue over a cut, creating smooth temporal continuity. (See pp. 273–275.) In addition, music could be more precisely timed to the action than was possible in live accompaniment. Max Steiner's scores for *The Most Dangerous Game* (1932) and *King Kong* (1933) showed that music could powerfully enhance both the image and spoken dialogue—sometimes amplifying frenzied action, sometimes quietly stressing a single sentence.

12.48

12.49

12.48–12.49 From booth to blimp. A posed publicity still demonstrated the limitations of early sound filming (12.48). A blimped camera during the early 1930s allowed more freedom of camera placement (12.49).

Studios, Genres, and Spectacle

Within the overall tradition of continuity style and classical narrative form, each of the large studios developed a distinctive approach. Thus MGM, for example, became the prestige studio, with a huge number of stars and technicians under long-term contract. MGM lavished money on settings, costumes, and special effects, as in *The Good Earth* (1937), with its locust attack, and *San Francisco* (1936),

CONNECT TO THE BLOG
www.davidbordwell.net/blog

Some of these early sound and color films can be hard to find, but we look at some DVD collections that provide lots of information and clips in "All singing! All dancing! All teaching!"

12.50 Studios specialize in genres. Heavy shadows, spiky shapes, and eccentric performances mix a menacing atmosphere with a touch of humor in Universal's *The Old Dark House*.

in which the great earthquake of 1906 is spectacularly re-created. Warner Bros., in spite of its success with sound, was still a relatively small studio and specialized in less expensive genre pictures. Its series of gangster films (*Little Caesar, Public Enemy*) and musicals (*42nd Street, Gold Diggers of 1933, Dames*) were among the studio's most successful products. Even lower on the ladder of prestige was Universal, which depended on imaginative filmmaking rather than established stars or expensive sets in its atmospheric horror films, such as *Frankenstein* (1931) and *The Old Dark House* (1932; **12.50**).

One major genre, the musical, became possible only with the introduction of sound. Indeed, the original intention of the Warners when they began their investment in sound equipment was to circulate vaudeville acts on film. Most musicals presented a linear plot with separate numbers inserted, although a few revue musicals simply strung together a series of numbers. One of the major studios, RKO, made a series of musicals starring Fred Astaire and Ginger Rogers: *Swing Time* (George Stevens, 1936) illustrates how a musical can be a classically constructed narrative (see pp. 345–346).

During the 1930s, color film stocks became widely used for the first time. In the 1920s, a small number of films had Technicolor sequences, but the process was crude, using only two colors in combination to create all other hues. The result tended to emphasize greenish-blue and pink tones; it was also too costly to use extensively **(12.51).** By the early 1930s, however, Technicolor had been improved. It now used three primary colors and thus could reproduce a large range of hues. Though still expensive, it was soon proved to add hugely to the appeal of many films. After *Becky Sharp* (1935), the first feature-length film to use the new Technicolor, and *The Trail of the Lonesome Pine* (1936), studios began using Technicolor extensively. The Technicolor process was used, for either camera originals or release prints, until the early 1970s. (For examples of Technicolor, see 2.17, 2.19, 2.20, 2.22–2.25; 4.2, 4.146; 5.7; 11.101–11.113.)

Deep Focus and Narrative Innovations

Technicolor needed a great deal of light on the set, so more powerful lighting units were introduced. Some cinematographers began to use the new units for black-and-white filming. These more powerful lamps, combined with faster film stocks, made it easier to achieve greater depth of field in the image. Many cinematographers stuck to the standard soft-focus style of the 1920s and 1930s, but others began to experiment.

By the late 1930s, there was a definite trend toward a deep-focus style. It was *Citizen Kane* that in 1941 brought deep focus strongly to the attention of spectators and filmmakers. Orson Welles's compositions placed the foreground figures close to the camera and the background figures deep in the space of the shot, and all were kept in sharp focus (5.48; 8.28–8.32, 8.37–8.42). In some cases, the image was achieved through matte work and rear projection, not cinematography on the set. Overall, *Citizen Kane* helped make deep focus a major creative option within classical Hollywood style.

Directors found that depth staging and deep-focus filming allowed them to create striking compositions and to sustain scenes in longer takes **(12.52).** The light necessary for deep focus tended to lend a hard-edged appearance to objects, a look well-suited to the stories of crime and pursuit that would eventually be called *film noir*. But like every creative choice, the new technique forced fresh decisions. If an object or a face was placed close to the foreground, cinematographers found it hard to keep the composition balanced and in focus when actors moved around the shot. The most famous deep-focus shots in *Citizen Kane* and other films tend to be fixed long takes with simple staging. As a result, many deep-focus images seem more static and enclosed than the fluid performances and framings of films like *His Girl Friday* (pp. 401–404).

12.51 Two-strip Technicolor. A color sequence from *Ben-Hur* (1925) captures mostly reddish-orange and green hues.

12.52 The spread of deep-focus cinematography. Many films using the technique soon appeared. *Citizen Kane's* cinematographer, Gregg Toland, worked on some of them, such as William Wyler's *The Little Foxes.*

12.53 Neo-noir pays homage to the past. A deep-focus composition in *The Usual Suspects* adapts Welles-Toland deep focus to the widescreen format.

During the same period, Hollywood was also broadening its narrative options. Flashbacks had been used since the 1910s, but they gained a new prominence in the 1940s. Films such as *The Long Night* (1947) and *The Big Clock* (1948) start from a point of crisis and go back in time to trace how events led up to it. Or there might be several flashbacks, threaded together by an investigation as in *Citizen Kane* or *The Killers* (1946). The flashback might replay an earlier scene, but now revealing unexpected information, as in the climax of *Mildred Pierce* (1945).

Along with flashbacks, screenwriters began experimenting with voice-over narration, already well established on radio but given a new power with the accompanying images. Both flashbacks and voice-over narration fed into a new emphasis on mental subjectivity. More than in the 1930s, films rendered dreams, hallucinations, and drunken or drug-induced visions. There are moments in *Murder, My Sweet* (1944) and *Possessed* (1947) that hark back to German Expressionism and French Impressionism, with subjective sound enhancing the imagery.

By assimilating sound and color to its system of visual storytelling, the Hollywood cinema laid the foundation of the popular film as we know it today. Later changes in technology, such as widescreen filming, multiple-track sound, computer-driven special effects, and digital capture, would build on this solid tradition **(12.53)**. For decades to follow, the formal and stylistic conventions elaborated in the Hollywood studios of the 1930s and 1940s would guide the creative choices of filmmakers. Those conventions would also become targets for filmmakers who wanted to try something different.

CONNECT TO THE BLOG
www.davidbordwell.net/blog

We examine deep-focus cinematography and staging in the 1930s and 1940s in "Foreground, background, playground" and "Problems, problems: Wyler's workarounds."

Italian Neorealism (1942–1951)

One of the most influential movements in film history, Neorealism has somewhat diffuse origins. The label first appeared in the writings of Italian critics of the 1940s. From one perspective, the term represented a younger generation's desire to break free of the conventions of ordinary Italian cinema. Under dictator Benito Mussolini, the motion picture industry had created colossal historical epics and sentimental upper-class melodramas, and many critics felt these to be artificial and decadent. Something closer to real life was needed. Some onlookers found that quality in French films of the 1930s, especially works by Jean Renoir. Other critics turned closer to home to praise films like Luchino Visconti's *Ossessione* (1942).

Today most historians believe that Neorealist filmmaking was not a complete break with Italian cinema under Mussolini. Pseudo-documentaries such as Roberto Rossellini's *White Ship* (1941), even though propagandistic, prepared the way for more forthright handling of contemporary events. Other current trends,

CONNECT TO THE BLOG
www.davidbordwell.net/blog

We consider 1940s flashback trickery in "Twice-Told Tales: *Mildred Pierce*," which includes a video analysis.

12.54

12.55

12.56

12.54–12.56 Filming in the streets. In one scene in *Open City*, Francesco is thrown into a truck by Nazi soldiers (12.54). His common-law wife Pina breaks through the guards (12.55), and a rough, bumpy shot taken from the truck shows her running after him (12.56).

such as regional dialect comedy and urban melodrama, encouraged directors and scriptwriters to turn toward realism. Overall, spurred by both foreign influences and indigenous traditions, the postwar period saw several filmmakers aiming to reveal contemporary social conditions. This trend became known as the Neorealist movement.

Leaving the Studio

Economic, political, and cultural factors helped Neorealism survive. Unlike the young Soviet filmmakers, nearly all the major Neorealists—Rossellini, Vittorio De Sica, Visconti, and others—came to the movement as experienced filmmakers. They had absorbed lessons from Hollywood and European film traditions. They knew one another, frequently shared scriptwriters and personnel, and gained public attention in the journals *Cinema* and *Bianco e Nero*. Before 1948, the Neorealist movement had enough friends in the government to be relatively free of censorship. There was as well an affinity between Neorealism and an Italian literary movement of the same period modeled on the *verismo* of the previous century. The result was an array of Italian films that gained worldwide recognition: Visconti's *La Terra Trema* (1947); Rossellini's *Rome Open City* (1945), *Paisan* (1946), and *Germany Year Zero* (1947); and De Sica's *Shoeshine* (1946) and *Bicycle Thieves* (1948).

Neorealism created a somewhat distinctive approach to film style. By 1945, the fighting had destroyed most of Cinecittà, the large Roman studio complex, so sets were in short supply and sound equipment was rare. As a result, Neorealist mise-en-scène relied on actual locales, and its photographic work tended toward the raw roughness of documentaries. Rossellini has told of buying bits of negative stock from street photographers, so that much of *Rome Open City* was shot on film with varying photographic qualities.

Shooting on the streets and in private buildings made Italian camera operators adept at cinematography that often avoided the three-point lighting system of Hollywood (4.70–4.72). Although Neorealist films often featured famous stage or film actors, non-actors were also recruited for their realistic looks and behavior. For the adult "star" of *Bicycle Thieves*, De Sica chose a factory worker: "The way he moved, the way he sat down, his gestures with those hands of a working man and not of an actor . . . everything about him was perfect." The Italian cinema had a long tradition of dubbing, so sound didn't have to be recorded on site. The ability to postsynchronize dialogue permitted the filmmakers to work on location with smaller crews and to move the camera freely. With a degree of improvisational freedom in the acting and setting went a certain flexibility of framing, well displayed in the death of Pina in *Rome Open City* **(12.54–12.56)** and the final sequence of *Germany Year Zero*. The tracking shots through the open-air bicycle market in *Bicycle Thieves* illustrate the possibilities that the Neorealist director found in returning to location filming.

A New Model of Storytelling

Just as influential was the Neorealist sense of narrative form. Reacting against the intricate plots found in light popular cinema, the Neorealists tended to loosen up narrative relations. The earliest major films of the movement, such as *Ossessione, Rome Open City,* and *Shoeshine,* contain relatively conventionally organized plots (albeit with unhappy endings). But the most formally innovative Neorealist films allow the intrusion of scenes that aren't motivated causally—that seem, in fact, to be accidents **(12.57).** The director may dwell on moments worth savoring for their own sake. A famous scene in De Sica's *Umberto D* (1951) records a pregnant housemaid grinding morning coffee. Her daily routine yields its own fascination, but the effect is very different from Hollywood's conception of what counts as drama.

Although the causes of characters' actions are usually seen as concretely economic and political (poverty, unemployment, exploitation), the effects are often fragmentary and inconclusive. Rossellini's *Paisan* is episodic, presenting six anecdotes of life in Italy during the Allied invasion. Often we are not told the outcome of an event, the consequence of a cause. In a harsh break with mainstream storytelling, Rossellini abruptly kills off one of his protagonists in *Rome Open City,* wiping out the film's romance plot.

Both the porous plot structure and the narration often refuse to provide an omniscient knowledge of events. The film seems to admit that the totality of reality is simply unknowable. This is especially evident in the films' endings. *Bicycle Thieves* concludes with the worker and his son wandering down the street, their stolen bicycle still missing, their future uncertain. *La Terra Trema* concludes with the suppression of the Sicilian fishermen's revolt against the merchants, but it hints that a future revolt might succeed. Neorealism's tendency toward slice-of-life plot construction gave many films of the movement an open-ended quality quite opposed to the tidy wrapup favored by American studio cinema.

12.57 The drama of accident. In *Bicycle Thieves,* the hero takes shelter along with a group of priests during a rain shower. The incident doesn't affect the plot and seems as casual as any moment in daily life.

The Movement's End and Its Legacy

As economic and cultural forces had sustained the Neorealist movement, so they helped bring it to an end. When Italy began to prosper after the war, the government looked askance at films so critical of contemporary society. After 1949, censorship and state pressures began to constrain the movement. Large-scale Italian film production began to reappear, and Neorealism no longer had the freedom permitted by small production companies. Neorealist directors, now famous, began to pursue more individualized concerns: Rossellini's investigation of Christian humanism and Western history, De Sica's sentimental romances, and Visconti's examination of upper-class milieus. Most historians date the end of the Neorealist movement with the public attacks on De Sica's *Umberto D* (1951). Nevertheless, Neorealist elements are still quite visible in the early works of Federico Fellini (*I Vitelloni,* 1954, is a good example) and Michelangelo Antonioni (*Cronaca di un amore,* 1951); both directors had worked on Neorealist films. Neorealist impulses periodically returned to Italian cinema, notably in the long career of Ermanno Olmi (*Il Posto, The Tree of the Wooden Clogs*).

The production strategies and artistic goals of this movement opened up a vast realm of creative choices. Throughout Latin America, the Middle East, and Asia, filmmakers followed the Neorealist model in rejecting polished studio production values. They realized that they could cast non-actors and let them perform in actual settings. They could rely on available light for shooting. Their screenplays didn't need intricate plotting and could incorporate the accidents and digressions of everyday life. The plot could even leave the story action unresolved at the end, the better to provoke the audience to weigh possible outcomes. The tenets of Neorealist theory and practice have formed a robust tradition for decades of non-Hollywood cinema. Today, filmmakers in many places continue to devise their own versions of Neorealism **(12.58).**

> ❝ The sentiment of [*Bicycle Thieves*] is expressed overtly. The feelings invoked are a natural consequence of the themes of the story and the point of view it is told from. It is a politically committed film, fueled by a quiet but burning passion. But it never lectures. It observes rather than explains.❞
>
> —Sally Potter, director, *Orlando*

12.58 Neorealism's legacy. Iranian filmmakers continue the Neorealist impulse: casual, anecdotal plots using non-actors to present social criticism. Samira Makhmalbaf's *The Apple* (1988) was based on a real incident, in which an unemployed father locked up his daughter for several years. The little girls and other family members played themselves.

The French New Wave (1959–1964)

The late 1950s and early 1960s saw the rise of a new generation of filmmakers around the world. In country after country, there emerged directors born before World War II but grown to adulthood in the postwar era of reconstruction and rising prosperity. Japan, Canada, England, Italy, Spain, Brazil, and the United States all had their new waves or young cinema groups—some trained in film schools, many allied with specialized film magazines, most in revolt against their elders in the industry. The most influential of these groups appeared in France.

Critics Become Moviemakers

In the mid-1950s, a group of young men who wrote for the Paris film journal *Cahiers du cinéma* made a habit of attacking the most artistically respected French filmmakers of the day. "I consider an adaptation of value," wrote François Truffaut, "only when written by a *man of the cinema.* Aurenche and Bost [the leading script-writers of the time] are essentially literary men and I reproach them here for being contemptuous of the cinema by underestimating it." Addressing 21 major directors, Jean-Luc Godard was more insulting: "Your camera movements are ugly because your subjects are bad, your casts act badly because your dialogue is worthless; in a word, you don't know how to create cinema because you no longer even know what it is." Truffaut and Godard, along with Claude Chabrol, Eric Rohmer, and Jacques Rivette, also praised directors considered somewhat outdated (Jean Renoir, Max Ophuls) or eccentric (Robert Bresson, Jacques Tati).

More important, the young men saw no contradiction in rejecting the French filmmaking establishment while loving blatantly commercial Hollywood. The young rebels of *Cahiers* claimed that in the works of certain directors—certain *auteurs* (authors)—artistry existed in the American cinema. An **auteur** usually did not literally write scripts but managed nonetheless to stamp his or her personality on studio products, transcending the constraints of Hollywood's standardized system. Howard Hawks, Otto Preminger, Samuel Fuller, Vincente Minnelli, Alfred Hitchcock—these were more than craftsmen. Each director's total output constituted a coherent world. Godard remarked, "We won the day in having it acknowledged in principle that a film by Hitchcock, for example, is as important as a book by Aragon. Film auteurs, thanks to us, have finally entered the history of art."

Writing criticism didn't satisfy these young men. They itched to make movies. Borrowing money from friends and filming on location, each started to shoot short films. By 1959, they had become a force to be reckoned with. In that year, Rivette filmed *Paris nous appartient* (*Paris Belongs to Us*); Godard made *À Bout de souffle* (*Breathless*); Chabrol made his second feature, *Les Cousins;* and in April, Truffaut's *Les Quatre cent coups* (*The 400 Blows*) won the Grand Prize at the Cannes Festival.

The novelty and youthful vigor of these directors led journalists to nickname them *la nouvelle vague*—the *New Wave.* Their output was staggering. All told, the five central directors made 32 feature films between 1959 and 1966; Godard and Chabrol made 11 apiece. So many films must of course be highly disparate, but there are enough similarities for us to identify a broadly distinctive New Wave approach to style and form.

A New Wave Style

The most obviously revolutionary quality of the New Wave films was their casual look. To proponents of the carefully polished French "cinema of quality," the young directors must have seemed hopelessly sloppy. The New Wave directors had admired the Neorealists (especially Rossellini) and, in opposition to studio filmmaking, took as their settings actual locales in and around Paris. Shooting on location became the norm **(12.59)**. Similarly, glossy studio lighting was replaced by available light and simple supplemental sources. Few postwar French films would have shown the dim apartments and grimy corridors featured in *Paris Belongs to Us.*

> " We were all critics before beginning to make films, and I loved all kinds of cinema—the Russians, the Americans, the Neorealists. It was the cinema that made us—or me, at least—want to make films. I knew nothing of life except through the cinema."
>
> —Jean-Luc Godard, director

12.59 **Location filming.** *Les Bonnes femmes:* While a serial killer stalks them, two of the heroines sit idly at work. Like many New Wave directors, Claude Chabrol followed the Neorealists in shooting on locations like this drab appliance shop.

Cinematography changed, too. The New Wave camera moves a great deal, panning and tracking to follow characters or to explore a locale. To make mobile shots cheaply on location demanded flexible, portable equipment. Fortunately, Éclair had recently developed a lightweight camera that could be handheld. (That the Éclair had been used primarily for documentary work accorded perfectly with the realistic mise-en-scene of the New Wave.) New Wave filmmakers were intoxicated with the new freedom offered by the handheld camera. In *The 400 Blows*, the camera explores a cramped apartment and rides a carnival centrifuge. In *Breathless*, the cinematographer held the camera while seated in a wheelchair to follow the hero's winding path through a travel agency (11.46).

One of the most salient features of New Wave films is their casual humor. These young men deliberately played with the medium. In Godard's *Band of Outsiders*, the three main characters resolve to be silent for a minute, and Godard dutifully shuts off *all* the sound. In Truffaut's *Shoot the Piano Player*, a character swears that he's not lying: "May my mother drop dead if I'm not telling the truth." Cut to a shot of an old lady keeling over.

Along with humor came esoteric references to other films, Hollywood or European. There are homages to admired auteurs: Godard characters allude to *Johnny Guitar* (Nicholas Ray), *Some Came Running* (Nicholas Minnelli), and "Arizona Jim" (from Renoir's *Crime of M. Lange*). In *Les Carabiniers*, Godard parodies Lumière, and in *Vivre sa vie*, he visually quotes *La Passion de Jeanne d'Arc* **(12.60, 12.61)**. Hitchcock is frequently cited in Chabrol's films, and Truffaut's *Les Mistons* re-creates a shot from a Lumière short. Such citations, the New Wave directors felt, acknowledged that cinema, like literature and painting, had lofty traditions that could be honored.

Neorealism Recast

New Wave films also pushed further the Neorealist experimentation with plot construction. In general, causal connections became quite loose. Is there actually a political conspiracy going on in *Paris Belongs to Us?* Why is Nana shot at the end of *Vivre sa vie?* In *Shoot the Piano Player*, the first sequence consists mainly of a conversation between the hero's brother and a man he accidentally meets on the street. The passerby laments his marital problems at some length. In a Hollywood film, he would become a major character, but here he departs and never reappears.

The films often lack goal-oriented protagonists. The heroes may drift aimlessly, engage in actions on the spur of the moment, or pass the time chatting in a café or going to movies. New Wave narratives also introduce startling shifts in tone, jolting our expectations. When two gangsters kidnap the hero and his girlfriend in *Shoot the Piano Player*, the whole group begins a comic discussion of sex. Discontinuous editing further disturbs narrative continuity; this tendency reaches its limit in Godard's jump cuts (6.151, 6.152; 11.51, 11.52).

Perhaps most important, the New Wave film typically ends ambiguously. Antoine in *The 400 Blows* reaches the sea in the last shot, but as he moves forward, Truffaut zooms in and freezes the frame, ending the film with the question of where Antoine will go from there (3.10). We've seen a similar lack of resolution in the final scene of *Breathless* (p. 420). In Chabrol's *Les Bonnes Femmes* and *Ophelia*, in Rivette's *Paris Belongs to Us*, and in nearly all the work of Godard and Truffaut in this period, the looseness of the causal chain leads to endings that remain defiantly open and uncertain.

Into the Mainstream and Beyond

The filmmakers were often bad mannered, and the films placed strong demands on the viewer, but the French film industry wasn't hostile to the New Wave. The decade 1947–1957 had been good to film production: The government supported

12.60

12.61

12.60–12.61 Classic film as a reference point. In Godard's *Vivre sa vie*, a clip from Dreyer's *The Passion of Joan of Arc* (12.60) provokes Nana's sympathy as she watches it (12.61). It also equates her with one of the great suffering heroines of silent cinema (see 4.46).

12.62 Borrowing from, and fighting, the New Wave. In spring 1995, a group of Danish directors founded a movement they called Dogme, to continue the impulse of the French New Wave. The group's manifesto laid down a series of rules, demanding that people shoot on location with a handheld camera and use no postproduction sound editing. One result was the second Dogme film, *The Idiots* (1998). It centered on a gang of young people who practice "spazzing"—going to public places and pretending to be physically or mentally handicapped, chiefly to test ordinary citizens' tolerance.

CONNECT TO THE BLOG
www.davidbordwell.net/blog

We consider Godard's highly original use of stereoscopic technology in "Adieu au language: 2 + 2 × 3D" and "Say hello to *Goodbye to Language*."

the industry through enforced quotas, banks had invested heavily, and there was a flourishing business of international coproductions. But in 1957, cinema attendance fell off drastically, chiefly because television became more widespread. By 1959, the industry was in a crisis. One solution was to encourage the independent financing of low-budget projects. New Wave directors shot films much more quickly and cheaply than did reigning directors. Moreover, the young directors helped one another out and reduced financial risk. By 1964, each New Wave director had his or her own production company, and the group had become absorbed into the film industry. By that time as well, the characteristic New Wave form and style had already become diffused and imitated (by, for instance, Tony Richardson in his 1963 English film *Tom Jones*). Most historians would argue that the movement, as a group initiative, had come to an end. Certainly, after 1968, the political upheavals in France drastically altered the personal relations among the directors.

New Wave figures remained powerful filmmakers for decades. Chabrol, Truffaut, and Rohmer became firmly entrenched in the French film industry, whereas Godard set up a facility in Switzerland, and Rivette began to create narratives of staggering complexity and length (such as *Out One,* originally about 12 hours long). Their films, though seldom popular, continued to be supported by government subsidies, international agencies, and private financing. They had, in a sense, become the sort of Old Guard that they had rebelled against. Yet many continued to produce provocative and influential films. Godard was one of the first filmmakers to embrace video as a medium, and in 2010 he released an HD feature, *Film Socialisme,* that remains as defiantly nonconformist as all his work. The same rebellious attitude is evident in *Goodbye to Language* (2014), which experiments with 3D.

The New Wave not only created several original and valuable films but also demonstrated that a stodgy film industry could gain new energy from talented, aggressive young people inspired by the sheer love of cinema. It has become the prototype of the fully self-conscious movement—aware of its place in film history, able to work with low budgets, and shrewd in its realization that media culture is always looking for the next big thing. The Danish Dogme 95 group attacked the French New Wave (it "proved to be a ripple that washed ashore and turned to muck"), but they followed the earlier generation in demanding a break with conformity **(12.62).** And the New Wave was not mere bluff. Like the Neorealists they admired, these young filmmakers showed that making unusual creative decisions could reveal new possibilities in the art of cinema.

The New Hollywood and Independent Filmmaking, 1970s–1980s

Hollywood filmmakers sustained their tradition during the 1930s and 1940s by assimilating the technological demands of sound and color. In the 1950s and 1960s, they faced greater difficulties. There were new technologies, such as widescreen and stereophonic sound, to master, but the real problems lay elsewhere. By government decree, the vertically integrated studios had been broken up in the late 1940s. Distributors could no longer own theaters or demand that exhibitors take weak films. This breakup coincided with a sharp drop in attendance as Americans turned to television and other leisure activities. Filmmakers responded by targeting certain market segments, like young people, and exploring previously forbidden content, like sex and drug use.

The Sound of Music (1965), Dr. Zhivago (1965), and a few other big films yielded huge profits, but these could not shore up the declining industry. Television networks, which had paid high prices to broadcast films after theatrical release, stopped bidding for pictures. American movie attendance flattened out at around 1 billion tickets per year. By 1969, Hollywood companies were losing over $200 million annually.

Blockbusters and Indie Pictures

The industry was saved by what has been called the blockbuster mentality. Along with the predictable favorites, like Disney animation, the top-ranking films of the period included some surprises: The Godfather (1972), The Exorcist (1973), American Graffiti (1973), Jaws (1975), Star Wars (1977), Close Encounters of the Third Kind (1977), and Superman (1978). Unlike most hits, these lacked established stars. They weren't based on Broadway musicals. They were in recognizable, even slightly down-market genres such as horror and science fiction, but they were enhanced by high production values and state-of-the-art special effects. Aimed at young audiences, they became "must-see" events, and many viewers returned again and again to their favorites. The 1970s blockbusters weren't usually designed to be colossal successes, but their box-office triumph convinced producers that a blockbuster could be engineered. In the process, Hollywood could be reinvented.

The studio-designed blockbusters came to be known as "tentpole" pictures because their profits sheltered other, smaller films. Studios spread their investment to star-driven romantic comedies, dramas, and adventure films. They continued to support, often by simply acquiring distribution rights, cheaper genre pictures likely to turn a profit. The studios also encouraged riskier fare that might win critical attention and awards. These might be prestige pictures like Sleuth (1972), or more controversial items like Taxi Driver (1976).

This division among blockbusters, program genre fare, Oscar bait, edgy experiments, and niche independents would roughly hold good from the 1970s through the 2010s. Tastes and trends would vary; The Matrix (1999) and Men in Black 3 (2012) tell more complex stories than The Empire Strikes Back (1980), but all show that science fiction, garlanded with top-flight special effects, was a steady source of blockbusters. Filmmakers might hop from one category to another. Spike Lee went from being a niche independent (She's Gotta Have It, 1986) to directing a prestige picture (Malcolm X, 1992), and then to more mainstream genre pictures (Clockers, 1995; Inside Man, 2006). Few would have predicted on the basis of Mean Streets (1973) and Raging Bull (1980) that Martin Scorsese would someday direct a children's 3D film budgeted at $150 million (Hugo, 2011). Regardless of such mixing and matching, the strategy of designing projects at different budget levels and for different tastes sustained the Hollywood tradition in the modern era.

The Rise of the Movie Brats

Nearly all the directors of Hollywood's golden age were dead or retired by 1975, so many major trends of that era sprang from young talent. A crucial feature set them apart from earlier American directors. Instead of coming up through the ranks of the studio system, most had gone to film schools. At New York University, the University of Southern California, and the University of California at Los Angeles, they had not only mastered the mechanics of production but also learned about film aesthetics and history. Like the French New Wave directors, the newcomers often had an encyclopedic knowledge of great movies and directors. As a result, they came to be known as the "movie brats." Whatever level of production they worked

> " I love the idea of not being an independent filmmaker. I've liked working within the system. And I've admired a lot of the older directors who were sort of 'directors for hire.' Like Victor Fleming was in a contract all those years to Metro and Selznick and Mayer . . . he made Captains Courageous. And you know, his most famous films: Wizard of Oz and Gone with the Wind."
> —Steven Spielberg, producer/director

> " To a whole generation, these [Hollywood classics] were more than just commodities. It was a part of who we are."
> —Martin Scorsese, director

12.63 Staging for multiple points of interest. In *Jaws*, Steven Spielberg displayed a flair for depth staging that has been a hallmark of his work ever since.

in, they were quite aware of the traditions that they inherited, and they set out to both extend the traditions and try something new.

So, for instance, when Steven Spielberg and George Lucas revived the science fiction genre, they did so in full awareness of film history. With *Close Encounters* and *E. T.: The Extraterrestrial* (1982), Spielberg defied the tradition of predatory alien invaders by presenting his creatures as lovable. With *Star Wars* and its sequels, George Lucas consciously revived the disreputable "rocket opera" of Flash Gordon serials and Saturday-matinee kiddie shows. Collaborating on *Raiders of the Lost Ark* (1981), Spielberg and Lucas updated the B-movie serial, giving preposterous plots the dazzle of modern action choreography. Spielberg also tried his hand at Oscar bait, with *The Color Purple* (1985), *Schindler's List* (1993), and other prestige projects. His Amblin company produced lively genre pictures such as *Poltergeist* (1982) and *Gremlins* (1984).

For the studio-oriented movie brats, it wasn't all nostalgia. To turn B-movie material into blockbusters and A-pictures, they called on sophisticated technique. Lucas developed motion-control techniques for filming miniatures for *Star Wars*, and his firm Industrial Light and Magic (ILM) became the leader in new special-effects technology. From *Jaws* onward, Spielberg used deep-focus tactics reminiscent of *Citizen Kane* (5.48, **12.63**). Spielberg and Lucas also led the move toward digital sound and high-quality theater reproduction technology. They wanted the modern equivalent of the showmanship that had characterized such 1950s innovations as Cinerama and 3D.

Other filmmakers sought to revive the old Hollywood at a lower budget level. Brian De Palma's admiration for Hitchcock led him to a series of horror films (*Carrie*, 1976) and thrillers (*Obsession*, 1976). *Dressed to Kill* (1980) reworked *Psycho*, while *Body Double* (1984) did the same for *Rear Window*. Peter Bogdanovich's *What's Up, Doc?* (1972) was an updating of screwball comedy, with particular reference to Howard Hawks's *Bringing Up Baby*. John Carpenter's *Assault on Precinct 13* (1976) derived partly from Hawks's *Rio Bravo;* the editing is credited to "John T. Chance," the character played by John Wayne in Hawks's Western.

Other Paths

For many critics, what made the 1970s an era of rejuvenation was the presence of *anti*-blockbusters, intimate dramas of ordinary people leading mundane lives. In *Five Easy Pieces* (1970), *The Last Picture Show* (1972), *The Last Detail* (1973), *Alice Doesn't Live Here Anymore* (1974), and other films, everyday crises and psychological tensions came to the fore. They gave American cinema a dose of social realism that had been missing from both old Hollywood and the "New Hollywood" of Spielberg, Lucas, and other movie brats. Some of these films traced their impulse to the work of John Cassavetes, who presented immediate and visceral confrontations in *Faces* (1968), *Husbands* (1970), and *A Woman under the Influence* (1974).

These small-scale dramas, backed by studios or independent companies, showed that American cinema could adapt the slice-of-life approach to narrative construction seen in Italian Neorealism. But the rationale wasn't wholly formal. Part of these films' appeal came from a sexual frankness that was made possible by the establishing of the film ratings system in 1968. Curses and obscenities, nudity, adulterous affairs, and simulated sex came into the mainstream, and these were motivated as elements of a cinema that dared to shatter classic Hollywood conventions of romance.

Narrative experiments were even more marked in other films of the 1970s. Some directors dreamed of making complex art films in the European mold. The best-known effort is probably Coppola's *The Conversation* (1974), a mystery-story reworking of Antonioni's *Blow-Up* (1966) that plays ambiguously between reality and hallucination (p. 301). Ventures into subjectivity, less clear-cut than the flashbacks and fantasies of the 1940s, were also seen in Robert Altman's *Images* (1972), Bob Fosse's *All That Jazz* (1979), and the opening of Coppola's *Apocalypse Now* (1979; 12.36). Echoing the New Wave were films in which the directors' love of cinema emerged as self-conscious reminders that the audience was watching a film. Dennis Hopper's *The Last Movie* (1971) interrupted its flow with a title, "SCENE MISSING." In Altman's *The Long Goodbye* (1973), Los Angeles detective Philip Marlowe seems aware that he's playing a hard-boiled detective but is not quite up to the part; the last shot shows him tap-dancing down a road to the tune of "Hooray for Hollywood."

Altman gave currency to another storytelling strategy, one we might call the "network narrative." "All-star" movies such as *Grand Hotel* (1932) had occasionally been made in the studio era, but *Nashville* (1975) and *A Wedding* (1978) took the principle of multiple protagonists and interwoven storylines to a new level. In these films, many characters converge in a single locale, such as a city or a social occasion, and then cross each others' paths, each one with individual concerns and no one emerging as a clear-cut hero or heroine. For Altman, the emphasis fell on chance encounters and incidents that might reveal character, rather than on a forward-moving, goal-driven plot.

Stylistically, the films in all these registers didn't challenge the core of the classic continuity system. Most filmmakers were content to employ it but inflect it in certain directions. It's in this period that we start to find that variant of the traditional 180° system we called intensified continuity in Chapter 6 (p. 246). Many filmmakers exploited the new resources of Dolby sound, which allowed for much greater dynamic range and permitted fine-grain detailing of the sound track. Altman pioneered a multiple-microphone recording technique that let him record, during a crowded scene, different conversations on different tracks and merge them into a dense mix that could stress or muffle certain lines.

The 1980s and After

With the colossal failure of *Heaven's Gate* (1980), studios lost faith in the auteur-driven blockbuster and turned control of such projects over to more tractable hands. More personal cinema survived, however, in the emerging realm of independent filmmaking. As usual, technology and money had a good deal to do with it.

During the 1980s, both cable television and home video, in the form of the videocassette tape, grew more popular. Small-budget filmmakers learned that they could finance a film by preselling the rights to video companies. In addition,

12.64

12.65

12.64–12.65 **1980s independents.** Wide-angle tracking shots follow crawling babies along the floor and under furniture in *Raising Arizona* (12.64) and Eva and Willie, the listless protagonists of *Stranger Than Paradise* (12.65): "These characters," Jarmusch explains, "move through the world of the film in a kind of random, aimless way, like looking for the next card game or something."

European television channels were eager for American films that were more afford-able than Hollywood blockbusters. Films could find funding through the so-called mini-majors, firms that had access to private capital and had solid distribution prospects. For these and other reasons, the 1980s saw a wave of independently made films that achieved fairly wide distribution.

This was the period that launched novelist John Sayles on a directing career that led to his exploration of U.S. social and political history (*The Return of the Secaucus Seven*, 1980; *Matewan*, 1987). Joel and Ethan Coen established their comic-grotesque vision of America and its film genres with *Blood Simple* (1984) and *Raising Arizona* (1987; **12.64**). Susan Seidelman's *Desperately Seeking Susan* (1985) featured popstar Madonna in a romantic comedy of mistaken identities. For many observers, this trend crystallized when Steven Soderbergh's *sex, lies, and videotape* (1989) won the top prize at the Sundance Film Festival, already emerg-ing as a showcase for off-Hollywood work. By the late 1980s there were 200–250 independent releases per year.

Several directors from independent film managed to shift into the mainstream, making medium-budget pictures with widely known stars. David Lynch moved from the midnight movie *Eraserhead* (1978) to the cult classic *Blue Velvet* (1986), and Canadian David Cronenberg, a specialist in low-budget horror films such as *Shivers* (1975), won wider recognition with *The Dead Zone* (1983) and *The Fly* (1986). Oliver Stone won Academy Awards for *Platoon* (1986), which propelled him into the bigger-budget realm. *She's Gotta Have It* gave Spike Lee access to studio financing for *Do The Right Thing* (1989) and other films. Lee's success paved the way for other African-American directors during the 1990s, a period that saw several minority and women directors starting careers in Hollywood or the independent realm.

Formally and stylistically, many 1980s films extended tendencies of the 1970s. David Lynch created disturbing, phantasmagoric narration in *Blue Velvet*. His exploration of subjectivity and primal, unconscious energies would become a hallmark of his career up through *Mulholland Dr.* (2001). *Stranger Than Paradise* presented a plot full of hesitations and down time, filmed in a rigorous fashion: one shot per scene, nearly always with the camera anchored to one spot **(12.65)**. Jarmusch's later *Mystery Train* (1989) experimented with multiple stories playing out simultaneously in different areas of Memphis, all linked by the moment of a gunshot.

Hollywood and Independents, To Be Continued

Much has happened since the 1980s, with studios sometimes courting independents and sometimes discouraging them, and animated features coming to play a bigger role at the box office. But many of the trends established in the 1970s persist. The major studios finance tentpole films, support star-driven comedies such as *The Heat* (2013), acquire genre projects as program filler, and occasionally turn a prestige picture such as *Lincoln* (2012) into a popular hit. Independent companies, or some "dependent" boutique branches of the studios, aim at ambitious genre pictures such as *Drive* (2011) and *Trance* (2013), along with Oscar bait. Other independent creators, such as Charlie Kaufman (*Synecdoche, New York*, 2008) and Miranda July (*You and Me and Everyone We Know*, 2005), survive on critics' accolades and foreign distribution.

As usual, every opportunity demands decisions. James Cameron, with *Titanic* (1997) and *Avatar* (2009), personifies the director who sees his future bound up with blockbusters. The movie brats' fondness for retooling genre pictures reappears in a younger generation's *Cloverfield* (2008) and *Source Code* (2011). *Old Joy* (2006), *Rachel Getting Married* (2008), *Frozen River* (2008), *The Kids Are All Right* (2010), and many other films continue the 1970s impulse toward friends-and-family dramas with social implications **(12.66).** At the microbudget level is the trend called Mumblecore, low-tech exercises in psychological observation, with loose plotting and performances that give off an air of improvisation.

As in the CinemaScope era, well-established directors championed new technology for exhibition. Tim Burton's *Batman Returns* (1992) became the first film mixed for Dolby Digital 5.1. Steven Spielberg's *Jurassic Park* marked the debut of DTS, which encoded audio information on compact discs synched with the projected images. By 2003, more than 65,000 screens across the globe had installed some type of digital sound. During the 2010s, director Peter Jackson's *Hobbit* trilogy showcased High Frame Rate (HFR) projection and Dolby Atmos.

At all these levels of production, we continue to see the reworking of narrative strategies in mainstream romances, science fiction tales, and crime thrillers (p. 332). M. Night Shyamalan followed Hitchcock in turning narrative subterfuge into a personal signature with films like *The Sixth Sense* (1999). Christopher Nolan experimented with juggled chronology and embedded narratives in his lower budget *Memento* (2001) and *The Prestige* (2006). When he shifted to making blockbusters—for example, in *Inception* (2010) and *Interstellar* (2014)—he continued to play with story time and probe alternate realities. The 1990s and 2000s also saw a burst of networked narratives such as *200 Cigarettes* (1999), *Thirteen Conversations about One Thing* (2001), and *Love Actually* (2003), with *Babel* (2006) taking the format to a global scale. Filmmakers continued to explore subjective storytelling as well. *Take Shelter* (2011) and *Beasts of the Southern Wild* (2012; **12.67**) showed that ambiguous plunges into memories, dreams, and hallucinations still offered powerful resources to enterprising directors.

Yet the urge to experiment was curtailed by a shrinking market. With tentpoles claiming the bulk of ticket sales, most studios shut down their specialty divisions during the 2000s and 2010s. An independent film's best chance for distribution was to be sold as "Oscar bait." Ava DuVernay's *Selma,* the biopic of civil rights leader Martin Luther King, had all the earmarks of a typical "Indiewood" project: a $20 million budget, a cast lacking big stars, and a relatively unknown director. Hoping for awards that would enhance box-office sales, Paramount opted to release *Selma* under its flagship label rather than its specialty division, Paramount Vantage.

In a climate that discouraged innovation in theatrical releases, it's not surprising that the 2000s saw network and cable television experimenting with narrative to a new extent. *The Wire, Six Feet Under, Damages, The Affair,* and other ambitious

CONNECT TO THE BLOG
www.davidbordwell.net/blog

Some independent filmmakers use sensationalism to call attention to their work. See "Visionary Outlaw Mavericks on the dark edge; or, Indie Guignol."

12.66

12.67

12.66–12.67 Narrative explorations. The first shot of Ramin Bahrani's *Goodbye Solo* (2008) avoids traditional exposition and plunges us into a scene that is already at a turning point: Solo is laughing at what his grizzled passenger has just asked him to do (12.66). *Beasts of the Southern Wild* (2012) depicts southern bayou life with a mixture of social realism and mythological fantasy (12.67).

CONNECT TO THE BLOG
www.davidbordwell.net/blog

The 50-year career of one direc-tor offers us a chance to survey changes in Hollywood and the independent scene in our entry, "Endurance: Survival lessons from Lumet."

series attracted admirers of independent cinema. Independent distributors began producing television shows, and directors often wound up working on high-profile cable series and streaming formats. Lena Dunham and Jill Soloway's modestly successful feature debuts gave them opportunities to create immensely popular television shows (*Girls*, *Transparent*). With most low-budget films finding their core audience watching at home on DVD and VOD, cable and Internet platforms ate away at the theatrical market. The changes generated more constraints, more opportunities, and more hard decisions for directors who wanted to tell stories outside the mainstream.

Hong Kong Cinema, 1980s–1990s

While independent directors were revamping American films in the 1980s, a young generation of directors in Hong Kong found footing in their industry and recast its traditional genres and creative methods. The result was a vigorous local tradition. Hong Kong's innovations in cinematic style and storytelling strongly influenced world filmmaking well into the 21st century.

A Local Tradition Goes Global

Although Hong Kong produced films in the silent era and during the 1930s, World War II halted production. When the industry revived in the 1950s, Shaw Brothers became the most powerful studio. Shaws owned theaters throughout East Asia and used Hong Kong as a production base for films in several languages, chiefly Mandarin Chinese. Shaws made films in many genres, but among its biggest successes were dynamic, gory swordfighting films (*wuxia pian,* or "tales of martial chivalry"). In the 1970s, another studio, Golden Harvest, triumphed with kung-fu films starring Bruce Lee. Although Lee completed only four martial-arts films before his death in 1973, he became the most famous Chinese actor of all time. Lee's graceful, almost feral presence brought Hong Kong cinema to worldwide attention and forever identified it with films of acrobatic and violent action.

Several major directors worked in this period. Most famous is King Hu, who started as a Shaws director. In films such as *Dragon Gate Inn* (1967) and *The Valiant Ones* (1975; 5.76), Hu reinvigorated the *wuxia pian* through graceful airborne swordplay and inventive cutting. Chang Cheh, another Shaws director, turned the swordplay film toward violent male melodrama (such as *The One-Armed Swordsman,* 1967) before specializing in flamboyant kung-fu films such as

Crippled Avengers (also called *Mortal Combat,* 1978). Neither King Hu nor Chang Cheh was a practitioner of martial arts, but Lau Kar-leung was a fight choreographer before becoming a full-fledged director. Lau created a string of inventive films (such as *36th Chamber of Shaolin,* 1978, and *The Eight-Diagram Pole Fighter,* 1983) that showcased a range of dazzling martial-arts techniques.

The New Generation: Two Schools

By the early 1980s, traditional kung-fu was fading in popularity, and Shaws turned from moviemaking to its lucrative television business. At the same time, a new generation of directors came forward. One group had little formal education but had grown up in the film industry, working as stuntmen and martial artists. Among those who became directors were choreographers Yuen Wo-ping and Yuen Kuei (*Yes, Madam!,* 1985). Sammo Hung choreographed, directed, and starred in many lively action films (such as *Eastern Condors,* 1987).

The most famous graduate of the studio system was Jackie Chan, who labored as a copy of Bruce Lee before finding his feet in comic kung-fu. With *Drunken Master* (1978, directed by Yuen Wo-ping), he became a star throughout Asia and gained the power to direct his own films. In the early 1980s, Chan and his colleagues realized that kung-fu could be incorporated into action movies in the Hollywood mold. Chan made the historical adventure *Project A* (1983, also starring Hung) and the contemporary cop drama *Police Story* (1985). These and others were huge hits across Asia, partly because of Chan's lovably goofy star persona and partly because of his resourceful and dangerous stunt scenes (6.49–6.51).

A second group of directors had more formal training, with many attending film schools in the United States or Britain. When Ann Hui, Allen Fong, and others returned to Hong Kong, they found work in television before moving on to feature filmmaking. For a time, they constituted a local art cinema, attracting attention at festivals with such films as Hui's *Boat People* (1982). But most of this group gravitated toward independent companies turning out comedies, dramas, and action films. Tsui Hark was the leader of this trend. As both director and producer, Tsui revived and reworked a range of genres: swordplay fantasy (*Zu: Warriors of the Magic Mountain,* 1979), romantic comedy (*Shanghai Blues,* 1984), historical adventure (*Peking Opera Blues,* 1986; **12.68**), supernatural romance (*A Chinese Ghost Story,* 1987, directed by Ching Siu-tung), and classic kung-fu (*Once upon a Time in China,* 1990).

Seeing the success that urban crime films were enjoying, Tsui partnered with John Woo on *A Better Tomorrow* (1986), a remake of a 1960s movie (**12.69**). Woo was something of an in-between figure, having been a successful studio comedy director during the 1970s. With Tsui as producer, *A Better Tomorrow* became Woo's comeback effort, one of the most successful Hong Kong films of the 1980s and a star-making vehicle for the charismatic Chow Yun-fat. Tsui, Woo, and Chow teamed again for a sequel and for the film that made Woo famous in the West, *The Killer* (1989), a lush and baroque story of the unexpected alliance between a hitman and a detective (**12.70**).

Story and Style

Hong Kong cinema of the 1980s and early 1990s simmered with almost reckless energy. The rushed production schedules didn't allow much time to prepare scripts, so the plots, borrowing freely from Chinese legend and Hollywood genres, tended to be less tightly unified than those in U.S. films. They avoided tight linkage of cause and effect in favor of a more casual, episodic construction—not, as in Italian Neorealism, to suggest the randomness of everyday life but

CONNECT TO THE BLOG
www.davidbordwell.net/blog

Two major directors are analyzed in "Sometimes a jump cut," on King Hu's editing, and "Lion, dancing: Lau Kar-leung."

CONNECT TO THE BLOG
www.davidbordwell.net/blog

We examine Hong Kong filmmaking style, and especially the work of Jackie Chan, in "Bond vs. Chan: Jackie shows how it's done."

12.68 Rhythmic staging. Abrupt movements into and out of the frame are characteristic of Hong Kong film style. In this shot from *Peking Opera Blues,* the sheriff and his captive rise into the foreground as the three heroines watch from the rear.

12.69

12.70

12.69–12.70 John Woo, influential stylist. A striking long shot as a hero walks to meet his fate in *A Better Tomorrow* suggests Woo's debt to the Western (12.69). The urban crime thriller often parallels cop and crook—a convention that *The Killer* boldly fulfills in presenting detective and hitman as mirror images (12.70).

rather to permit chases and fights to be inserted easily. Whereas action sequences were meticulously choreographed, connecting scenes were often improvised and shot quickly. Similarly, the kung-fu films had often bounced between pathos and silly comedy, and this tendency to mix tones continued through the 1980s. Because of rushed shooting, the plots often end abruptly, with a big action set-piece but little in the nature of a mood-setting epilogue. One of Tsui's innovations was to provide more satisfying conclusions, as in the lilting railroad station finale of *Shanghai Blues.*

At the level of visual style, Hong Kong directors brought the action film to a new pitch of excitement. Gunmen (and gunwomen) leaped and fired in slow motion, hovering in midair like 1970s swordfighters and kung-fu warriors. Directors also developed florid color designs, with rich reds, blues, and yellows glowing out of smoky nightclubs or narrow alleyways. Well into the 2000s, unrealistically tinted mood lighting was a trademark of Hong Kong cinema **(12.71).** Above all, everything was sacrificed to constant motion; even in dialogue scenes, the camera and the characters seldom stood still.

Aiming to energize the viewer, the new action directors built on the innovations of King Hu and his contemporaries. They developed a staccato cutting technique based on the tempo of martial-arts routines and Peking Opera displays, alternating rapid movement with sudden pauses. If shot composition was kept simple, an action

12.71 Hong Kong stylization. Blocks of colored light enhance a gun battle in *The Longest Nite* (1998).

12.72

12.73

12.74

12.72–12.74 Rhythmic editing and movement. During a fight scene in *Yes, Madam!* Michele Yeoh swings swiftly around, in a shot only 7 frames long (12.72). In two more shots, 12.73 and 12.74, she knocks the villain spinning (15 frames), and drops smoothly into a relaxed posture on the rail (17 frames). Her stillness at the end of the shot provides a pause before she launches another assault.

could be cut to flow across shots very rapidly, while one shot could accentuate a moment of stillness **(12.72–12.74).** Most Hong Kong directors were unaware of the Soviet Montage movement, but in their efforts to arouse viewers through expressive movement and editing, they were reviving ideas of concern to those 1920s filmmakers.

Legacy Overseas

The 1990s brought the golden age of Hong Kong action cinema to a close. Jackie Chan, John Woo, Chow Yun-fat, Sammo Hung, and action star Jet Li began working in Hollywood, with Yuen Wo-ping designing the action choreography for *The Matrix* (1999) and *Crouching Tiger, Hidden Dragon* (2000). A recession after Hong Kong's 1997 handover to China depressed the local film industry. As Hollywood began imitating Hong Kong movies, local audiences developed a taste for U.S. films. At the same time, the art-cinema wing became more ambitious, and festivals rewarded the offbeat works of Wong Kar-wai (see the analysis of *Chungking Express,* pp. 428–432). The action tradition was maintained by only a few directors such as Johnnie To, whose laconic film noir *The Mission* (1999) brought a leanness and pictorial abstraction to the gangster genre.

The legions of American fans of Hong Kong films included Quentin Tarantino, who paid homage to the Asian action cinema in *Kill Bill, Volumes 1 and 2* (2003–2004). He mixed together elements of Japanese swordplay, anime, and low-budget European thrillers, but his allegiance to Hong Kong's tradition shone through **(12.75).** Just as other countries' cinemas borrow from Hollywood, Hollywood selectively absorbed Hong Kong's innovations in staging and cutting action.

Tarantino was a film fan from childhood. He watched old movies on TV, recent releases in theaters, and anything that caught his fancy on VHS. Like every

 CONNECT TO THE BLOG
www.davidbordwell.net/blog

A week-long series of blog entries devoted to Hong Kong film starts with "PLANET HONG KONG now in cyberspace." "PLANET HONG KONG: The dragon dances" is devoted to analyzing Hong Kong action scenes. "*The Grandmaster*: Moving forward, turning back" discusses a major film Wong Kar-wai made after *Chungking Express,* and "Mixing business with pleasure: Johnnie To's *Drug War*" examines a crime thriller set in mainland China.

12.75 *Kill Bill* and Hong Kong cinema. Although the weaponry in this fight consists mostly of samurai swords, director Tarantino pays tribute to the Hong Kong tradition: Yuen Woo-ping serves as martial-arts choreographer and the heroine wears Bruce Lee's signature yellow track suit.

filmmaker, he started as a film viewer; like many filmmakers, he was keen to explore the entire range of film history. Asked what he does in his spare time, he replied, "What you'd expect—read, listen to music, hang out with friends, watch my video and DVD collection. Get obsessions about this or that. I'm a film historian so I'm always trying to feed my brain."

Just as anyone who thinks, talks, and writes analytically about movies is doing film criticism, Tarantino is right to suggest that seeking out older films and letting them feed your brain is a step toward doing film history. The films he sees nourish his passion to create films himself. Even if you don't follow that career path, thinking like a filmmaker includes opening yourself up to the vast variety of films made in different times and places. By considering what artistic choices were available, by recognizing the creative decisions made by filmmakers who have come before us, we become more sensitive to every movie we see. To fully appreciate the films we watch now, we need to be aware that their makers are struggling with the same problems and decisions that appear at every moment of film history. Technology, tastes, and received traditions offer both opportunities and constraints—sometimes opportunities *within* constraints.

By looking at films from a historical angle, we realize that filmmakers have always been as fascinated by the power of movies as we are today. As Wölfflin says, not everything may be possible at all times. Still, some filmmakers always try to push the boundaries of what *is* possible, and others show us new possibilities in what seems familiar. Their hard work and imaginative energies have given us richer experiences of the art of cinema.

GLOSSARY

abstract form   A type of filmic organization in which the parts relate to one another through repetition and variation of such visual qualities as shape, color, rhythm, and direction of movement.

Academy ratio   The standardized shape of the film frame established by the Academy of Motion Picture Arts and Sciences. In the original ratio, the frame was $1^1/_3$ times as wide as it was high (1.33:1); later the width was normalized at 1.85 times the height (1.85:1).

aerial perspective   A cue for suggesting depth in the image by presenting objects in the distance less distinctly than those in the foreground.

anamorphic lens   A lens for making widescreen films using regular *Academy ratio* frame size. The camera lens takes in a wide field of view and squeezes it onto the frame, and a similar projector lens unsqueezes the image onto a wide theater screen.

angle of framing   The position of the frame in relation to the subject it shows: above it, looking down (a high angle); horizontal, on the same level (a straight-on angle); below it, looking up (a low angle). Also called *camera angle*.

animation   Any process whereby artificial movement is created by photographing a series of drawings (see also *cel animation*), objects, or computer images one by one. Small changes in position, recorded frame by frame, create the illusion of movement.

aspect ratio   The relationship of the frame's width to its height. The standard *Academy ratio* is currently 1.85:1.

associational form   A type of organization in which the film's parts are juxtaposed to suggest similarities, contrasts, concepts, emotions, and expressive qualities.

asynchronous sound   Sound that is not matched temporally with the movements occurring in the image, as when dialogue is out of synchronization with lip movements.

auteur   The presumed or actual author of a film, usually identified as the director; also sometimes used in an evaluative sense to distinguish good filmmakers (*auteurs*) from bad ones.

axis of action   In the *continuity editing* system, the imaginary line that passes through the main actors or the principal movement. The axis of action defines the spatial relations of all the elements of the scene as being to the right or left. The camera is not supposed to cross the axis at a cut and thus reverse those spatial relations. The axis of action is also called the 180° line. See also *180° system, screen direction*.

backlighting   Illumination cast onto the figures in the scene from the side opposite the camera, usually creating a thin outline of highlighting on those figures.

Blu-ray disc (or **BD**)   A high-definition digital medium for home video, similar to a DVD but having a higher storage capacity and producing a higher-resolution image.

boom   A pole on which a microphone can be suspended above the scene being filmed and that is used to change the microphone's position as the action shifts.

camera angle   See *angle of framing*.

canted framing   A view in which the frame is not level; either the right or the left side is lower than the other, causing objects in the scene to appear slanted out of an upright position.

categorical form   A type of filmic organization in which the parts treat distinct subsets of a topic. For example, a film about the United States might be organized into 50 parts, each devoted to a state.

cel animation   Animation that uses a series of drawings on pieces of celluloid, called *cels* for short. Slight changes between the drawings combine to create an illusion of movement.

CGI   Computer-generated imagery: using digital software systems to create figures, settings, or other material in the frame.

cheat cut   In the *continuity editing* system, a cut that presents continuous time from shot to shot but that mismatches the positions of figures or objects.

cinematography   A general term for all the manipulations of the film strip by the camera in the shooting phase and by the laboratory in the developing phase.

close-up   A framing in which the scale of the object shown is relatively large; most commonly, a person's head seen from the neck up, or an object of a comparable size that fills most of the screen.

closure   The degree to which the ending of a narrative film reveals the effects of all the causal events and resolves (or "closes off") all lines of action.

constructive editing   Editing that suggests a scene's space by providing only portions of it, without an establishing shot.

continuity editing   A system of cutting to maintain continuous and clear narrative action. Continuity editing relies on matching screen direction, position, and temporal relations from shot to shot. For specific techniques of continuity editing, see *axis of action, crosscutting, cut-in, establishing shot, eyeline match, match on action, reestablishing shot, screen direction, shot/reverse shot*.

contrast   In cinematography, the difference between the brightest and the darkest areas within the frame.

crane shot   A shot with a change in framing accomplished by placing the camera above the subject and moving through the air in any direction.

crosscutting   Editing that alternates shots of two or more lines of action occurring in different places, usually simultaneously.

cut   (1) In filmmaking, the joining of two strips of film together with a splice. (2) In the finished film, an instantaneous change from one framing to another. See also *jump cut*.

cut-in   An instantaneous shift from a distant framing to a closer view of some portion of the same space.

cutscenes   Parts of a videogame over which the player has no control. They appear at the start of a game to help prepare the player for the next turn and as transitional material that links one level of the game to the next. Cutscenes are also known as "in-game cinematics" or "in-game movies," terms that hint at their underlying similarities with film.

deep focus   A use of the camera lens and lighting that keeps objects in both close and distant planes in sharp focus.

deep space   An arrangement of mise-en-scene elements so that there is a considerable distance between the plane closest to the camera and the one farthest away. Any or all of these planes may be in focus. See also *shallow space.*

depth of field   The measurements of the closest and farthest planes in front of the camera lens between which everything will be in sharp focus. A depth of field from 5 to 16 feet, for example, would mean everything closer than 5 feet and farther than 16 feet would be out of focus.

dialogue overlap   In editing a scene, arranging the cut so that a bit of dialogue coming from shot A is heard under a shot that shows another character or another element in the scene.

diegesis   In a narrative film, the world of the film's story. The diegesis includes events that are presumed to have occurred and actions and spaces not shown onscreen. See also *diegetic sound, nondiegetic insert, nondiegetic sound.*

diegetic sound   Any voice, musical passage, or sound effect presented as originating from a source within the film's world. See also *nondiegetic sound.*

digital intermediate   A strip of film is developed and scanned, frame by frame, to create a digital copy of sequence or a whole movie. The digital copy is manipulated with software. When finished, it is scanned frame by frame onto a strip of negative film, which will be used to make prints to send to theaters.

digital resolution   The detailed clarity of a digital image, typically measured by the number or density of pixels. The common professional image resolutions are measured at horizontal resolutions of 1280, 2K, and 4K.

direct sound   Music, noise, and speech recorded from the event at the moment of filming; opposite of *postsynchronization.*

discontinuity editing   Any alternative system of joining shots together using techniques unacceptable within *continuity editing* principles. Possibilities include mismatching of temporal and spatial relations, violations of the *axis of action,* and concentration on graphic relationships. See also *elliptical editing, graphic match, intellectual montage, jump cut, nondiegetic insert, overlapping editing.*

dissolve   A transition between two shots during which the first image gradually disappears while the second image gradually appears; for a moment, the two images blend in *superimposition.*

distance of framing   The apparent distance of the frame from the mise-en-scene elements; also called camera distance and shot scale. See also *close-up, extreme close-up, extreme long shot, medium close-up, medium shot, plan américain.*

distribution   One of the three branches of the film industry; the process of marketing the film and supplying copies to exhibition venues. See also *exhibition, production.*

dolly   A camera support with wheels, used in making *tracking shots.*

dubbing   The process of replacing part or all of the voices on the sound track in order to correct mistakes or rerecord dialogue. See also *postsynchronization.*

duration   In a narrative film, the aspect of temporal manipulation that involves the time span presented in the *plot* and assumed to operate in the *story.* See also *frequency, order.*

DVD   Short for digital versatile disc or digital video disc, a home-video device containing moving-image content and played on a dedicated player or a game console or computer.

editing   (1) In filmmaking, the task of selecting and joining camera takes. (2) In the finished film, the set of techniques that governs the relations among shots.

ellipsis   In a narrative film, the shortening of *plot* duration achieved by omitting some *story* duration. See also *elliptical editing, viewing time.*

elliptical editing   Shot transitions that omit parts of an event, causing an *ellipsis* in plot duration.

equivalents   Storytelling techniques, devices, or formal elements that are shared across media.

establishing shot   A shot, usually involving a distant framing, that shows the spatial relations among the important figures, objects, and setting in a scene.

exhibition   One of the three branches of the film industry; the process of showing the finished film to audiences. See also *distribution, production.*

exposure   The adjustment of the camera mechanism in order to control how much light strikes each frame of film passing through the aperture.

external diegetic sound   Sound represented as coming from a physical source within the story space that we assume characters in the scene also hear. See also *internal diegetic sound.*

extreme close-up   A framing in which the scale of the object shown is very large; most commonly, a small object or a part of the body.

extreme long shot   A framing in which the scale of the object shown is very small; a building, landscape, or crowd of people will fill the screen.

eyeline match   A cut obeying the *axis of action* principle, in which the first shot shows a person looking off in one direction and the second shows a nearby space containing what he or she sees. If the person looks left, the following shot should imply that the looker is offscreen right.

fade   (1) *Fade-in:* a dark screen that gradually brightens as a shot appears. (2) *Fade-out:* a shot that gradually disappears as the screen darkens. Occasionally, fade-outs brighten to pure white or to a color.

fidelity   The degree to which a film adaptation remains faithful to either the narrative details or the spirit of its source material.

fill light   Illumination from a source less bright than the *key light,* used to soften deep shadows in a scene. See also *three-point lighting.*

film noir   "Dark film," a term applied by French critics to a type of American film, usually in the detective or thriller genres, with low-key lighting and a somber mood.

film stock   The strip of material on which a series of still photographs is registered; it consists of a clear base coated on one side with a light-sensitive emulsion.

filter   A piece of glass or gelatin placed in front of the camera or printer lens to alter the quality or quantity of light striking the film in the aperture.

flashback   An alteration of *story* order in which the *plot* moves back to show events that have taken place earlier than ones already shown.

flashforward   An alteration of story order in which the plot presentation moves forward to future events and then returns to the present.

focal length   The distance from the center of the lens to the point at which the light rays meet in sharp focus. The focal length determines the perspective relations of the space represented on the flat screen. See also *normal lens, telephoto lens, wide-angle lens.*

focus   The degree to which light rays coming from the same part of an object through different parts of the lens reconverge at the same point on the film frame, creating sharp outlines and distinct textures.

following shot   A shot with framing that shifts to keep a moving figure onscreen.

form   The overall system of relationships among the parts of a film.

frame   A single image on the strip of film. When a series of frames is projected onto a screen in quick succession, an illusion of movement is created.

frame rate   In shooting, the number of frames exposed per second; in projection, the number of frames thrown on the screen per second. If the two are the same, the speed of the action appears normal, whereas a disparity creates slow or fast motion. The standard rate in sound cinema is 24 frames per second (fps) for both shooting and projection, although some European films aiming at television broadcast are shot at 25 fps. In video, common frame rates are 23.98 fps, 24 fps, 25 fps, 30 fps, and 60 fps.

framing   The use of the edges of the film frame to select and to compose what will be visible onscreen.

frequency   In a narrative film, the aspect of temporal manipulation that involves the number of times any *story* event is shown in the *plot.* See also *duration, order.*

front projection   A composite process whereby footage meant to appear as the background of a shot is projected from the front onto a screen; figures in the foreground are filmed in front of the screen as well. This is the opposite of *rear projection.*

frontal lighting   Illumination directed into the scene from a position near the camera.

frontality   In staging, the positioning of figures so that they face the viewer.

function   The role or effect of any element within the film's form.

gauge   The width of the film strip, measured in millimeters.

genres   Types of films that audiences and filmmakers recognize by their familiar narrative conventions. Common genres are musical, gangster, and science fiction films.

graphic match   Two successive shots joined so as to create a strong similarity of compositional elements (e.g., color, shape).

handheld camera   The use of the camera operator's body as a camera support, either holding it by hand or using a harness.

hard lighting   Illumination that creates sharp-edged shadows.

height of framing   The distance of the camera above the ground, regardless of the *angle of framing.*

high-key lighting   Illumination that creates comparatively little contrast between the light and dark areas of the shot. Shadows are fairly transparent and brightened by *fill light.*

ideology   A relatively coherent system of values, beliefs, or ideas shared by some social group and often taken for granted as natural or inherently true.

intellectual montage   The juxtaposition of a series of images to create an abstract idea not present in any one image.

internal diegetic sound   Sound represented as coming from the mind of a character within the story space. Although we and the character can hear it, we assume that the other characters cannot. See also *external diegetic sound.*

interpretation   The viewer's activity of analyzing the implicit and symptomatic meanings suggested in a film. See also *meaning.*

iris   A round, moving *mask* that can close down to end a scene (iris-out) or emphasize a detail, or that can open to begin a scene (iris-in) or to reveal more space around a detail.

jump cut   An elliptical cut that appears to be an interruption of a single shot. Either the figures seem to change instantly against a constant background, or the background changes instantly while the figures remain constant. See also *ellipsis.*

key light   In the three-point lighting system, the brightest illumination coming into the scene. See also *backlighting, fill light, three-point lighting.*

lens   A shaped piece of transparent material (usually glass) with either or both sides curved to gather and focus light rays. Most camera and projector lenses place a series of lenses within a metal tube to form a compound lens.

linearity   In a narrative, the clear motivation of a series of causes and effects that progress without significant digressions, delays, or irrelevant actions.

long shot   A framing in which the scale of the object shown is small; a standing human figure would appear nearly the height of the screen.

long take   A shot that continues for an unusually lengthy time before the transition to the next shot.

low-key lighting   Illumination that creates strong contrast between light and dark areas of the shot, with deep shadows and little *fill light.*

mask   An opaque screen placed in the camera or printer that blocks part of the frame off and changes the shape of the photographed image, leaving part of the frame a solid color. As seen on the screen, most masks are black, although they can be white or colored.

masking   In exhibition, stretches of black fabric that frame the theater screen. Masking can be adjusted according to the *aspect ratio* of the film to be projected.

match on action   A continuity cut that splices two different views of the same action together at the same moment in the movement, making it seem to continue uninterrupted.

matte work   A type of *process shot* in which different areas of the image (usually actors and setting) are photographed separately and combined in laboratory work.

meaning   (1) Referential meaning: allusion to particular items of knowledge outside the film that the viewer is expected to recognize. (2) Explicit meaning: significance presented overtly, usually in language and often near the film's beginning or end. (3) Implicit meaning: significance left tacit, for the viewer to discover upon analysis or reflection. (4) Symptomatic meaning: significance that the film divulges, often against its will, by virtue of its historical or social context.

medium close-up   A framing in which the scale of the object shown is fairly large; a human figure seen from the chest up would fill most of the screen.

medium long shot   A framing at a distance that makes an object about 4 or 5 feet high appear to fill most of the screen vertically. See also *plan américain,* the special term for a medium long shot depicting human figures.

medium shot   A framing in which the scale of the object shown is of moderate size; a human figure seen from the waist up would fill most of the screen.

mise-en-scene   All of the elements placed in front of the camera to be photographed: the settings and props, lighting, costumes and makeup, and figure behavior.

mixing   Combining two or more sound tracks by recording them onto a single one.

mobile frame   The effect on the screen of the moving camera, a *zoom lens,* or certain *special effects*; the framing shifts in relation to the scene being photographed. See also *crane shot, pan, tilt, tracking shot.*

monochromatic color design   Color design that emphasizes a narrow set of shades of a single color.

montage   (1) A synonym for *editing.* (2) An approach to editing developed by the Soviet filmmakers of the 1920s; it emphasizes dynamic, often discontinuous, relationships between shots and the juxtaposition of images to create ideas not present in either shot by itself. See also *discontinuity editing, intellectual montage.*

montage sequence   A segment of a film that summarizes a topic or compresses a passage of time into brief symbolic or typical images. Frequently, *dissolves, fades, superimpositions,* and *wipes* are used to link the images in a montage sequence.

motif   An element in a film that is repeated in a significant way.

motion capture   In digital filmmaking, the recording of patterns of movement of a figure. Small reflective markers are placed at key points on a person, animal, or object. These are recorded by a special camera and provide a record of the motion but not the appearance of the subject. From that record, animation software can imbue other creatures with the same patterns of motion. When the markers are placed on an actor's face, the recording is often called *performance capture.*

motion control   A computerized method of planning and repeating camera movements on miniatures, models, and process work.

motivation   The justification given in the film for the presence of an element. This may be an appeal to the viewer's knowledge of the real world, to *genre* conventions, to narrative causality, or to a stylistic pattern within the film.

narration   The process through which the *plot* conveys or withholds *story* information. The narration can be more or less restricted to character knowledge and more or less deep in presenting characters' perceptions and thoughts.

narrative form   A type of filmic organization in which the parts relate to one another through a series of causally related events taking place in time and space.

nondiegetic insert   A shot or series of shots cut into a sequence, showing objects that are represented as being outside the world of the narrative.

nondiegetic sound   Sound, such as mood music or a narrator's commentary, represented as coming from a source outside the space of the narrative.

nonsimultaneous sound   Diegetic sound that comes from a source in time either earlier or later than the images it accompanies.

normal lens   A lens that shows objects without severely exaggerating or reducing the depth of the scene's planes. In 35mm filming, a normal lens has a *focal length* between 35 and 50mm. See also *telephoto lens, wide-angle lens.*

offscreen sound   Simultaneous sound from a source assumed to be in the space of the scene but outside what is visible onscreen.

offscreen space   The six areas blocked from being visible on the screen but still part of the space of the scene: to each side and above and below the frame, behind the set, and behind the camera. See also *space.*

180° system   The continuity approach to editing dictates that the camera should stay on one side of the action to ensure consistent left-right spatial relations between elements from shot to shot. The 180° line is the same as the *axis of action.* See also *continuity editing, screen direction.*

order   In a narrative film, the aspect of temporal manipulation that involves the sequence in which the chronological events of the *story* are arranged in the *plot.* See also *duration, frequency.*

overlap   A cue for suggesting represented depth in the film image by placing objects partly in front of more distant ones.

overlapping editing   Cuts that repeat part or all of an action, thus expanding its viewing time and plot duration.

pan   A camera movement with the camera body turning to the right or left. On the screen, it produces a mobile framing that scans the space horizontally.

performance capture   See *motion capture.*

pixels   Short for "picture elements." The small glowing dots that make up the image on a television monitor or computer screen; also visible in digital theatrical projection. Changes in color and brightness of the array of pixels create moving images on these devices.

pixillation   A form of single-frame animation in which three-dimensional objects, often people, are made to move in staccato bursts through the use of stop-action cinematography.

plan américain   A framing in which the scale of the object shown is moderately small; the human figure seen from the shins to the head would fill most of the screen. This is sometimes referred to as a *medium long shot,* especially when human figures are not shown.

plan-séquence   A French term for a scene handled in a single shot, usually a *long take.*

plot   In a narrative film, all the events that are directly presented to us, including their causal relations, chronological order, duration, frequency, and spatial locations; opposed to *story,* which is the viewer's imaginary construction of all the events in the narrative. See also *duration, ellipsis, flashback, flashforward, frequency, order, viewing time.*

point-of-view shot (POV shot)   A shot taken with the camera placed approximately where the character's eyes would be, showing what the character would see; usually cut in before or after a shot of the character looking.

postproduction   The phase of film production that assembles the images and sounds into the finished film.

postsynchronization   The process of adding sound to images after they have been shot and assembled. This can include *dubbing* of voices, as well as inserting diegetic music or sound effects. It is the opposite of *direct sound.*

preproduction   The phase of filmmaking that prepares for production on the basis of a screenplay, design, and financing.

previsualization   A computer-generated early version of a film or sequence, with simplified images. Filmmakers use it to plan such aspects as framing, lens length, settings, and staging. Often referred to as a *previz* or *previs,* this tool is most common on large-budget, special-effects-heavy projects.

process shot   Any shot involving rephotography to combine two or more images into one or to create a special effect; also called composite shot. See also *matte work, rear projection, special effects.*

production   One of the three branches of the film industry; the process of creating the film. See also *distribution, exhibition.*

racking focus   Shifting the area of sharp focus from one plane to another during a shot; the effect on the screen is called rack-focus.

ramping   Changing the speed of photographed motion within a single shot, as when the action in a fight scene suddenly goes from regular speed to slow motion and back. This effect can be achieved during shooting or postproduction.

rate   In shooting, the number of frames exposed per second; in projection, the number of frames thrown on the screen per second. If the two are the same, the speed of the action will appear normal, whereas a disparity will create slow or fast motion. The standard rate in sound cinema is 24 frames per second for both shooting and projection.

rear projection   A technique for combining a foreground action with a background action filmed earlier. The foreground is filmed in a studio, against a screen; the background imagery is projected from behind the screen. The opposite of *front projection.*

reestablishing shot   A return to a view of an entire space after a series of closer shots following the *establishing shot.*

reframing   Short panning or tilting movements to adjust for the figures' movements, keeping them onscreen or centered.

rhetorical form   A type of filmic organization in which the parts create and support an argument.

rhythm   The perceived rate and regularity of sounds, series of shots, and movements within the shots. Rhythmic factors include beat (or pulse), accent (or stress), and tempo (or pace).

rotoscope   A machine that projects live-action motion picture frames one by one onto a drawing pad so that an animator can trace the figures in each frame. The aim is to achieve more realistic movement in an animated film.

scene   A segment in a narrative film that takes place in one time and space or that uses crosscutting to show two or more simultaneous actions.

screen direction   The right-left relationships in a scene, set up in an establishing shot and determined by the position of characters and objects in the frame, by the directions of movement, and by the characters' eyelines. *Continuity editing* will attempt to keep screen direction consistent between shots. See also *axis of action, eyeline match, 180° system.*

segmentation   The process of dividing a film into parts for analysis.

sensor   A chip designed to capture visual information in digital form. It is located behind the lens in a digital motion-picture camera.

sequence   Term commonly used for a moderately large segment of film, involving one complete stretch of action; in a narrative film, often equivalent to a *scene.*

shallow focus   A restricted *depth of field,* which keeps only one plane in sharp focus; the opposite of *deep focus.*

shallow space   Staging the action in relatively few planes of depth; the opposite of *deep space.*

shot   (1) In shooting, one uninterrupted run of the camera to expose a series of frames; also called a *take.* (2) In the finished film, one uninterrupted image, whether or not there is mobile framing.

shot/reverse shot   Two or more shots edited together that alternate characters, typically in a conversation situation. In *continuity editing,* characters in one framing usually look left; in the other framing, right. Over-the-shoulder framings are common in shot/reverse-shot editing.

side lighting (sidelight)   Lighting coming from one side of a person or an object, usually to create a sense of volume, to bring out surface tensions, or to fill in areas left shadowed by light from another source.

simultaneous sound   Diegetic sound that is represented as occurring at the same time in the story as the image it accompanies.

size diminution   A cue for suggesting represented depth in the image by showing objects that are farther away as smaller than foreground objects.

soft lighting   Illumination that avoids harsh bright and dark areas, creating a gradual transition from highlights to shadows.

sound bridge   (1) At the beginning of one scene, the sound from the previous scene carries over briefly before the sound from the new scene begins. (2) At the end of one scene, the sound from the next scene is heard, leading into that scene.

sound over   Any sound that is not represented as coming from the space and time of the images on the screen. This includes both nondiegetic sounds and nonsimultaneous diegetic sound. See also *nondiegetic sound, nonsimultaneous sound.*

sound perspective   The sense of a sound's position in space, yielded by volume, timbre, pitch, and, in stereophonic reproduction systems, binaural information.

space   Any film displays a two-dimensional graphic space, the flat composition of the image. In films that depict recognizable objects, figures, and locales, a three-dimensional space is represented as well. At any moment, three-dimensional space may be directly depicted, as onscreen space or suggested, as *offscreen space.* In narrative film, we can also distinguish between story space—the locale of the totality of the action (whether shown or not)—and plot space—the locales visibly and audibly represented in the scenes.

special effects   A general term for various photographic manipulations that create fictitious spatial relations in the shot, such as *superimposition, matte work,* and *rear projection.*

story   In a narrative film, all the events that we see and hear, plus all those that we infer or assume to have occurred, arranged in their presumed causal relations, chronological order, duration, frequency, and spatial locations; opposed to *plot,* which is the film's actual presentation of events in the story. See also *duration, ellipsis, frequency, order, space, viewing time.*

storyboard   A tool used in planning film production, consisting of comic-strip-like drawings of individual shots or phases of shots with descriptions written below each drawing.

style   The repeated and salient uses of film techniques characteristic of a single film or a group of films (for example, a film-maker's work or a national movement).

superimposition   The exposure of more than one image on the same film strip or in the same shot.

synchronous sound   Sound that is matched temporally with the movements occurring in the images, as when dialogue corresponds to lip movements.

take   In filmmaking, the shot produced by one uninterrupted run of the camera. One shot in the final film may be chosen from among several takes of the same action.

technique   Any aspect of the film medium that can be chosen and manipulated in making a film.

telephoto lens   A lens of long focal length that affects a scene's perspective by enlarging distant planes and making them seem close to the foreground planes; in 35mm filming, a lens with a *focal length* of 75mm or more. See also *normal lens, wide-angle lens.*

3D computer animation   Digitally generated series of images that imitate the rounded look of people, puppets, or models (not to be confused with stereoscopic 3D images viewed through glasses).

three-point lighting   A common arrangement using three directions of light on a scene: from behind the subjects (*backlighting*), from one bright source (*key light*), and from a less bright source balancing the key light (*fill light*).

tilt   A camera movement with the camera body swiveling upward or downward on a stationary support. It produces a mobile framing that scans the space vertically.

top lighting   Lighting coming from above a person or an object, usually in order to outline the upper areas of the figure or to separate it more clearly from the background.

tracking shot   A mobile framing that travels through space forward, backward, or laterally. See also *crane shot, pan,* and *tilt.*

transmedia storytelling   Storytelling that occurs across different media platforms, such as films, comic books, and novels, but that derives from a single intellectual property. Each platform is expected to add some unique narrative material.

2D computer animation   Digitally generated series of images that give the appearance of flat drawings or paintings.

typage   A performance technique of Soviet Montage cinema. The actor's appearance and behavior are presented as typical of a social class or other group.

underlighting   Illumination from a point below the figures in the scene.

unity   The degree to which a film's parts relate systematically to one another and provide motivations for all the elements included.

variation   In film form, the return of an element with notable changes.

viewing time   The length of time it takes to watch a film when it is projected at the appropriate speed.

whip pan   An extremely fast movement of the camera from side to side, which briefly causes the image to blur into a set of indistinct horizontal streaks. Often an imperceptible cut joins two whip pans to create a trick transition between scenes.

wide-angle lens   A lens of short focal length that affects a scene's perspective by distorting straight lines near the edges of the frame and by exaggerating the distance between foreground and background planes. In 35mm filming, a wide-angle lens has a *focal length* of 35mm or less. See also *normal lens, telephoto lens.*

wipe   A transition between shots in which a line passes across the screen, eliminating one shot as it goes and replacing it with the next one.

zoom lens   A lens with a focal length that can be changed during a shot. A shift toward the *telephoto-lens* range enlarges the image and flattens its planes together, giving an impression of magnifying the scene's space; a shift toward the *wide-angle* range does the opposite.

CREDITS

Note: Page numbers in italics indicate illustrations.

Mc
Graw
Hill
Education